THE POEMS OF
JOHN DRYDEN

THE POEMS OF
JOHN DRYDEN

EDITED BY

JAMES KINSLEY

VOLUME IV

OXFORD
AT THE CLARENDON PRESS
1958

Oxford University Press, Amen House, London E.C.4

GLASGOW NEW YORK TORONTO MELBOURNE WELLINGTON
BOMBAY CALCUTTA MADRAS KARACHI KUALA LUMPUR
CAPE TOWN IBADAN NAIROBI ACCRA

PRINTED IN GREAT BRITAIN
AT THE UNIVERSITY PRESS, OXFORD
BY CHARLES BATEY, PRINTER TO THE UNIVERSITY

CONTENTS

VOLUME IV

FABLES

Ancient and *Modern*;

Translated into Verse,

from

Homer, Ovid, Boccace and Chaucer:

with Original Poems.

Nunc ultrò ad Cineres ipsius & ossa parentis
(Haud equidem sine mente, reor, sine numine divum)
Adsumus.   Virg. Æn. lib. 5.

Fables. Text from the first edition, 1700 (F)

TO HIS GRACE
The Duke of Ormond

My LORD,

SOME Estates are held in *England*, by paying a Fine at the change of every Lord: I have enjoy'd the Patronage of your Family, from the time of your excellent Grandfather to this present Day. I have dedicated the Lives of *Plutarch* to the first Duke; and have celebrated the Memory of your Heroick Father. Tho' I am very short of the Age of *Nestor*, yet 5 I have liv'd to a third Generation of your House; and by your Grace's Favour am admitted still to hold from you by the same Tenure.

I am not vain enough to boast that I have deserv'd the value of so Illustrious a Line; but my Fortune is the greater, that for three Descents they have been pleas'd to distinguish my Poems from those of other 10 Men; and have accordingly made me their peculiar Care. May it be permitted me to say, That as your Grandfather and Father were cherish'd and adorn'd with Honours by two successive Monarchs, so I have been esteem'd, and patronis'd, by the Grandfather, the Father, and the Son, descended from one of the most Ancient, most Con- 15 spicuous, and most Deserving Families in *Europe*.

'Tis true, that by delaying the Payment of my last Fine, when it was due by your Grace's Accession to the Titles, and Patrimonies of your House, I may seem in rigour of Law to have made a forfeiture of my Claim, yet my Heart has always been devoted to your Service: And 20 since you have been graciously pleas'd, by your permission of this Address, to accept the tender of my Duty, 'tis not yet too late to lay these Poems at your Feet.

The World is sensible that you worthily succeed, not only to the Honours of your Ancestors, but also to their Virtues. The long Chain 25 of Magnanimity, Courage, easiness of Access, and desire of doing Good, even to the Prejudice of your Fortune, is so far from being broken in your Grace, that the precious Metal yet runs pure to the newest Link of it: Which I will not call the last, because I hope and pray, it may descend to late Posterity: And your flourishing Youth, and that of your 30 excellent Dutchess, are happy Omens of my Wish.

'Tis observ'd by *Livy* and by others, That some of the noblest *Roman* Families retain'd a resemblance of their Ancestry, not only in their Shapes and Features, but also in their Manners, their Qualities, and the

distinguishing Characters of their Minds: Some Lines were noted for 35
a stern, rigid Virtue, salvage, haughty, parcimonious and unpopular:
Others were more sweet, and affable; made of a more pliant Past,
humble, courteous, and obliging; studious of doing charitable Offices,
and diffusive of the Goods which they enjoy'd. The last of these is the
proper and indelible Character of your Grace's Family. God Almighty 40
has endu'd you with a Softness, a Beneficence, an attractive Behaviour
winning on the Hearts of others; and so sensible of their Misery, that
the Wounds of Fortune, seem not inflicted on them but on your self.
You are so ready to redress, that you almost prevent their Wishes, and
always exceed their Expectations: As if what was yours, was not your 45
own, and not given you to possess, but to bestow on wanting Merit.
But this is a Topick which I must cast in Shades, lest I offend your
Modesty, which is so far from being ostentatious of the Good you do,
that it blushes even to have it known: And therefore I must leave you
to the Satisfaction and Testimony of your own Conscience, which 50
though it be a silent Panegyrick, is yet the best.

You are so easy of Access, that *Poplicola* was not more, whose Doors
were open'd on the Outside to save the People even the common
Civility of asking entrance; where all were equally admitted; where
nothing that was reasonable was deny'd; where Misfortune was a 55
powerful Recommendation, and where (I can scarce forbear saying) that
Want it self was a powerful Mediator, and was next to Merit.

The History of *Peru* assures us, That their *Inca's* above all their Titles,
esteem'd that the highest, which call'd them Lovers of the Poor: A
Name more glorious, than the *Felix, Pius,* and *Augustus* of the *Roman* 60
Emperors; which were Epithets of Flattery, deserv'd by few of them;
and not running in a Blood like the perpetual Gentleness, and inherent
Goodness of the *ORMOND* Family.

Gold, as it is the purest, so it is the softest, and most ductile of all
Metals: Iron, which is the hardest, gathers Rust, corrodes its self; and 65
is therefore subject to Corruption: It was never intended for Coins and
Medals, or to bear the Faces and Inscriptions of the Great. Indeed 'tis
fit for Armour, to bear off Insults, and preserve the Wearer in the Day
of Battle: But the Danger once repell'd, 'tis laid aside by the Brave, as
a Garment too rough for civil Conversation; a necessary Guard in War, 70
but too harsh and cumbersome in Peace, and which keeps off the embraces of a more human Life.

For this Reason, my Lord, though you have Courage in a heroical
Degree, yet I ascribe it to you, but as your second Attribute: Mercy,

Beneficence, and Compassion, claim Precedence, as they are first in the 75
divine Nature. An intrepid Courage, which is inherent in your Grace,
is at best but a Holiday-kind of Virtue, to be seldom exercis'd, and never
but in Cases of Necessity: Affability, Mildness, Tenderness, and a
Word, which I would fain bring back to its original Signification of
Virtue, I mean good Nature, are of daily use: They are the Bread of 80
Mankind, and Staff of Life: Neither Sighs, nor Tears, nor Groans, nor
Curses of the vanquish'd, follow Acts of Compassion, and of Charity:
But a sincere Pleasure, and Serenity of Mind, in him who performs an
Action of Mercy, which cannot suffer the Misfortunes of another, with-
out redress; least they should bring a kind of Contagion along with 85
them, and pollute the Happiness which he enjoys.

Yet since the perverse Tempers of Mankind, since Oppression on one
side, and Ambition on the other, are sometimes the unavoidable Occasions of War; that Courage, that Magnanimity, and Resolution, which
is born with you, cannot be too much commended: And here it grieves 90
me that I am scanted in the pleasure of dwelling on many of your
Actions: But αἰδέομαι Τρῶας is an Expression which *Tully* often uses,
when he would do what he dares not, and fears the Censure of the
Romans.

I have sometimes been forc'd to amplify on others; but here, where 95
the Subject is so fruitful, that the Harvest overcomes the Reaper, I am
shorten'd by my Chain, and can only see what is forbidden me to reach:
Since it is not permitted me to commend you, according to the extent
of my Wishes, and much less is it in my Power to make my Commendations equal to your Merits.   100

Yet in this Frugality of your Praises, there are some Things which I
cannot omit, without detracting from your Character. You have so
form'd your own Education, as enables you to pay the Debt you owe
your Country; or more properly speaking, both your Countries: Because you were born, I may almost say in Purple at the Castle of *Dublin,* 105
when your Grandfather was Lord-Lieutenant, and have since been bred
in the Court of *England.*

If this Address had been in Verse, I might have call'd you as *Claudian*
calls *Mercury, Numen commune, Gemino faciens commercia mundo.* The better
to satisfy this double Obligation you have early cultivated the Genius 110
you have to Arms, that when the Service of *Britain* or *Ireland* shall require your Courage, and your Conduct, you may exert them both to
the Benefit of either Country. You began in the Cabinet what you afterwards practis'd in the Camp; and thus both *Lucullus* and *Cæsar* (to omit

a crowd of shining *Romans*) form'd themselves to the War by the Study 115
of History; and by the Examples of the greatest Captains, both of *Greece*
and *Italy*, before their time. I name those two Commanders in particular, because they were better read in Chronicle than any of the
Roman Leaders; and that *Lucullus* in particular, having only the Theory
of War from Books, was thought fit, without Practice, to be sent into 120
the Field, against the most formidable Enemy of *Rome*. *Tully* indeed was
call'd the learn'd Consul in derision; but then he was not born a Soldier:
His Head was turn'd another way: When he read the Tacticks he was
thinking on the Bar, which was his Field of Battle. The Knowledge of
Warfare is thrown away on a General who dares not make use of what 125
he knows. I commend it only in a Man of Courage and of Resolution;
in him it will direct his Martial Spirit; and teach him the way to the
best Victories, which are those that are least bloody, and which tho'
atchiev'd by the Hand, are manag'd by the Head. Science distinguishes
a Man of Honour from one of those Athletick Brutes whom undeservedly 130
we call Heroes. Curs'd be the Poet, who first honour'd with that Name
a meer *Ajax*, a Man-killing Ideot. The *Ulysses* of *Ovid* upbraids his Ignorance, that he understood not the Shield for which he pleaded: There
was engraven on it, Plans of Cities, and Maps of Countries, which *Ajax*
could not comprehend, but look'd on them as stupidly as his Fellow- 135
Beast the Lion. But on the other side, your Grace has given your self the
Education of his Rival; you have studied every Spot of Ground in
Flanders, which for these ten Years past has been the Scene of Battles and
of Sieges. No wonder if you perform'd your Part with such Applause
on a Theater which you understood so well. 140

   If I design'd this for a Poetical Encomium, it were easy to enlarge on
so copious a Subject; but confining my self to the Severity of Truth,
and to what is becoming me to say, I must not only pass over many
Instances of your Military Skill, but also those of your assiduous Diligence in the War; and of your Personal Bravery, attended with an 145
ardent Thirst of Honour; a long Train of Generosity; Profuseness of
doing Good; a Soul unsatisfy'd with all it has done; and an unextinguish'd Desire of doing more. But all this is Matter for your own His-
torians; I am, as *Virgil* says, *Spatiis exclusus iniquis.*

   Yet not to be wholly silent of all your Charities I must stay a little 150
on one Action, which preferr'd the Relief of Others, to the Consideration of your Self. When, in the Battle of *Landen*, your Heat of Courage
(a Fault only pardonable to your Youth) had transported you so far
before your Friends, that they were unable to follow, much less to

succour you; when you were not only dangerously, but in all appear- 155
ance mortally wounded; when in that desperate Condition you were
made Prisoner, and carried to *Namur* at that time in Possession of the
French; then it was, my Lord, that you took a considerable Part of what
was remitted to you of your own Revenues, and as a memorable Instance of your Heroick Charity, put it into the Hands of Count *Guiscard*, 160
who was Governor of the Place, to be distributed among your Fellow-
Prisoners. The *French* Commander, charm'd with the greatness of your
Soul, accordingly consign'd it to the Use for which it was intended by
the Donor: By which means the Lives of so many miserable Men were
sav'd, and a comfortable Provision made for their Subsistance, who had 165
otherwise perish'd, had not you been the Companion of their Misfortune: or rather sent by Providence, like another *Joseph*, to keep out
Famine from invading those, whom in Humility you call'd your Brethren. How happy was it for those poor Creatures, that your Grace was
made their Fellow-Sufferer? And how glorious for You, that you chose 170
to want rather than not relieve the Wants of others? The Heathen Poet,
in commending the Charity of *Dido* to the *Trojans*, spoke like a Christian: *Non ignara mali miseris, succurrere disco.* All Men, even those of a
different Interest, and contrary Principles, must praise this Action, as
the most eminent for Piety, not only in this degenerate Age, but almost 175
in any of the former; when Men were made *de meliore luto*; when Examples of Charity were frequent, and when there were in being, *Teucri
pulcherrima proles, Magnanimi Heroes nati melioribus annis.* No Envy can
detract from this; it will shine in History; and like Swans, grow
whiter the longer it endures: And the Name of *O R M O N D* will be 180
more celebrated in his Captivity, than in his greatest Triumphs.

But all Actions of your Grace are of a piece; as Waters keep the
Tenour of their Fountains: your Compassion is general, and has the
same Effect as well on Enemies as Friends. 'Tis so much in your
Nature to do Good, that your Life is but one continued Act of placing 185
Benefits on many; as the Sun is always carrying his Light to some Part
or other of the World: And were it not that your Reason guides you
where to give, I might almost say that you could not help bestowing
more, than is consisting with the Fortune of a private Man, or with the
Will of any but an *Alexander*. 190

What Wonder is it then, that being born for a Blessing to Mankind,
your suppos'd Death in that Engagement, was so generally lamented
through the Nation? The Concernment for it was as universal as the

Dedication. 156 wounded;] wounded, F

Loss: And though the Gratitude might be counterfeit in some, yet the Tears of all were real: Where every Man deplor'd his private Part in 195 that Calamity, and even those who had not tasted of your Favours, yet built so much on the Fame of your Beneficence, that they bemoan'd the Loss of their Expectations.

This brought the untimely Death of your Great Father into fresh remembrance; as if the same Decree had pass'd on two short successive 200 Generations of the Virtuous; and I repeated to my self the same Verses, which I had formerly apply'd to him: *Ostendunt terris hunc tantum fata, nec ultra, esse sinunt.* But to the Joy not only of all good Men, but of Mankind in general, the unhappy Omen took not place. You are still living to enjoy the Blessings and Applause of all the Good you have 205 perform'd, the Prayers of Multitudes whom you have oblig'd, for your long Prosperity; and that your Power of doing generous and charitable Actions, may be as extended as your Will; which is by none more zealously desir'd than by

Your GRACE's most humble,
most oblig'd, and most
obedient Servant,

John Dryden.

PREFACE

'TIS with a Poet, as with a Man who designs to build, and is very exact, as he supposes, in casting up the Cost beforehand: But, generally speaking, he is mistaken in his Account, and reckons short of the Expence he first intended: He alters his Mind as the Work proceeds, and will have this or that Convenience more, of which he had not 5 thought when he began. So has it hapned to me; I have built a House, where I intended but a Lodge: Yet with better Success than a certain Nobleman, who beginning with a Dog-kennil, never liv'd to finish the Palace he had contriv'd.

From translating the First of *Homer's Iliads*, (which I intended as an 10 Essay to the whole Work) I proceeded to the Translation of the Twelfth Book of *Ovid's Metamorphoses*, because it contains, among other Things, the Causes, the Beginning, and Ending, of the *Trojan* War: Here I ought in reason to have stopp'd; but the Speeches of *Ajax* and *Ulysses* lying next in my way, I could not balk 'em. When I had compass'd them, I 15 was so taken with the former Part of the Fifteenth Book, (which is the Master-piece of the whole *Metamorphoses*) that I enjoyn'd my self the pleasing Task of rendring it into *English*. And now I found, by the Number of my Verses, that they began to swell into a little Volume; which gave me an Occasion of looking backward on some Beauties of 20 my Author, in his former Books: There occur'd to me the Hunting of the Boar, *Cinyras* and *Myrrha*, the good-natur'd Story of *Baucis* and *Philemon*, with the rest, which I hope I have translated closely enough, and given them the same Turn of Verse, which they had in the Original; and this, I may say without vanity, is not the Talent of every Poet: 25 He who has arriv'd the nearest to it, is the Ingenious and Learned *Sandys*, the best Versifier of the former Age; if I may properly call it by that Name, which was the former Part of this concluding Century. For *Spencer* and *Fairfax* both flourish'd in the Reign of Queen *Elizabeth*: Great Masters in our Language; and who saw much farther into the 30 Beauties of our Numbers, than those who immediately followed them. *Milton* was the Poetical Son of *Spencer*, and Mr. *Waller* of *Fairfax*; for we have our Lineal Descents and Clans, as well as other Families: *Spencer* more than once insinuates, that the Soul of *Chaucer* was transfus'd into his Body; and that he was begotten by him Two hundred years after 35 his Decease. *Milton* has acknowledg'd to me, that *Spencer* was his Original; and many besides my self have heard our famous *Waller* own, that he deriv'd the Harmony of his Numbers from the *Godfrey of Bulloign*, which was turn'd into *English* by Mr. *Fairfax*. But to return: Having done with *Ovid* for this time, it came into my mind, that our old *English* 40 Poet *Chaucer* in many Things resembled him, and that with no disadvantage on the Side of the Modern Author, as I shall endeavour to prove when I compare them: And as I am, and always have been studious to promote the Honour of my Native Country, so I soon resolv'd to put their Merits to the Trial, by turning some of the *Canterbury* Tales 45 into our Language, as it is now refin'd: For by this Means both the Poets being set in the same Light, and dress'd in the same *English* Habit, Story to be compar'd with Story, a certain Judgment may be made betwixt them, by the Reader, without obtruding my Opinion on him: Or if I seem partial to my Country-man, and Predecessor in the Laurel, 50 the Friends of Antiquity are not few: And besides many of the Learn'd, *Ovid* has almost all the *Beaux*, and the whole Fair Sex, his declar'd Patrons. Perhaps I have assum'd somewhat more to my self than they allow me; because I have adventur'd to sum up the Evidence: But the Readers are the Jury; and their Privilege remains entire to decide 55 according to the Merits of the Cause: Or, if they please to bring it to

Preface. 52 Sex,] Sex F

another Hearing, before some other Court. In the mean time, to follow the Thrid of my Discourse, (as Thoughts, according to Mr. *Hobbs*, have always some Connexion) so from *Chaucer* I was led to think on *Boccace*, who was not only his Contemporary, but also pursu'd the same Studies; 60 wrote Novels in Prose, and many Works in Verse; particularly is said to have invented the Octave Rhyme, or *Stanza* of Eight Lines, which ever since has been maintain'd by the Practice of all *Italian* Writers, who are, or at least assume the Title of *Heroick Poets*: He and *Chaucer*, among other Things, had this in common, that they refin'd their Mother- 65 Tongues; but with this difference, that *Dante* had begun to file their Language, at least in Verse, before the time of *Boccace*, who likewise receiv'd no little Help from his Master *Petrarch*: But the Reformation of their Prose was wholly owing to *Boccace* himself; who is yet the Standard of Purity in the *Italian* Tongue; though many of his Phrases 70 are become obsolete, as in process of Time it must needs happen. *Chaucer* (as you have formerly been told by our learn'd Mr. *Rhymer*) first adorn'd and amplified our barren Tongue from the *Provencall*, which was then the most polish'd of all the Modern Languages: But this Subject has been copiously treated by that great Critick, who 75 deserves no little Commendation from us his Countrymen. For these Reasons of Time, and Resemblance of Genius, in *Chaucer* and *Boccace*, I resolv'd to join them in my present Work; to which I have added some Original Papers of my own; which whether they are equal or inferiour to my other Poems, an Author is the most improper Judge; 80 and therefore I leave them wholly to the Mercy of the Reader: I will hope the best, that they will not be condemn'd; but if they should, I have the Excuse of an old Gentleman, who mounting on Horseback before some Ladies, when I was present, got up somewhat heavily, but desir'd of the Fair Spectators, that they would count Fourscore and 85 eight before they judg'd him. By the Mercy of God, I am already come within Twenty Years of his Number, a Cripple in my Limbs, but what Decays are in my Mind, the Reader must determine. I think my self as vigorous as ever in the Faculties of my Soul, excepting only my Memory, which is not impair'd to any great degree; and if I lose not 90 more of it, I have no great reason to complain. What Judgment I had, increases rather than diminishes; and Thoughts, such as they are, come crowding in so fast upon me, that my only Difficulty is to chuse or to reject; to run them into Verse, or to give them the other Harmony of Prose. I have so long studied and practis'd both, that they are grown 95

95 Prose.] Prose, F

into a Habit, and become familiar to me. In short, though I may lawfully plead some part of the old Gentleman's Excuse; yet I will reserve it till I think I have greater need, and ask no Grains of Allowance for the Faults of this my present Work, but those which are given of course to Humane Frailty. I will not trouble my Reader with the shortness of 100 Time in which I writ it; or the several Intervals of Sickness: They who think too well of their own Performances, are apt to boast in their Prefaces how little Time their Works have cost them; and what other Business of more importance interfer'd: But the Reader will be as apt to ask the Question, Why they allow'd not a longer Time to make their 105 Works more perfect? and why they had so despicable an Opinion of their Judges, as to thrust their indigested Stuff upon them, as if they deserv'd no better?

With this Account of my present Undertaking, I conclude the first Part of this Discourse: In the second Part, as at a second Sitting, though 110 I alter not the Draught, I must touch the same Features over again, and change the Dead-colouring of the Whole. In general I will only say, that I have written nothing which savours of Immorality or Profaneness; at least, I am not conscious to my self of any such Intention. If there happen to be found an irreverent Expression, or a Thought too wanton, 115 they are crept into my Verses through my Inadvertency: If the Searchers find any in the Cargo, let them be stav'd or forfeited, like Counterbanded Goods; at least, let their Authors be answerable for them, as being but imported Merchandise, and not of my own Manufacture. On the other Side, I have endeavour'd to chuse such Fables, both Ancient 120 and Modern, as contain in each of them some instructive Moral, which I could prove by Induction, but the Way is tedious; and they leap foremost into sight, without the Reader's Trouble of looking after them. I wish I could affirm with a safe Conscience, that I had taken the same Care in all my former Writings; for it must be own'd, that supposing 125 Verses are never so beautiful or pleasing, yet if they contain any thing which shocks Religion, or Good Manners, they are at best, what *Horace* says of good Numbers without good Sense, *Versus inopes rerum, nugæque canoræ:* Thus far, I hope, I am Right in Court, without renouncing to my other Right of Self-defence, where I have been wrongfully accus'd, 130 and my Sense wire-drawn into Blasphemy or Bawdry, as it has often been by a Religious Lawyer, in a late Pleading against the Stage; in which he mixes Truth with Falshood, and has not forgotten the old Rule, of calumniating strongly, that something may remain.

I resume the Thrid of my Discourse with the first of my Translations, 135 which was the First _Iliad_ of _Homer_. If it shall please God to give me longer Life, and moderate Health, my Intentions are to translate the whole _Ilias_; provided still, that I meet with those Encouragements from the Publick, which may enable me to proceed in my Undertaking with some Chearfulness. And this I dare assure the World before-hand, that 140 I have found by Trial, _Homer_ a more pleasing Task than _Virgil_, (though I say not the Translation will be less laborious.) For the _Grecian_ is more according to my Genius, than the _Latin_ Poet. In the Works of the two Authors we may read their Manners, and natural Inclinations, which are wholly different. _Virgil_ was of a quiet, sedate Temper; _Homer_ was 145 violent, impetuous, and full of Fire. The chief Talent of _Virgil_ was Propriety of Thoughts, and Ornament of Words: _Homer_ was rapid in his Thoughts, and took all the Liberties both of Numbers, and of Expressions, which his Language, and the Age in which he liv'd allow'd him: _Homer_'s Invention was more copious, _Virgil_'s more confin'd: So 150 that if _Homer_ had not led the Way, it was not in _Virgil_ to have begun Heroick Poetry: For, nothing can be more evident, than that the _Roman_ Poem is but the Second Part of the _Ilias_; a Continuation of the same Story: And the Persons already form'd: The Manners of _Æneas_, are those of _Hector_ superadded to those which _Homer_ gave him. The 155 Adventures of _Ulysses_ in the _Odysseis_, are imitated in the first Six Books of _Virgil_'s _Æneis_: And though the Accidents are not the same, (which would have argu'd him of a servile, copying, and total Barrenness of Invention) yet the Seas were the same, in which both the _Heroes_ wander'd; and _Dido_ cannot be deny'd to be the Poetical Daughter of _Calypso_. 160 The Six latter Books of _Virgil_'s Poem, are the Four and twenty _Iliads_ contracted: A Quarrel occasion'd by a Lady, a Single Combate, Battels fought, and a Town besieg'd. I say not this in derogation to _Virgil_, neither do I contradict any thing which I have formerly said in his just Praise: For his _Episodes_ are almost wholly of his own Invention; and the 165 Form which he has given to the Telling, makes the Tale his own, even though the Original Story had been the same. But this proves, however, that _Homer_ taught _Virgil_ to design: And if Invention be the first Vertue of an Epick Poet, then the _Latin_ Poem can only be allow'd the second Place. Mr. _Hobbs_, in the Preface to his own bald Translation of the _Ilias_, 170 (studying Poetry as he did Mathematicks, when it was too late) Mr. _Hobbs_, I say, begins the Praise of _Homer_ where he should have ended it. He tells us, that the first Beauty of an Epick Poem consists in Diction, that is, in the Choice of Words, and Harmony of Numbers: Now, the Words are the Colouring of the Work, which in the Order of Nature 175 is last to be consider'd. The Design, the Disposition, the Manners, and the Thoughts, are all before it: Where any of those are wanting or imperfect, so much wants or is imperfect in the Imitation of Humane Life; which is in the very Definition of a Poem. Words indeed, like glaring Colours, are the first Beauties that arise, and strike the Sight; 180 but if the Draught be false or lame, the Figures ill dispos'd, the Manners obscure or inconsistent, or the Thoughts unnatural, then the finest Colours are but Dawbing, and the Piece is a beautiful Monster at the best. Neither *Virgil* nor *Homer* were deficient in any of the former Beauties; but in this last, which is Expression, the *Roman* Poet is at least 185 equal to the *Grecian*, as I have said elsewhere; supplying the Poverty of his Language, by his Musical Ear, and by his Diligence. But to return: Our two Great Poets, being so different in their Tempers, one Cholerick and Sanguin, the other Phlegmatick and Melancholick; that which makes them excel in their several Ways, is, that each of them has fol- 190 low'd his own natural Inclination, as well in Forming the Design, as in the Execution of it. The very *Heroes* shew their Authors: *Achilles* is hot, impatient, revengeful, *Impiger, iracundus, inexorabilis, acer*, &c. *Æneas* patient, considerate, careful of his People, and merciful to his Enemies; ever submissive to the Will of Heaven, *quo fata trahunt retrahuntque*, 195 *sequamur*. I could please my self with enlarging on this Subject, but am forc'd to defer it to a fitter Time. From all I have said, I will only draw this Inference, That the Action of *Homer* being more full of Vigour than that of *Virgil*, according to the Temper of the Writer, is of consequence more pleasing to the Reader. One warms you by Degrees; the other 200 sets you on fire all at once, and never intermits his Heat. 'Tis the same Difference which *Longinus* makes betwixt the Effects of Eloquence in *Demosthenes*, and *Tully*. One persuades; the other commands. You never cool while you read *Homer*, even not in the Second Book, (a graceful Flattery to his Countrymen;) but he hastens from the Ships, and con- 205 cludes not that Book till he has made you an Amends by the violent playing of a new Machine. From thence he hurries on his Action with Variety of Events, and ends it in less Compass than Two Months. This Vehemence of his, I confess, is more suitable to my Temper: and there- fore I have translated his First Book with greater Pleasure than any 210 Part of *Virgil*: But it was not a Pleasure without Pains: The continual Agitations of the Spirits, must needs be a Weakning of any Constitu- tion, especially in Age: and many Pauses are required for Refreshment betwixt the Heats; the *Iliad* of its self being a third part longer than all *Virgil's* Works together. 215

This is what I thought needful in this Place to say of *Homer*. I proceed to *Ovid*, and *Chaucer*; considering the former only in relation to the latter. With *Ovid* ended the Golden Age of the *Roman* Tongue: From *Chaucer* the Purity of the *English* Tongue began. The Manners of the Poets were not unlike: Both of them were well-bred, well-natur'd, 220 amorous, and Libertine, at least in their Writings, it may be also in their Lives. Their Studies were the same, Philosophy, and Philology. Both of them were knowing in Astronomy, of which *Ovid's* Books of the *Roman* Feasts, and *Chaucer's* Treatise of the *Astrolabe*, are sufficient Witnesses. But *Chaucer* was likewise an Astrologer, as were *Virgil, Horace,* 225 *Persius,* and *Manilius.* Both writ with wonderful Facility and Clearness; neither were great Inventors: For *Ovid* only copied the *Grecian* Fables; and most of *Chaucer's* Stories were taken from his *Italian* Contemporaries, or their Predecessors: *Boccace* his *Decameron* was first publish'd; and from thence our *Englishman* has borrow'd many of his *Canterbury* Tales: 230 Yet that of *Palamon* and *Arcite* was written in all probability by some *Italian* Wit, in a former Age; as I shall prove hereafter: The Tale of *Grizild* was the Invention of *Petrarch*; by him sent to *Boccace*; from whom it came to *Chaucer*: *Troilus* and *Cressida* was also written by a *Lombard* Author; but much amplified by our *English* Translatour, as 235 well as beautified; the Genius of our Countrymen in general being rather to improve an Invention, than to invent themselves; as is evident not only in our Poetry, but in many of our Manufactures. I find I have anticipated already, and taken up from *Boccace* before I come to him: But there is so much less behind; and I am of the Temper of most 240 Kings, *who love to be in Debt*, are all for present Money, no matter how they pay it afterwards: Besides, the Nature of a Preface is rambling; never wholly out of the Way, nor in it. This I have learn'd from the Practice of honest *Montaign*, and return at my pleasure to *Ovid* and *Chaucer*, of whom I have little more to say. Both of them built on the 245 Inventions of other Men; yet since *Chaucer* had something of his own, as *The Wife of Baths Tale, The Cock and the Fox*, which I have translated, and some others, I may justly give our Countryman the Precedence in that Part; since I can remember nothing of *Ovid* which was wholly his. Both of them understood the Manners; under which Name I compre- 250 hend the Passions, and, in a larger Sense, the Descriptions of Persons, and their very Habits: For an Example, I see *Baucis* and *Philemon* as perfectly before me, as if some ancient Painter had drawn them; and all the Pilgrims in the *Canterbury* Tales, their Humours, their Features, and the very Dress, as distinctly as if I had supp'd with them at the *Tabard* in 255

Southwark: Yet even there too the Figures of *Chaucer* are much more lively, and set in a better Light: Which though I have not time to prove; yet I appeal to the Reader, and am sure he will clear me from Partiality. The Thoughts and Words remain to be consider'd, in the Comparison of the two Poets; and I have sav'd my self one half of that Labour, by 260 owning that *Ovid* liv'd when the *Roman* Tongue was in its Meridian; *Chaucer*, in the Dawning of our Language: Therefore that Part of the Comparison stands not on an equal Foot, any more than the Diction of *Ennius* and *Ovid*; or of *Chaucer*, and our present *English*. The Words are given up as a Post not to be defended in our Poet, because he wanted 265 the Modern Art of Fortifying. The Thoughts remain to be consider'd: And they are to be measur'd only by their Propriety; that is, as they flow more or less naturally from the Persons describ'd, on such and such Occasions. The Vulgar Judges, which are Nine Parts in Ten of all Nations, who call Conceits and Jingles Wit, who see *Ovid* full of them, 270 and *Chaucer* altogether without them, will think me little less than mad, for preferring the *Englishman* to the *Roman*: Yet, with their leave, I must presume to say, that the Things they admire are only glittering Trifles, and so far from being Witty, that in a serious Poem they are nauseous, because they are unnatural. Wou'd any Man who is ready to die for 275 Love, describe his Passion like *Narcissus*? Wou'd he think of *inopem me copia fecit*, and a Dozen more of such Expressions, pour'd on the Neck of one another, and signifying all the same Thing? If this were Wit, was this a Time to be witty, when the poor Wretch was in the Agony of Death? This is just *John Littlewit* in *Bartholomew Fair*, who had a Con- 280 ceit (as he tells you) left him in his Misery; a miserable Conceit. On these Occasions the Poet shou'd endeavour to raise Pity: But instead of this, *Ovid* is tickling you to laugh. *Virgil* never made use of such Machines, when he was moving you to commiserate the Death of *Dido*: He would not destroy what he was building. *Chaucer* makes *Arcite* 285 violent in his Love, and unjust in the Pursuit of it: Yet when he came to die, he made him think more reasonably: He repents not of his Love, for that had alter'd his Character; but acknowledges the Injustice of his Proceedings, and resigns *Emilia* to *Palamon*. What would *Ovid* have done on this Occasion? He would certainly have made *Arcite* witty on 290 his Death-bed. He had complain'd he was farther off from Possession, by being so near, and a thousand such Boyisms, which *Chaucer* rejected as below the Dignity of the Subject. They who think otherwise, would by the same Reason prefer *Lucan* and *Ovid* to *Homer* and *Virgil*, and *Martial* to all Four of them. As for the Turn of Words, in which *Ovid* 295 particularly excels all Poets; they are sometimes a Fault, and sometimes a Beauty, as they are us'd properly or improperly; but in strong Passions always to be shunn'd, because Passions are serious, and will admit no Playing. The *French* have a high Value for them; and I confess, they are often what they call Delicate, when they are introduc'd with Judgment; 300 but *Chaucer* writ with more Simplicity, and follow'd Nature more closely, than to use them. I have thus far, to the best of my Knowledge, been an upright Judge betwixt the Parties in Competition, not medling with the Design nor the Disposition of it; because the Design was not their own; and in the disposing of it they were equal. It remains that 305 I say somewhat of *Chaucer* in particular.

In the first place, As he is the Father of *English* Poetry, so I hold him in the same Degree of Veneration as the *Grecians* held *Homer*, or the *Romans Virgil*: He is a perpetual Fountain of good Sense; learn'd in all Sciences; and therefore speaks properly on all Subjects: As he knew 310 what to say, so he knows also when to leave off; a Continence which is practis'd by few Writers, and scarcely by any of the Ancients, excepting *Virgil* and *Horace*. One of our late great Poets is sunk in his Reputation, because he cou'd never forgive any Conceit which came in his way; but swept like a Drag-net, great and small. There was plenty 315 enough, but the Dishes were ill sorted; whole Pyramids of Sweet-meats, for Boys and Women; but little of solid Meat, for Men: All this proceeded not from any want of Knowledge, but of Judgment; neither did he want that in discerning the Beauties and Faults of other Poets; but only indulg'd himself in the Luxury of Writing; and perhaps knew it 320 was a Fault, but hop'd the Reader would not find it. For this Reason, though he must always be thought a great Poet, he is no longer esteem'd a good Writer: And for Ten Impressions, which his Works have had in so many successive Years, yet at present a hundred Books are scarcely purchas'd once a Twelvemonth: For, as my last Lord 325 *Rochester* said, though somewhat profanely, *Not being of God, he could not stand.*

Chaucer follow'd Nature every where; but was never so bold to go beyond her: And there is a great Difference of being *Poeta* and *nimis Poeta*, if we may believe *Catullus*, as much as betwixt a modest Behaviour 330 and Affectation. The Verse of *Chaucer*, I confess, is not Harmonious to us; but 'tis like the Eloquence of one whom *Tacitus* commends, it was *auribus istius temporis accommodata:* They who liv'd with him, and some time after him, thought it Musical; and it continues so even in our Judgment, if compar'd with the Numbers of *Lidgate* and *Gower* his Con- 335 temporaries: There is the rude Sweetness of a *Scotch* Tune in it, which is natural and pleasing, though not perfect. 'Tis true, I cannot go so far as he who publish'd the last Edition of him; for he would make us believe the Fault is in our Ears, and that there were really Ten Syllables in a Verse where we find but Nine: But this Opinion is not worth con- 340 futing; 'tis so gross and obvious an Errour, that common Sense (which is a Rule in every thing but Matters of Faith and Revelation) must convince the Reader, that Equality of Numbers in every Verse which we call *Heroick*, was either not known, or not always practis'd in *Chaucer*'s Age. It were an easie Matter to produce some thousands of 345 his Verses, which are lame for want of half a Foot, and sometimes a whole one, and which no Pronunciation can make otherwise. We can only say, that he liv'd in the Infancy of our Poetry, and that nothing is brought to Perfection at the first. We must be Children before we grow Men. There was an *Ennius*, and in process of Time a *Lucilius*, and 350 a *Lucretius*, before *Virgil* and *Horace*; even after *Chaucer* there was a *Spencer*, a *Harrington*, a *Fairfax*, before *Waller* and *Denham* were in being: And our Numbers were in their Nonage till these last appear'd. I need say little of his Parentage, Life, and Fortunes: They are to be found at large in all the Editions of his Works. He was employ'd abroad, and 355 favour'd by *Edward* the Third, *Richard* the Second, and *Henry* the Fourth, and was Poet, as I suppose, to all Three of them. In *Richard*'s Time, I doubt, he was a little dipt in the Rebellion of the Commons; and being Brother-in-Law to *John of Ghant*, it was no wonder if he follow'd the Fortunes of that Family; and was well with *Henry* the Fourth when he 360 had depos'd his Predecessor. Neither is it to be admir'd, that *Henry*, who was a wise as well as a valiant Prince, who claim'd by Succession, and was sensible that his Title was not sound, but was rightfully in *Mortimer*, who had married the Heir of *York*; it was not to be admir'd, I say, if that great Politician should be pleas'd to have the greatest Wit of 365 those Times in his Interests, and to be the Trumpet of his Praises. *Augustus* had given him the Example, by the Advice of *Mæcenas*, who recommended *Virgil* and *Horace* to him; whose Praises help'd to make him Popular while he was alive, and after his Death have made him Precious to Posterity. As for the Religion of our Poet, he seems to have some 370 little Byas towards the Opinions of *Wickliff*, after *John of Ghant* his Patron; somewhat of which appears in the Tale of *Piers Plowman*: Yet I cannot blame him for inveighing so sharply against the Vices of the Clergy in his Age: Their Pride, their Ambition, their Pomp, their Avarice, their Worldly Interest, deserv'd the Lashes which he gave 375

them, both in that, and in most of his *Canterbury Tales*: Neither has his
Contemporary *Boccace*, spar'd them. Yet both those Poets liv'd in much
esteem, with good and holy Men in Orders: For the Scandal which
is given by particular Priests, reflects not on the Sacred Function.
Chaucer's *Monk*, his *Chanon*, and his *Fryar*, took not from the Character 380
of his *Good Parson*. A Satyrical Poet is the Check of the Laymen, on bad
Priests. We are only to take care, that we involve not the Innocent with
the Guilty in the same Condemnation. The Good cannot be too much
honour'd, nor the Bad too coursly us'd: For the Corruption of the Best,
becomes the Worst. When a Clergy-man is whipp'd, his Gown is first 385
taken off, by which the Dignity of his Order is secur'd: If he be wrongfully accus'd, he has his Action of Slander; and 'tis at the Poet's Peril,
if he transgress the Law. But they will tell us, that all kind of Satire,
though never so well deserv'd by particular Priests, yet brings the
whole Order into Contempt. Is then the Peerage of *England* any thing 390
dishonour'd, when a Peer suffers for his Treason? If he be libell'd, or
any way defam'd, he has his *Scandalum Magnatum* to punish the Offendor.
They who use this kind of Argument, seem to be conscious to themselves of somewhat which has deserv'd the Poet's Lash; and are less
concern'd for their Publick Capacity, than for their Private: At least, 395
there is Pride at the bottom of their Reasoning. If the Faults of Men
in Orders are only to be judg'd among themselves, they are all in some
sort Parties: For, since they say the Honour of their Order is concern'd
in every Member of it, how can we be sure, that they will be impartial
Judges? How far I may be allow'd to speak my Opinion in this Case, 400
I know not: But I am sure a Dispute of this Nature caus'd Mischief in
abundance betwixt a King of *England* and an Archbishop of *Canterbury*;
one standing up for the Laws of his Land, and the other for the Honour
(as he call'd it) of God's Church; which ended in the Murther of the
Prelate, and in the whipping of his Majesty from Post to Pillar for his 405
Penance. The Learn'd and Ingenious Dr. *Drake* has sav'd me the Labour
of inquiring into the Esteem and Reverence which the Priests have had
of old; and I would rather extend than diminish any part of it: Yet I
must needs say, that when a Priest provokes me without any Occasion
given him, I have no Reason, unless it be the Charity of a *Christian*, to 410
forgive him: *Prior læsit* is Justification sufficient in the Civil Law. If I
answer him in his own Language, Self-defence, I am sure, must be
allow'd me; and if I carry it farther, even to a sharp Recrimination,
somewhat may be indulg'd to Humane Frailty. Yet my Resentment
has not wrought so far, but that I have follow'd *Chaucer* in his Character 415

of a Holy Man, and have enlarg'd on that Subject with some Pleasure, reserving to my self the Right, if I shall think fit hereafter, to describe another sort of Priests, such as are more easily to be found than the Good Parson; such as have given the last Blow to Christianity in this Age, by a Practice so contrary to their Doctrine. But this will keep cold 420 till another time. In the mean while, I take up *Chaucer* where I left him. He must have been a Man of a most wonderful comprehensive Nature, because, as it has been truly observ'd of him, he has taken into the Compass of his *Canterbury Tales* the various Manners and Humours (as we now call them) of the whole *English* Nation, in his Age. Not a single 425 Character has escap'd him. All his Pilgrims are severally distinguish'd from each other; and not only in their Inclinations, but in their very Phisiognomies and Persons. *Baptista Porta* could not have describ'd their Natures better, than by the Marks which the Poet gives them. The Matter and Manner of their Tales, and of their Telling, are so suited 430 to their different Educations, Humours, and Callings, that each of them would be improper in any other Mouth. Even the grave and serious Characters are distinguish'd by their several sorts of Gravity: Their Discourses are such as belong to their Age, their Calling, and their Breeding; such as are becoming of them, and of them only. Some of his 435 Persons are Vicious, and some Vertuous; some are unlearn'd, or (as *Chaucer* calls them) Lewd, and some are Learn'd. Even the Ribaldry of the Low Characters is different: The *Reeve*, the *Miller*, and the *Cook*, are several Men, and distinguish'd from each other, as much as the mincing Lady Prioress, and the broad-speaking gap-tooth'd Wife of *Bathe*. But 440 enough of this: There is such a Variety of Game springing up before me, that I am distracted in my Choice, and know not which to follow. 'Tis sufficient to say according to the Proverb, that here is God's Plenty. We have our Fore-fathers and Great Grand-dames all before us, as they were in *Chaucer*'s Days; their general Characters are still remain- 445 ing in Mankind, and even in *England*, though they are call'd by other Names than those of *Moncks*, and *Fryars*, and *Chanons*, and *Lady Abbesses*, and *Nuns*: For Mankind is ever the same, and nothing lost out of Nature, though every thing is alter'd. May I have leave to do my self the Justice, (since my Enemies will do me none, and are so far from granting 450 me to be a good Poet, that they will not allow me so much as to be a Christian, or a Moral Man) may I have leave, I say, to inform my Reader, that I have confin'd my Choice to such Tales of *Chaucer*, as savour nothing of Immodesty. If I had desir'd more to please than to instruct, the *Reve*, the *Miller*, the *Shipman*, the *Merchant*, the *Sumner*, and 455 above all, the *Wife of Bathe,* in the Prologue to her Tale, would have procur'd me as many Friends and Readers, as there are *Beaux* and Ladies of Pleasure in the Town. But I will no more offend against Good Manners: I am sensible as I ought to be of the Scandal I have given by my loose Writings; and make what Reparation I am able, by this 460 Publick Acknowledgment. If any thing of this Nature, or of Profaneness, be crept into these Poems, I am so far from defending it, that I disown it. *Totum hoc indictum volo. Chaucer* makes another manner of Apologie for his broad-speaking, and *Boccace* makes the like; but I will follow neither of them. Our Country-man, in the end of his Characters, before the 465 *Canterbury Tales,* thus excuses the Ribaldry, which is very gross, in many of his Novels.

> *But first, I pray you, of your courtesy,*
> *That ye ne arrete it nought my villany,*
> *Though that I plainly speak in this mattere* 470
> *To tellen you her words, and eke her chere:*
> *Ne though I speak her words properly,*
> *For this ye knowen as well as I,*
> *Who shall tellen a tale after a man*
> *He mote rehearse as nye, as ever He can:* 475
> *Everich word of it been in his charge,*
> All speke he, never so rudely, ne large.
> *Or else he mote tellen his tale untrue,*
> *Or feine things, or find words new:*
> *He may not spare, altho he were his brother,* 480
> *He mote as well say o word as another.*
> Christ *spake himself full broad in holy Writ,*
> *And well I wote no Villany is it.*
> *Eke* Plato *saith, who so can him rede,*
> *The words mote been Cousin to the dede.* 485

Yet if a Man should have enquir'd of *Boccace* or of *Chaucer,* what need they had of introducing such Characters, where obscene Words were proper in their Mouths, but very undecent to be heard; I know not what Answer they could have made: For that Reason, such Tales shall be left untold by me. You have here a *Specimen* of *Chaucer*'s Language, 490 which is so obsolete, that his Sense is scarce to be understood; and you have likewise more than one Example of his unequal Numbers, which were mention'd before. Yet many of his Verses consist of Ten

Syllables, and the Words not much behind our present *English*: As for Example, these two Lines, in the Description of the Carpenter's 495 Young Wife:

> *Wincing she was, as is a jolly Colt,*
> *Long as a Mast, and upright as a Bolt.*

I have almost done with *Chaucer*, when I have answer'd some Objections relating to my present Work. I find some People are offended that 500 I have turn'd these Tales into modern *English*; because they think them unworthy of my Pains, and look on *Chaucer* as a dry, old-fashion'd Wit, not worth receiving. I have often heard the late Earl of *Leicester* say, that Mr. *Cowley* himself was of that opinion; who having read him over at my Lord's Request, declar'd he had no Taste of him. I dare not 505 advance my Opinion against the Judgment of so great an Author: But I think it fair, however, to leave the Decision to the Publick: Mr. *Cowley* was too modest to set up for a Dictatour; and being shock'd perhaps with his old Style, never examin'd into the depth of his good Sense. *Chaucer*, I confess, is a rough Diamond, and must first be polish'd e'er 510 he shines. I deny not likewise, that living in our early Days of Poetry, he writes not always of a piece; but sometimes mingles trivial Things, with those of greater Moment. Sometimes also, though not often, he runs riot, like *Ovid*, and knows not when he has said enough. But there are more great Wits, beside *Chaucer*, whose Fault is their Excess of 515 Conceits, and those ill sorted. An Author is not to write all he can, but only all he ought. Having observ'd this Redundancy in *Chaucer*, (as it is an easie Matter for a Man of ordinary Parts to find a Fault in one of greater) I have not ty'd my self to a Literal Translation; but have often omitted what I judg'd unnecessary, or not of Dignity enough to appear 520 in the Company of better Thoughts. I have presum'd farther in some Places, and added somewhat of my own where I thought my Author was deficient, and had not given his Thoughts their true Lustre, for want of Words in the Beginning of our Language. And to this I was the more embolden'd, because (if I may be permitted to say it of my self) 525 I found I had a Soul congenial to his, and that I had been conversant in the same Studies. Another Poet, in another Age, may take the same Liberty with my Writings; if at least they live long enough to deserve Correction. It was also necessary sometimes to restore the Sense of *Chaucer*, which was lost or mangled in the Errors of the Press: Let this 530 Example suffice at present; in the Story of *Palamon* and *Arcite*, where

531 present;] present F

the Temple of *Diana* is describ'd, you find these Verses, in all the
Editions of our Author:

> *There saw I* Danè *turned unto a Tree,*
> *I mean not the Goddess* Diane,   535
> *But* Venus *Daughter, which that hight* Danè.

Which after a little Consideration I knew was to be reform'd into this
Sense, that *Daphne* the Daughter of *Peneus* was turn'd into a Tree. I durst
not make thus bold with *Ovid*, lest some future *Milbourn* should arise,
and say, I varied from my Author, because I understood him not.   540
  But there are other Judges who think I ought not to have translated
Chaucer into *English*, out of a quite contrary Notion: They suppose there
is a certain Veneration due to his old Language; and that it is little less
than Profanation and Sacrilege to alter it. They are farther of opinion,
that somewhat of his good Sense will suffer in this Transfusion, and 545
much of the Beauty of his Thoughts will infallibly be lost, which appear
with more Grace in their old Habit. Of this Opinion was that excellent Person, whom I mention'd, the late Earl of *Leicester*, who valu'd
Chaucer as much as Mr. *Cowley* despis'd him. My Lord dissuaded me
from this Attempt, (for I was thinking of it some Years before his 550
Death) and his Authority prevail'd so far with me, as to defer my
Undertaking while he liv'd, in deference to him: Yet my Reason was
not convinc'd with what he urg'd against it. If the first End of a Writer
be to be understood, then as his Language grows obsolete, his Thoughts
must grow obscure, *multa renascentur quæ nunc cecidere; cadentque quæ nunc* 555
sunt in honore vocabula, si volet usus, quem penes arbitrium est & jus & norma
loquendi. When an ancient Word for its Sound and Significancy deserves
to be reviv'd, I have that reasonable Veneration for Antiquity, to
restore it. All beyond this is Superstition. Words are not like Land-
marks, so sacred as never to be remov'd: Customs are chang'd, and even 560
Statutes are silently repeal'd, when the Reason ceases for which they
were enacted. As for the other Part of the Argument, that his Thoughts
will lose of their original Beauty, by the innovation of Words; in the
first place, not only their Beauty, but their Being is lost, where they
are no longer understood, which is the present Case. I grant, that some- 565
thing must be lost in all Transfusion, that is, in all Translations; but
the Sense will remain, which would otherwise be lost, or at least be
maim'd, when it is scarce intelligible; and that but to a few. How few
are there who can read *Chaucer*, so as to understand him perfectly? And
if imperfectly, then with less Profit, and no Pleasure. 'Tis not for the 570

Use of some old *Saxon* Friends, that I have taken these Pains with him: Let them neglect my Version, because they have no need of it. I made it for their sakes who understand Sense and Poetry, as well as they; when that Poetry and Sense is put into Words which they understand. I will go farther, and dare to add, that what Beauties I lose in some Places, I 575 give to others which had them not originally: But in this I may be partial to my self; let the Reader judge, and I submit to his Decision. Yet I think I have just Occasion to complain of them, who because they understand *Chaucer*, would deprive the greater part of their Country-men of the same Advantage, and hoord him up, as Misers do their 580 Grandam Gold, only to look on it themselves, and hinder others from making use of it. In sum, I seriously protest, that no Man ever had, or can have, a greater Veneration for *Chaucer*, than my self. I have trans-lated some part of his Works, only that I might perpetuate his Memory, or at least refresh it, amongst my Countrymen. If I have alter'd him any 585 where for the better, I must at the same time acknowledge, that I could have done nothing without him: *Facile est inventis addere*, is no great Commendation; and I am not so vain to think I have deserv'd a greater. I will conclude what I have to say of him singly, with this one Remark: A Lady of my Acquaintance, who keeps a kind of Correspondence with 590 some Authors of the Fair Sex in *France*, has been inform'd by them, that *Mademoiselle de Scudery*, who is as old as *Sibyl*, and inspir'd like her by the same God of Poetry, is at this time translating *Chaucer* into modern *French*. From which I gather, that he has been formerly translated into the old *Provencall*, (for, how she should come to understand Old *English*, 595 I know not.) But the Matter of Fact being true, it makes me think, that there is something in it like Fatality; that after certain Periods of Time, the Fame and Memory of Great Wits should be renew'd, as *Chaucer* is both in *France* and *England*. If this be wholly Chance, 'tis extraordinary; and I dare not call it more, for fear of being tax'd with Superstition.   600

    Boccace comes last to be consider'd, who living in the same Age with *Chaucer*, had the same Genius, and follow'd the same Studies: Both writ Novels, and each of them cultivated his Mother-Tongue: But the great-est Resemblance of our two Modern Authors being in their familiar Style, and pleasing way of relating Comical Adventures, I may pass it 605 over, because I have translated nothing from *Boccace* of that Nature. In the serious Part of Poetry, the Advantage is wholly on *Chaucer*'s Side; for though the *Englishman* has borrow'd many Tales from the *Italian*, yet it appears, that those of *Boccace* were not generally of his own making, but taken from Authors of former Ages, and by him only modell'd: So 610 that what there was of Invention in either of them, may be judg'd equal. But *Chaucer* has refin'd on *Boccace*, and has mended the Stories which he has borrow'd, in his way of telling; though Prose allows more Liberty of Thought, and the Expression is more easie, when unconfin'd by Numbers. Our Countryman carries Weight, and yet wins the Race at 615 disadvantage. I desire not the Reader should take my Word; and therefore I will set two of their Discourses on the same Subject, in the same Light, for every Man to judge betwixt them. I translated *Chaucer* first, and amongst the rest, pitch'd on the Wife of *Bath*'s Tale; not daring, as I have said, to adventure on her Prologue; because 'tis too licentious: 620 There *Chaucer* introduces an old Woman of mean Parentage, whom a youthful Knight of Noble Blood was forc'd to marry, and consequently loath'd her: The Crone being in bed with him on the wedding Night, and finding his Aversion, endeavours to win his Affection by Reason, and speaks a good Word for her self, (as who could blame her?) in hope 625 to mollifie the sullen Bridegroom. She takes her Topiques from the Benefits of Poverty, the Advantages of old Age and Ugliness, the Vanity of Youth, and the silly Pride of Ancestry and Titles without inherent Vertue, which is the true Nobility. When I had clos'd *Chaucer*, I return'd to *Ovid*, and translated some more of his Fables; and by this time had 630 so far forgotten the Wife of *Bath*'s Tale, that when I took up *Boccace*, unawares I fell on the same Argument of preferring Virtue to Nobility of Blood, and Titles, in the Story of *Sigismonda*; which I had certainly avoided for the Resemblance of the two Discourses, if my Memory had not fail'd me. Let the Reader weigh them both; and if he thinks me 635 partial to *Chaucer*, 'tis in him to right *Boccace.*

I prefer in our Countryman, far above all his other Stories, the Noble Poem of *Palamon* and *Arcite*, which is of the *Epique* kind, and perhaps not much inferiour to the *Ilias* or the *Æneis*: the Story is more pleasing than either of them, the Manners as perfect, the Diction as poetical, the 640 Learning as deep and various; and the Disposition full as artful: only it includes a greater length of time; as taking up seven years at least; but *Aristotle* has left undecided the Duration of the Action; which yet is easily reduc'd into the Compass of a year, by a Narration of what preceded the Return of *Palamon* to *Athens*. I had thought for the Honour of 645 our Nation, and more particularly for his, whose Laurel, tho' unworthy, I have worn after him, that this Story was of *English* Growth, and *Chaucer*'s own: But I was undeceiv'd by *Boccace*; for casually looking on the End of his seventh *Giornata*, I found *Dioneo* (under which name he shadows himself) and *Fiametta* (who represents his Mistress, the natural 650

Daughter of *Robert* King of *Naples*) of whom these Words are spoken. *Dioneo e Fiametta gran pezza cantarono insieme d'Arcita, e di Palamone:* by which it appears that this Story was written before the time of *Boccace*; but the Name of its Author being wholly lost, *Chaucer* is now become an Original; and I question not but the Poem has receiv'd many Beauties 655 by passing through his Noble Hands. Besides this Tale, there is another of his own Invention, after the manner of the *Provencalls*, call'd *The Flower and the Leaf*; with which I was so particularly pleas'd, both for the Invention and the Moral; that I cannot hinder my self from recommending it to the Reader. 660

   As a Corollary to this Preface, in which I have done Justice to others, I owe somewhat to my self: not that I think it worth my time to enter the Lists with one *M*——, or one *B*——, but barely to take notice, that such Men there are who have written scurrilously against me without any Provocation. *M*——, who is in Orders, pretends amongst the rest 665 this Quarrel to me, that I have fallen foul on Priesthood; If I have, I am only to ask Pardon of good Priests, and am afraid his part of the Reparation will come to little. Let him be satisfied that he shall not be able to force himself upon me for an Adversary. I contemn him too much to enter into Competition with him. His own Translations of *Virgil* have 670 answer'd his Criticisms on mine. If (as they say, he has declar'd in Print) he prefers the Version of *Ogilby* to mine, the World has made him the same Compliment: For 'tis agreed on all hands, that he writes even below *Ogilby*: That, you will say, is not easily to be done; but what cannot *M*—— bring about? I am satisfy'd however, that while he and 675 I live together, I shall not be thought the worst Poet of the Age. It looks as if I had desir'd him underhand to write so ill against me: But upon my honest Word I have not brib'd him to do me this Service, and am wholly guiltless of his Pamphlet. 'Tis true I should be glad, if I could persuade him to continue his good Offices, and write such another 680 Critique on any thing of mine: For I find by Experience he has a great Stroke with the Reader, when he condemns any of my Poems to make the World have a better Opinion of them. He has taken some Pains with my Poetry; but no body will be persuaded to take the same with his. If I had taken to the Church (as he affirms, but which was never in my 685 Thoughts) I should have had more Sense, if not more Grace, than to have turn'd my self out of my Benefice by writing Libels on my Parishioners. But his Account of my Manners and my Principles, are of a Piece with his Cavils and his Poetry: And so I have done with him for ever. 690

As for the City Bard, or Knight Physician, I hear his Quarrel to me is, that I was the Author of *Absalom and Achitophel,* which he thinks is a little hard on his Fanatique Patrons in *London.*

But I will deal the more civilly with his two Poems, because nothing ill is to be spoken of the Dead: And therefore Peace be to the *Manes* of 695 his *Arthurs.* I will only say that it was not for this Noble Knight that I drew the Plan of an Epick Poem on King *Arthur* in my Preface to the Translation of *Juvenal.* The Guardian Angels of Kingdoms were Machines too ponderous for him to manage; and therefore he rejected them as *Dares* did the Whirl-bats of *Eryx* when they were thrown before 700 him by *Entellus*: Yet from that Preface he plainly took his Hint: For he began immediately upon the Story; though he had the Baseness not to acknowledge his Benefactor; but in stead of it, to traduce me in a Libel.

I shall say the less of Mr. *Collier,* because in many Things he has tax'd me justly; and I have pleaded Guilty to all Thoughts and Expressions 705 of mine, which can be truly argu'd of Obscenity, Profaneness, or Immorality; and retract them. If he be my Enemy, let him triumph; if he be my Friend, as I have given him no Personal Occasion to be otherwise, he will be glad of my Repentance. It becomes me not to draw my Pen in the Defence of a bad Cause, when I have so often drawn it for a good 710 one. Yet it were not difficult to prove, that in many Places he has perverted my Meaning by his Glosses; and interpreted my Words into Blasphemy and Baudry, of which they were not guilty. Besides that, he is too much given to Horse-play in his Raillery; and comes to Battel, like a Dictatour from the Plough. I will not say, *The Zeal of God's House* 715 *has eaten him up;* but I am sure it has devour'd some Part of his Good Manners and Civility. It might also be doubted, whether it were altogether Zeal, which prompted him to this rough manner of Proceeding; perhaps it became not one of his Function to rake into the Rubbish of Ancient and Modern Plays; a Divine might have employ'd 720 his Pains to better purpose, than in the Nastiness of *Plautus* and *Aristophanes*; whose Examples, as they excuse not me, so it might be possibly suppos'd, that he read them not without some Pleasure. They who have written Commentaries on those Poets, or on *Horace, Juvenal,* and *Martial,* have explain'd some Vices, which without their Inter- 725 pretation had been unknown to Modern Times. Neither has he judg'd impartially betwixt the former Age and us.

There is more Baudry in one Play of *Fletcher*'s, call'd *The Custom of the Country,* than in all ours together. Yet this has been often acted on the

692 *Achitophel*] *Architophel* F

Stage in my remembrance. Are the Times so much more reform'd now, 730 than they were Five and twenty Years ago? If they are, I congratulate the Amendment of our Morals. But I am not to prejudice the Cause of my Fellow-Poets, though I abandon my own Defence: They have some of them answer'd for themselves, and neither they nor I can think Mr. *Collier* so formidable an Enemy, that we should shun him. He has 735 lost Ground at the latter end of the Day, by pursuing his Point too far, like the Prince of *Condé* at the Battel of *Senneph*: From Immoral Plays, to No Plays; *ab abusu ad usum, non valet consequentia.* But being a Party, I am not to erect my self into a Judge. As for the rest of those who have written against me, they are such Scoundrels, that they deserve not the 740 least Notice to be taken of them. *B*—— and *M*—— are only distin-guish'd from the Crowd, by being remember'd to their Infamy.

———————*Demetri, Teque Tigelli*
Discipularum inter jubeo plorare cathedras.

TO HER GRACE
THE DUTCHESS OF ORMOND,
With the following POEM of
Palamon and Arcite, from CHAUCER

MADAM,

THE Bard who first adorn'd our Native Tongue
Tun'd to his *British* Lyre this ancient Song:
Which *Homer* might without a Blush reherse,
And leaves a doubtful Palm in *Virgil*'s Verse:
He match'd their Beauties, where they most excell; 5
Of Love sung better, and of Arms as well.
Vouchsafe, Illustrious *Ormond*, to behold
What Pow'r the Charms of Beauty had of old;
Nor wonder if such Deeds of Arms were done,
Inspir'd by two fair Eyes, that sparkled like your own. 10
If *Chaucer* by the best Idea wrought,
And Poets can divine each others Thought,
The fairest Nymph before his Eyes he set;
And then the fairest was *Plantagenet*;
Who three contending Princes made her Prize, 15
And rul'd the Rival-Nations with her Eyes:

Who left Immortal Trophies of her Fame,
And to the Noblest Order gave the Name.
　　Like Her, of equal Kindred to the Throne,
You keep her Conquests, and extend your own: 20
As when the Stars, in their Etherial Race,
At length have roll'd around the Liquid Space,
At certain Periods they resume their Place,
From the same Point of Heav'n their Course advance,
And move in Measures of their former Dance;   25
Thus, after length of Ages, she returns,
Restor'd in you, and the same Place adorns;
Or you perform her Office in the Sphere,
Born of her Blood, and make a new Platonick Year.
　　O true *Plantagenet*, O Race Divine,   30
(For Beauty still is fatal to the Line,)
Had *Chaucer* liv'd that Angel-Face to view,
Sure he had drawn his *Emily* from You:
Or had You liv'd, to judge the doubtful Right,
Your Noble *Palamon* had been the Knight: 35
And Conqu'ring *Theseus* from his Side had sent
Your Gen'rous Lord, to guide the *Theban* Government.
　　Time shall accomplish that; and I shall see
A *Palamon* in Him, in You an *Emily*.
　　Already have the Fates your Path prepar'd,   40
And sure Presage your future Sway declar'd:
When Westward, like the Sun, you took your Way,
And from benighted *Britain* bore the Day,
Blue *Triton* gave the Signal from the Shore,
The ready *Nereids* heard, and swam before   45
To smooth the Seas; a soft *Etesian* Gale
But just inspir'd, and gently swell'd the Sail;
Portunus took his Turn, whose ample Hand
Heav'd up the lighten'd Keel, and sunk the Sand,
And steer'd the sacred Vessel safe to Land.   50
The Land, if not restrain'd, had met Your Way,
Projected out a Neck, and jutted to the Sea.
Hibernia, prostrate at Your Feet, ador'd,
In You, the Pledge of her expected Lord;
Due to her Isle; a venerable Name;   55
His Father and his Grandsire known to Fame:

Aw'd by that House, accustom'd to command,
The sturdy *Kerns* in due Subjection stand;
Nor hear the Reins in any Foreign Hand.

   At Your Approach, they crowded to the Port;   60
And scarcely Landed, You create a Court:
As *Ormond*'s Harbinger, to You they run;
For *Venus* is the Promise of the *Sun*.

   The Waste of Civil Wars, their Towns destroy'd,
Pales unhonour'd, *Ceres* unemploy'd,   65
Were all forgot; and one Triumphant Day
Wip'd all the Tears of three Campaigns away.
Blood, Rapines, Massacres, were cheaply bought,
So mighty Recompence Your Beauty brought.

   As when the Dove returning, bore the Mark   70
Of Earth restor'd to the long-lab'ring Ark,
The Relicks of Mankind, secure of Rest,
Op'd ev'ry Window to receive the Guest,
And the fair Bearer of the Message bless'd;
So, when You came, with loud repeated Cries,   75
The Nation took an Omen from your Eyes,
And God advanc'd his Rainbow in the Skies,
To sign inviolable Peace restor'd;
The Saints with solemn Shouts proclaim'd the new accord.

   When at Your second Coming You appear,   80
(For I foretell that Millenary Year)
The sharpen'd Share shall vex the Soil no more,
But Earth unbidden shall produce her Store:
The Land shall laugh, the circling Ocean smile,
And Heav'ns Indulgence bless the Holy Isle.   85

   Heav'n from all Ages has reserv'd for You
That happy Clyme, which Venom never knew;
Or if it had been there, Your Eyes alone
Have Pow'r to chase all Poyson, but their own.

   Now in this Interval, which Fate has cast   90
Betwixt Your Future Glories, and Your Past,
This Pause of Pow'r, 'tis *Irelands* Hour to mourn;
While *England* celebrates Your safe Return,
By which You seem the Seasons to command,
And bring our Summers back to their forsaken Land.   95

The Vanquish'd Isle our Leisure must attend,
Till the Fair Blessing we vouchsafe to send;
Nor can we spare You long, though often we may lend.
The Dove was twice employ'd abroad, before
The World was dry'd; and she return'd no more.   100
 Nor dare we trust so soft a Messenger,
New from her Sickness, to that Northern Air;
Rest here a while, Your Lustre to restore,
That they may see You as You shone before:
For yet, th' Eclipse not wholly past, You wade   105
Thro' some Remains, and Dimness of a Shade.
 A Subject in his Prince may claim a Right,
Nor suffer him with Strength impair'd to fight;
Till Force returns, his Ardour we restrain,
And curb his Warlike Wish to cross the Main.   110
 Now past the Danger, let the Learn'd begin
Th' Enquiry, where Disease could enter in;
How those malignant Atoms forc'd their Way,
What in the faultless Frame they found to make their Prey?
Where ev'ry Element was weigh'd so well,   115
That Heav'n alone, who mix'd the Mass, could tell
Which of the Four Ingredients could rebel;
And where, imprison'd in so sweet a Cage,
A Soul might well be pleas'd to pass an Age.
 And yet the fine Materials made it weak;   120
Porcelain by being Pure, is apt to break:
Ev'n to Your Breast the Sickness durst aspire;
And forc'd from that fair Temple to retire,
Profanely set the Holy Place on Fire.
In vain Your Lord like young *Vespasian* mourn'd,   125
When the fierce Flames the Sanctuary burn'd:
And I prepar'd to pay in Verses rude
A most detested Act of Gratitude:
Ev'n this had been Your Elegy, which now
Is offer'd for Your Health, the Table of my Vow.   130
 Your Angel sure our *Morley*'s Mind inspir'd,
To find the Remedy Your Ill requir'd;
As once the *Macedon*, by *Jove*'s Decree,
Was taught to dream an Herb for *Ptolomee*:

To the Dutchess. 102 Sickness,] Sickness F

Or Heav'n, which had such Over-cost bestow'd,   135
As scarce it could afford to Flesh and Blood,
So lik'd the Frame, he would not work anew,
To save the Charges of another You.
Or by his middle Science did he steer,
And saw some great contingent Good appear,   } 140
Well worth a Miracle to keep You here:
And for that End, preserv'd the precious Mould,
Which all the future *Ormonds* was to hold;
And meditated in his better Mind
An Heir from You, who may redeem the failing Kind.   145
    Bless'd be the Pow'r which has at once restor'd
The Hopes of lost Succession to Your Lord,
Joy to the first, and last of each Degree,
Vertue to Courts, and what I long'd to see,   } 150
To You the Graces, and the Muse to me.
    O Daughter of the Rose, whose Cheeks unite
The diff'ring Titles of the Red and White;
Who Heav'ns alternate Beauty well display,
The Blush of Morning, and the Milky Way;
Whose Face is Paradise, but fenc'd from Sin: 155
For God in either Eye has plac'd a Cherubin.
    All is Your Lord's alone; ev'n absent, He
Employs the Care of Chast *Penelope.*
For him You waste in Tears Your Widow'd Hours,
For him Your curious Needle paints the Flow'rs: 160
Such Works of Old Imperial Dames were taught;
Such for *Ascanius*, fair *Elisa* wrought.
    The soft Recesses of Your Hours improve
The Three fair Pledges of Your Happy Love:
All other Parts of Pious Duty done,   165
You owe Your *Ormond* nothing but a Son:
To fill in future Times his Father's Place,
And wear the Garter of his Mother's Race.

PALAMON AND ARCITE:

Or, The Knight's Tale, from CHAUCER.
In Three Books.

BOOK I

I N Days of old, there liv'd, of mighty Fame
 A valiant Prince; and *Theseus* was his Name:
A Chief, who more in Feats of Arms excell'd
The Rising nor the Setting Sun beheld.
Of *Athens* he was Lord; much Land he won,　　　　　5
And added Foreign Countrys to his Crown:
In *Scythia* with the Warriour Queen he strove,
Whom first by Force he conquer'd, then by Love;
He brought in Triumph back the beauteous Dame,
With whom her Sister, fair *Emilia*, came.　　　　　10
With Honour to his Home let *Theseus* ride, ⎫
With Love to Friend, and Fortune for his Guide, ⎬
And his victorious Army at his Side. ⎭
I pass their warlike Pomp, their proud Array,
Their Shouts, their Songs, their Welcome on the Way:　15
But, were it not too long, I would recite ⎫
The Feats of *Amazons*, the fatal Fight ⎬
Betwixt the hardy Queen, and *Heroe* Knight. ⎭
The Town besieg'd, and how much Blood it cost
The Female Army, and th' *Athenian* Host;　　　　　20
The Spousals of *Hippolita* the Queen;
What Tilts, and Turneys at the Feast were seen;
The Storm at their Return, the Ladies Fear:
But these and other Things I must forbear.
The Field is spacious I design to sow,　　　　　25
With Oxen far unfit to draw the Plow:
The Remnant of my Tale is of a length
To tire your Patience, and to waste my Strength;
And trivial Accidents shall be forborn,
That others may have time to take their Turn;　　　30
As was at first enjoin'd us by mine Host: ⎫
That he whose Tale is best, and pleases most, ⎬
Should win his Supper at our common Cost. ⎭

And therefore where I left, I will pursue
This ancient Story, whether false or true, } 35
In hope it may be mended with a new.
The Prince I mention'd, full of high Renown,
In this Array drew near th' *Athenian* Town;
When in his Pomp and utmost of his Pride,
Marching, he chanc'd to cast his Eye aside, 40
And saw a Quire of mourning Dames, who lay
By Two and Two across the common Way:
At his Approach they rais'd a rueful Cry,
And beat their Breasts, and held their Hands on high,
Creeping and crying, till they seiz'd at last 45
His Coursers Bridle, and his Feet embrac'd.

Tell me, said *Theseus*, what and whence you are,
And why this Funeral Pageant you prepare?
Is this the Welcome of my worthy Deeds,
To meet my Triumph in Ill-omen'd Weeds? 50
Or envy you my Praise, and would destroy
With Grief my Pleasures, and pollute my Joy?
Or are you injur'd, and demand Relief?
Name your Request, and I will ease your Grief.

The most in Years of all the Mourning Train 55
Began; (but sounded first away for Pain)
Then scarce recover'd, spoke: Nor envy we
Thy great Renown, nor grudge thy Victory;
'Tis thine, O King, th' Afflicted to redress,
And Fame has fill'd the World with thy Success: 60
We wretched Women sue for that alone,
Which of thy Goodness is refus'd to none:
Let fall some Drops of Pity on our Grief,
If what we beg be just, and we deserve Relief:
For none of us, who now thy Grace implore, 65
But held the Rank of Sovereign Queen before;
Till, thanks to giddy Chance, which never bears
That Mortal Bliss should last for length of Years,
She cast us headlong from our high Estate,
And here in hope of thy Return we wait: 70
And long have waited in the Temple nigh,
Built to the gracious Goddess *Clemency*.
But rev'rence thou the Pow'r whose Name it bears,

Relieve th' Oppress'd, and wipe the Widows Tears.
I, wretched I, have other Fortune seen,   75
The Wife of *Capaneus*, and once a Queen:
At *Thebes* he fell; curs'd be the fatal Day!
And all the rest thou seest in this Array,
To make their moan, their Lords in Battel lost
Before that Town besieg'd by our Confed'rate Host: 80
But *Creon*, old and impious, who commands
The *Theban* City, and usurps the Lands,
Denies the Rites of Fun'ral Fires to those
Whose breathless Bodies yet he calls his Foes.
Unburn'd, unbury'd, on a Heap they lie;   85
Such is their Fate, and such his Tyranny;
No Friend has leave to bear away the Dead,
But with their Lifeless Limbs his Hounds are fed:
At this she skriek'd aloud, the mournful Train
Echo'd her Grief, and grov'ling on the Plain,   90
With Groans, and Hands upheld, to move his Mind,
Besought his Pity to their helpless Kind!
    The Prince was touch'd, his Tears began to flow,
And, as his tender Heart would break in two,
He sigh'd; and could not but their Fate deplore,   95
So wretched now, so fortunate before.
Then lightly from his lofty Steed he flew,
And raising one by one the suppliant Crew,
To comfort each, full solemnly he swore,
That by the Faith which Knights to Knighthood bore,   100
And what e'er else to Chivalry belongs,
He would not cease, till he reveng'd their Wrongs:
That *Greece* shou'd see perform'd what he declar'd,
And cruel *Creon* find his just Reward.
He said no more, but shunning all Delay,   105
Rode on; nor enter'd *Athens* on his Way:
But left his Sister and his Queen behind,
And wav'd his Royal Banner in the Wind:
Where in an *Argent* Field the God of War
Was drawn triumphant on his Iron Carr;   110
Red was his Sword, and Shield, and whole Attire,
And all the Godhead seem'd to glow with Fire;
Ev'n the Ground glitter'd where the Standard flew,

And the green Grass was dy'd to sanguin Hue.
High on his pointed Lance his Pennon bore 115
His *Cretan* Fight, the conquer'd *Minotaure*:
The Soldiers shout around with generous Rage,
And in that Victory, their own presage.
He prais'd their Ardour: inly pleas'd to see
His Host the Flow'r of *Grecian* Chivalry. 120
All Day he march'd; and all th' ensuing Night;
And saw the City with returning Light.
The Process of the War I need not tell,
How *Theseus* conquer'd, and how *Creon* fell:
Or after, how by Storm the Walls were won, 125
Or how the Victor sack'd and burn'd the Town:
How to the Ladies he restor'd again
The Bodies of their Lords in Battel slain:
And with what ancient Rites they were interr'd;
All these to fitter time shall be deferr'd: 130
I spare the Widows Tears, their woful Cries
And Howling at their Husbands Obsequies;
How *Theseus* at these Fun'rals did assist,
And with what Gifts the mourning Dames dismiss'd.
  Thus when the Victor Chief had *Creon* slain, 135
And conquer'd *Thebes*, he pitch'd upon the Plain
His mighty Camp, and when the Day return'd,
The Country wasted, and the Hamlets burn'd;
And left the Pillagers, to Rapine bred,
Without Controul to strip and spoil the Dead: 140
  There, in a Heap of Slain, among the rest
Two youthful Knights they found beneath a Load oppress'd
Of slaughter'd Foes, whom first to Death they sent,
The Trophies of their Strength, a bloody Monument.
Both fair, and both of Royal Blood they seem'd, 145
Whom Kinsmen to the Crown the Heralds deem'd;
That Day in equal Arms they fought for Fame;
Their Swords, their Shields, their Surcoats were the same.
Close by each other laid they press'd the Ground,
Their manly Bosoms pierc'd with many a griesly Wound; 150
Nor well alive, nor wholly dead they were,
But some faint Signs of feeble Life appear:
The wandring Breath was on the Wing to part,

Weak was the Pulse, and hardly heav'd the Heart.
These two were Sisters Sons; and *Arcite* one,   155
Much fam'd in Fields, with valiant *Palamon.*
From These their costly Arms the Spoilers rent,
And softly both convey'd to *Theseus* Tent;
Whom known of *Creon*'s Line, and cur'd with care,
He to his City sent as Pris'ners of the War,   160
Hopeless of Ransom, and condemn'd to lie
In Durance, doom'd a lingring Death to die.
     This done, he march'd away with warlike Sound,
And to his *Athens* turn'd with Laurels crown'd,
Where happy long he liv'd, much lov'd, and more renown'd.   165
But in a Tow'r, and never to be loos'd,
The woful captive Kinsmen are enclos'd;
     Thus Year by Year they pass, and Day by Day,
Till once ('twas on the Morn of chearful *May*)
The young *Emilia,* fairer to be seen   170
Than the fair Lilly on the Flow'ry Green,
More fresh than *May* her self in Blossoms new
(For with the Rosie Colour strove her Hue)
Wak'd as her Custom was before the Day,
To do th' Observance due to sprightly *May*:   175
For sprightly *May* commands our Youth to keep
The Vigils of her Night, and breaks their sluggard Sleep:
Each gentle Breast with kindly Warmth she moves;
Inspires new Flames, revives extinguish'd Loves.
In this Remembrance *Emily* e'er Day   180
Arose, and dress'd her self in rich Array;
Fresh as the Month, and as the Morning fair:
Adown her Shoulders fell her length of Hair:
A Ribband did the braided Tresses bind,
The rest was loose, and wanton'd in the Wind: 185
Aurora had but newly chas'd the Night,
And purpl'd o'er the Sky with blushing Light,
When to the Garden-walk she took her way,
To sport and trip along in Cool of Day,
And offer Maiden Vows in honour of the *May*.   190
     At ev'ry Turn, she made a little Stand,
And thrust among the Thorns her Lilly Hand

Palamon and Arcite. Book I. 179 Loves.] Loves; F

To draw the Rose, and ev'ry Rose she drew
She shook the Stalk, and brush'd away the Dew:
Then party-colour'd Flow'rs of white and red   195
She wove, to make a Garland for her Head:
This done, she sung and caroll'd out so clear,
That Men and Angels might rejoice to hear.
Ev'n wondring *Philomel* forgot to sing;
And learn'd from Her to welcome in the Spring.   200
The Tow'r, of which before was mention made,
Within whose Keep the captive Knights were laid,
Built of a large Extent, and strong withal,
Was one Partition of the Palace Wall:
The Garden was enclos'd within the Square   205
Where young *Emilia* took the Morning-Air.
　It happen'd *Palamon* the Pris'ner Knight,
Restless for Woe, arose before the Light,
And with his Jaylor's leave desir'd to breathe
An Air more wholesom than the Damps beneath.   210
This granted, to the Tow'r he took his way,
Cheer'd with the Promise of a glorious Day:
Then cast a languishing Regard around,
And saw with hateful Eyes the Temples crown'd
With golden Spires, and all the Hostile Ground.   215
He sigh'd, and turn'd his Eyes, because he knew
'Twas but a larger Jayl he had in view:
Then look'd below, and from the Castles height
Beheld a nearer and more pleasing Sight:
The Garden, which before he had not seen,   220
In Springs new Livery clad of White and Green,
Fresh Flow'rs in wide *Parterres*, and shady Walks between.
This view'd, but not enjoy'd, with Arms across
He stood, reflecting on his Country's Loss;
Himself an Object of the Publick Scorn,   225
And often wish'd he never had been born.
At last (for so his Destiny requir'd)
With walking giddy, and with thinking tir'd,
He thro' a little Window cast his Sight,
Tho' thick of Bars, that gave a scanty Light: 230
But ev'n that Glimmering serv'd him to descry
Th' inevitable Charms of *Emily*.

Scarce had he seen, but seiz'd with sudden Smart,
Stung to the Quick, he felt it at his Heart;
Struck blind with overpowering Light he stood,   235
Then started back amaz'd, and cry'd aloud.
    Young *Arcite* heard; and up he ran with haste,
To help his Friend, and in his Arms embrac'd;
And ask'd him why he look'd so deadly wan,
And whence, and how his change of Cheer began?   240
Or who had done th' Offence? But if, said he,
Your Grief alone is hard Captivity;
For Love of Heav'n, with Patience undergo
A cureless Ill, since Fate will have it so:
So stood our *Horoscope* in Chains to lie,   245
And *Saturn* in the Dungeon of the Sky,
Or other baleful Aspect, rul'd our Birth,
When all the friendly Stars were under Earth:
Whate'er betides, by Destiny 'tis done;
And better bear like Men, than vainly seek to shun.   250
Nor of my Bonds, said *Palamon* again,
Nor of unhappy Planets I complain;
But when my mortal Anguish caus'd my Cry,
That Moment I was hurt thro' either Eye;
Pierc'd with a Random-shaft, I faint away   255
And perish with insensible Decay:
A Glance of some new Goddess gave the Wound,
Whom, like *Acteon*, unaware I found.
Look how she walks along yon shady Space,
Not *Juno* moves with more Majestick Grace;   260
And all the *Cyprian* Queen is in her Face.
If thou art *Venus*, (for thy Charms confess
That Face was form'd in Heav'n) nor art thou less;
Disguis'd in Habit, undisguis'd in Shape,
O help us Captives from our Chains to scape;   265
But if our Doom be past in Bonds to lie
For Life, and in a loathsom Dungeon die;
Then be thy Wrath appeas'd with our Disgrace,
And shew Compassion to the *Theban* Race,
Oppress'd by Tyrant Pow'r! While yet he spoke,   270
Arcite on *Emily* had fix'd his Look;
The fatal Dart a ready Passage found,

And deep within his Heart infix'd the Wound:
So that if *Palamon* were wounded sore,
Arcite was hurt as much as he, or more: 275
Then from his inmost Soul he sigh'd, and said,
The Beauty I behold has struck me dead:
Unknowingly she strikes; and kills by chance;
Poyson is in her Eyes, and Death in ev'ry Glance.
O, I must ask; nor ask alone, but move   280
Her Mind to Mercy, or must die for Love.
   Thus *Arcite*: And thus *Palamon* replies,
(Eager his Tone, and ardent were his Eyes.)
Speak'st thou in earnest, or in jesting Vein?
Jesting, said *Arcite*, suits but ill with Pain.   285
It suits far worse (said *Palamon* again,
And bent his Brows) with Men who Honour weigh,
Their Faith to break, their Friendship to betray;
But worst with Thee, of Noble Lineage born,
My Kinsman, and in Arms my Brother sworn.   290
Have we not plighted each our holy Oath,
That one shou'd be the Common Good of both?
One Soul shou'd both inspire, and neither prove
His Fellows Hindrance in pursuit of Love?
To this before the Gods we gave our Hands,   295
And nothing but our Death can break the Bands.
This binds thee, then, to farther my Design;
As I am bound by Vow to farther thine:
Nor canst, nor dar'st thou, Traytor, on the Plain
Appeach my Honour, or thy own maintain,   300
Since thou art of my Council, and the Friend
Whose Faith I trust, and on whose Care depend:
And would'st thou court my Ladies Love, which I
Much rather than release, would chuse to die?
But thou false *Arcite* never shalt obtain   305
Thy bad Pretence; I told thee first my Pain:
For first my Love began e'er thine was born;
Thou, as my Council, and my Brother sworn,
Art bound t' assist my Eldership of Right,
Or justly to be deem'd a perjur'd Knight.   310
   Thus *Palamon*: But *Arcite* with disdain
In haughty Language thus reply'd again:

Forsworn thy self: The Traytor's odious Name
I first return, and then disprove thy Claim.
If Love be Passion, and that Passion nurst   315
With strong Desires, I lov'd the Lady first.
Canst thou pretend Desire, whom Zeal inflam'd
To worship, and a Pow'r Cœlestial nam'd?
Thine was Devotion to the Blest above,
I saw the Woman, and desir'd her Love;   320
First own'd my Passion, and to thee commend
Th' important Secret, as my chosen Friend.
Suppose (which yet I grant not) thy Desire
A Moment elder than my Rival Fire;
Can Chance of seeing first thy Title prove?   325
And know'st thou not, no Law is made for Love?
Law is to Things which to free Choice relate;
Love is not in our Choice, but in our Fate:
Laws are but positive: Loves Pow'r we see
Is Natures Sanction, and her first Decree.   330
Each Day we break the Bond of Humane Laws
For Love, and vindicate the Common Cause.
Laws for Defence of Civil Rights are plac'd,
Love throws the Fences down, and makes a general Waste:
Maids, Widows, Wives, without distinction fall;   335
The sweeping Deluge, Love, comes on, and covers all.
If then the Laws of Friendship I transgress,   ⎫
I keep the Greater, while I break the Less;   ⎬
And both are mad alike, since neither can possess.   ⎭
Both hopeless to be ransom'd, never more   340
To see the Sun, but as he passes o'er.
Like *Esop*'s Hounds contending for the Bone,
Each pleaded Right, and wou'd be Lord alone:
The fruitless Fight continu'd all the Day;
A Cur came by, and snatch'd the Prize away.   345
As Courtiers therefore justle for a Grant,
And when they break their Friendship, plead their Want,
So thou, if Fortune will thy Suit advance,
Love on; nor envy me my equal Chance:
For I must love, and am resolv'd to try   350
My Fate, or failing in th' Adventure die.

342 *new paragraph in* F

Great was their Strife, which hourly was renew'd,
Till each with mortal Hate his Rival view'd:
Now Friends no more, nor walking Hand in Hand;
But when they met, they made a surly Stand; 355
And glar'd like angry Lions as they pass'd,
And wish'd that ev'ry Look might be their last.
    It chanc'd at length, *Perithous* came, t' attend
This worthy *Theseus*, his familiar Friend:
Their Love in early Infancy began, 360
And rose as Childhood ripen'd into Man.
Companions of the War; and lov'd so well,
That when one dy'd, as ancient Stories tell,
His Fellow to redeem him went to Hell.
    But to pursue my Tale; to welcome home 365
His Warlike Brother, is *Perithous* come:
Arcite of *Thebes* was known in Arms long since,
And honour'd by this young *Thessalian* Prince.
Theseus, to gratifie his Friend and Guest,
Who made our *Arcite*'s Freedom his Request, 370
Restor'd to Liberty the Captive Knight,
But on these hard Conditions I recite:
That if hereafter *Arcite* shou'd be found
Within the Compass of *Athenian* Ground,
By Day or Night, or on whate'er Pretence, 375
His Head shou'd pay the Forfeit of th' Offence.
To this, *Perithous* for his Friend, agreed,
And on his Promise was the Pris'ner freed.
    Unpleas'd and pensive hence he takes his way,
At his own Peril; for his Life must pay. 380
Who now but *Arcite* mourns his bitter Fate,
Finds his dear Purchase, and repents too late?
What have I gain'd, he said, in Prison pent,
If I but change my Bonds for Banishment?
And banish'd from her Sight, I suffer more 385
In Freedom, than I felt in Bonds before;
Forc'd from her Presence, and condemn'd to live:
Unwelcom Freedom, and unthank'd Reprieve:
Heav'n is not but where *Emily* abides,
And where she's absent, all is Hell besides. 390
Next to my Day of Birth, was that accurst

Which bound my Friendship to *Perithous* first:
Had I not known that Prince, I still had been
In Bondage, and had still *Emilia* seen:
For tho' I never can her Grace deserve,   395
'Tis Recompence enough to see and serve.
O *Palamon*, my Kinsman and my Friend,
How much more happy Fates thy Love attend!
Thine is th' Adventure; thine the Victory:
Well has thy Fortune turn'd the Dice for thee: 400
Thou on that Angels Face maist feed thy Eyes,
In Prison, no; but blissful Paradise!
Thou daily seest that Sun of Beauty shine,
And lov'st at least in Loves extreamest Line.
I mourn in Absence, Loves Eternal Night,   405
And who can tell but since thou hast her Sight,
And art a comely, young, and valiant Knight,
Fortune (a various Pow'r) may cease to frown,
And by some Ways unknown thy Wishes crown:
But I, the most forlorn of Humane Kind,   410
Nor Help can hope, nor Remedy can find;
But doom'd to drag my loathsom Life in Care,
For my Reward, must end it in Despair.
Fire, Water, Air, and Earth, and Force of Fates
That governs all, and Heav'n that all creates,   415
Nor Art, nor Natures Hand can ease my Grief,
Nothing but Death, the Wretches last Relief:
Then farewel Youth, and all the Joys that dwell
With Youth and Life, and Life it self farewell.
    But why, alas! do mortal Men in vain   420
Of Fortune, Fate, or Providence complain?
God gives us what he knows our Wants require,
And better Things than those which we desire:
Some pray for Riches; Riches they obtain;
But watch'd by Robbers, for their Wealth are slain: 425
Some pray from Prison to be freed; and come
When guilty of their Vows, to fall at home;
Murder'd by those they trusted with their Life,
A favour'd Servant, or a Bosom Wife.
Such dear-bought Blessings happen ev'ry Day,   430
Because we know not for what Things to pray.

Like drunken Sots about the Streets we roam;
Well knows the Sot he has a certain Home;
Yet knows not how to find th' uncertain Place,
And blunders on, and staggers ev'ry Pace. 435
Thus all seek Happiness; but few can find,
For far the greater Part of Men are blind.
This is my Case, who thought our utmost Good
Was in one Word of Freedom understood:
The fatal Blessing came: From Prison free, 440
I starve abroad, and lose the Sight of *Emily.*
    Thus *Arcite*; but if *Arcite* thus deplore
His Suff'rings, *Palamon* yet suffers more.
For when he knew his Rival freed and gone,
He swells with Wrath; he makes outrageous Moan: 445
He frets, he fumes, he stares, he stamps the Ground;
The hollow Tow'r with Clamours rings around:
With briny Tears he bath'd his fetter'd Feet,
And dropp'd all o'er with Agony of Sweat.
Alas! he cry'd, I Wretch in Prison pine, 450
Too happy Rival, while the Fruit is thine:
Thou liv'st at large, thou draw'st thy Native Air,
Pleas'd with thy Freedom, proud of my Despair:
Thou may'st, since thou hast Youth and Courage join'd,
A sweet Behaviour, and a solid Mind, 455
Assemble ours, and all the *Theban* Race,
To vindicate on *Athens* thy Disgrace.
And after (by some Treaty made) possess
Fair *Emily*, the Pledge of lasting Peace.
So thine shall be the beauteous Prize, while I 460
Must languish in Despair, in Prison die.
Thus all th' Advantage of the Strife is thine,
Thy Portion double Joys, and double Sorrows mine.
    The Rage of Jealousie then fir'd his Soul,
And his Face kindl'd like a burning Coal: 465
Now cold Despair, succeeding in her stead,
To livid Paleness turns the glowing Red.
His Blood scarce Liquid, creeps within his Veins,
Like Water, which the freezing Wind constrains.
Then thus he said; Eternal Deities, 470
Who rule the World with absolute Decrees,

And write whatever Time shall bring to pass
With Pens of Adamant, on Plates of Brass;
What is the Race of Humane Kind your Care
Beyond what all his Fellow-Creatures are?   475
He with the rest is liable to Pain,
And like the Sheep, his Brother-Beast, is slain.
Cold, Hunger, Prisons, Ills without a Cure,
All these he must, and guiltless oft, endure:
Or does your Justice, Pow'r, or Prescience fail,   480
When the Good suffer, and the Bad prevail?
What worse to wretched Vertue could befall,
If Fate, or giddy Fortune govern'd all?
Nay, worse than other Beasts is our Estate;
Them, to pursue their Pleasures you create;   485
We, bound by harder Laws, must curb our Will,
And your Commands, not our Desires fulfil:
Then when the Creature is unjustly slain,
Yet after Death at least he feels no Pain;
But Man in Life surcharg'd with Woe before,   490
Not freed when dead, is doom'd to suffer more.
A Serpent shoots his Sting at unaware;
An ambush'd Thief forelays a Traveller;
The Man lies murder'd, while the Thief and Snake,
One gains the Thickets, and one thrids the Brake.   495
This let Divines decide; but well I know,
Iust, or unjust, I have my Share of Woe:
Through *Saturn* seated in a luckless Place,
And *Juno*'s Wrath, that persecutes my Race;
Or *Mars* and *Venus* in a Quartil, move   500
My Pangs of Jealousie for *Arcite*'s Love.
   Let *Palamon* oppress'd in Bondage mourn,
While to his exil'd Rival we return.
By this the Sun declining from his Height,
The Day had shortned to prolong the Night: 505
The lengthen'd Night gave length of Misery
Both to the Captive Lover, and the Free.
For *Palamon* in endless Prison mourns,
And *Arcite* forfeits Life if he returns.
The Banish'd never hopes his Love to see,   510
Nor hopes the Captive Lord his Liberty:

'Tis hard to say who suffers greater Pains,
One sees his Love, but cannot break his Chains:
One free, and all his Motions uncontroul'd,
Beholds whate'er he wou'd, but what he wou'd behold.   515
Judge as you please, for I will haste to tell
What Fortune to the banish'd Knight befel.
When *Arcite* was to *Thebes* return'd again,
The Loss of her he lov'd renew'd his Pain;
What could be worse, than never more to see   520
His Life, his Soul, his charming *Emily*?
He rav'd with all the Madness of Despair,
He roar'd, he beat his Breast, he tore his Hair.
Dry Sorrow in his stupid Eyes appears,
For wanting Nourishment, he wanted Tears: 525
His Eye-balls in their hollow Sockets sink,
Bereft of Sleep; he loaths his Meat and Drink.
He withers at his Heart, and looks as wan
As the pale Spectre of a murder'd Man:
That Pale turns Yellow, and his Face receives   530
The faded Hue of sapless Boxen Leaves:
In solitary Groves he makes his Moan,
Walks early out, and ever is alone.
Nor mix'd in Mirth, in youthful Pleasure shares,
But sighs when Songs and Instruments he hears: 535
His Spirits are so low, his Voice is drown'd,
He hears as from afar, or in a Swound,
Like the deaf Murmurs of a distant Sound:
Uncomb'd his Locks, and squalid his Attire,
Unlike the Trim of Love and gay Desire;   540
But full of museful Mopings, which presage
The loss of Reason, and conclude in Rage.
    This when he had endur'd a Year and more,
Now wholly chang'd from what he was before,
It happen'd once, that slumbring as he lay,   545
He dreamt (his Dream began at Break of Day)
That *Hermes* o'er his Head in Air appear'd,
And with soft Words his drooping Spirits cheer'd:
His Hat, adorn'd with Wings, disclos'd the God,
And in his Hand he bore the Sleep-compelling Rod: 550
Such as he seem'd, when at his Sire's Command

On *Argus* Head he laid the Snaky Wand:
Arise, he said, to conqu'ring *Athens* go,
There Fate appoints an End of all thy Woe.
The Fright awaken'd *Arcite* with a Start,   555
Against his Bosom bounc'd his heaving Heart;
But soon he said, with scarce-recover'd Breath,
And thither will I go, to meet my Death,
Sure to be slain; but Death is my Desire,
Since in *Emilia*'s Sight I shall expire.   560
By chance he spy'd a Mirrour while he spoke,
And gazing there beheld his alter'd Look;
Wondring, he saw his Features and his Hue
So much were chang'd, that scarce himself he knew.
A sudden Thought then starting in his Mind,   565
Since I in *Arcite* cannot *Arcite* find,
The World may search in vain with all their Eyes,
But never penetrate through this Disguise.
Thanks to the Change which Grief and Sickness give,
In low Estate I may securely live,   570
And see unknown my Mistress Day by Day:
He said; and cloth'd himself in course Array;
A lab'ring Hind in shew: Then forth he went,
And to th' *Athenian* Tow'rs his Journey bent:
One Squire attended in the same Disguise,   575
Made conscious of his Master's Enterprize.
Arriv'd at *Athens*, soon he came to Court,
Unknown, unquestion'd in that thick Resort;
Proff'ring for Hire his Service at the Gate,
To drudge, draw Water, and to run or wait.   580
    So fair befel him, that for little Gain
He serv'd at first *Emilia*'s Chamberlain;
And watchful all Advantages to spy,
Was still at Hand, and in his Master's Eye;
And as his Bones were big, and Sinews strong,   585
Refus'd no Toil that could to Slaves belong;
But from deep Wells with Engines Water drew,
And us'd his Noble Hands the Wood to hew.
He pass'd a Year at least attending thus
On *Emily*, and call'd *Philostratus*.   590

552 Wand:] Wand; F

But never was there Man of his Degree
So much esteem'd, so well belov'd as he.
So gentle of Condition was he known,
That through the Court his Courtesie was blown:
All think him worthy of a greater Place,   595
And recommend him to the Royal Grace;
That exercis'd within a higher Sphere,
His Vertues more conspicuous might appear.
Thus by the general Voice was *Arcite* prais'd,
And by Great *Theseus* to high Favour rais'd;   600
Among his Menial Servants first enroll'd,
And largely entertain'd with Sums of Gold:
Besides what secretly from *Thebes* was sent,
Of his own Income, and his Annual Rent.
This well employ'd, he purchas'd Friends and Fame,   605
But cautiously conceal'd from whence it came.
Thus for three Years he liv'd with large Increase,
In Arms of Honour, and Esteem in Peace;
To *Theseus* Person he was ever near,
And *Theseus* for his Vertues held him dear.   610

PALAMON AND ARCITE:
Or, The Knight's Tale.

BOOK II

WHILE *Arcite* lives in Bliss, the Story turns
    Where hopeless *Palamon* in Prison mourns.
For six long Years immur'd, the captive Knight
Had dragg'd his Chains, and scarcely seen the Light:
Lost Liberty, and Love at once he bore;   5
His Prison pain'd him much, his Passion more:
Nor dares he hope his Fetters to remove,
Nor ever wishes to be free from Love.
    But when the sixth revolving Year was run,
And *May* within the *Twins* receiv'd the Sun,   10
Were it by Chance, or forceful Destiny,
Which forms in Causes first whate'er shall be,
Assisted by a Friend one Moonless Night,

This *Palamon* from Prison took his Flight:
A pleasant Beverage he prepar'd before   15
Of Wine and Honey mix'd, with added Store
Of *Opium*; to his Keeper this he brought,
Who swallow'd unaware the sleepy Draught,
And snor'd secure till Morn, his Senses bound
In Slumber, and in long Oblivion drown'd.   20
Short was the Night, and careful *Palamon*
Sought the next Covert e'er the Rising Sun.
A thick spread Forest near the City lay,
To this with lengthen'd Strides he took his way,
(For far he cou'd not fly, and fear'd the Day:)   25
Safe from Pursuit, he meant to shun the Light,
Till the brown Shadows of the friendly Night
To *Thebes* might favour his intended Flight.
When to his Country come, his next Design
Was all the *Theban* Race in Arms to join,   30
And war on *Theseus*, till he lost his Life,
Or won the Beauteous *Emily* to Wife.
Thus while his Thoughts the lingring Day beguile,
To gentle *Arcite* let us turn our Style;
Who little dreamt how nigh he was to Care,   35
Till treacherous Fortune caught him in the Snare.
The Morning-Lark, the Messenger of Day,
Saluted in her Song the Morning gray;
And soon the Sun arose with Beams so bright,
That all th' Horizon laugh'd to see the joyous Sight;   40
He with his tepid Rays the Rose renews,
And licks the dropping Leaves, and dries the Dews;
When *Arcite* left his Bed, resolv'd to pay
Observance to the Month of merry *May*:
Forth on his fiery Steed betimes he rode,   45
That scarcely prints the Turf on which he trod:
At ease he seem'd, and pransing o'er the Plains,
Turn'd only to the Grove his Horses Reins,
The Grove I nam'd before; and lighting there,
A Woodbind Garland sought to crown his Hair;   50
Then turn'd his Face against the rising Day,
And rais'd his Voice to welcom in the *May*.
  For thee, sweet Month, the Groves green Liv'ries wear:

If not the first, the fairest of the Year:
For thee the Graces lead the dancing Hours,   55
And Nature's ready Pencil paints the Flow'rs:
When thy short Reign is past, the Fev'rish Sun
The sultry Tropick fears, and moves more slowly on.
So may thy tender Blossoms fear no Blite,
Nor Goats with venom'd Teeth thy Tendrils bite,   60
As thou shalt guide my wandring Feet to find
The fragrant Greens I seek, my Brows to bind.

   His Vows address'd, within the Grove he stray'd, ⎫
Till Fate, or Fortune, near the Place convey'd   ⎬
His Steps where secret *Palamon* was laid.   ⎭ 65
Full little thought of him the gentle Knight,   ⎫
Who flying Death had there conceal'd his Flight,   ⎬
In Brakes and Brambles hid, and shunning Mortal Sight. ⎭
And less he knew him for his hated Foe,
But fear'd him as a Man he did not know.   70
But as it has been said of ancient Years,
That Fields are full of Eyes, and Woods have Ears;
For this the Wise are ever on their Guard,
For, Unforeseen, they say, is unprepar'd.
Uncautious *Arcite* thought himself alone,   75
And less than all suspected *Palamon*,
Who listning heard him, while he search'd the Grove,
And loudly sung his Roundelay of Love.
But on the sudden stopp'd, and silent stood,
(As Lovers often muse, and change their Mood;)   80
Now high as Heav'n, and then as low as Hell;
Now up, now down, as Buckets in a Well:
For *Venus*, like her Day, will change her Cheer,
And seldom shall we see a *Friday* clear.
Thus *Arcite* having sung, with alter'd Hue   85
Sunk on the Ground, and from his Bosom drew
A desp'rate Sigh, accusing Heav'n and Fate,
And angry *Juno's* unrelenting Hate.
Curs'd be the Day when first I did appear;   ⎫
Let it be blotted from the Calendar,   ⎬ 90
Lest it pollute the Month, and poison all the Year. ⎭
Still will the jealous Queen pursue our Race?
Cadmus is dead, the *Theban* City *was*:

Yet ceases not her Hate: For all who come
From *Cadmus* are involv'd in *Cadmus* Doom.   95
I suffer for my Blood: Unjust Decree!
That punishes another's Crime on me.
In mean Estate I serve my mortal Foe,
The Man who caus'd my Countrys Overthrow.
This is not all; for *Juno*, to my shame,   100
Has forc'd me to forsake my former Name;
Arcite I was, *Philostratus* I am.
That Side of Heav'n is all my Enemy:
Mars ruin'd *Thebes*; his Mother ruin'd me.
Of all the Royal Race remains but one   105
Beside my self, th' unhappy *Palamon*,
Whom *Theseus* holds in Bonds, and will not free;
Without a Crime, except his Kin to me.
Yet these, and all the rest I cou'd endure;
But Love's a Malady without a Cure: 110
Fierce Love has pierc'd me with his fiery Dart,
He fries within, and hisses at my Heart.
Your Eyes, fair *Emily*, my Fate pursue;
I suffer for the rest, I die for you.
Of such a Goddess no Time leaves Record,   115
Who burn'd the Temple where she was ador'd:
And let it burn, I never will complain,
Pleas'd with my Suff'rings, if you knew my Pain.
    At this a sickly Qualm his Heart assail'd,
His Ears ring inward, and his Senses fail'd.   120
No Word miss'd *Palamon* of all he spoke,
But soon to deadly Pale he chang'd his Look:
He trembl'd ev'ry Limb, and felt a Smart,
As if cold Steel had glided through his Heart;
Nor longer staid, but starting from his Place,   125
Discover'd stood, and shew'd his hostile Face:
False Traytor *Arcite*, Traytor to thy Blood,
Bound by thy sacred Oath to seek my Good,
Now art thou found forsworn, for *Emily*;
And dar'st attempt her Love, for whom I die.   130
So hast thou cheated *Theseus* with a Wile,
Against thy Vow, returning to beguile
Under a borrow'd Name: As false to me,

So false thou art to him who set thee free:
But rest assur'd, that either thou shalt die,   135
Or else renounce thy Claim in *Emily*:
For though unarm'd I am, and (freed by Chance)
Am here without my Sword, or pointed Lance;
Hope not, base Man, unquestion'd hence to go,
For I am *Palamon* thy mortal Foe.   140
    Arcite, who heard his Tale, and knew the Man,
His Sword unsheath'd, and fiercely thus began:
Now by the Gods, who govern Heav'n above,
Wert thou not weak with Hunger, mad with Love,
That Word had been thy last, or in this Grove   145
This Hand should force thee to renounce thy Love.
The Surety which I gave thee, I defie;
Fool, not to know that Love endures no Tie,
And *Jove* but laughs at Lovers Perjury.
Know I will serve the Fair in thy despight;   150
But since thou art my Kinsman, and a Knight,
Here, have my Faith, to morrow in this Grove
Our Arms shall plead the Titles of our Love:
And Heav'n so help my Right, as I alone
Will come, and keep the Cause and Quarrel both unknown;   155
With Arms of Proof both for my self and thee;
Chuse thou the best, and leave the worst to me.
And, that at better ease, thou maist abide,
Bedding and Clothes I will this Night provide,
And needful Sustenance, that thou maist be   160
A Conquest better won, and worthy me.
His Promise *Palamon* accepts; but pray'd,
To keep it better than the first he made.
Thus fair they parted till the Morrows Dawn,
For each had laid his plighted Faith to pawn.   165
Oh Love! Thou sternly dost thy Pow'r maintain,
And wilt not bear a Rival in thy Reign,
Tyrants and thou all Fellowship disdain.
This was in *Arcite* prov'd, and *Palamon*,
Both in Despair, yet each would love alone.   170
Arcite return'd, and, as in Honour ty'd,
His Foe with Bedding, and with Food supply'd;
Then, e'er the Day, two Suits of Armour sought,

Which born before him on his Steed he brought:
Both were of shining Steel, and wrought so pure,   175
As might the Strokes of two such Arms endure.
Now, at the Time, and in th' appointed Place,
The Challenger, and Challeng'd, Face to Face,
Approach; each other from afar they knew,
And from afar their Hatred chang'd their Hue.   180
So stands the *Thracian* Heardsman with his Spear,
Full in the Gap, and hopes the hunted Bear,
And hears him rustling in the Wood, and sees
His Course at Distance by the bending Trees;
And thinks, Here comes my mortal Enemy,   185
And either he must fall in Fight, or I:
This while he thinks, he lifts aloft his Dart;
A gen'rous Chilness seizes ev'ry Part;
The Veins pour back the Blood, and fortifie the Heart.

    Thus pale they meet; their Eyes with Fury burn;   190
None greets; for none the Greeting will return:
But in dumb Surliness, each arm'd with Care
His Foe profest, as Brother of the War:
Then both, no Moment lost, at once advance
Against each other, arm'd with Sword and Lance: 195
They lash, they foin, they pass, they strive to bore
Their Corslets, and the thinnest Parts explore.
Thus two long Hours in equal Arms they stood,
And wounded, wound; till both were bath'd in Blood;
And not a Foot of Ground had either got,   200
As if the World depended on the Spot.
Fell *Arcite* like an angry Tyger far'd,
And like a Lion *Palamon* appear'd:
Or as two Boars whom Love to Battel draws,
With rising Bristles, and with froathy Jaws,   205
Their adverse Breasts with Tusks oblique they wound;
With Grunts and Groans the Forest rings around.
So fought the Knights, and fighting must abide,
Till Fate an Umpire sends their Diff'rence to decide.
The Pow'r that ministers to God's Decrees,   210
And executes on Earth what Heav'n foresees,
Call'd Providence, or Chance, or fatal Sway,
Comes with resistless Force, and finds or makes her Way.

Nor Kings, nor Nations, nor united Pow'r
One Moment can retard th' appointed Hour.　　　　215
And some one Day, some wondrous Chance appears,
Which happen'd not in Centuries of Years:
For sure, whate'er we Mortals hate or love,
Or hope, or fear, depends on Pow'rs above;
They move our Appetites to Good or Ill,　　　　220
And by Foresight necessitate the Will.
In *Theseus* this appears; whose youthful Joy
Was Beasts of Chase in Forests to destroy;
This gentle Knight, inspir'd by jolly *May*,
Forsook his easie Couch at early Day,　　　　225
And to the Wood and Wilds pursu'd his Way.
Beside him rode *Hippolita* the Queen,
And *Emily* attir'd in lively Green:
With Horns, and Hounds, and all the tuneful Cry,
To hunt a Royal Hart within the Covert nigh:　　　　230
And as he follow'd *Mars* before, so now
He serves the Goddess of the Silver Bow.
The Way that *Theseus* took was to the Wood
Where the two Knights in cruel Battel stood:
The Laund on which they fought, th' appointed Place　　　　235
In which th' uncoupl'd Hounds began the Chace.
Thither forth-right he rode to rowse the Prey,
That shaded by the Fern in Harbour lay;
And thence dislodg'd, was wont to leave the Wood,
For open Fields, and cross the Crystal Flood.　　　　240
Approach'd, and looking underneath the Sun,
He saw proud *Arcite*, and fierce *Palamon*,
In mortal Battel doubling Blow on Blow,
Like Lightning flam'd their Fauchions to and fro,
And shot a dreadful Gleam; so strong they strook,　　　　245
There seem'd less Force requir'd to fell an Oak:
He gaz'd with Wonder on their equal Might,
Look'd eager on, but knew not either Knight:
Resolv'd to learn, he spurr'd his fiery Steed
With goring Rowels, to provoke his Speed.　　　　250
The Minute ended that began the Race,
So soon he was betwixt 'em on the Place;
And with his Sword unsheath'd, on pain of Life

Commands both Combatants to cease their Strife:
Then with imperious Tone pursues his Threat;   255
What are you? Why in Arms together met?
How dares your Pride presume against my Laws,
As in a listed Field to fight your Cause?
Unask'd the Royal Grant; no Marshal by,
As Knightly Rites require; nor Judge to try?   260
Then *Palamon*, with scarce recover'd Breath,
Thus hasty spoke; We both deserve the Death,
And both wou'd die; for look the World around,
A Pair so wretched is not to be found.
Our Life's a Load; encumber'd with the Charge,   265
We long to set th' imprison'd Soul at large.
Now as thou art a Sovereign Judge, decree
The rightful Doom of Death to him and me,
Let neither find thy Grace; for Grace is Cruelty.
Me first, O kill me first; and cure my Woe: 270
Then sheath the Sword of Justice on my Foe:
Or kill him first; for when his Name is heard,
He foremost will receive his due Reward.
Arcite of *Thebes* is he; thy mortal Foe,
On whom thy Grace did Liberty bestow,   275
But first contracted, that if ever found
By Day or Night upon th' *Athenian* Ground,
His Head should pay the Forfeit: See return'd
The perjur'd Knight, his Oath and Honour scorn'd.
For this is he, who with a borrow'd Name   280
And profer'd Service, to thy Palace came,
Now call'd *Philostratus*: retain'd by thee,
A Traytor trusted, and in high Degree,
Aspiring to the Bed of beauteous *Emily*.
My Part remains: From *Thebes* my Birth I own,   285
And call my self th' unhappy *Palamon*.
Think me not like that Man; since no Disgrace
Can force me to renounce the Honour of my Race.
Know me for what I am: I broke thy Chain,
Nor promis'd I thy Pris'ner to remain: 290
The Love of Liberty with Life is giv'n,
And Life it self th' inferiour Gift of Heaven.
Thus without Crime I fled; but farther know,

I with this *Arcite* am thy mortal Foe:
Then give me Death, since I thy Life pursue,   295
For Safeguard of thy self, Death is my Due.
More would'st thou know? I love bright *Emily*,
And for her Sake, and in her Sight will die:
But kill my Rival too; for he no less
Deserves; and I thy righteous Doom will bless,   } 300
Assur'd that what I lose, he never shall possess.
To this reply'd the stern *Athenian* Prince,
And sow'rly smild, In owning your Offence
You judge your self; and I but keep Record
In place of Law, while you pronounce the Word.   305
Take your Desert, the Death you have decreed;
I seal your Doom, and ratifie the Deed.
By *Mars*, the Patron of my Arms, you die.
   He said; dumb Sorrow seiz'd the Standers by.
The Queen above the rest, by Nature Good,   310
(The Pattern form'd of perfect Womanhood)
For tender Pity wept: When she began,
Through the bright Quire th' infectious Vertue ran.
All dropp'd their Tears, ev'n the contended Maid;
And thus among themselves they softly said: 315
What Eyes can suffer this unworthy Sight!
Two Youths of Royal Blood, renown'd in Fight,
The Mastership of Heav'n in Face and Mind,
And Lovers, far beyond their faithless Kind;
See their wide streaming Wounds; they neither came   320
From Pride of Empire, nor desire of Fame:
Kings fight for Kingdoms, Madmen for Applause;
But Love for Love alone; that crowns the Lover's Cause.
This Thought, which ever bribes the beauteous Kind,
Such Pity wrought in ev'ry Ladies Mind,   325
They left their Steeds, and prostrate on the Place,
From the fierce King, implor'd th' Offenders Grace.
   He paus'd a while, stood silent in his Mood,
(For yet, his Rage was boiling in his Blood)
But soon his tender Mind th' Impression felt,   330
(As softest Metals are not slow to melt
And Pity soonest runs in gentle Minds:)
Then reasons with himself; and first he finds

His Passion cast a Mist before his Sense,
And either made, or magnifi'd th' Offence.   335
Offence! of what? to whom? Who judg'd the Cause?
The Pris'ner freed himself by Natures Laws:
Born free, he sought his Right: The Man he freed
Was perjur'd, but his Love excus'd the Deed:
Thus pond'ring, he look'd under with his Eyes,   340
And saw the Womens Tears, and heard their Cries;
Which mov'd Compassion more: He shook his Head,
And softly sighing to himself, he said,
    Curse on th' unpard'ning Prince, whom Tears can draw
To no Remorse; who rules by Lions Law;   345
And deaf to Pray'rs, by no Submission bow'd,
Rends all alike; the Penitent, and Proud:
At this, with Look serene, he rais'd his Head,
Reason resum'd her Place, and Passion fled:
Then thus aloud he spoke: The Pow'r of Love,   350
In Earth, and Seas, and Air, and Heav'n above,
Rules, unresisted, with an awful Nod;
By daily Miracles declar'd a God:
He blinds the Wise, gives Eye-sight to the Blind;
And moulds and stamps anew the Lover's Mind.   355
Behold that *Arcite*, and this *Palamon*,
Freed from my Fetters, and in Safety gone,
What hinder'd either in their Native Soil
At ease to reap the Harvest of their Toil?
But Love, their Lord, did otherwise ordain,   360
And brought 'em in their own despite again,
To suffer Death deserv'd; for well they know,
'Tis in my Pow'r, and I their deadly Foe;
The Proverb holds, That to be wise and love,
Is hardly granted to the Gods above.   365
See how the Madmen bleed: Behold the Gains
With which their Master, Love, rewards their Pains:
For sev'n long Years, on Duty ev'ry Day,
Lo their Obedience, and their Monarch's Pay:
Yet, as in Duty bound, they serve him on,   370
And ask the Fools, they think it wisely done:
Nor Ease, nor Wealth, nor Life it self regard,
For 'tis their Maxim, Love is Love's Reward.

This is not all; the Fair for whom they strove
Nor knew before, nor could suspect their Love,   375
Nor thought, when she beheld the Fight from far,
Her Beauty was th' Occasion of the War.
But sure a gen'ral Doom on Man is past,
And all are Fools and Lovers, first or last:
This both by others and my self I know,   380
For I have serv'd their Sovereign, long ago.
Oft have been caught within the winding Train
Of Female Snares, and felt the Lovers Pain,
And learn'd how far the God can Humane Hearts constrain.
To this Remembrance, and the Pray'rs of those   385
Who for th' offending Warriors interpose,
I give their forfeit Lives; on this accord,
To do me Homage as their Sov'reign Lord;
And as my Vassals, to their utmost Might,
Assist my Person, and assert my Right.   390
This, freely sworn, the Knights their Grace obtain'd;
Then thus the King his secret Thoughts explain'd:
If Wealth, or Honour, or a Royal Race,
Or each, or all, may win a Ladies Grace,
Then either of you Knights may well deserve   395
A Princess born; and such is she you serve:
For *Emily* is Sister to the Crown,
And but too well to both her Beauty known:
But shou'd you combate till you both were dead,
Two Lovers cannot share a single Bed: 400
As therefore both are equal in Degree,
The Lot of both be left to Destiny.
Now hear th' Award, and happy may it prove
To her, and him who best deserves her Love.
Depart from hence in Peace, and free as Air,   405
Search the wide World, and where you please repair;
But on the Day when this returning Sun
To the same Point through ev'ry Sign has run,
Then each of you his Hundred Knights shall bring,
In Royal Lists, to fight before the King;   410
And then, the Knight whom Fate or happy Chance
Shall with his Friends to Victory advance,
And grace his Arms so far in equal Fight,

From out the Bars to force his Opposite,
Or kill, or make him Recreant on the Plain, 415
The Prize of Valour and of Love shall gain;
The vanquish'd Party shall their Claim release,
And the long Jars conclude in lasting Peace.
The Charge be mine t' adorn the chosen Ground,
The Theatre of War, for Champions so renown'd; 420
And take the Patrons Place of either Knight,
With Eyes impartial to behold the Fight;
And Heav'n of me so judge, as I shall judge aright.
If both are satisfi'd with this Accord,
Swear by the Laws of Knighthood on my Sword. 425
　　Who now but *Palamon* exults with Joy?
And ravish'd *Arcite* seems to touch the Sky:
The whole assembl'd Troop was pleas'd as well,
Extol'd th' Award, and on their Knees they fell
To bless the gracious King. The Knights with Leave 430
Departing from the Place, his last Commands receive;
On *Emily* with equal Ardour look,
And from her Eyes their Inspiration took.
From thence to *Thebes* old Walls pursue their Way,
Each to provide his Champions for the Day. 435
　　It might be deem'd on our Historian's Part,
Or too much Negligence, or want of Art,
If he forgot the vast Magnificence
Of Royal *Theseus*, and his large Expence.
He first enclos'd for Lists a level Ground, 440
The whole Circumference a Mile around:
The Form was Circular; and all without
A Trench was sunk, to Moat the Place about.
Within, an Amphitheatre appear'd,
Rais'd in Degrees; to sixty Paces rear'd: 445
That when a Man was plac'd in one Degree,
Height was allow'd for him above to see.
　　Eastward was built a Gate of Marble white;
The like adorn'd the Western opposite.
A nobler Object than this Fabrick was, 450
Rome never saw; nor of so vast a Space.
For, rich with Spoils of many a conquer'd Land,

Book II. 444 Within,] Within; F

All Arts and Artists *Theseus* could command;
Who sold for Hire, or wrought for better Fame:
The Master-Painters, and the Carvers came.   455
So rose within the Compass of the Year
An Ages Work, a glorious Theatre.
Then, o'er its Eastern Gate was rais'd above
A Temple, sacred to the Queen of Love;
An Altar stood below: On either Hand   460
A Priest with Roses crown'd, who held a Myrtle Wand.
    The Dome of *Mars* was on the Gate oppos'd,
And on the North a Turret was enclos'd,
Within the Wall, of Alabaster white,
And crimson Coral, for the Queen of Night,   } 465
Who takes in Sylvan Sports her chaste Delight.
    Within these Oratories might you see
Rich Carvings, Pourtraitures, and Imagery:
Where ev'ry Figure to the Life express'd
The Godhead's Pow'r to whom it was address'd.   470
In *Venus* Temple, on the Sides were seen
The broken Slumbers of inamour'd Men:
Pray'rs that ev'n spoke, and Pity seem'd to call,
And issuing Sighs that smoak'd along the Wall.
Complaints, and hot Desires, the Lover's Hell,   475
And scalding Tears, that wore a Channel where they fell:
And all around were Nuptial Bonds, the Ties   }
Of Loves Assurance, and a Train of Lies,
That, made in Lust, conclude in Perjuries.
Beauty, and Youth, and Wealth, and Luxury,   480
And spritely Hope, and short-enduring Joy;
And Sorceries to raise th' Infernal Pow'rs,
And Sigils fram'd in Planetary Hours:
Expence, and After-thought, and idle Care,
And Doubts of motley Hue, and dark Despair: 485
Suspicions, and fantastical Surmise,
And Jealousie suffus'd, with Jaundice in her Eyes;
Discolouring all she view'd, in Tawney dress'd;
Down-look'd, and with a Cuckow on her Fist.
Oppos'd to her, on t'other side, advance   490
The costly Feast, the Carol, and the Dance,
Minstrels, and Musick, Poetry, and Play,

And Balls by Night, and Turnaments by Day.
All these were painted on the Wall, and more;
With Acts, and Monuments of Times before: 495
And others added by Prophetick Doom,
And Lovers yet unborn, and Loves to come:
For there, th' *Idalian* Mount, and *Citheron*,
The Court of *Venus*, was in Colours drawn:
Before the Palace-gate, in careless Dress,   500
And loose Array, sat Portress Idleness:
There, by the Fount, *Narcissus* pin'd alone;
There *Samson* was; with wiser *Solomon*,
And all the mighty Names by Love undone:
Medea's Charms were there, *Circean* Feasts,   505
With Bowls that turn'd inamour'd Youth to Beasts.
Here might be seen, that Beauty, Wealth, and Wit,
And Prowess, to the Pow'r of Love submit:
The spreading Snare for all Mankind is laid;
And Lovers all betray, and are betray'd.   510
The Goddess self, some noble Hand had wrought;
Smiling she seem'd, and full of pleasing Thought:
From Ocean as she first began to rise,
And smooth'd the ruffl'd Seas, and clear'd the Skies;
She trode the Brine all bare below the Breast,   515
And the green Waves, but ill conceal'd the rest;
A Lute she held; and on her Head was seen
A Wreath of Roses red, and Myrtles green:
Her Turtles fann'd the buxom Air above;
And, by his Mother, stood an Infant-Love: 520
With Wings unfledg'd; his Eyes were banded o'er;
His Hands a Bow, his Back a Quiver bore,
Supply'd with Arrows bright and keen, a deadly Store.
    But in the Dome of mighty *Mars* the Red,
With diff'rent Figures all the Sides were spread: 525
This Temple, less in Form, with equal Grace
Was imitative of the first in *Thrace*:
For that cold Region was the lov'd Abode,
And Sov'reign Mansion of the Warriour-God.
The Landscape was a Forest wide and bare;   530
Where neither Beast, nor Humane Kind repair;
The Fowl, that scent afar, the Borders fly,

And shun the bitter Blast, and wheel about the Sky.
A Cake of Scurf lies baking on the Ground,
And prickly Stubs, instead of Trees, are found;   535
Or Woods with Knots and Knares, deform'd and old;
Headless the most, and hideous to behold:
A ratling Tempest through the Branches went,
That stripp'd 'em bare, and one sole way they bent.
Heav'n froze above, severe, the Clouds congeal,   540
And through the Crystal Vault appear'd the standing Hail.
Such was the Face without, a Mountain stood
Threatning from high, and overlook'd the Wood:
Beneath the lowring Brow, and on a Bent,
The Temple stood of *Mars* Armipotent: 545
The Frame of burnish'd Steel, that cast a Glare
From far, and seem'd to thaw the freezing Air.
A streight, long Entry, to the Temple led,
Blind with high Walls; and Horrour over Head:
Thence issu'd such a Blast, and hollow Rore,   550
As threaten'd from the Hinge, to heave the Door;
In, through that Door, a Northern Light there shone;
'Twas all it had, for Windows there were none.
The Gate was Adamant; Eternal Frame!
Which hew'd by *Mars* himself, from *Indian* Quarries came,   555
The Labour of a God; and all along
Tough Iron Plates were clench'd to make it strong.
A Tun about, was ev'ry Pillar there;
A polish'd Mirrour shone not half so clear.
There saw I how the secret Fellon wrought,   ⎫   560
And Treason lab'ring in the Traytor's Thought;   ⎬
And Midwife Time the ripen'd Plot to Murder brought.   ⎭
There, the Red Anger dar'd the Pallid Fear;
Next stood Hypocrisie, with holy Lear:
Soft, smiling, and demurely looking down,   565
But hid the Dagger underneath the Gown:
Th' assassinating Wife, the Houshold Fiend;
And far the blackest there, the Traytor-Friend.
On t'other Side there stood Destruction bare;
Unpunish'd Rapine, and a Waste of War.   570
Contest, with sharpen'd Knives in Cloysters drawn,

536 Knots and Knares,] Knots, and Knares *F*

And all with Blood bespread the holy Lawn.
Loud Menaces were heard, and foul Disgrace,
And bawling Infamy, in Language base;
Till Sense was lost in Sound, and Silence fled the Place.   575
The Slayer of Himself yet saw I there,
The Gore congeal'd was clotter'd in his Hair:
With Eyes half clos'd, and gaping Mouth he lay,
And grim, as when he breath'd his sullen Soul away.
In midst of all the Dome, Misfortune sat,   580
And gloomy Discontent, and fell Debate:
And Madness laughing in his ireful Mood;
And arm'd Complaint on Theft; and Cries of Blood.
There was the murder'd Corps, in Covert laid,
And Violent Death in thousand Shapes display'd: 585
The City to the Soldier's Rage resign'd:
Successless Wars, and Poverty behind:
Ships burnt in Fight, or forc'd on Rocky Shores,
And the rash Hunter strangled by the Boars:
The new-born Babe by Nurses overlaid;   590
And the Cook caught within the raging Fire he made.
All Ills of *Mars* his Nature, Flame and Steel:
The gasping Charioteer, beneath the Wheel
Of his own Car; the ruin'd House that falls
And intercepts her Lord betwixt the Walls: 595
The whole Division that to *Mars* pertains,
All Trades of Death that deal in Steel for Gains,
Were there: The Butcher, Armourer, and Smith,
Who forges sharpen'd Fauchions, or the Scythe.
The scarlet Conquest on a Tow'r was plac'd,   600
With Shouts, and Soldiers Acclamations grac'd:
A pointed Sword hung threatning o'er his Head,
Sustain'd but by a slender Twine of Thred.
There saw I *Mars* his *Ides*, the *Capitol*,
The Seer in vain foretelling *Cæsar*'s Fall,   605
The last *Triumvirs*, and the Wars they move,
And *Antony*, who lost the World for Love.
These, and a thousand more, the Fane adorn;
Their Fates were painted e'er the Men were born,
All copied from the Heav'ns, and ruling Force   610
Of the Red Star, in his revolving Course.

The Form of *Mars* high on a Chariot stood,
All sheath'd in Arms, and gruffly look'd the God:
Two Geomantick Figures were display'd
Above his Head, a *Warriour and a Maid,   *Rubeus, & 615
One when Direct, and one when Retrograde.   *Puella.*

   Tir'd with Deformities of Death, I haste
To the third Temple of *Diana* chaste;
A Sylvan Scene with various Greens was drawn,
Shades on the Sides, and on the midst a Lawn: 620
The Silver *Cynthia*, with her Nymphs around,
Pursu'd the flying Deer, the Woods with Horns resound:
Calistho there stood manifest of Shame,
And turn'd a Bear, the Northern Star became:
Her Son was next, and by peculiar Grace   625
In the cold Circle held the second Place:
The Stag *Acteon* in the Stream had spy'd
The naked Huntress, and, for seeing, dy'd:
His Hounds, unknowing of his Change, pursue
The Chace, and their mistaken Master slew.   630
Peneian Daphne too was there to see
Apollo's Love before, and now his Tree:
Th' adjoining Fane th' assembl'd *Greeks* express'd,
And hunting of the *Caledonian* Beast.
Oenides Valour, and his envy'd Prize;   635
The fatal Pow'r of *Atalanta*'s Eyes;
Diana's Vengeance on the Victor shown,
The Murdress Mother, and consuming Son.
The *Volscian* Queen extended on the Plain;
The Treason punish'd, and the Traytor slain.   640
The rest were various Huntings, well design'd,
And Salvage Beasts destroy'd, of ev'ry Kind:
The graceful Goddess was array'd in Green;
About her Feet were little Beagles seen,
That watch'd with upward Eyes the Motions of their Queen. 645
Her Legs were Buskin'd, and the Left before,
In act to shoot, a Silver Bow she bore,
And at her Back a painted Quiver wore.
She trod a wexing Moon, that soon wou'd wane,
And drinking borrow'd Light, be fill'd again: 650
With down-cast Eyes, as seeming to survey

The dark Dominions, her alternate Sway.
Before her stood a Woman in her Throws,
And call'd *Lucina*'s Aid, her Burden to disclose.
All these the Painter drew with such Command,   655
That Nature snatch'd the Pencil from his Hand,
Asham'd and angry that his Art could feign
And mend the Tortures of a Mothers Pain.
Theseus beheld the Fanes of ev'ry God,
And thought his mighty Cost was well bestow'd: 660
So Princes now their Poets should regard;
But few can write, and fewer can reward.
     The Theater thus rais'd, the Lists enclos'd,
And all with vast Magnificence dispos'd,
We leave the Monarch pleas'd, and haste to bring   665
The Knights to combate; and their Arms to sing.

PALAMON AND ARCITE:
Or, The Knight's Tale.

BOOK III

THE Day approach'd when Fortune shou'd decide
     Th' important Enterprize, and give the Bride;
For now, the Rivals round the World had sought,
And each his Number, well appointed, brought.
The Nations far and near, contend in Choice,   5
And send the Flow'r of War by Publick Voice;
That after, or before, were never known
Such Chiefs; as each an Army seem'd alone:
Beside the Champions; all of high Degree,
Who Knighthood lov'd, and Deeds of Chivalry,   10
Throng'd to the Lists, and envy'd to behold
The Names of others, not their own inroll'd.
Nor seems it strange; for ev'ry Noble Knight,
Who loves the Fair, and is endu'd with Might,
In such a Quarrel wou'd be proud to fight.   15
There breaths not scarce a Man on *British* Ground
(An Isle for Love, and Arms of old renown'd)
But would have sold his Life to purchase Fame,

To *Palamon* or *Arcite* sent his Name:
And had the Land selected of the best,   20
Half had come hence, and let the World provide the rest.
A hundred Knights with *Palamon* there came,
Approv'd in Fight, and Men of mighty Name;
Their Arms were sev'ral, as their Nations were,
But furnish'd all alike with Sword and Spear.   25
Some wore Coat-armour, imitating Scale;
And next their Skins were stubborn Shirts of Mail.
Some wore a Breastplate and a light Juppon,
Their Horses cloth'd with rich Caparison:
Some for Defence would Leathern Bucklers use,   30
Of folded Hides; and others Shields of Pruce.
One hung a Poleax at his Saddle-bow,
And one a heavy Mace, to stun the Foe:
One for his Legs and Knees provided well,
With *Jambeux* arm'd, and double Plates of Steel: 35
This on his Helmet wore a Ladies Glove,
And that a Sleeve embroider'd by his Love.
  With *Palamon*, above the rest in Place,
Lycurgus came, the surly King of *Thrace*;
Black was his Beard, and manly was his Face: 40
The Balls of his broad Eyes roll'd in his Head,
And glar'd betwixt a Yellow and a Red:
He look'd a Lion with a gloomy Stare,
And o'er his Eye-brows hung his matted Hair:
Big-bon'd, and large of Limbs, with Sinews strong,   45
Broad-shoulder'd, and his Arms were round and long.
Four Milk-white Bulls (the *Thracian* Use of old)
Were yok'd to draw his Car of burnish'd Gold.
Upright he stood, and bore aloft his Shield,
Conspicuous from afar, and over-look'd the Field.   50
His Surcoat was a Bear-skin on his Back;
His Hair hung long behind, and glossy Raven-black.
His ample Forehead bore a Coronet
With sparkling Diamonds, and with Rubies set:
Ten Brace, and more, of Greyhounds, snowy fair,   55
And tall as Stags, ran loose, and cours'd around his Chair,
A Match for Pards in flight, in grappling, for the Bear:
With Golden Muzzles all their Mouths were bound,

And Collars of the same their Necks surround.
Thus thro' the Fields *Lycurgus* took his way;   60
His hundred Knights attend in Pomp and proud Array.
   To match this Monarch, with strong *Arcite* came
Emetrius King of *Inde*, a mighty Name,
On a Bay Courser, goodly to behold,
The Trappings of his Horse emboss'd with barb'rous Gold.   65
Not *Mars* bestrode a Steed with greater Grace;
His Surcoat o'er his Arms was Cloth of *Thrace*,
Adorn'd with Pearls, all Orient, round, and great;
His Saddle was of Gold, with Emeralds set.
His Shoulders large, a Mantle did attire,   70
With Rubies thick, and sparkling as the Fire:
His Amber-colour'd Locks in Ringlets run,
With graceful Negligence, and shone against the Sun.
His Nose was Aquiline, his Eyes were blue,
Ruddy his Lips, and fresh and fair his Hue: 75
Some sprinkled Freckles on his Face were seen,
Whose Dusk set off the Whiteness of the Skin:
His awful Presence did the Crowd surprize,
Nor durst the rash Spectator meet his Eyes,
Eyes that confess'd him born for Kingly Sway,   80
So fierce, they flash'd intolerable Day.
His Age in Nature's youthful Prime appear'd,
And just began to bloom his yellow Beard.
Whene'er he spoke, his Voice was heard around,
Loud as a Trumpet, with a Silver Sound.   85
A Laurel wreath'd his Temples, fresh, and green;
And Myrtle-sprigs, the Marks of Love, were mix'd between.
Upon his Fist he bore, for his Delight,
An Eagle well reclaim'd, and Lilly-white.
   His hundred Knights attend him to the War,   90
All arm'd for Battel; save their Heads were bare.
Words, and Devices blaz'd on ev'ry Shield,
And pleasing was the Terrour of the Field.
For Kings, and Dukes, and Barons you might see,
Like sparkling Stars, though diff'rent in Degree,   } 95
All for th' Increase of Arms, and Love of Chivalry.
Before the King, tame Leopards led the way,
And Troops of Lions innocently play.

So *Bacchus* through the conquer'd *Indies* rode,
And Beasts in Gambols frisk'd before their honest God.   100
    In this Array the War of either Side
Through *Athens* pass'd with Military Pride.
At Prime, they enter'd on the *Sunday* Morn;
Rich Tap'stry spread the Streets, and Flow'rs the Posts adorn.
The Town was all a Jubilee of Feasts;   105
So *Theseus* will'd, in Honour of his Guests:
Himself with open Arms the Kings embrac'd,
Then all the rest in their Degrees were grac'd.
No Harbinger was needful for the Night,
For ev'ry House was proud to lodge a Knight.   110
    I pass the Royal Treat, nor must relate
The Gifts bestow'd, nor how the Champions sate;
Who first, who last, or how the Knights address'd
Their Vows, or who was fairest at the Feast;
Whose Voice, whose graceful Dance did most surprise,   115
Soft am'rous Sighs, and silent Love of Eyes.
The Rivals call my Muse another way,
To sing their Vigils for th' ensuing Day.
    'Twas ebbing Darkness, past the Noon of Night;
And *Phospher* on the Confines of the Light,   120
Promis'd the Sun; e'er Day began to spring
The tuneful Lark already stretch'd her Wing,
And flick'ring on her Nest, made short Essays to sing:
When wakeful *Palamon*, preventing Day,
Took, to the Royal Lists, his early way,   125
To *Venus* at her Fane, in her own House to pray.
There, falling on his Knees before her Shrine,
He thus implor'd with Pray'rs her Pow'r Divine.
Creator *Venus*, Genial Pow'r of Love,
The Bliss of Men below, and Gods above,   130
Beneath the sliding Sun thou runn'st thy Race,
Dost fairest shine, and best become thy Place.
For thee the Winds their Eastern Blasts forbear,
Thy Month reveals the Spring, and opens all the Year.

Book III. 104 Posts] Pots F. *See Commentary*   119 *Editor's paragraph. In F a new*
paragraph opens at l. 124   121 Sun;] Sun, F   123 sing:] sing. F

Thee, Goddess, thee the Storms of Winter fly, 135
Earth smiles with Flow'rs renewing; laughs the Sky,
And Birds to Lays of Love their tuneful Notes apply.
For thee the Lion loaths the Taste of Blood,
And roaring hunts his Female through the Wood:
For thee the Bulls rebellow through the Groves, 140
And tempt the Stream, and snuff their absent Loves.
'Tis thine, whate'er is pleasant, good, or fair:
All Nature is thy Province, Life thy Care;
Thou mad'st the World, and dost the World repair.
Thou Gladder of the Mount of *Cytheron*, 145
Increase of *Jove*, Companion of the Sun;
If e'er *Adonis* touch'd thy tender Heart,
Have pity, Goddess, for thou know'st the Smart:
Alas! I have not Words to tell my Grief;
To vent my Sorrow wou'd be some Relief: 150
Light Suff'rings give us leisure to complain;
We groan, but cannot speak, in greater Pain.
O Goddess, tell thy self what I would say,
Thou know'st it, and I feel too much to pray.
So grant my Suit, as I enforce my Might, 155
In Love to be thy Champion, and thy Knight;
A Servant to thy Sex, a Slave to thee,
A Foe profest to barren Chastity.
Nor ask I Fame or Honour of the Field,
Nor chuse I more to vanquish, than to yield: 160
In my Divine *Emilia* make me blest,
Let Fate, or partial Chance, dispose the rest:
Find thou the Manner, and the Means prepare;
Possession, more than Conquest, is my Care.
Mars is the Warriour's God; in him it lies, 165
On whom he favours, to confer the Prize;
With smiling Aspect you serenely move
In your fifth Orb, and rule the Realm of Love.
The Fates but only spin the courser Clue,
The finest of the Wooll is left for you. 170
Spare me but one small Portion of the Twine,
And let the Sisters cut below your Line:
The rest among the Rubbish may they sweep,
Or add it to the Yarn of some old Miser's Heap.

But if you this ambitious Pray'r deny,   175
(A Wish, I grant, beyond Mortality)
Then let me sink beneath proud *Arcite*'s Arms,
And I once dead, let him possess her Charms.
   Thus ended he; then, with Observance due,
The sacred Incence on her Altar threw: 180
The curling Smoke mounts heavy from the Fires;
At length it catches Flame, and in a Blaze expires;
At once the gracious Goddess gave the Sign,
Her Statue shook, and trembl'd all the Shrine:
Pleas'd *Palamon* the tardy *Omen* took: 185
For, since the Flames pursu'd the trailing Smoke,
He knew his Boon was granted; but the Day
To distance driv'n, and Joy adjourn'd with long Delay.
   Now Morn with Rosie Light had streak'd the Sky,
Up rose the Sun, and up rose *Emily*;   190
Address'd her early Steps to *Cynthia*'s Fane,
In State attended by her Maiden Train,
Who bore the Vests that Holy Rites require,
Incence, and od'rous Gums, and cover'd Fire.
The plenteous Horns with pleasant Mead they crown,   195
Nor wanted ought besides in honour of the Moon.
Now while the Temple smoak'd with hallow'd Steam,
They wash the Virgin in a living Stream;
The secret Ceremonies I conceal:
Uncouth; perhaps unlawful to reveal: 200
But such they were as Pagan Use requir'd,
Perform'd by Women when the Men retir'd,
Whose Eyes profane, their chast mysterious Rites
Might turn to Scandal, or obscene Delights.
Well-meaners think no Harm; but for the rest,   205
Things Sacred they pervert, and Silence is the best.
Her shining Hair, uncomb'd, was loosly spread,
A Crown of Mastless Oak adorn'd her Head:
When to the Shrine approach'd, the spotless Maid
Had kindling Fires on either Altar laid: 210
(The Rites were such as were observ'd of old,
By *Statius* in his *Theban* Story told.)
Then kneeling with her Hands across her Breast,

209 approach'd,] approach'd *F*   Maid] Maid, *F*

Thus lowly she preferr'd her chast Request.
    O Goddess, Haunter of the Woodland Green, 215
To whom both Heav'n and Earth and Seas are seen;
Queen of the nether Skies, where half the Year
Thy Silver Beams descend, and light the gloomy Sphere;
Goddess of Maids, and conscious of our Hearts,
So keep me from the Vengeance of thy Darts, 220
Which *Niobe*'s devoted Issue felt,
When hissing through the Skies the feather'd Deaths were dealt:
As I desire to live a Virgin-life,
Nor know the Name of Mother or of Wife.
Thy Votress from my tender Years I am, 225
And love, like thee, the Woods and Sylvan Game.
Like Death, thou know'st, I loath the Nuptial State,
And Man, the Tyrant of our Sex, I hate,
A lowly Servant, but a lofty Mate.
Where Love is Duty, on the Female Side; 230
On theirs meer sensual Gust, and sought with surly Pride.
Now by thy triple Shape, as thou art seen
In Heav'n, Earth, Hell, and ev'ry where a Queen,
Grant this my first Desire; let Discord cease,
And make betwixt the Rivals lasting Peace: 235
Quench their hot Fire, or far from me remove
The Flame, and turn it on some other Love.
Or if my frowning Stars have so decreed,
That one must be rejected, one succeed,
Make him my Lord within whose faithful Breast 240
Is fix'd my Image, and who loves me best.
But, oh! ev'n that avert! I chuse it not,
But take it as the least unhappy Lot.
A Maid I am, and of thy Virgin-Train;
Oh, let me still that spotless Name retain! 245
Frequent the Forests, thy chast Will obey,
And only make the Beasts of Chace my Prey!
    The Flames ascend on either Altar clear,
While thus the blameless Maid address'd her Pray'r.
When lo! the burning Fire that shone so bright, 250
Flew off, all sudden, with extinguish'd Light,
And left one Altar dark, a little space;
Which turn'd self-kindl'd, and renew'd the Blaze:

That other Victour-Flame a Moment stood,
Then fell, and lifeless left th' extinguish'd Wood;　　　255
For ever lost, th' irrevocable Light
Forsook the blackning Coals, and sunk to Night:
At either End it whistled as it flew,
And as the Brands were green, so dropp'd the Dew;
Infected as it fell with Sweat of Sanguin Hue.　　　260
　　The Maid from that ill *Omen* turn'd her Eyes,
And with loud Shrieks and Clamours rent the Skies,
Nor knew what signifi'd the boding Sign,
But found the Pow'rs displeas'd, and fear'd the Wrath Divine.
　　Then shook the Sacred Shrine, and sudden Light　　　265
Sprung through the vaulted Roof, and made the Temple bright.
The Pow'r, behold! the Pow'r in Glory shone,
By her bent Bow, and her keen Arrows known:
The rest, a Huntress issuing from the Wood,
Reclining on her Cornel Spear she stood.　　　270
Then gracious thus began; Dismiss thy Fear,
And Heav'ns unchang'd Decrees attentive hear:
More pow'rful Gods have torn thee from my Side,
Unwilling to resign, and doom'd a Bride:
The two contending Knights are weigh'd above;　　　275
One *Mars* protects, and one the Queen of Love:
But which the Man, is in the Thund'rer's Breast,
This he pronounc'd, 'tis he who loves thee best.
The Fire that once extinct, reviv'd again,
Foreshews the Love allotted to remain.　　　280
Farewell, she said, and vanish'd from the Place;
The Sheaf of Arrows shook, and rattl'd in the Case.
Agast at this, the Royal Virgin stood,
Disclaim'd, and now no more a Sister of the Wood:
But to the parting Goddess thus she pray'd;　　　285
Propitious still be present to my Aid,
Nor quite abandon your once favour'd Maid.
Then sighing she return'd; but smil'd betwixt,
With Hopes, and Fears, and Joys with Sorrows mixt.
　　The next returning Planetary Hour　　　290
Of *Mars*, who shar'd the Heptarchy of Pow'r,
His Steps bold *Arcite* to the Temple bent,
T' adore with Pagan Rites the Pow'r Armipotent:

Then prostrate, low before his Altar lay,
And rais'd his manly Voice, and thus began to pray.   295
Strong God of Arms, whose Iron Scepter sways
The freezing North, and *Hyperborean* Seas,
And *Scythian* Colds, and *Thracia*'s Wintry Coast,
Where stand thy Steeds, and thou art honour'd most:
There most; but ev'ry where thy Pow'r is known,   300
The Fortune of the Fight is all thy own:
Terrour is thine, and wild Amazement flung
From out thy Chariot, withers ev'n the Strong:
And Disarray and shameful Rout ensue,
And Force is added to the fainting Crew.   305
Acknowledg'd as thou art, accept my Pray'r,
If ought I have atchiev'd deserve thy Care:
If to my utmost Pow'r with Sword and Shield
I dar'd the Death, unknowing how to yield,
And falling in my Rank, still kept the Field: 310
Then let my Arms prevail, by thee sustain'd,
That *Emily* by Conquest may be gain'd.
Have pity on my Pains; nor those unknown
To *Mars*, which when a Lover, were his own.
Venus, the Publick Care of all above,   315
Thy stubborn Heart has softned into Love:
Now by her Blandishments and pow'rful Charms
When yielded, she lay curling in thy Arms,
Ev'n by thy Shame, if Shame it may be call'd,
When *Vulcan* had thee in his Net inthrall'd;   320
O envy'd Ignominy, sweet Disgrace,
When ev'ry God that saw thee, wish'd thy Place!
By those dear Pleasures, aid my Arms in Fight,
And make me conquer in my Patron's Right:
For I am young, a Novice in the Trade,   325
The Fool of Love, unpractis'd to persuade;
And want the soothing Arts that catch the Fair,
But caught my self, lie strugling in the Snare:
And she I love, or laughs at all my Pain,
Or knows her Worth too well; and pays me with Disdain. 330
For sure I am, unless I win in Arms,
To stand excluded from *Emilia*'s Charms:
Nor can my Strength avail, unless by thee

Endu'd with Force, I gain the Victory:
Then for the Fire which warm'd thy gen'rous Heart,   335
Pity thy Subject's Pains, and equal Smart.
So be the Morrows Sweat and Labour mine,
The Palm and Honour of the Conquest thine:
Then shall the War, and stern Debate, and Strife
Immortal, be the Bus'ness of my Life;   340
And in thy Fane, the dusty Spoils among,
High on the burnish'd Roof, my Banner shall be hung;
Rank'd with my Champions Bucklers, and below
With Arms revers'd, th' Atchievements of my Foe:
And while these Limbs the Vital Spirit feeds,   345
While Day to Night, and Night to Day succeeds,
Thy smoaking Altar shall be fat with Food
Of Incence, and the grateful Steam of Blood;
Burnt Off'rings Morn and Ev'ning shall be thine;
And Fires eternal in thy Temple shine.   350
This Bush of yellow Beard, this Length of Hair,
Which from my Birth inviolate I bear,
Guiltless of Steel, and from the Razour free,
Shall fall a plenteous Crop, reserv'd for thee.
So may my Arms with Victory be blest,   355
I ask no more; let Fate dispose the rest.
　　The Champion ceas'd; there follow'd in the Close
A hollow Groan, a murm'ring Wind arose,
The Rings of Ir'n, that on the Doors were hung,
Sent out a jarring Sound, and harshly rung: 360
The bolted Gates flew open at the Blast,
The Storm rush'd in; and *Arcite* stood agast:
The Flames were blown aside, yet shone they bright,
Fann'd by the Wind, and gave a ruffl'd Light:
　　Then from the Ground a Scent began to rise,   365
Sweet-smelling, as accepted Sacrifice:
This *Omen* pleas'd, and as the Flames aspire
With od'rous Incence *Arcite* heaps the Fire:
Nor wanted Hymns to *Mars*, or Heathen Charms:
At length the nodding Statue clash'd his Arms,   370
And with a sullen Sound, and feeble Cry,
Half sunk, and half pronounc'd the Word of Victory.
For this, with Soul devout, he thank'd the God,

And of Success secure, return'd to his Abode.

   These Vows thus granted, rais'd a Strife above,   375
Betwixt the God of War, and Queen of Love.
She granting first, had Right of Time to plead;
But he had granted too, nor would recede.
Jove was for *Venus*; but he fear'd his Wife,
And seem'd unwilling to decide the Strife;   380
Till *Saturn* from his Leaden Throne arose,
And found a Way the Diff'rence to compose:
Though sparing of his Grace, to Mischief bent,
He seldom does a Good with good Intent.
Wayward, but wise; by long Experience taught   385
To please both Parties, for ill Ends, he sought:
For this Advantage Age from Youth has won,
As not to be outridden, though outrun.
By Fortune he was now to *Venus* Trin'd,
And with stern *Mars* in *Capricorn* was join'd: 390
Of him disposing in his own Abode,
He sooth'd the Goddess, while he gull'd the God:
Cease, Daughter, to complain; and stint the Strife;
Thy *Palamon* shall have his promis'd Wife:
And *Mars*, the Lord of Conquest, in the Fight   395
With Palm and Laurel shall adorn his Knight.
Wide is my Course, nor turn I to my Place
Till length of Time, and move with tardy Pace.
Man feels me, when I press th' Etherial Plains,
My Hand is heavy, and the Wound remains.   400
Mine is the Shipwreck, in a Watry Sign;
And in an Earthy, the dark Dungeon mine.
Cold shivering Agues, melancholy Care,
And bitter blasting Winds, and poison'd Air,
Are mine, and wilful Death, resulting from Despair.   405
The throtling Quinsey 'tis my Star appoints,
And Rheumatisms I send to rack the Joints:
When Churls rebel against their Native Prince,
I arm their Hands, and furnish the Pretence;
And housing in the Lion's hateful Sign,   410
Bought Senates, and deserting Troops are mine.
Mine is the privy Pois'ning, I command
Unkindly Seasons, and ungrateful Land.

By me Kings Palaces are push'd to Ground,
And Miners, crush'd beneath their Mines are found.　　415
'Twas I slew *Samson*, when the Pillar'd Hall
Fell down, and crush'd the Many with the Fall.
My Looking is the Sire of Pestilence,
That sweeps at once the People and the Prince.
Now weep no more, but trust thy Grandsire's Art;　　420
Mars shall be pleas'd, and thou perform thy Part.
'Tis ill, though diff'rent your Complexions are,
The Family of Heav'n for Men should war.
Th' Expedient pleas'd, where neither lost his Right:
Mars had the Day, and *Venus* had the Night.　　425
The Management they left to *Chronos* Care;
Now turn we to th' Effect, and sing the War.
　　In *Athens*, all was Pleasure, Mirth, and Play,
All proper to the Spring, and spritely *May*:
Which ev'ry Soul inspir'd with such Delight,　　430
'Twas Justing all the Day, and Love at Night.
Heav'n smil'd, and gladded was the Heart of Man;
And *Venus* had the World, as when it first began.
At length in Sleep their Bodies they compose,
And dreamt the future Fight, and early rose.　　435
　　Now scarce the dawning Day began to spring,
As at a Signal giv'n, the Streets with Clamours ring:
At once the Crowd arose; confus'd and high
Ev'n from the Heav'n was heard a shouting Cry;
For *Mars* was early up, and rowz'd the Sky.　　440
The Gods came downward to behold the Wars,
Sharpning their Sights, and leaning from their Stars.
The Neighing of the gen'rous Horse was heard,
For Battel by the busie Groom prepar'd:
Rustling of Harness, ratling of the Shield,　　445
Clatt'ring of Armour, furbish'd for the Field.
Crowds to the Castle mounted up the Street,
Batt'ring the Pavement with their Coursers Feet:
The greedy Sight might there devour the Gold
Of glittring Arms, too dazling to behold;　　450
And polish'd Steel that cast the View aside,
And Crested Morions, with their Plumy Pride.

Knights, with a long Retinue of their Squires,
In gawdy Liv'ries march, and quaint Attires.
One lac'd the Helm, another held the Lance: 455
A third the shining Buckler did advance.
The Courser paw'd the Ground with restless Feet,
And snorting foam'd, and champ'd the Golden Bit.
The Smiths and Armourers on Palfreys ride,
Files in their Hands, and Hammers at their Side,   } 460
And Nails for loosen'd Spears, and Thongs for Shields provide.
The Yeomen guard the Streets, in seemly Bands;
And Clowns come crowding on, with Cudgels in their Hands.
    The Trumpets, next the Gate, in order plac'd,
Attend the Sign to sound the Martial Blast: 465
The Palace-yard is fill'd with floating Tides,
And the last Comers bear the former to the Sides.
The Throng is in the midst: The common Crew
Shut out, the Hall admits the better Few.
In Knots they stand, or in a Rank they walk,   470
Serious in Aspect, earnest in their Talk:
Factious, and fav'ring this or t'other Side,
As their strong Fancies, and weak Reason, guide:
Their Wagers back their Wishes: Numbers hold
With the fair freckl'd King, and Beard of Gold: 475
So vig'rous are his Eyes, such Rays they cast,
So prominent his Eagles Beak is plac'd.
But most their Looks on the black Monarch bend,
His rising Muscles, and his Brawn commend;
His double-biting Ax, and beamy Spear,   480
Each asking a Gygantick Force to rear.
All spoke as partial Favour mov'd the Mind;
And safe themselves, at others Cost divin'd.
    Wak'd by the Cries, th' *Athenian* Chief arose,
The Knightly Forms of Combate to dispose;   485
And passing through th' obsequious Guards, he sate
Conspicuous on a Throne, sublime in State;
There, for the two contending Knights he sent:
Arm'd *Cap-a-pe*, with Rev'rence low they bent;
He smil'd on both, and with superiour Look   490
Alike their offer'd Adoration took.
The People press on ev'ry Side to see

Their awful Prince, and hear his high Decree.
Then signing to the Heralds with his Hand,
They gave his Orders from their lofty Stand.   495
Silence is thrice enjoin'd; then thus aloud
The King at Arms bespeaks the Knights and listning Crowd.
    Our Sovereign Lord has ponder'd in his Mind
The Means to spare the Blood of gentle Kind;
And of his Grace, and in-born Clemency,   500
He modifies his first severe Decree;
The keener Edge of Battel to rebate,
The Troops for Honour fighting, not for Hate.
He wills, not Death shou'd terminate their Strife;
And Wounds, if Wounds ensue, be short of Life.   505
But issues, e'er the Fight, his dread Command,
That Slings afar, and Ponyards Hand to Hand,
Be banish'd from the Field; that none shall dare
With shortned Sword to stab in closer War;
But in fair Combate fight with manly Strength,   510
Nor push with biting Point, but strike at length.
The Turney is allow'd but one Career,
Of the tough Ash, with the sharp-grinded Spear.
But Knights unhors'd may rise from off the Plain,
And fight on Foot, their Honour to regain.   515
Nor, if at Mischief taken, on the Ground
Be slain, but Pris'ners to the Pillar bound,
At either Barrier plac'd; nor (Captives made,)
Be freed, or arm'd anew the Fight invade.
The Chief of either Side, bereft of Life,   520
Or yielded to his Foe, concludes the Strife.
Thus dooms the Lord: Now valiant Knights and young,
Fight each his fill with Swords and Maces long.
    The Herald ends: The vaulted Firmament
With loud Acclaims, and vast Applause is rent: 525
Heav'n guard a Prince so gracious and so good,
So just, and yet so provident of Blood!
This was the gen'ral Cry. The Trumpets sound,
And Warlike Symphony is heard around.
The marching Troops through *Athens* take their way,   530
The great Earl-Marshal orders their Array.
The Fair from high the passing Pomp behold;

A Rain of Flow'rs is from the Windows roll'd.
The Casements are with Golden Tissue spread,
And Horses Hoofs, for Earth, on Silken Tap'stry tread.   535
The King goes midmost, and the Rivals ride
In equal Rank, and close his either Side.
Next after these, there rode the Royal Wife,
With *Emily*, the Cause, and the Reward of Strife.
The following Cavalcade, by Three and Three,   540
Proceed by Titles marshall'd in Degree.
Thus through the Southern Gate they take their Way,
And at the Lists arriv'd e'er Prime of Day.
There, parting from the King, the Chiefs divide,
And wheeling East and West, before their Many ride.   545
Th' *Athenian* Monarch mounts his Throne on high,
And after him the Queen, and *Emily*:
Next these, the Kindred of the Crown are grac'd
With nearer Seats, and Lords by Ladies plac'd.
Scarce were they seated, when with Clamours loud   550
In rush'd at once a rude promiscuous Crowd:
The Guards, and then each other overbare,
And in a Moment throng the spacious Theatre.
Now chang'd the jarring Noise to Whispers low,
As Winds forsaking Seas more softly blow;   555
When at the Western Gate, on which the Car
Is plac'd aloft, that bears the God of War,
Proud *Arcite* entring arm'd before his Train,
Stops at the Barrier, and divides the Plain.
Red was his Banner, and display'd abroad   560
The bloody Colours of his Patron God.
    At that self-moment enters *Palamon*
The Gate of *Venus*, and the Rising Sun;
Wav'd by the wanton Winds, his Banner flies,
All Maiden White, and shares the Peoples Eyes.   565
From East to West, look all the World around,
Two Troops so match'd were never to be found:
Such Bodies built for Strength, of equal Age,
In Stature siz'd; so proud an Equipage:
The nicest Eye cou'd no Distinction make,   570
Where lay th' Advantage, or what Side to take.

560 abroad] abroad, *F*

Thus rang'd, the Herald for the last proclaims
A Silence, while they answer'd to their Names:
For so the King decreed, to shun with Care
The Fraud of Musters false, the common Bane of War.   575
The Tale was just, and then the Gates were clos'd;
And Chief to Chief, and Troop to Troop oppos'd.
The Heralds last retir'd, and loudly cry'd,
The Fortune of the Field be fairly try'd.
    At this, the Challenger with fierce Defie   } 580
His Trumpet sounds; the Challeng'd makes Reply: }
With Clangour rings the Field, resounds the vaulted Sky. }
Their Vizors clos'd, their Lances in the Rest,
Or at the Helmet pointed, or the Crest;
They vanish from the Barrier, speed the Race,   585
And spurring see decrease the middle Space.
A Cloud of Smoke envellops either Host,
And all at once the Combatants are lost:
Darkling they join adverse, and shock unseen,
Coursers with Coursers justling, Men with Men: 590
As lab'ring in Eclipse, a while they stay,
Till the next Blast of Wind restores the Day.
They look anew: The beauteous Form of Fight
Is chang'd, and War appears a grizly Sight.
Two Troops in fair Array one Moment show'd,   595
The next, a Field with fallen Bodies strow'd:
Not half the Number in their Seats are found,
But Men and Steeds lie grov'ling on the Ground.
The Points of Spears are stuck within the Shield,
The Steeds without their Riders scour the Field.   600
The Knights unhors'd, on Foot renew the Fight;
The glitt'ring Fauchions cast a gleaming Light:
Hauberks and Helms are hew'd with many a Wound;
Out spins the streaming Blood, and dies the Ground.
The mighty Maces with such haste descend,   605
They break the Bones, and make the solid Armour bend.
This thrusts amid the Throng with furious Force;
Down goes, at once, the Horseman and the Horse:
That Courser stumbles on the fallen Steed,
And floundring, throws the Rider o'er his Head.   610
One rolls along, a Foot-ball to his Foes;

One with a broken Truncheon deals his Blows.
This halting, this disabl'd with his Wound,
In Triumph led, is to the Pillar bound,
Where by the King's Award he must abide: 615
There goes a Captive led on t'other Side.
By Fits they cease; and leaning on the Lance,
Take Breath a while, and to new Fight advance.
    Full oft the Rivals met, and neither spar'd
His utmost Force, and each forgot to ward.   620
The Head of this was to the Saddle bent,
That other backward to the Crupper sent:
Both were by Turns unhors'd; the jealous Blows
Fall thick and heavy, when on Foot they close.
So deep their Fauchions bite, that ev'ry Stroke   625
Pierc'd to the Quick; and equal Wounds they gave and took.
Born far asunder by the Tides of Men,
Like Adamant and Steel they meet agen.
    So when a Tyger sucks the Bullock's Blood,
A famish'd Lion issuing from the Wood   630
Roars Lordly fierce, and challenges the Food.
Each claims Possession, neither will obey,
But both their Paws are fasten'd on the Prey:
They bite, they tear; and while in vain they strive,
The Swains come arm'd between, and both to distance drive. 635
    At length, as Fate foredoom'd, and all things tend
By Course of Time to their appointed End;
So when the Sun to West was far declin'd,
And both afresh in mortal Battel join'd,
The strong *Emetrius* came in *Arcite*'s Aid,   640
And *Palamon* with Odds was overlaid:
For turning short, he struck with all his Might
Full on the Helmet of th' unwary Knight.
Deep was the Wound; he stagger'd with the Blow,
And turn'd him to his unexpected Foe;   645
Whom with such Force he struck, he fell'd him down,
And cleft the Circle of his Golden Crown.
But *Arcite*'s Men, who now prevail'd in Fight,
Twice Ten at once surround the single Knight:
O'erpowr'd at length, they force him to the Ground,   650
Unyielded as he was, and to the Pillar bound;

And King *Lycurgus*, while he fought in vain
His Friend to free, was tumbl'd on the Plain.
    Who now laments but *Palamon*, compell'd
No more to try the Fortune of the Field!   655
And worse than Death, to view with hateful Eyes
His Rival's Conquest, and renounce the Prize!
    The Royal Judge on his Tribunal plac'd,
Who had beheld the Fight from first to last,
Bad cease the War; pronouncing from on high   660
Arcite of *Thebes* had won the beauteous *Emily*.
The Sound of Trumpets to the Voice reply'd,
And round the Royal Lists the Heralds cry'd,
Arcite of *Thebes* has won the beauteous Bride.
    The People rend the Skies with vast Applause;   665
All own the Chief, when Fortune owns the Cause.
Arcite is own'd ev'n by the Gods above,
And conqu'ring *Mars* insults the Queen of Love.
So laugh'd he, when the rightful *Titan* fail'd,
And *Jove*'s usurping Arms in Heav'n prevail'd.   670
Laugh'd all the Pow'rs who favour Tyranny;
And all the Standing Army of the Sky.
But *Venus* with dejected Eyes appears,
And weeping, on the Lists, distill'd her Tears;
Her Will refus'd, which grieves a Woman most,   675
And in her Champion foil'd, the Cause of Love is lost.
Till *Saturn* said, Fair Daughter, now be still,
The blustring Fool has satisfi'd his Will:
His Boon is giv'n; his Knight has gain'd the Day,
But lost the Prize, th' Arrears are yet to pay.   680
Thy Hour is come, and mine the Care shall be
To please thy Knight, and set thy Promise free.
    Now while the Heralds run the Lists around,
And *Arcite*, *Arcite*, Heav'n and Earth resound;
A Miracle (nor less it could be call'd)   685
Their Joy with unexpected Sorrow pall'd.
The Victor Knight had laid his Helm aside,
Part for his Ease, the greater part for Pride:
Bare-headed, popularly low he bow'd,
And paid the Salutations of the Crowd.   690
Then spurring at full speed, ran endlong on

Where *Theseus* sat on his Imperial Throne;
Furious he drove, and upward cast his Eye,
Where next the Queen was plac'd his *Emily*;
Then passing, to the Saddle-bow he bent,   695
A sweet Regard the gracious Virgin lent:
(For Women, to the Brave an easie Prey,
Still follow Fortune, where she leads the Way:)
Just then, from Earth sprung out a flashing Fire,
By *Pluto* sent, at *Saturn*'s bad Desire;   700
The startling Steed was seiz'd with sudden Fright,
And, bounding, o'er the Pummel cast the Knight:
Forward he flew, and pitching on his Head,
He quiver'd with his Feet, and lay for Dead.
Black was his Count'nance in a little space,   705
For all the Blood was gather'd in his Face.
Help was at Hand; they rear'd him from the Ground,
And from his cumbrous Arms his Limbs unbound;
Then lanc'd a Vein, and watch'd returning Breath;
It came, but clogg'd with Symptoms of his Death.   710
The Saddle-bow the Noble Parts had prest,
All bruis'd and mortifi'd his Manly Breast.
Him still entranc'd, and in a Litter laid,
They bore from Field, and to his Bed convey'd.
At length he wak'd, and with a feeble Cry,   715
The Word he first pronounc'd was *Emily*.
    Mean time the King, though inwardly he mourn'd,
In Pomp triumphant to the Town return'd,
Attended by the Chiefs, who fought the Field;
(Now friendly mix'd, and in one Troop compell'd.)   720
Compos'd his Looks to counterfeited Cheer,
And bade them not for *Arcite*'s Life to fear.
But that which gladded all the Warriour Train,
Though most were sorely wounded, none were slain.
The Surgeons soon despoil'd 'em of their Arms,   725
And some with Salves they cure, and some with Charms.
Foment the Bruises, and the Pains asswage,
And heal their inward Hurts with Sov'reign Draughts of Sage.
The King in Person visits all around,
Comforts the Sick, congratulates the Sound;   730
Honours the Princely Chiefs, rewards the rest,

And holds for thrice three Days a Royal Feast.
None was disgrac'd; for Falling is no Shame;
And Cowardice alone is Loss of Fame.
The vent'rous Knight is from the Saddle thrown;   735
But 'tis the Fault of Fortune, not his own.
If Crowns and Palms the conqu'ring Side adorn,
The Victor under better Stars was born:
The brave Man seeks not popular Applause,
Now overpow'r'd with Arms, deserts his Cause;   740
Unsham'd, though foil'd, he does the best he can;
Force is of Brutes, but Honour is of Man.
    Thus *Theseus* smil'd on all with equal Grace;
And each was set according to his Place.
With ease were reconcil'd the diff'ring Parts,   745
For Envy never dwells in Noble Hearts.
At length they took their Leave, the Time expir'd;
Well pleas'd; and to their sev'ral Homes retir'd.
    Mean while the Health of *Arcite* still impairs;
From Bad proceeds to Worse, and mocks the Leaches Cares: 750
Swoln is his Breast, his inward Pains increase,
All Means are us'd, and all without Success.
The clotted Blood lies heavy on his Heart,
Corrupts, and there remains in spite of Art:
Nor breathing Veins, nor Cupping will prevail;   755
All outward Remedies and inward fail:
The Mold of Natures Fabrick is destroy'd,
Her Vessels discompos'd, her Vertue void:
The Bellows of his Lungs begins to swell: ⎫
All out of frame is ev'ry secret Cell,   ⎬ 760
Nor can the Good receive, nor Bad expel.   ⎭
Those breathing Organs thus within opprest,
With Venom soon distend the Sinews of his Breast.
Nought profits him to save abandon'd Life,
Nor Vomits upward aid, nor downward Laxatife.   765
The midmost Region batter'd, and destroy'd,
When Nature cannot work, th' Effect of Art is void.
For Physick can but mend our crazie State,
Patch an old Building, not a new create.

Arcite is doom'd to die in all his Pride,   770
Must leave his Youth, and yield his beauteous Bride,
Gain'd hardly, against Right, and unenjoy'd.
When 'twas declar'd, all Hope of Life was past,
Conscience, that of all Physick works the last,
Caus'd him to send for *Emily* in haste.   775
With her, at his desire, came *Palamon*;
Then on his Pillow rais'd, he thus begun.
No Language can express the smallest part
Of what I feel, and suffer in my Heart,
For you, whom best I love and value most;   780
But to your Service I bequeath my Ghost;
Which from this mortal Body when unty'd,
Unseen, unheard, shall hover at your Side;
Nor fright you waking, nor your Sleep offend,
But wait officious, and your Steps attend: 785
How I have lov'd, excuse my faltring Tongue,
My Spirit's feeble, and my Pains are strong:
This I may say, I only grieve to die
Because I lose my charming *Emily*:
To die, when Heav'n had put you in my Pow'r,   790
Fate could not chuse a more malicious Hour!
What greater Curse cou'd envious Fortune give,
Than just to die, when I began to live!
Vain Men, how vanishing a Bliss we crave,
Now warm in Love, now with'ring in the Grave!   795
Never, O never more to see the Sun!
Still dark, in a damp Vault, and still alone!
This Fate is common; but I lose my Breath
Near Bliss, and yet not bless'd before my Death.
Farewell; but take me dying in your Arms,   800
'Tis all I can enjoy of all your Charms:
This Hand I cannot but in Death resign;
Ah, could I live! But while I live 'tis mine.
I feel my End approach, and thus embrac'd,
Am pleas'd to die; but hear me speak my last.   805
Ah! my sweet Foe, for you, and you alone,
I broke my Faith with injur'd *Palamon*.
But Love the Sense of Right and Wrong confounds,

787 Spirit's] Spirits F

Strong Love and proud Ambition have no Bounds.
And much I doubt, shou'd Heav'n my Life prolong,   810
I shou'd return to justifie my Wrong:
For while my former Flames remain within,
Repentance is but want of Pow'r to sin.
With mortal Hatred I pursu'd his Life,
Nor he, nor you, were guilty of the Strife;   815
Nor I, but as I lov'd: Yet all combin'd,
Your Beauty, and my Impotence of Mind;
And his concurrent Flame, that blew my Fire;
For still our Kindred Souls had one Desire.
He had a Moments Right in point of Time;   820
Had I seen first, then his had been the Crime.
Fate made in mine, and justified his Right;
Nor holds this Earth a more deserving Knight,
For Vertue, Valour, and for Noble Blood,
Truth, Honour, all that is compriz'd in Good;   825
So help me Heav'n, in all the World is none
So worthy to be lov'd as *Palamon.*
He loves you too; with such a holy Fire,
As will not, cannot but with Life expire:
Our vow'd Affections both have often try'd,   830
Nor any Love but yours cou'd ours divide.
Then by my Loves inviolable Band,
By my long Suff'ring, and my short Command,
If e'er you plight your Vows when I am gone,
Have pity on the faithful *Palamon.*   835
   This was his last; for Death came on amain,
And exercis'd below, his Iron Reign;
Then upward, to the Seat of Life he goes;
Sense fled before him, what he touch'd he froze:
Yet cou'd he not his closing Eyes withdraw,   840
Though less and less of *Emily* he saw:
So, speechless, for a little space he lay;
Then grasp'd the Hand he held, and sigh'd his Soul away.
   But whither went his Soul, let such relate
Who search the Secrets of the future State: 845
Divines can say but what themselves believe;
Strong Proofs they have, but not demonstrative:
For, were all plain, then all Sides must agree,

And Faith it self be lost in Certainty.
To live uprightly then is sure the best,   850
To save our selves, and not to damn the rest.
The Soul of *Arcite* went, where Heathens go,
Who better live than we, though less they know.
    In *Palamon* a manly Grief appears;
Silent, he wept, asham'd to shew his Tears: 855
Emilia shriek'd but once, and then oppress'd
With Sorrow, sunk upon her Lovers Breast:
Till *Theseus* in his Arms convey'd with Care,
Far from so sad a Sight, the swooning Fair.
'Twere loss of Time her Sorrow to relate;   860
Ill bears the Sex a youthful Lover's Fate,
When just approaching to the Nuptial State.
But like a low-hung Cloud, it rains so fast,
That all at once it falls, and cannot last.
The Face of Things is chang'd, and *Athens* now,   865
That laugh'd so late, becomes the Scene of Woe:
Matrons and Maids, both Sexes, ev'ry State,
With Tears lament the Knight's untimely Fate.
Not greater Grief in falling *Troy* was seen
For *Hector*'s Death; but *Hector* was not then.   870
Old Men with Dust deform'd their hoary Hair,
The Women beat their Breasts, their Cheeks they tear.
Why would'st thou go, with one Consent they cry,
When thou hadst Gold enough, and *Emily*!
    Theseus himself, who shou'd have cheer'd the Grief   875
Of others, wanted now the same Relief.
Old *Egeus* only could revive his Son,
Who various Changes of the World had known;
And strange Vicissitudes of Humane Fate,
Still alt'ring, never in a steady State: 880
Good after Ill, and after Pain, Delight;
Alternate, like the Scenes of Day and Night:
Since ev'ry Man who lives, is born to die,
And none can boast sincere Felicity.
With equal Mind, what happens, let us bear,   885
Nor joy, nor grieve too much for Things beyond our Care.
Like Pilgrims, to th' appointed Place we tend;
The World's an Inn, and Death the Journeys End.

Ev'n Kings but play; and when their Part is done,
Some other, worse or better, mount the Throne. 890
With Words like these the Crowd was satisfi'd,
And so they would have been, had *Theseus* dy'd.
  But he, their King, was lab'ring in his Mind,
A fitting Place for Fun'ral Pomps to find,
Which were in Honour of the Dead design'd. 895
And after long Debate, at last he found
(As Love it self had mark'd the Spot of Ground)
That Grove for ever green, that conscious Lawnd,
Where he with *Palamon* fought Hand to Hand:
That where he fed his amorous Desires 900
With soft Complaints, and felt his hottest Fires,
There other Flames might waste his Earthly Part,
And burn his Limbs, where Love had burn'd his Heart.
  This once resolv'd, the Peasants were enjoin'd
Sere Wood, and Firs, and dodder'd Oaks to find. 905
With sounding Axes to the Grove they go,
Fell, split, and lay the Fewel on a Row,
Vulcanian Food: A Bier is next prepar'd,
On which the lifeless Body should be rear'd,
Cover'd with Cloth of Gold, on which was laid 910
The Corps of *Arcite*, in like Robes array'd.
White Gloves were on his Hands, and on his Head
A Wreath of Laurel, mix'd with Myrtle, spread.
A Sword keen-edg'd within his Right he held,
The warlike Emblem of the conquer'd Field: 915
Bare was his manly Visage on the Bier;
Menac'd his Count'nance; ev'n in Death severe.
Then to the Palace-Hall they bore the Knight,
To lie in solemn State, a Publick Sight.
Groans, Cries, and Howlings fill the crowded Place, 920
And unaffected Sorrow sat on ev'ry Face.
Sad *Palamon* above the rest appears,
In Sable Garments, dew'd with gushing Tears:
His Auburn Locks on either Shoulder flow'd,
Which to the Fun'ral of his Friend he vow'd: 925
But *Emily*, as Chief, was next his Side,
A Virgin-Widow, and a *Mourning Bride*.

904 This] This, F

And that the Princely Obsequies might be
Perform'd according to his high Degree,
The Steed that bore him living to the Fight, 930
Was trapp'd with polish'd Steel, all shining bright,
And cover'd with th' Atchievements of the Knight.
The Riders rode abreast, and one his Shield,
His Lance of Cornel-wood another held;
The third his Bow, and, glorious to behold, 935
The costly Quiver, all of burnish'd Gold.
The Noblest of the *Grecians* next appear,
And weeping, on their Shoulders bore the Bier;
With sober Pace they march'd, and often staid,
And through the Master-Street the Corps convey'd. 940
The Houses to their Tops with Black were spread,
And ev'n the Pavements were with Mourning hid.
The Right-side of the Pall old *Egeus* kept,
And on the Left the Royal *Theseus* wept:
Each bore a Golden Bowl of Work Divine, 945
With Honey fill'd, and Milk, and mix'd with ruddy Wine.
Then *Palamon* the Kinsman of the Slain,
And after him appear'd th' Illustrious Train:
To grace the Pomp, came *Emily* the Bright,
With cover'd Fire, the Fun'ral Pile to light. 950
With high Devotion was the Service made,
And all the Rites of Pagan-Honour paid:
So lofty was the Pile, a *Parthian* Bow,
With Vigour drawn, must send the Shaft below.
The Bottom was full twenty Fathom broad, 955
With crackling Straw beneath in due Proportion strow'd.
The Fabrick seem'd a Wood of rising Green,
With Sulphur and Bitumen cast between,
To feed the Flames: The Trees were unctuous Fir,
And Mountain-Ash, the Mother of the Spear; 960
The Mourner Eugh, and Builder Oak were there:
The Beech, the swimming Alder, and the Plane,
Hard Box, and Linden of a softer Grain,
And Laurels, which the Gods for Conqu'ring Chiefs ordain.
How they were rank'd, shall rest untold by me, 965
With nameless Nymphs that liv'd in ev'ry Tree;
Nor how the Dryads, and the Woodland Train,

Disherited, ran howling o'er the Plain:
Nor how the Birds to Foreign Seats repair'd,
Or Beasts, that bolted out, and saw the Forest bar'd: 970
Nor how the Ground, now clear'd, with gastly Fright
Beheld the sudden Sun, a Stranger to the Light.
   The Straw, as first I said, was laid below;
Of Chips and Sere-wood was the second Row;
The third of Greens, and Timber newly fell'd;   975
The fourth high Stage the fragrant Odours held,
And Pearls, and Precious Stones, and rich Array;
In midst of which, embalm'd, the Body lay.
The Service sung, the Maid with mourning Eyes
The Stubble fir'd; the smouldring Flames arise: 980
This Office done, she sunk upon the Ground;
But what she spoke, recover'd from her Swoond,
I want the Wit in moving Words to dress;
But by themselves the tender Sex may guess.
While the devouring Fire was burning fast,   985
Rich Jewels in the Flame the Wealthy cast;
And some their Shields, and some their Lances threw,
And gave the Warriour's Ghost a Warriour's Due.
Full Bowls of Wine, of Honey, Milk, and Blood,
Were pour'd upon the Pile of burning Wood,   990
And hissing Flames receive, and hungry lick the Food.
Then thrice the mounted Squadrons ride around
The Fire, and *Arcite*'s Name they thrice resound:
Hail, and Farewell, they shouted thrice amain,
Thrice facing to the Left, and thrice they turn'd again: 995
Still as they turn'd, they beat their clatt'ring Shields;
The Women mix their Cries; and Clamour fills the Fields.
The warlike Wakes continu'd all the Night,
And Fun'ral Games were plaid at new-returning Light:
Who naked wrestl'd best, besmear'd with Oil,   1000
Or who with Gantlets gave or took the Foil,
I will not tell you, nor wou'd you attend;
But briefly haste to my long Stories End.
   I pass the rest; the Year was fully mourn'd,
And *Palamon* long since to *Thebes* return'd,   1005
When, by the *Grecians* general Consent,
At *Athens Theseus* held his Parliament:

Among the Laws that pass'd, it was decreed,
That conquer'd *Thebes* from Bondage shou'd be freed;
Reserving Homage to th' *Athenian* Throne,   101
To which the Sov'reign summon'd *Palamon*.
Unknowing of the Cause, he took his Way,
Mournful in Mind, and still in Black Array.

The Monarch mounts the Throne, and plac'd on high,
Commands into the Court the beauteous *Emily*:   101
So call'd, she came; the Senate rose, and paid
Becoming Rev'rence to the Royal Maid.
And first soft Whispers through th' Assembly went:
With silent Wonder then they watch'd th' Event:
All hush'd, the King arose with awful Grace,   102
Deep Thought was in his Breast, and Counsel in his Face.
At length he sigh'd; and having first prepar'd
Th' attentive Audience, thus his Will declar'd.

The Cause and Spring of Motion, from above
Hung down on Earth the Golden Chain of Love: 102
Great was th' Effect, and high was his Intent,
When Peace among the jarring Seeds he sent.
Fire, Flood, and Earth, and Air by this were bound,
And Love, the common Link, the new Creation crown'd.
The Chain still holds; for though the Forms decay,   103
Eternal Matter never wears away:
The same First Mover certain Bounds has plac'd,
How long those perishable Forms shall last;
Nor can they last beyond the Time assign'd
By that All-seeing, and All-making Mind: 103
Shorten their Hours they may; for Will is free;
But never pass th' appointed Destiny.
So Men oppress'd, when weary of their Breath,
Throw off the Burden, and subborn their Death.
Then since those Forms begin, and have their End,   104
On some unalter'd Cause they sure depend:
Parts of the Whole are we; but God the Whole;
Who gives us Life, and animating Soul.
For Nature cannot from a Part derive
That Being, which the Whole can only give: 104
He perfect, stable; but imperfect We,
Subject to Change, and diff'rent in Degree.

Plants, Beasts, and Man; and as our Organs are,
We more or less of his Perfection share.
But by a long Descent, th' Etherial Fire   1050
Corrupts; and Forms, the mortal Part, expire:
As he withdraws his Vertue, so they pass,
And the same Matter makes another Mass:
This Law th' Omniscient Pow'r was pleas'd to give,
That ev'ry Kind should by Succession live;   1055
That Individuals die, his Will ordains;
The propagated Species still remains.
The Monarch Oak, the Patriarch of the Trees,
Shoots rising up, and spreads by slow Degrees:
Three Centuries he grows, and three he stays,   1060
Supreme in State; and in three more decays:
So wears the paving Pebble in the Street,
And Towns and Tow'rs their fatal Periods meet.
So Rivers, rapid once, now naked lie,
Forsaken of their Springs; and leave their Channels dry.   1065
So Man, at first a Drop, dilates with Heat,
Then form'd, the little Heart begins to beat;
Secret he feeds, unknowing in the Cell;
At length, for Hatching ripe, he breaks the Shell,
And struggles into Breath, and cries for Aid;   1070
Then, helpless, in his Mothers Lap is laid.
He creeps, he walks, and issuing into Man,
Grudges their Life, from whence his own began.
Retchless of Laws, affects to rule alone,
Anxious to reign, and restless on the Throne: 1075
First vegetive, then feels, and reasons last;
Rich of Three Souls, and lives all three to waste.
Some thus; but thousands more in Flow'r of Age:
For few arrive to run the latter Stage.
Sunk in the first, in Battel some are slain,   1080
And others whelm'd beneath the stormy Main.
What makes all this, but *Jupiter* the King,
At whose Command we perish, and we spring?
Then 'tis our best, since thus ordain'd to die,
To make a Vertue of Necessity.   1085
Take what he gives, since to rebel is vain;

1055 live;] live, F

The Bad grows better, which we well sustain:
And cou'd we chuse the Time, and chuse aright,
'Tis best to die, our Honour at the height.
When we have done our Ancestors no Shame,   1090
But serv'd our Friends, and well secur'd our Fame;
Then should we wish our happy Life to close,
And leave no more for Fortune to dispose:
So should we make our Death a glad Relief,
From future Shame, from Sickness, and from Grief: 1095
Enjoying while we live the present Hour,
And dying in our Excellence, and Flow'r.
Then round our Death-bed ev'ry Friend shou'd run,
And joy us of our Conquest, early won:
While the malicious World with envious Tears   1100
Shou'd grudge our happy End, and wish it Theirs.
Since then our *Arcite* is with Honour dead,
Why shou'd we mourn, that he so soon is freed,
Or call untimely, what the Gods decreed?
With Grief as just, a Friend may be deplor'd,   1105
From a foul Prison to free Air restor'd.
Ought he to thank his Kinsman, or his Wife,
Cou'd Tears recall him into wretched Life!
Their Sorrow hurts themselves; on him is lost;
And worse than both, offends his happy Ghost.   1110
What then remains, but after past Annoy,
To take the good Vicissitude of Joy?
To thank the gracious Gods for what they give,
Possess our Souls, and while we live, to live?
Ordain we then two Sorrows to combine,   1115
And in one Point th' Extremes of Grief to join;
That thence resulting Joy may be renew'd,
As jarring Notes in Harmony conclude.
Then I propose, that *Palamon* shall be
In Marriage join'd with beauteous *Emily*;   1120
For which already I have gain'd th' Assent
Of my free People in full Parliament.
Long Love to her has born the faithful Knight,
And well deserv'd, had Fortune done him Right:
'Tis time to mend her Fault; since *Emily*   1125
By *Arcite*'s Death from former Vows is free:

If you, Fair Sister, ratifie th' Accord,
And take him for your Husband, and your Lord.
'Tis no Dishonour to confer your Grace
On one descended from a Royal Race: 1130
And were he less, yet Years of Service past
From grateful Souls exact Reward at last:
Pity is Heav'ns and yours: Nor can she find
A Throne so soft as in a Womans Mind.
 . He said; she blush'd; and as o'eraw'd by Might,   1135
Seem'd to give *Theseus*, what she gave the Knight.
Then turning to the *Theban*, thus he said;
Small Arguments are needful to persuade
Your Temper to comply with my Command;
And speaking thus, he gave *Emilia*'s Hand.   1140
Smil'd *Venus*, to behold her own true Knight
Obtain the Conquest, though he lost the Fight,
And bless'd with Nuptial Bliss the sweet laborious Night.
Eros, and *Anteros*, on either Side,
One fir'd the Bridegroom, and one warm'd the Bride; 1145
And long-attending *Hymen* from above
Showr'd on the Bed the whole *Idalian* Grove.
All of a Tenour was their After-Life,
No Day discolour'd with Domestick Strife;
No Jealousie, but mutual Truth believ'd,   1150
Secure Repose, and Kindness undeceiv'd.
Thus Heav'n, beyond the Compass of his Thought,
Sent him the Blessing he so dearly bought.
 So may the Queen of Love long Duty bless,
And all true Lovers find the same Success.   1155

To my Honour'd Kinsman, JOHN DRIDEN, OF CHESTERTON IN THE COUNTY OF HUNTINGDON, ESQUIRE

How Bless'd is He, who leads a Country Life,
Unvex'd with anxious Cares, and void of Strife!
Who studying Peace, and shunning Civil Rage,
Enjoy'd his Youth, and now enjoys his Age:

All who deserve his Love, he makes his own;   5
And, to be lov'd himself, needs only to be known.
  Just, Good, and Wise, contending Neighbours come,   ⎫
From your Award, to wait their final Doom;   ⎬
And, Foes before, return in Friendship home.   ⎭
Without their Cost, you terminate the Cause;   10
And save th' Expence of long Litigious Laws:
Where Suits are travers'd; and so little won,
That he who conquers, is but last undone:
Such are not your Decrees; but so design'd,   ⎫
The Sanction leaves a lasting Peace behind;   ⎬ 15
Like your own Soul, Serene; a Pattern of your Mind.   ⎭
  Promoting Concord, and composing Strife,
Lord of your self, uncumber'd with a Wife;
Where, for a Year, a Month, perhaps a Night,
Long Penitence succeeds a short Delight: 20
Minds are so hardly match'd, that ev'n the first,
Though pair'd by Heav'n, in Paradise, were curs'd.
For Man and Woman, though in one they grow,
Yet, first or last, return again to Two.
He to God's Image, She to His was made;   25
So, farther from the Fount, the Stream at random stray'd.
  How cou'd He stand, when put to double Pain,
He must a Weaker than himself sustain!
Each might have stood perhaps; but each alone;
Two Wrestlers help to pull each other down.   30
  Not that my Verse wou'd blemish all the Fair;   ⎫
But yet, if *some* be Bad, 'tis Wisdom to beware;   ⎬
And better shun the Bait, than struggle in the Snare.   ⎭
Thus have you shunn'd, and shun the married State,
Trusting as little as you can to Fate.   35
  No Porter guards the Passage of your Door;
T' admit the Wealthy, and exclude the Poor:
For God, who gave the Riches, gave the Heart
To sanctifie the Whole, by giving Part:
Heav'n, who foresaw the Will, the Means has wrought,   40
And to the Second Son, a Blessing brought:
The First-begotten had his Father's Share;
But you, like *Jacob*, are *Rebecca*'s Heir.

                    To John Driden. 7 come,] come F

So may your Stores, and fruitful Fields increase;
And ever be you bless'd, who live to bless.   45
As *Ceres* sow'd, where e'er her Chariot flew;
As Heav'n in Desarts rain'd the Bread of Dew,
So free to Many, to Relations most,
You feed with Manna your own *Israel*-Host.

    With Crowds attended of your ancient Race,   50
You seek the Champian-Sports, or Sylvan-Chace:
With well-breath'd Beagles, you surround the Wood;
Ev'n then, industrious of the Common Good:
And often have you brought the wily Fox
To suffer for the Firstlings of the Flocks;   55
Chas'd ev'n amid the Folds; and made to bleed,
Like Felons, where they did the murd'rous Deed.
This fiery Game, your active Youth maintain'd;
Not yet, by Years extinguish'd, though restrain'd:
You season still with Sports your serious Hours;   60
For Age but tastes of Pleasures, Youth devours.
The Hare, in Pastures or in Plains is found,
Emblem of Humane Life, who runs the Round;
And, after all his wand'ring Ways are done, ⎫
His Circle fills, and ends where he begun, ⎬ 65
Just as the Setting meets the Rising Sun. ⎭

    Thus Princes ease their Cares: But happier he,
Who seeks not Pleasure thro' Necessity,
Than such as once on slipp'ry Thrones were plac'd;
And chasing, sigh to think themselves are chas'd.   70

    So liv'd our Sires, e'er Doctors learn'd to kill,
And multiply'd with theirs, the Weekly Bill:
The first Physicians by Debauch were made:
Excess began, and Sloth sustains the Trade.
Pity the gen'rous Kind their Cares bestow   75
To search forbidden Truths; (a Sin to know:)
To which, if Humane Science cou'd attain,
The Doom of Death, pronounc'd by God, were vain.
In vain the Leech wou'd interpose Delay;
Fate fastens first, and vindicates the Prey.   80
What Help from Arts Endeavours can we have! ⎫
Guibbons but guesses, nor is sure to save: ⎬
But *Maurus* sweeps whole Parishes, and Peoples ev'ry Grave. ⎭

And no more Mercy to Mankind will use,
Than when he robb'd and murder'd *Maro*'s Muse.   85
Wou'dst thou be soon dispatch'd, and perish whole?
Trust *Maurus* with thy Life, and *M-lb—rn* with thy Soul.
　By Chace our long-liv'd Fathers earn'd their Food;
Toil strung the Nerves, and purifi'd the Blood:
But we, their Sons, a pamper'd Race of Men,   90
Are dwindl'd down to threescore Years and ten.
Better to hunt in Fields, for Health unbought,
Than fee the Doctor for a nauseous Draught.
The Wise, for Cure, on Exercise depend;
God never made his Work, for Man to mend.   95
　The Tree of Knowledge, once in *Eden* plac'd,
Was easie found, but was forbid the Taste:
O, had our Grandsire walk'd without his Wife,
He first had sought the better Plant of Life!
Now, both are lost: Yet, wandring in the dark,   100
Physicians for the Tree, have found the Bark:
They, lab'ring for Relief of Humane Kind,
With sharpen'd Sight some Remedies may find; ⎫
Th' Apothecary-Train is wholly blind. ⎭
From Files, a Random-*Recipe* they take,   105
And Many Deaths of One Prescription make.
Garth, gen'rous as his Muse, prescribes and gives;
The Shop-man sells; and by Destruction lives:
Ungrateful Tribe! who, like the Viper's Brood,
From Med'cine issuing, suck their Mother's Blood!   110
Let These obey; and let the Learn'd prescribe;
That Men may die, without a double Bribe:
Let Them, but under their Superiours kill;
When Doctors first have sign'd the bloody Bill:
He scapes the best, who Nature to repair,   115
Draws Phisick from the Fields, in Draughts of Vital Air.
　You hoard not Health, for your own private Use;
But on the Publick spend the rich Produce:
When, often urg'd, unwilling to be Great,
Your Country calls you from your lov'd Retreat,   120
And sends to Senates, charg'd with Common Care,
Which none more shuns; and none can better bear.

Where cou'd they find another form'd so fit,
To poise, with solid Sense, a spritely Wit!
Were these both wanting, (as they both abound)   125
Where cou'd so firm Integrity be found?
    Well-born, and Wealthy; wanting no Support,
You steer betwixt the Country and the Court:
Nor gratifie whate'er the Great desire,
Nor grudging give, what Publick Needs require.   130
Part must be left, a Fund when Foes invade;
And Part employ'd to roll the Watry Trade:
Ev'n *Canaans* happy Land, when worn with Toil,
Requir'd a Sabbath-Year, to mend the meagre Soil.
    Good Senators, (and such are you,) so give,   135
That Kings may be supply'd, the People thrive.
And He, when Want requires, is truly Wise,
Who slights not Foreign Aids, nor over-buys;
But, on our Native Strength, in time of need, relies.
Munster was bought, we boast not the Success;   140
Who fights for Gain, for greater, makes his Peace.
    Our Foes, compell'd by Need, have Peace embrac'd:
The Peace both Parties want, is like to last:
Which, if secure, securely we may trade;
Or, not secure, shou'd never have been made.   145
Safe in our selves, while on our selves we stand,
The Sea is ours, and that defends the Land.
Be, then, the Naval Stores the Nations Care,
New Ships to build, and batter'd to repair.
    Observe the War, in ev'ry Annual Course;   150
What has been done, was done with *British* Force:
Namur Subdu'd, is *England*'s Palm alone;
The Rest Besieg'd; but we Constrain'd the Town:
We saw th' Event that follow'd our Success;
France, though pretending Arms, pursu'd the Peace;   155
Oblig'd, by one sole Treaty, to restore
What Twenty Years of War had won before.
Enough for *Europe* has our *Albion* fought:
Let us enjoy the Peace our Blood has bought.
When once the *Persian* King was put to Flight,   160
The weary *Macedons* refus'd to fight:
Themselves their own Mortality confess'd;

And left the Son of *Jove*, to quarrel for the rest.
 Ev'n Victors are by Victories undone;
Thus *Hannibal*, with Foreign Laurels won,   165
To *Carthage* was recall'd, too late to keep his own.
While sore of Battel, while our Wounds are green,
Why shou'd we tempt the doubtful Dye agen?
In Wars renew'd, uncertain of Success,
Sure of a Share, as Umpires of the Peace.   170
 A Patriot, both the King and Country serves;
Prerogative, and Privilege preserves:
Of Each, our Laws the certain Limit show;
One must not ebb, nor t'other overflow:
Betwixt the Prince and Parliament we stand;   175
The Barriers of the State on either Hand:
May neither overflow, for then they drown the Land.
When both are full, they feed our bless'd Abode;
Like those, that water'd once, the Paradise of God.
 Some Overpoise of Sway, by Turns they share; 180
In Peace the People, and the Prince in War:
Consuls of mod'rate Pow'r in Calms were made;
When the *Gauls* came, one sole Dictator sway'd.
 Patriots, in Peace, assert the Peoples Right;
With noble Stubbornness resisting Might: 185
No Lawless Mandates from the Court receive,
Nor lend by Force; but in a Body give.
Such was your gen'rous Grandsire; free to grant
In Parliaments, that weigh'd their Prince's Want:
But so tenacious of the Common Cause,   190
As not to lend the King against his Laws.
And, in a lothsom Dungeon doom'd to lie,
In Bonds retain'd his Birthright Liberty,
And sham'd Oppression, till it set him free.
 O true Descendent of a Patriot Line,   195
Who, while thou shar'st their Lustre, lend'st 'em thine,
Vouchsafe this Picture of thy Soul to see;
'Tis so far Good, as it resembles thee:
The Beauties to th' Original I owe;
Which, when I miss, my own Defects I show: 200
Nor think the Kindred-Muses thy Disgrace;
A Poet is not born in ev'ry Race.

Two of a House, few Ages can afford;
One to perform, another to record.
Praise-worthy Actions are by thee embrac'd;   205
And 'tis my Praise, to make thy Praises last.
For ev'n when Death dissolves our Humane Frame,
The Soul returns to Heav'n, from whence it came;
Earth keeps the Body, Verse preserves the Fame.

MELEAGER AND ATALANTA,
Out of the Eighth Book of
OVID'S Metamorphosis

CONNEXION to the Former STORY

Ovid, *having told how* Theseus *had freed* Athens *from the Tribute of Children,* (*which was impos'd on them by* Minos *King of* Creta) *by killing the* Minotaur, *here makes a Digression to the Story of* Meleager *and* Atalanta, *which is one of the most inartificial Connexions in all the* Metamorphoses: *For he only says, that* Theseus *obtain'd such Honour from that Combate, that* 5 *all* Greece *had recourse to him in their Necessities; and, amongst others,* Calydon, *though the* Heroe *of that Country, Prince* Meleager, *was then living.*

FROM him, the *Caledonians* sought Relief;
   Tho' valiant *Meleagrus* was their Chief.
The Cause, a Boar, who ravag'd far and near:
Of *Cynthia's* Wrath, th' avenging Minister.
For *Oeneus* with Autumnal Plenty bless'd,   5
By Gifts to Heav'n his Gratitude express'd:
Cull'd Sheafs, to *Ceres*; to *Lyæus*, Wine;
To *Pan*, and *Pales*, offer'd Sheep and Kine;
And Fat of Olives, to *Minerva's* Shrine.
Beginning from the Rural Gods, his Hand   10
Was lib'ral to the Pow'rs of high Command:
Each Deity in ev'ry Kind was bless'd,
Till at *Diana's* Fane th' invidious Honour ceas'd.
   Wrath touches ev'n the Gods; the Queen of Night
Fir'd with Disdain, and jealous of her Right,   15

Unhonour'd though I am, at least, said she,
Not unreveng'd that impious Act shall be.
Swift as the Word, she sped the Boar away,
With Charge on those devoted Fields to prey.
No larger Bulls th' *Ægyptian* Pastures feed,   20
And none so large *Sicilian* Meadows breed:
His Eye-balls glare with Fire suffus'd with Blood;
His Neck shoots up a thick-set thorny Wood;
His bristled Back a Trench impal'd appears,
And stands erected, like a Field of Spears.   25
Froth fills his Chaps, he sends a grunting Sound,
And part he churns, and part befoams the Ground.
For Tusks with *Indian* Elephants he strove,
And *Jove*'s own Thunder from his Mouth he drove.
He burns the Leaves; the scorching Blast invades   30
The tender Corn, and shrivels up the Blades:
Or suff'ring not their yellow Beards to rear,
He tramples down the Spikes, and intercepts the Year.
In vain the Barns expect their promis'd Load,
Nor Barns at home, nor Reeks are heap'd abroad: 35
In vain the Hinds the Threshing-Floor prepare,
And exercise their Flails in empty Air.
With Olives ever-green the Ground is strow'd,
And Grapes ungather'd shed their gen'rous Blood.
Amid the Fold he rages, nor the Sheep   40
Their Shepherds, nor the Grooms their Bulls can keep.
    From Fields to Walls the frighted Rabble run,
Nor think themselves secure within the Town:
Till *Meleagros*, and his chosen Crew,
Contemn the Danger, and the Praise pursue.   45
Fair *Leda*'s Twins (in time to Stars decreed)
One fought on Foot, one curb'd the fiery Steed;
Then issu'd forth fam'd *Jason* after These,
Who mann'd the foremost Ship that sail'd the Seas;
Then *Theseus* join'd with bold *Perithous* came;   50
A single Concord in a double Name:
The *Thestian* Sons, *Idas* who swiftly ran,
And *Ceneus*, once a Woman, now a Man.
Lynceus, with Eagles Eyes, and Lions Heart;
Leucippus, with his never-erring Dart;   55

Acastus, Phileus, Phœnix, Telamon,
Echion, Lelex, and *Eurytion,*
Achilles Father, and Great *Phocus* Son;
Dryas the Fierce, and *Hippasus* the Strong;
With twice old *Iolas,* and *Nestor* then but young.   60
Laertes active, and *Ancæus* bold;
Mopsus the Sage, who future Things foretold;
And t'other Seer, yet by his Wife* unsold.   * *Amphiaraus.*
A thousand others of immortal Fame;
Among the rest, fair *Atalanta* came,   65
Grace of the Woods: A Diamond Buckle bound
Her Vest behind, that else had flow'd upon the Ground,
And shew'd her buskin'd Legs; her Head was bare,
But for her Native Ornament of Hair;
Which in a simple Knot was ty'd above,   70
Sweet Negligence! unheeded Bait of Love!
Her sounding Quiver, on her Shoulder ty'd,
One Hand a Dart, and one a Bow supply'd.
Such was her Face, as in a Nymph display'd
A fair fierce Boy, or in a Boy betray'd   75
The blushing Beauties of a modest Maid.
The *Caledonian* Chief at once the Dame
Beheld, at once his Heart receiv'd the Flame,
With Heav'ns averse. O happy Youth, he cry'd,
For whom thy Fates reserve so fair a Bride!   80
He sigh'd, and had no leisure more to say;
His Honour call'd his Eyes another way,
And forc'd him to pursue the now neglected Prey.
    There stood a Forest on a Mountains Brow,
Which over-look'd the shaded Plains below.   85
No sounding Ax presum'd those Trees to bite;
Coeval with the World, a venerable Sight.
The *Heroes* there arriv'd, some spread around
The Toils; some search the Footsteps on the Ground:
Some from the Chains the faithful Dogs unbound.   90
Of Action eager, and intent in Thought,
The Chiefs their honourable Danger sought:
A Valley stood below; the common Drain
Of Waters from above, and falling Rain:
The Bottom was a moist and marshy Ground,   95

Whose Edges were with bending Oziers crown'd:
The knotty Bulrush next in Order stood,
And all within of Reeds a trembling Wood.
    From hence the Boar was rows'd, and sprung amain
Like Lightning sudden, on the Warriour-Train;   100
Beats down the Trees before him, shakes the Ground,
The Forest echoes to the crackling Sound;
Shout the fierce Youth, and Clamours ring around.
All stood with their protended Spears prepar'd,
With broad Steel Heads, and brandish'd Weapons glar'd.   105
The Beast impetuous with his Tusks aside
Deals glancing Wounds; the fearful Dogs divide:
All spend their Mouth aloof, but none abide.
Echion threw the first, but miss'd his Mark,
And stuck his Boar-spear on a Maples Bark.   110
Then *Jason*: and his Javelin seem'd to take,
But fail'd with over-force, and whiz'd above his Back.
Mopsus was next; but e'er he threw, address'd
To *Phœbus*, thus: O Patron, help thy Priest:
If I adore, and ever have ador'd   115
Thy Pow'r Divine, thy present Aid afford;
That I may reach the Beast. The God allow'd
His Pray'r, and smiling, gave him what he cou'd:
He reach'd the Savage, but no Blood he drew,
Dian, unarm'd the Javelin as it flew.   120
    This chaf'd the Boar, his Nostrils Flames expire,
And his red Eye-balls roll with living Fire.
Whirl'd from a Sling, or from an Engine thrown,
Amid the Foes, so flies a mighty Stone,
As flew the Beast: The Left Wing put to flight,   125
The Chiefs o'er-born, he rushes on the Right.
Empalamos and *Pelagon* he laid
In Dust, and next to Death, but for their Fellows Aid.
Onesimus far'd worse, prepar'd to fly,
The fatal Fang drove deep within his Thigh,   130
And cut the Nerves: The Nerves no more sustain
The Bulk; the Bulk unprop'd, falls headlong on the Plain.
    Nestor had fail'd the Fall of *Troy* to see,
But leaning on his Lance, he vaulted on a Tree;
Then gath'ring up his Feet, look'd down with Fear,   135

And thought his monstrous Foe was still too near.
Against a Stump his Tusk the Monster grinds,
And in the sharpen'd Edge new Vigour finds;
Then, trusting to his Arms, young *Othrys* found,
And ranch'd his Hips with one continu'd Wound.   140
Now *Leda*'s Twins, the future Stars, appear;
White were their Habits, white their Horses were:
Conspicuous both, and both in act to throw,
Their trembling Lances brandish'd at the Foe:
Nor had they miss'd; but he to Thickets fled,   145
Conceal'd from aiming Spears, not pervious to the Steed.
But *Telamon* rush'd in, and happ'd to meet
A rising Root, that held his fastned Feet;
So down he fell; whom, sprawling on the Ground,
His Brother from the Wooden Gyves unbound.   150
   Mean time the Virgin-Huntress was not slow
T' expel the Shaft from her contracted Bow:
Beneath his Ear the fastned Arrow stood,
And from the Wound appear'd the trickling Blood.
She blush'd for Joy: But *Meleagros* rais'd   155
His voice with loud Applause, and the fair Archer prais'd.
He was the first to see, and first to show
His Friends the Marks of the successful Blow.
Nor shall thy Valour want the Praises due,
He said; a vertuous Envy seiz'd the Crew.   160
They shout; the Shouting animates their Hearts,
And all at once employ their thronging Darts:
But out of Order thrown, in Air they joyn;
And Multitude makes frustrate the Design.
With both his Hands the proud *Anceus* takes,   165
And flourishes his double-biting Ax:
Then forward to his Fate, he took a Stride
Before the rest, and to his Fellows cry'd,
Give place, and mark the diff'rence, if you can,
Between a Woman Warriour, and a Man;   170
The Boar is doom'd; nor though *Diana* lend
Her Aid, *Diana* can her Beast defend.
Thus boasted he; then stretch'd, on Tiptoe stood,
Secure to make his empty Promise good.
But the more wary Beast prevents the Blow,   175

And upward rips the Groin of his audacious Foe.
Ancæus talls; his Bowels from the Wound
Rush out, and clotter'd Blood distains the Ground.
    Perithous, no small Portion of the War
Press'd on, and shook his Lance: To whom from far   180
Thus *Theseus* cry'd; O stay, my better Part,
My more than Mistress; of my Heart, the Heart.
The Strong may fight aloof; *Anceus* try'd
His Force too near, and by presuming dy'd:
He said, and while he spake his Javelin threw,   185
Hissing in Air th' unerring Weapon flew;
But on an Arm of Oak, that stood betwixt
The Marks-man and the Mark, his Lance he fixt.
    Once more bold *Jason* threw, but fail'd to wound
The Boar, and slew an undeserving Hound;   190
And through the Dog the Dart was nail'd to Ground.
    Two Spears from *Meleager*'s Hand were sent,
With equal Force, but various in th' Event:
The first was fix'd in Earth, the second stood
On the Boars bristled Back, and deeply drank his Blood. 195
Now while the tortur'd Salvage turns around,
And flings about his Foam, impatient of the Wound,
The Wounds great Author close at Hand, provokes
His Rage, and plyes him with redoubled Strokes;
Wheels as he wheels; and with his pointed Dart   200
Explores the nearest Passage to his Heart.
Quick, and more quick he spins in giddy Gires,
Then falls, and in much Foam his Soul expires.
This Act with Shouts Heav'n high the friendly Band
Applaud, and strain in theirs the Victour Hand.   205
Then all approach the Slain with vast Surprize,
Admire on what a Breadth of Earth he lies,
And scarce secure, reach out their Spears afar,
And blood their Points, to prove their Partnership **of War.**
    But he, the conqu'ring Chief, his Foot impress'd   210
On the strong Neck of that destructive Beast;
And gazing on the Nymph with ardent Eyes,
Accept, said he, fair *Nonacrine*, my Prize,
And, though inferiour, suffer me to join

My Labours, and my Part of Praise with thine: 215
At this presents her with the Tusky Head
And Chine, with rising Bristles roughly spread.
Glad, she receiv'd the Gift; and seem'd to take
With double Pleasure, for the Giver's sake.
The rest were seiz'd with sullen Discontent,   220
And a deaf Murmur through the Squadron went:
All envy'd; but the *Thestyan* Brethren show'd
The least Respect, and thus they vent their Spleen aloud:
Lay down those honour'd Spoils, nor think to share,
Weak Woman as thou art, the Prize of War: 225
Ours is the Title, thine a foreign Claim,
Since *Meleagros* from our Lineage came.
Trust not thy Beauty; but restore the Prize,
Which he, besotted on that Face and Eyes,
Would rend from us: At this, inflam'd with Spite,   230
From her they snatch the Gift, from him the Givers Right.
    But soon th' impatient Prince his Fauchion drew,
And cry'd, Ye Robbers of another's Due,
Now learn the Diff'rence, at your proper Cost,
Betwixt true Valour, and an empty Boast.   235
At this advanc'd, and sudden as the Word,
In proud *Plexippus* Bosom plung'd the Sword:
Toxeus amaz'd, and with Amazement slow,
Or to revenge, or ward the coming Blow,
Stood doubting; and, while doubting thus he stood,   240
Receiv'd the Steel bath'd in his Brother's Blood.
    Pleas'd with the first, unknown the second News,
Althea, to the Temples, pays their Dues,
For her Son's Conquest; when at length appear
Her griesly Brethren stretch'd upon the Bier: } 245
Pale at the sudden Sight, she chang'd her Cheer,
And with her Cheer her Robes; but hearing tell
The Cause, the Manner, and by whom they fell,
'Twas Grief no more, or Grief and Rage were one
Within her Soul; at last 'twas Rage alone;   250
Which burning upwards in succession dries
The Tears that stood consid'ring in her Eyes.
    There lay a Log unlighted on the Hearth,

237 *Plexippus*] *Ploxippus* F   253 Hearth,] Hearth: F

When she was lab'ring in the Throws of Birth
For th' unborn Chief; the Fatal Sisters came,   255
And rais'd it up, and toss'd it on the Flame:
Then on the Rock a scanty Measure place
Of Vital Flax, and turn'd the Wheel apace;
And turning sung, To this red Brand and thee,
O new-born Babe, we give an equal Destiny: 260
So vanish'd out of View. The frighted Dame
Sprung hasty from her Bed, and quench'd the Flame:
The Log in secret lock'd, she kept with Care,
And that, while thus preserv'd, preserv'd her Heir.
This Brand she now produc'd; and first she strows   265
The Hearth with Heaps of Chips, and after blows,
Thrice heav'd her Hand, and heav'd, she thrice repress'd: ⎫
The Sister and the Mother long contest   ⎬
Two doubtful Titles in one tender Breast: ⎭
And now her Eyes and Cheeks with Fury glow,   270
Now pale her Cheeks, her Eyes with Pity flow:
Now lowring Looks presage approaching Storms,
And now prevailing Love her Face reforms:
Resolv'd, she doubts again; the Tears she dry'd
With burning Rage, are by new Tears supply'd;   275
And as a Ship, which Winds and Waves assail,   ⎫
Now with the Current drives, now with the Gale,   ⎬
Both opposite, and neither long prevail: ⎭
She feels a double Force, by Turns obeys
Th' imperious Tempest, and th' impetuous Seas: 280
So fares *Althæa*'s Mind; she first relents
With Pity, of that Pity then repents:
Sister and Mother long the Scales divide,
But the Beam nodded on the Sisters side.
Sometimes she softly sigh'd, then roar'd aloud;   285
But Sighs were stifl'd in the Cries of Blood.
    The pious, impious Wretch at length decreed,
To please her Brother's Ghost, her Son shou'd bleed:
And when the Fun'ral Flames began to rise,
Receive, she said, a Sisters Sacrifice;   290
A Mothers Bowels burn: High in her Hand
Thus while she spoke, she held the fatal Brand;

255 Chief;] Chief, F

Then thrice before the kindled Pyle she bow'd,
And the three Furies thrice invok'd aloud:
Come, come, revenging Sisters, come and view   295
A Sister paying her dead Brothers Due:
A Crime I punish, and a Crime commit;
But Blood for Blood, and Death for Death is fit:
Great Crimes must be with greater Crimes repaid,
And second Funerals on the former laid.   300
Let the whole Houshold in one Ruine fall,
And may *Diana*'s Curse o'ertake us all.
Shall Fate to happy *Oeneus* still allow
One Son, while *Thestius* stands depriv'd of two?
Better three lost, than one unpunish'd go.   305
Take then, dear Ghosts, (while yet admitted new
In Hell you wait my Duty) take your Due:
A costly Off'ring on your Tomb is laid,
When with my Blood the Price of yours is paid.
    Ah! Whither am I hurried? Ah! forgive,   310
Ye Shades, and let your Sisters Issue live:
A Mother cannot give him Death, though he
Deserves it, he deserves it not from me.
    Then shall th' unpunish'd Wretch insult the Slain,
Triumphant live, nor only live, but reign?   315
While you, thin Shades, the Sport of Winds, are toss'd
O'er dreery Plains, or tread the burning Coast.
I cannot, cannot bear; 'tis past, 'tis done;
Perish this impious, this detested Son:
Perish his Sire, and perish I withal;   320
And let the Houses Heir, and the hop'd Kingdom fall.
    Where is the Mother fled, her pious Love,
And where the Pains with which ten Months I strove!
Ah! hadst thou dy'd, my Son, in Infant-years,
Thy little Herse had been bedew'd with Tears.   325
    Thou liv'st by me; to me thy Breath resign;
Mine is the Merit, the Demerit thine.
Thy Life by double Title I require;
Once giv'n at Birth, and once preserv'd from Fire:
One Murder pay, or add one Murder more,   330
And me to them who fell by thee restore.
    I wou'd, but cannot: My Son's Image stands

Before my Sight; and now their angry Hands
My Brothers hold, and Vengeance these exact,
This pleads Compassion, and repents the Fact.   335
     He pleads in vain, and I pronounce his Doom:
My Brothers, though unjustly, shall o'ercome.
But having paid their injur'd Ghosts their Due,
My Son requires my Death, and mine shall his pursue.
     At this, for the last time she lifts her Hand,   340
Averts her Eyes, and, half unwilling, drops the Brand.
The Brand, amid the flaming Fewel thrown,
Or drew, or seem'd to draw a dying Groan:
The Fires themselves but faintly lick'd their Prey,
Then loath'd their impious Food, and wou'd have shrunk away.   345
     Just then the *Heroe* cast a doleful Cry,
And in those absent Flames began to fry:
The blind Contagion rag'd within his Veins;
But he with manly Patience bore his Pains:
He fear'd not Fate, but only griev'd to die   350
Without an honest Wound, and by a Death so dry.
Happy *Ancæus*, thrice aloud he cry'd,
With what becoming Fate in Arms he dy'd!
Then call'd his Brothers, Sisters, Sire, around,
And her to whom his Nuptial Vows were bound;   355
Perhaps his Mother; a long Sigh he drew,
And his Voice failing, took his last Adieu:
For as the Flames augment, and as they stay
At their full Height, then languish to decay,
They rise, and sink by Fits; at last they soar   360
In one bright Blaze, and then descend no more:
Just so his inward Heats at height, impair,
Till the last burning Breath shoots out the Soul in Air.
     Now lofty *Calidon* in Ruines lies;
All Ages, all Degrees unsluice their Eyes;   }   365
And Heav'n and Earth resound with Murmurs, Groans, and Cries.
Matrons and Maidens beat their Breasts, and tear
Their Habits, and root up their scatter'd Hair:
The wretched Father, Father now no more,
With Sorrow sunk, lies prostrate on the Floor,   370
Deforms his hoary Locks with Dust obscene,
And curses Age, and loaths a Life prolong'd with Pain.

By Steel her stubborn Soul his Mother freed,
And punish'd on her self her impious Deed.
  Had I a hundred Tongues, a Wit so large   375
As cou'd their hundred Offices discharge;
Had *Phœbus* all his *Helicon* bestow'd
In all the Streams inspiring all the God;
Those Tongues, that Wit, those Streams, that God, in vain
Wou'd offer to describe his Sisters pain: 380
They beat their Breasts with many a bruizing Blow,
Till they turn'd livid, and corrupt the Snow.
The Corps they cherish, while the Corps remains,
And exercise and rub with fruitless Pains;
And when to Fun'ral Flames 'tis born away,   385
They kiss the Bed on which the Body lay:
And when those Fun'ral Flames no longer burn,
(The Dust compos'd within a pious Urn)
Ev'n in that Urn their Brother they confess,
And hug it in their Arms, and to their Bosoms press.   390
  His Tomb is rais'd; then, stretch'd along the Ground,
Those living Monuments his Tomb surround:
Ev'n to his Name, inscrib'd, their Tears they pay,
Till Tears and Kisses wear his Name away.
  But *Cynthia* now had all her Fury spent,   395
Not with less Ruine than a Race, content:
Excepting *Gorge*, perish'd all the Seed,
And *Her whom Heav'n for *Hercules* decreed.   *Dejanira.
Satiate at last, no longer she pursu'd
The weeping Sisters; but with Wings endu'd,   400
And Horny Beaks, and sent to flit in Air;
Who yearly round the Tomb in Feather'd Flocks repair.

SIGISMONDA AND GUISCARDO,
FROM BOCCACE

WHILE *Norman Tancred* in *Salerno* reign'd,
  The Title of a Gracious Prince he gain'd;
Till turn'd a Tyrant in his latter Days,
He lost the Lustre of his former Praise;

And from the bright Meridian where he stood,   5
Descending, dipp'd his Hands in Lovers Blood.
     This Prince, of Fortunes Favour long possess'd,
Yet was with one fair Daughter only bless'd;
And bless'd he might have been with her alone:
But oh! how much more happy, had he none!   10
She was his Care, his Hope, and his Delight,
Most in his Thought, and ever in his Sight:
Next, nay beyond his Life, he held her dear;
She liv'd by him, and now he liv'd in her.
For this, when ripe for Marriage, he delay'd   15
Her Nuptial Bands, and kept her long a Maid,
As envying any else should share a Part
Of what was his, and claiming all her Heart.
At length, as Publick Decency requir'd,
And all his Vassals eagerly desir'd,   20
With Mind averse, he rather underwent
His Peoples Will, than gave his own Consent:
So was she torn, as from a Lover's Side,
And made almost in his despite a Bride.
     Short were her Marriage-Joys; for in the Prime   25
Of Youth, her Lord expir'd before his time:
And to her Father's Court, in little space
Restor'd anew, she held a higher Place;
More lov'd, and more exalted into Grace.
This Princess fresh and young, and fair, and wise,   30
The worshipp'd Idol of her Father's Eyes,
Did all her Sex in ev'ry Grace exceed,
And had more Wit beside than Women need.
     Youth, Health, and Ease, and most an amorous Mind,
To second Nuptials had her Thoughts inclin'd: 35
And former Joys had left a secret Sting behind.
But prodigal in ev'ry other Grant,
Her Sire left unsupply'd her only Want;
And she, betwixt her Modesty and Pride,
Her Wishes, which she could not help, would hide.   40
     Resolv'd at last to lose no longer Time,
And yet to please her self without a Crime,
She cast her Eyes around the Court, to find
A worthy Subject suiting to her Mind,

To him in holy Nuptials to be ty'd,   45
A seeming Widow, and a secret Bride.
Among the Train of Courtiers, one she found
With all the Gifts of bounteous Nature crown'd,
Of gentle Blood; but one whose niggard Fate
Had set him far below her high Estate;   50
Guiscard his Name was call'd, of blooming Age,
Now Squire to *Tancred*, and before his Page:
To him, the Choice of all the shining Crowd,
Her Heart the noble *Sigismonda* vow'd.

   Yet hitherto she kept her Love conceal'd,   55
And with close Glances ev'ry Day beheld
The graceful Youth; and ev'ry Day increas'd
The raging Fire that burn'd within her Breast:
Some secret Charm did all his Acts attend,
And what his Fortune wanted, hers could mend: 60
Till, as the Fire will force its outward way,
Or, in the Prison pent, consume the Prey;
So long her earnest Eyes on his were set,
At length their twisted Rays together met;
And he, surpriz'd with humble Joy, survey'd   65
One sweet Regard, shot by the Royal Maid:
Not well assur'd, while doubtful Hopes he nurs'd,
A second Glance came gliding like the first;
And he who saw the Sharpness of the Dart,
Without Defence receiv'd it in his Heart.   70
In Publick though their Passion wanted Speech,
Yet mutual Looks interpreted for each:
Time, Ways, and Means of Meeting were deny'd;
But all those Wants ingenious Love supply'd.
Th' inventive God, who never fails his Part,   75
Inspires the Wit, when once he warms the Heart.

   When *Guiscard* next was in the Circle seen,
Where *Sigismonda* held the Place of Queen,
A hollow Cane within her Hand she brought,
But in the Concave had enclos'd a Note: 80
With this she seem'd to play, and, as in sport,
Toss'd to her Love, in presence of the Court;
Take it, she said; and when your Needs require,
This little Brand will serve to light your Fire.

He took it with a Bow, and soon divin'd   85
The seeming Toy was not for nought design'd:
But when retir'd, so long with curious Eyes
He view'd the Present, that he found the Prize.
Much was in little writ; and all convey'd
With cautious Care, for fear to be betray'd   90
By some false Confident, or Fav'rite Maid.
The Time, the Place, the Manner how to meet,
Were all in punctual Order plainly writ:
But since a Trust must be, she thought it best
To put it out of Laymens Pow'r at least,   95
And for their solemn Vows prepar'd a Priest.
    Guiscard (her secret Purpose understood)
With Joy prepar'd to meet the coming Good;
Nor Pains nor Danger was resolv'd to spare,
But use the Means appointed by the Fair.   100
    Near the proud Palace of *Salerno* stood
A Mount of rough Ascent, and thick with Wood;
Through this a Cave was dug with vast Expence,
The Work it seem'd of some suspicious Prince,
Who, when abusing Pow'r with lawless Might,   105
From Publick Justice would secure his Flight.
The Passage made by many a winding Way,
Reach'd ev'n the Room in which the Tyrant lay.
Fit for his Purpose, on a lower Floor
He lodg'd, whose Issue was an Iron Door,   110
From whence, by Stairs descending to the Ground,
In the blind Grot a safe Retreat he found.
Its Outlet ended in a Brake o'ergrown
With Brambles, choak'd by Time, and now unknown.
A Rift there was, which from the Mountains Height   115
Convey'd a glimm'ring and malignant Light,
A Breathing-place to draw the Damps away,
A Twilight of an intercepted Day.
The Tyrants Den, whose Use though lost to Fame,
Was now th' Apartment of the Royal Dame;   120
The Cavern only to her Father known,
By him was to his Darling-Daughter shown.
    Neglected long she let the Secret rest,

Till Love recall'd it to her lab'ring Breast,
And hinted as the Way by Heav'n design'd   125
The Teacher, by the Means he taught, to blind.
What will not Women do, when Need inspires
Their Wit, or Love their Inclination fires!
Though Jealousie of State th' Invention found,
Yet Love refin'd upon the former Ground.   130
That Way, the Tyrant had reserv'd, to fly
Pursuing Hate, now serv'd to bring two Lovers nigh.
     The Dame, who long in vain had kept the Key,
Bold by Desire, explor'd the secret Way;
Now try'd the Stairs, and wading through the Night,   135
Search'd all the deep Recess, and issu'd into Light.
All this her Letter had so well explain'd,
Th' instructed Youth might compass what remain'd:
The Cavern-mouth alone was hard to find,
Because the Path disus'd, was out of mind: 140
But in what Quarter of the Cops it lay,
His Eye by certain Level could survey:
Yet (for the Wood perplex'd with Thorns he knew)
A Frock of Leather o'er his Limbs he drew:
And thus provided, search'd the Brake around,   145
Till the choak'd Entry of the Cave he found.
     Thus, all prepar'd, the promis'd Hour arriv'd,
So long expected, and so well contriv'd:
With Love to Friend, th' impatient Lover went,
Fenc'd from the Thorns, and trod the deep Descent.   150
The conscious Priest, who was suborn'd before,
Stood ready posted at the Postern-door;
The Maids in distant Rooms were sent to rest,
And nothing wanted but th' invited Guest.
He came, and knocking thrice, without delay,   155
The longing Lady heard, and turn'd the Key;
At once invaded him with all her Charms,
And the first Step he made, was in her Arms:
The Leathern Out-side, boistrous as it was,
Gave way, and bent beneath her strict Embrace: 160
On either Side the Kisses flew so thick,
That neither he nor she had Breath to speak.
The holy Man amaz'd at what he saw,

Made haste to sanctifie the Bliss by Law;
And mutter'd fast the Matrimony o're,   165
For fear committed Sin should get before.
His Work perform'd, he left the Pair alone,
Because he knew he could not go too soon;
His Presence odious, when his Task was done.
What Thoughts he had, beseems not me to say;   170
Though some surmise he went to fast and pray,
And needed both, to drive the tempting Thoughts away.

   The Foe once gone, they took their full Delight;
'Twas restless Rage, and Tempest all the Night:
For greedy Love each Moment would employ,   175
And grudg'd the shortest Pauses of their Joy.

   Thus were their Loves auspiciously begun,
And thus with secret Care were carried on.
The Stealth it self did Appetite restore,
And look'd so like a Sin, it pleas'd the more.   180

   The Cave was now become a common Way,
The Wicket often open'd, knew the Key:
Love rioted secure, and long enjoy'd,
Was ever eager, and was never cloy'd.

   But as Extremes are short, of Ill and Good,   185
And Tides at highest Mark regorge the Flood;
So Fate, that could no more improve their Joy,
Took a malicious Pleasure to destroy.

   Tancred, who fondly lov'd, and whose Delight
Was plac'd in his fair Daughters daily Sight,   190
Of Custom, when his State-Affairs were done,
Would pass his pleasing Hours with her alone:
And, as a Father's Privilege allow'd,
Without Attendance of th' officious Crowd.

   It happen'd once, that when in Heat of Day   195
He try'd to sleep, as was his usual Way,
The balmy Slumber fled his wakeful Eyes,
And forc'd him, in his own despite, to rise:
Of Sleep forsaken, to relieve his Care,
He sought the Conversation of the Fair: 200
But with her Train of Damsels she was gone,
In shady Walks the scorching Heat to shun:
He would not violate that sweet Recess,

And found besides a welcome Heaviness
That seiz'd his Eyes; and Slumber, which forgot   205
When call'd before to come, now came unsought.
From Light retir'd, behind his Daughters Bed,
He for approaching Sleep compos'd his Head;
A Chair was ready, for that Use design'd,
So quilted, that he lay at ease reclin'd;   210
The Curtains closely drawn, the Light to skreen,
As if he had contriv'd to lie unseen:
Thus cover'd with an artificial Night,
Sleep did his Office soon, and seal'd his Sight.

    With Heav'n averse, in this ill-omen'd Hour   215
Was *Guiscard* summon'd to the secret Bow'r,
And the fair Nymph, with Expectation fir'd,
From her attending Damsels was retir'd:
For, true to Love, she measur'd Time so right,
As not to miss one Moment of Delight.   220
The Garden, seated on the level Floor,
She left behind, and locking ev'ry Door,
Thought all secure; but little did she know,
Blind to her Fate, she had inclos'd her Foe.
Attending *Guiscard*, in his Leathern Frock,   225
Stood ready, with his thrice-repeated Knock:
Thrice with a doleful Sound the jarring Grate
Rung deaf, and hollow, and presag'd their Fate.
The Door unlock'd, to known Delight they haste,
And panting in each others Arms, embrac'd;   230
Rush to the conscious Bed, a mutual Freight,
And heedless press it with their wonted Weight.

    The sudden Bound awak'd the sleeping Sire,
And shew'd a Sight no Parent can desire:
His opening Eyes at once with odious View   235
The Love discover'd, and the Lover knew:
He would have cry'd; but hoping that he dreamt,
Amazement ty'd his Tongue, and stopp'd th' Attempt.
Th' ensuing Moment all the Truth declar'd,
But now he stood collected, and prepar'd;   240
For Malice and Revenge had put him on his Guard.

So, like a Lion that unheeded lay,
Dissembling Sleep, and watchful to betray,
With inward Rage he meditates his Prey.
The thoughtless Pair, indulging their Desires,   245
Alternate, kindl'd, and then quench'd their Fires;
Nor thinking in the Shades of Death they play'd,
Full of themselves, themselves alone survey'd,
And, too secure, were by themselves betray'd.
Long time dissolv'd in Pleasure thus they lay,   250
Till Nature could no more suffice their Play;
Then rose the Youth, and through the Cave again
Return'd; the Princess mingl'd with her Train.
    Resolv'd his unripe Vengeance to defer,
The Royal Spy, when now the Coast was clear,   255
Sought not the Garden, but retir'd unseen,
To brood in secret on his gather'd Spleen,
And methodize Revenge: To Death he griev'd;
And, but he saw the Crime, had scarce believ'd.
Th' Appointment for th' ensuing Night he heard;   260
And therefore in the Cavern had prepar'd
Two brawny Yeomen of his trusty Guard.
    Scarce had unwary *Guiscard* set his Foot
Within the farmost Entrance of the Grot,
When these in secret Ambush ready lay,   265
And rushing on the sudden seiz'd the Prey:
Encumber'd with his Frock, without Defence,
An easie Prize, they led the Pris'ner thence,
And, as commanded, brought before the Prince.
The gloomy Sire, too sensible of Wrong   270
To vent his Rage in Words, restrain'd his Tongue;
And only said, Thus Servants are preferr'd,
And trusted, thus their Sov'reigns they reward.
Had I not seen, had not these Eyes receiv'd
Too clear a Proof, I could not have believ'd.   275
    He paus'd, and choak'd the rest. The Youth, who saw
His forfeit Life abandon'd to the Law,
The Judge th' Accuser, and th' Offence to him
Who had both Pow'r and Will t' avenge the Crime,
No vain Defence prepar'd; but thus reply'd,   280

254 defer,] defer *F*   279 Crime,] Crime; *F*

The Faults of Love by Love are justifi'd:
With unresisted Might the Monarch reigns,
He levels Mountains, and he raises Plains;
And not regarding Diff'rence of Degree,
Abas'd your Daughter, and exalted me.   285
   This bold Return with seeming Patience heard,
The Pris'ner was remitted to the Guard.
The sullen Tyrant slept not all the Night,
But lonely walking by a winking Light,
Sobb'd, wept, and groan'd, and beat his wither'd Breast,   290
But would not violate his Daughters Rest;
Who long expecting lay, for Bliss prepar'd,
Listning for Noise, and griev'd that none she heard;
Oft rose, and oft in vain employ'd the Key,
And oft accus'd her Lover of Delay;   295
And pass'd the tedious Hours in anxious Thoughts away.
   The Morrow came; and at his usual Hour
Old *Tancred* visited his Daughters Bow'r;
Her Cheek (for such his Custom was) he kiss'd,
Then bless'd her kneeling, and her Maids dismiss'd.   300
The Royal Dignity thus far maintain'd,
Now left in private, he no longer feign'd;
But all at once his Grief and Rage appear'd,
And Floods of Tears ran trickling down his Beard.
   O *Sigismonda*, he began to say: 305
Thrice he began, and thrice was forc'd to stay,
Till Words with often trying found their Way:
I thought, O *Sigismonda*, (But how blind
Are Parents Eyes, their Childrens Faults to find!)
Thy Vertue, Birth, and Breeding were above   310
A mean Desire, and vulgar Sense of Love:
Nor less than Sight and Hearing could convince
So fond a Father, and so just a Prince,
Of such an unforeseen, and unbeliev'd Offence.
Then what indignant Sorrow must I have,   315
To see thee lie subjected to my Slave!
A Man so smelling of the Peoples Lee,
The Court receiv'd him first for Charity;
And since with no Degree of Honour grac'd,
But only suffer'd, where he first was plac'd: 320

A grov'ling Insect still; and so design'd
By Natures Hand, nor born of Noble Kind:
A Thing, by neither Man nor Woman priz'd,
And scarcely known enough, to be despis'd.
To what has Heav'n reserv'd my Age? Ah! why   325
Should Man, when Nature calls, not chuse to die,
Rather than stretch the Span of Life, to find
Such Ills as Fate has wisely cast behind,
For those to feel, whom fond Desire to live
Makes covetous of more than Life can give!   330
Each has his Share of Good; and when 'tis gone,
The Guest, though hungry, cannot rise too soon.
But I, expecting more, in my own wrong
Protracting Life, have liv'd a Day too long.
If Yesterday cou'd be recall'd again,   335
Ev'n now would I conclude my happy Reign:
But 'tis too late, my glorious Race is run,
And a dark Cloud o'ertakes my setting Sun.
Hadst thou not lov'd, or loving sav'd the Shame,
If not the Sin, by some Illustrious Name,   340
This little Comfort had reliev'd my Mind,
'Twas frailty, not unusual to thy Kind:
But thy low Fall beneath thy Royal Blood,
Shews downward Appetite to mix with Mud:
Thus not the least Excuse is left for thee,   345
Nor the least Refuge for unhappy me.
    For him I have resolv'd: whom by Surprize
I took, and scarce can call it, in Disguise:
For such was his Attire, as with Intent
Of Nature, suited to his mean Descent: 350
The harder Question yet remains behind,
What Pains a Parent and a Prince can find
To punish an Offence of this degenerate Kind.
    As I have lov'd, and yet I love thee more
Than ever Father lov'd a Child before;   355
So, that Indulgence draws me to forgive:
Nature, that gave thee Life, would have thee live.
But, as a Publick Parent of the State,
My Justice, and thy Crime, requires thy Fate.
Fain would I chuse a middle Course to steer;   360

Nature's too kind, and Justice too severe:
Speak for us both, and to the Balance bring
On either side, the Father, and the King.
Heav'n knows, my Heart is bent to favour thee;
Make it but scanty weight, and leave the rest to me.   365
　　Here stopping with a Sigh, he pour'd a Flood
Of Tears, to make his last Expression good.
　　She, who had heard him speak, nor saw alone
The secret Conduct of her Love was known;
But he was taken who her Soul possess'd,   370
Felt all the Pangs of Sorrow in her Breast:
And little wanted, but a Womans Heart
With Cries, and Tears, had testifi'd her Smart:
But in-born Worth, that Fortune can controul,
New strung, and stiffer bent her softer Soul;   375
The *Heroine* assum'd the Womans Place,
Confirm'd her Mind, and fortifi'd her Face:
Why should she beg, or what cou'd she pretend,
When her stern Father had condemn'd her Friend!
Her Life she might have had; but her Despair   380
Of saving his, had put it past her Care:
Resolv'd on Fate, she would not lose her Breath
But rather than not die, sollicit Death.
Fix'd on this Thought, she not as Women use,
Her Fault by common Frailty would excuse;   385
But boldly justifi'd her Innocence,
And while the Fact was own'd, deny'd th' Offence:
Then with dry Eyes, and with an open Look,
She met his Glance mid-way, and thus undaunted spoke.
　　Tancred, I neither am dispos'd to make   390
Request for Life, nor offer'd Life to take:
Much less deny the Deed; but least of all
Beneath pretended Justice weakly fall.
My Words to sacred Truth shall be confin'd,
My Deeds shall shew the Greatness of my Mind.   395
That I have lov'd, I own; that still I love,
I call to Witness all the Pow'rs above:
Yet more I own: To *Guiscard*'s Love I give
The small remaining Time I have to live;
And if beyond this Life Desire can be,   400

Not Fate it self shall set my Passion free.
  This first avow'd; nor Folly warp'd my Mind,
Nor the frail Texture of the Female Kind
Betray'd my Vertue: For, too well I knew
What Honour was, and Honour had his Due: 40
Before the Holy Priest my Vows were ty'd,
So came I not a Strumpet, but a Bride;
This for my Fame: and for the Publick Voice:
Yet more, his Merits justifi'd my Choice;
Which had they not, the first Election thine,   41
That Bond dissolv'd, the next is freely mine:
Or grant I err'd, (which yet I must deny,)
Had Parents pow'r ev'n second Vows to tie,
Thy little Care to mend my Widow'd Nights
Has forc'd me to recourse of Marriage-Rites,   41
To fill an empty Side, and follow known Delights.
What have I done in this, deserving Blame?
State-Laws may alter: Nature's are the same;
Those are usurp'd on helpless Woman-kind,
Made without our Consent, and wanting Pow'r to bind.   42
  Thou, *Tancred*, better should'st have understood,
That as thy Father gave thee Flesh and Blood,
So gav'st thou me: Not from the Quarry hew'd,
But of a softer Mould, with Sense endu'd;
Ev'n softer than thy own, of suppler Kind,   42
More exquisite of Taste, and more than Man refin'd.
Nor need'st thou by thy Daughter to be told,
Though now thy spritely Blood with Age be cold,
Thou hast been young; and canst remember still,
That when thou hadst the Pow'r, thou hadst the Will;   43
And from the past Experience of thy Fires,
Canst tell with what a Tide our strong Desires
Come rushing on in Youth, and what their Rage requires.
  And grant thy Youth was exercis'd in Arms,
When Love no leisure found for softer Charms;   43
My tender Age in Luxury was train'd,
With idle Ease and Pageants entertain'd;
My Hours my own, my Pleasures unrestrain'd.
So bred, no wonder if I took the Bent
That seem'd ev'n warranted by thy Consent;   44

For, when the Father is too fondly kind,
Such Seed he sows, such Harvest shall he find.
Blame then thy self, as Reason's Law requires,
(Since Nature gave, and thou foment'st my Fires;)
If still those Appetites continue strong, 445
Thou maist consider, I am yet but young:
Consider too, that having been a Wife,
I must have tasted of a better Life,
And am not to be blam'd, if I renew,
By lawful Means, the Joys which then I knew. 450
Where was the Crime, if Pleasure I procur'd,
Young, and a Woman, and to Bliss inur'd?
That was my Case, and this is my Defence;
I pleas'd my self, I shunn'd Incontinence,
And, urg'd by strong Desires, indulg'd my Sense. 455
    Left to my self, I must avow, I strove
From publick Shame to screen my secret Love,
And, well acquainted with thy Native Pride,
Endeavour'd, what I could not help, to hide;
For which, a Womans Wit an easie Way supply'd. 460
How this, so well contriv'd, so closely laid,
Was known to thee, or by what Chance betray'd,
Is not my Care: To please thy Pride alone,
I could have wish'd it had been still unknown.
    Nor took I *Guiscard* by blind Fancy led, 465
Or hasty Choice, as many Women wed;
But with delib'rate Care, and ripen'd Thought,
At leisure first design'd, before I wrought:
On him I rested, after long Debate,
And not without consid'ring, fix'd my Fate: 470
His Flame was equal, though by mine inspir'd;
(For so the Diff'rence of our Birth requir'd:)
Had he been born like me, like me his Love
Had first begun, what mine was forc'd to move:
But thus beginning, thus we persevere; 475
Our Passions yet continue what they were,
Nor length of Trial makes our Joys the less sincere.
    At this my Choice, though not by thine allow'd,
(Thy Judgment herding with the common Crowd)
Thou tak'st unjust Offence; and, led by them, 480

Dost less the Merit, than the Man esteem.
Too sharply, *Tancred*, by thy Pride betray'd,
Hast thou against the Laws of Kind inveigh'd;
For all th' Offence is in Opinion plac'd,
Which deems high Birth by lowly Choice debas'd: 485
This Thought alone with Fury fires thy Breast,
(For Holy Marriage justifies the rest)
That I have sunk the Glories of the State,
And mix'd my Blood with a Plebeian Mate:
In which I wonder thou shouldst oversee   490
Superiour Causes, or impute to me
The Fault of Fortune, or the Fates Decree.
Or call it Heav'ns Imperial Pow'r alone,
Which moves on Springs of Justice, though unknown;
Yet this we see, though order'd for the best,   495
The Bad exalted, and the Good oppress'd;
Permitted Laurels grace the Lawless Brow,
Th' Unworthy rais'd, the Worthy cast below.
    But leaving that: Search we the secret Springs,
And backward trace the Principles of Things;   500
There shall we find, that when the World began,
One common Mass compos'd the Mould of Man;
One Paste of Flesh on all Degrees bestow'd,
And kneaded up alike with moistning Blood.
The same Almighty Pow'r inspir'd the Frame   505
With kindl'd Life, and form'd the Souls the same:
The Faculties of Intellect, and Will,
Dispens'd with equal Hand, dispos'd with equal Skill,
Like Liberty indulg'd with Choice of Good or Ill.
Thus born alike, from Vertue first began   510
The Diff'rence that distinguish'd Man from Man:
He claim'd no Title from Descent of Blood,
But that which made him Noble, made him Good:
Warm'd with more Particles of Heav'nly Flame,
He wing'd his upward Flight, and soar'd to Fame;   515
The rest remain'd below, a Tribe without a Name.
    This Law, though Custom now diverts the Course,
As Natures Institute, is yet in force;
Uncancell'd, tho disus'd: And he whose Mind
Is Vertuous, is alone of Noble Kind.   520

Though poor in Fortune, of Celestial Race;
And he commits the Crime, who calls him Base.
   Now lay the Line; and measure all thy Court,
By inward Vertue, not external Port,
And find whom justly to prefer above   525
The Man on whom my Judgment plac'd my Love:
So shalt thou see his Parts, and Person shine;
And thus compar'd, the rest a base degen'rate Line.
Nor took I, when I first survey'd thy Court,
His Valour, or his Vertues on Report;   530
But trusted what I ought to trust alone,
Relying on thy Eyes, and not my own;
Thy Praise (and Thine was then the Publick Voice)
First recommended *Guiscard* to my Choice:
Directed thus by thee, I look'd, and found   535
A Man, I thought, deserving to be crown'd;
First by my Father pointed to my Sight,
Nor less conspicuous by his Native Light:
His Mind, his Meen, the Features of his Face,
Excelling all the rest of Humane Race: 540
These were thy Thoughts, and thou could'st judge aright,
Till Int'rest made a Jaundice in thy Sight.
   Or shou'd I grant, thou didst not rightly see;
Then thou wert first deceiv'd, and I deceiv'd by thee.
But if thou shalt alledge, through Pride of Mind,   545
Thy Blood with one of base Condition join'd,
'Tis false; for 'tis not Baseness to be Poor;
His Poverty augments thy Crime the more;
Upbraids thy Justice with the scant Regard
Of Worth: Whom Princes praise, they shou'd reward.   550
Are these the Kings intrusted by the Crowd
With Wealth, to be dispens'd for Common Good?
The People sweat not for their King's Delight,
T' enrich a Pimp, or raise a Parasite;
Theirs is the Toil; and he who well has serv'd   555
His Country, has his Countrys Wealth deserv'd.
   Ev'n mighty Monarchs oft are meanly born,
And Kings by Birth, to lowest Rank return;
All subject to the Pow'r of giddy Chance,
For Fortune can depress, or can advance: 560

But true Nobility, is of the Mind,
Not giv'n by Chance, and not to Chance resign'd.
　For the remaining Doubt of thy Decree,
What to resolve, and how dispose of me,
Be warn'd to cast that useless Care aside,   565
My self alone, will for my self provide:
If in thy doting, and decrepit Age,
Thy Soul, a Stranger in thy Youth to Rage,
Begins in cruel Deeds to take Delight,
Gorge with my Blood thy barb'rous Appetite;   570
For I so little am dispos'd to pray
For Life, I would not cast a Wish away.
Such as it is, th' Offence is all my own;
And what to *Guiscard* is already done,
Or to be done, is doom'd by thy Decree,   575
That, if not executed first by thee,
Shall on my Person be perform'd by me.
　　Away, with Women weep, and leave me here,
Fix'd, like a Man to die, without a Tear;
Or save, or slay us both this present Hour,   580
'Tis all that Fate has left within thy Pow'r.
　　She said: Nor did her Father fail to find,
In all she spoke, the Greatness of her Mind;
Yet thought she was not obstinate to die,
Nor deem'd the Death she promis'd was so nigh: 585
Secure in this Belief, he left the Dame,
Resolv'd to spare her Life, and save her Shame;
But that detested Object to remove,
To wreak his Vengeance, and to cure her Love.
　　Intent on this, a secret Order sign'd,   590
The Death of *Guiscard* to his Guards enjoin'd;
Strangling was chosen, and the Night the Time,
A mute Revenge, and blind as was the Crime:
His faithful Heart, a bloody Sacrifice,
Torn from his Breast, to glut the Tyrant's Eyes,   595
Clos'd the severe Command: For, (Slaves to Pay)
What Kings decree, the Soldier must obey:
Wag'd against Foes; and, when the Wars are o'er,
Fit only to maintain Despotick Pow'r:
Dang'rous to Freedom, and desir'd alone   600

By Kings, who seek an Arbitrary Throne:
Such were these Guards; as ready to have slain
The Prince himself, allur'd with greater gain:
So was the Charge perform'd with better Will,
By Men inur'd to Blood, and exercis'd in Ill.   605
   Now, though the sullen Sire had eas'd his Mind,
The Pomp of his Revenge was yet behind,
A Pomp prepar'd to grace the Present he design'd.
A Goblet rich with Gems, and rough with Gold,
Of Depth, and Breadth, the precious Pledge to hold,   610
With cruel Care he chose: The hollow Part
Inclos'd; the Lid conceal'd the Lover's Heart:
Then of his trusted Mischiefs, one he sent,
And bad him with these Words the Gift present;
Thy Father sends thee this, to cheer thy Breast,   615
And glad thy Sight with what thou lov'st the best;
As thou hast pleas'd his Eyes, and joy'd his Mind,
With what he lov'd the most of Humane Kind.
   E'er this the Royal Dame, who well had weigh'd
The Consequence of what her Sire had said,   620
Fix'd on her Fate, against th' expected Hour,
Procur'd the Means to have it in her Pow'r:
For this, she had distill'd, with early Care,
The Juice of Simples, friendly to Despair,
A Magazine of Death; and thus prepar'd,   625
Secure to die, the fatal Message heard:
Then smil'd severe; nor with a troubl'd Look,
Or trembling Hand, the Fun'ral Present took;
Ev'n kept her Count'nance, when the Lid remov'd,
Disclos'd the Heart, unfortunately lov'd: 630
She needed not be told within whose Breast
It lodg'd; the Message had explain'd the rest.
Or not amaz'd, or hiding her Surprize,
She sternly on the Bearer fix'd her Eyes:
Then thus; Tell *Tancred*, on his Daughters part,   635
The Gold, though precious, equals not the Heart:
But he did well to give his best; and I,
Who wish'd a worthier Urn, forgive his Poverty.
   At this, she curb'd a Groan, that else had come,
And pausing, view'd the Present in the Tomb: 640

Then, to the Heart ador'd, devoutly glew'd
Her Lips, and raising it, her Speech renew'd;
Ev'n from my Day of Birth, to this, the Bound
Of my unhappy Being, I have found
My Father's Care, and Tenderness express'd: 645
But this last Act of Love excels the rest:
For this so dear a Present, bear him back
The best Return that I can live to make.

   The Messenger dispatch'd, again she view'd
The lov'd Remains, and sighing, thus pursu'd;   650
Source of my Life, and Lord of my Desires,
In whom I liv'd, with whom my Soul expires;
Poor Heart, no more the Spring of Vital Heat,
Curs'd be the Hands that tore thee from thy Seat!
The Course is finish'd, which thy Fates decreed,   655
And thou, from thy Corporeal Prison freed:
Soon hast thou reach'd the Goal with mended Pace,
A World of Woes dispatch'd in little space:
Forc'd by thy Worth, thy Foe in Death become
Thy Friend, has lodg'd thee in a costly Tomb;   660
There yet remain'd thy Fun'ral Exequies,
The weeping Tribute of thy Widows Eyes,
And those, indulgent Heav'n has found the way
That I, before my Death, have leave to pay.
My Father ev'n in Cruelty is kind,   } 665
Or Heav'n has turn'd the Malice of his Mind
To better Uses than his Hate design'd;   }
And made th' Insult which in his Gift appears,
The Means to mourn thee with my pious Tears;
Which I will pay thee down, before I go,   670
And save my self the Pains to weep below,
If Souls can weep; though once I meant to meet
My Fate with Face unmov'd, and Eyes unwet,
Yet since I have thee here in narrow Room,
My Tears shall set thee first afloat within thy Tomb: 675
Then (as I know thy Spirit hovers nigh)
Under thy friendly Conduct will I fly
To Regions unexplor'd, secure to share   }
Thy State; nor Hell shall Punishment appear;
And Heav'n is double Heav'n, if thou art there.   } 680

She said: Her brim-full Eyes, that ready stood,
And only wanted Will to weep a Flood,
Releas'd their watry Store, and pour'd amain,
Like Clouds low hung, a sober Show'r of Rain;
Mute solemn Sorrow, free from Female Noise,   685
Such as the Majesty of Grief destroys:
For, bending o'er the Cup, the Tears she shed
Seem'd by the Posture to discharge her Head,
O'er-fill'd before; and oft (her Mouth apply'd
To the cold Heart) she kiss'd at once, and cry'd.   690
Her Maids, who stood amaz'd, nor knew the Cause
Of her Complaining, nor whose Heart it was;
Yet all due Measures of her Mourning kept,
Did Office at the Dirge, and by Infection wept;
And oft enquir'd th' Occasion of her Grief,   695
(Unanswer'd but by Sighs) and offer'd vain Relief.
At length, her Stock of Tears already shed,
She wip'd her Eyes, she rais'd her drooping Head,
And thus pursu'd: O ever faithful Heart,
I have perform'd the Ceremonial Part,   700
The Decencies of Grief: It rests behind,
That as our Bodies were, our Souls be join'd:
To thy whate'er abode, my Shade convey,
And as an elder Ghost, direct the way.
She said; and bad the Vial to be brought,   705
Where she before had brew'd the deadly Draught,
First pouring out the med'cinable Bane,
The Heart, her Tears had rins'd, she bath'd again;
Then down her Throat the Death securely throws,
And quaffs a long Oblivion of her Woes.   710
   This done, she mounts the Genial Bed, and there,
(Her Body first compos'd with honest Care,)
Attends the welcom Rest: Her Hands yet hold
Close to her Heart, the Monumental Gold;
Nor farther Word she spoke, but clos'd her Sight,   715
And quiet, sought the Covert of the Night.
   The Damsels, who the while in Silence mourn'd,
Not knowing, nor suspecting Death suborn'd,
Yet, as their Duty was, to *Tancred* sent,
Who, conscious of th' Occasion, fear'd th' Event.   720

Alarm'd, and with presaging Heart he came,
And drew the Curtains, and expos'd the Dame
To loathsom Light: then with a late Relief
Made vain Efforts, to mitigate her Grief.
She, what she could, excluding Day, her Eyes   725
Kept firmly seal'd, and sternly thus replies:
    Tancred, restrain thy Tears, unsought by me,
And Sorrow, unavailing now to thee:
Did ever Man before, afflict his Mind,
To see th' Effect of what himself design'd?   730
Yet if thou hast remaining in thy Heart
Some Sense of Love, some unextinguish'd Part
Of former Kindness, largely once profess'd,
Let me by that adjure thy harden'd Breast,
Not to deny thy Daughters last Request: 735
The secret Love, which I so long enjoy'd,
And still conceal'd, to gratifie thy Pride,
Thou hast disjoin'd; but, with my dying Breath,
Seek not, I beg thee, to disjoin our Death:
Where-e'er his Corps by thy Command is laid,   740
Thither let mine in publick be convey'd;
Expos'd in open View, and Side by Side,
Acknowledg'd as a Bridegroom and a Bride.
    The Prince's Anguish hinder'd his Reply:
And she, who felt her Fate approaching nigh,   745
Seiz'd the cold Heart, and heaving to her Breast,
Here, precious Pledge, she said, securely rest:
These Accents were her last; the creeping Death
Benum'd her Senses first, then stopp'd her Breath.
    Thus she for Disobedience justly dy'd;   750
The Sire was justly punish'd for his Pride:
The Youth, least guilty, suffer'd for th' Offence
Of Duty violated to his Prince;
Who late repenting of his cruel Deed,
One common Sepulcher for both decreed;   755
Intomb'd the wretched Pair in Royal State,
And on their Monument inscrib'd their Fate.

BAUCIS AND PHILEMON,
Out of the Eighth Book of
OVID'S Metamorphoses

The Author pursuing the Deeds of Theseus; *relates how He, with his Friend* Perithous, *were invited by* Achelous, *the River-God, to stay with him, till his Waters were abated.* Achelous *entertains them with a Relation of his own Love to* Perimele, *who was chang'd into an Island by* Neptune, *at his Request.* Perithous, *being an Atheist, derides the Legend, and denies the* 5 *Power of the Gods, to work that Miracle.* Lelex, *another Companion of* Theseus, *to confirm the Story of* Achelous, *relates another Metamorphosis of* Baucis *and* Philemon, *into Trees; of which he was partly an Eye-witness.*

THUS *Achelous* ends: His Audience hear,
　With admiration, and admiring, fear
The Pow'rs of Heav'n; except *Ixion*'s Son,
Who laugh'd at all the Gods, believ'd in none:
He shook his impious Head, and thus replies, 5
These Legends are no more than pious Lies:
You attribute too much to Heavenly Sway,
To think they give us Forms, and take away.
　The rest of better Minds, their Sense declar'd
Against this Doctrine, and with Horrour heard. 10
Then *Lelex* rose, an old experienc'd Man,
And thus with sober Gravity began:
Heav'ns Pow'r is Infinite: Earth, Air, and Sea,
The Manufacture Mass, the making Pow'r obey:
By Proof to clear your Doubt; In *Phrygian* Ground 15
Two neighb'ring Trees, with Walls encompass'd round,
Stand on a mod'rate Rise, with wonder shown,
One a hard Oak, a softer Linden one:
I saw the Place and them, by *Pittheus* sent
To *Phrygian* Realms, my Grandsire's Government. 20
Not far from thence is seen a Lake, the Haunt
Of Coots, and of the fishing Cormorant:
Here *Jove* with *Hermes* came; but in Disguise
Of mortal Men conceal'd their Deities;
One laid aside his Thunder, one his Rod; 25
And many toilsom Steps together trod:

For Harbour at a thousand Doors they knock'd,
Not one of all the thousand but was lock'd.
At last an hospitable House they found,
A homely Shed; the Roof, not far from Ground,   } 30
Was thatch'd with Reeds, and Straw together bound.
There *Baucis* and *Philemon* liv'd, and there
Had liv'd long marry'd, and a happy Pair:
Now old in Love, though little was their Store,
Inur'd to Want, their Poverty they bore,   } 35
Nor aim'd at Wealth, professing to be poor.
For Master or for Servant here to call,
Was all alike, where only Two were All.
Command was none, where equal Love was paid,
Or rather both commanded, both obey'd.   40
     From lofty Roofs the Gods repuls'd before,
Now stooping, enter'd through the little Door:
The Man (their hearty Welcome first express'd)
A common Settle drew for either Guest,
Inviting each his weary Limbs to rest.   } 45
But e'er they sat, officious *Baucis* lays
Two Cushions stuff'd with Straw, the Seat to raise;
Course, but the best she had; then rakes the Load
Of Ashes from the Hearth, and spreads abroad
The living Coals; and, lest they shou'd expire,   50
With Leaves and Barks she feeds her Infant-fire:
It smoaks; and then with trembling Breath she blows,
Till in a chearful Blaze the Flames arose.
With Brush-wood and with Chips she strengthens these,
And adds at last the Boughs of rotten Trees.   55
The Fire thus form'd, she sets the Kettle on,
(Like burnish'd Gold the little Seether shone)
Next took the Coleworts which her Husband got
From his own Ground, (a small well-water'd Spot;)
She stripp'd the Stalks of all their Leaves; the best   60
She cull'd, and then with handy-care she dress'd.
High o'er the Hearth a Chine of Bacon hung;
Good old *Philemon* seiz'd it with a Prong,
And from the sooty Rafter drew it down,
Then cut a Slice, but scarce enough for one;   65

Baucis and Philemon. 30 Shed;] Shed, F

Yet a large Portion of a little Store,
Which for their Sakes alone he wish'd were more.
This in the Pot he plung'd without delay,
To tame the Flesh, and drain the Salt away.
The Time between, before the Fire they sat, 70
And shorten'd the Delay by pleasing Chat.
  A Beam there was, on which a Beechen Pail
Hung by the Handle, on a driven Nail:
This fill'd with Water, gently warm'd, they set
Before their Guests; in this they bath'd their Feet, 75
And after with clean Towels dry'd their Sweat:
This done, the Host produc'd the genial Bed,
Sallow the Feet, the Borders, and the Sted,
Which with no costly Coverlet they spread;
But course old Garments, yet such Robes as these 80
They laid alone, at Feasts, on Holydays.
The good old Huswife tucking up her Gown,
The Table sets; th' invited Gods lie down.
The Trivet-Table of a Foot was lame,
A Blot which prudent *Baucis* overcame, 85
Who thrusts beneath the limping Leg, a Sherd,
So was the mended Board exactly rear'd:
Then rubb'd it o'er with newly-gather'd Mint,
A wholesom Herb, that breath'd a grateful Scent.
Pallas began the Feast, where first was seen 90
The party-colour'd Olive, Black, and Green:
Autumnal Cornels next in order serv'd,
In Lees of Wine well pickl'd, and preserv'd.
A Garden-Sallad was the third Supply,
Of Endive, Radishes, and Succory: 95
Then Curds and Cream, the Flow'r of Country-Fare,
And new-laid Eggs, which *Baucis* busie Care
Turn'd by a gentle Fire, and roasted rear.
All these in Earthen Ware were serv'd to Board;
And next in place, an Earthen Pitcher stor'd 100
With Liquor of the best the Cottage cou'd afford.
This was the Tables Ornament, and Pride,
With Figures wrought: Like Pages at his Side
Stood Beechen Bowls; and these were shining clean,

100 stor'd] stor'd, F

Vernish'd with Wax without, and lin'd within.   105
By this the boiling Kettle had prepar'd,
And to the Table sent the smoaking Lard;
On which with eager Appetite they dine,
A sav'ry Bit, that serv'd to rellish Wine:
The Wine it self was suiting to the rest,   110
Still working in the Must, and lately press'd.
The Second Course succeeds like that before,
Plums, Apples, Nuts, and of their Wintry Store,
Dry Figs, and Grapes, and wrinkl'd Dates were set
In Canisters, t' enlarge the little Treat: 115
All these a Milk-white Honey-comb surround,
Which in the midst the Country-Banquet crown'd:
But the kind Hosts their Entertainment grace
With hearty Welcom, and an open Face:
In all they did, you might discern with ease,   120
A willing Mind, and a Desire to please.
    Mean time the Beechen Bowls went round, and still
Though often empty'd, were observ'd to fill;
Fill'd without Hands, and of their own accord
Ran without Feet, and danc'd about the Board.   125
Devotion seiz'd the Pair, to see the Feast
With Wine, and of no common Grape, increas'd;
And up they held their Hands, and fell to Pray'r,
Excusing as they cou'd, their Country Fare.
    One Goose they had, ('twas all they cou'd allow) ⎫   130
A wakeful Cent'ry, and on Duty now,   ⎬
Whom to the Gods for Sacrifice they vow: ⎭
Her, with malicious Zeal, the Couple view'd;
She ran for Life, and limping they pursu'd:
Full well the Fowl perceiv'd their bad intent,   135
And wou'd not make her Masters Compliment;
But persecuted, to the Pow'rs she flies,
And close between the Legs of *Jove* she lies:
He with a gracious Ear the Suppliant heard,
And sav'd her Life; then what he was declar'd,   140
And own'd the God. The Neighbourhood, said he,
Shall justly perish for Impiety:
You stand alone exempted; but obey
With speed, and follow where we lead the way:

Leave these accurs'd; and to the Mountains Height   145
Ascend; nor once look backward in your Flight.
  They haste, and what their tardy Feet deny'd,
The trusty Staff (their better Leg) supply'd.
An Arrows Flight they wanted to the Top,
And there secure, but spent with Travel, stop;   150
Then turn their now no more forbidden Eyes;
Lost in a Lake the floated Level lies:
A Watry Desart covers all the Plains,
Their Cot alone, as in an Isle, remains:
Wondring with weeping Eyes, while they deplore   155
Their Neighbours Fate, and Country now no more,
Their little Shed, scarce large enough for Two,
Seems, from the Ground increas'd, in Height and Bulk to grow.
A stately Temple shoots within the Skies,
The Crotches of their Cot in Columns rise: 160
The Pavement polish'd Marble they behold,
The Gates with Sculpture grac'd, the Spires and Tiles of Gold.
  Then thus the Sire of Gods, with Look serene,
Speak thy Desire, thou only Just of Men;
And thou, O Woman, only worthy found   165
To be with such a Man in Marriage bound.
  A while they whisper; then to *Jove* address'd,
Philemon thus prefers their joint Request.
We crave to serve before your sacred Shrine,
And offer at your Altars Rites Divine: 170
And since not any Action of our Life
Has been polluted with Domestick Strife,
We beg one Hour of Death; that neither she
With Widows Tears may live to bury me,
Nor weeping I, with wither'd Arms may bear   175
My breathless *Baucis* to the Sepulcher.
  The Godheads sign their Suit. They run their Race
In the same Tenor all th' appointed Space:
Then, when their Hour was come, while they relate
These past Adventures at the Temple-gate,   180
Old *Baucis* is by old *Philemon* seen
Sprouting with sudden Leaves of spritely Green:
Old *Baucis* look'd where old *Philemon* stood,
And saw his lengthen'd Arms a sprouting Wood:

New Roots their fasten'd Feet begin to bind,   185
Their Bodies stiffen in a rising Rind:
Then e'er the Bark above their Shoulders grew,
They give and take at once their last Adieu:
At once, Farewell, O faithful Spouse, they said;
At once th' incroaching Rinds their closing Lips invade.   190
Ev'n yet, an ancient *Tyanæan* shows
A spreading Oak, that near a Linden grows;
The Neighbourhood confirm the Prodigie,
Grave Men, not vain of Tongue, or like to lie.
I saw my self the Garlands on their Boughs,   195
And Tablets hung for Gifts of granted Vows;
And off'ring fresher up, with pious Pray'r,
The Good, said I, are God's peculiar Care,
And such as honour Heav'n, shall heav'nly Honour share.

PYGMALION AND THE STATUE,
Out of the Tenth Book of
OVID'S Metamorphoses

The Propætides, *for their impudent Behaviour, being turn'd into Stone by*
Venus, Pygmalion, *Prince of* Cyprus, *detested all Women for their Sake,
and resolv'd never to marry: He falls in love with a Statue of his own making,
which is chang'd into a Maid, whom he marries. One of his Descendants is*
Cinyras, *the Father of* Myrrha; *the Daughter incestuously loves her own* 5
*Father; for which she is chang'd into the Tree which bears her Name. These
two Stories immediately follow each other, and are admirably well connected.*

*P*YGMALION loathing their lascivious Life,
Abhorr'd all Womankind, but most a Wife:
So single chose to live, and shunn'd to wed,
Well pleas'd to want a Consort of his Bed.
Yet fearing Idleness, the Nurse of Ill,   5
In Sculpture exercis'd his happy Skill;
And carv'd in Iv'ry such a Maid, so fair,
As Nature could not with his Art compare,
Were she to work; but in her own Defence
Must take her Pattern here, and copy hence.   10

Pleas'd with his Idol, he commends, admires,
Adores; and last, the Thing ador'd, desires.
A very Virgin in her Face was seen,
And had she mov'd, a living Maid had been:
One wou'd have thought she cou'd have stirr'd; but strove   15
With Modesty, and was asham'd to move.
Art hid with Art, so well perform'd the Cheat,
It caught the Carver with his own Deceit:
He knows 'tis Madness, yet he must adore,
And still the more he knows it, loves the more: 20
The Flesh, or what so seems, he touches oft,
Which feels so smooth, that he believes it soft.
Fir'd with this Thought, at once he strain'd the Breast,
And on the Lips a burning Kiss impress'd.
'Tis true, the harden'd Breast resists the Gripe,   25
And the cold Lips return a Kiss unripe:
But when, retiring back, he look'd agen,
To think it Iv'ry, was a Thought too mean:
So wou'd believe she kiss'd, and courting more,
Again embrac'd her naked Body o'er;   30
And straining hard the Statue, was afraid
His Hands had made a Dint, and hurt his Maid:
Explor'd her, Limb by Limb, and fear'd to find
So rude a Gripe had left a livid Mark behind:
With Flatt'ry now, he seeks her Mind to move,   35
And now with Gifts, (the pow'rful Bribes of Love:)
He furnishes her Closet first; and fills
The crowded Shelves with Rarities of Shells;
Adds Orient Pearls, which from the Conchs he drew,
And all the sparkling Stones of various Hue: 40
And Parrots, imitating Humane Tongue,
And Singing-birds in Silver Cages hung;
And ev'ry fragrant Flow'r, and od'rous Green,
Were sorted well, with Lumps of Amber laid between:
Rich, fashionable Robes her Person deck,   45
Pendants her Ears, and Pearls adorn her Neck:
Her taper'd Fingers too with Rings are grac'd,
And an embroider'd Zone surrounds her slender Waste.
Thus like a Queen array'd, so richly dress'd,
Beauteous she shew'd, but naked shew'd the best.   50

Then, from the Floor, he rais'd a Royal Bed,
With Cov'rings of *Sydonian* Purple spread:
The Solemn Rites perform'd, he calls her Bride,
With Blandishments invites her to his Side,
And as she were with Vital Sense possess'd,   55
Her Head did on a plumy Pillow rest.
 The Feast of *Venus* came, a Solemn Day,
To which the *Cypriots* due Devotion pay;
With gilded Horns, the Milk-white Heifers led,
Slaughter'd before the sacred Altars, bled: 60
Pygmalion off'ring, first, approach'd the Shrine,
And then with Pray'rs implor'd the Pow'rs Divine,
Almighty Gods, if all we Mortals want,
If all we can require, be yours to grant;
Make this fair Statue mine, he wou'd have said,   ⎫ 65
But chang'd his Words, for shame; and only pray'd,   ⎬
Give me the Likeness of my Iv'ry Maid.   ⎭
 The Golden Goddess, present at the Pray'r,
Well knew he meant th' inanimated Fair,
And gave the Sign of granting his Desire;   70
For thrice in chearful Flames ascends the Fire.
The Youth, returning to his Mistress, hies,   ⎫
And impudent in Hope, with ardent Eyes,   ⎬
And beating Breast, by the dear Statue lies.   ⎭
He kisses her white Lips, renews the Bliss,   75
And looks, and thinks they redden at the Kiss;
He thought them warm before: Nor longer stays,
But next his Hand on her hard Bosom lays:
Hard as it was, beginning to relent,
It seem'd, the Breast beneath his Fingers bent;   80
He felt again, his Fingers made a Print,
'Twas Flesh, but Flesh so firm, it rose against the Dint:
The pleasing Task he fails not to renew;
Soft, and more soft at ev'ry Touch it grew;
Like pliant Wax, when chafing Hands reduce   85
The former Mass to Form, and frame for Use.
He would believe, but yet is still in pain,   ⎫
And tries his Argument of Sense again,   ⎬
Presses the Pulse, and feels the leaping Vein.   ⎭
Convinc'd, o'erjoy'd, his studied Thanks and Praise,   90

To her who made the Miracle, he pays:
Then Lips to Lips he join'd; now freed from Fear,
He found the Savour of the Kiss sincere:
At this the waken'd Image op'd her Eyes,
And view'd at once the Light and Lover, with surprize.   95
The Goddess present at the Match she made,
So bless'd the Bed, such Fruitfulness convey'd,
That e'er ten Moons had sharpen'd either Horn,
To crown their Bliss, a lovely Boy was born;
Paphos his Name, who grown to Manhood, wall'd   100
The City *Paphos*, from the Founder call'd.

CINYRAS AND MYRRHA,
Out of the Tenth Book ot
OVID'S Metamorphoses

There needs no Connection of this Story with the Former; for the Beginning of
This immediately follows the End of the Last: The Reader is only to take
notice, that Orpheus, *who relates both, was by Birth a* Thracian; *and his*
Country far distant from Cyprus *where* Myrrha *was born, and from* Arabia
whither she fled. You will see the Reason of this Note, soon after the first Lines 5
of this Fable.

NOR him alone produc'd the fruitful Queen;
But *Cinyras*, who like his Sire had been
A happy Prince, had he not been a Sire.
Daughters and Fathers from my Song retire;
I sing of Horrour; and could I prevail,   5
You shou'd not hear, or not believe my Tale.
Yet if the Pleasure of my Song be such,
That you will hear, and credit me too much,
Attentive listen to the last Event,
And with the Sin believe the Punishment: 10
Since Nature cou'd behold so dire a Crime,
I gratulate at least my Native Clime,
That such a Land, which such a Monster bore,
So far is distant from our *Thracian* Shore.
Let *Araby* extol her happy Coast,   15
Her Cinamon, and sweet *Amomum* boast,

Her fragrant Flow'rs, her Trees with precious Tears, ⎫
Her second Harvests, and her double Years; |
How can the Land be call'd so bless'd that *Myrrha* bears? ⎭
Nor all her od'rous Tears can cleanse her Crime,   20
Her Plant alone deforms the happy Clime:
Cupid denies to have inflam'd thy Heart,
Disowns thy Love, and vindicates his Dart:
Some Fury gave thee those infernal Pains,
And shot her venom'd Vipers in thy Veins.   25
To hate thy Sire, had meritted a Curse;
But such an impious Love deserv'd a worse.
The Neighb'ring Monarchs, by thy Beauty led,
Contend in Crowds, ambitious of thy Bed:
The World is at thy Choice; except but one,   30
Except but him thou canst not chuse alone.
She knew it too, the miserable Maid,   ⎫
E'er impious Love her better Thoughts betray'd, |
And thus within her secret Soul she said: ⎭
Ah *Myrrha*! whither wou'd thy Wishes tend?   35
Ye Gods, ye sacred Laws, my Soul defend
From such a Crime, as all Mankind detest,
And never lodg'd before in Humane Breast!
But is it Sin? Or makes my Mind alone
Th' imagin'd Sin? For Nature makes it none.   40
What Tyrant then these envious Laws began,
Made not for any other Beast, but Man!
The Father-Bull his Daughter may bestride,
The Horse may make his Mother-Mare a Bride;
What Piety forbids the lusty Ram   45
Or more salacious Goat, to rut their Dam?
The Hen is free to wed the Chick she bore,
And make a Husband, whom she hatch'd before.
All Creatures else are of a happier Kind,   ⎫
Whom nor ill-natur'd Laws from Pleasure bind, | 50
Nor Thoughts of Sin disturb their Peace of mind. ⎭
But Man, a Slave of his own making lives;
The Fool denies himself what Nature gives:
Too busie Senates, with an over-care
To make us better than our Kind can bear,   55
Have dash'd a Spice of Envy in the Laws,

And straining up too high, have spoil'd the Cause.
Yet some wise Nations break their cruel Chains,
And own no Laws, but those which Love ordains:
Where happy Daughters with their Sires are join'd,   60
And Piety is doubly paid in Kind.
O that I had been born in such a Clime,
Not here, where 'tis the Country makes the Crime!
But whither wou'd my impious Fancy stray?
Hence Hopes, and ye forbidden Thoughts away!   65
His Worth deserves to kindle my Desires,
But with the Love, that Daughters bear to Sires.
Then had not *Cinyras* my Father been,
What hinder'd *Myrrha*'s Hopes to be his Queen?
But the Perverseness of my Fate is such,   70
That he's not mine, because he's mine too much:
Our Kindred-Blood debars a better Tie;
He might be nearer, were he not so nigh.
Eyes and their Objects never must unite,
Some Distance is requir'd to help the Sight: 75
Fain wou'd I travel to some Foreign Shore,
Never to see my Native Country more,
So might I to my self my self restore;
So might my Mind these impious Thoughts remove,
And ceasing to behold, might cease to love.   80
But stay I must, to feed my famish'd Sight,
To talk, to kiss; and more, if more I might:
More, impious Maid! What more canst thou design,
To make a monstrous Mixture in thy Line,
And break all Statutes Humane and Divine?   85
Canst thou be call'd (to save thy wretched Life)
Thy Mother's Rival, and thy Father's Wife?
Confound so many sacred Names in one,
Thy Brother's Mother, Sister to thy Son!
And fear'st thou not to see th' Infernal Bands,   90
Their Heads with Snakes, with Torches arm'd their Hands;
Full at thy Face, th' avenging Brands to bear,
And shake the Serpents from their hissing Hair?
But thou in time th' increasing Ill controul,
Nor first debauch the Body by the Soul;   95
Secure the sacred Quiet of thy Mind,

And keep the Sanctions Nature has design'd.
Suppose I shou'd attempt, th' Attempt were vain,
No Thoughts like mine his sinless Soul profane:
Observant of the Right; and O, that he   100
Cou'd cure my Madness, or be mad like me!
Thus she: But *Cinyras* who daily sees
A Crowd of Noble Suitors at his Knees,
Among so many, knew not whom to chuse,
Irresolute to grant, or to refuse.   105
But having told their Names, enquir'd of her,
Who pleas'd her best, and whom she would prefer?
The blushing Maid stood silent with Surprize,
And on her Father fix'd her ardent Eyes,
And looking sigh'd, and as she sigh'd, began   110
Round Tears to shed, that scalded as they ran.
The tender Sire, who saw her blush, and cry,
Ascrib'd it all to Maiden-modesty,
And dry'd the falling Drops, and yet more kind,
He stroak'd her Cheeks, and holy Kisses join'd.   115
She felt a secret Venom fire her Blood,
And found more Pleasure than a Daughter shou'd;
And, ask'd again, what Lover of the Crew
She lik'd the best, she answer'd, One like you.
Mistaking what she meant, her pious Will   120
He prais'd, and bad her so continue still:
The Word of Pious heard, she blush'd with shame
Of secret Guilt, and cou'd not bear the Name.
   'Twas now the mid of Night, when Slumbers close
Our Eyes, and sooth our Cares with soft Repose;   125
But no Repose cou'd wretched *Myrrha* find,
Her Body rouling, as she rould her Mind:
Mad with Desire, she ruminates her Sin,
And wishes all her Wishes o'er again:
Now she despairs, and now resolves to try;   130
Wou'd not, and wou'd again, she knows not why;
Stops, and returns, makes and retracts the Vow;
Fain wou'd begin, but understands not how.
As when a Pine is hew'd upon the Plains,
And the last mortal Stroke alone remains,   135
Lab'ring in Pangs of Death, and threatning all,

This way, and that she nods, consid'ring where to fall:
So *Myrrha*'s Mind, impell'd on either Side,
Takes ev'ry Bent, but cannot long abide:
Irresolute on which she shou'd relie,   140
At last unfix'd in all, is only fix'd to die;
On that sad Thought she rests, resolv'd on Death,
She rises, and prepares to choak her Breath:
Then while about the Beam her Zone she ties,
Dear *Cinyras*, farewell, she softly cries;   145
For thee I die, and only wish to be
Not hated, when thou know'st I die for thee:
Pardon the Crime, in pity to the Cause:
This said, about her Neck the Noose she draws.
The Nurse, who lay without, her faithful Guard,   150
Though not the Words, the Murmurs overheard,
And Sighs, and hollow Sounds: Surpriz'd with Fright,
She starts, and leaves her Bed, and springs a Light;
Unlocks the Door, and entring out of Breath,
The Dying saw, and Instruments of Death;   155
She shrieks, she cuts the Zone, with trembling haste,
And in her Arms, her fainting Charge embrac'd:
Next, (for she now had leisure for her Tears)
She weeping ask'd, in these her blooming Years,
What unforeseen Misfortune caus'd her Care,   160
To loath her Life, and languish in Despair!
The Maid, with down-cast Eyes, and mute with Grief
For Death unfinish'd, and ill-tim'd Relief,
Stood sullen to her Suit: The Beldame press'd
The more to know, and bar'd her wither'd Breast,   165
Adjur'd her by the kindly Food she drew
From those dry Founts, her secret Ill to shew.
Sad *Myrrha* sigh'd, and turn'd her Eyes aside;
The Nurse still urg'd, and wou'd not be deny'd:
Nor only promis'd Secresie; but pray'd   170
She might have leave to give her offer'd Aid.
Good-will, she said, my want of Strength supplies,
And Diligence shall give, what Age denies:
If strong Desires thy Mind to Fury move,
With Charms, and Med'cines, I can cure thy Love: 175
If envious Eyes their hurtful Rays have cast,

More pow'rful Verse shall free thee from the Blast:
If Heav'n offended sends thee this Disease,
Offended Heav'n with Pray'rs we can appease.
What then remains, that can these Cares procure?   180
Thy House is flourishing, thy Fortune sure:
Thy careful Mother yet in Health survives,
And, to thy Comfort, thy kind Father lives.
The Virgin started at her Father's Name,
And sigh'd profoundly, conscious of the Shame: 185
Nor yet the Nurse her impious Love divin'd;
But yet surmis'd, that Love disturb'd her Mind:
Thus thinking, she pursu'd her Point, and laid
And lull'd within her Lap the mourning Maid;
Then softly soothed her thus, I guess your Grief: 190
You love, my Child; your Love shall find Relief.
My long-experienc'd Age shall be your Guide;
Relie on that, and lay Distrust aside:
No Breath of Air shall on the Secret blow,
Nor shall (what most you fear) your Father know.   195
Struck once again, as with a Thunder-clap,
The guilty Virgin bounded from her Lap,
And threw her Body prostrate on the Bed,
And, to conceal her Blushes, hid her Head:
There silent lay, and warn'd her with her Hand   200
To go: But she receiv'd not the Command;
Remaining still importunate to know:
Then *Myrrha* thus; Or ask no more, or go:
I prethee go, or staying spare my Shame;
What thou wou'dst hear, is impious ev'n to name.   205
At this, on high the Beldame holds her Hands,
And trembling, both with Age, and Terrour, stands;
Adjures, and falling at her Feet intreats,
Sooths her with Blandishments, and frights with Threats,
To tell the Crime intended, or disclose   210
What Part of it she knew, if she no farther knows.
And last; if conscious to her Counsel made,
Confirms anew the Promise of her Aid.
Now *Myrrha* rais'd her Head; but soon oppress'd
With Shame, reclin'd it on her Nurses Breast;   215
Bath'd it with Tears, and strove to have confess'd:

Twice she began, and stopp'd; again she try'd;
The falt'ring Tongue its Office still deny'd.
At last her Veil before her Face she spread,
And drew a long preluding Sigh, and said,   } 220
O happy Mother, in thy Marriage-bed!
Then groan'd, and ceas'd; the good Old Woman shook,
Stiff were her Eyes, and ghastly was her Look:
Her hoary Hair upright with Horrour stood,
Made (to her Grief) more knowing than she wou'd: 225
Much she reproach'd, and many Things she said,
To cure the Madness of th' unhappy Maid:
In vain: For *Myrrha* stood convict of Ill;
Her Reason vanquish'd, but unchang'd her Will:
Perverse of Mind, unable to reply;   230
She stood resolv'd or to possess, or die.
At length the Fondness of a Nurse prevail'd
Against her better Sense, and Vertue fail'd:
Enjoy, my Child, since such is thy Desire,
Thy Love, she said; she durst not say, thy Sire.   235
Live, though unhappy, live on any Terms:
Then with a second Oath her Faith confirms.
   The Solemn Feast of *Ceres* now was near,
When long white Linen Stoles the Matrons wear;
Rank'd in Procession walk the pious Train,   240
Off'ring First-fruits, and Spikes of yellow Grain:
For nine long Nights the Nuptial-Bed they shun,
And sanctifying Harvest, lie alone.
   Mix'd with the Crowd, the Queen forsook her Lord,
And *Ceres* Pow'r with secret Rites ador'd: 245
The Royal Couch now vacant for a time,
The crafty Crone, officious in her Crime,
The curst Occasion took: The King she found
Easie with Wine, and deep in Pleasures drown'd,
Prepar'd for Love: The Beldame blew the Flame,   250
Confess'd the Passion, but conceal'd the Name.
Her Form she prais'd; the Monarch ask'd her Years,
And she reply'd, The same thy *Myrrha* bears.
Wine and commended Beauty fir'd his Thought;
Impatient, he commands her to be brought.   255

Cinyras and Myrrha. 235 Sire.] Sire, F

Pleas'd with her Charge perform'd, she hies her home,
And gratulates the Nymph, the Task was overcome.
Myrrha was joy'd the welcom News to hear;
But clogg'd with Guilt, the Joy was unsincere:
So various, so discordant is the Mind,   260
That in our Will, a diff'rent Will we find.
Ill she presag'd, and yet pursu'd her Lust;
For guilty Pleasures give a double Gust.
'Twas Depth of Night: *Arctophylax* had driv'n
His lazy Wain half round the Northern Heav'n;   265
When *Myrrha* hasten'd to the Crime desir'd,
The Moon beheld her first, and first retir'd:
The Stars amaz'd, ran backward from the Sight,
And (shrunk within their Sockets) lost their Light.
Icarius first withdraws his holy Flame: 270
The Virgin Sign, in Heav'n the second Name,
Slides down the Belt, and from her Station flies,
And Night with Sable Clouds involves the Skies.
Bold *Myrrha* still pursues her black Intent;
She stumbl'd thrice, (an Omen of th' Event;)   275
Thrice shriek'd the Fun'ral Owl, yet on she went,
Secure of Shame, because secure of Sight;
Ev'n bashful Sins are impudent by Night.
Link'd Hand in Hand, th' Accomplice, and the Dame,
Their Way exploring, to the Chamber came: 280
The Door was ope, they blindly grope their Way,
Where dark in Bed th' expecting Monarch lay:
Thus far her Courage held, but here forsakes;
Her faint Knees knock at ev'ry Step she makes.
The nearer to her Crime, the more within   285
She feels Remorse, and Horrour of her Sin;
Repents too late her criminal Desire,
And wishes, that unknown she cou'd retire.
Her, lingring thus, the Nurse (who fear'd Delay
The fatal Secret might at length betray)   290
Pull'd forward, to compleat the Work begun,
And said to *Cinyras*, Receive thy own:
Thus saying, she deliver'd Kind to Kind,
Accurs'd, and their devoted Bodies join'd.
The Sire, unknowing of the Crime, admits   295

His Bowels, and profanes the hallow'd Sheets;
He found she trembl'd, but believ'd she strove
With Maiden-Modesty, against her Love,
And sought with flatt'ring Words vain Fancies to remove.
Perhaps he said, My Daughter, cease thy Fears, 300
(Because the Title suited with her Years;)
And Father, she might whisper him agen,
That Names might not be wanting to the Sin.
Full of her Sire, she left th' incestuous Bed,
And carry'd in her Womb the Crime she bred: 305
Another, and another Night she came;
For frequent Sin had left no Sense of Shame:
Till *Cinyras* desir'd to see her Face,
Whose Body he had held in close Embrace,
And brought a Taper; the Revealer, Light, 310
Expos'd both Crime, and Criminal to Sight:
Grief, Rage, Amazement, cou'd no Speech afford,
But from the Sheath he drew th' avenging Sword;
The Guilty fled: The Benefit of Night,
That favour'd first the Sin, secur'd the Flight. 315
Long wandring through the spacious Fields, she bent
Her Voyage to th' *Arabian* Continent;
Then pass'd the Region which *Panchæa* join'd,
And flying left the Palmy Plains behind.
Nine times the Moon had mew'd her Horns; at length 320
With Travel weary, unsupply'd with Strength,
And with the Burden of her Womb oppress'd,
Sabæan Fields afford her needful Rest:
There, loathing Life, and yet of Death afraid,
In anguish of her Spirit, thus she pray'd. 325
Ye Pow'rs, if any so propitious are
T' accept my Penitence, and hear my Pray'r;
Your Judgments, I confess, are justly sent;
Great Sins deserve as great a Punishment:
Yet since my Life the Living will profane, 330
And since my Death the happy Dead will stain,
A middle State your Mercy may bestow,
Betwixt the Realms above, and those below:
Some other Form to wretched *Myrrha* give,
Nor let her wholly die, nor wholly live. 335

The Pray'rs of Penitents are never vain;
At least, she did her last Request obtain:
For while she spoke, the Ground began to rise,
And gather'd round her Feet, her Leggs, and Thighs;
Her Toes in Roots descend, and spreading wide,   340
A firm Foundation for the Trunk provide:
Her solid Bones convert to solid Wood,
To Pith her Marrow, and to Sap her Blood:
Her Arms are Boughs, her Fingers change their Kind,
Her tender Skin is harden'd into Rind.   345
And now the rising Tree her Womb invests,
Now, shooting upwards still, invades her Breasts,
And shades the Neck; when, weary with Delay,
She sunk her Head within, and met it half the Way.
And though with outward Shape she lost her Sense,   350
With bitter Tears she wept her last Offence;
And still she weeps, nor sheds her Tears in vain;
For still the precious Drops her Name retain.
Mean time the mis-begotten Infant grows,
And, ripe for Birth, distends with deadly Throws   355
The swelling Rind, with unavailing Strife,
To leave the wooden Womb, and pushes into Life.
The Mother-Tree, as if oppress'd with Pain,
Writhes here and there, to break the Bark, in vain;
And, like a Lab'ring Woman, wou'd have pray'd,   360
But wants a Voice to call *Lucina*'s Aid:
The bending Bole sends out a hollow Sound,
And trickling Tears fall thicker on the Ground.
The mild *Lucina* came uncall'd, and stood
Beside the struggling Boughs, and heard the groaning Wood: 365
Then reach'd her Midwife-Hand, to speed the Throws,
And spoke the pow'rful Spells that Babes to Birth disclose.
The Bark divides, the living Load to free,
And safe delivers the Convulsive Tree.
The ready Nymphs receive the crying Child,   370
And wash him in the Tears the Parent-Plant distill'd.
They swath'd him with their Scarfs; beneath him spread
The Ground with Herbs; with Roses rais'd his Head.
The lovely Babe was born with ev'ry Grace,
Ev'n Envy must have prais'd so fair a Face: 375

Such was his Form, as Painters when they show
Their utmost Art, on naked Loves bestow:
And that their Arms no Diff'rence might betray,
Give him a Bow, or his from *Cupid* take away.
Time glides along, with undiscover'd haste,   380
The Future but a Length behind the past;
So swift are Years: The Babe whom just before
His Grandsire got, and whom his Sister bore;
The Drop, the Thing which late the Tree inclos'd,
And late the yawning Bark to Life expos'd;   385
A Babe, a Boy, a beauteous Youth appears,
And lovelier than himself at riper Years.
Now to the Queen of Love he gave Desires,
And, with her Pains, reveng'd his Mother's Fires.

THE FIRST BOOK OF HOMER'S ILIAS

THE ARGUMENT

Chryses, *Priest of* Apollo, *brings Presents to the* Grecian *Princes, to ransom
his Daughter* Chryseis, *who was Prisoner in the Fleet.* Agamemnon, *the
General, whose Captive and Mistress the young Lady was, refuses to deliver
her, threatens the Venerable Old Man, and dismisses him with Contumely.
The Priest craves Vengeance of his God; who sends a Plague among the* Greeks: 5
Which occasions Achilles, *their Great Champion, to summon a Council of the
Chief Officers: He encourages* Calchas, *the High Priest and Prophet, to tell
the Reason, why the Gods were so much incens'd against them.* Calchas *is
fearful of provoking* Agamemnon, *till* Achilles *engages to protect him:
Then, embolden'd by the* Heroe, *he accuses the General as the Cause of all,* 10
*by detaining the Fair Captive, and refusing the Presents offer'd for her
Ransom. By this Proceeding,* Agamemnon *is oblig'd, against his Will, to
restore* Chryseis, *with Gifts, that he might appease the Wrath of* Phœbus;
but, at the same time, to revenge himself on Achilles, *sends to seize his Slave*
Briseis. Achilles, *thus affronted, complains to his Mother* Thetis; *and begs* 15
*her to revenge his Injury, not only on the General, but on all the Army, by
giving Victory to the* Trojans, *till the ungrateful King became sensible of
his Injustice. At the same time, he retires from the Camp to his Ships, and
withdraws his Aid from his Country-men.* Thetis *prefers her Son's Petition
to* Jupiter, *who grants her Sute.* Juno *suspects her Errand, and quarrels with* 20

her Husband, for his Grant; till Vulcan *reconciles his Parents with a Bowl of* Nectar, *and sends them peaceably to Bed.*

THE Wrath of *Peleus* Son, O Muse, resound;
  Whose dire Effects the *Grecian* Army found:
And many a Heroe, King, and hardy Knight,
Were sent, in early Youth, to Shades of Night:
Their Limbs a Prey to Dogs and Vulturs made;   5
So was the Sov'reign Will of *Jove* obey'd:
From that ill-omen'd Hour when Strife begun,
Betwixt *Atrides* Great, and *Thetis* God-like Son.
    What Pow'r provok'd, and for what Cause, relate,
Sow'd, in their Breasts, the Seeds of stern Debate: 10
Jove's and *Latona's* Son his Wrath express'd,
In Vengeance of his violated Priest,
Against the King of Men; who swoln with Pride,
Refus'd his Presents, and his Pray'rs deny'd.
For this the God a swift Contagion spread   15
Amid the Camp; where Heaps on Heaps lay dead.
    For Venerable *Chryses* came to buy,
With Gold and Gifts of Price, his Daughters Liberty.
Suppliant before the *Grecian* Chiefs he stood;
Awful, and arm'd with Ensigns of his God: 20
Bare was his hoary Head; one holy Hand
Held forth his Laurel Crown, and one his Sceptre of Command.
His Suit was common; but above the rest,
To both the Brother-Princes thus address'd:
    Ye Sons of *Atreus*, and ye *Grecian* Pow'rs,   25
So may the Gods who dwell in Heav'nly Bow'rs
Succeed your Siege, accord the Vows you make,
And give you *Troys* Imperial Town to take;
So, by their happy Conduct, may you come
With Conquest back to your sweet Native Home;   30
As you receive the Ransom which I bring,
(Respecting *Jove*, and the far-shooting King,)
And break my Daughters Bonds, at my desire;
And glad with her Return her grieving Sire.
    With Shouts of loud Acclaim the *Greeks* decree   35
To take the Gifts, to set the Damsel free.

The First Book &c.   1 Peleus] Peleu's F

The King of Men alone with Fury burn'd;
And haughty, these opprobrious Words return'd:
Hence, Holy Dotard, and avoid my Sight,
E'er Evil intercept thy tardy Flight: 40
Nor dare to tread this interdicted Strand,
Lest not that idle Sceptre in thy Hand,
Nor thy God's Crown, my vow'd Revenge withstand.
Hence on thy Life: The Captive-Maid is mine;
Whom not for Price or Pray'rs I will resign: 45
Mine she shall be, till creeping Age and Time
Her Bloom have wither'd, and consum'd her Prime:
Till then my Royal Bed she shall attend;
And having first adorn'd it, late ascend:
This, for the Night; by Day, the Web and Loom   50
And homely Houshold-task, shall be her Doom,
Far from thy lov'd Embrace, and her sweet Native Home.
He said: The helpless Priest reply'd no more,
But sped his Steps along the hoarse-resounding Shore:
Silent he fled; secure at length he stood,   55
Devoutly curs'd his Foes, and thus invok'd his God.
   O Source of Sacred Light, attend my Pray'r,
God with the Silver Bow, and Golden Hair;
Whom *Chrysa, Cilla, Tenedos* obeys,
And whose broad Eye their happy Soil surveys: 60
If, *Smintheus,* I have pour'd before thy Shrine
The Blood of Oxen, Goats, and ruddy Wine,
And Larded Thighs on loaded Altars laid,
Hear, and my just Revenge propitious aid.
Pierce the proud *Greeks,* and with thy Shafts attest   65
How much thy Pow'r is injur'd in thy Priest.
   He pray'd, and *Phœbus* hearing, urg'd his Flight,
With Fury kindled, from *Olympus* Height;
His Quiver o'er his ample Shoulders threw;
His Bow twang'd, and his Arrows rattl'd as they flew.   70
Black as a stormy Night, he rang'd around
The Tents, and compass'd the devoted Ground.
Then with full Force his deadly Bowe he bent,
And Feather'd Fates among the Mules and Sumpters sent:
Th' Essay of Rage, on faithful Dogs the next;   75
And last, in Humane Hearts his Arrows fix'd.

The God nine Days the *Greeks* at Rovers kill'd,
Nine Days the Camp with Fun'ral Fires was fill'd;
The Tenth, *Achilles*, by the Queens Command,
Who bears Heav'ns awful Sceptre in her Hand,   80
A Council summon'd: for the Goddess griev'd
Her favour'd Hoast shou'd perish unreliev'd.

   The Kings, assembl'd, soon their Chief inclose;
Then from his Seat the Goddess-born arose,
And thus undaunted spoke: What now remains,   85
But that once more we tempt the watry Plains,
And wandring homeward, seek our Safety hence,
In Flight at least if we can find Defence?
Such Woes at once encompass us about,
The Plague within the Camp, the Sword without.   90
Consult, O King, the Prophets of th' event:
And whence these Ills, and what the Gods intent,
Let them by Dreams explore; for Dreams from *Jove* are sent.
What want of offer'd Victims, what Offence
In Fact committed cou'd the Sun incense,   95
To deal his deadly Shafts? What may remove
His settled Hate, and reconcile his Love?
That he may look propitious on our Toils;
And hungry Graves no more be glutted with our Spoils.

   Thus to the King of Men the Hero spoke,   100
Then *Calchas* the desir'd Occasion took:
Calchas the sacred Seer, who had in view
Things present and the past; the Things to come foreknew.
Supream of Augurs, who by *Phœbus* taught
The *Grecian* Pow'rs to *Troy*'s Destruction brought.   105
Skill'd in the secret Causes of their Woes,
The Reverend Priest in graceful Act arose:
And thus bespoke *Pelides*: Care of *Jove*,
Favour'd of all th' Immortal Pow'rs above;
Wou'dst thou the Seeds deep sown of Mischief know,   110
And why, provok'd *Apollo* bends his Bow?
Plight first thy Faith, inviolably true,
To save me from those Ills, that may ensue.

   For I shall tell ungrateful Truths, to those
Whose boundless Pow'r of Life and Death dispose.   11

     104 Augurs] *Angurs* F

And Sov'reigns ever jealous of their State,
Forgive not those whom once they mark for Hate;
Ev'n tho' th' Offence they seemingly digest,
Revenge, like Embers, rak'd within their Breast,
Bursts forth in Flames; whose unresisted Pow'r   120
Will seize th' unwary Wretch and soon devour.
Such, and no less is he, on whom depends
The sum of Things; and whom my Tongue of force offends.
Secure me then from his foreseen Intent,
That what his Wrath may doom, thy Valour may prevent.   125
    To this the stern *Achilles* made Reply:
Be bold; and on my plighted Faith rely,
To speak what *Phœbus* has inspir'd thy Soul
For common Good; and speak without controul.
His Godhead I invoke, by him I swear,   130
That while my Nostrils draw this vital Air,
None shall presume to violate those Bands;
Or touch thy Person with unhallow'd Hands:
Ev'n not the King of Men that all commands.
    At this, resuming Heart, the Prophet said: 135
Nor Hecatombs unslain, nor Vows unpaid,
On *Greeks*, accurs'd, this dire Contagion bring;
Or call for Vengeance from the Bowyer King;
But he the Tyrant, whom none dares resist,
Affronts the Godhead in his injur'd Priest: 140
He keeps the Damsel Captive in his Chain,
And Presents are refus'd, and Pray'rs preferr'd in vain.
For this th' avenging Pow'r employs his Darts;
And empties all his Quiver in our Hearts.
Thus will persist, relentless in his Ire,   145
Till the fair Slave be render'd to her Syre:
And Ransom-free restor'd to his Abode,
With Sacrifice to reconcile the God:
Then he, perhaps, atton'd by Pray'r, may cease
His Vengeance justly vow'd; and give the Peace.   150
    Thus having said he sate: Thus answer'd then
Upstarting from his Throne, the King of Men,
His Breast with Fury fill'd, his Eyes with Fire;
Which rowling round, he shot in Sparkles on the Sire:

153 fill'd,] fill'd **F**

Augur of Ill, whose Tongue was never found   155
Without a Priestly Curse or boding Sound;
For not one bless'd Event foretold to me
Pass'd through that Mouth, or pass'd unwillingly.
And now thou dost with Lies the Throne invade,
By Practice harden'd in thy sland'ring Trade.   160
Obtending Heav'n, for what e'er Ills befal;
And sputtring under specious Names thy Gall.
Now *Phœbus* is provok'd; his Rites and Laws
Are in his Priest profan'd, and I the Cause:
Since I detain a Slave, my Sov'reign Prize;   165
And sacred Gold, your Idol-God, despise.
I love her well: And well her Merits claim,
To stand preferr'd before my *Grecian* Dame:
Not *Clytemnestra*'s self in Beauties Bloom
More charm'd, or better ply'd the various Loom: 170
Mine is the Maid; and brought in happy Hour
With every Houshold-grace adorn'd, to bless my Nuptial Bow'r.
Yet shall she be restor'd; since publick Good
For private Int'rest ought not be withstood,
To save th' Effusion of my People's Blood.   175
But Right requires, if I resign my own,
I shou'd not suffer for your sakes alone:
Alone excluded from the Prize I gain'd,
And by your common Suffrage have obtain'd.
The Slave without a Ransom shall be sent: 180
It rests for you to make th' Equivalent.
  To this the fierce *Thessalian* Prince reply'd:
O first in Pow'r, but passing all in Pride,
Griping, and still tenacious of thy Hold,
Would'st thou the *Grecian* Chiefs, though largely Sould,   185
Shou'd give the Prizes they had gain'd before;
And with their Loss thy Sacrilege restore?
Whate'er by force of Arms the Soldier got,
Is each his own, by dividend of Lot:
Which to resume, were both unjust, and base: 190
Not to be born but by a servile Race.
But this we can: If *Saturn*'s Son bestows
The Sack of *Troy*, which he by Promise owes;

     192 Son] Son, F

Then shall the conquering *Greeks* thy Loss restore,
And with large Int'rest, make th' advantage more.   195
    To this *Atrides* answer'd, Though thy Boast
Assumes the foremost Name of all our Host,
Pretend not, mighty Man, that what is mine
Controll'd by thee, I tamely shou'd resign.
Shall I release the Prize I gain'd by Right,   200
In taken Towns, and many a bloody Fight,
While thou detain'st *Briseis* in thy Bands,
By priestly glossing on the God's Commands?
Resolve on this, (a short Alternative)
Quit mine, or, in exchange, another give;   205
Else I, assure thy Soul, by Sov'reign Right
Will seize thy Captive in thy own Despight.
Or from stout *Ajax*, or *Ulysses*, bear
What other Prize my Fancy shall prefer:
Then softly murmur, or aloud complain,   210
Rage as you please, you shall resist in vain.
But more of this, in proper Time and Place,
To Things of greater moment let us pass.
A Ship to sail the sacred Seas prepare;
Proud in her Trim; and put on board the Fair,   } 215
With Sacrifice and Gifts, and all the pomp of Pray'r.
The Crew well chosen, the Command shall be
In *Ajax*; or if other I decree,   }
In *Creta*'s King, or *Ithacus*, or if I please in Thee: }
Most fit thy self to see perform'd th' intent   } 220
For which my Pris'ner from my Sight is sent;
(Thanks to thy pious Care) that *Phœbus* may relent.   }
    At this, *Achilles* roul'd his furious Eyes,
Fix'd on the King askant; and thus replies.
O, Impudent, regardful of thy own,   225
Whose Thoughts are center'd on thy self alone,
Advanc'd to Sovereign Sway, for better Ends
Than thus like abject Slaves to treat thy Friends.
What *Greek* is he, that urg'd by thy Command,
Against the *Trojan* Troops will lift his Hand?   230
Not I: Nor such inforc'd Respect I owe;
Nor *Pergamus* I hate, nor *Priam* is my Foe.

What Wrong from *Troy* remote, cou'd I sustain,
To leave my fruitful Soil, and happy Reign,
And plough the Surges of the stormy Main?   235
Thee, frontless Man, we follow'd from afar;
Thy Instruments of Death, and Tools of War.
Thine is the Triumph; ours the Toil alone:
We bear thee on our Backs, and mount thee on the Throne.
For thee we fall in Fight; for thee redress   240
Thy baffled Brother; not the Wrongs of *Greece*.
And now thou threaten'st with unjust Decree,
To punish thy affronting Heav'n, on me.
To seize the Prize which I so dearly bought;
By common Suffrage giv'n, confirm'd by Lot.   245
Mean Match to thine: For still above the rest,
Thy hook'd rapacious Hands usurp the best.
Though mine are first in Fight, to force the Prey;
And last sustain the Labours of the Day.
Nor grudge I thee, the much the *Grecians* give;   250
Nor murm'ring take the little I receive.
Yet ev'n this little, thou, who woud'st ingross
The whole, Insatiate, envy'st as thy Loss.
Know, then, for *Phthya*, fix'd is my return:
Better at home my ill-paid Pains to mourn,   255
Than from an Equal here sustain the publick Scorn.
    The King, whose Brows with shining Gold were bound;
Who saw his Throne with scepter'd Slaves incompass'd round,
Thus answer'd stern! Go, at thy Pleasure, go:
We need not such a Friend, nor fear we such a Foe.   260
There will not want to follow me in Fight:
Jove will assist, and *Jove* assert my Right.
But thou of all the Kings (his Care below)
Art least at my Command, and most my Foe.
Debates, Dissentions, Uproars are thy Joy;   265
Provok'd without Offence, and practis'd to destroy.
Strength is of Brutes; and not thy Boast alone;
At least 'tis lent from Heav'n; and not thy own.
Fly then, ill-manner'd, to thy Native Land,
And there, thy Ant-born *Myrmidons* command.   270
But mark this Menace; since I must resign
My black-ey'd Maid, to please the Pow'rs divine:

(A well-rigg'd Vessel in the Port attends,
Man'd at my Charge! commanded by my Friends;)
The Ship shall waft her to her wish'd Abode,   275
Full fraught with holy Bribes to the far-shooting God.
This thus dispatch'd, I owe my self the Care,
My Fame and injur'd Honour to repair:
From thy own Tent, proud Man, in thy despight,
This Hand shall ravish thy pretended Right.   280
Briseis shall be mine, and thou shalt see,
What odds of awful Pow'r I have on thee:
That others at thy cost may learn the diff'rence of degree.

    At this th' Impatient Hero sowrly smil'd:
His Heart, impetuous in his Bosom boil'd,   285
And justled by two Tides of equal sway,
Stood, for a while, suspended in his way.
Betwixt his Reason, and his Rage untam'd;
One whisper'd soft, and one aloud reclaim'd:
That only counsell'd to the safer side;   290
This to the Sword, his ready Hand apply'd.
Unpunish'd to support th' Affront was hard:
Nor easy was th' Attempt to force the Guard.
But soon the thirst of Vengeance fir'd his Blood:
Half shone his Faulchion, and half sheath'd it stood.   295

    In that nice moment, *Pallas*, from above,
Commission'd by th' Imperial Wife of *Jove*,
Descended swift: (the white arm'd Queen was loath
The Fight shou'd follow; for she favour'd both:)
Just as in Act he stood, in Clouds inshrin'd,   300
Her Hand she fasten'd on his Hair behind;
Then backward by his yellow Curls she drew:
To him, and him alone confess'd in view.
Tam'd by superiour Force he turn'd his Eyes
Aghast at first, and stupid with Surprize: 305
But by her sparkling Eyes, and ardent Look,
The Virgin-Warrior known, he thus bespoke.

    Com'st thou, Celestial, to behold my Wrongs?
Then view the Vengeance which to Crimes belongs.

    Thus He. The blue-ey'd Goddess thus rejoin'd: 310
I come to calm thy turbulence of Mind,

    311 Mind,] Mind. F

If Reason will resume her soveraign Sway,
And sent by *Juno*, her Commands obey.
Equal she loves you both, and I protect:
Then give thy Guardian Gods their due respect;   315
And cease Contention; be thy Words severe,
Sharp as he merits: But the Sword forbear.
An Hour unhop'd already wings her way,
When he his dire Affront shall dearly pay:
When the proud King shall sue, with trebble Gain,   320
To quit thy Loss, and conquer thy Disdain.
But thou secure of my unfailing Word,
Compose thy swelling Soul; and sheath the Sword.
     The Youth thus answer'd mild; Auspicious Maid,
Heav'ns will be mine; and your Commands obey'd.   325
The Gods are just, and when subduing Sense,
We serve their Pow'rs, provide the Recompence.
He said; with surly Faith believ'd her Word,
And, in the Sheath, reluctant, plung'd the Sword.
Her Message done, she mounts the bless'd Abodes,   330
And mix'd among the Senate of the Gods.
     At her departure his Disdain return'd:
The Fire she fan'd, with greater Fury burn'd;
Rumbling within till thus it found a vent:
Dastard, and Drunkard, Mean and Insolent: 335
Tongue-valiant Hero, Vaunter of thy Might,
In Threats the foremost, but the lag in Fight;
When did'st thou thrust amid the mingled Preace,
Content to bid the War aloof in Peace?
Arms are the Trade of each *Plebeyan* Soul;   340
'Tis Death to fight; but Kingly to controul.
Lord-like at ease, with arbitrary Pow'r,
To peel the Chiefs, the People to devour.
These, Traitor, are thy Tallents; safer far
Than to contend in Fields, and Toils of War.   345
Nor coud'st thou thus have dar'd the common Hate,
Were not their Souls as abject as their State.
But, by this Scepter, solemnly I swear,
(Which never more green Leaf or growing Branch shall bear:
Torn from the Tree, and giv'n by *Jove* to those   350
Who Laws dispence and mighty Wrongs oppose)

That when the *Grecians* want my wonted Aid,
No Gift shall bribe it, and no Pray'r persuade.
When *Hector* comes, the Homicide, to wield
His conquering Arms, with Corps to strow the Field;   355
Then shalt thou mourn thy Pride; and late confess,
My Wrong repented when 'tis past redress:
He said: And with Disdain in open view,
Against the Ground his golden Scepter threw;
Then sate: with boiling Rage *Atrides* burn'd: 360
And Foam betwixt his gnashing Grinders churn'd.
    But from his Seat the *Pylian* Prince arose,
With Reas'ning mild, their Madness to compose:
Words, sweet as Hony, from his Mouth distill'd;
Two Centuries already he fulfill'd;   365
And now began the third; unbroken yet:
Once fam'd for Courage; still in Council great.
    What worse, he said, can *Argos* undergo,
What can more gratify the *Phrygian* Foe,
Than these distemper'd Heats? If both the Lights   370
Of *Greece* their private Int'rest disunites!
Believe a Friend, with thrice your Years increas'd,
And let these youthful Passions be repress'd:
I flourish'd long before your Birth; and then
Liv'd equal with a Race of braver Men,   375
Than these dim Eyes shall e'er behold agen.
Ceneus and *Dryas*, and, excelling them,
Great *Theseus*, and the force of greater *Polypheme*.
With these I went, a Brother of the War,
Their Dangers to divide; their Fame to share.   380
Nor idle stood with unassisting Hands,
When salvage Beasts, and Men's more salvage Bands,
Their virtuous Toil subdu'd: Yet those I sway'd,
With pow'rful Speech: I spoke and they obey'd.
If such as those, my Councils cou'd reclaim,   385
Think not, young Warriors, your diminish'd Name,
Shall lose of Lustre, by subjecting Rage
To the cool Dictates of experienc'd Age.
Thou, King of Men, stretch not thy sovereign Sway
Beyond, the Bounds free Subjects can obey: 390

355 Field;] Field: *F*   359 threw;] threw. *F*   360 sate:] sate, *F*

But let *Pelides* in his Prize rejoice,
Atchiev'd in Arms, allow'd by publick Voice.
Nor Thou, brave Champion, with his Pow'r contend,
Before whose Throne, ev'n Kings their lower'd Scepters bend.
The Head of Action He, and Thou the Hand,   395
Matchless thy Force; but mightier his Command:
Thou first, O King, release the rights of Sway,
Pow'r, self-restrain'd, the People best obey.
Sanctions of Law from Thee derive their Source;
Command thy Self, whom no Commands can force.   400
The Son of *Thetis* Rampire of our Host,
Is worth our Care to keep; nor shall my Pray'rs be lost.
    Thus *Nestor* said, and ceas'd: *Atrides* broke
His Silence next; but ponder'd e'er he spoke.
Wise are thy Words, and glad I would obey,   405
But this proud Man affects Imperial Sway.
Controlling Kings, and trampling on our State
His Will is Law; and what he wills is Fate.
The Gods have giv'n him Strength: But whence the Style,
Of lawless Pow'r assum'd, or Licence to revile?   410
    Achilles, cut him short; and thus reply'd:
My Worth allow'd in Words, is in effect deny'd.
For who but a Poltron, possess'd with Fear,
Such haughty Insolence, can tamely bear?
Command thy Slaves: My freeborn Soul disdains   41
A Tyrant's Curb; and restiff breaks the Reins.
Take this along; that no Dispute shall rise
(Though mine the Woman) for my ravish'd Prize:
But she excepted, as unworthy Strife,
Dare not, I charge thee dare not, on thy Life,   42
Touch ought of mine beside, by Lot my due,
But stand aloof, and think profane to view:
This Fauchion, else, not hitherto withstood,
These hostile Fields shall fatten with thy Blood.
    He said; and rose the first; the Council broke;   42
And all their grave Consults dissolv'd in Smoke.
    The Royal Youth retir'd, on Vengeance bent,
Patroclus follow'd silent to his Tent.
    Mean time, the King with Gifts a Vessel stores;
Supplies the Banks with twenty chosen Oars: 43

And next, to reconcile the shooter God,
Within her hollow Sides the Sacrifice he stow'd:
Chryseis last was set on board; whose Hand
Ulysses took, intrusted with Command;
They plow the liquid Seas; and leave the less'ning Land.   435
   Atrides then his outward Zeal to boast,
Bade purify the Sin-polluted Host.
With perfect Hecatombs the God they grac'd;
Whose offer'd Entrails in the Main were cast.
Black Bulls, and bearded Goats on Altars lie;   440
And clouds of sav'ry stench, involve the Sky.
These Pomps the Royal Hypocrite design'd,
For Shew: But harbour'd Vengeance in his Mind:
Till holy Malice, longing for a vent,
At length, discover'd his conceal'd Intent.   445
Talthybius, and *Eurybates* the just,
Heralds of Arms, and Ministers of Trust,
He call'd; and thus bespoke: Haste hence your way;
And from the Goddess-born demand his Prey.
If yielded, bring the Captive: If deny'd,   450
The King (so tell him) shall chastise his Pride:
And with arm'd Multitudes in Person come
To vindicate his Pow'r, and justify his Doom.
   This hard Command unwilling they obey,
And o'er the barren Shore pursue their way,   455
Where quarter'd in their Camp, the fierce *Thessalians* lay.
Their Sov'reign seated on his Chair, they find;
His pensive Cheek upon his Hand reclin'd,
And anxious Thoughts revolving in his Mind.
With gloomy Looks he saw them entring in   460
Without Salute: Nor durst they first begin,
Fearful of rash Offence and Death foreseen.
He soon the Cause divining, clear'd his Brow;
And thus did liberty of Speech allow.
   Interpreters of Gods and Men, be bold: 465
Awful your Character, and uncontroll'd;
Howe'er unpleasing, be the News you bring,
I blame not you, but your Imperious King.
You come, I know, my Captive to demand;

   446 just,] just *F*   466 uncontroll'd;] uncontroll'd, *F*

Patroclus, give her, to the Herald's Hand.   470
But you, authentick Witnesses I bring,
Before the Gods, and your ungrateful King,
Of this my Manifest: That never more
This Hand shall combate on the crooked Shore:
No, let the *Grecian* Pow'rs oppress'd in Fight,   475
Unpity'd perish in their Tyrants sight.
Blind of the future and by Rage misled,
He pulls his Crimes upon his People's Head.
Forc'd from the Field in Trenches to contend,
And his Insulted Camp from Foes defend.   480
He said, and soon obeying his intent,
Patroclus brought *Briseis* from her Tent;
Then to th' intrusted Messengers resign'd:
She wept, and often cast her Eyes behind;
Forc'd from the Man she lov'd: They led her thence,   485
Along the Shore a Pris'ner to their Prince.
     Sole on the barren Sands the suff'ring Chief
Roar'd out for Anguish, and indulg'd his Grief.
Cast on his Kindred Seas a stormy Look,
And his upbraided Mother thus bespoke.   490
     Unhappy Parent, of a short-liv'd Son,
Since *Jove* in pity by thy Pray'rs was won
To grace my small Remains of Breath with Fame,
Why loads he this imbitter'd Life with Shame?
Suff'ring his King of Men to force my Slave,   495
Whom well deserv'd in War, the *Grecians* gave.
     Set by old Ocean's side the Goddess heard;
Then from the sacred Deep her Head she rear'd:
Rose like a Morning-mist; and thus begun
To sooth the Sorrows of her plaintive Son.   500
Why cry's my Care, and why conceals his Smart?
Let thy afflicted Parent, share her part.
     Then, sighing from the bottom of his Breast,
To the Sea-Goddess thus the Goddess-born address'd.
Thou know'st my Pain, which telling but recals: 505
By force of Arms we raz'd the *Theban* Walls;
The ransack'd City, taken by our Toils,
We left, and hither brought the golden Spoils:

484 behind;] behind: *F*   501 Smart?] Smart, *F*   502 part.] part? *F*

Equal we shar'd them; but before the rest,
The proud Prerogative had seiz'd the best.   510
Chryseis was the greedy Tyrant's Prize,
Chryseis rosy Cheek'd with charming Eyes.
Her Syre, *Apollo*'s Priest, arriv'd to buy
With proffer'd Gifts of Price, his Daughter's liberty.
Suppliant before the *Grecians* Chiefs he stood,   515
Awful, and arm'd with Ensigns of his God:
Bare was his hoary Head, one holy Hand
Held forth his Lawrel-Crown, and one, his Scepter of Command.
His Suit was common, but above the rest
To both the Brother-Princes was address'd.   520
With Shouts of loud Acclaim the *Greeks* agree
To take the Gifts, to set the Pris'ner free.
Not so the Tyrant, who with scorn the Priest
Receiv'd, and with opprobrious Words dismiss'd.
The good old Man, forlorn of human Aid,   525
For Vengeance to his heav'nly Patron pray'd:
The Godhead gave a favourable Ear,
And granted all to him he held so dear;
In an ill hour his piercing Shafts he sped;
And heaps on heaps of slaughter'd *Greeks* lay dead,   530
While round the Camp he rang'd: At length arose
A Seer who well divin'd; and durst disclose
The Source of all our Ills: I took the Word;
And urg'd the sacred Slave to be restor'd,
The God appeas'd: The swelling Monarch storm'd;   535
And then, the Vengeance, vow'd; he since perform'd:
The *Greeks* 'tis true, their Ruin to prevent
Have to the Royal Priest, his Daughter sent;
But from their haughty King his Heralds came
And seiz'd by his Command, my Captive Dame,   540
By common Suffrage given; but, thou, be won,
If in thy Pow'r, t' avenge thy injur'd Son:
Ascend the Skies; and supplicating move
Thy just Complaint, to Cloud-compelling *Jove*.
If thou by either Word or Deed hast wrought   545
A kind remembrance in his grateful Thought,

517 Hand] Hand, *F*   525 forlorn] forlorn, *F*   530 dead,] dead. *F*
541 won,] won *F*   542 If] If, *F*   543 move] move, *F*

Urge him by that: For often hast thou said
Thy Pow'r was once not useless in his Aid.
When He who high above the Highest reigns,
Surpriz'd by Traytor-Gods, was bound in Chains.   550
When *Juno*, *Pallas*, with Ambition fir'd,
And his blue Brother of the Seas conspir'd.
Thou freed'st the Soveraign from unworthy Bands,
Thou brought'st *Briareus* with his hundred Hands,
(So call'd in Heav'n, but mortal Men below   555
By his terrestrial Name, *Ægeon* know:
Twice stronger than his Syre, who sate above,
Assessor to the Throne of thundring *Jove*.)
The Gods, dismay'd at his approach, withdrew
Nor durst their unaccomplish'd Crime, pursue.   560
That Action to his grateful Mind recal;
Embrace his Knees, and at his Footstool fall:
That now if ever, he will aid our Foes;
Let *Troy*'s triumphant Troops the Camp inclose:
Ours beaten to the Shore, the Siege forsake;   565
And what their King deserves with him partake.
That the proud Tyrant at his proper cost,
May learn the value of the Man he lost.
    To whom the Mother-Goddess thus reply'd,
Sigh'd e'er she spoke, and while she spoke she cry'd,   570
Ah wretched me! by Fates averse, decreed,
To bring thee forth with Pain, with care to breed!
Did envious Heav'n not otherwise ordain,
Safe in thy hollow Ships thou shou'd'st remain;
Nor ever tempt the fatal Field again.   575
But now thy Planet sheds his pois'nous Rays:
And short, and full of Sorrow are thy Days.
For what remains, to Heav'n I will ascend,
And at the Thund'rer's Throne thy Suit commend.
'Till then, secure in Ships, abstain from Fight;   580
Indulge thy Grief in Tears, and vent thy Spight.
For yesterday the Court of Heav'n with *Jove*,
Remov'd: 'Tis dead Vacation now above.
Twelve Days the Gods their solemn Revels keep,
And quaff with blameless *Ethiops* in the Deep.   585

557 above,] above *F*   565 forsake] fasake *F*

Return'd from thence, to Heav'n my Flight I take,
Knock at the brazen Gates, and Providence awake.
Embrace his Knees, and suppliant to the Sire,
Doubt not I will obtain the grant of thy desire.

She said: And parting left him on the place,   590
Swoln with Disdain, resenting his Disgrace:
Revengeful Thoughts revolving in his Mind,
He wept for Anger and for Love he pin'd.

Mean time with prosperous Gales, *Ulysses* brought
The Slave, and Ship with Sacrifices fraught,   595
To *Chrysa*'s Port: Where entring with the Tide
He drop'd his Anchors, and his Oars he ply'd.
Furl'd every Sail, and drawing down the Mast,
His Vessel moor'd; and made with Haulsers fast.
Descending on the Plain, ashore they bring   600
The Hecatomb to please the shooter King.
The Dame before an Altars holy Fire,
Ulysses led; and thus bespoke her Sire.

Reverenc'd be thou, and be thy God ador'd:
The King of Men thy Daughter has restor'd;   605
And sent by me with Presents and with Pray'r;
He recommends him to thy pious Care.
That *Phœbus* at thy Sute his Wrath may cease,
And give the penitent Offenders Peace.

He said, and gave her to her Father's Hands,   610
Who glad receiv'd her, free from servile Bands.
This done, in Order they with sober Grace
Their Gifts around the well-built Altar place.
Then wash'd, and took the Cakes; while *Chryses* stood
With Hands upheld, and thus invok'd his God.   615

God, of the Silver Bow, whose Eyes survey
The sacred *Cilla*, thou whose awful Sway
Chrysa the bless'd, and *Tenedos* obey:
Now hear, as thou before my Pray'r hast heard,
Against the *Grecians*, and their Prince, preferr'd: 620
Once thou hast honour'd, honour once again
Thy Priest; nor let his second Vows be vain.
But from th' afflicted Host and humbled Prince,
Avert thy Wrath, and cease thy Pestilence.

612 Grace] Grace, F

Apollo heard, and conquering his Disdain, 625
Unbent his Bow and *Greece* respir'd again.
  Now when the solemn Rites of Pray'r were past,
Their salted Cakes on crackling Flames they cast.
Then, turning back, the Sacrifice they sped:
The fatted Oxen slew, and flea'd the Dead. 630
Chop'd off their nervous Thighs, and next prepar'd
T' involve the lean in Cauls, and mend with Lard.
Sweet-breads and Collops, were with Skewers prick'd
About the Sides; inbibing what they deck'd.
The Priest with holy Hands was seen to tine 635
The cloven Wood, and pour the ruddy Wine.
The Youth approach'd the Fire and as it burn'd
On five sharp Broachers rank'd, the Roast they turn'd:
These Morsels stay'd their Stomachs; then the rest
They cut in Legs and Fillets for the Feast; 640
Which drawn and serv'd, their Hunger they appease
With sav'ry Meat, and set their Minds at ease.
  Now when the rage of Eating was repell'd,
The Boys with generous Wine the Goblets fill'd.
The first Libations to the Gods they pour: 645
And then with Songs indulge the Genial Hour.
Holy Debauch! Till Day to Night they bring,
With Hymns and *Pæans* to the Bowyer King.
At Sun-set to their Ship they make return,
And snore secure on Decks, till rosy Morn. 650
  The Skies with dawning Day were purpled o'er;
Awak'd, with lab'ring Oars they leave the Shore:
The Pow'r appeas'd, with Winds suffic'd the Sail,
The bellying Canvass strutted with the Gale;
The Waves indignant roar with surly Pride, 655
And press against the Sides, and beaten off divide.
They cut the foamy way, with Force impell'd
Superiour, till the *Trojan* Port they held:
Then hauling on the Strand their Gally Moor,
And pitch their Tents along the crooked Shore. 660
  Mean time the Goddess-born, in secret pin'd;
Nor visited the Camp, nor in the Council join'd,
But keeping close, his gnawing Heart he fed
With hopes of Vengeance on the Tyrant's Head:

And wish'd for bloody Wars and mortal Wounds,   665
And of the *Greeks* oppress'd in Fight, to hear the dying Sounds.
    Now, when twelve Days compleat had run their Race,
The Gods bethought them of the Cares belonging to their place.
Jove at their Head ascending from the Sea,
A shoal of puny Pow'rs attend his way.   670
Then *Thetis* not unmindful of her Son
Emerging from the Deep, to beg her Boon,
Pursu'd their Track; and waken'd from his rest,
Before the Soveraign stood a Morning Guest.
Him in the Circle but apart, she found: 675
The rest at awful distance stood around.
She bow'd, and e'er she durst her Sute begin,
One Hand embrac'd his Knees, one prop'd his Chin.
Then thus. If I, Celestial Sire, in aught
Have serv'd thy Will, or gratify'd thy Thought,   680
One glimpse of Glory to my Issue give;
Grac'd for the little time he has to live.
Dishonour'd by the King of Men he stands:
His rightful Prize is ravish'd from his Hands.
But thou, O Father, in my Son's Defence,   685
Assume thy Pow'r, assert thy Providence.
Let *Troy* prevail, till *Greece* th' Affront has paid,
With doubled Honours; and redeem'd his Aid.
    She ceas'd, but the consid'ring God was mute:
'Till she resolv'd to win, renew'd her Sute: 690
Nor loos'd her Hold, but forc'd him to reply,
Or grant me my Petition, or deny:
Jove cannot fear: Then tell me to my Face
That I, of all the Gods am least in grace.
This I can bear: The Cloud-Compeller mourn'd,   695
And sighing, first, this Answer he return'd.
    Know'st thou what Clamors will disturb my Reign,
What my stun'd Ears from *Juno* must sustain?
In Council she gives Licence to her Tongue,
Loquacious, Brawling, ever in the wrong.   700
And now she will my partial Pow'r upbraid,
If alienate from *Greece*, I give the *Trojans* Aid.
But thou depart, and shun her jealous Sight,
The Care be mine, to do *Pelides* right.

Go then, and on the Faith of *Jove* rely;   705
When nodding to thy Sute, he bows the Sky.
This ratifies th' irrevocable Doom:
The Sign ordain'd, that what I will shall come:
The Stamp of Heav'n, and Seal of Fate: He said,
And shook the sacred Honours of his Head.   710
With Terror trembled Heav'ns subsiding Hill:
And from his shaken Curls Ambrosial Dews distil.
The Goddess goes exulting from his Sight,
And seeks the Seas profound; and leaves the Realms of Light.
    He moves into his Hall: The Pow'rs resort,   715
Each from his House to fill the Soveraign's Court.
Nor waiting Summons, nor expecting stood;
But met with Reverence, and receiv'd the God.
He mounts the Throne; and *Juno* took her place:
But sullen Discontent sate lowring on her Face.   720
With jealous Eyes, at distance she had seen,
Whisp'ring with *Jove* the Silver-footed Queen;
Then, impotent of Tongue (her Silence broke)
Thus turbulent in rattling Tone she spoke.
    Author of Ills, and close Contriver *Jove*,   725
Which of thy Dames, what Prostitute of Love,
Has held thy Ear so long and begg'd so hard
For some old Service done, some new Reward?
Apart you talk'd, for that's your special care
The Consort never must the Council share.   730
One gracious Word is for a Wife too much:
Such is a Marriage-Vow, and *Jove*'s own Faith is such.
    Then thus the Sire of Gods, and Men below,
What I have hidden, hope not thou to know.
Ev'n Goddesses are Women: And no Wife   735
Has Pow'r to regulate her Husband's Life:
Counsel she may; and I will give thy Ear
The Knowledge first, of what is fit to hear.
What I transact with others, or alone,
Beware to learn; nor press too near the Throne.   740
    To whom the Goddess with the charming Eyes,
What hast thou said, O Tyrant of the Skies,
When did I search the Secrets of thy Reign,
Though priviledg'd to know, but priviledg'd in vain?

But well thou dost, to hide from common Sight   745
Thy close Intrigues, too bad to bear the Light.
Nor doubt I, but the Silver-footed Dame,
Tripping from Sea, on such an Errand came,
To grace her Issue, at the *Grecians* Cost,
And for one peevish Man destroy an Host.   750
　　To whom the Thund'rer made this stern Reply;
My Houshold Curse, my lawful Plague, the Spy
Of *Jove*'s Designs, his other squinting Eye;
Why this vain prying, and for what avail?
Jove will be Master still and *Juno* fail.   755
Shou'd thy suspicious Thoughts divine aright,
Thou but becom'st more odious to my Sight,
For this Attempt: uneasy Life to me
Still watch'd, and importun'd, but worse for thee.
Curb that impetuous Tongue, before too late   760
The Gods behold, and tremble at thy Fate.
Pitying, but daring not in thy Defence,
To lift a Hand against Omnipotence.
　　This heard, the Imperious Queen sate mute with Fear;
Nor further durst incense the gloomy Thunderer.   765
Silence was in the Court at this Rebuke:
Nor cou'd the Gods abash'd, sustain their Sov'reigns Look.
　　The Limping Smith, observ'd the sadden'd Feast;
And hopping here and there (himself a Jest)
Put in his Word, that neither might offend;   770
To *Jove* obsequious, yet his Mother's Friend.
What end in Heav'n will be of civil War,
If Gods of Pleasure will for Mortals jar?
Such Discord but disturbs our Jovial Feast;
One Grain of Bad, embitters all the best.   775
Mother, tho' wise your self, my Counsel weigh;
'Tis much unsafe my Sire to disobey.
Not only you provoke him to your Cost,
But Mirth is marr'd, and the good Chear is lost.
Tempt not his heavy Hand; for he has Pow'r   780
To throw you Headlong, from his Heav'nly Tow'r.
But one submissive Word, which you let fall,
Will make him in good Humour with us All.
　　He said no more but crown'd a Bowl, unbid:

The laughing Nectar overlook'd the Lid: 785
Then put it to her Hand; and thus pursu'd,
This cursed Quarrel be no more renew'd.
Be, as becomes a Wife, obedient still;
Though griev'd, yet subject to her Husband's Will.
I wou'd not see you beaten; yet affraid   790
Of *Jove*'s superiour Force, I dare not aid.
Too well I know him, since that hapless Hour
When I, and all the Gods employ'd our Pow'r
To break your Bonds: Me by the Heel he drew;
And o'er Heav'n's Battlements with Fury threw.   795
All Day I fell; My Flight at Morn begun,
And ended not but with the setting Sun.
Pitch'd on my Head, at length the *Lemnian*-ground
Receiv'd my batter'd Skull, the *Sinthians* heal'd my Wound.
    At *Vulcan*'s homely Mirth his Mother smil'd,   800
And smiling took the Cup the Clown had fill'd.
The Reconciler Bowl, went round the Board,
Which empty'd, the rude Skinker still restor'd.
Loud Fits of Laughter seiz'd the Guests, to see
The limping God so deft at his new Ministry.   805
The Feast continu'd till declining Light:
They drank, they laugh'd, they lov'd, and then 'twas Night.
Nor wanted tuneful Harp, nor vocal Quire;
The Muses sung; *Apollo* touch'd the Lyre.
Drunken at last, and drowsy they depart,   810
Each to his House; Adorn'd with labour'd Art
Of the lame Architect: The thund'ring God
Ev'n he withdrew to rest, and had his Load.
His swimming Head to needful Sleep apply'd;
And *Juno* lay unheeded by his Side.   815

788 still;] still F   798 *Lemnian*-ground] *Lemnian*-ground, F

THE COCK and the FOX:
OR, THE TALE OF THE NUN'S PRIEST,
FROM CHAUCER

THERE liv'd, as Authors tell, in Days of Yore,
A Widow somewhat old, and very poor:
Deep in a Dell her Cottage lonely stood,
Well thatch'd, and under covert of a Wood.
This Dowager, on whom my Tale I found,   5
Since last she laid her Husband in the Ground,
A simple sober Life, in patience led,
And had but just enough to buy her Bread:
But Huswifing the little Heav'n had lent,
She duly paid a Groat for Quarter-Rent;   10
And pinch'd her Belly with her Daughters two,
To bring the Year about with much ado.
The Cattel in her Homestead were three Sows,
An Ewe call'd *Mally*; and three brinded Cows.
Her Parlor-Window stuck with Herbs around,   15
Of sav'ry Smell; and Rushes strew'd the Ground.
A Maple-Dresser, in her Hall she had,
On which full many a slender Meal she made:
For no delicious Morsel pass'd her Throat;
According to her Cloth she cut her Coat: 20
No paynant Sawce she knew, no costly Treat,
Her Hunger gave a Relish to her Meat:
A sparing Diet did her Health assure;
Or sick, a Pepper-Posset was her Cure.
Before the Day was done her Work she sped,   25
And never went by Candle-light to Bed:
With Exercise she sweat ill Humors out,
Her Dancing was not hinder'd by the Gout.
Her Poverty was glad; her Heart content,
Nor knew she what the Spleen or Vapors meant.   30
Of Wine she never tasted through the Year,
But White and Black was all her homely Chear;
Brown Bread, and Milk, (but first she skim'd her Bowls)

The Cock and the Fox. 3 Dell] Cell *F. See Commentary*   11 Daughters] Daughter *F*

And Rashers of sindg'd Bacon, on the Coals.
On Holy-Days, an Egg or two at most;   35
But her Ambition never reach'd to roast.
   A Yard she had with Pales enclos'd about,
Some high, some low, and a dry Ditch without.
Within this Homestead, liv'd without a Peer,
For crowing loud, the noble Chanticleer: 40
So hight her Cock, whose singing did surpass
The merry Notes of Organs at the Mass.
More certain was the crowing of a Cock
To number Hours, than is an Abbey-clock;
And sooner than the Mattin-Bell was rung,   45
He clap'd his Wings upon his Roost, and sung:
For when Degrees fifteen ascended right,
By sure Instinct he knew 'twas One at Night.
High was his Comb, and Coral-red withal,
In dents embattel'd like a Castle-Wall;   50
His Bill was Raven-black, and shon like Jet,
Blue were his Legs, and Orient were his Feet:
White were his Nails, like Silver to behold,
His Body glitt'ring like the burnish'd Gold.
   This gentle Cock for solace of his Life,   55
Six Misses had beside his lawful Wife;
Scandal that spares no King, tho' ne'er so good,
Says, they were all of his own Flesh and Blood:
His Sisters both by Sire, and Mother's side,
And sure their likeness show'd them near ally'd.   60
But make the worst, the Monarch did no more,
Than all the *Ptolomeys* had done before:
When Incest is for Int'rest of a Nation,
'Tis made no Sin by Holy Dispensation.
Some Lines have been maintain'd by this alone,   65
Which by their common Ugliness are known.
   But passing this as from our Tale apart,
Dame Partlet was the Soveraign of his Heart:
Ardent in Love, outragious in his Play,
He feather'd her a hundred times a Day: 70
And she that was not only passing fair,
But was withal discreet, and debonair,

62 Ptolomeys] Ptolomey's F

Resolv'd the passive Doctrin to fulfil
Tho' loath: And let him work his wicked Will.
At Board and Bed was affable and kind,   75
According as their Marriage-Vow did bind,
And as the Churches Precept had enjoin'd.
Ev'n since she was a Sennight old, they say
Was chast, and humble to her dying Day,
Nor Chick nor Hen was known to disobey.   80
    By this her Husband's Heart she did obtain,
What cannot Beauty, join'd with Virtue, gain!
She was his only Joy, and he her Pride,
She, when he walk'd, went pecking by his side;
If spurning up the Ground, he sprung a Corn,   85
The Tribute in his Bill to her was born.
But oh! what Joy it was to hear him sing
In Summer, when the Day began to spring,
Stretching his Neck, and warbling in his Throat,
Solus cum Sola, then was all his Note.   90
For in the Days of Yore, the Birds of Parts
Were bred to Speak, and Sing, and learn the lib'ral Arts.
    It happ'd that perching on the Parlor-beam
Amidst his Wives he had a deadly Dream;
Just at the Dawn, and sigh'd, and groan'd so fast,   95
As ev'ry Breath he drew wou'd be his last.
Dame Partlet, ever nearest to his Side,
Heard all his piteous Moan, and how he cry'd
For Help from Gods and Men: And sore aghast
She peck'd and pull'd, and waken'd him at last.   100
Dear Heart, said she, for Love of Heav'n declare
Your Pain, and make me Partner of your Care.
You groan, Sir, ever since the Morning-light,
As something had disturb'd your noble Spright.
    And Madam, well I might, said Chanticleer,   105
Never was *Shrovetide*-Cock in such a fear.
Ev'n still I run all over in a Sweat,
My Princely Senses not recover'd yet.
For such a Dream I had of dire Portent,
That much I fear my Body will be shent: 110
It bodes I shall have Wars and woful Strife,
Or in a loathsom Dungeon end my Life.

Know Dame, I dreamt within my troubled Breast,
That in our Yard, I saw a murd'rous Beast,
That on my Body would have made Arrest.   115
With waking Eyes I ne'er beheld his Fellow,
His Colour was betwixt a Red and Yellow:
Tipp'd was his Tail, and both his pricking Ears
With black; and much unlike his other Hairs:
The rest, in shape a Beagle's Whelp throughout,   120
With broader Forehead, and a sharper Snout:
Deep in his Front were sunk his glowing Eyes,
That yet methinks I see him with Surprize.
Reach out your Hand, I drop with clammy Sweat,
And lay it to my Heart, and feel it beat.   125

    Now fy for Shame, quoth she, by Heav'n above,
Thou hast for ever lost thy Ladies Love;
No Woman can endure a Recreant Knight,
He must be bold by Day, and free by Night:
Our Sex desires a Husband or a Friend,   130
Who can our Honour and his own defend;
Wise, Hardy, Secret, lib'ral of his Purse:
A Fool is nauseous, but a Coward worse:
No bragging Coxcomb, yet no baffled Knight,
How dar'st thou talk of Love, and dar'st not Fight?   135
How dar'st thou tell thy Dame thou art affer'd,
Hast thou no manly Heart, and hast a Beard?

    If ought from fearful Dreams may be divin'd,
They signify a Cock of Dunghill-kind.
All Dreams, as in old *Gallen* I have read,   140
Are from Repletion and Complexion bred:
From rising Fumes of indigested Food,
And noxious Humors that infect the Blood:
And sure, my Lord, if I can read aright,
These foolish Fancies you have had to Night   145
Are certain Symptoms (in the canting Style)
Of boiling Choler, and abounding Bile:
This yellow Gaul that in your Stomach floats,
Ingenders all these visionary Thoughts.
When Choler overflows, then Dreams are bred   150
Of Flames and all the Family of Red;

145 to Night] to Night; F

Red Dragons, and red Beasts in sleep we view;
For Humors are distinguish'd by their Hue.
From hence we dream of Wars and Warlike Things,
And Wasps and Hornets with their double Wings.   155
    Choler adust congeals our Blood with Fear;
Then black Bulls toss us, and black Devils tear.
In sanguine airy Dreams aloft we bound,
With Rhumes oppress'd we sink in Rivers drown'd.
    More I could say, but thus conclude my Theme,   160
The dominating Humour makes the Dream.
Cato was in his time accounted Wise,
And he condemns them all for empty Lies.
Take my Advice, and when we fly to Ground
With Laxatives preserve your Body sound,   165
And purge the peccant Humors that abound.
I should be loath to lay you on a Bier;
And though there lives no 'Pothecary near,
I dare for once prescribe for your Disease,
And save long Bills, and a damn'd Doctor's Fees.   170
    Two Soveraign Herbs, which I by practise know,
And both at Hand, (for in our Yard they grow;)
On peril of my Soul shall rid you wholly
Of yellow Choler, and of Melancholy:
You must both Purge, and Vomit; but obey,   175
And for the love of Heav'n make no delay.
Since hot and dry in your Complexion join,
Beware the Sun when in a vernal Sign;
For when he mounts exalted in the Ram,
If then he finds your Body in a Flame,   180
Replete with Choler, I dare lay a Groat,
A Tertian Ague is at least your Lot.
Perhaps a Fever (which the Gods forefend)
May bring your Youth to some untimely end.
And therefore, Sir, as you desire to live,   185
A Day or two before your Laxative,
Take just three Worms, nor over nor above,
Because the Gods unequal Numbers love.
These Digestives prepare you for your Purge,
Of Fumetery, Centaury, and Spurge,   190
And of Ground-Ivy add a Leaf, or two,

All which within our Yard or Garden grow.
Eat these, and be, my Lord, of better Cheer,
Your Father's Son was never born to fear.
     Madam, quoth he, Grammercy for your Care,   195
But *Cato*, whom you quoted, you may spare:
'Tis true, a wise, and worthy Man he seems,
And (as you say) gave no belief to Dreams:
But other Men of more Authority,
And by th' Immortal Pow'rs as wise as He   200
Maintain, with sounder Sense, that Dreams forbode;
For *Homer* plainly says they come from God.
Nor *Cato* said it: But some modern Fool,
Impos'd in *Cato*'s Name on Boys at School.
     Believe me, Madam, Morning Dreams foreshow   205
Th' events of Things, and future Weal or Woe:
Some Truths are by Reason to be try'd,
But we have sure Experience for our Guide.
An ancient Author, equal with the best,
Relates this Tale of Dreams among the rest.   210
     Two Friends, or Brothers, with devout Intent,
On some far Pilgrimage together went.
It happen'd so that when the Sun was down,
They just arriv'd by twilight at a Town;
That Day had been the baiting of a Bull,   215
'Twas at a Feast, and ev'ry Inn so full;
That no void Room in Chamber, or on Ground,
And but one sorry Bed was to be found:
And that so little it would hold but one,
Though till this Hour they never lay alone.   220
     So were they forc'd to part; one stay'd behind,
His Fellow sought what Lodging he could find:
At last he found a Stall where Oxen stood,
And that he rather chose than lie abroad.
'Twas in a farther Yard without a Door,   225
But for his ease, well litter'd was the Floor.
     His Fellow, who the narrow Bed had kept,
Was weary, and without a Rocker slept:
Supine he snor'd; but in the dead of Night,
He dreamt his Friend appear'd before his Sight,   230

Who with a ghastly Look and doleful Cry,
Said help me Brother, or this Night I die:
Arise, and help, before all Help be vain,
Or in an Oxes Stall I shall be slain.

    Rowz'd from his Rest he waken'd in a start, 235
Shiv'ring with Horror, and with aking Heart;
At length to cure himself by Reason tries;
'Twas but a Dream, and what are Dreams but Lies?
So thinking chang'd his Side, and clos'd his Eyes.
His Dream returns; his Friend appears again, 240
The Murd'rers come; now help, or I am slain:
'Twas but a Vision still, and Visions are but vain.

    He dreamt the third: But now his Friend appear'd
Pale, naked, pierc'd with Wounds, with Blood besmear'd:
Thrice warn'd awake, said he; Relief is late, 245
The Deed is done; but thou revenge my Fate:
Tardy of Aid, unseal thy heavy Eyes,
Awake, and with the dawning Day arise:
Take to the Western Gate thy ready way,
For by that Passage they my Corps convey: 250
My Corpse is in a Tumbril laid; among
The Filth, and Ordure, and enclos'd with Dung.
That Cart arrest, and raise a common Cry,
For sacred hunger of my Gold I die;
Then shew'd his grisly Wounds; and last he drew 255
A piteous Sigh; and took a long Adieu.

    The frighted Friend arose by break of Day,
And found the Stall where late his Fellow lay.
Then of his impious Host enquiring more,
Was answer'd that his Guest was gone before: 260
Muttring he went, said he, by Morning-light,
And much complain'd of his ill Rest by Night.
This rais'd Suspicion in the Pilgrim's Mind;
Because all Hosts are of an evil Kind,
And oft, to share the Spoil, with Robbers join'd. 265

    His Dream confirm'd his Thought: with troubled Look
Strait to the Western-Gate his way he took.
There, as his Dream foretold, a Cart he found,
That carry'd Composs forth to dung the Ground.
This, when the Pilgrim saw, he stretch'd his Throat, 270

And cry'd out Murther, with a yelling Note.
My murther'd Fellow in this Cart lies dead,
Vengeance and Justice on the Villain's Head.
You, Magistrates, who sacred Laws dispense,
On you I call to punish this Offence.   275
   The Word thus giv'n, within a little space,
The Mob came roaring out, and throng'd the Place.
All in a trice they cast the Cart to Ground,
And in the Dung the murther'd Body found;
Though breathless, warm, and reeking from the Wound.   280
Good Heav'n, whose darling Attribute we find
Is boundless Grace, and Mercy to Mankind,
Abhors the Cruel; and the Deeds of Night
By wond'rous Ways reveals in open Light:
Murther may pass unpunished for a time,   285
But tardy Justice will o'ertake the Crime.
And oft a speedier Pain the Guilty feels;
The Hue and Cry of Heav'n pursues him at the Heels,
Fresh from the Fact; as in the present Case;
The Criminals are seiz'd upon the Place: 290
Carter and Host confronted Face to Face.
Stiff in denial, as the Law appoints
On Engins they distend their tortur'd Joints:
So was Confession forc'd, th' Offence was known,
And publick Justice on th' Offenders done.   295
   Here may you see that Visions are to dread:
And in the Page that follows this; I read
Of two young Merchants, whom the hope of Gain
Induc'd in Partnership to cross the Main:
Waiting till willing Winds their Sails supply'd,   300
Within a Trading-Town they long abide,
Full fairly situate on a Haven's side.
   One Evening it befel that looking out,
The Wind they long had wish'd was come about:
Well pleas'd they went to Rest; and if the Gale   305
'Till Morn continu'd, both resolv'd to sail.
But as together in a Bed they lay,
The younger had a Dream at break of Day.

A Man, he thought, stood frowning at his side;
Who warn'd him for his Safety to provide, }310
Not put to Sea, but safe on Shore abide.
I come, thy Genius, to command thy stay;
Trust not the Winds, for fatal is the Day,
And Death unhop'd attends the watry way.
   The Vision said: And vanish'd from his sight, 315
The Dreamer waken'd in a mortal Fright:
Then pull'd his drowzy Neighbour, and declar'd
What in his Slumber he had seen, and heard.
His Friend smil'd scornful, and with proud contempt
Rejects as idle what his Fellow dreamt. 320
Stay, who will stay: For me no Fears restrain,
Who follow *Mercury* the God of Gain:
Let each Man do as to his Fancy seems,
I wait, not I, till you have better Dreams.
Dreams are but Interludes, which Fancy makes, 325
When Monarch-Reason sleeps, this Mimick wakes:
Compounds a Medley of disjointed Things,
A Mob of Coblers, and a Court of Kings:
Light Fumes are merry, grosser Fumes are sad;
Both are the reasonable Soul run mad: 330
And many monstrous Forms in sleep we see,
That neither were, nor are, nor e'er can be.
Sometimes, forgotten Things long cast behind
Rush forward in the Brain, and come to mind.
The Nurses Legends are for Truths receiv'd, 335
And the Man dreams but what the Boy believ'd.
   Sometimes we but rehearse a former Play,
The Night restores our Actions done by Day;
As Hounds in sleep will open for their Prey.
In short, the Farce of Dreams is of a piece, 340
Chimera's all; and more absurd, or less:
You, who believe in Tales, abide alone,
What e'er I get this Voyage is my own.
   Thus while he spoke he heard the shouting Crew
That call'd aboard, and took his last adieu. 345
The Vessel went before a merry Gale,
And for quick Passage put on ev'ry Sail:
But when least fear'd, and ev'n in open Day,

The Mischief overtook her in the way:
Whether she sprung a Leak, I cannot find,   35
Or whether she was overset with Wind;
Or that some Rock below, her bottom rent,
But down at once with all her Crew she went;
Her Fellow Ships from far her Loss descry'd;
But only she was sunk, and all were safe beside.   35

By this Example you are taught again,
That Dreams and Visions are not always vain:
But if, dear Partlet, you are yet in doubt,
Another Tale shall make the former out.

    Kenelm the Son of *Kenulph*, *Mercia*'s King,   30
Whose holy Life the Legends loudly sing,
Warn'd, in a Dream, his Murther did foretel
From Point to Point as after it befel:
All Circumstances to his Nurse he told,
(A Wonder, from a Child of sev'n Years old:)   34
The Dream with Horror heard, the good old Wife
From Treason counsell'd him to guard his Life:
But close to keep the Secret in his Mind,
For a Boy's Vision small Belief would find.
The pious Child, by Promise bound, obey'd,   3
Nor was the fatal Murther long delay'd:
By *Quenda* slain he fell before his time,
Made a young Martyr by his Sister's Crime.
The Tale is told by venerable *Bede*,
Which, at your better leisure, you may read.   3

    Macrobius too relates the Vision sent
To the great *Scipio* with the fam'd event,
Objections makes, but after makes Replies,
And adds, that Dreams are often Prophecies.

    Of *Daniel*, you may read in Holy Writ,   3
Who, when the King his Vision did forget,
Cou'd Word for Word the wond'rous Dream repeat.
Nor less of Patriarch *Joseph* understand
Who by a Dream inslav'd th' *Egyptian* Land,
The Years of Plenty and of Dearth foretold,
When for their Bread, their Liberty they sold.
Nor must th' exalted Buttler be forgot,
Nor he whose Dream presag'd his hanging Lot.

And did not *Cræsus* the same Death foresee,
Rais'd in his Vision on a lofty Tree?   390
The Wife of *Hector* in his utmost Pride,
Dreamt of his Death the Night before he dy'd:
Well was he warn'd from Battle to refrain,
But Men to Death decreed are warn'd in vain:
He dar'd the Dream, and by his fatal Foe was slain.   395

   Much more I know, which I forbear to speak,
For see the ruddy Day begins to break:
Let this suffice, that plainly I foresee
My Dream was bad, and bodes Adversity:
But neither Pills nor Laxatives I like,   400
They only serve to make a well-man sick:
Of these his Gain the sharp Phisician makes,
And often gives a Purge, but seldom takes:
They not correct, but poyson all the Blood,
And ne'er did any but the Doctors good.   405
Their Tribe, Trade, Trinkets, I defy them all,
With ev'ry Work of 'Pothecary's Hall.

   These melancholy Matters I forbear:
But let me tell Thee, Partlet mine, and swear,
That when I view the Beauties of thy Face,   410
I fear not Death, nor Dangers, nor Disgrace:
So may my Soul have Bliss, as when I spy
The Scarlet Red about thy Partridge Eye,
While thou art constant to thy own true Knight,
While thou art mine, and I am thy delight,   415
All Sorrows at thy Presence take their flight.
For true it is, as *in Principio*,
Mulier est hominis confusio.
Madam, the meaning of this Latin is,
That Woman is to Man his Soveraign Bliss.   420
For when by Night I feel your tender Side,
Though for the narrow Perch I cannot ride,
Yet I have such a Solace in my Mind,
That all my boding Cares are cast behind:
And ev'n already I forget my Dream;   425
He said, and downward flew from off the Beam.
For Day-light now began apace to spring,
The Thrush to whistle, and the Lark to sing.

Then crowing clap'd his Wings, th' appointed call
To chuck his Wives together in the Hall.   430
  By this the Widow had unbarr'd the Door,
And Chanticleer went strutting out before,
With Royal Courage, and with Heart so light,
As shew'd he scorn'd the Visions of the Night.
Now roaming in the Yard he spurn'd the Ground,   435
And gave to Partlet the first Grain he found.
Then often feather'd her with wanton Play,
And trod her twenty times e'er prime of Day;
And took by turns and gave so much delight,
Her Sisters pin'd with Envy at the sight.   440
  He chuck'd again, when other Corns he found,
And scarcely deign'd to set a Foot to Ground.
But swagger'd like a Lord about his Hall,
And his sev'n Wives came running at his call.
  'Twas now the Month in which the World began,   445
(If *March* beheld the first created Man:)
And since the vernal Equinox, the Sun,
In *Aries* twelve Degrees, or more had run,
When casting up his Eyes against the Light,
Both Month, and Day, and Hour he measur'd right;   450
And told more truly, than th' Ephemeris,
For Art may err, but Nature cannot miss.
  Thus numb'ring Times, and Seasons in his Breast,
His second crowing the third Hour confess'd.
Then turning, said to Partlet, See, my Dear,   455
How lavish Nature has adorn'd the Year;
How the pale Primrose, and blue Violet spring,
And Birds essay their Throats disus'd to sing:
All these are ours; and I with pleasure see
Man strutting on two Legs, and aping me!   460
An unfledg'd Creature, of a lumpish frame,
Indew'd with fewer Particles of Flame:
Our Dame sits couring o'er a Kitchin-fire,
I draw fresh Air, and Nature's Works admire:
And ev'n this Day, in more delight abound,   465
Than since I was an Egg, I ever found.
  The time shall come when Chanticleer shall wish
His Words unsaid, and hate his boasted Bliss:

The crested Bird shall by Experience know,
Jove made not him his Master-piece below;   470
And learn the latter end of Joy is Woe.
The Vessel of his Bliss to Dregs is run,
And Heav'n will have him tast his other Tun.
    Ye Wise draw near, and hearken to my Tale,
Which proves that oft the Proud by Flatt'ry fall: 475
The Legend is as true I undertake
As *Tristram* is, and *Launcelot* of the Lake:
Which all our Ladies in such rev'rence hold,
As if in Book of Martyrs it were told.
    A Fox full fraught with seeming Sanctity,   480
That fear'd an Oath, but like the Devil, would lie,
Who look'd like Lent, and had the holy Leer,
And durst not sin before he say'd his Pray'r:
This pious Cheat that never suck'd the Blood,
Nor chaw'd the Flesh of Lambs but when he cou'd,   485
Had pass'd three Summers in the neighb'ring Wood;
And musing long, whom next to circumvent,
On Chanticleer his wicked Fancy bent:
And in his high Imagination cast,
By Stratagem to gratify his Tast.   490
    The Plot contriv'd, before the break of Day,
Saint *Reynard* through the Hedge had made his way;
The Pale was next, but proudly with a bound
He lept the Fence of the forbidden Ground:
Yet fearing to be seen, within a Bed   495
Of Colworts he conceal'd his wily Head;
There sculk'd till Afternoon, and watch'd his time,
(As Murd'rers use) to perpetrate his Crime.
    O Hypocrite, ingenious to destroy,
O Traytor, worse than *Sinon* was to *Troy*;   500
O vile Subverter of the *Gallick* Reign,
More false than *Gano* was to *Charlemaign*!
O Chanticleer, in an unhappy Hour
Did'st thou forsake the Safety of thy Bow'r:
Better for Thee thou had'st believ'd thy Dream,   505
And not that Day descended from the Beam!
    But here the Doctors eagerly dispute:
Some hold Predestination absolute:

Some Clerks maintain, that Heav'n at first foresees,
And in the virtue of Foresight decrees. 510
If this be so, then Prescience binds the Will,
And Mortals are not free to Good or Ill:
For what he first foresaw, he must ordain,
Or its eternal Prescience may be vain:
As bad for us as Prescience had not bin: 515
For first, or last, he's Author of the Sin.
And who says that, let the blaspheming Man
Say worse ev'n of the Devil, if he can.
For how can that Eternal Pow'r be just
To punish Man, who Sins because he must? 520
Or, how can He reward a vertuous Deed,
Which is not done by us; but first decreed?
 I cannot boult this Matter to the Bran,
As *Bradwardin* and holy *Austin* can:
If Prescience can determine Actions so 525
That we must do, because he did foreknow;
Or that foreknowing, yet our choice is free,
Not forc'd to Sin by strict necessity:
This strict necessity they simple call,
Another sort there is conditional. 530
The first so binds the Will, that Things foreknown
By Spontaneity, not Choice, are done.
Thus Galley-Slaves tug willing, at their Oar, ⎫
Consent to work, in prospect of the Shore; ⎬ 53
But wou'd not work at all, if not constrain'd before. ⎭
That other does not Liberty constrain,
But Man may either act, or may refrain.
Heav'n made us Agents free to Good or Ill,
And forc'd it not, tho' he foresaw the Will.
Freedom was first bestow'd on human Race, 54
And Prescience only held the second place.
 If he could make such Agents wholly free,
I not dispute; the Point's too high for me;
For Heav'n's unfathom'd Pow'r what Man can sound,
Or put to his Omnipotence a Bound? 54

He made us to his Image all agree;
That Image is the Soul, and that must be,
Or not the Maker's Image, or be free.
But whether it were better Man had been
By Nature bound to Good, not free to Sin,   550
I wave, for fear of splitting on a Rock,
The Tale I tell is only of a Cock;
Who had not run the hazard of his Life
Had he believ'd his Dream, and not his Wife:
For Women, with a mischief to their Kind,   555
Pervert, with bad Advice, our better Mind.
A Woman's Counsel brought us first to Woe,
And made her Man his Paradice forego,
Where at Heart's ease he liv'd; and might have bin
As free from Sorrow as he was from Sin.   560
For what the Devil had their Sex to do,
That, born to Folly, they presum'd to know,
And could not see the Serpent in the Grass?
But I my self presume, and let it pass.
Silence in times of Suff'ring is the best,   565
'Tis dang'rous to disturb a Hornet's Nest.
In other Authors you may find enough,
But all they say of Dames is idle Stuff.
Legends of lying Wits together bound,
The Wife of *Bath* would throw 'em to the Ground: 570
These are the Words of Chanticleer, not mine,
I honour Dames, and think their Sex divine.
Now to continue what my Tale begun.
Lay Madam Partlet basking in the Sun,
Breast-high in Sand: Her Sisters in a row,   575
Enjoy'd the Beams above, the Warmth below.
The Cock that of his Flesh was ever free,
Sung merrier than the Mermaid in the Sea:
And so befel, that as he cast his Eye,
Among the Colworts on a Butterfly,   580
He saw false *Reynard* where he lay full low,
I need not swear he had no list to Crow:
But cry'd Cock, Cock, and gave a suddain start,
As sore dismaid and frighted at his Heart.
For Birds and Beasts, inform'd by Nature, know   585

Kinds opposite to theirs, and fly their Foe.
So, Chanticleer, who never saw a Fox,
Yet shun'd him as a Sailor shuns the Rocks.
    But the false Loon who cou'd not work his Will
By open Force, employ'd his flatt'ring Skill;   590
I hope, my Lord, said he, I not offend,
Are you afraid of me, that am your Friend?
I were a Beast indeed to do you wrong,
I, who have lov'd and honour'd you so long:
Stay, gentle Sir, nor take a false Alarm,   595
For on my Soul I never meant you harm.
I come no Spy, nor as a Traytor press,
To learn the Secrets of your soft Recess:
Far be from *Reynard* so prophane a Thought,
But by the sweetness of your Voice was brought: 600
For, as I bid my Beads, by chance I heard,
The Song as of an Angel in the Yard:
A Song that wou'd have charm'd th' infernal Gods,
And banish'd Horror from the dark Abodes:
Had *Orpheus* sung it in the neather Sphere,   605
So much the Hymn had pleas'd the Tyrant's Ear,
The Wife had been detain'd, to keep the Husband there.
    My Lord, your Sire familiarly I knew,
A Peer deserving such a Son, as you:
He, with your Lady-Mother (whom Heav'n rest)   610
Has often grac'd my House, and been my Guest:
To view his living Features does me good,
For I am your poor Neighbour in the Wood;
And in my Cottage shou'd be proud to see
The worthy Heir of my Friend's Family.   615
    But since I speak of Singing let me say,
As with an upright Heart I safely may,
That, save your self, there breaths not on the Ground,
One like your Father for a Silver sound.
So sweetly wou'd he wake the Winter-day,   620
That Matrons to the Church mistook their way,
And thought they heard the merry Organ play.
And he to raise his Voice with artful Care,
(What will not Beaux attempt to please the Fair?)

      599 so] to F   605 *Orpheus*] Orphans F

On Tiptoe stood to sing with greater Strength,   625
And stretch'd his comely Neck at all the length:
And while he pain'd his Voice to pierce the Skies,
As Saints in Raptures use, would shut his Eyes,
That the sound striving through the narrow Throat,
His winking might avail, to mend the Note.   630
By this, in Song, he never had his Peer,
From sweet *Cecilia* down to Chanticleer;
Not *Maro*'s Muse who sung the mighty Man,
Nor *Pindar*'s heav'nly Lyre, nor *Horace* when a Swan.
Your Ancestors proceed from Race divine,   635
From *Brennus* and *Belinus* is your Line:
Who gave to sov'raign *Rome* such loud Alarms,
That ev'n the Priests were not excus'd from Arms.
   Besides, a famous Monk of modern times,
Has left of Cocks recorded in his Rhimes,   640
That of a Parish-Priest the Son and Heir,
(When Sons of Priests were from the Proverb clear)
Affronted once a Cock of noble Kind,
And either lam'd his Legs, or struck him blind;
For which the Clerk his Father was disgrac'd,   645
And in his Benefice another plac'd.
Now sing, my Lord, if not for love of me,
Yet for the sake of sweet Saint Charity;
Make Hills, and Dales, and Earth and Heav'n rejoice,
And emulate your Father's Angel-voice.   650
   The Cock was pleas'd to hear him speak so fair,
And proud beside, as solar People are:
Nor cou'd the Treason from the Truth descry,
So was he ravish'd with this Flattery:
So much the more as from a little Elf,   655
He had a high Opinion of himself:
Though sickly, slender, and not large of Limb,
Concluding all the World was made for him.
   Ye Princes rais'd by Poets to the Gods,
And *Alexander'd* up in lying Odes,   660
Believe not ev'ry flatt'ring Knave's report,
There's many a *Reynard* lurking in the Court;
And he shall be receiv'd with more regard
And list'ned to, than modest Truth is heard.

This Chanticleer of whom the Story sings,   665
Stood high upon his Toes, and clap'd his Wings;
Then stretch'd his Neck, and wink'd with both his Eyes;
Ambitious, as he sought, th' Olympick Prize.
But while he pain'd himself to raise his Note,
False *Reynard* rush'd, and caught him by the Throat.   670
Then on his Back he laid the precious Load,
And sought his wonted shelter of the Wood;
Swiftly he made his way, the Mischief done,
Of all unheeded, and pursu'd by none.

Alas, what stay is there in human State,   675
Or who can shun inevitable Fate?
The Doom was written, the Decree was past,
E'er the Foundations of the World were cast!
In *Aries* though the Sun exalted stood,
His Patron-Planet to procure his good;   680
Yet *Saturn* was his mortal Foe, and he
In *Libra* rais'd, oppos'd the same Degree:
The Rays both good and bad, of equal Pow'r,
Each thwarting other made a mingled Hour.

On *Friday*-morn he dreamt this direful Dream,   685
Cross to the worthy Native, in his Scheme!
Ah blissful *Venus*, Goddess of Delight,
How cou'd'st thou suffer thy devoted Knight,
On thy own Day to fall by Foe oppress'd,
The wight of all the World who serv'd thee best?   690
Who true to Love, was all for Recreation,
And minded not the Work of Propagation.
Gaufride, who could'st so well in Rhime complain,
The Death of *Richard* with an Arrow slain,
Why had not I thy Muse, or thou my Heart,   695
To sing this heavy Dirge with equal Art!
That I like thee on *Friday* might complain;
For on that Day was *Ceur de Lion* slain.

Not louder Cries when *Ilium* was in Flames,
Were sent to Heav'n by woful *Trojan* Dames,   700
When *Pyrrhus* toss'd on high his burnish'd Blade,
And offer'd *Priam* to his Father's Shade,
Than for the Cock the widow'd Poultry made.
Fair Partlet first, when he was born from sight,

With soveraign Shrieks bewail'd her Captive Knight.   705
Far lowder than the *Carthaginian* Wife,
When *Asdrubal* her Husband lost his Life,
When she beheld the smouldring Flames ascend,
And all the *Punick* Glories at an end:
Willing into the Fires she plung'd her Head,   710
With greater Ease than others seek their Bed.
Not more aghast the Matrons of Renown,
When Tyrant *Nero* burn'd th' Imperial Town,
Shriek'd for the downfal in a doleful Cry,
For which their guiltless Lords were doom'd to die.   715
    Now to my Story I return again.
The trembling Widow, and her Daughters twain,
This woful cackling Cry with Horror heard,
Of those distracted Damsels in the Yard;
And starting up beheld the heavy Sight,   720
How *Reynard* to the Forest took his Flight,
And cross his Back as in triumphant Scorn,
The Hope and Pillar of the House was born.
    The Fox, the wicked Fox, was all the Cry,
Out from his House ran ev'ry Neighbour nigh: 725
The Vicar first, and after him the Crew,
With Forks and Staves the Fellon to pursue.
Ran *Coll* our Dog, and *Talbot* with the Band,
And *Malkin*, with her Distaff in her Hand:
Ran Cow and Calf, and Family of Hogs,   730
In Panique Horror of pursuing Dogs,
With many a deadly Grunt and doleful Squeak
Poor Swine, as if their pretty Hearts would break.
The Shouts of Men, the Women in dismay,
With Shrieks augment the Terror of the Day.   735
The Ducks that heard the Proclamation cry'd,
And fear'd a Persecution might betide,
Full twenty Mile from Town their Voyage take,
Obscure in Rushes of the liquid Lake.
The Geese fly o'er the Barn; the Bees in Arms,   740
Drive headlong from their Waxen Cells in Swarms.
Jack Straw at *London*-stone with all his Rout
Struck not the City with so loud a Shout;

Not when with *English* Hate they did pursue
A *French* Man, or an unbelieving *Jew*:   745
Not when the Welkin rung with one and all;   ⎫
And Echoes bounded back from *Fox*'s Hall;   ⎬
Earth seem'd to sink beneath, and Heav'n above to fall. ⎭
With Might and Main they chas'd the murd'rous Fox,
With brazen Trumpets, and inflated Box,   750
To kindle *Mars* with military Sounds,
Nor wanted Horns t' inspire sagacious Hounds.
   But see how Fortune can confound the Wise,
And when they least expect it, turn the Dice.
The Captive Cock, who scarce cou'd draw his Breath,   755
And lay within the very Jaws of Death;
Yet in this Agony his Fancy wrought
And Fear supply'd him with this happy Thought:
Yours is the Prize, victorious Prince, said he,
The Vicar my defeat, and all the Village see.   760
Enjoy your friendly Fortune while you may,
And bid the Churls that envy you the Prey,
Call back their mungril Curs, and cease their Cry,   ⎫
See Fools, the shelter of the Wood is nigh,   ⎬
And Chanticleer in your despight shall die.   ⎭   765
He shall be pluck'd, and eaten to the Bone.
   'Tis well advis'd, in Faith it shall be done;
This *Reynard* said: but as the Word he spoke,
The Pris'ner with a Spring from Prison broke:
Then stretch'd his feather'd Fans with all his might,   770
And to the neighb'ring Maple wing'd his flight.
   Whom when the Traytor safe on Tree beheld,
He curs'd the Gods, with Shame and Sorrow fill'd;
Shame for his Folly; Sorrow out of time,
For Plotting an unprofitable Crime: 775
Yet mast'ring both, th' Artificer of Lies
Renews th' Assault, and his last Batt'ry tries.
   Though I, said he, did ne'er in Thought offend,
How justly may my Lord suspect his Friend?
Th' appearance is against me, I confess,   780
Who seemingly have put you in Distress:
You, if your Goodness does not plead my Cause,

756 Death;] Death: F

May think I broke all hospitable Laws,
To bear you from your Palace-yard by Might,
And put your noble Person in a Fright: 785
This, since you take it ill, I must repent,
Though Heav'n can witness with no bad intent,
I practis'd it, to make you taste your Cheer,
With double Pleasure first prepar'd by fear.
So loyal Subjects often seize their Prince,   790
Forc'd (for his Good) to seeming Violence,
Yet mean his sacred Person not the least Offence.
Descend; so help me *Jove* as you shall find
That *Reynard* comes of no dissembling Kind.
    Nay, quoth the Cock; but I beshrew us both,   795
If I believe a Saint upon his Oath:
An honest Man may take a Knave's Advice,
But Idiots only will be couzen'd twice:
Once warn'd is well bewar'd: No flatt'ring Lies
Shall sooth me more to sing with winking Eyes,   800
And open Mouth, for fear of catching Flies.
Who Blindfold walks upon a Rivers brim
When he should see, has he deserv'd to swim?
Better, Sir Cock, let all Contention cease,
Come down, said *Reynard*, let us treat of Peace.   805
A Peace with all my Soul, said Chanticleer;
But with your Favour, I will treat it here:
And least the Truce with Treason should be mixt,
'Tis my concern to have the Tree betwixt.

The MORAL

    In this plain Fable you th' Effect may see   810
Of Negligence, and fond Credulity:
And learn besides of Flatt'rers to beware,
Then most pernicious when they speak too fair.
The Cock and Fox, the Fool and Knave imply;
The Truth is moral, though the Tale a Lie.   815
Who spoke in Parables, I dare not say;
But sure, he knew it was a pleasing way,
Sound Sense, by plain Example, to convey.

And in a Heathen Author we may find,
That Pleasure with Instruction should be join'd: 820
So take the Corn, and leave the Chaff behind.

THEODORE AND HONORIA,
FROM BOCCACE

OF all the Cities in *Romanian* Lands,
 The chief, and most renown'd *Ravenna* stands:
Adorn'd in ancient Times with Arms and Arts,
And rich Inhabitants, with generous Hearts.
But *Theodore* the Brave, above the rest,   5
With Gifts of Fortune, and of Nature bless'd,
The foremost Place, for Wealth and Honour held,
And all in Feats of Chivalry excell'd.
 This noble Youth to Madness lov'd a Dame,
Of high Degree, *Honoria* was her Name: 10
Fair as the Fairest, but of haughty Mind,
And fiercer than became so soft a kind;
Proud of her Birth; (for equal she had none;)
The rest she scorn'd; but hated him alone.
His Gifts, his constant Courtship, nothing gain'd; 15
For she, the more he lov'd, the more disdain'd:
He liv'd with all the Pomp he cou'd devise,
At Tilts and Turnaments obtain'd the Prize,
But found no favour in his Ladies Eyes:
Relentless as a Rock, the lofty Maid   20
Turn'd all to Poyson that he did, or said:
Nor Pray'rs, nor Tears, nor offer'd Vows could move;
The Work went backward; and the more he strove
T' advance his Sute, the farther from her Love.
 Weary'd at length, and wanting Remedy,   25
He doubted oft, and oft resolv'd to die.
But Pride stood ready to prevent the Blow,
For who would die to gratify a Foe?
His generous Mind disdain'd so mean a Fate;
That pass'd, his next Endeavour was to Hate.   30

But vainer that Relief than all the rest,
The less he hop'd with more Desire possess'd;
Love stood the Siege, and would not yield his Breast.
  Change was the next, but change deceiv'd his Care,   35
He sought a Fairer, but found none so Fair.
He would have worn her out by slow degrees,
As Men by Fasting starve th' untam'd Disease:
But present Love requir'd a present Ease.
Looking he feeds alone his famish'd Eyes,
Feeds lingring Death, but looking not he dies.   40
Yet still he chose the longest way to Fate,
Wasting at once his Life, and his Estate.
  His Friends beheld, and pity'd him in vain,
For what Advice can ease a Lover's Pain!
Absence, the best Expedient they could find   45
Might save the Fortune, if not cure the Mind:
This Means they long propos'd, but little gain'd,
Yet after much pursuit, at length obtain'd.
  Hard, you may think it was, to give consent,
But, struggling with his own Desires, he went: 50
With large Expence, and with a pompous Train,
Provided, as to visit *France* or *Spain*,
Or for some distant Voyage o'er the Main.
But Love had clipp'd his Wings, and cut him short,
Confin'd within the purlieus of his Court: 55
Three Miles he went, nor farther could retreat;
His Travels ended at his Country-Seat:
To *Chassis* pleasing Plains he took his way,
There pitch'd his Tents, and there resolv'd to stay.
  The Spring was in the Prime; the neighb'ring Grove,   60
Supply'd with Birds, the Choristers of Love:
Musick unbought, that minister'd Delight
To Morning-walks, and lull'd his Cares by Night:
There he discharg'd his Friends; but not th' Expence
Of frequent Treats, and proud Magnificence.   65
He liv'd as Kings retire, though more at large,
From publick Business, yet with equal Charge;
With House, and Heart still open to receive;
As well content, as Love would give him leave:

Theodore and Honoria. 62 Delight] Delight, F

He would have liv'd more free; but many a Guest,   70
Who could forsake the Friend, pursu'd the Feast.
  It happ'd one Morning, as his Fancy led,
Before his usual Hour, he left his Bed;
To walk within a lonely Lawn, that stood
On ev'ry side surrounded by the Wood: 75
Alone he walk'd, to please his pensive Mind,
And sought the deepest Solitude to find:
'Twas in a Grove of spreading Pines he stray'd;
The Winds, within the quiv'ring Branches plaid,
And Dancing-Trees a mournful Musick made.   80
The Place it self was suiting to his Care,
Uncouth, and Salvage, as the cruel Fair.
He wander'd on, unknowing where he went,
Lost in the Wood, and all on Love intent:
The Day already half his Race had run,   85
And summon'd him to due Repast at Noon,
But Love could feel no Hunger but his own.
  While list'ning to the murm'ring Leaves he stood,
More than a Mile immers'd within the Wood,
At once the Wind was laid; the whisp'ring sound   90
Was dumb; a rising Earthquake rock'd the Ground:
With deeper Brown the Grove was overspred:
A suddain Horror seiz'd his giddy Head,
And his Ears tinckled, and his Colour fled.
Nature was in alarm; some Danger nigh   95
Seem'd threaten'd, though unseen to mortal Eye:
Unus'd to fear, he summon'd all his Soul
And stood collected in himself, and whole;
Not long: For soon a Whirlwind rose around,
And from afar he heard a screaming sound,   100
As of a Dame distress'd, who cry'd for Aid,
And fill'd with loud Laments the secret Shade.
  A Thicket close beside the Grove there stood
With Breers, and Brambles choak'd, and dwarfish Wood:
From thence the Noise: Which now approaching near   105
With more distinguish'd Notes invades his Ear:
He rais'd his Head, and saw a beauteous Maid,
With Hair dishevell'd, issuing through the Shade;

Stripp'd of her Cloaths, and e'en those Parts reveal'd,
Which modest Nature keeps from Sight conceal'd.   110
Her Face, her Hands, her naked Limbs were torn,
With passing through the Brakes, and prickly Thorn:
Two Mastiffs gaunt and grim, her Flight pursu'd,
And oft their fasten'd Fangs in Blood embru'd:
Oft they came up and pinch'd her tender Side,   115
Mercy, O Mercy, Heav'n, she ran, and cry'd;
When Heav'n was nam'd they loos'd their Hold again,
Then sprung she forth, they follow'd her amain.
  Not far behind, a Knight of swarthy Face,
High on a Coal-black Steed pursu'd the Chace;   120
With flashing Flames his ardent Eyes were fill'd,
And in his Hands a naked Sword he held:
He chear'd the Dogs to follow her who fled,
And vow'd Revenge on her devoted Head.
  As *Theodore* was born of noble Kind,   125
The brutal Action rowz'd his manly Mind:
Mov'd with unworthy Usage of the Maid,
He, though unarm'd, resolv'd to give her Aid.
A Saplin Pine he wrench'd from out the Ground,
The readiest Weapon that his Fury found.   130
Thus furnish'd for Offence, he cross'd the way
Betwixt the graceless Villain, and his Prey.
  The Knight came thund'ring on, but from afar
Thus in imperious Tone forbad the War:
Cease, *Theodore*, to proffer vain Relief,   135
Nor stop the vengeance of so just a Grief;
But give me leave to seize my destin'd Prey,
And let eternal Justice take the way:
I but revenge my Fate; disdain'd, betray'd,
And suff'ring Death for this ungrateful Maid.   140
  He say'd; at once dismounting from the Steed;
For now the Hell-hounds with superiour Speed
Had reach'd the Dame, and fast'ning on her Side,
The Ground with issuing Streams of Purple dy'd.
Stood *Theodore* surpriz'd in deadly Fright,   145
With chatt'ring Teeth and bristling Hair upright;
Yet arm'd with inborn Worth, What e'er, said he,
Thou art, who know'st me better than I thee;

Or prove thy rightful Cause, or be defy'd:
The Spectre, fiercely staring, thus reply'd.   150
 Know, *Theodore*, thy Ancestry I claim,
And *Guido Cavalcanti* was my Name.
One common Sire our Fathers did beget,
My Name and Story some remember yet:
Thee, then a Boy, within my Arms I laid,   155
When for my Sins I lov'd this haughty Maid;
Not less ador'd in Life, nor serv'd by Me,
Than proud *Honoria* now is lov'd by Thee.
What did I not her stubborn Heart to gain?
But all my Vows were answer'd with Disdain;   160
She scorn'd my Sorrows, and despis'd my Pain.
Long time I dragg'd my Days in fruitless Care,
Then loathing Life, and plung'd in deep Despair,
To finish my unhappy Life, I fell
On this sharp Sword, and now am damn'd in Hell. 165
 Short was her Joy; for soon th' insulting Maid
By Heav'n's Decree in the cold Grave was laid,
And as in unrepenting Sin she dy'd,
Doom'd to the same bad Place, is punish'd for her Pride;
Because she deem'd I well deserv'd to die,   170
And made a Merit of her Cruelty.
There, then, we met; both try'd and both were cast,
And this irrevocable Sentence pass'd;
That she whom I so long pursu'd in vain,
Should suffer from my Hands a lingring Pain: 175
Renew'd to Life, that she might daily die,
I daily doom'd to follow, she to fly;
No more a Lover but a mortal Foe,
I seek her Life (for Love is none below:)
As often as my Dogs with better speed   180
Arrest her Flight, is she to Death decreed.
Then with this fatal Sword on which I dy'd,
I pierce her open'd Back or tender Side,
And tear that harden'd Heart from out her Breast,
Which, with her Entrails, makes my hungry Hounds a Feast. 185
Nor lies she long, but as her Fates ordain,
Springs up to Life, and fresh to second Pain,
Is sav'd to Day, to Morrow to be slain.

This, vers'd in Death, th' infernal Knight relates,
And then for Proof fulfill'd their common Fates;   190
Her Heart and Bowels through her Back he drew,
And fed the Hounds that help'd him to pursue.
Stern look'd the Fiend, as frustrate of his Will
Not half suffic'd, and greedy yet to kill.
And now the Soul expiring through the Wound,   195
Had left the Body breathless on the Ground,
When thus the grisly Spectre spoke again:
Behold the Fruit of ill-rewarded Pain:
As many Months as I sustain'd her Hate,
So many Years is she condemn'd by Fate   200
To daily Death; and ev'ry several Place,
Conscious of her Disdain, and my Disgrace,
Must witness her just Punishment; and be
A Scene of Triumph and Revenge to me.
As in this Grove I took my last Farewel,   205
As on this very spot of Earth I fell,
As *Friday* saw me die, so she my Prey
Becomes ev'n here, on this revolving Day.
    Thus while he spoke, the Virgin from the Ground
Upstarted fresh, already clos'd the Wound,   210
And unconcern'd for all she felt before
Precipitates her Flight along the Shore:
The Hell-hounds, as ungorg'd with Flesh and Blood
Pursue their Prey, and seek their wonted Food:
The Fiend remounts his Courser; mends his Pace,   215
And all the Vision vanish'd from the Place.
    Long stood the noble Youth oppress'd with Awe,
And stupid at the wond'rous Things he saw
Surpassing common Faith; transgressing Nature's Law.
He would have been asleep, and wish'd to wake,   220
But Dreams, he knew, no long Impression make,
Though strong at first: If Vision, to what end,
But such as must his future State portend?
His Love the Damsel, and himself the Fiend.
But yet reflecting that it could not be   225
From Heav'n, which cannot impious Acts decree,
Resolv'd within himself to shun the Snare

193 Stern] Stern'd F

Which Hell for his Distruction did prepare;
And as his better Genius should direct
From an ill Cause to draw a good effect.   23

 Inspir'd from Heav'n he homeward took his way,
Nor pall'd his new Design with long delay:
But of his Train a trusty Servant sent;
To call his Friends together at his Tent.
They came, and usual Salutations paid,   23
With Words premeditated thus he said:
What you have often counsell'd, to remove
My vain pursuit of unregarded Love;
By Thrift my sinking Fortune to repair,
Tho' late, yet is at last become my Care: 2.
My Heart shall be my own; my vast Expence
Reduc'd to bounds, by timely Providence:
This only I require; invite for me
Honoria, with her Father's Family,
Her Friends, and mine; the Cause I shall display, 2
On *Friday* next, for that's th' appointed Day.

 Well pleas'd were all his Friends, the Task was light;
The Father, Mother, Daughter, they invite;
Hardly the Dame was drawn to this repast;
But yet resolv'd, because it was the last.   2
The Day was come; the Guests invited came,
And, with the rest, th' inexorable Dame:
A Feast prepar'd with riotous Expence,
Much Cost, more Care, and most Magnificence.
The Place ordain'd was in that haunted Grove, 2
Where the revenging Ghost pursu'd his Love:
The Tables in a proud Pavilion spred,
With Flow'rs below, and Tissue overhead:
The rest in rank; *Honoria* chief in place, ⎫
Was artfully contriv'd to set her Face   ⎬ 2
To front the Thicket, and behold the Chace. ⎭
The Feast was serv'd; the time so well forecast,
That just when the Dessert, and Fruits were plac'd,
The Fiend's Alarm began; the hollow sound ⎫
Sung in the Leaves, the Forest shook around, ⎬
Air blacken'd; rowl'd the Thunder; groan'd the Ground.⎭

238 unregarded] unreguarded *F*

Nor long before the loud Laments arise,
Of one distress'd, and Mastiffs mingled Cries;
And first the Dame came rushing through the Wood,
And next the famish'd Hounds that sought their Food   } 270
And grip'd her Flanks, and oft essay'd their Jaws in Blood.
Last came the Fellon on the Sable Steed,
Arm'd with his naked Sword, and urg'd his Dogs to speed:
She ran, and cry'd; her Flight directly bent,
(A Guest unbidden) to the fatal Tent,   } 275
The Scene of Death, and Place ordain'd for Punishment.
Loud was the Noise, aghast was every Guest,
The Women shriek'd, the Men forsook the Feast;
The Hounds at nearer distance hoarsly bay'd;
The Hunter close pursu'd the visionary Maid,   } 280
She rent the Heav'n with loud Laments, imploring Aid.
    The Gallants to protect the Ladies right,
Their Fauchions brandish'd at the grisly Spright;
High on his Stirups, he provok'd the Fight.   }
Then on the Crowd he cast a furious Look,   285
And wither'd all their Strength before he strook:
Back on your Lives; let be, said he, my Prey,
And let my Vengeance take the destin'd way.
Vain are your Arms, and vainer your Defence,
Against th' eternal Doom of Providence: 290
Mine is th' ungrateful Maid by Heav'n design'd:
Mercy she would not give, nor Mercy shall she find.
At this the former Tale again he told
With thund'ring Tone, and dreadful to behold:
Sunk were their Hearts with Horror of the Crime,   295
Nor needed to be warn'd a second time,
But bore each other back; some knew the Face,
And all had heard the much lamented Case,   }
Of him who fell for Love, and this the fatal Place.
    And now th' infernal Minister advanc'd,   300
Seiz'd the due Victim, and with Fury lanch'd
Her Back, and piercing through her inmost Heart,
Drew backward, as before, th' offending part.
The reeking Entrails next he tore away,
And to his meagre Mastiffs made a Prey: 305

280 close] clos'd F

The pale Assistants, on each other star'd
With gaping Mouths for issuing Words prepar'd;
The still-born sounds upon the Palate hung,
And dy'd imperfect on the faltring Tongue.
The Fright was general; but the Female Band   31
(A helpless Train) in more Confusion stand;
With Horror shuddring, on a heap they run,
Sick at the sight of hateful Justice done;
For Conscience rung th' Alarm, and made the Case their own.

   So spread upon a Lake with upward Eye   31
A plump of Fowl behold their Foe on high,
They close their trembling Troop; and all attend
On whom the sowsing Eagle will descend.
   But most the proud *Honoria* fear'd th' event,
And thought to her alone the Vision sent.   32
Her Guilt presents to her distracted Mind
Heav'ns Justice, *Theodore*'s revengeful Kind,
And the same Fate to the same Sin assign'd;
Already sees her self the Monster's Prey,
And feels her Heart, and Entrails torn away.   32
'Twas a mute Scene of Sorrow, mix'd with fear,
Still on the Table lay th' unfinish'd Cheer;
The Knight, and hungry Mastiffs stood around,
The mangled Dame lay breathless on the Ground:
When on a suddain reinspired with Breath,   3
Again she rose, again to suffer Death;
Nor stay'd the Hell-hounds, nor the Hunter stay'd,
But follow'd, as before, the flying Maid:
Th' Avenger took from Earth th' avenging Sword,
And mounting light as Air, his Sable Steed he spurr'd: 3
The Clouds dispell'd, the Sky resum'd her Light,
And Nature stood recover'd of her Fright.
   But Fear, the last of Ills, remain'd behind,
And Horror heavy sat on ev'ry Mind.
Nor *Theodore* incourag'd more his Feast,   3
But sternly look'd, as hatching in his Breast
Some deep Design, which when *Honoria* view'd,
The fresh Impulse her former Fright renew'd:
She thought her self the trembling Dame who fled,

And him the grisly Ghost that spurr'd th' infernal Steed: 345
The more dismay'd, for when the Guests withdrew,
Their courteous Host saluting all the Crew
Regardless pass'd her o'er; nor grac'd with kind adieu.
That Sting infix'd within her haughty Mind,
The downfal of her Empire she divin'd;   350
And her proud Heart with secret Sorrow pin'd.
Home as they went, the sad Discourse renew'd
Of the relentless Dame to Death pursu'd,
And of the Sight obscene so lately view'd.
None durst arraign the righteous Doom she bore,   355
Ev'n they who pity'd most yet blam'd her more:
The Parallel they needed not to name,
But in the Dead they damn'd the living Dame.
   At ev'ry little Noise she look'd behind,
For still the Knight was present to her Mind: 360
And anxious oft she started on the way,
And thought the Horseman-Ghost came thundring for his Prey.
Return'd, she took her Bed, with little Rest,
But in short Slumbers dreamt the Funeral Feast:
Awak'd, she turn'd her Side, and slept again;   365
The same black Vapors mounted in her Brain,
And the same Dreams return'd with double Pain.
   Now forc'd to wake because afraid to sleep
Her Blood all Fever'd, with a furious Leap
She sprung from Bed, distracted in her Mind,   370
And fear'd, at ev'ry Step, a twitching Spright behind.
Darkling and desp'rate with a stagg'ring pace,
Of Death afraid, and conscious of Disgrace;
Fear, Pride, Remorse, at once her Heart assail'd,
Pride put Remorse to flight, but Fear prevail'd.   375
Friday, the fatal Day, when next it came,
Her Soul forethought the Fiend would change his Game,
And her pursue, or *Theodore* be slain,
And two Ghosts join their Packs to hunt her o'er the Plain.
   This dreadful Image so possess'd her Mind,   380
That desp'rate any Succour else to find,
She ceas'd all farther hope; and now began

346 withdrew,] withdrew *F*   347 Crew] Crew, *F*   365 Side,] Side; *F*
again;] again, *F*

To make reflection on th' unhappy Man.
Rich, Brave, and Young, who past expression lov'd,
Proof to Disdain; and not to be remov'd: 385
Of all the Men respected, and admir'd,
Of all the Dames, except her self, desir'd.
Why not of her? Preferr'd above the rest
By him with Knightly Deeds, and open Love profess'd?
So had another been; where he his Vows address'd.   390
This quell'd her Pride, yet other Doubts remain'd,
That once disdaining she might be disdain'd:
The Fear was just, but greater Fear prevail'd,
Fear of her Life by hellish Hounds assail'd:
He took a low'ring leave; but who can tell,   395
What outward Hate, might inward Love conceal?
Her Sexes Arts she knew, and why not then,
Might deep dissembling have a place in Men?
Here Hope began to dawn; resolv'd to try,
She fix'd on this her utmost Remedy;   400
Death was behind, but hard it was to die.
'Twas time enough at last on Death to call,
The Precipice in sight: A Shrub was all,
That kindly stood betwixt to break the fatal fall.
     One Maid she had, belov'd above the rest,   405
Secure of her, the Secret she confess'd:
And now the chearful Light her Fears dispell'd,
She with no winding turns the Truth conceal'd,
But put the Woman off, and stood reveal'd:
With Faults confess'd commission'd her to go,   410
If Pity yet had place, and reconcile her Foe:
The welcom Message made, was soon receiv'd;
'Twas what he wish'd, and hop'd, but scarce believ'd;
Fate seem'd a fair occasion to present,
He knew the Sex, and fear'd she might repent,   415
Should he delay the moment of Consent.
There yet remain'd to gain her Friends (a Care
The modesty of Maidens well might spare;)
But she with such a Zeal the Cause embrac'd,
(As Women where they will, are all in hast)   420
That Father, Mother, and the Kin beside,
Were overborn by fury of the Tide:

With full consent of all, she chang'd her State,
Resistless in her Love, as in her Hate.
  By her Example warn'd, the rest beware;   425
More Easy, less Imperious, were the Fair;
And that one Hunting which the Devil design'd,
For one fair Female, lost him half the Kind.

CEYX AND ALCYONE

CONNECTION OF THIS FABLE WITH THE FORMER

Ceyx, *the Son of* Lucifer, (*the Morning Star*) *and King of* Trachin *in*
Thessaly, *was married to* Alcyone *Daughter to* Æolus *God of the Winds.*
Both the Husband and the Wife lov'd each other with an entire Affection.
Dædalion, *the Elder Brother of* Ceyx (*whom he succeeded*) *having been*
turn'd into a Falcon by Apollo, *and* Chione, Dædalion's *Daughter, slain* 5
by Diana; Ceyx *prepares a Ship to sail to* Claros *there to consult the Oracle*
of Apollo, *and* (*as* Ovid *seems to intimate*) *to enquire how the Anger of the*
Gods might be atton'd.

THESE Prodigies afflict the pious Prince,
  But more perplex'd with those that happen'd since,
He purposes to seek the *Clarian* God,
Avoiding *Delphos*, his more fam'd Abode;
Since *Phlegyan* Robbers made unsafe the Road.   5
Yet cou'd he not from her he lov'd so well
The fatal Voyage, he resolv'd, conceal;
But when she saw her Lord prepar'd to part,
A deadly Cold ran shiv'ring to her Heart:
Her faded Cheeks are chang'd to Boxen Hue,   10
And in her Eyes the Tears are ever new:
She thrice assay'd to Speak; her Accents hung
And faltring dy'd unfinish'd on her Tongue,
Or vanish'd into Sighs: With long delay
Her Voice return'd; and found the wonted way.   15
  Tell me, my Lord, she said, what Fault unknown
Thy once belov'd *Alcyone* has done?
Whether, ah whether is thy Kindness gone!

Ceyx and Alcyone. Connection. 6 Diana;] Diana. F

Can *Ceyx* then sustain to leave his Wife,
And unconcern'd forsake the Sweets of Life?   20
What can thy Mind to this long Journey move,
Or need'st thou absence to renew thy Love?
Yet, if thou go'st by Land, tho' Grief possess
My Soul ev'n then, my Fears will be the less.
But ah! be warn'd to shun the Watry Way,   25
The Face is frightful of the stormy Sea.
For late I saw a-drift disjointed Planks,
And empty Tombs erected on the Banks.
Nor let false Hopes to trust betray thy Mind,
Because my Sire in Caves constrains the Wind,   30
Can with a Breath their clam'rous Rage appease,
They fear his Whistle, and forsake the Seas;
Not so, for once indulg'd, they sweep the Main;
Deaf to the Call, or hearing hear in vain;
But bent on Mischief bear the Waves before,   35
And not content with Seas insult the Shoar,
When Ocean, Air, and Earth, at once ingage
And rooted Forrests fly before their Rage:
At once the clashing Clouds to Battle move,
And Lightnings run across the Fields above: 40
I know them well, and mark'd their rude Comport,
While yet a Child, within my Father's Court:
In times of Tempest they command alone,
And he but sits precarious on the Throne:
The more I know, the more my Fears augment,   45
And Fears are oft prophetick of th' event.
But if not Fears, or Reasons will prevail,
If Fate has fix'd thee obstinate to sail,
Go not without thy Wife, but let me bear
My part of Danger with an equal share,   } 50
And present, what I suffer only fear:
Then o'er the bounding Billows shall we fly,
Secure to live together, or to die.

    These Reasons mov'd her starlike Husband's Heart,
But still he held his Purpose to depart: 55
For as he lov'd her equal to his Life,
He wou'd not to the Seas expose his Wife;
Nor cou'd be wrought his Voyage to refrain,

But sought by Arguments to sooth her Pain:
Nor these avail'd; at length he lights on one,   60
With which, so difficult a Cause he won:
My Love, so short an absence cease to fear,
For by my Father's holy Flame, I swear,
Before two Moons their Orb with Light adorn,
If Heav'n allow me Life, I will return.   65
    This Promise of so short a stay prevails;
He soon equips the Ship, supplies the Sails,
And gives the Word to launch; she trembling views
This pomp of Death, and parting Tears renews:
Last with a Kiss, she took a long farewel,   70
Sigh'd, with a sad Presage, and swooning fell:
While *Ceyx* seeks Delays, the lusty Crew
Rais'd on their Banks their Oars in order drew
To their broad Breasts; the Ship with fury flew.
    The Queen recover'd rears her humid Eyes,   75
And first her Husband on the Poop espies
Shaking his Hand at distance on the Main;
She took the Sign; and shook her Hand again.
Still as the Ground recedes, contracts her View
With sharpen'd Sight, till she no longer knew   80
The much-lov'd Face; that Comfort lost supplies
With less, and with the Galley feeds her Eyes;
The Galley born from view by rising Gales
She follow'd with her Sight the flying Sails:
When ev'n the flying Sails were seen no more   85
Forsaken of all Sight, she left the Shoar.
    Then on her Bridal-Bed her Body throws,
And sought in sleep her weary'd Eyes to close:
Her Husband's Pillow, and the Widow'd part
Which once he press'd, renew'd the former Smart.   90
    And now a Breeze from Shoar began to blow,
The Sailors ship their Oars, and cease to row;
Then hoist their Yards a-trip, and all their Sails
Let fall, to court the Wind, and catch the Gales:
By this the Vessel half her Course had run,   95
And as much rested till the rising Sun;
Both Shores were lost to Sight, when at the close

73 drew] drew, F   74 Breasts;] Breasts, F

Of Day, a stiffer Gale at East arose:
The Sea grew White, the rowling Waves from far
Like Heralds first denounce, the Wat'ry War.   100
   This seen, the Master soon began to cry,
Strike, strike the Top-sail; let the Main-sheet fly,
And furl your Sails: The Winds repel the sound,
And in the Speaker's Mouth the Speech is drown'd.
Yet of their own accord, as Danger taught   105
Each in his way, officiously they wrought;
Some stow their Oars, or stop the leaky Sides,
Another bolder yet the Yard bestrides,
And folds the Sails; a fourth with Labour, laves
Th' intruding Seas, and Waves ejects on Waves.   110
   In this Confusion while their Work they ply,
The Winds augment the Winter of the Sky,
And wage intestine Wars; the suff'ring Seas
Are toss'd, and mingled as their Tyrants please.
The Master wou'd command, but in despair   115
Of Safety, stands amaz'd with stupid Care,
Nor what to bid, or what forbid he knows,
Th' ungovern'd Tempest to such Fury grows:
Vain is his Force, and vainer is his Skill;
With such a Concourse comes the Flood of Ill: 120
The Cries of Men are mix'd with rattling Shrowds;
Seas dash on Seas, and Clouds encounter Clouds:
At once from East to West, from Pole to Pole,
The forky Lightnings flash, the roaring Thunders roul.
   Now Waves on Waves ascending scale the Skies,   125
And in the Fires above, the Water fries:
When yellow Sands are sifted from below,
The glitt'ring Billows give a golden Show:
And when the fouler bottom spews the Black,
The *Stygian* Dye the tainted Waters take: 130
Then frothy White appear the flatted Seas,
And change their Colour, changing their Disease.
Like various Fits the *Trachin* Vessel finds,
And now sublime, she rides upon the Winds;
As from a lofty Summet looks from high,   135
And from the Clouds beholds the neather Sky;

109 laves] laves, F

Now from the depth of Hell they lift their Sight,
And at a distance see superiour Light:
The lashing Billows make a loud report
And beat her Sides, as batt'ring Rams, a Fort: 140
Or as a Lyon, bounding in his way
With Force augmented bears against his Prey;
Sidelong to seize; or unappal'd with fear
Springs on the Toils, and rushes on the Spear:
So Seas impell'd by Winds with added Pow'r   145
Assault the Sides, and o'er the Hatches tow'r.
    The Planks (their pitchy Cov'ring wash'd away)
Now yield; and now a yawning Breach display:
The roaring Waters with a hostile Tide
Rush through the Ruins of her gaping Side.   150
Mean time in Sheets of Rain the Sky descends,
And Ocean swell'd with Waters upwards tends,
One rising, falling one, the Heav'ns, and Sea
Meet at their Confines, in the middle Way:
The Sails are drunk with Show'rs, and drop with Rain,   155
Sweet Waters mingle with the briny Main.
No Star appears to lend his friendly Light:
Darkness and Tempest make a double Night.
But flashing Fires disclose the Deep by turns,
And while the Light'nings blaze, the Water burns.   160
    Now all the Waves, their scatter'd Force unite,
And as a Soldier, foremost in the Fight
Makes way for others: And an Host alone
Still presses on, and urging gains the Town;
So while th' invading Billows come a-brest,   165
The Hero tenth advanc'd before the rest,
Sweeps all before him with impetuous Sway,
And from the Walls descends upon the Prey;
Part following enter, part remain without,
With Envy hear their Fellows conqu'ring Shout: 170
And mount on others Backs, in hope to share
The City, thus become the Seat of War.
    An universal Cry resounds aloud,
The Sailors run in heaps, a helpless Crowd;
Art fails, and Courage falls, no Succour near;   175

As many Waves, as many Deaths appear.
One weeps, and yet despairs of late Relief;
One cannot weep, his Fears congeal his Grief,
But stupid, with dry Eyes expects his Fate:
One with loud Shrieks laments his lost Estate,   180
And calls those happy whom their Funerals wait.
This Wretch with Pray'rs, and Vows the Gods implores,
And ev'n the Sky's he cannot see, adores.
That other on his Friends his Thoughts bestows,
His careful Father, and his faithful Spouse.   185
The covetous Worldling in his anxious Mind
Thinks only on the Wealth he left behind.
    All *Ceyx* his *Alcyone* employs,
For her he grieves, yet in her absence joys:
His Wife he wishes, and wou'd still be near,   190
Not her with him, but wishes him with her:
Now with last Looks he seeks his Native Shoar,
Which Fate has destin'd him to see no more;
He sought, but in the dark tempestuous Night
He knew not whether to direct his Sight.   195
So whirl the Seas, such Darkness blinds the Sky,
That the black Night receives a deeper Dye.
    The giddy Ship ran round; the Tempest tore
Her Mast, and over-board the Rudder bore.
One Billow mounts; and with a scornful Brow   200
Proud of her Conquest gain'd insults the Waves below;
Nor lighter falls, than if some Gyant tore
Pyndus and *Athos*, with the Freight they bore,
And toss'd on Seas; press'd with the pondrous Blow
Down sinks the Ship within th' Abyss below: 205
Down with the Vessel sink into the Main
The many, never more to rise again.
Some few on scatter'd Planks with fruitless Care
Lay hold, and swim, but while they swim, despair.
    Ev'n he who late a Scepter did command   210
Now grasps a floating Fragment in his Hand,
And while he struggles on the stormy Main,
Invokes his Father, and his Wife's, in vain;
But yet his Consort is his greatest Care;

176 appear.] appear, F   203 bore,] bore: F

Alcyone he names amidst his Pray'r,   215
Names as a Charm against the Waves, and Wind;
Most in his Mouth, and ever in his Mind:
Tir'd with his Toyl, all hopes of Safety past,
From Pray'rs to Wishes he descends at last:
That his dead Body wafted to the Sands,   220
Might have its Burial from her Friendly Hands.
As oft as he can catch a gulp of Air,
And peep above the Seas, he names the Fair,
And ev'n when plung'd beneath, on her he raves,
Murm'ring *Alcyone* below the Waves: 225
At last a falling Billow stops his Breath,
Breaks o'er his Head, and whelms him underneath.
Bright *Lucifer* unlike himself appears
That Night, his heav'nly Form obscur'd with Tears,
And since he was forbid to leave the Skies,   230
He muffled with a Cloud his mournful Eyes.
   Mean time *Alcyone* (his Fate unknown)
Computes how many Nights he had been gone,
Observes the waning Moon with hourly view,
Numbers her Age, and wishes for a new;   235
Against the promis'd Time provides with care,
And hastens in the Woof the Robes he was to wear:
And for her Self employs another Loom,
New-dress'd to meet her Lord returning home,
Flatt'ring her Heart with Joys that never were to come: 240
She fum'd the Temples with an odrous Flame,
And oft before the sacred Altars came,
To pray for him, who was an empty Name.
All Pow'rs implor'd, but far above the rest
To *Juno* she her pious Vows address'd,   245
Her much-lov'd Lord from Perils to protect
And safe o'er Seas his Voyage to direct:
Then pray'd that she might still possess his Heart,
And no pretending Rival share a part;
This last Petition heard of all her Pray'r,   250
The rest dispers'd by Winds were lost in Air.
   But she, the Goddess of the Nuptial-Bed,
Tir'd with her vain Devotions for the Dead,

Resolv'd the tainted Hand should be repell'd
Which Incense offer'd, and her Altar held: 255
Then *Iris* thus bespoke; Thou faithful Maid
By whom thy Queen's Commands are well convey'd,
Hast to the House of Sleep, and bid the God
Who rules the Night by Visions with a Nod,
Prepare a Dream, in Figure and in Form   260
Resembling him who perish'd in the Storm;
This Form before *Alcyone* present,
To make her certain of the sad Event.

     Indu'd with Robes of various Hew she flies,
And flying draws an Arch, (a segment of the Skies:)   265
Then leaves her bending Bow, and from the steep
Descends to search the silent House of Sleep.

     Near the *Cymmerians*, in his dark Abode
Deep in a Cavern, dwells the drowzy God;
Whose gloomy Mansion nor the rising Sun   270
Nor setting, visits, nor the lightsome Noon:
But lazy Vapors round the Region fly,
Perpetual Twilight, and a doubtful Sky;
No crowing Cock does there his Wings display
Nor with his horny Bill provoke the Day: 275
Nor watchful Dogs, nor the more wakeful Geese,
Disturb with nightly Noise the sacred Peace:
Nor Beast of Nature, nor the Tame are nigh,
Nor Trees with Tempests rock'd, nor human Cry,
But safe Repose without an air of Breath   280
Dwells here, and a dumb Quiet next to Death.

     An Arm of *Lethe* with a gentle flow
Arising upwards from the Rock below,
The Palace moats, and o'er the Pebbles creeps
And with soft Murmers calls the coming Sleeps: 285
Around its Entry nodding Poppies grow,
And all cool Simples that sweet Rest bestow;
Night from the Plants their sleepy Virtue drains,
And passing sheds it on the silent Plains:
No Door there was th' unguarded House to keep,   290
On creaking Hinges turn'd, to break his Sleep.

     But in the gloomy Court was rais'd a Bed
Stuff'd with black Plumes, and on an Ebon-sted:

Black was the Cov'ring too, where lay the God
And slept supine, his Limbs display'd abroad: 295
About his Head fantastick Visions fly,
Which various Images of Things supply,
And mock their Forms, the Leaves on Trees not more;
Nor bearded Ears in Fields, nor Sands upon the Shore.
    The Virgin entring bright indulg'd the Day   300
To the brown Cave, and brush'd the Dreams away:
The God disturb'd with this new glare of Light
Cast sudden on his Face, unseal'd his Sight,
And rais'd his tardy Head, which sunk agen,
And sinking on his Bosom knock'd his Chin;   305
At length shook off himself; and ask'd the Dame,
(And asking yawn'd) for what intent she came?
    To whom the Goddess thus: O sacred Rest,
Sweet pleasing Sleep, of all the Pow'rs the best!
O Peace of Mind, repairer of Decay,   310
Whose Balm renews the Limbs to Labours of the Day,
Care shuns thy soft approach, and sullen flies away!
Adorn a Dream, expressing human Form,
The Shape of him who suffer'd in the Storm,
And send it flitting to the *Trachin* Court,   315
The Wreck of wretched *Ceyx* to report:
Before his Queen bid the pale Spectre stand,
Who begs a vain Relief at *Juno*'s Hand.
She said, and scarce awake her Eyes cou'd keep,
Unable to support the fumes of Sleep: 320
But fled returning by the way she went,
And swerv'd along her Bow with swift ascent.
    The God uneasy till he slept again
Resolv'd at once to rid himself of Pain;
And tho' against his Custom, call'd aloud,   325
Exciting *Morpheus* from the sleepy Crowd:
Morpheus of all his numerous Train express'd
The Shape of Man, and imitated best;
The Walk, the Words, the Gesture cou'd supply,
The Habit mimick, and the Mien bely;   330
Plays well, but all his Action is confin'd;
Extending not beyond our human kind.

311 Balm] Balms F

Another Birds, and Beasts, and Dragons apes,
And dreadful Images, and Monster shapes:
This Demon, *Icelos*, in Heav'ns high Hall   33
The Gods have nam'd; but Men *Phobetor* call:
A third is *Phantasus*, whose Actions roul
On meaner Thoughts, and Things devoid of Soul;
Earth, Fruits and Flow'rs, he represents in Dreams,
And solid Rocks unmov'd, and running Streams: 3
These three to Kings, and Chiefs their Scenes display,
The rest before th' ignoble Commons play:
Of these the chosen *Morpheus* is dispatch'd,
Which done, the lazy Monarch overwatch'd
Down from his propping Elbow drops his Head,   3
Dissolv'd in Sleep, and shrinks within his Bed.

    Darkling the Demon glides for Flight prepar'd,
So soft that scarce his fanning Wings are heard.
To *Trachin*, swift as Thought, the flitting Shade
Through Air his momentary Journey made: 3
Then lays aside the steerage of his Wings,
Forsakes his proper Form, assumes the Kings;
And pale as Death despoil'd of his Array
Into the Queen's Apartment takes his way,
And stands before the Bed at dawn of Day: 3
Unmov'd his Eyes, and wet his Beard appears;
And shedding vain, but seeming real Tears;
The briny Water dropping from his Hairs;
Then staring on her with a ghastly Look
And hollow Voice, he thus the Queen bespoke.

    Know'st thou not me? Not yet unhappy Wife?
Or are my Features perish'd with my Life?
Look once again, and for thy Husband lost,
Lo all that's left of him, thy Husband's Ghost!
Thy Vows for my return were all in vain;
The stormy South o'ertook us in the Main;
And never shalt thou see thy living Lord again.
Bear witness Heav'n I call'd on Thee in Death,
And while I call'd, a Billow stop'd my Breath:
Think not that flying Fame reports my Fate;
I present, I appear, and my own Wreck relate.

    347 Darkling] *Darkling* F   352 Kings;] Kings? F

Rise wretched Widow, rise, nor undeplor'd
Permit my Ghost to pass the *Stygian* Ford:
But rise, prepar'd in Black, to mourn thy perish'd Lord.

   Thus said the Player-God; and adding Art   375
Of Voice and Gesture, so perform'd his part,
She thought (so like her Love the Shade appears)
That *Ceyx* spake the Words, and *Ceyx* shed the Tears:
She groan'd, her inward Soul with Grief opprest,
She sigh'd, she wept; and sleeping beat her Breast: 380
Then stretch'd her Arms t' embrace his Body bare,
Her clasping Arms inclose but empty Air:
At this not yet awake she cry'd, O stay,
One is our Fate, and common is our way!
So dreadful was the Dream, so loud she spoke,   385
That starting sudden up, the Slumber broke:
Then cast her Eyes around in hope to view
Her vanish'd Lord, and find the Vision true:
For now the Maids, who waited her Commands,
Ran in with lighted Tapers in their Hands.   390
Tir'd with the Search, not finding what she seeks,
With cruel Blows she pounds her blubber'd Cheeks:
Then from her beaten Breast the Linnen tare,
And cut the golden Caull that bound her Hair.
Her Nurse demands the Cause; with louder Cries,   395
She prosecutes her Griefs, and thus replies.

   No more *Alcyone*; she suffer'd Death
With her lov'd Lord, when *Ceyx* lost his Breath:
No Flatt'ry, no false Comfort, give me none,
My Shipwreck'd *Ceyx* is for ever gone: 400
I saw, I saw him manifest in view,
His Voice, his Figure, and his Gestures knew:
His Lustre lost, and ev'ry living Grace,
Yet I retain'd the Features of his Face;
Tho' with pale Cheeks, wet Beard, and dropping Hair,   405
None but my *Ceyx* cou'd appear so fair:
I would have strain'd him with a strict Embrace,
But through my Arms he slip'd, and vanish'd from the Place:
There, ev'n just there he stood; and as she spoke
Where last the Spectre was, she cast her Look: 410

395 Cause;] Cause F. *See Commentary*

Fain wou'd she hope, and gaz'd upon the Ground
If any printed Footsteps might be found.
    Then sigh'd and said; This I too well foreknew,
And, my prophetick Fear presag'd too true:
'Twas what I beg'd when with a bleeding Heart   41
I took my leave, and suffer'd Thee to part;
Or I to go along, or Thou to stay,
Never, ah never to divide our way!
Happier for me, that all our Hours assign'd
Together we had liv'd; e'en not in Death disjoin'd!   42
So had my *Ceyx* still been living here,
Or with my *Ceyx* I had perish'd there:
Now I die absent, in the vast profound;
And Me without my Self the Seas have drown'd:
The Storms were not so cruel; should I strive   42
To lengthen Life, and such a Grief survive;
But neither will I strive, nor wretched Thee
In Death forsake, but keep thee Company.
If not one common Sepulcher contains
Our Bodies, or one Urn, our last Remains,   4
Yet *Ceyx* and *Alcyone* shall join,
Their Names remember'd in one common Line.
    No farther Voice her mighty Grief affords,
For Sighs come rushing in betwixt her Words,
And stop'd her Tongue, but what her Tongue deny'd   4
Soft Tears, and Groans, and dumb Complaints supply'd.
    'Twas Morning; to the Port she takes her way,
And stands upon the Margin of the Sea:
That Place, that very Spot of Ground she sought,
Or thither by her Destiny was brought;
Where last he stood: And while she sadly said   ⎫
'Twas here he left me, lingring here delay'd   ⎬
His parting Kiss; and there his Anchors weigh'd: ⎭
    Thus speaking, while her Thoughts past Actions trace,
And call to mind admonish'd by the Place,
Sharp at her utmost Ken she cast her Eyes,
And somewhat floating from afar descries:
It seem'd a Corps adrift, to distant Sight,
But at a distance who could judge aright?

442 delay'd] delay'd, *F*   443 weigh'd:] weigh'd. *F*

It wafted nearer yet, and then she knew 450
That what before she but surmis'd, was true.
A Corps it was, but whose it was, unknown,
Yet mov'd, howe'er, she made the Case her own:
Took the bad Omen of a shipwreck'd Man,
As for a Stranger wept, and thus began. 455
 Poor Wretch, on stormy Seas to lose thy Life,
Unhappy thou, but more thy widdow'd Wife!
At this she paus'd; for now the flowing Tide
Had brought the Body nearer to the side:
The more she looks, the more her Fears increase, 460
At nearer Sight; and she's her self the less:
Now driv'n ashore, and at her Feet it lies,
She knows too much, in knowing whom she sees:
Her Husband's Corps; at this she loudly shrieks,
'Tis he, 'tis he, she cries, and tears her Cheeks, 465
Her Hair, her Vest, and stooping to the Sands
About his Neck she cast her trembling Hands.
 And is it thus, O dearer than my Life,
Thus, thus return'st Thou to thy longing Wife!
She said, and to the neighb'ring Mole she strode, 470
(Rais'd there to break th' Incursions of the Flood;)
 Headlong from hence to plunge her self she springs,
But shoots along supported on her Wings,
A Bird new-made about the Banks she plies,
Not far from Shore; and short Excursions tries; 475
Nor seeks in Air her humble Flight to raise,
Content to skim the Surface of the Seas:
Her Bill, tho' slender, sends a creaking Noise,
And imitates a lamentable Voice:
Now lighting where the bloodless Body lies, 480
She with a Funeral Note renews her Cries.
At all her stretch her little Wings she spread,
And with her feather'd Arms embrac'd the Dead:
Then flick'ring to his palid Lips, she strove
To print a Kiss, the last essay of Love: 485
Whether the vital Touch reviv'd the Dead,
Or that the moving Waters rais'd his Head
To meet the Kiss, the Vulgar doubt alone;
For sure a present Miracle was shown.

The Gods their Shapes to Winter-Birds translate,   490
But both obnoxious to their former Fate.
Their conjugal Affection still is ty'd,
And still the mournful Race is multiply'd:
They bill, they tread; *Alcyone* compress'd
Sev'n Days sits brooding on her floating Nest: 495
A wintry Queen: Her Sire at length is kind,
Calms ev'ry Storm, and hushes ev'ry Wind;
Prepares his Empire for his Daughter's Ease,
And for his hatching Nephews smooths the Seas.

THE FLOWER AND THE LEAF:
OR, THE LADY IN THE ARBOUR.
A VISION

Now turning from the wintry Signs, the Sun
His Course exalted through the Ram had run:
And whirling up the Skies, his Chariot drove
Through *Taurus*, and the lightsome Realms of Love;
Where *Venus* from her Orb descends in Show'rs   5
To glad the Ground, and paint the Fields with Flow'rs:
When first the tender Blades of Grass appear,
And Buds that yet the blast of *Eurus* fear,
Stand at the door of Life; and doubt to cloath the Year;
Till gentle Heat, and soft repeated Rains,   10
Make the green Blood to dance within their Veins:
Then, at their Call, embolden'd out they come,
And swell the Gems, and burst the narrow Room;
Broader and broader yet, their Blooms display,
Salute the welcome Sun, and entertain the Day.   15
Then from their breathing Souls the Sweets repair
To scent the Skies, and purge th' unwholsome Air:
Joy spreads the Heart, and with a general Song,
Spring issues out, and leads the jolly Months along.
In that sweet Season, as in Bed I lay,   20
And sought in Sleep to pass the Night away,
I turn'd my weary Side, but still in vain,
Tho' full of youthful Health, and void of Pain:

Cares I had none, to keep me from my Rest,
For Love had never enter'd in my Breast;   25
I wanted nothing Fortune could supply,
Nor did she Slumber till that hour deny:
I wonder'd then, but after found it true,
Much Joy had dry'd away the balmy Dew:
Sea's wou'd be Pools, without the brushing Air,   } 30
To curl the Waves; and sure some little Care
Shou'd weary Nature so, to make her want repair.   }

　　When Chaunticleer the second Watch had sung,
Scorning the Scorner Sleep from Bed I sprung.
And dressing, by the Moon, in loose Array,   } 35
Pass'd out in open Air, preventing Day,
And sought a goodly Grove as Fancy led my way.   }
Strait as a Line in beauteous Order stood
Of Oaks unshorn a venerable Wood;
Fresh was the Grass beneath, and ev'ry Tree   40
At distance planted in a due degree,
Their branching Arms in Air with equal space
Stretch'd to their Neighbours with a long Embrace:
And the new Leaves on ev'ry Bough were seen,
Some ruddy-colour'd, some of lighter green.   45
The painted Birds, Companions of the Spring,
Hopping from Spray to Spray, were heard to sing;
Both Eyes and Ears receiv'd a like Delight,
Enchanting Musick, and a charming Sight.
On *Philomel* I fix'd my whole Desire;   50
And list'n'd for the Queen of all the Quire;
Fain would I hear her heav'nly Voice to sing;
And wanted yet an Omen to the Spring.
　　Attending long in vain; I took the way,
Which through a Path, but scarcely printed, lay;   55
In narrow Mazes oft it seem'd to meet,
And look'd, as lightly press'd, by Fairy Feet.
Wandring I walk'd alone, for still methought
To some strange End so strange a Path was wrought:
At last it led me where an Arbour stood,   60
The sacred Receptacle of the Wood:
This Place unmark'd though oft I walk'd the Green,
In all my Progress I had never seen:

And seiz'd at once with Wonder and Delight,
Gaz'd all arround me, new to the transporting Sight.   65
'Twas bench'd with Turf, and goodly to be seen,
The thick young Grass arose in fresher Green:
The Mound was newly made, no Sight cou'd pass
Betwixt the nice Partitions of the Grass;
The well-united Sods so closely lay;   70
And all arround the Shades defended it from Day.
For Sycamours with Eglantine were spread,
A Hedge about the Sides, a Covering over Head.
And so the fragrant Brier was wove between,
The Sycamour and Flow'rs were mix'd with Green,   75
That Nature seem'd to vary the Delight;
And satisfy'd at once the Smell and Sight.
The Master Work-man of the Bow'r was known
Through Fairy-Lands, and built for *Oberon*;
Who twining Leaves with such Proportion drew,   80
They rose by Measure, and by Rule they grew:
No mortal Tongue can half the Beauty tell;
For none but Hands divine could work so well.
Both Roof and Sides were like a Parlour made,
A soft Recess, and a cool Summer shade;   85
The Hedge was set so thick, no Foreign Eye
The Persons plac'd within it could espy:
But all that pass'd without with Ease was seen,
As if nor Fence nor Tree was plac'd between.
'Twas border'd with a Field; and some was plain   90
With Grass; and some was sow'd with rising Grain.
That (now the Dew with Spangles deck'd the Ground:)
A sweeter spot of Earth was never found.
I look'd, and look'd, and still with new Delight;
Such Joy my Soul, such Pleasures fill'd my Sight: 95
And the fresh Eglantine exhal'd a Breath;
Whose Odours were of Pow'r to raise from Death:
Nor sullen Discontent, nor anxious Care,
Ev'n tho' brought thither, could inhabit there:
But thence they fled as from their mortal Foe;   1
For this sweet Place cou'd only Pleasure know.
   Thus, as I mus'd, I cast aside my Eye

The Flower and the Leaf. 75 Green,] Green. F

And saw a Medlar-Tree was planted nigh;
The spreading Branches made a goodly Show,
And full of opening Blooms was ev'ry Bough: 105
A Goldfinch there I saw with gawdy Pride
Of painted Plumes, that hopp'd from side to side,
Still pecking as she pass'd; and still she drew
The Sweets from ev'ry Flow'r, and suck'd the Dew:
Suffic'd at length, she warbled in her Throat,   110
And tun'd her Voice to many a merry Note,
But indistinct, and neither Sweet nor Clear,
Yet such as sooth'd my Soul, and pleas'd my Ear.
    Her short Performance was no sooner try'd,
When she I sought, the Nightingale reply'd: 115
So sweet, so shrill, so variously she sung,
That the Grove eccho'd, and the Valleys rung:
And I so ravish'd with her heav'nly Note
I stood intranc'd, and had no room for Thought.
But all o'er-pou'r'd with Extasy of Bliss,   120
Was in a pleasing Dream of Paradice;
At length I wak'd; and looking round the Bow'r
Search'd ev'ry Tree, and pry'd on ev'ry Flow'r,
If any where by chance I might espy
The rural Poet of the Melody: 125
For still methought she sung not far away;
At last I found her on a Lawrel Spray,
Close by my Side she sate, and fair in Sight,
Full in a Line, against her opposite;
Where stood with Eglantine the Lawrel twin'd: 130
And both their native Sweets were well conjoin'd.
    On the green Bank I sat, and listen'd long;
(Sitting was more convenient for the Song!)
Nor till her Lay was ended could I move,
But wish'd to dwell for ever in the Grove.   135
Only methought the time too swiftly pass'd,
And ev'ry Note I fear'd wou'd be the last.
My Sight, and Smell, and Hearing were employ'd,
And all three Senses in full Gust enjoy'd.
And what alone did all the rest surpass,   140
The sweet Possession of the Fairy Place;
Single, and conscious to my Self alone,

Of Pleasures to th' excluded World unknown.
Pleasures which no where else, were to be found,
And all *Elysium* in a spot of Ground.   145
   Thus while I sat intent to see and hear,
And drew Perfumes of more than vital Air,
All suddenly I heard th' approaching sound
Of vocal Musick, on th' enchanted Ground:
An Host of Saints it seem'd, so full the Quire;   150
As if the Bless'd above did all conspire,
To join their Voices, and neglect the Lyre.
At length there issu'd from the Grove behind
A fair Assembly of the Female Kind:
A Train less fair, as ancient Fathers tell,   155
Seduc'd the Sons of Heaven to rebel.
I pass their Forms, and ev'ry charming Grace,
Less than an Angel wou'd their Worth debase:
But their Attire like Liveries of a kind,
All rich and rare, is fresh within my Mind.   160
In Velvet white as Snow the Troop was gown'd,
The Seams with sparkling Emeralds, set around;
Their Hoods and Sleeves the same: And purfled o'er
With Diamonds, Pearls, and all the shining store
Of Eastern Pomp: Their long descending Train   165
With Rubies edg'd, and Saphires, swept the Plain:
High on their Heads, with Jewels richly set
Each Lady wore a radiant Coronet.
Beneath the Circles, all the Quire was grac'd
With Chaplets green on their fair Foreheads plac'd.   170
Of Lawrel some, of Woodbine many more;
And Wreaths of *Agnus castus*, others bore:
These last who with those Virgin Crowns were dress'd,
Appear'd in higher Honour than the rest.
They danc'd around, but in the midst was seen   175
A Lady of a more majestique Mien;
By Stature, and by Beauty mark'd their Sovereign Queen.
   She in the midst began with sober Grace;
Her Servants Eyes were fix'd upon her Face:
And as she mov'd or turn'd her Motions view'd,   180
Her Measures kept, and Step by Step pursu'd.

Methought she trod the Ground with greater Grace,
With more of Godhead shining in her Face;
And as in Beauty she surpass'd the Quire,
So, nobler than the rest, was her Attire.   185
A Crown of ruddy Gold inclos'd her Brow,
Plain without Pomp, and Rich without a Show:
A Branch of *Agnus castus* in her Hand,
She bore aloft (her Scepter of Command;)
Admir'd, ador'd by all the circling Crowd,   190
For wheresoe'er she turn'd her Face, they bow'd:
And as she danc'd, a Roundelay she sung,
In honour of the Lawrel, ever young:
She rais'd her Voice on high, and sung so clear, ⎫
The Fawns came scudding from the Groves to hear: ⎬ 195
And all the bending Forest lent an Ear.   ⎭
At ev'ry Close she made, th' attending Throng
Reply'd, and bore the Burden of the Song:
So just, so small, yet in so sweet a Note,
It seem'd the Musick melted in the Throat.   200
   Thus dancing on, and singing as they danc'd,
They to the middle of the Mead advanc'd:
Till round my Arbour, a new Ring they made,
And footed it about the secret Shade:
O'erjoy'd to see the jolly Troop so near,   205
But somewhat aw'd I shook with holy Fear;
Yet not so much, but that I noted well
Who did the most in Song, or Dance excel.
   Not long I had observ'd, when from afar
I heard a suddain Symphony of War;   210
The neighing Coursers, and the Soldiers cry,
And sounding Trumps that seem'd to tear the Sky:
I saw soon after this, behind the Grove
From whence the Ladies did in order move,
Come issuing out in Arms a Warrior-Train,   215
That like a Deluge pour'd upon the Plain:
On barbed Steeds they rode in proud Array,
Thick as the College of the Bees in *May*,
When swarming o'er the dusky Fields they fly,
New to the Flow'rs, and intercept the Sky.   220
So fierce they drove, their Coursers were so fleet,

That the Turf trembled underneath their Feet.
   To tell their costly Furniture were long,
The Summers Day wou'd end before the Song:
To purchase but the Tenth of all their Store,   225
Would make the mighty *Persian* Monarch poor.
Yet what I can, I will; before the rest
The Trumpets issu'd in white Mantles dress'd:
A numerous Troop, and all their Heads around
With Chaplets green of Cerrial-Oak were crown'd,   230
And at each Trumpet was a Banner bound;
Which waving in the Wind display'd at large
Their Master's Coat of Arms, and Knightly Charge.
Broad were the Banners, and of snowy Hue,
A purer Web the Silk-worm never drew.   235
The chief about their Necks, the Scutcheons wore,
With Orient Pearls and Jewels pouder'd o'er:
Broad were their Collars too, and ev'ry one
Was set about with many a costly Stone.
Next these of Kings at Arms a goodly Train,   240
In proud Array came prancing o'er the Plain:
Their Cloaks were Cloth of Silver mix'd with Gold,
And Garlands green arround their Temples roll'd:
Rich Crowns were on their royal Scutcheons plac'd
With Saphires, Diamonds, and with Rubies grac'd.   245
And as the Trumpets their appearance made,
So these in Habits were alike array'd;
But with a Pace more sober, and more slow:
And twenty, Rank in Rank, they rode a-row.
The Pursevants came next in number more;   250
And like the Heralds each his Scutcheon bore:
Clad in white Velvet all their Troop they led,
With each an Oaken Chaplet on his Head.
   Nine royal Knights in equal Rank succeed,
Each Warrior mounted on a fiery Steed: 255
In golden Armour glorious to behold;
The Rivets of their Arms were nail'd with Gold.
Their Surcoats of white Ermin-Fur were made;
With Cloth of Gold between that cast a glitt'ring Shade.
The Trappings of their Steeds were of the same;   260
The golden Fringe ev'n set the Ground on flame;

And drew a precious Trail: A Crown divine
Of Lawrel did about their Temples twine.
   Three Henchmen were for ev'ry Knight assign'd,
All in rich Livery clad, and of a kind: 265
White Velvet, but unshorn, for Cloaks they wore,
And each within his Hand a Truncheon bore:
The foremost held a Helm of rare Device;
A Prince's Ransom wou'd not pay the Price.
The second bore the Buckler of his Knight,   270
The third of Cornel-Wood a Spear upright,
Headed with piercing Steel, and polish'd bright.
Like to their Lords their Equipage was seen,
And all their Foreheads crown'd with Garlands green.
   And after these came arm'd with Spear and Shield   275
An Host so great, as cover'd all the Field:
And all their Foreheads, like the Knights before,
With Lawrels ever green were shaded o'er,
Or Oak, or other Leaves of lasting kind,
Tenacious of the Stem and firm against the Wind.   280
Some in their Hands besides the Lance and Shield,
The Boughs of Woodbind or of Hauthorn held,
Or Branches for their mistique Emblems took,
Of Palm, of Lawrel, or of Cerrial Oak.
   Thus marching to the Trumpets lofty sound   285
Drawn in two Lines adverse they wheel'd around,
And in the middle Meadow took their Ground.
Among themselves the Turney they divide,
In equal Squadrons, rang'd on either side.
Then turn'd their Horses Heads, and Man to Man,   290
And Steed to Steed oppos'd, the Justs began.
They lightly set their Lances in the rest,
And, at the Sign, against each other press'd:
They met, I sitting at my Ease beheld
The mix'd Events, and Fortunes of the Field.   295
Some broke their Spears, some tumbled Horse and Man,
And round the Fields the lighten'd Coursers ran.
An Hour and more like Tides, in equal sway
They rush'd, and won by turns, and lost the Day:

At length the Nine (who still together held)   300
Their fainting Foes to shameful Flight compell'd,
And with resistless Force, o'er-ran the Field.
Thus, to their Fame, when finish'd was the Fight,
The Victors from their lofty Steeds alight:
Like them dismounted all the Warlike Train,   305
And two by two proceeded o'er the Plain:
Till to the fair Assembly they advanc'd,
Who near the secret Arbour sung and danc'd.

  The Ladies left their Measures at the Sight,
To meet the Chiefs returning from the Fight,   310
And each with open Arms embrac'd her chosen Knight.
Amid the Plain a spreading Lawrel stood,
The Grace and Ornament of all the Wood:
That pleasing Shade they sought, a soft retreat
From suddain *April* Show'rs, a Shelter from the Heat.   315
Her leavy Arms with such extent were spread,
So near the Clouds was her aspiring Head,
That Hosts of Birds, that wing the liquid Air,
Perch'd in the Boughs, had nightly Lodging there.
And Flocks of Sheep beneath the Shade from far   320
Might hear the ratling Hail, and wintry War;
From Heav'ns Inclemency here found retreat,
Enjoy'd the cool, and shun'd the scorching Heat:
A hundred Knights might there at Ease abide;
And ev'ry Knight a Lady by his side: 325
The Trunk it self such Odours did bequeath,
That a Moluccan Breeze to these was common Breath.
The Lords, and Ladies here approaching, paid
Their Homage, with a low Obeisance made:
And seem'd to venerate the sacred Shade.   330
These Rites perform'd, their Pleasures they pursue,
With Songs of Love, and mix with Measures new;
Around the holy Tree their Dance they frame,
And ev'ry Champion leads his chosen Dame.

  I cast my Sight upon the farther Field,   335
And a fresh Object of Delight beheld:
For from the Region of the West I heard
New Musick sound, and a new Troop appear'd;

301 Flight] Fight *F*   314 retreat] retreat, *F*

Of Knights, and Ladies mix'd a jolly Band,
But all on Foot they march'd, and Hand in Hand. 340
   The Ladies dress'd in rich Symarrs were seen
Of *Florence* Satten, flow'r'd with White and Green,
And for a Shade betwixt the bloomy Gridelin.
The Borders of their Petticoats below
Were guarded thick with Rubies on a-row; 345
And ev'ry Damsel wore upon her Head
Of Flow'rs a Garland blended White and Red.
Attir'd in Mantles all the Knights were seen,
That gratify'd the View with chearful Green:
Their Chaplets of their Ladies Colours were 350
Compos'd of White and Red to shade their shining Hair.
Before the merry Troop the Minstrels play'd,
All in their Masters Liveries were array'd:
And clad in Green, and on their Temples wore
The Chaplets White and Red their Ladies bore. 355
Their Instruments were various in their kind,
Some for the Bow, and some for breathing Wind:
The Sawtry, Pipe, and Hautbois noisy band,
And the soft Lute trembling beneath the touching Hand.
A Tuft of Daisies on a flow'ry Lay 360
They saw, and thitherward they bent their way:
To this both Knights and Dames their Homage made,
And due Obeisance to the Daisy paid.
And then the Band of Flutes began to play,
To which a Lady sung a Virelay; 365
And still at ev'ry close she wou'd repeat
The Burden of the Song, *The Daisy is so sweet.*
The Daisy is so sweet when she begun,
The Troop of Knights and Dames continu'd on.
The Concert and the Voice so charm'd my Ear, 370
And sooth'd my Soul, that it was Heav'n to hear.
   But soon their Pleasure pass'd: At Noon of Day,
The Sun with sultry Beams began to play:
Not *Syrius* shoots a fiercer Flame from high,
When with his pois'nous Breath he blasts the Sky: 375

353 Masters] Master's *F*   354 wore] wore, *F*   368 *Editor's italics*
372 Day,] Day; *F*

Then droop'd the fading Flow'rs (their Beauty fled)
And clos'd their sickly Eyes, and hung the Head;
And, rivell'd up with Heat, lay dying in their Bed.
The Ladies gasp'd, and scarcely could respire;
The Breath they drew, no longer Air, but Fire;   380
The fainty Knights were scorch'd; and knew not where
To run for Shelter, for no Shade was near.
And after this the gath'ring Clouds amain,
Pour'd down a Storm of rattling Hail and Rain.
And Lightning flash'd betwixt: The Field, and Flow'rs   385
Burnt up before, were bury'd in the Show'rs.
The Ladies, and the Knights no Shelter nigh,
Bare to the Weather, and the wintry Sky,
Were dropping wet, disconsolate and wan,
And through their thin Array receiv'd the Rain.   390
    While those in White protected by the Tree
Saw pass the vain Assault, and stood from Danger free.
But as Compassion mov'd their gentle Minds,
When ceas'd the Storm, and silent were the Winds,
Displeas'd at what, not suff'ring they had seen,   395
They went to chear the Faction of the Green:
The Queen in white Array before her Band,
Saluting, took her Rival by the Hand;
So did the Knights and Dames, with courtly Grace
And with Behaviour sweet their Foes embrace.   400
Then thus the Queen with Lawrel on her Brow,
Fair Sister I have suffer'd in your Woe:
Nor shall be wanting ought within my Pow'r
For your Relief in my refreshing Bow'r.
That other answer'd with a lowly Look,   405
And soon the gracious Invitation took:
For ill at ease both she and all her Train
The scorching Sun had born, and beating Rain.
Like Courtesy was us'd by all in White,
Each Dame a Dame receiv'd, and ev'ry Knight a Knight.   410
The Lawrel-Champions with their Swords invade
The neighb'ring Forests where the Justs were made,
And Serewood from the rotten Hedges took,
And Seeds of Latent-Fire from Flints provoke:

411 invade] invade, F

A chearful Blaze arose, and by the Fire,   415
They warm'd their frozen Feet, and dry'd their wet Attire.
Refresh'd with Heat the Ladies sought around
For virtuous Herbs which gather'd from the Ground
They squeez'd the Juice; and cooling Ointment made,
Which on their Sun-burnt Cheeks, and their chapt Skins they laid: 420
Then sought green Salads which they bad 'em eat,
A Soveraign Remedy for inward Heat.
   The Lady of the Leaf ordain'd a Feast,
And made the Lady of the Flow'r her Guest:
When lo, a Bow'r ascended on the Plain,   425
With suddain Seats adorn'd, and large for either Train.
This Bow'r was near my pleasant Arbour plac'd,
That I could hear and see whatever pass'd:
The Ladies sat, with each a Knight between
Distinguish'd by their Colours White and Green: 430
The vanquish'd Party with the Victors join'd,
Nor wanted sweet Discourse, the Banquet of the Mind.
Mean time the Minstrels play'd on either side
Vain of their Art, and for the Mast'ry vy'd:
The sweet Contention lasted for an Hour,   435
And reach'd my secret Arbour from the Bow'r.
   The Sun was set; and *Vesper* to supply
His absent Beams, had lighted up the Sky:
When *Philomel*, officious all the Day
To sing the Service of th' ensuing *May*,   440
Fled from her Lawrel Shade, and wing'd her Flight
Directly to the Queen array'd in White:
And hopping sate familiar on her Hand,
A new Musitian, and increas'd the Band.
   The Goldfinch, who to shun the scalding Heat,   445
Had chang'd the Medlar for a safer Seat,
And hid in Bushes scap'd the bitter Show'r,
Now perch'd upon the Lady of the Flow'r;
And either Songster holding out their Throats,
And folding up their Wings renew'd their Notes: 450
As if all Day, preluding to the Fight,
They only had rehears'd, to sing by Night.
The Banquet ended, and the Battle done,
They danc'd by Star-light and the friendly Moon:

And when they were to part, the Laureat Queen,   455
Supply'd with Steeds the Lady of the Green.
Her, and her Train conducting on the way
The Moon to follow, and avoid the Day.
   This when I saw, inquisitive to know
The secret Moral of the Mystique Show,   460
I started from my Shade in hopes to find
Some Nymph to satisfy my longing Mind:
And as my fair Adventure fell, I found
A Lady all in White with Lawrel crown'd
Who clos'd the Rear, and softly pac'd along,   465
Repeating to her self the former Song.
With due respect my Body I inclin'd,
As to some Being of Superiour Kind,
And made my Court, according to the Day,
Wishing her Queen and Her a happy *May*.   470
Great Thanks my Daughter, with a gracious Bow
She said; and I who much desir'd to know
Of whence she was, yet fearful how to break
My Mind, adventur'd humbly thus to speak.
Madam, Might I presume and not offend,   475
So may the Stars and shining Moon attend
Your Nightly Sports, as you vouchsafe to tell,
What Nymphs they were who mortal Forms excel,
And what the Knights who fought in listed Fields so well.
   To this the Dame reply'd, Fair Daughter know   480
That what you saw, was all a Fairy Show:
And all those airy Shapes you now behold
Were humane Bodies once, and cloath'd with earthly Mold:
Our Souls not yet prepar'd for upper Light,
Till Doomsday wander in the Shades of Night;   485
This only Holiday of all the Year,
We priviledg'd in Sun-shine may appear:
With Songs and Dance we celebrate the Day,
And with due Honours usher in the *May*.
At other Times we reign by Night alone,   490
And posting through the Skies pursue the Moon:
But when the Morn arises, none are found;
For cruel *Demogorgon* walks the round,
And if he finds a Fairy lag in Light,

He drives the Wretch before; and lashes into Night.   495
   All Courteous are by Kind; and ever proud
With friendly Offices to help the Good.
In every Land we have a larger Space
Than what is known to you of mortal Race:
Where we with Green adorn our Fairy Bow'rs,   500
And ev'n this Grove unseen before, is ours.
Know farther; Ev'ry Lady cloath'd in White,
And, crown'd with Oak and Lawrel ev'ry Knight,
Are Servants to the Leaf, by Liveries known
Of Innocence; and I my self am one.   505
Saw you not Her so graceful to behold
In white Attire, and crown'd with Radiant Gold:
The Soveraign Lady of our Land is She,
Diana call'd, the Queen of Chastity:
And, for the spotless Name of Maid she bears,   510
That *Agnus castus* in her Hand appears:
And all her Train with leavy Chaplets crown'd
Were for unblam'd Virginity renown'd:
But those the chief and highest in Command
Who bear those holy Branches in their Hand: 515
The Knights adorn'd with Lawrel-Crowns, are they
Whom Death nor Danger ever cou'd dismay,
Victorious Names, who made the World obey:
Who while they liv'd, in Deeds of Arms excell'd,
And after Death for Deities were held.   520
But those who wear the Woodbine on their Brow
Were Knights of Love, who never broke their Vow:
Firm to their plighted Faith, and ever free
From Fears and fickle Chance, and Jealousy.
The Lords and Ladies, who the Woodbine bear,   525
As true as *Tristram*, and *Isotta* were.
   But what are those said I, th' unconquer'd Nine
Who crown'd with Lawrel-Wreaths in golden Armour shine?
And who the Knights in Green, and what the Train
Of Ladies dress'd with Daisies on the Plain?   530
Why both the Bands in Worship disagree,
And some adore the Flow'r, and some the Tree?
   Just is your Suit, fair Daughter, said the Dame,
Those lawrell'd Chiefs were Men of mighty Fame;

Nine Worthies were they call'd of diff'rent Rites,   535
Three Jews, three Pagans, and three Christian Knights.
These, as you see, ride foremost in the Field,
As they the foremost Rank of Honour held,
And all in Deeds of Chivalry excell'd.
Their Temples wreath'd with Leafs, that still renew;   540
For deathless Lawrel is the Victor's due:
Who bear the Bows were Knights in *Arthur*'s Reign,
Twelve they, and twelve the Peers of *Charlemain*:
For Bows the Strength of brawny Arms imply,
Emblems of Valour, and of Victory.   545
Behold an Order yet of newer Date
Doubling their Number, equal in their State;
Our *England*'s Ornament, the Crown's Defence,
In Battle brave, Protectors of their Prince.
Unchang'd by Fortune, to their Soveraign true,   550
For which their manly Legs are bound with Blue.
These, of the Garter call'd, of Faith unstain'd,
In fighting Fields the Lawrel have obtain'd,
And well repaid those Honours which they gain'd.
The Lawrel-Wreaths were first by *Cæsar* worn,   555
And still they *Cæsar*'s Successors adorn:
One Leaf of this is Immortality,
And more of Worth, than all the World can buy.
   One Doubt remains, said I, the Dames in Green,
What were their Qualities, and who their Queen?   560
Flora commands, said she, those Nymphs and Knights,
Who liv'd in slothful Ease, and loose Delights:
Who never Acts of Honour durst pursue,
The Men inglorious Knights, the Ladies all untrue:
Who nurs'd in Idleness, and train'd in Courts,   565
Pass'd all their precious Hours in Plays, and Sports,
Till Death behind came stalking on, unseen,
And wither'd (like the Storm) the freshness of their Green.
These, and their Mates, enjoy the present Hour,
And therefore pay their Homage to the Flow'r.   570
But Knights in Knightly Deeds should persevere,
And still continue what at first they were;
Continue, and proceed in Honours fair Career.
No room for Cowardise, or dull delay;

From Good to Better they should urge their way.   575
For this with golden Spurs the Chiefs are grac'd,
With pointed Rowels arm'd to mend their haste;
For this with lasting Leaves their Brows are bound;
For Lawrel is the Sign of Labour crown'd;
Which bears the bitter Blast, nor shaken falls to Ground: 580
From Winter-Winds it suffers no decay,
For ever fresh and fair, and ev'ry Month is *May*.
Ev'n when the vital Sap retreats below,
Ev'n when the hoary Head is hid in Snow;
The Life is in the Leaf, and still between   585
The Fits of falling Snows, appears the streaky Green.
Not so the Flow'r which lasts for little space
A short-liv'd Good, and an uncertain Grace;
This way and that the feeble Stem is driv'n,
Weak to sustain the Storms, and Injuries of Heav'n.   590
Prop'd by the Spring, it lifts aloft, the Head,
But of a sickly Beauty, soon to shed;
In Summer living, and in Winter dead.
For Things of tender Kind for Pleasure made
Shoot up with swift Increase, and suddain are decay'd.   595
    With humble Words, the wisest I could frame,
And profer'd Service I repaid the Dame:
That of her Grace she gave her Maid to know
The secret meaning of this moral Show.
And she to prove what Profit I had made,   600
Of mystique Truth, in Fables first convey'd,
Demanded, till the next returning *May*,
Whether the Leaf or Flow'r I would obey?
I chose the Leaf; she smil'd with sober Chear,
And wish'd me fair Adventure for the Year.   605
And gave me Charms and Sigils, for Defence
Against ill Tongues that scandal Innocence:
But I, said she, my Fellows must pursue,
Already past the Plain, and out of view.
    We parted thus; I homeward sped my way,   610
Bewilder'd in the Wood till Dawn of Day:
And met the merry Crew who danc'd about the *May*.
Then late refresh'd with Sleep I rose to write
The visionary Vigils of the Night:

Blush, as thou may'st, my little Book for Shame,
Nor hope with homely Verse to purchase Fame;
For such thy Maker chose; and so design'd
Thy simple Style to sute thy lowly Kind.

THE TWELFTH BOOK OF OVID
HIS METAMORPHOSES, Wholly Translated

CONNECTION TO THE END OF THE
ELEVENTH BOOK

Æsacus, *the Son of* Priam, *loving a Country-Life, forsakes the Court: Living obscurely, he falls in Love with a Nymph; who flying from him, was kill'd by a Serpent; for Grief of this, he wou'd have drown'd himself; but by the pity of the Gods, is turn'd into a Cormorant.* Priam, *not hearing of* Æsacus, *believes him to be dead, and raises a Tomb to preserve his Memory. By this Transition,* 5 *which is one of the finest in all* Ovid, *the Poet naturally falls into the Story of the* Trojan *War, which is summ'd up, in the present Book, but so very briefly, in many Places, that* Ovid *seems more short than* Virgil, *contrary to his usual Style. Yet the House of Fame, which is here describ'd, is one of the most beautiful Pieces in the whole* Metamorphoses. *The Fight of* Achilles 10 *and* Cygnus, *and the Fray betwixt the* Lapythæ *and* Centaurs, *yield to no other part of this Poet: And particularly the Loves and Death of* Cyllarus *and* Hylonome, *the Male and Female* Centaur, *are wonderfully moving.*

*P*RIAM, to whom the Story was unknown,
As dead, deplor'd his Metamorphos'd Son:
A Cenotaph his Name and Title kept,
And *Hector* round the Tomb, with all his Brothers wept.
   This pious Office *Paris* did not share,   5
Absent alone; and Author of the War,
Which, for the *Spartan* Queen, the *Grecians* drew
T' avenge the Rape; and *Asia* to subdue.
   A thousand Ships were man'd, to sail the Sea:
Nor had their just Resentments found delay,   10
Had not the Winds and Waves, oppos'd their way.
At *Aulis*, with United Pow'rs they meet,
But there, Cross-winds or Calms, detain'd the Fleet.

Now, while they raise an Altar on the Shore,
And *Jove* with solemn Sacrifice adore;   15
A boding Sign the Priests and People see:
A Snake of size immense, ascends a Tree.
And in the leavy Summet, spy'd a Neast,
Which, o'er her Callow young, a Sparrow press'd.
Eight were the Birds unfledg'd; their Mother flew;   20
And hover'd round her Care; but still in view:
Till the fierce Reptile first devour'd the Brood;
Then siez'd the flutt'ring Dam, and drunk her Blood.
This dire Ostent, the fearful People view;
Calchas alone, by *Phœbus* taught, foreknew   25
What Heav'n decreed; and with a smiling Glance,
Thus gratulates to *Greece* her happy Chance.
O *Argives* we shall Conquer: *Troy* is ours,
But long Delays shall first afflict our Pow'rs:
Nine Years of Labour, the nine Birds portend;   30
The Tenth shall in the Town's Destruction end.
    The Serpent, who his Maw obscene had fill'd,
The Branches in his curl'd Embraces held:
But, as in Spires he stood, he turn'd to Stone:
The stony Snake retain'd the Figure still his own.   35
    Yet, not for this, the Wind-bound Navy weigh'd,
Slack were their Sails; and *Neptune* disobey'd.
Some thought him loath the Town shou'd be destroy'd,
Whose Building had his Hands divine employ'd:
Not so the Seer; who knew, and known foreshow'd,   40
The Virgin *Phœbe*, with a Virgin's Blood
Must first be reconcil'd; the common Cause
Prevail'd; and Pity yielding to the Laws,
Fair *Iphigenia* the devoted Maid
Was, by the weeping Priests, in Linnen-Robes array'd;   45
All mourn her Fate; but no Relief appear'd:
The Royal Victim bound, the Knife already rear'd:
When that offended Pow'r, who caus'd their Woe,
Relenting ceas'd her Wrath; and stop'd the coming Blow.
A Mist before the Ministers she cast;   50
And, in the Virgin's room, a Hind she plac'd.
Th' Oblation slain, and *Phœbe* reconcil'd,
The Storm was hush'd, and dimpled Ocean smil'd:

A favourable Gale arose from Shore,
Which to the Port desir'd, the *Grecian* Gallies bore.   55
   Full in the midst of this Created Space,
Betwixt Heav'n, Earth and Skies, there stands a Place,
Confining on all three; with triple Bound;
Whence all Things, though remote, are view'd around;
And thither bring their Undulating Sound.   } 60
The Palace of loud Fame; her Seat of Pow'r;
Plac'd on the Summet of a lofty Tow'r;
A thousand winding Entries long and wide,
Receive of fresh Reports a flowing Tide.
A thousand Crannies in the Walls are made;   65
Nor Gate nor Bars exclude the busy Trade.
'Tis built of Brass the better to diffuse
The spreading Sounds, and multiply the News:
Where Eccho's, in repeated Eccho's play:
A Mart for ever full; and open Night and Day.   70
Nor Silence is within, nor Voice express,
But a deaf Noise of Sounds that never cease.
Confus'd, and Chiding, like the hollow Roar
Of Tides, receding from th' insulted Shore.
Or like the broken Thunder, heard from far,   75
When *Jove* to distance drives the rowling War.
The Courts are fill'd with a tumultuous Din
Of Crowds, or issuing forth, or entring in:
A thorough fare of News: Where some devise
Things never heard; some mingle Truth with Lies: 80
The troubled Air with empty Sounds they beat:
Intent to hear; and eager to repeat.
Error sits brooding there; with added Train
Of vain Credulity; and Joys as vain:
Suspicion, with Sedition join'd, are near;   85
And Rumors rais'd, and Murmurs mix'd, and Panique Fear.
Fame sits aloft; and sees the subject Ground;
And Seas about, and Skies above; enquiring all around.
   The Goddess gives th' Alarm; and soon is known
The *Grecian* Fleet, descending on the Town.   90
Fix'd on Defence the *Trojans* are not slow
To guard their Shore, from an expected Foe.

    The Twelfth Book. 57 Skies,] Skies; F

They meet in Fight: By *Hector*'s fatal Hand
Protesilaus falls; and bites the Strand;
Which with expence of Blood the *Grecians* won;   95
And prov'd the Strength unknown of *Priam*'s Son.
And to their Cost the *Trojan* Leaders felt
The *Grecian* Heroes; and what Deaths they dealt.
    From these first Onsets, the *Sigæan* Shore
Was strew'd with Carcasses; and stain'd with Gore: 100
Neptunian Cygnus, Troops of *Greeks* had slain;
Achilles in his Carr had scow'r'd the Plain;
And clear'd the *Trojan* Ranks: Where e'er he fought,
Cygnus, or *Hector*, through the Fields he sought:
Cygnus he found; on him his Force essay'd: 105
For *Hector* was to the tenth Year delay'd.
His white man'd Steeds, that bow'd beneath the Yoke
He chear'd to Courage, with a gentle Stroke;
Then urg'd his fiery Chariot on the Foe;
And rising, shook his Lance; in act to throw.   110
But first, he cry'd, O Youth be proud to bear
Thy Death, enobled, by *Pelides* Spear.
The Lance pursu'd the Voice without delay;
Nor did th' whizzing Weapon miss the way:
But pierc'd his Cuirass, with such Fury sent;   115
And sign'd his Bosom with a Purple dint.
At this the Seed of *Neptune*; Goddess-born,
For Ornament, not Use, these Arms are worn;
This Helm, and heavy Buckler I can spare;
As only Decorations of the War: 120
So *Mars* is arm'd for Glory, not for Need.
'Tis somewhat more from *Neptune* to proceed,
Than from a Daughter of the Sea to spring:
Thy Sire is Mortal; mine is Ocean's King.
Secure of Death, I shou'd contemn thy Dart,   125
Tho' naked; and impassible depart:
He said, and threw: The trembling Weapon pass'd ⎫
Through nine Bull-hides, each under other plac'd, ⎬
On his broad Shield; and stuck within the last. ⎭
Achilles wrench'd it out; and sent again   130

94 Strand;] Strand: F   101 *Neptunian*] *Neptuman* F   102 Plain;] Plain: F
128 plac'd,] plac'd; F

The hostile Gift: The hostile Gift was vain.
He try'd a third, a tough well-chosen Spear,
Th' inviolable Body stood sincere;
Though *Cygnus* then did no Defence provide,
But scornful offer'd his unshielded Side.   13﹕

  Not otherwise th' impatient Hero far'd,
Than as a Bull, incompass'd with a Guard
Amid the *Circus* roars: Provok'd from far
By sight of Scarlet, and a sanguine War:
They quit their Ground; his bended Horns elude;   14﹖
In vain pursuing, and in vain pursu'd.

  Before to farther Fight he wou'd advance,
He stood considering, and survey'd his Lance.
Doubts if he wielded not a Wooden Spear
Without a Point: He look'd, the Point was there   14
This is my Hand, and this my Lance he se'd;
By which so many thousand Foes are dead.
O whether is their usual Virtue fled!
I had it once; and the *Lyrnessian* Wall,
And *Tenedos* confess'd it in their fall.   1﹕
Thy Streams, *Caicus*, rowl'd a Crimson-Flood;
And *Thebes* ran Red with her own Natives Blood.
Twice *Telephus* employ'd this piercing Steel,
To wound him first, and afterward to heal.
The Vigour of this Arm, was never vain;   1﹒
And that my wonted Prowess I retain,
Witness these heaps of Slaughter on the Plain.
He said; and doubtful of his former Deeds,
To some new trial of his Force proceeds.
He chose *Menœtes* from among the rest;   1
At him he lanch'd his Spear; and pierc'd his Breast:
On the hard Earth, the *Lycian* knock'd his Head;
And lay supine; and forth the Spirit fled.

  Then thus the Hero; neither can I blame;
The Hand, or Javelin; both are still the same.   1
The same I will employ against this Foe;
And wish but with the same Success to throw.
So spoke the Chief; and while he spoke he threw;
The Weapon with unerring Fury flew!

    132 third,] third; F   158 Deeds,] Deeds; F

At his left Shoulder aim'd: Nor entrance found;   170
But back, as from a Rock, with swift rebound
Harmless return'd: A bloody Mark appear'd,
Which with false Joy, the flatter'd Hero chear'd.
Wound there was none; the Blood that was in view,
The Lance before from slain *Menœtes* drew.   175

    Headlong he leaps from off his lofty Car,
And in close Fight on foot renews the War.
Raging with high Disdain, repeats his Blows;
Nor Shield nor Armour can their Force oppose;
Huge Cantlets of his Buckler strew the Ground,   180
And no Defence in his bor'd Arms is found.
But on his Flesh, no Wound or Blood is seen;
The Sword it self, is blunted on the Skin.

    This vain Attempt the Chief no longer bears;
But round his hollow Temples and his Ears   185
His Buckler beats: The Son of *Neptune*, stun'd
With these repeated Buffets, quits his Ground;
A sickly Sweat succeeds; and Shades of Night:
Inverted Nature swims before his Sight:
Th' insulting Victor presses on the more,   190
And treads the Steps the vanquish'd trod before.
Nor Rest, nor Respite gives: A Stone there lay,
Behind his trembling Foe; and stop'd his way.
Achilles took th' Advantage which he found,
O'er-turn'd, and push'd him backward on the Ground.   195
His Buckler held him under, while he press'd
With both his Knees above, his panting Breast.
Unlac'd his Helm: About his Chin the Twist
He ty'd; and soon the strangled Soul dismiss'd.

    With eager haste he went to strip the Dead: 200
The vanish'd Body from his Arms was fled.
His Sea-God Sire t' immortalize his Fame,
Had turn'd it to the Bird, that bears his Name.

    A Truce succeeds the Labours of this Day,
And Arms suspended with a long delay.   205
While *Trojan* Walls are kept with Watch and Ward,
The *Greeks* before their Trenches, mount the Guard;

The Feast approach'd; when to the blue-Ey'd Maid
His Vows for *Cygnus* slain the Victor paid,
And a white Heyfer, on her Altar laid.   2}
The reeking Entrails on the Fire they threw;
And to the Gods the grateful Odour flew:
Heav'n had its part in Sacrifice: The rest
Was broil'd and roasted for the future Feast.
The chief invited Guests, were set around: 2}
And Hunger first asswag'd, the Bowls were crown'd,
Which in deep Draughts, their Cares and Labours drown'd.}
The mellow Harp did not their Ears employ:
And mute was all the Warlike Symphony:
Discourse, the Food of Souls, was their Delight,   2
And pleasing Chat, prolong'd the Summers-night.
The Subject, Deeds of Arms; and Valour shown
Or on the *Trojan* side, or on their own.
Of Dangers undertaken, Fame atchiev'd;
They talk'd by turns; the Talk by turns reliev'd.   2
What Things but these, cou'd fierce *Achilles* tell,
Or what cou'd fierce *Achilles* hear so well?
The last great Act perform'd, of *Cygnus* slain,
Did most the Martial Audience entertain:
Wondring to find a Body, free by Fate   2
From Steel; and which cou'd ev'n that Steel rebate:
Amaz'd, their Admiration they renew;
And scarce *Pelides* cou'd believe it true.
    Then *Nestor*, thus: What once this Age has known,
In fated *Cygnus*, and in him alone,   2
Those Eyes have seen in *Cæneus* long before,
Whose Body, not a thousand Swords cou'd bore.
Cæneus, in Courage, and in Strength excell'd;
And still his *Othrys*, with his Fame is fill'd:
But what did most his Martial Deeds adorn,   2
(Though since he chang'd his Sex) a Woman born.
    A Novelty so strange, and full of Fate,
His list'ning Audience ask'd him to relate.
Achilles, thus commends their common Sute;
O Father, first for Prudence in repute,   2
Tell, with that Eloquence, so much thy own,

239 *Othrys*] Othry's F

What thou hast heard, or what of *Cæneus* known:
What was he, whence his change of Sex begun,
What Trophies, join'd in Wars with thee, he won?
Who conquer'd him, and in what fatal Strife   250
The Youth without a Wound, cou'd lose his Life?
   Neleides then; though tardy Age, and Time
Have shrunk my Sinews, and decay'd my Prime:
Though much I have forgotten of my Store,
Yet not exhausted, I remember more.   255
Of all that Arms atchiev'd, or Peace design'd,
That Action still is fresher in my Mind
Than ought beside. If Reverend Age can give
To Faith a Sanction, in my third I live.
   'Twas in my second Cent'ry, I survey'd   260
Young *Cænis*, then a fair *Thessalian* Maid:
Cænis the bright, was born to high Command;
A Princess; and a Native of thy Land,
Divine *Achilles*; every Tongue proclaim'd
Her Beauty; and her Eyes all Hearts inflam'd.   265
Peleus, thy Sire, perhaps had sought her Bed;
Among the rest; but he had either led
Thy Mother then; or was by Promise ty'd:
But she to him, and all alike her Love deny'd.
   It was her Fortune once, to take her way   270
Along the sandy Margin of the Sea:
The Pow'r of Ocean view'd her as she pass'd,
And lov'd as soon as seen, by Force embrac'd.
So Fame reports. Her Virgin-Treasure seiz'd,
And his new Joys, the Ravisher so pleas'd,   275
That thus, transported, to the Nymph he cry'd;
Ask what thou wilt, no Pray'r shall be deny'd.
This also Fame relates: The haughty Fair
Who not the Rape, ev'n of a God cou'd bear,
This Answer, proud, return'd: To mighty Wrongs   280
A mighty Recompence, of right, belongs.
Give me no more to suffer such a Shame;
But change the Woman, for a better Name,
One Gift for all: She said; and while she spoke,
A stern, majestick, manly Tone she took.   285
     283 Name,] Name. F

A Man she was: And as the Godhead swore,
To *Cæneus* turn'd, who *Cænis* was before.
   To this the Lover adds without request:
No force of Steel shou'd violate his Breast.
Glad of the Gift, the new-made Warrior goes: 29•
And Arms among the *Greeks*; and longs for equal Foes.
   Now brave *Perithous*, bold *Ixion*'s Son,
The Love of fair *Hippodame* had won.
The Cloud-begotten Race half Men, half Beast,
Invited, came to grace the Nuptial Feast: 29•
In a cool Cave's recess, the Treat was made,
Whose entrance, Trees with spreading Boughs o'ershade.
They sate: And summon'd by the Bridegroom, came
To mix with those the *Lapythæan* Name:
Nor wanted I: The Roofs with Joy resound: 30•
And *Hymen, Io Hymen*, rung around.
Rais'd Altars shone with holy Fires; the Bride,
Lovely her self (and lovely by her side
A bevy of bright Nimphs, with sober Grace,)
Came glitt'ring like a Star; and took her Place.   30•
Her heav'nly Form beheld, all wish'd her Joy;
And little wanted, but in vain, their Wishes all employ.
   For One, most Brutal, of the Brutal Brood,
Or whether Wine or Beauty fir'd his Blood,
Or both at once; beheld with lustful Eyes   31•
The Bride; at once resolv'd to make his Prize.
Down went the Board; and fastning on her Hair,
He seiz'd with sudden Force the frighted Fair.
'Twas *Eurytus* began: His bestial Kind
His Crime pursu'd; and each as pleas'd his Mind,   31•
Or her, whom Chance presented, took: The Feast
An Image of a taken Town express'd.
   The Cave resounds with Female Shrieks; we rise,
Mad with Revenge, to make a swift Reprise:
And *Theseus* first; what Frenzy has possess'd   3:
O *Eurytus*, he cry'd, thy brutal Breast,
To wrong *Perithous*, and not him alone,
But while I live, two Friends conjoyn'd in one?
   To justify his Threat, he thrusts aside
The Crowd of Centaurs; and redeems the Bride: 3:

The Monster nought reply'd: For Words were vain;
And Deeds cou'd only Deeds unjust maintain:
But answers with his Hand; and forward press'd,
With Blows redoubled, on his Face and Breast.
An ample Goblet stood, of antick Mold,   330
And rough with Figures of the rising Gold;
The Hero snatch'd it up: And toss'd in Air,
Full at the Front of the foul Ravisher.
He falls; and falling vomits forth a Flood
Of Wine, and Foam and Brains, and mingled Blood.   335
Half roaring, and half neighing through the Hall,
Arms, Arms, the double form'd with Fury call;
To wreak their Brother's death: A Medley-Flight
Of Bowls and Jars, at first supply the Fight.
Once Instruments of Feasts; but now of Fate;   340
Wine animates their Rage, and arms their Hate.
   Bold *Amycus*, from the robb'd Vestry brings
The Chalices of Heav'n; and holy Things
Of precious Weight: A Sconce, that hung on high,
With Tapers fill'd, to light the Sacristy,   345
Torn from the Cord, with his unhallow'd Hand
He threw amid the *Lapythæan* Band.
On *Celadon* the Ruin fell; and left
His Face of Feature and of Form bereft:
So, when some brawny Sacrificer knocks   350
Before an Altar led, an offer'd Oxe,
His Eye-balls rooted out, are thrown to Ground;
Nis Nose dismantled, in his Mouth is found,
His Jaws, Cheeks, Front, one undistinguish'd Wound.
   This, *Belates*, th' Avenger, cou'd not brook;   355
But, by the Foot a Maple-board he took;
And hurl'd at *Amycus*; his Chin it bent
Against his Chest, and down the Centaur sent:
Whom sputtring bloody Teeth, the second Blow
Of his drawn Sword, dispatch'd to Shades below.   360
   Grineus was near; and cast a furious Look
On the side Altar, cens'd with sacred Smoke,
And bright with flaming Fires; the Gods, he cry'd,
Have with their holy Trade, our Hands supply'd:

330 Mold,] Mold: *F*   347 Band.] Band, *F*

Why use we not their Gifts? Then from the Floor   365
An Altar-Stone he heav'd, with all the Load it bore:
Altar and Altars freight together flew,
Where thickest throng'd the *Lapythæan* Crew:
And *Broteas*, and at once, *Oryus* slew.
Oryus Mother, *Mycale*, was known   370
Down from her Sphere, to draw the lab'ring Moon.
    Exadius cry'd, unpunish'd shall not go
This Fact, if Arms are found against the Foe.
He look'd about, where on a Pine were spred
The votive Horns of a Stags branching Head: 375
At *Grineus* these he throws; so just they fly,
That the sharp Antlers stuck in either Eye:
Breathless and Blind he fell; with Blood besmear'd;
His Eye-balls beaten out, hung dangling on his Beard.
Fierce *Rhœtus*, from the Hearth a burning Brand   380
Selects, and whirling waves; till, from his Hand
The Fire took Flame; then dash'd it from the right,
On fair *Charaxus* Temples; near the Sight:
The whistling Pest came on; and pierc'd the Bone,
And caught the yellow Hair, that shrievel'd while it shone.   385
Caught, like dry Stubble fir'd; or like Seerwood;
Yet from the Wound ensu'd no Purple Flood;
But look'd a bubbling Mass, of frying Blood.
His blazing Locks, sent forth a crackling Sound;
And hiss'd, like red hot Iron, within the Smithy drown'd.   390
The wounded Warrior shook his flaming Hair,
Then (what a Team of Horse cou'd hardly rear)
He heaves the Threshold-Stone; but cou'd not throw;
The Weight it self, forbad the threaten'd Blow,
Which dropping from his lifted Arms, came down,   395
Full on *Cometes* Head; and crush'd his Crown.
Nor *Rhœtus* then retain'd his Joy; but se'd;
So by their Fellows may our Foes be sped;
Then, with redoubled Strokes he plies his Head:
The burning Lever, not deludes his Pains;   400
But drives the batter'd Skull, within the Brains.
    Thus flush'd, the Conqueror, with Force renew'd,
Evagrus, Dryas, Corythus, pursu'd:

First, *Corythus*, with downy Cheeks, he slew;
Whose fall, when fierce *Evagrus* had in view,　　405
He cry'd, what Palm is from a beardless Prey?
Rhœtus prevents what more he had to say;
And drove within his Mouth the fiery Death,
Which enter'd hissing in, and choak'd his Breath.
At *Dryas* next he flew: But weary Chance　　410
No longer wou'd the same Success advance.
For while he whirl'd in fiery Circles round
The Brand, a sharpen'd Stake strong *Dryas* found;
And in the Shoulder's Joint inflicts the Wound.
The Weapon stuck; which roaring out with Pain,　　415
He drew; nor longer durst the Fight maintain,
But turn'd his Back, for fear; and fled amain.
With him fled *Orneus*, with like Dread possess'd;
Thaumas, and *Medon* wounded in the Breast;
And *Mermeros* in the late Race renown'd,　　420
Now limping ran, and tardy with his Wound.
Pholus and *Melaneus* from Fight withdrew,
And *Abas* maim'd, who Boars encountring slew:
And Augur *Astylos*, whose Art in vain
From Fight dissuaded the four-footed Train,　　425
Now beat the Hoof with *Nessus* on the Plain;
But to his Fellow cry'd, be safely slow,
Thy Death deferr'd is due to great *Alcides* Bow.
　　Mean time strong *Dryas* urg'd his Chance so well,
That *Lycidas*, *Areos*, *Imbreus* fell;　　430
All, one by one, and fighting Face to Face:
Crenæus fled, to fall with more Disgrace:
For, fearful, while he look'd behind, he bore
Betwixt his Nose and Front, the Blow before.
Amid the Noise and Tumult of the Fray,　　435
Snoring, and drunk with Wine, *Aphidas* lay.
Ev'n then the Bowl within his Hand he kept:
And on a Bear's rough Hide securely slept.
Him *Phorbas* with his flying Dart, transfix'd;
Take thy next Draught, with *Stygian* Waters mix'd,　　440
And sleep thy fill, th' insulting Victor cry'd;

424 Augur] *Augur F*　　vain] vain, *F*　　425 dissuaded] dissuaded, *F*
Train,] Train; *F*　　441 fill,] fill *F*
917.19.**IV**　　　　R

Surpris'd with Death unfelt, the Centaur dy'd;
The ruddy Vomit, as he breath'd his Soul,
Repass'd his Throat; and fill'd his empty Bowl.

    I saw *Petræus* Arms, employ'd around   445
A well-grown Oak, to root it from the Ground.
This way, and that, he wrench'd the fibrous Bands;
The Trunk, was like a Sapling in his Hands
And still obey'd the Bent: While thus he stood,
Perithous Dart drove on; and nail'd him to the Wood.   450
Lycus, and *Chromys* fell by him oppress'd:
Helops and *Dictys* added to the rest
A nobler Palm: *Helops* through either Ear
Transfix'd, receiv'd the penetrating Spear.
This, *Dictys* saw; and seiz'd with suddain Fright   } 455
Leapt headlong from the Hill of steepy height;
And crush'd an Ash beneath, that cou'd not bear his weight. }
The shatter'd Tree receives his fall; and strikes
Within his full-blown Paunch, the sharpen'd Spikes.
Strong *Aphareus* had heav'd a mighty Stone,   460
The Fragment of a Rock; and wou'd have thrown;
But *Theseus* with a Club of harden'd Oak,   }
The Cubit-bone of the bold Centaur broke;
And left him maim'd; nor seconded the Stroke.   }
Then leapt on tall *Bianor*'s Back: (Who bore   465
No mortal Burden but his own, before.)
Press'd with his Knees his Sides; the double Man
His speed with Spurs increas'd, unwilling ran.
One Hand the Hero fasten'd on his Locks;
His other ply'd him with repeated Strokes.   470
The Club rung round his Ears, and batter'd Brows;
He falls; and lashing up his Heels, his Rider throws.

    The same *Herculean* Arms, *Nedymnus* wound;
And lay by him *Lycotas* on the Ground.
And *Hippasus*, whose Beard his Breast invades;   475
And *Ripheus*, haunter of the Woodland Shades:
And *Tereus* us'd with Mountain-Bears to strive;
And from their Dens to draw th' indignant Beasts alive.

    Demoleon cou'd not bear this hateful Sight,
Or the long Fortune of th' *Athenian* Knight: 480
But pull'd with all his Force, to disengage

From Earth a Pine; the Product of an Age:
The Root stuck fast: The broken Trunk he sent
At *Theseus*: *Theseus* frustrates his Intent,
And leaps aside; by *Pallas* warn'd, the Blow   485
To shun: (for so he said; and we believ'd it so.)
Yet not in vain, th' enormous Weight was cast;
Which *Crantor*'s Body sunder'd at the Waist.
Thy Father's Squire, *Achilles*, and his Care;
Whom Conquer'd in the *Dolopeian* War,   490
Their King, his present Ruin to prevent,
A Pledge of Peace implor'd, to *Peleus* sent.
    Thy Sire, with grieving Eyes, beheld his Fate;
And cry'd, not long, lov'd *Crantor*, shalt thou wait
Thy vow'd Revenge. At once he said, and threw   495
His Ashen-Spear; which quiver'd as it flew;
With all his Force and all his Soul apply'd;
The sharp Point enter'd in the Centaur's Side:
Both Hands, to wrench it out, the Monster join'd;
And wrench'd it out; but left the Steel behind.   500
Stuck in his Lungs it stood: Inrag'd he rears
His Hoofs, and down to Ground thy Father bears.
Thus trampled under Foot, his Shield defends
His Head; his other Hand the Lance protends.
Ev'n while he lay extended on the Dust,   505
He sped the Centaur, with one single Thrust.
Two more, his Lance before transfix'd from far;
And two, his Sword had slain, in closer War.
To these was added *Dorylas*: Who spread
A Bull's two goring Horns around his Head.   510
With these he push'd; in Blood already dy'd:
Him, fearless, I approach'd; and thus defy'd:
Now Monster, now, by Proof it shall appear,
Whether thy Horns, are sharper or my Spear.
At this, I threw: For want of other Ward,   515
He lifted up his Hand, his Front to guard.
His Hand it pass'd: And fix'd it to his Brow:
Loud Shouts of ours, attend the lucky Blow.

491 prevent,] prevent F

Him *Peleus* finish'd, with a second Wound,
Which through the Navel pierc'd: He reel'd around;   520
And drag'd his dangling Bowels on the Ground.
Trod what he drag'd; and what he trod he crush'd:
And to his Mother-Earth, with empty Belly rush'd.
   Nor cou'd thy Form, O *Cyllarus*, foreslow
Thy Fate; (if Form to Monsters Men allow:)   525
Just bloom'd thy Beard: Thy Beard of golden Hew:
Thy Locks in golden Waves, about thy Shoulders flew.
Sprightly thy Look: Thy Shapes in ev'ry part
So clean, as might instruct the Sculptor's Art;
As far as Man extended: Where began   530
The Beast, the Beast was equal to the Man.
Add but a Horses Head and Neck; and he,
O *Castor*, was a Courser worthy thee.
So was his Back proportion'd for the Seat;
So rose his brawny Chest; so swiftly mov'd his Feet.   535
Coal-black his Colour, but like Jet it shone;
His Legs and flowing Tail, were White alone.
Belov'd by many Maidens of his Kind;
But fair *Hylonome*, possess'd his Mind:
Hylonome, for Features, and for Face   540
Excelling all the Nymphs of double Race:
Nor less her Blandishments, than Beauty move;
At once both loving, and confessing Love.
For him she dress'd: For him with Female Care
She comb'd, and set in Curls, her auborn Hair.   545
Of Roses, Violets, and Lillies mix'd
And Sprigs of flowing Rosemary betwixt
She form'd the Chaplet, that adorn'd her Front:
In Waters of the *Pagasæan* Fount,
And in the Streams that from the Fountain play,   550
She wash'd her Face; and bath'd her twice a Day.
The Scarf of Furs, that hung below her Side,
Was Ermin, or the Panther's spotted Pride;
Spoils of no common Beast: With equal Flame
They lov'd: Their *Sylvan* Pleasures were the same: 555
All Day they hunted: And when Day expir'd,

519 Wound,] Wound: *F*   529 clean,] clean; *F*   Art;] Art: *F*
536 Colour,] Colour; *F*   shone;] shone, *F*   539 fair] fair, *F*

Together to some shady Cave retir'd:
Invited to the Nuptials, both repair:
And Side by Side, they both ingage in War.
   Uncertain from what Hand, a flying Dart   560
At *Cyllarus* was sent; which pierc'd his Heart.
The Javelin drawn from out the mortal Wound,
He faints with staggring Steps; and seeks the Ground:
The Fair, within her Arms receiv'd his fall,
And strove his wandring Spirits to recal: 565
And while her Hand the streaming Blood oppos'd,
Join'd Face to Face, his Lips with hers she clos'd.
Stiffled with Kisses, a sweet Death he dies;
She fills the Fields with undistinguish'd Cries:
At least her Words, were in her Clamour drown'd;   570
For my stun'd Ears receiv'd no vocal Sound.
In madness of her Grief, she seiz'd the Dart
New-drawn, and reeking from her Lover's Heart;
To her bare Bosom the sharp Point apply'd;
And wounded fell; and falling by his Side,   575
Embrac'd him in her Arms; and thus embracing, dy'd.
   Ev'n still methinks, I see *Phæocomes*;
Strange was his Habit; and as odd his Dress.
Six Lion's Hides, with Thongs together fast,
His upper part defended to his Waist: 580
And where Man ended, the continued Vest,
Spread on his Back, the Houss and Trappings of a Beast.
A Stump too heavy for a Team to draw,
(It seems a Fable, tho' the Fact I saw;)
He threw at *Pholon*; the descending Blow   585
Divides the Skull, and cleaves his Head in two.
The Brains, from Nose and Mouth, and either Ear
Came issuing out, as through a Colendar
The curdled Milk: or from the Press the Whey
Driv'n down by Weights above, is drain'd away.   590
   But him, while stooping down to spoil the Slain,
Pierc'd through the Paunch, I tumbled on the Plain.
Then *Chthonyus*, and *Teleboas* I slew:
A Fork the former arm'd; a Dart his Fellow threw.
The Javelin wounded me; (behold the Skar.)   595

581 where] where, *F*   583 draw,] draw; *F*

Then was my time to seek the *Trojan* War;
Then I was *Hector*'s Match in open Field;
But he was then unborn; at least a Child:
Now, I am nothing. I forbear to tell
By *Periphantas* how *Pyretus* fell,   600
The Centaur by the Knight: Nor will I stay
On *Amphyx*, or what Deaths he dealt that Day:
What Honour, with a pointless Lance he won,
Stuck in the front of a four-footed Man.
What Fame young *Macareus* obtain'd in Fight: 605
Or dwell on *Nessus*, now return'd from Flight.
How Prophet *Mopsus*, not alone devin'd,
Whose Valour equall'd his foreseeing Mind.
    Already *Cæneus*, with his conquering Hand,
Had slaughter'd five the boldest of their Band.   610
Pyrachmus, *Helymus*, *Antimachus*,
Bromus the Brave, and stronger *Stiphelus*,
Their Names I number'd, and remember well,
No Trace remaining, by what Wounds they fell.
    Latreus, the bulkiest of the double Race,   615
Whom the spoil'd Arms of slain *Halesus* grace,
In Years retaining still his Youthful Might,
Though his black Hairs were interspers'd with White,
Betwixt th' imbattled Ranks, began to prance,
Proud of his Helm, and *Macedonian* Lance;   620
And rode the Ring around; that either Hoast
Might hear him, while he made this empty Boast.
And from a Strumpet shall we suffer Shame,
For *Cænis* still, not *Cæneus* is thy Name:
And still the Native Softness of thy Kind   625
Prevails; and leaves the Woman in thy Mind?
Remember what thou wert; what Price was paid
To change thy Sex: To make thee not a Maid;
And but a Man in shew: Go, Card and Spin;
And leave the Business of the War to Men.   630
    While thus the Boaster exercis'd his Pride
The fatal Spear of *Cæneus* reach'd his Side:
Just in the mixture of the Kinds it ran;
Betwixt the neather Beast, and upper Man:

600 fell,] fell. F   615 Race,] Race F   634 Beast] Breast F

The Monster mad with Rage, and stung with Smart,   635
His Lance directed at the Hero's Heart:
It strook: But bounded from his harden'd Breast,
Like Hail from Tiles, which the safe House invest.
Nor seem'd the Stroke with more effect to come,
Than a small Pebble falling on a Drum.   640
He next his Fauchion try'd, in closer Fight;
But the keen Fauchion, had no Pow'r to bite.
He thrust; the blunted Point return'd again:
Since downright Blows, he cry'd, and Thrusts are vain,
I'll prove his Side: In strong Embraces held   645
He prov'd his Side; his Side the Sword repell'd:
His hollow Belly eccho'd to the Stroke;
Untouch'd his Body, as a solid Rock;
Aim'd at his Neck at last, the Blade in Shivers broke.

   Th' Impassive Knight stood Idle, to deride   650
His Rage, and offer'd oft his naked Side:
At length, Now Monster, in thy turn he cry'd
Try thou the Strength of *Cæneus*: At the Word
He thrust; and in his Shoulder plung'd the Sword.
Then writh'd his Hand; and as he drove it down,   655
Deep in his Breast, made many Wounds in one.

   The Centaurs saw inrag'd, th' unhop'd Success;
And rushing on, in Crowds, together press;
At him, and him alone, their Darts they threw:
Repuls'd they from his fated Body flew.   660
Amaz'd they stood; till *Monychus* began,
O Shame, a Nation conquer'd by a Man!
A Woman-Man; yet more a Man is He,
Than all our Race; and what He was, are We.
Now, what avail our Nerves? The united Force,   665
Of two the strongest Creatures, Man and Horse:
Nor Goddess-born; nor of *Ixion*'s Seed
We seem; (a Lover built for *Juno*'s Bed;)
Master'd by this half Man. Whole Mountains throw
With Woods at once, and bury him below.   670
This only way remains. Nor need we doubt
To choak the Soul within; though not to force it out.
Heap Weights, instead of Wounds: He chanc'd to see
Where Southern Storms had rooted up a Tree;

This, rais'd from Earth, against the Foe he threw; 675
Th' Example shewn, his Fellow-Brutes pursue.
With Forest-loads the Warrior they invade;
Othrys and *Pelion* soon were void of Shade;
And spreading Groves were naked Mountains made.
Press'd with the Burden, *Cæneus* pants for Breath; 680
And on his Shoulders bears the Wooden Death.
To heave th' intolerable Weight he tries;
At length it rose above his Mouth and Eyes:
Yet still he heaves: And strugling with Despair,
Shakes all aside; and gains a gulp of Air: 685
A short Relief, which but prolongs his Pain;
He faints by Fits; and then respires again:
At last, the Burden only nods above,
As when an Earthquake stirs th' *Idæan* Grove.
Doubtful his Death: He suffocated seem'd, 690
To most; but otherwise our *Mopsus* deem'd.
Who said he saw a yellow Bird arise
From out the Pile, and cleave the liquid Skies:
I saw it too: With golden Feathers bright;
Nor e're before, beheld so strange a Sight. 695
Whom *Mopsus* viewing, as it soar'd around
Our Troop, and heard the Pinions rattling Sound,
All hail he cry'd, thy Countries Grace and Love;
Once first of Men below; now first of Birds above.
Its Author to the Story gave Belief: 700
For us, our Courage was increas'd by Grief:
Asham'd to see a single Man, pursu'd
With Odds, to sink beneath a Multitude:
We push'd the Foe; and forc'd to shameful Flight;
Part fell; and part escap'd by favour of the Night. 705
   This Tale by *Nestor* told, did much displease
Tlepolemus, the Seed of *Hercules*:
For, often he had heard his Father say,
That he himself was present at the Fray;
And more than shar'd the Glories of the Day. 710
   Old Chronicle, he said, among the rest,
You might have nam'd *Alcides* at the least:
Is he not worth your Praise? The *Pylian* Prince

681 Wooden] Wooden, *F*

Sigh'd e'er he spoke; then made this proud Defence.
My former Woes in long Oblivion drown'd, 715
I wou'd have lost; but you renew the Wound:
Better to pass him o'er, than to relate
The Cause I have your mighty Sire to hate.
His Fame has fill'd the World, and reach'd the Sky;
(Which, Oh, I wish with Truth, I cou'd deny!) 720
We praise not *Hector*; though his Name, we know
Is great in Arms; 'tis hard to praise a Foe.

He, your Great Father, levell'd to the Ground
Messenia's Tow'rs: Nor better Fortune found
Elis, and *Pylos*; that a neighb'ring State 725
And this my own: Both guiltless of their Fate.

To pass the rest, twelve wanting one, he slew;
My Brethren, who their Birth from *Neleus* drew.
All Youths of early Promise, had they liv'd;
By him they perish'd: I alone surviv'd. 730
The rest were easy Conquest: But the Fate
Of *Periclymenos*, is wondrous to relate.
To him, our common Grandsire of the Main
Had giv'n to change his Form; and chang'd, resume again.
Vary'd at Pleasure, every Shape he try'd; 735
And in all Beasts *Alcides* still defy'd:
Vanquish'd on Earth, at length he soar'd above;
Chang'd to the Bird, that bears the Bolt of *Jove*.
The new-dissembled Eagle, now endu'd
With Beak and Pounces, *Hercules* pursu'd: 740
And cuff'd his manly Cheeks, and tore his Face;
Then, safe retir'd, and tour'd in empty space.
Alcides bore not long his flying Foe;
But bending his inevitable Bow,
Reach'd him in Air, suspended as he stood; 745
And in his Pinion fix'd the feather'd Wood.
Light was the Wound; but in the Sinew hung
The Point; and his disabled Wing unstrung.
He wheel'd in Air, and stretch'd his Vans in vain;
His Vans no longer cou'd his Flight sustain: 750
For while one gather'd Wind, one unsupply'd
Hung drooping down; nor pois'd his other Side.

733 Main] Main, F   747 hung] hung, F

He fell: The Shaft that slightly was impress'd,
Now from his heavy Fall with weight increas'd,
Drove through his Neck, aslant; he spurns the Ground; 755
And the Soul issues through the Weazon's Wound.
 Now, brave Commander of the *Rhodian* Seas,
What Praise is due from me, to *Hercules*?
Silence is all the Vengeance I decree
For my slain Brothers; but 'tis Peace with thee. 760
 Thus with a flowing Tongue old *Nestor* spoke:
Then, to full Bowls each other they provoke:
At length, with Weariness, and Wine oppress'd,
They rise from Table; and withdraw to Rest.
 The Sire of *Cygnus*, Monarch of the Main, } 765
Mean time, laments his Son, in Battle slain:
And vows the Victor's Death; nor vows in vain. }
For nine long Years the smoother'd Pain he bore;
(*Achilles* was not ripe for Fate, before:)
Then when he saw the promis'd Hour was near, 770
He thus bespoke the God, that guides the Year.
Immortal Offspring of my Brother *Jove*;
My brightest Nephew, and whom best I love,
Whose Hands were join'd with mine, to raise the Wall
Of tottring *Troy*, now nodding to her fall, 775
Dost thou not mourn our Pow'r employ'd in vain;
And the Defenders of our City slain?
To pass the rest, cou'd noble *Hector* lie
Unpity'd, drag'd around his Native *Troy*?
And yet the Murd'rer lives: Himself by far 780
A greater Plague, than all the wastful War:
He lives; the proud *Pelides* lives to boast
Our Town destroy'd, our common Labour lost!
O, cou'd I meet him! But I wish too late:
To prove my Trident is not in his Fate! 785
But let him try (for that's allow'd) thy Dart,
And pierce his only penetrable Part.
 Apollo bows to the superiour Throne;
And to his Uncle's Anger, adds his own.
Then in a Cloud involv'd, he takes his Flight, 790
Where *Greeks* and *Trojans* mix'd in mortal Fight;

And found out *Paris*, lurking where he stood,
And stain'd his Arrows with *Plebeyan* Blood:
Phœbus to him alone the God confess'd,
Then to the recreant Knight, he thus address'd.   795
Dost thou not blush, to spend thy Shafts in vain
On a degenerate, and ignoble Train?
If Fame, or better Vengeance be thy Care,
There aim: And with one Arrow, end the War.
    He said; and shew'd from far the blazing Shield   800
And Sword, which but *Achilles* none cou'd weild;
And how he mov'd a God, and mow'd the standing Field.
The Deity himself directs aright
Th' invenom'd Shaft; and wings the fatal Flight.
    Thus fell the foremost of the *Grecian* Name;   805
And He, the base Adult'rer, boasts the Fame.
A Spectacle to glad the *Trojan* Train;
And please old *Priam*, after *Hector* slain.
If by a Female Hand he had foreseen
He was to die, his Wish had rather been   810
The Lance and double Axe of the fair Warriour Queen.
    And now the Terror of the *Trojan* Field,
The *Grecian* Honour, Ornament, and Shield,
High on a Pile, th' Unconquer'd Chief is plac'd,
The God that arm'd him first, consum'd at last.   815
Of all the Mighty Man, the small Remains
A little Urn, and scarcely fill'd, contains.
Yet great in *Homer*, still *Achilles* lives;
And equal to himself, himself survives.
    His Buckler owns its former Lord; and brings   820
New cause of Strife, betwixt contending Kings;
Who Worthiest after him, his Sword to weild,
Or wear his Armour, or sustain his Shield.
Ev'n *Diomede* sate Mute, with down-cast Eyes;
Conscious of wanted Worth to win the Prize: 825
Nor *Menelas* presum'd these Arms to claim,
Nor He the King of Men, a greater Name.
Two Rivals only rose: *Laertes* Son,
And the vast Bulk of *Ajax Telamon*:
The King, who cherish'd each, with equal Love,   830

And, from himself all Envy wou'd remove,
Left both to be determin'd by the Laws;
And to the *Grecian* Chiefs, transferr'd the Cause.

THE SPEECHES OF AJAX AND ULYSSES
FROM Ovid's Metamorphoses Book XIII

THE Chiefs were set; the Soldiers crown'd the Field:
To these the Master of the sevenfold Shield,
Upstarted fierce: And kindled with Disdain
Eager to speak, unable to contain
His boiling Rage, he rowl'd his Eyes around   5
The Shore, and *Grecian* Gallies hall'd a-ground.
Then stretching out his Hands, O *Jove*, he cry'd,
Must then our Cause before the Fleet be try'd?
And dares *Ulysses* for the Prize contend,
In sight of what he durst not once defend?   10
But basely fled that memorable Day,
When I from *Hector*'s Hands redeem'd the flaming Prey.
So much 'tis safer at the noisy Bar
With Words to flourish than ingage in War.
By different Methods we maintain our Right,   15
Nor am I made to Talk, nor he to Fight.
In bloody Fields I labour to be great;
His Arms are a smooth Tongue; and soft Deceit:
Nor need I speak my Deeds, for those you see,
The Sun and Day are Witnesses for me.   20
Let him who fights unseen relate his own,
And vouch the silent Stars, and conscious Moon;
Great is the Prize demanded, I confess,
But such an abject Rival makes it less;
That Gift, those Honours, he but hop'd to gain   25
Can leave no room for *Ajax* to be vain:
Losing he wins, because his Name will be
Enobled by Defeat, who durst contend with me.
Were my known Valour question'd, yet my Blood
Without that Plea wou'd make my Title good: 30
My Sire was *Telamon* whose Arms, employ'd
With *Hercules*, these *Trojan* Walls destroy'd;

And who before with *Jason*, sent from *Greece*
In the first Ship brought home the Golden Fleece:
Great *Telamon* from *Æacus* derives   35
His Birth (th' Inquisitor of guilty lives
In Shades below where *Sysiphus* whose Son
This Thief is thought rouls up the restless heavy Stone.)
Just *Æacus* the King of Gods, above
Begot: Thus *Ajax* is the third from *Jove*.   40
Nor shou'd I seek advantage from my Line,
Unless (*Achilles*) it were mix'd with thine:
As next of Kin *Achilles* Arms I claim,
This Fellow wou'd ingraft a Foreign Name
Upon our Stock, and the *Sysiphian* Seed   45
By Fraud and Theft asserts his Father's Breed:
Then must I lose these Arms, because I came
To fight uncall'd, a voluntary Name,
Nor shun'd the Cause, but offer'd you my Aid,
While he long lurking was to War betray'd: 50
Forc'd to the Field he came, but in the Reer;
And feign'd Distraction to conceal his Fear:
Till one more cunning caught him in the Snare;
(Ill for himself) and drag'd him into War.
Now let a Hero's Arms a Coward vest,   55
And he who shun'd all Honours, gain the best:
And let me stand excluded from my Right
Rob'd of my Kinsman's Arms, who first appear'd in Fight.
Better for us at home had he remain'd
Had it been true, the Madness which he feign'd,   60
Or so believ'd; the less had been our Shame,
The less his counsell'd Crime which brands the *Grecian* Name;
Nor *Philoctetes* had been left inclos'd
In a bare Isle to Wants and Pains expos'd,
Where to the Rocks, with solitary Groans   65
His Suff'rings and our Baseness he bemoans;
And wishes (so may Heav'n his Wish fulfill)
The due Reward to him who caus'd his Ill.
Now he with us to *Troy*'s Destruction sworn
Our Brother of the War, by whom are born   70
Alcides Arrows, pent in narrow Bounds

The Speeches of Ajax and Ulysses. 44 Name] Name, F

With Cold and Hunger pinch'd, and pain'd with Wounds,
To find him Food and Cloathing must employ
Against the Birds the Shafts due to the Fate of *Troy*.
Yet still he lives, and lives from Treason free,   75
Because he left *Ulysses* Company:
Poor *Palamede* might wish, so void of Aid,
Rather to have been left, than so to Death betray'd:
The Coward bore the Man immortal Spight,
Who sham'd him out of Madness into Fight: 80
Nor daring otherwise to vent his Hate
Accus'd him first of Treason to the State;
And then for proof produc'd the golden Store,
Himself had hidden in his Tent before:
Thus of two Champions he depriv'd our Hoast,   85
By Exile one, and one by Treason lost.
Thus fights *Ulysses*, thus his Fame extends,
A formidable Man, but to his Friends:
Great, for what Greatness is in Words and Sound,
Ev'n faithful *Nestor* less in both is found: 90
But that he might without a Rival reign,
He left this faithful *Nestor* on the Plain;
Forsook his Friend ev'n at his utmost Need,
Who tir'd, and tardy with his wounded Steed
Cry'd out for Aid, and call'd him by his Name;   95
But Cowardice has neither Ears nor Shame:
Thus fled the good old Man, bereft of Aid,
And for as much as lay in him, betray'd:
That this is not a Fable forg'd by me,
Like one of his, an *Ulyssean* Lie,   100
I vouch ev'n *Diomede*, who tho' his Friend
Cannot that Act excuse, much less defend:
He call'd him back aloud, and tax'd his Fear;
And sure enough he heard, but durst not hear.
     The Gods with equal Eyes on Mortals look,   10
He justly was forsaken, who forsook:
Wanted that Succour he refused to lend,
Found ev'ry Fellow such another Friend:
No wonder, if he roar'd that all might hear;
His Elocution was increas'd by fear: 1

I heard, I ran, I found him out of Breath,
Pale, trembling, and half dead, with fear of Death.
Though he had judg'd himself by his own Laws,
And stood condemn'd, I help'd the common Cause:
With my broad Buckler hid him from the Foe;   115
(Ev'n the Shield trembled as he lay below;)
And from impending Fate the Coward freed:
Good Heav'n forgive me for so bad a Deed!
If still he will persist, and urge the Strife,
First let him give me back his forfeit Life: 120
Let him return to that opprobrious Field;
Again creep under my protecting Shield:
Let him lie wounded, let the Foe be near,
And let his quiv'ring Heart confess his Fear;
There put him in the very Jaws of Fate;   125
And let him plead his Cause in that Estate:
And yet when snatch'd from Death, when from below
My lifted Shield I loos'd, and let him go:
Good Heav'ns how light he rose, with what a bound
He sprung from Earth, forgetful of his Wound;   130
How fresh, how eager then his Feet to ply,
Who had not Strength to stand, had Speed to fly!
    Hector came on, and brought the Gods along;
Fear seiz'd alike the Feeble and the Strong:
Each *Greek* was an *Ulysses*; such a Dread   135
Th' approach, and ev'n the sound of *Hector* bred:
Him, flesh'd with Slaughter, and with Conquest crown'd,
I met, and over-turn'd him to the Ground;
When after, matchless as he deem'd, in Might,
He challeng'd all our Hoast to single Fight;   140
All Eyes were fix'd on me: The Lots were thrown;
But for your Champion I was wish'd alone:
Your Vows were heard, we Fought, and neither yield;
Yet I return'd unvanquish'd from the Field.
With *Jove* to friend th' insulting *Trojan* came,   145
And menac'd us with Force, our Fleet with Flame:
Was it the Strength of this Tongue-valiant Lord,
In that black Hour, that sav'd you from the Sword?
Or was my Breast expos'd alone, to brave
A thousand Swords, a thousand Ships to save?   150

The hopes of your return! And can you yield,
For a sav'd Fleet, less than a single Shield?
Think it no Boast, O *Grecians*, if I deem
These Arms want *Ajax*, more than *Ajax* them;
Or, I with them an equal Honour share;   155
They honour'd to be worn, and I to wear.
Will he compare my Courage with his Slight?
As well he may compare the Day with Night.
Night is indeed the Province of his Reign:
Yet all his dark Exploits no more contain   160
Than a Spy taken, and a Sleeper slain,
A Priest made Pris'ner, *Pallas* made a Prey,
But none of all these Actions done by Day:
Nor ought of these was done, and *Diomed* away.
If on such petty Merits you confer   165
So vast a Prize, let each his Portion share;
Make a just Dividend; and if not all,
The greater part to *Diomed* will fall.
But why, for *Ithacus* such Arms as those,
Who naked and by Night invades his Foes?   170
The glitt'ring Helm by Moonlight will proclaim
The latent Robber, and prevent his Game:
Nor cou'd he hold his tott'ring Head upright
Beneath that Motion, or sustain the Weight;
Nor that right Arm cou'd toss the beamy Lance;   175
Much less the left that ampler Shield advance;
Pond'rous with precious Weight, and rough with Cost
Of the round World in rising Gold emboss'd.
That Orb would ill become his Hand to wield,
And look as for the Gold he stole the Shield;   180
Which, shou'd your error on the Wretch bestow,
It would not frighten, but allure the Foe:
Why asks he, what avails him not in Fight,
And wou'd but cumber and retard his Flight,
In which his only Excellence is plac'd?   185
You give him Death, that intercept his hast.
Add, that his own is yet a Maiden-Shield,
Nor the least Dint has suffer'd in the Field,
Guiltless of Fight: Mine batter'd, hew'd, and bor'd,

161 slain,] slain. F   185 plac'd?] plac'd, F   186 hast.] hast? F

Worn out of Service, must forsake his Lord.   190
What farther need of Words our Right to scan?
My Arguments are Deeds, let Action speak the Man.
Since from a Champion's Arms the Strife arose,
So cast the glorious Prize amid the Foes:
Then send us to redeem both Arms and Shield,   195
And let him wear who wins 'em in the Field.
   He said: A Murmur from the Multitude,
Or somewhat like a stiffled Shout ensu'd!
Till from his Seat arose *Laertes* Son,
Look'd down awhile, and paus'd e'er he begun;   200
Then to th' expecting Audience rais'd his Look,
And not without prepar'd Attention spoke:
Soft was his Tone, and sober was his Face;
Action his Words, and Words his Action grace.
   If Heav'n, my Lords, had heard our common Pray'r,   205
These Arms had caus'd no Quarrel for an Heir;
Still great *Achilles* had his own possess'd,
And we with great *Achilles* had been bless'd;
But since hard Fate, and Heav'ns severe Decree
Have ravish'd him away from you and me,   210
(At this he sigh'd, and wip'd his Eyes, and drew
Or seem'd to draw some Drops of kindly Dew)
Who better can succeed *Achilles* lost,
Than He who gave *Achilles* to your Hoast?
This only I request, that neither He   215
May gain, by being what he seems to be,
A stupid Thing, nor I may lose the Prize,
By having Sense, which Heav'n to him denies:
Since, great or small, the Talent I enjoy'd
Was ever in the common Cause employ'd: 220
Nor let my Wit, and wonted Eloquence
Which often has been us'd in your Defence
And in my own, this only time be brought
To bear against my self, and deem'd a Fault.
Make not a Crime, where Nature made it none;   225
For ev'ry Man may freely use his own.
The Deeds of long descended Ancestors
Are but by grace of Imputation ours,

     191 scan?] scan; *F*   192 Man.] Man? *F*

Theirs in effect; but since he draws his Line
From *Jove*, and seems to plead a Right Divine,   230
From *Jove*, like him, I claim my Pedigree;
And am descended in the same degree:
My Sire *Laertes* was *Arcesius* Heir,
Arcesius was the Son of *Jupiter*:
No Paricide, no banish'd Man is known,   235
In all my Line: Let him excuse his own.
Hermes ennobles too, my Mother's Side,
By both my Parents to the Gods ally'd;
But not because that on the Female Part
My Blood is better, dare I claim Desert,   240
Or that my Sire from Paricide is free;
But judge by Merit betwixt Him and Me:
The Prize be to the best; provided yet,
That *Ajax* for a while his Kin forget;
And his great Sire, and greater Uncles, Name,   245
To fortify by them his feeble Claim:
Be Kindred and Relation laid aside,
And Honours Cause by Laws of Honour try'd:
For if he plead Proximity of Blood;
That empty Title is with Ease withstood.   250
Peleus, the Hero's Sire, more nigh than he,
And *Pyrrhus*, his undoubted Progeny,
Inherit first these Trophies of the Field;
To *Scyros*, or to *Phthya*, send the Shield:
And *Teucer* has an Uncle's Right; yet he   255
Waves his Pretensions, nor contends with me.
    Then since the Cause on pure Desert is plac'd,
Whence shall I take my rise, what reckon last?
I not presume on ev'ry Act to dwell,
But take these few, in order as they fell.   260
    Thetis, who knew the Fates, apply'd her Care
To keep *Achilles* in disguise from War;
And till the threat'ning Influence were past,
A Woman's Habit on the Hero cast:
All Eyes were couzen'd by the borrow'd Vest,   265
And *Ajax* (never wiser than the rest)
Found no *Pelides* there: At length I came

251 he,] he F   254 *Phthya*] *Pthya* F

With proffer'd Wares to this pretended Dame;
She not discover'd by her Mien or Voice,
Betray'd her Manhood by her manly Choice;   270
And while on Female Toys her Fellows look,
Grasp'd in her Warlike Hand, a Javelin shook,
Whom by this Act reveal'd I thus bespoke:
O Goddess born! resist not Heav'ns Decree,
The fall of *Ilium*, is reserv'd for Thee;   275
Then seiz'd him, and produc'd in open Light,
Sent blushing to the Field the fatal Knight.
Mine then are all his Actions of the War,
Great *Telephus* was conquer'd by my Spear
And after cur'd: To me the *Thebans* owe,   280
Lesbos, and *Tenedos*, their overthrow;
Syros and *Cylla*! Not on all to dwell,
By me *Lyrnesus*, and strong *Chrysa* fell:
And since I sent the Man who *Hector* slew,
To me the noble *Hector*'s Death is due: 285
Those Arms I put into his living Hand,
Those Arms, *Pelides* dead, I now demand.
   When *Greece* was injur'd in the *Spartan* Prince,
And met at *Aulis* to revenge th' Offence,
'Twas a dead Calm, or adverse Blasts that reign'd,   290
And in the Port the Wind-bound Fleet detain'd:
Bad Signs were seen, and Oracles severe
Were daily thunder'd in our General's Ear;
That by his Daughter's Blood we must appease
Diana's kindled Wrath, and free the Seas.   295
Affection, Int'rest, Fame, his Heart assail'd;
But soon the Father o'er the King prevail'd:
Bold, on himself he took the pious Crime,
As angry with the Gods, as they with him.
No Subject cou'd sustain their Sov'raign's Look,   300
Till this hard Enterprize I undertook:
I only durst th' Imperial Pow'r controul,
And undermin'd the Parent in his Soul;
Forc'd him t' exert the King for common Good,
And pay our Ransom with his Daughters Blood.   305
Never was Cause more difficult to plead,

268 Dame;] Dame, F   284 slew,] slew: F

Than where the Judge against himself decreed:
Yet this I won by dint of Argument;
The Wrongs his injur'd Brother underwent;
And his own Office sham'd him to consent.   310
    'Twas harder yet to move the Mother's Mind,
And to this heavy Task was I design'd:
Reasons against her Love I knew were vain;
I circumvented whom I could not gain:
Had *Ajax* been employ'd, our slacken'd Sails   315
Had still at *Aulis* waited happy Gales.
    Arriv'd at *Troy*, your choice was fix'd on me
A fearless Envoy, fit for a bold Embassy:
Secure, I enter'd through the hostile Court,
Glitt'ring with Steel, and crowded with Resort: 320
There, in the midst of Arms, I plead our Cause,
Urge the foul Rape, and violated Laws;
Accuse the Foes, as Authors of the Strife,
Reproach the Ravisher, demand the Wife.
Priam, *Antenor*, and the wiser few   325
I mov'd; but *Paris* and his lawless Crew
Scarce held their Hands, and lifted Swords: But stood
In Act to quench their impious Thirst of Blood:
This *Menelaus* knows; expos'd to share
With me the rough Preludium of the War.   330
    Endless it were to tell what I have done,
In Arms, or Council, since the Siege begun:
The first Encounters past, the Foe repell'd,
They skulk'd within the Town, we kept the Field.
War seem'd asleep for nine long Years; at length   335
Both Sides resolv'd to push, we try'd our Strength.
Now what did *Ajax* while our Arms took Breath,
Vers'd only in the gross mechanick Trade of Death?
If you require my Deeds, with ambush'd Arms
I trap'd the Foe, or tir'd with false Alarms;   340
Secur'd the Ships, drew Lines along the Plain,
The Fainting chear'd, chastis'd the Rebel-train,
Provided Forage, our spent Arms renew'd,
Employ'd at home, or sent abroad, the common Cause pursu'd.
    The King, deluded in a Dream by *Jove*,   345

333 Encounters] Encounter's *F*   335 Years;] Years, *F*

Despair'd to take the Town, and order'd to remove.
What Subject durst arraign the Pow'r supreme,
Producing *Jove* to justify his Dream?
Ajax might wish the Soldiers to retain
From shameful Flight, but Wishes were in vain: 350
As wanting of effect had been his Words,
Such as of course his thundring Tongue affords.
But did this Boaster threaten, did he pray,
Or by his own Example urge their stay?
None, none of these, but ran himself away.   355
I saw him run, and was asham'd to see;
Who ply'd his Feet so fast to get aboard as He?
Then speeding through the Place, I made a stand,
And loudly cry'd, O base, degenerate Band,
To leave a Town already in your Hand!   360
After so long expence of Blood, for Fame,
To bring home nothing but perpetual Shame!
These Words, or what I have forgotten since,
(For Grief inspir'd me then with Eloquence)
Reduc'd their Minds; they leave the crowded Port,   365
And to their late forsaken Camp resort:
Dismay'd the Council met: This Man was there,
But mute, and not recover'd of his Fear.
Thersites tax'd the King, and loudly rail'd,
But his wide opening Mouth with Blows I seal'd.   370
Then rising I excite their Souls to Fame,
And kindle sleeping Virtue into Flame.
From thence, whatever he perform'd in Fight
Is justly mine, who drew him back from Flight.
   Which of the *Grecian* Chiefs consorts with Thee?   375
But *Diomede*, desires my Company,
And still communicates his Praise with me.
As guided by a God, secure he goes,
Arm'd with my Fellowship amid the Foes;
And sure no little Merit I may boast,   380
Whom such a Man selects from such an Hoast;
Unforc'd by Lots I went without affright,
To dare with him the Dangers of the Night:
On the same Errand sent, we met the Spy,

Of *Hector*, double-tongu'd, and us'd to lie;   385
Him I dispatch'd, but not till undermin'd,
I drew him first to tell what treacherous *Troy* design'd:
My Task perform'd, with Praise I had retir'd,
But not content with this, to greater Praise aspir'd.
Invaded *Rhœsus*, and his *Thracian* Crew,   390
And him, and his, in their own Strength I slew:
Return'd a Victor all my Vows compleat,
With the King's Chariot, in his Royal Seat:
Refuse me now his Arms, whose fiery Steeds
Were promis'd to the Spy for his Nocturnal Deeds: 395
And let dull *Ajax* bear away my Right,
When all his Days out-ballance this one Night.
   Nor fought I Darkling still: The Sun beheld
With slaughter'd *Lycians* when I strew'd the Field:
You saw, and counted as I pass'd along,   400
Alastor, *Cromyus*, *Ceranos* the Strong,
Alcander, *Prytanis*, and *Halius*,
Noemon, *Charopes*, and *Ennomus*;
Choon, *Chersidamas*; and five beside
Men of obscure Descent, but Courage try'd: 405
All these this Hand laid breathless on the Ground;
Nor want I Proofs of many a manly Wound:
All honest, all before: Believe not me,
Words may deceive, but credit what you see.
   At this he bar'd his Breast, and show'd his Scars,   410
As of a furrow'd Field, well plough'd with Wars;
Nor is this Part unexercis'd, said he;
That Gyant-bulk of his from Wounds is free:
Safe in his Shield he fears no Foe to try,
And better manages his Blood than I: 415
But this avails me not; our Boaster strove
Not with our Foes alone, but partial *Jove*,
To save the Fleet: This I confess is true,
(Nor will I take from any Man his due:)
But thus assuming all, he robs from you.   420
Some part of Honour to your share will fall,
He did the best indeed, but did not all.
Patroclus in *Achilles* Arms, and thought
The Chief he seem'd, with equal Ardour fought;

Preserv'd the Fleet, repell'd the raging Fire,   425
And forc'd the fearful *Trojans* to retire.

But *Ajax* boasts, that he was only thought
A Match for *Hector*, who the Combat sought:
Sure he forgets the King, the Chiefs, and Me:
All were as eager for the Fight as He: 430
He but the ninth, and not by publick Voice,
Or ours preferr'd, was only Fortunes choice:
They fought; nor can our Hero boast the Event,
For *Hector* from the Field, unwounded went.

Why am I forc'd to name that fatal Day,   435
That snatch'd the Prop and Pride of *Greece* away?
I saw *Pelides* sink, with pious Grief,
And ran in vain, alas, to his Relief;
For the brave Soul was fled: Full of my Friend
I rush'd amid the War his Relicks to defend: 440
Nor ceas'd my Toil till I redeem'd the Prey,
And loaded with *Achilles*, march'd away:
Those Arms, which on these Shoulders then I bore,
'Tis just you to these Shoulders should restore.
You see I want not Nerves, who cou'd sustain   445
The pond'rous Ruins of so great a Man:
Or if in others equal Force you find,
None is endu'd with a more grateful Mind.

Did *Thetis* then, ambitious in her Care,
These Arms thus labour'd for her Son prepare;   450
That *Ajax* after him the heav'nly Gift shou'd wear.
For that dull Soul to stare with stupid Eyes,
On the learn'd unintelligible Prize!
What are to him the Sculptures of the Shield,
Heav'ns Planets, Earth, and Oceans watry Field?   455
The *Pleiads*, *Hyads*; less, and greater Bear,
Undipp'd in Seas; *Orion*'s angry Star;
Two diff'ring Cities, grav'd on either Hand;
Would he wear Arms he cannot understand?

Beside, what wise Objections he prepares   460
Against my late accession to the Wars?
Does not the Fool perceive his Argument
Is with more force against *Achilles* bent?

437 sink, with] sink: With *F*   457 Star;] Star, *F*

For if Dissembling be so great a Crime,
The Fault is common, and the same in him: 46
And if he taxes both of long delay,
My Guilt is less who sooner came away.
His pious Mother anxious for his Life,
Detain'd her Son, and me, my pious Wife.
To them the Blossoms of our Youth were due,   47
Our riper Manhood we reserv'd for you.
But grant me guilty, 'tis not much my care,
When with so great a Man my Guilt I share:
My Wit to War the matchless Hero brought,
But by this Fool I never had been caught.   47

   Nor need I wonder, that on me he threw
Such foul Aspersions, when he spares not you:
If *Palamede* unjustly fell by me,
Your Honour suffer'd in th' unjust Decree:
I but accus'd, you doom'd: And yet he dy'd,   48
Convinc'd of Treason, and was fairly try'd:
You heard not he was false; your Eyes beheld
The Traytor manifest; the Bribe reveal'd.

   That *Philoctetes* is on *Lemnos* left
Wounded, forlorn, of human Aid bereft,   48
Is not my Crime, or not my Crime alone,
Defend your Justice, for the Fact's your own:
'Tis true, th' Advice was mine; that staying there
He might his weary Limbs with rest repair,
From a long Voyage free, and from a longer War.   49
He took the Counsel, and he lives at least;
Th' event declares I counsell'd for the best:
Though Faith is all, in Ministers of State;
For who can promise to be fortunate?
Now since his Arrows are the Fate of *Troy*,   4
Do not my Wit, or weak Address employ;
Send *Ajax* there, with his persuasive Sense
To mollify the Man, and draw him thence:
But *Xanthus* shall run backward; *Ida* stand
A leafless Mountain; and the *Grecian* Band   5
Shall fight for *Troy*; if when my Counsel fail,
The Wit of heavy *Ajax* can prevail.

   Hard *Philoctetes*, exercise thy Spleen,

Against thy Fellows, and the King of Men;
Curse my devoted Head, above the rest,   505
And wish in Arms to meet me Breast to Breast:
Yet I the dang'rous Task will undertake
And either die my self, or bring thee back.
   Nor doubt the same Success, as when before
The *Phrygian* Prophet to these Tents I bore,   510
Surpriz'd by Night, and forc'd him to declare
In what was plac'd the fortune of the War,
Heav'ns dark Decrees, and Answers to display,
And how to take the Town, and where the Secret lay:
Yet this I compass'd, and from *Troy* convey'd   515
The fatal Image of their Guardian-Maid;
That Work was mine; for *Pallas*, though our Friend,
Yet while she was in *Troy* did *Troy* defend.
Now what has *Ajax* done, or what design'd,
A noisy Nothing, and an empty Wind?   520
If he be what he promises in Show,
Why was I sent, and why fear'd he to go?
Our boasting Champion thought the Task not light
To pass the Guards, commit himself to Night;
Not only through a hostile Town to pass,   525
But scale, with steep ascent, the sacred Place;
With wand'ring Steps to search the Cittadel,
And from the Priests their Patroness to steal:
Then through surrounding Foes to force my way,
And bear in Triumph home the heav'nly Prey;   530
Which had I not: *Ajax* in vain had held,
Before that monst'rous Bulk, his sev'nfold Shield.
That Night to conquer *Troy* I might be said,
When *Troy* was liable to Conquest made.
   Why point'st thou to my Partner of the War?   535
Tydides had indeed a worthy share
In all my Toil, and Praise; but when thy Might
Our Ships protected, did'st thou singly fight?
All join'd, and thou of many wert but one;
I ask'd no Friend, nor had, but him alone: 540
Who, had he not been well assur'd, that Art
And Conduct were of War the better part,
And more avail'd than Strength, my valiant Friend

Had urg'd a better Right, than *Ajax* can pretend:
As good at least *Euripylus* may claim,   545
And the more moderate *Ajax* of the Name:
The *Cretan* King, and his brave Charioteer,
And *Menelaus* bold with Sword and Spear:
All these had been my Rivals in the Shield,
And yet all these to my Pretensions yield.   550
Thy boist'rous Hands are then of use, when I
With this directing Head those Hands apply.
Brawn without Brain is thine: My prudent Care
Foresees, provides, administers the War:
Thy Province is to Fight; but when shall be   555
The time to Fight, the King consults with me:
No dram of Judgment with thy Force is join'd,
Thy Body is of Profit, and my Mind.
But how much more the Ship her Safety owes
To him who steers, than him that only rows,   560
By how much more the Captain merits Praise
Than he who Fights, and Fighting but obeys;
By so much greater is my Worth than thine,
Who can'st but execute what I design.
What gain'st thou brutal Man, if I confess   565
Thy Strength superiour when thy Wit is less?
Mind is the Man: I claim my whole Desert,
From the Mind's Vigour, and th' immortal part.
    But you, O *Grecian* Chiefs, reward my Care,
Be grateful to your Watchman of the War: 570
For all my Labours in so long a space,
Sure I may plead a Title to your Grace:
Enter the Town; I then unbarr'd the Gates,
When I remov'd their tutelary Fates.
By all our common hopes, if hopes they be   575
Which I have now reduc'd to Certainty;
By falling *Troy*, by yonder tott'ring Tow'rs,
And by their taken Gods, which now are ours;
Or if there yet a farther Task remains,
To be perform'd by Prudence or by Pains;   580
If yet some desperate Action rests behind
That asks high Conduct, and a dauntless Mind;
If ought be wanting to the *Trojan* Doom

Which none but I can manage and o'ercome,
Award, those Arms I ask, by your Decree: 585
Or give to this what you refuse to me.
   He ceas'd: And ceasing with Respect he bow'd,
And with his Hand at once the fatal Statue show'd.
Heav'n, Air and Ocean rung, with loud Applause,
And by the general Vote he gain'd his Cause.   590
Thus Conduct won the Prize, when Courage fail'd,
And Eloquence o'er brutal Force prevail'd.

The Death of Ajax

   He who cou'd often, and alone withstand
The Foe, the Fire, and *Jove*'s own partial Hand,
Now cannot his unmaster'd Grief sustain,   595
But yields to Rage, to Madness, and Disdain;
Then snatching out his Fauchion, Thou, said He,
Art mine; *Ulysses* lays no claim to Thee.
O often try'd, and ever trusty Sword,
Now do thy last kind Office to thy Lord: 600
'Tis *Ajax*, who requests thy Aid, to show
None but himself, himself cou'd overthrow:
He said, and with so good a Will to die
Did to his Breast the fatal Point apply,
It found his Heart, a way till then unknown,   605
Where never Weapon enter'd, but his own.
No Hands cou'd force it thence, so fix'd it stood
Till out it rush'd, expell'd by Streams of spouting Blood.
The fruitful Blood produc'd a Flow'r, which grew ⎫
On a green Stem; and of a Purple Hue: ⎬ 610
Like his, whom unaware *Apollo* slew: ⎭
Inscrib'd in both, the Letters are the same,
But those express the Grief, and these the Name.

THE WIFE OF BATH HER TALE

IN Days of Old when *Arthur* fill'd the Throne,
Whose Acts and Fame to Foreign Lands were blown;
The King of Elfs and little Fairy Queen
Gamboll'd on Heaths, and danc'd on ev'ry Green.

And where the jolly Troop had led the round
The Grass unbidden rose, and mark'd the Ground:
Nor darkling did they dance, the Silver Light
Of *Phœbe* serv'd to guide their Steps aright,
And, with their Tripping pleas'd, prolong'd the Night.
Her Beams they follow'd, where at full she plaid,
Nor longer than she shed her Horns they staid,
From thence with airy Flight to Foreign Lands convey'd.
Above the rest our *Britain* held they dear,
More solemnly they kept their Sabbaths here,
And made more spacious Rings, and revell'd half the Year.
   I speak of ancient Times, for now the Swain
Returning late may pass the Woods in vain,
And never hope to see the nightly Train:
In vain the Dairy now with Mints is dress'd,
The Dairy-Maid expects no Fairy Guest,
To skim the Bowls and after pay the Feast.
She sighs and shakes her empty Shoes in vain,
No Silver Penny to reward her Pain:
For Priests with Pray'rs, and other godly Geer,
Have made the merry Goblins disappear;
And where they plaid their merry Pranks before,
Have sprinkled Holy Water on the Floor:
And Fry'rs that through the wealthy Regions run
Thick as the Motes, that twinkle in the Sun;
Resort to Farmers rich, and bless their Halls
And exorcise the Beds, and cross the Walls:
This makes the Fairy Quires forsake the Place,
When once 'tis hallow'd with the Rites of Grace:
But in the Walks where wicked Elves have been,
The Learning of the Parish now is seen,
The Midnight Parson posting o'er the Green,
With Gown tuck'd up to Wakes; for *Sunday* next,
With humming Ale encouraging his Text;
Nor wants the holy Leer to Country-Girl betwixt.
From Fiends and Imps he sets the Village free,
There haunts not any Incubus, but He.
The Maids and Women need no Danger fear
To walk by Night, and Sanctity so near:

The Wife of Bath Her Tale. 36 Green,] Green. F

For by some Haycock or some shady Thorn
He bids his Beads both Even-song and Morn.   45
    It so befel in this King *Arthur*'s Reign,
A lusty Knight was pricking o'er the Plain;
A Batchelor he was, and of the courtly Train.
It happen'd as he rode, a Damsel gay
In Russet-Robes to Market took her way;   50
Soon on the Girl he cast an amorous Eye,
So strait she walk'd, and on her Pasterns high:
If seeing her behind he lik'd her Pace,
Now turning short he better lik'd her Face:
He lights in hast, and full of Youthful Fire,   55
By Force accomplish'd his obscene Desire:
This done away he rode, not unespy'd,
For swarming at his Back the Country cry'd;
And once in view they never lost the Sight,
But seiz'd, and pinion'd brought to court the Knight.   60
    Then Courts of Kings were held in high Renown,
E'er made the common Brothels of the Town:
There, Virgins honourable Vows receiv'd,
But chast as Maids in Monasteries liv'd:
The King himself to Nuptial Ties a Slave,   65
No bad Example to his Poets gave:
And they not bad, but in a vicious Age,
Had not to please the Prince debauch'd the Stage.
    Now what shou'd *Arthur* do? He lov'd the Knight,
But Soveraign Monarchs are the Source of Right: 70
Mov'd by the Damsels Tears and common Cry,
He doom'd the brutal Ravisher to die.
But fair *Geneura* rose in his Defence,
And pray'd so hard for Mercy from the Prince;
That to his Queen the King th' Offender gave,   75
And left it in her Pow'r to Kill or Save:
This gracious Act the Ladies all approve,
Who thought it much a Man should die for Love.
And with their Mistress join'd in close Debate,
(Covering their Kindness with dissembled Hate;)   80
If not to free him, to prolong his Fate.
At last agreed they call'd him by consent

Before the Queen and Female Parliament.
And the fair Speaker rising from her Chair,
Did thus the Judgment of the House declare.   8
    Sir Knight, tho' I have ask'd thy Life, yet still
Thy Destiny depends upon my Will:
Nor hast thou other Surety than the Grace
Not due to thee from our offended Race.
But as our Kind is of a softer Mold,   9
And cannot Blood without a Sigh behold,
I grant thee Life; reserving still the Pow'r
To take the Forfeit when I see my Hour:
Unless thy Answer to my next Demand
Shall set Thee free from our avenging Hand;   9
The Question, whose Solution I require,
Is *what the Sex of Women most desire?*
In this Dispute thy Judges are at Strife;
Beware; for on thy Wit depends thy Life.
Yet (lest surpriz'd, unknowing what to say
Thou damn thy self) we give thee farther Day:
A Year is thine to wander at thy Will;
And learn from others if thou want'st the Skill.
But, our Proffer not to hold in Scorn,
Good Sureties will we have for thy return;
That at the time prefix'd thou shalt obey,
And at thy Pledges Peril keep thy Day.
    Woe was the Knight at this severe Command!
But well he knew 'twas bootless to withstand:
The Terms accepted as the Fair ordain,
He put in Bail for his return again.
And promis'd Answer at the Day assign'd,
The best, with Heav'ns Assistance, he could find.
    His Leave thus taken, on his Way he went
With heavy Heart, and full of Discontent,
Misdoubting much, and fearful of th' Event.
'Twas hard the Truth of such a Point to find,
As was not yet agreed among the Kind.
Thus on he went; still anxious more and more,

97 Is] *Is F*   104 our Proffer not to hold *Ed. conj.*: not to hold our Proffer *F*: not to hold our Proffer turn'd *1713*: not to hold our proffer'd turn *Warton, Scott*: not to hold our proffer for *Christie*: not to hold our proffer'd boon *Noyes*: not to hold our Proffer as *Sargeaunt*. *See Commentary*

Ask'd all he met; and knock'd at ev'ry Door;   120
Enquir'd of Men; but made his chief Request
To learn from Women what they lov'd the best.
They answer'd each according to her Mind;
To please her self, not all the Female Kind.
One was for Wealth, another was for Place: 125
Crones old and ugly, wish'd a better Face.
The Widow's Wish was oftentimes to Wed;
The wanton Maids were all for Sport a Bed.
Some said the Sex were pleas'd with handsom Lies,
And some gross Flatt'ry lov'd without disguise: 130
Truth is, says one, he seldom fails to win
Who Flatters well, for that's our darling Sin.
But long Attendance, and a duteous Mind,
Will work ev'n with the wisest of the Kind.
One thought the Sexes prime Felicity   135
Was from the Bonds of Wedlock to be free:
Their Pleasures, Hours, and Actions all their own,
And uncontroll'd to give Account to none.
Some wish a Husband-Fool; but such are curst,
For Fools perverse, of Husbands are the worst: 140
All Women wou'd be counted Chast and Wise,
Nor should our Spouses see, but with our Eyes;
For Fools will prate; and tho' they want the Wit
To find close Faults, yet open Blots will hit:
Tho' better for their Ease to hold their Tongue,   145
For Womankind was never in the Wrong.
So Noise ensues, and Quarrels last for Life;
The Wife abhors the Fool, the Fool the Wife.
And some Men say that great Delight have we,
To be for Truth extoll'd, and Secrecy: 150
And constant in one Purpose still to dwell;
And not our Husband's Counsels to reveal.
But that's a Fable; for our Sex is frail,
Inventing rather than not tell a Tale.
Like leaky Sives no Secrets we can hold: 155
Witness the famous Tale that *Ovid* told.
   Midas the King, as in his Book appears,
By *Phœbus* was endow'd with Asses Ears,
Which under his long Locks, he well conceal'd,

(As Monarch's Vices must not be reveal'd)   160
For fear the People have 'em in the Wind,
Who long ago were neither Dumb nor Blind;
Nor apt to think from Heav'n their Title springs,
Since *Jove* and *Mars* left off begetting Kings.
This *Midas* knew; and durst communicate   165
To none but to his Wife, his Ears of State:
One must be trusted, and he thought her fit,
As passing prudent; and a parlous Wit.
To this sagacious Confessor he went,
And told her what a Gift the Gods had sent: 170
But told it under Matrimonial Seal,
With strict Injunction never to reveal.
The Secret heard she plighted him her Troth,
(And sacred sure is every Woman's Oath)
The royal Malady should rest unknown   175
Both for her Husband's Honour and her own:
But ne'ertheless she pin'd with Discontent;
The Counsel rumbled till it found a vent.
The Thing she knew she was oblig'd to hide;
By Int'rest and by Oath the Wife was ty'd;   180
But if she told it not the Woman dy'd.
Loath to betray a Husband and a Prince,
But she must burst, or blab; and no pretence
Of Honour ty'd her Tongue from Self-defence.
A marshy Ground commodiously was near,   185
Thither she ran, and held her Breath for fear,
Lest if a Word she spoke of any Thing,
That Word might be the Secret of the King.
Thus full of Counsel to the Fen she went,
Grip'd all the way, and longing for a vent: 190
Arriv'd, by pure Necessity compell'd,
On her majestick mary-bones she kneel'd:
Then to the Waters-brink she laid her Head,
And, as a Bittour bumps within a Reed,
To thee alone, O Lake, she said, I tell   195
(And as thy Queen command thee to conceal)
Beneath his Locks the King my Husband wears
A goodly Royal pair of Asses Ears:
Now I have eas'd my Bosom of the Pain

Till the next longing Fit return again!   200
   Thus through a Woman was the Secret known;
Tell us, and in effect you tell the Town:
But to my Tale: The Knight with heavy Cheer,
Wandring in vain had now consum'd the Year:
One Day was only left to solve the Doubt,   205
Yet knew no more than when he first set out.
But home he must: And as th' Award had been,
Yield up his Body Captive to the Queen.
In this despairing State he hap'd to ride
As Fortune led him, by a Forest-side: 210
Lonely the Vale, and full of Horror stood
Brown with the shade of a religious Wood:
When full before him at the Noon of night,
(The Moon was up and shot a gleamy Light)
He saw a Quire of Ladies in a round,   215
That featly footing seem'd to skim the Ground:
Thus dancing Hand in Hand, so light they were,
He knew not where they trod, on Earth or Air.
At speed he drove, and came a suddain Guest,
In hope where many Women were, at least,   220
Some one by chance might answer his Request.
But faster than his Horse the Ladies flew,
And in a trice were vanish'd out of view.
   One only Hag remain'd: But fowler far
Than Grandame Apes in *Indian* Forests are: 225
Against a wither'd Oak she lean'd her weight,
Prop'd on her trusty Staff, not half upright,
And drop'd an awkard Court'sy to the Knight.
Then said, What make you Sir so late abroad
Without a Guide, and this no beaten Road?   230
Or want you ought that here you hope to find,
Or travel for some Trouble in your Mind?
The last I guess; and, if I read aright,
Those of our Sex are bound to serve a Knight:
Perhaps good Counsel may your Grief asswage,   235
Then tell your Pain: For Wisdom is in Age.
   To this the Knight: Good Mother, wou'd you know
The secret Cause and Spring of all my Woe?

207 been,] been F

My Life must with to Morrow's Light expire,
Unless I tell, what Women most desire: 240
Now cou'd you help me at this hard Essay,
Or for your inborn Goodness, or for Pay:
Yours is my Life, redeem'd by your Advice,
Ask what you please, and I will pay the Price:
The proudest Kerchief of the Court shall rest   24
Well satisfy'd of what they love the best.
Plight me thy Faith, quoth she: That what I ask,
Thy Danger over, and perform'd the Task;
That shalt thou give for Hire of thy Demand,
Here take thy Oath; and seal it on my Hand;   250
I warrant thee on Peril of my Life,
Thy Words shall please both Widow, Maid and Wife.
      More Words there needed not to move the Knight
To take her Offer, and his Truth to plight.
With that she spread her Mantle on the Ground,   25
And first enquiring whether he was bound,
Bade him not fear, tho' long and rough the Way,
At Court he should arrive e'er break of Day:
His Horse should find the way without a Guide,
She said: With Fury they began to ride,   260
He on the midst, the Beldam at his Side.
The Horse, what Devil drove I cannot tell,
But only this, they sped their Journey well:
And all the way the Crone inform'd the Knight,
How he should answer the Demand aright.   260
      To Court they came: The News was quickly spread
Of his returning to redeem his Head.
The Female Senate was assembled soon,
With all the Mob of Women in the Town:
The Queen sate Lord Chief Justice of the Hall,   27
And bad the Cryer cite the Criminal.
The Knight appear'd; and Silence they proclaim,
Then first the *Culprit* answer'd to his Name:
And after Forms of Laws, was last requir'd
To name the Thing that Women most desir'd.   27
      Th' Offender, taught his Lesson by the way,
And by his Counsel order'd what to say,

247 ask,] ask F

Thus bold began; My Lady Liege, said he,
What all your Sex desire is *Soveraignty*.
The Wife affects her Husband to command,   280
All must be hers, both Mony, House, and Land.
The Maids are Mistresses ev'n in their Name;
And of their Servants full Dominion claim.
This, at the Peril of my Head, I say
A blunt plain Truth, the Sex aspires to sway,   } 285
You to rule all; while we, like Slaves, obey.

    There was not one or Widow, Maid, or Wife,
But said the Knight had well deserv'd his Life.
Ev'n fair *Geneura*, with a Blush confess'd,
The Man had found what Women love the best.   290

    Upstarts the Beldam, who was there unseen,
And Reverence made, accosted thus the Queen.
My Liege, said she, before the Court arise,
May I poor Wretch find Favour in your Eyes;
To grant my just Request: 'Twas I who taught   295
The Knight this Answer, and inspir'd his Thought.
None but a Woman could a Man direct
To tell us Women, what we most affect.
But first I swore him on his Knightly Troth,
(And here demand performance of his Oath)   300
To grant the Boon that next I should desire;
He gave his Faith, and I expect my Hire:
My Promise is fulfill'd: I sav'd his Life,
And claim his Debt to take me for his Wife.
The Knight was ask'd, nor cou'd his Oath deny,   305
But hop'd they would not force him to comply.
The Women, who would rather wrest the Laws,
Than let a Sister-Plantiff lose the Cause,
(As Judges on the Bench more gracious are,
And more attent to Brothers of the Bar)   310
Cry'd one, and all, the Suppliant should have Right,
And to the Grandame-Hag adjudg'd the Knight.

    In vain he sigh'd, and oft with Tears desir'd,
Some reasonable Sute, might be requir'd.
But still the Crone was constant to her Note;   315
The more he spoke, the more she stretch'd her Throat.

    294 Eyes;] Eyes: F

In vain he proffer'd all his Goods, to save
His Body, destin'd to that living Grave.
The liquorish Hag rejects the Pelf with scorn:
And nothing but the Man would serve her turn.   320
Not all the Wealth of Eastern Kings, said she,
Have Pow'r to part my plighted Love, and me:
And Old, and Ugly as I am, and Poor;
Yet never will I break the Faith I swore;
For mine thou art by Promise, during Life,   325
And I thy loving and obedient Wife.

   My Love! Nay rather my Damnation Thou,
Said he: Nor am I bound to keep my Vow:
The Fiend thy Sire has sent thee from below,
Else how cou'dst thou my secret Sorrows know?   330
Avaunt old Witch, for I renounce thy Bed:
The Queen may take the Forfeit of my Head,
E'er any of my Race so foul a Crone shall wed.

   Both heard, the Judge pronounc'd against the Knight;
So was he Marry'd in his own despight;   335
And all Day after hid him as an Owl,
Not able to sustain a Sight so foul.
Perhaps the Reader thinks I do him wrong
To pass the Marriage-Feast, and Nuptial Song:
Mirth there was none, the Man was *a-la-mort*:   340
And little Courage had to make his Court.
To Bed they went, the Bridegroom and the Bride:
Was never such an ill-pair'd Couple ty'd.
Restless he toss'd and tumbled to and fro,
And rowl'd, and wriggled further off; for Woe.   345
The good old Wife lay smiling by his Side,
And caught him in her quiv'ring Arms, and cry'd,
When you my ravish'd Predecessor saw,
You were not then become this Man of Straw;
Had you been such, you might have scap'd the Law.   350
Is this the Custom of King *Arthur*'s Court?
Are all Round-Table Knights of such a sort?
Remember I am she who sav'd your Life,
Your loving, lawful, and complying Wife:
Not thus you swore in your unhappy Hour,   355
Nor I for this return employ'd my Pow'r.

In time of Need I was your faithful Friend;
Nor did I since, nor ever will offend.
Believe me my lov'd Lord, 'tis much unkind;
What Fury has possess'd your alter'd Mind?   360
Thus on my Wedding-night—Without Pretence—
Come turn this way, or tell me my Offence.
If not your Wife, let Reasons Rule persuade,
Name but my Fault, amends shall soon be made.
    Amends! Nay that's impossible, said he,   365
What change of Age, or Ugliness can be!
Or, could *Medea*'s Magick mend thy Face,
Thou art descended from so mean a Race,
That never Knight was match'd with such Disgrace.
What wonder, Madam, if I move my Side,   370
When if I turn, I turn to such a Bride?
    And is this all that troubles you so sore!
    And what the Devil cou'dst thou wish me more?
Ah *Benedicite*, reply'd the Crone:
Then cause of just Complaining have you none.   375
The Remedy to this were soon apply'd,
Wou'd you be like the Bridegroom to the Bride.
But, for you say a long descended Race,
And Wealth, and Dignity, and Pow'r, and Place,
Make Gentlemen, and that your high Degree   380
Is much disparag'd to be match'd with me;
Know this, my Lord, Nobility of Blood
Is but a glitt'ring, and fallacious Good:
The Nobleman is he whose noble Mind
Is fill'd with inborn Worth, unborrow'd from his Kind.   385
The King of Heav'n was in a Manger laid;
And took his Earth but from an humble Maid:
Then what can Birth, or mortal Men bestow,
Since Floods no higher than their Fountains flow.
We who for Name, and empty Honour strive,   390
Our true Nobility from him derive.
Your Ancestors who puff your Mind with Pride,
And vast Estates to mighty Titles ty'd,
Did not your Honour, but their own advance,
For Virtue comes not by Inheritance.   395
If you tralineate from your Father's Mind,

What are you else but of a Bastard-kind?
Do, as your great Progenitors have done,
And by their Virtues prove your self their Son.
No Father can infuse, or Wit, or Grace,   400
A Mother comes across, and marrs the Race.
A Grandsire, or a Grandame taints the Blood;
And seldom three Descents continue Good.
Were Virtue by Descent, a noble Name
Cou'd never villanize his Father's Fame: 405
But as the first, the last of all the Line,
Wou'd like the Sun ev'n in Descending shine.
Take Fire; and bear it to the darkest House,
Betwixt King *Arthur*'s Court and *Caucasus*,
If you depart, the Flame shall still remain,   410
And the bright Blaze enlighten all the Plain:
Nor, till the Fewel perish, can decay,
By Nature form'd on Things combustible to prey.
Such is not Man, who mixing better Seed
With worse, begets a base, degenerate Breed: 415
The Bad corrupts the Good, and leaves behind
No trace of all the great Begetter's Mind.
The Father sinks within his Son, we see,
And often rises in the third Degree;
If better Luck, a better Mother give: 420
Chance gave us being, and by Chance we live.
Such as our Atoms were, ev'n such are we,
Or call it Chance, or strong Necessity.
Thus, loaded with dead weight, the Will is free.
And thus it needs must be: For Seed conjoin'd   425
Lets into Nature's Work th' imperfect Kind:
But Fire, th' enliv'ner of the general Frame
Is one, its Operation still the same.
Its Principle is in it self: While ours
Works as Confederates War, with mingled Pow'rs: 430
Or Man, or Woman, which soever fails:
And, oft, the Vigour of the Worse prevails.
Æther with Sulphur blended, alters hue,
And casts a dusky gleam of *Sodom* blue.
Thus in a Brute, their ancient Honour ends,   435

406 first,] first *F*   426 Lets] Let's *F*   430 Confederates] Confederate's *F*

And the fair Mermaid in a Fish descends:
The Line is gone; no longer Duke or Earl;
But by himself degraded turns a Churl.
Nobility of Blood is but Renown
Of thy great Fathers by their Virtue known,   440
And a long trail of Light, to thee descending down.
If in thy Smoke it ends: Their Glories shine;
But Infamy and Villanage are thine.
Then what I said before, is plainly show'd,
That true Nobility proceeds from God: 445
Not left us by Inheritance, but giv'n
By Bounty of our Stars, and Grace of Heav'n.
Thus from a Captive *Servius Tullus* rose,
Whom for his Virtues, the first *Romans* chose:
Fabritius from their Walls repell'd the Foe,   450
Whose noble Hands had exercis'd the Plough.
From hence, my Lord, and Love, I thus conclude,
That tho' my homely Ancestors, were rude,
Mean as I am, yet I may have the Grace,
To make you Father of a generous Race: 455
And Noble then am I, when I begin
In Virtue cloath'd, to cast the Rags of Sin:
If Poverty be my upbraided Crime,
And you believe in Heav'n; there was a time,
When He, the great Controller of our Fate   460
Deign'd to be Man; and liv'd in low Estate:
Which he who had the World at his dispose,
If Poverty were Vice, wou'd never choose.
Philosophers have said, and Poets sing,
That a glad Poverty's an honest Thing.   465
Content is Wealth, the Riches of the Mind;
And happy He who can that Treasure find.
But the base Miser starves amidst his Store,
Broods on his Gold, and griping still at more
Sits sadly pining, and believes he's Poor.   470
The ragged Beggar, tho' he wants Relief,
Has not to lose, and sings before the Thief.
Want is a bitter, and a hateful Good,
Because its Virtues are not understood:
Yet many Things impossible to Thought   475

Have been by Need to full Perfection brought:
The daring of the Soul proceeds from thence,
Sharpness of Wit, and active Diligence:
Prudence at once, and Fortitude it gives,
And if in patience taken mends our Lives;   480
For ev'n that Indigence that brings me low
Makes me my self; and Him above to know.
A Good which none would challenge, few would choose,
A fair Possession, which Mankind refuse.

   If we from Wealth to Poverty descend,   485
Want gives to know the Flatt'rer from the Friend.
If I am Old, and Ugly, well for you,
No leud Adult'rer will my Love pursue.
Nor Jealousy the Bane of marry'd Life,
Shall haunt you, for a wither'd homely Wife: 490
For Age, and Ugliness, as all agree,
Are the best Guards of Female Chastity.

   Yet since I see your Mind is Worldly bent,
I'll do my best to further your Content.
And therefore of two Gifts in my dispose,   495
Think e'er you speak, I grant you leave to choose:
Wou'd you I should be still Deform'd, and Old,
Nauseous to Touch, and Loathsome to Behold;
On this Condition, to remain for Life
A careful, tender and obedient Wife,   500
In all I can contribute to your Ease,
And not in Deed or Word, or Thought displease?
Or would you rather have me Young and Fair,
And take the Chance that happens to your share?
Temptations are in Beauty, and in Youth,   505
And how can you depend upon my Truth?
Now weigh the Danger, with the doubtful Bliss,
And thank your self, if ought should fall amiss.

   Sore sigh'd the Knight, who this long Sermon heard,
At length considering all, his Heart he chear'd: 510
And thus reply'd, My Lady, and my Wife,
To your wise Conduct I resign my Life:
Choose you for me, for well you understand
The future Good and Ill, on either Hand:
But if an humble Husband may request,   515

Provide, and order all Things for the best;
Your's be the Care to profit, and to please:
And let your Subject-Servant take his Ease.
   Then thus in Peace, quoth she, concludes the Strife,
Since I am turn'd the Husband, you the Wife: 520
The Matrimonial Victory is mine,
Which having fairly gain'd, I will resign;
Forgive, if I have said, or done amiss,
And seal the Bargain with a Friendly Kiss:
I promis'd you but one Content to share,   525
But now I will become both Good, and Fair.
No Nuptial Quarrel shall disturb your Ease,
The Business of my Life shall be to please:
And for my Beauty that, as Time shall try;
But draw the Curtain first, and cast your Eye.   530
   He look'd, and saw a Creature heav'nly Fair,
In bloom of Youth, and of a charming Air.
With Joy he turn'd, and seiz'd her Iv'ry Arm;
And like *Pygmalion* found the Statue warm.
Small Arguments there needed to prevail,   535
A Storm of Kisses pour'd as thick as Hail.
   Thus long in mutual Bliss they lay embrac'd,
And their first Love continu'd to the last:
One Sun-shine was their Life; no Cloud between;
Nor ever was a kinder Couple seen.   540
   And so may all our Lives like their's be led;
Heav'n send the Maids young Husbands, fresh in Bed:
May Widows Wed as often as they can,
And ever for the better change their Man.
And some devouring Plague pursue their Lives,   545
Who will not well be govern'd by their Wives.

OF THE PYTHAGOREAN PHILOSOPHY
From Ovid's Metamorphoses Book XV

The Fourteenth Book concludes with the Death and Deification of Romulus:
The Fifteenth begins with the Election of Numa *to the Crown of* Rome. *On
this Occasion,* Ovid *following the Opinion of some Authors, makes* Numa *the*

543 often as they] often they F

Schollar of Pythagoras; *and to have begun his Acquaintance with that*
Philosopher at Crotona, *a Town in* Italy; *from thence he makes a Digression* 5
to the Moral and Natural Philosophy of Pythagoras: *On both which our*
Author enlarges; and which are, the most learned and beautiful Parts of the
whole Metamorphoses.

A KING is sought to guide the growing State,
　One able to support the Publick Weight,
And fill the Throne where *Romulus* had sat.
Renown, which oft bespeaks the Publick Voice,
Had recommended *Numa* to their choice:　　　　　　　　5
A peaceful, pious Prince; who not content
To know the *Sabine* Rites, his Study bent
To cultivate his Mind: To learn the Laws
Of Nature, and explore their hidden Cause.
Urg'd by this Care, his Country he forsook,　　　　　　10
And to *Crotona* thence, his Journey took.
Arriv'd, he first enquir'd the Founder's Name,
Of this new Colony; and whence he came.
Then thus a Senior of the Place replies,
(Well read, and curious of Antiquities)　　　　　　　15
'Tis said; *Alcides* hither took his way,
From *Spain*, and drove along his conquer'd Prey;
Then leaving in the Fields his grazing Cows,
He sought himself some hospitable House:
Good *Croton* entertain'd his Godlike Guest;　　　　　20
While he repair'd his weary Limbs with rest.
The Hero, thence departing, bless'd the Place;
And here, he said, in Times revolving Race
A rising Town shall take his Name from thee;
Revolving Time fulfill'd the Prophecy:　　　　　　　25
For *Myscelos*, the justest Man on Earth,
Alemon's Son, at *Argos* had his Birth:
Him *Hercules*, arm'd with his Club of Oak
O'ershadow'd in a Dream, and thus bespoke;
Go, leave thy Native Soil, and make Abode　　　　　30
Where *Æsaris* rowls down his rapid Flood;
He said; and Sleep forsook him, and the God.
Trembling he wak'd, and rose with anxious Heart;
His Country Laws, forbad him to depart;

What shou'd he do? 'Twas Death to go away,   35
And the God menac'd if he dar'd to stay:
All Day he doubted, and when Night came on,
Sleep, and the same forewarning Dream begun:
Once more the God stood threatning o'er his Head;
With added Curses if he disobey'd.   40
Twice warn'd, he study'd Flight; but wou'd convey
At once his Person, and his Wealth away:
Thus while he linger'd, his Design was heard;
A speedy Process form'd, and Death declar'd.
Witness there needed none of his Offence,   45
Against himself the Wretch was Evidence:
Condemn'd, and destitute of human Aid,
To him, for whom he suffer'd, thus he pray'd.
    O Pow'r who hast deserv'd in Heav'n a Throne
Not giv'n, but by thy Labours made thy own,   50
Pity thy Suppliant, and protect his Cause,
Whom thou hast made obnoxious to the Laws.
    A Custom was of old, and still remains;
Which Life or Death by Suffrages ordains;
White Stones and Black within an Urn are cast,   55
The first absolve, but Fate is in the last.
The Judges to the common Urn bequeath
Their Votes, and drop the Sable Signs of Death;
The Box receives all Black, but pour'd from thence
The Stones came candid forth: The Hue of Innocence.   60
Thus *Alemonides* his Safety won,
Preserv'd from Death by *Alcumena*'s Son:
Then to his Kinsman-God his Vows he pays,
And cuts with prosp'rous Gales th' *Ionian* Seas:
He leaves *Tarentum* favour'd by the Wind,   65
And *Thurine* Bays, and *Temises* behind;
Soft *Sybaris*, and all the Capes that stand
Along the Shore, he makes in sight of Land;
Still doubling, and still coasting, till he found
The Mouth of *Æsaris*, and promis'd Ground,   70
Then saw where on the Margin of the Flood
The Tomb, that held the Bones of *Croton* stood:
Here, by the God's Command, he built and wall'd
The Place predicted; and *Crotona* call'd:

Thus Fame from time to time delivers down   75
The sure Tradition of th' *Italian* Town.
    Here dwelt the Man divine whom *Samos* bore,
But now Self-banish'd from his Native Shore,
Because he hated Tyrants, nor cou'd bear
The Chains which none but servile Souls will wear: 80
He, tho' from Heav'n remote, to Heav'n cou'd move,
With Strength of Mind, and tread th' Abyss above;
And penetrate with his interiour Light
Those upper Depths, which Nature hid from Sight:
And what he had observ'd, and learnt from thence,   85
Lov'd in familiar Language to dispence.
    The Crowd with silent Admiration stand
And heard him, as they heard their God's Command;
While he discours'd of Heav'ns mysterious Laws,
The World's Original, and Nature's Cause;   90
And what was God, and why the fleecy Snows
In silence fell, and rattling Winds arose;
What shook the stedfast Earth, and whence begun
The dance of Planets round the radiant Sun;
If Thunder was the Voice of angry *Jove*,   95
Or Clouds with Nitre pregnant burst above:
Of these, and Things beyond the common reach
He spoke, and charm'd his Audience with his Speech.
    He first the tast of Flesh from Tables drove,
And argu'd well, if Arguments cou'd move.   100
O Mortals! from your Fellow's Blood abstain,
Nor taint your Bodies with a Food profane:
While Corn and Pulse by Nature are bestow'd,
And planted Orchards bend their willing Load;
While labour'd Gardens wholsom Herbs produce,   105
And teeming Vines afford their generous Juice:
Nor tardier Fruits of cruder Kind are lost,
But tam'd with Fire, or mellow'd by the Frost:
While Kine to Pails distended Udders bring,
And Bees their Hony redolent of Spring: 110
While Earth not only can your Needs supply,
But lavish of her Store, provides for Luxury;
A guiltless Feast administers with Ease,
And without Blood is prodigal to please.

Wild Beasts their Maws with their slain Brethren fill;   115
And yet not all, for some refuse to kill:
Sheep, Goats, and Oxen, and the nobler Steed
On Browz and Corn, and flow'ry Meadows feed.
Bears, Tygers, Wolves, the Lion's angry Brood,
Whom Heav'n endu'd with Principles of Blood,   120
He wisely sundred from the rest, to yell
In Forests, and in lonely Caves to dwell,
Where stronger Beasts oppress the weak by Might,
And all in Prey, and Purple Feasts delight.
　　O impious use! to Nature's Laws oppos'd,   125
Where Bowels are in other Bowels clos'd:
Where fatten'd by their Fellow's Fat they thrive;
Maintain'd by Murder, and by Death they live.
'Tis then for nought that Mother Earth provides
The Stores of all she shows, and all she hides,   130
If Men with fleshy Morsels must be fed,
And chaw with bloody Teeth the breathing Bread:
What else is this but to devour our Guests,
And barb'rously renew *Cyclopean* Feasts!
We, by destroying Life, our Life sustain;   135
And gorge th' ungodly Maw with Meats obscene.
　　Not so the Golden Age, who fed on Fruit,
Nor durst with bloody Meals their Mouths pollute.
Then Birds in airy space might safely move,
And timerous Hares on Heaths securely rove: 140
Nor needed Fish the guileful Hooks to fear,
For all was peaceful; and that Peace sincere.
Whoever was the Wretch (and curs'd be He)
That envy'd first our Food's simplicity;
Th' essay of bloody Feasts on Brutes began,   145
And after forg'd the Sword to murther Man.
Had he the sharpen'd Steel alone employ'd,
On Beasts of Prey that other Beasts destroy'd,
Or Man invaded with their Fangs and Paws,
This had been justify'd by Nature's Laws,   150
And Self-defence: But who did Feasts begin
Of Flesh, he stretch'd Necessity to Sin.
To kill Man-killers, Man has lawful Pow'r,

Of the Pythagorean Philosophy. 145 Brutes] Bruits F

But not th' extended Licence, to devour.
   Ill Habits gather by unseen degrees, 15
As Brooks make Rivers, Rivers run to Seas.
The Sow, with her broad Snout for rooting up
Th' intrusted Seed, was judg'd to spoil the Crop,
And intercept the sweating Farmer's hope:
The cov'tous Churl of unforgiving kind, 16
Th' Offender to the bloody Priest resign'd:
Her Hunger was no Plea: For that she dy'd.
The Goat came next in order, to be try'd:
The Goat had cropt the tendrills of the Vine:
In vengeance Laity, and Clergy join, 16
Where one had lost his Profit, one his Wine.
Here was at least, some shadow of Offence:
The Sheep was sacrific'd on no pretence,
But meek, and unresisting Innocence.
A patient, useful Creature, born to bear 1
The warm and woolly Fleece, that cloath'd her Murderer,
And daily to give down the Milk she bred,
A Tribute for the Grass on which she fed.
Living, both Food and Rayment she supplies,
And is of least advantage when she dies. 1
   How did the toiling Oxe his Death deserve,
A downright simple Drudge, and born to serve?
O Tyrant! with what Justice can'st thou hope
The promise of the Year, a plenteous Crop;
When thou destroy'st thy lab'ring Steer, who till'd,
And plough'd with Pains, thy else ungrateful Field?
From his yet reeking Neck to draw the Yoke,
That Neck, with which the surly Clods he broke;
And to the Hatchet yield thy Husband-Man,
Who finish'd Autumn and the Spring began!
   Nor this alone! but Heav'n it self to bribe,
We to the Gods our impious Acts ascribe:
First recompence with Death their Creatures Toil,
Then call the Bless'd above to share the Spoil:
The fairest Victim must the Pow'rs appease,
(So fatal 'tis sometimes too much to please!)
A purple Fillet his broad Brows adorns,

160 cov'tous] covet'ous F   170 bear] bear, F

With flow'ry Garlands crown'd, and gilded Horns:
He hears the murd'rous Pray'r the Priest prefers,
But understands not, 'tis his Doom he hears: 195
Beholds the Meal betwixt his Temples cast,
(The Fruit and Product of his Labours past;)
And in the Water views perhaps the Knife
Uplifted, to deprive him of his Life;
Then broken up alive his Entrails sees,   200
Torn out for Priests t' inspect the God's Decrees.
    From whence, O mortal Men, this gust of Blood
Have you deriv'd, and interdicted Food?
Be taught by me this dire Delight to shun,
Warn'd by my Precepts, by my Practice won: 205
And when you eat the well deserving Beast,
Think, on the Lab'rer of your Field, you feast!
    Now since the God inspires me to proceed,
Be that, whate'er inspiring Pow'r, obey'd.
For I will sing of mighty Mysteries,   ⎫ 210
Of Truths conceal'd before, from human Eyes,   ⎬
Dark Oracles unveil, and open all the Skies.   ⎭
Pleas'd as I am to walk along the Sphere
Of shining Stars, and travel with the Year,
To leave the heavy Earth, and scale the height   215
Of *Atlas*, who supports the heav'nly weight;
To look from upper Light, and thence survey
Mistaken Mortals wandring from the way,
And wanting Wisdom, fearful for the state
Of future Things, and trembling at their Fate!   220
    Those I would teach; and by right Reason bring
To think of Death, as but an idle Thing.
Why thus affrighted at an empty Name,
A Dream of Darkness, and fictitious Flame?
Vain Themes of Wit, which but in Poems pass,   225
And Fables of a World, that never was!
What feels the Body when the Soul expires,
By time corrupted, or consum'd by Fires?
Nor dies the Spirit, but new Life repeats
In other Forms, and only changes Seats.   230
    Ev'n I, who these mysterious Truths declare,
Was once *Euphorbus* in the *Trojan* War;

My Name and Lineage I remember well,
And how in Fight by *Sparta*'s King I fell.
In *Argive Juno*'s Fane I late beheld   235
My Buckler hung on high, and own'd my former Shield.
   Then, Death, so call'd, is but old Matter dress'd
In some new Figure, and a vary'd Vest:
Thus all Things are but alter'd, nothing dies;
And here and there th' unbodied Spirit flies,   240
By Time, or Force, or Sickness dispossest,
And lodges, where it lights, in Man or Beast;
Or hunts without, till ready Limbs it find,
And actuates those according to their kind;
From Tenement to Tenement is toss'd;   245
The Soul is still the same, the Figure only lost:
And, as the soften'd Wax new Seals receives,
This Face assumes, and that Impression leaves;
Now call'd by one, now by another Name;
The Form is only chang'd, the Wax is still the same: 250
So Death, so call'd, can but the Form deface,
Th' immortal Soul flies out in empty space;
To seek her Fortune in some other Place.
   Then let not Piety be put to flight,
To please the tast of Glutton-Appetite;   255
But suffer inmate Souls secure to dwell,
Lest from their Seats your Parents you expel;
With rabid Hunger feed upon your kind,
Or from a Beast dislodge a Brother's Mind.
   And since, like *Tiphys* parting from the Shore,   260
In ample Seas I sail, and Depths untry'd before,
This let me further add, that Nature knows
No stedfast Station, but, or Ebbs, or Flows:
Ever in motion; she destroys her old,
And casts new Figures in another Mold.   265
Ev'n Times are in perpetual Flux; and run
Like Rivers from their Fountain rowling on;
For Time no more than Streams, is at a stay:
The flying Hour is ever on her way;
And as the Fountain still supplies her store,   270
The Wave behind impels the Wave before;

Thus in successive Course the Minutes run,
And urge their Predecessor Minutes on,
Still moving, ever new: For former Things
Are set aside, like abdicated Kings: 275
And every moment alters what is done,
And innovates some Act till then unknown.
　　Darkness we see emerges into Light,
And shining Suns descend to Sable Night;
Ev'n Heav'n it self receives another die,   280
When weari'd Animals in Slumbers lie,
Of Midnight Ease: Another when the gray
Of Morn preludes the Splendor of the Day.
The disk of *Phœbus* when he climbs on high,
Appears at first but as a bloodshot Eye;   285
And when his Chariot downward drives to Bed,
His Ball is with the same Suffusion red;
But mounted high in his Meridian Race
All bright he shines, and with a better Face:
For there, pure Particles of *Æther* flow,   290
Far from th' Infection of the World below.
　　Nor equal Light th' unequal Moon adorns,
Or in her wexing or her waning Horns.
For ev'ry Day she wanes, her Face is less,
But gath'ring into Globe, she fattens at increase.   295
　　Perceiv'st thou not the process of the Year,
How the four Seasons in four Forms appear,
Resembling human Life in ev'ry Shape they wear?
Spring first, like Infancy, shoots out her Head,
With milky Juice requiring to be fed: 300
Helpless, tho' fresh, and wanting to be led.
The green Stem grows in Stature and in Size,
But only feeds with hope the Farmer's Eyes;
Then laughs the childish Year with Flourets crown'd,
And lavishly perfumes the Fields around,   305
But no substantial Nourishment receives,
Infirm the Stalks, unsolid are the Leaves.
　　Proceeding onward whence the Year began
The Summer grows adult, and ripens into Man.
This Season, as in Men, is most repleat,   310
With kindly Moisture, and prolifick Heat.

Autumn succeeds, a sober tepid Age,
Not froze with Fear, nor boiling into Rage;
More than mature, and tending to decay,
When our brown Locks repine to mix with odious Grey.   315

     Last Winter creeps along with tardy pace,
Sour is his Front, and furrow'd is his Face;
His Scalp if not dishonour'd quite of Hair,
The ragged Fleece is thin, and thin is worse than bare.

     Ev'n our own Bodies daily change receive,   320
Some part of what was theirs before, they leave;
Nor are to Day what Yesterday they were;
Nor the whole same to Morrow will appear.

     Time was, when we were sow'd, and just began
From some few fruitful Drops, the promise of a Man;   325
Then Nature's Hand (fermented as it was)
Moulded to Shape the soft, coagulated Mass;
And when the little Man was fully form'd,
The breathless Embryo with a Spirit warm'd;
But when the Mothers Throws begin to come,   330
The Creature, pent within the narrow Room,
Breaks his blind Prison, pushing to repair
His stiffled Breath, and draw the living Air;
Cast on the Margin of the World he lies,
A helpless Babe, but by Instinct he cries.   335
He next essays to walk, but downward press'd
On four Feet imitates his Brother Beast:
By slow degrees he gathers from the Ground
His Legs, and to the rowling Chair is bound;
Then walks alone; a Horseman now become   340
He rides a Stick, and travels round the Room:
In time he vaunts among his youthful Peers,
Strong-bon'd, and strung with Nerves, in pride of Years,
He runs with Mettle his first merry Stage,   ⎫
Maintains the next abated of his Rage,   ⎬ 345
But manages his Strength, and spares his Age.   ⎭
Heavy the third, and stiff, he sinks apace,
And tho' 'tis down-hill all, but creeps along the Race.
Now sapless on the verge of Death he stands,
Contemplating his former Feet, and Hands;   350

And *Milo*-like, his slacken'd Sinews sees,
And wither'd Arms, once fit to cope with *Hercules*,
Unable now to shake, much less to tear the Trees.
    So *Helen* wept when her too faithful Glass
Reflected to her Eyes the ruins of her Face: 355
Wondring what Charms her Ravishers cou'd spy,
To force her twice, or ev'n but once enjoy!
    Thy Teeth, devouring Time, thine, envious Age,
On Things below still exercise your Rage:
With venom'd Grinders you corrupt your Meat,   360
And then at lingring Meals, the Morsels eat.
    Nor those, which Elements we call, abide,
Nor to this Figure, nor to that are ty'd:
For this eternal World is said of Old
But four prolifick Principles to hold,   365
Four different Bodies; two to Heaven ascend,
And other two down to the Center tend:
Fire first with Wings expanded mounts on high,
Pure, void of weight, and dwells in upper Sky;
Then Air, because unclogg'd in empty space   370
Flies after Fire, and claims the second Place:
But weighty Water as her Nature guides,
Lies on the lap of Earth; and Mother Earth subsides.
    All Things are mix'd of these, which all contain,
And into these are all resolv'd again: 375
Earth rarifies to Dew; expanded more,
The subtil Dew in Air begins to soar;
Spreads as she flies, and weary of her Name
Extenuates still, and changes into Flame;
Thus having by degrees Perfection won,   380
Restless they soon untwist the Web they spun,
And Fire begins to lose her radiant Hue,
Mix'd with gross Air, and Air descends to Dew:
And Dew condensing, does her Form forego,
And sinks, a heavy lump of Earth below.   385
    Thus are their Figures never at a stand,
But chang'd by Nature's innovating Hand;
All Things are alter'd, nothing is destroy'd,
The shifted Scene, for some new Show employ'd.

       376 Dew;] Dew, F

Then to be born, is to begin to be   390
Some other Thing we were not formerly:
And what we call to Die, is not t' appear,
Or be the Thing that formerly we were.
Those very Elements which we partake,
Alive, when Dead some other Bodies make: 395
Translated grow, have Sense, or can Discourse,
But Death on deathless Substance has no force.
    That Forms are chang'd I grant; that nothing can
Continue in the Figure it began:
The Golden Age, to Silver was debas'd: 400
To Copper that; our Mettal came at last.
    The Face of Places, and their Forms decay;
And that is solid Earth, that once was Sea:
Seas in their turn retreating from the Shore,
Make solid Land, what Ocean was before;   405
And far from Strands are Shells of Fishes found,
And rusty Anchors fix'd on Mountain-Ground:
And what were Fields before, now wash'd and worn
By falling Floods from high, to Valleys turn,
And crumbling still descend to level Lands;   410
And Lakes, and trembling Bogs are barren Sands:
And the parch'd Desart floats in Streams unknown;
Wondring to drink of Waters not her own.
    Here Nature living Fountains ope's; and there
Seals up the Wombs where living Fountains were;   415
Or Earthquakes stop their ancient Course, and bring
Diverted Streams to feed a distant Spring.
So *Lycus*, swallow'd up, is seen no more,
But far from thence knocks out another Door.
Thus *Erasinus* dives; and blind in Earth   420
Runs on, and gropes his way to second Birth,
Starts up in *Argos* Meads, and shakes his Locks,
Around the Fields, and fattens all the Flocks.
So *Mysus* by another way is led,
And, grown a River now disdains his Head: 425
Forgets his humble Birth, his Name forsakes,
And the proud Title of *Caicus* takes.
Large *Amenane*, impure with yellow Sands,
Runs rapid often, and as often stands,

And here he threats the drunken Fields to drown; 430
And there his Dugs deny to give their Liquor down.
   Anigros once did wholsome Draughts afford,
But now his deadly Waters are abhorr'd:
Since, hurt by *Hercules*, as Fame resounds,
The Centaurs, in his current wash'd their Wounds. 435
The Streams of *Hypanis* are sweet no more,
But brackish lose the tast they had before.
Antissa, *Pharos*, *Tyre*, in Seas were pent,
Once Isles, but now increase the Continent;
While the *Leucadian* Coast, main Land before, 440
By rushing Seas is sever'd from the Shore.
So *Zancle* to th' *Italian* Earth was ty'd,
And Men once walk'd where Ships at Anchor ride.
Till *Neptune* overlook'd the narrow way,
And in disdain pour'd in the conqu'ring Sea. 445
   Two Cities that adorn'd th' *Achaian* Ground,
Buris and *Helice*, no more are found,
But whelm'd beneath a Lake are sunk and drown'd;
And Boatsmen through the Chrystal Water show
To wond'ring Passengers the Walls below. 450
   Near *Trœzen* stands a Hill, expos'd in Air
To Winter-Winds, of leafy Shadows bare:
This once was level Ground: But (strange to tell)
Th' included Vapors, that in Caverns dwell,
Lab'ring with Cholick Pangs, and close confin'd, 455
In vain sought issue for the rumbling Wind:
Yet still they heav'd for vent, and heaving still
Inlarg'd the Concave, and shot up the Hill;
As Breath extends a Bladder, or the Skins
Of Goats are blown t' inclose the hoarded Wines: 460
The Mountain yet retains a Mountain's Face,
And gather'd Rubbish heals the hollow space.
   Of many Wonders, which I heard or knew,
Retrenching most, I will relate but few:
What, are not Springs with Qualities oppos'd, 465
Endu'd at Seasons, and at Seasons lost?
Thrice in a Day thine, *Ammon*, change their Form,
Cold at high Noon, at Morn and Evening warm:
Thine, *Athaman*, will kindle Wood, if thrown

On the pil'd Earth, and in the waning Moon.   470
The *Thracians* have a Stream, if any try
The tast, his harden'd Bowels petrify;
Whate'er it touches it converts to Stones,
And makes a Marble Pavement where it runs.

    Crathis, and *Sybaris* her Sister Flood,   475
That slide through our *Calabrian* Neighbour Wood,
With Gold and Amber die the shining Hair,
And thither Youth resort; (for who wou'd not be Fair?)

    But stranger Virtues yet in Streams we find,
Some change not only Bodies, but the Mind: 480
Who has not heard of *Salmacis* obscene,
Whose Waters into Women soften Men?
Or *Æthyopian* Lakes which turn the Brain
To Madness, or in heavy Sleep constrain?
Clytorian Streams the love of Wine expel,   485
(Such is the Virtue of th' abstemious Well;)
Whether the colder Nymph that rules the Flood
Extinguishes, and balks the drunken God;
Or that *Melampus* (so have some assur'd)
When the mad *Prœtides* with Charms he cur'd;   490
And pow'rful Herbs, both Charms and Simples cast
Into th' sober Spring, where still their Virtues last.

    Unlike Effects *Lyncestis* will produce,
Who drinks his Waters, tho' with moderate use,
Reels as with Wine, and sees with double Sight: 495
His Heels too heavy, and his Head too light.
Ladon, once *Pheneos*, an *Arcadian* Stream,
(Ambiguous in th' Effects, as in the Name)
By Day is wholsom Bev'rage; but is thought
By Night infected, and a deadly Draught.   500

    Thus running Rivers, and the standing Lake
Now of these Virtues, now of those partake:
Time was (and all Things Time and Fate obey)
When fast *Ortygia* floated on the Sea:
Such were *Cyanean* Isles, when *Tiphys* steer'd   505
Betwixt their Streights and their Collision fear'd;
They swam where now they sit; and firmly join'd
Secure of rooting up, resist the Wind.

Nor *Ætna* vomiting sulphureous Fire
Will ever belch; for Sulphur will expire,　　　　510
(The Veins exhausted of the liquid Store:)
Time was she cast no Flames; in time will cast no more.
　　For whether Earth's an Animal, and Air
Imbibes, her Lungs with coolness to repair,
And what she sucks remits; she still requires　　　515
Inlets for Air, and Outlets for her Fires;
When tortur'd with convulsive Fits she shakes,
That motion choaks the vent till other vent she makes:
Or when the Winds in hollow Caves are clos'd,
And subtil Spirits find that way oppos'd,　　　　520
They toss up Flints in Air; the Flints that hide
The Seeds of Fire, thus toss'd in Air, collide,
Kindling the Sulphur, till the Fewel spent
The Cave is cool'd, and the fierce Winds relent.
Or whether Sulphur, catching Fire, feeds on　　　525
Its unctuous Parts, till all the Matter gone
The Flames no more ascend; for Earth supplies
The Fat that feeds them; and when Earth denies
That Food, by length of Time consum'd, the Fire
Famish'd for want of Fewel must expire.　　　　530
　　A Race of Men there are, as Fame has told,
Who shiv'ring suffer *Hyperborean* Cold,
Till nine times bathing in *Minerva*'s Lake,
Soft Feathers, to defend their naked Sides, they take.
'Tis said, the *Scythian* Wives (believe who will)　　535
Transform themselves to Birds by Magick Skill;
Smear'd over with an Oil of wond'rous Might,
That adds new Pinions to their airy Flight.
　　But this by sure Experiment we know,
That living Creatures from Corruption grow:　　　540
Hide in a hollow Pit a slaughter'd Steer,
Bees from his putrid Bowels will appear;
Who like their Parents haunt the Fields, and bring
Their Hony-Harvest home, and hope another Spring.
The Warlike-Steed is multiply'd we find,　　　　545
To Wasps and Hornets of the Warrior Kind.

Cut from a Crab his crooked Claws, and hide
The rest in Earth, a Scorpion thence will glide
And shoot his Sting, his Tail in Circles toss'd
Refers the Limbs his backward Father lost.   550
And Worms, that stretch on Leaves their filmy Loom,
Crawl from their Bags, and Butterflies become.
Ev'n Slime begets the Frog's loquacious Race:
Short of their Feet at first, in little space
With Arms and Legs endu'd, long leaps they take,   555
Rais'd on their hinder part, and swim the Lake,
And Waves repel: For Nature gives their Kind
To that intent, a length of Legs behind.
     The Cubs of Bears, a living lump appear,
When whelp'd, and no determin'd Figure wear.   560
Their Mother licks 'em into Shape, and gives
As much of Form, as she her self receives.
     The Grubs from their sexangular abode
Crawl out unfinish'd, like the Maggot's Brood:
Trunks without Limbs; till time at leisure brings   565
The Thighs they wanted, and their tardy Wings.
     The Bird who draws the Carr of *Juno*, vain
Of her crown'd Head, and of her Starry Train;
And he that bears th' Artillery of *Jove*,
The strong-pounc'd Eagle, and the billing Dove;   570
And all the feather'd Kind, who cou'd suppose
(But that from sight the surest Sense he knows)
They from th' included Yolk, not ambient White arose.
     There are who think the Marrow of a Man,
Which in the Spine, while he was living ran;   575
When dead, the Pith corrupted will become
A Snake, and hiss within the hollow Tomb.
     All these receive their Birth from other Things;
But from himself the *Phœnix* only springs:
Self-born, begotten by the Parent Flame   580
In which he burn'd, another and the same;
Who not by Corn or Herbs his Life sustains,
But the sweet Essence of *Amomum* drains:
And watches the rich Gums *Arabia* bears,
While yet in tender Dew they drop their Tears.   585
He, (his five Cent'ries of Life fulfill'd)

His Nest on Oaken Boughs begins to build,
Or trembling tops of Palm, and first he draws
The Plan with his broad Bill, and crooked Claws,
Nature's Artificers; on this the Pile   590
Is form'd, and rises round, then with the Spoil
Of *Casia*, *Cynamon*, and Stems of *Nard*,
(For softness strew'd beneath,) his Fun'ral Bed is rear'd:
Fun'ral and Bridal both; and all around
The Borders with corruptless Myrrh are crown'd,   595
On this incumbent; till ætherial Flame
First catches, then consumes the costly Frame:
Consumes him too, as on the Pile he lies;
He liv'd on Odours, and in Odours dies.

    An Infant-*Phœnix* from the former springs   600
His Father's Heir, and from his tender Wings
Shakes off his Parent Dust, his Method he pursues,
And the same Lease of Life on the same Terms renews.
When grown to Manhood he begins his reign,
And with stiff Pinions can his Flight sustain,   605
He lightens of its Load, the Tree that bore
His Father's Royal Sepulcher before,
And his own Cradle: (This with pious Care
Plac'd on his Back) he cuts the buxome Air,
Seeks the Sun's City, and his sacred Church,   610
And decently lays down his Burden in the Porch.
    A Wonder more amazing wou'd we find?
Th' *Hyæna* shows it, of a double kind,
Varying the Sexes in alternate Years,
In one begets, and in another bears.   615
The thin *Camelion* fed with Air, receives
The colour of the Thing to which he cleaves.
    India when conquer'd, on the conqu'ring God
For planted Vines the sharp-ey'd *Lynx* bestow'd,
Whose Urine shed, before it touches Earth,   620
Congeals in Air, and gives to Gems their Birth.
So *Coral* soft, and white in Oceans Bed,
Comes harden'd up in Air, and glows with Red.
    All changing Species should my Song recite;
Before I ceas'd, wou'd change the Day to Night.   625

608 (This with] This (with F   620 Urine shed,] Urine, shed F

Nations and Empires flourish, and decay,
By turns command, and in their turns obey;
Time softens hardy People, Time again
Hardens to War a soft, unwarlike Train.
Thus *Troy* for ten long Years her Foes withstood,   63
And daily bleeding bore th' expence of Blood:
Now for thick Streets it shows an empty space,
Or only fill'd with Tombs of her own perish'd Race,
Her self becomes the Sepulcher of what she was.

    Mycene, *Sparta*, *Thebes* of mighty Fame,   63
Are vanish'd out of Substance into Name.
And *Dardan Rome* that just begins to rise,
On *Tiber*'s Banks, in time shall mate the Skies;
Widening her Bounds, and working on her way;
Ev'n now she meditates Imperial Sway: 64
Yet this is change, but she by changing thrives,
Like Moons new-born, and in her Cradle strives
To fill her Infant-Horns; an Hour shall come
When the round World shall be contain'd in *Rome*.

    For thus old Saws foretel, and *Helenus*   64
Anchises drooping Son enliven'd thus;
When *Ilium* now was in a sinking State;
And he was doubtful of his future Fate:
O Goddess born, with thy hard Fortune strive,
Troy never can be lost, and thou alive.   6
Thy Passage thou shalt free through Fire and Sword,
And *Troy* in Foreign Lands shall be restor'd.
In happier Fields a rising Town I see,
Greater than what e'er was, or is, or e'er shall be:
And Heav'n yet owes the World a Race deriv'd from Thee. 6
Sages, and Chiefs of other Lineage born
The City shall extend, extended shall adorn:
But from *Julus* he must draw his Birth,
By whom thy *Rome* shall rule the conquer'd Earth:
Whom Heav'n will lend Mankind on Earth to reign,   6
And late require the precious Pledge again.
This *Helenus* to great *Æneas* told,
Which I retain, e'er since in other Mould
My Soul was cloath'd; and now rejoice to view

658 Birth] Breath F. *See Commentary*   663 Mould] Mould: F

My Country Walls rebuilt, and *Troy* reviv'd anew, 665
Rais'd by the fall: Decreed by Loss to Gain;
Enslav'd but to be free, and conquer'd but to reign.
   'Tis time my hard mouth'd Coursers to controul,
Apt to run Riot, and transgress the Goal:
And therefore I conclude, whatever lies 670
In Earth, or flits in Air, or fills the Skies,
All suffer change, and we, that are of Soul
And Body mix'd, are Members of the whole.
Then, when our Sires, or Grandsires shall forsake
The Forms of Men, and brutal Figures take, 675
Thus hous'd, securely let their Spirits rest,
Nor violate thy Father in the Beast.
Thy Friend, thy Brother, any of thy Kin,
If none of these, yet there's a Man within:
O spare to make a *Thyestæan* Meal, 680
T' inclose his Body, and his Soul expel.
   Ill Customs by degrees to Habits rise,
Ill Habits soon become exalted Vice:
What more advance can Mortals make in Sin
So near Perfection, who with Blood begin? 685
Deaf to the Calf that lies beneath the Knife,
Looks up, and from her Butcher begs her Life:
Deaf to the harmless Kid, that e'er he dies }
All Methods to procure thy Mercy tries,
And imitates in vain thy Children's Cries. } 690
Where will he stop, who feeds with Houshold Bread,
Then eats the Poultry which before he fed?
Let plough thy Steers; that when they lose their Breath
To Nature, not to thee they may impute their Death.
Let Goats for Food their loaded Udders lend, 695
And Sheep from Winter-cold thy Sides defend;
But neither Sprindges, Nets, nor Snares employ,
And be no more Ingenious to destroy.
Free as in Air, let Birds on Earth remain,
Nor let insidious Glue their Wings constrain; 700
Nor opening Hounds the trembling Stag affright,
Nor purple Feathers intercept his Flight:
Nor Hooks conceal'd in Baits for Fish prepare,

670 lies] lies, F

Nor Lines to heave 'em twinkling up in Air.
   Take not away the Life you cannot give: 70
For all Things have an equal right to live.
Kill noxious Creatures, where 'tis Sin to save;
This only just Prerogative we have:
But nourish Life with vegetable Food,
And shun the sacrilegious tast of Blood.   71
   These Precepts by the *Samian* Sage were taught,
Which Godlike *Numa* to the *Sabines* brought,
And thence transferr'd to *Rome*, by Gift his own:
A willing People, and an offer'd Throne.
O happy Monarch, sent by Heav'n to bless   71
A Salvage Nation with soft Arts of Peace,
To teach Religion, Rapine to restrain,
Give Laws to Lust, and Sacrifice ordain:
Himself a Saint, a Goddess was his Bride,
And all the Muses o'er his Acts preside.   72

THE CHARACTER OF A GOOD PARSON;
Imitated from CHAUCER, And Inlarg'd

A PARISH-PRIEST, was of the Pilgrim-Train:
   An Awful, Reverend, and Religious Man.
His Eyes diffus'd a venerable Grace,
And Charity it self was in his Face.
Rich was his Soul, though his Attire was poor;   5
(As God had cloath'd his own Embassador;)
For such, on Earth, his bless'd Redeemer bore.
Of Sixty Years he seem'd; and well might last
To Sixty more, but that he liv'd too fast;
Refin'd himself to Soul, to curb the Sense;   1
And made almost a Sin of Abstinence.
Yet, had his Aspect nothing of severe,
But such a Face as promis'd him sincere.
Nothing reserv'd or sullen was to see:
But sweet Regards; and pleasing Sanctity: 1
Mild was his Accent, and his Action free.

With Eloquence innate his Tongue was arm'd;
Tho' harsh the Precept, yet the Preacher charm'd.
For, letting down the golden Chain from high,
He drew his Audience upward to the Sky: 20
And oft, with holy Hymns, he charm'd their Ears:
(A Musick more melodious than the Spheres.)
For *David* left him, when he went to rest,
His Lyre; and after him, he sung the best.
He bore his great Commission in his Look: 25
But sweetly temper'd Awe; and soften'd all he spoke.
He preach'd the Joys of Heav'n, and Pains of Hell; ⎫
And warn'd the Sinner with becoming Zeal;   ⎬
But on Eternal Mercy lov'd to dwell.   ⎭
He taught the Gospel rather than the Law: 30
And forc'd himself to drive; but lov'd to draw.
For Fear but freezes Minds; but Love, like Heat,
Exhales the Soul sublime, to seek her Native Seat.
  To Threats, the stubborn Sinner oft is hard:
Wrap'd in his Crimes, against the Storm prepar'd;   35
But, when the milder Beams of Mercy play,
He melts, and throws his cumb'rous Cloak away.
  Lightnings and Thunder (Heav'ns Artillery)
As Harbingers before th' Almighty fly:
Those, but proclaim his Stile, and disappear;   40
The stiller Sound succeeds; and God is there.
  The Tythes, his Parish freely paid, he took;
But never Su'd; or Curs'd with Bell and Book.
With Patience bearing wrong; but off'ring none:
Since every Man is free to lose his own.   45
The Country-Churles, according to their Kind,
(Who grudge their Dues, and love to be behind,)
The less he sought his Off'rings, pinch'd the more;
And prais'd a Priest, contented to be Poor.
  Yet, of his little, he had some to spare,   50
To feed the Famish'd, and to cloath the Bare:
For Mortify'd he was, to that degree,
A poorer than himself, he wou'd not see.
True Priests, he said, and Preachers of the Word,
Were only Stewards of their Soveraign Lord;   55
Nothing was theirs; but all the publick Store:

Intrusted Riches, to relieve the Poor.
Who, shou'd they steal, for want of his Relief,
He judg'd himself Accomplice with the Thief.
Wide was his Parish; not contracted close   60
In Streets, but here and there a straggling House;
Yet still he was at Hand, without Request
To serve the Sick; to succour the Distress'd:
Tempting, on Foot, alone, without affright,
The Dangers of a dark, tempestuous Night.   65
All this, the good old Man, perform'd alone,
Nor spar'd his Pains; for Curate he had none.
Nor durst he trust another with his Care;
Nor rode himself to *Pauls*, the publick Fair,
To chaffer for Preferment with his Gold,   70
Where Bishopricks, and *sine Cures* are sold.
But duly watch'd his Flock, by Night and Day;
And from the prowling Wolf, redeem'd the Prey;
And hungry sent the wily Fox away.
The Proud he tam'd, the Penitent he chear'd: 75
Nor to rebuke the rich Offender fear'd.
His Preaching much, but more his Practice wrought;
(A living Sermon of the Truths he taught;)
For this by Rules severe his Life he squar'd:
That all might see the Doctrin which they heard.   80
For Priests, he said, are Patterns for the rest:
(The Gold of Heav'n, who bear the God Impress'd:)
But when the precious Coin is kept unclean,
The Soveraign's Image is no longer seen.
If they be foul, on whom the People trust,   85
Well may the baser Brass, contract a Rust.
The Prelate, for his Holy Life he priz'd;
The worldly Pomp of Prelacy despis'd.
His Saviour came not with a gawdy Show;
Nor was his Kingdom of the World below.   90
Patience in Want, and Poverty of Mind,
These Marks of Church and Churchmen he design'd,
And living taught; and dying left behind.
The Crown he wore was of the pointed Thorn:
In Purple he was Crucify'd, not born.   95
They who contend for Place and high Degree,

Are not his Sons, but those of *Zebadee*.
    Not, but he knew the Signs of Earthly Pow'r
Might well become St. *Peter*'s Successor:
The Holy Father holds a double Reign,   100
The Prince may keep his Pomp; the Fisher must be plain.
    Such was the Saint; who shone with every Grace:
Reflecting, *Moses*-like, his Maker's Face.
God, saw his Image lively was express'd;
And his own Work, as in Creation bless'd.   105
    The Tempter saw him too, with envious Eye;
And, as on *Job*, demanded leave to try.
He took the time when *Richard* was depos'd:
And High and Low, with happy *Harry* clos'd.
This Prince, tho' great in Arms, the Priest withstood: 110
Near tho' he was, yet not the next of Blood.
Had *Richard* unconstrain'd, resign'd the Throne:
A King can give no more than is his own:
The Title stood entail'd, had *Richard* had a Son.
    Conquest, an odious Name, was laid aside,   115
Where all submitted; none the Battle try'd.
The senseless Plea of Right by Providence,
Was, by a flatt'ring Priest, invented since:
And lasts no longer than the present sway;
But justifies the next who comes in play.   120
    The People's Right remains; let those who dare
Dispute their Pow'r, when they the Judges are.
    He join'd not in their Choice; because he knew
Worse might, and often did from Change ensue.
Much to himself he thought; but little spoke: 125
And, Undepriv'd, his Benefice forsook.
    Now, through the Land, his Cure of Souls he stretch'd:
And like a Primitive Apostle preach'd.
Still Chearful; ever Constant to his Call;
By many follow'd; Lov'd by most, Admir'd by All.   130
With what he beg'd, his Brethren he reliev'd;
And gave the Charities himself receiv'd.
Gave, while he Taught; and Edify'd the more,
Because he shew'd by Proof, 'twas easy to be Poor.
    He went not, with the Crowd, to see a Shrine;   135
But fed us by the way, with Food divine.

In deference to his Virtues, I forbear
To shew you, what the rest in Orders were:
This Brillant, is so Spotless, and so Bright,
He needs no Foyl: But shines by his own proper Light.   14⟨

THE MONUMENT OF A FAIR MAIDEN
LADY, Who dy'd at *Bath*, and is there Interr'd

BELOW this Marble Monument, is laid
All that Heav'n wants of this Celestial Maid.
Preserve, O sacred Tomb, thy Trust consign'd:
The Mold was made on purpose for the Mind:
And she wou'd lose, if at the latter Day   5
One Atom cou'd be mix'd, of other Clay.
Such were the Features of her heav'nly Face,
Her Limbs were form'd with such harmonious Grace,
So faultless was the Frame, as if the Whole
Had been an Emanation of the Soul;   10
Which her own inward Symmetry reveal'd;
And like a Picture shone, in Glass Anneal'd.
Or like the Sun eclips'd, with shaded Light:
Too piercing, else, to be sustain'd by Sight.
Each Thought was visible that rowl'd within: 15
As through a Crystal Case, the figur'd Hours are seen.
And Heav'n did this transparent Veil provide,
Because she had no guilty Thought to hide.
All white, a Virgin-Saint, she sought the Skies:
For Marriage, tho' it sullies not, it dies.   20
High tho' her Wit, yet Humble was her Mind;
As if she cou'd not, or she wou'd not find
How much her Worth transcended all her Kind.
Yet she had learn'd so much of Heav'n below,
That when arriv'd, she scarce had more to know: 2⟨
But only to refresh the former Hint;
And read her Maker in a fairer Print.
So Pious, as she had no time to spare
For human Thoughts, but was confin'd to Pray'r.

The Monument, &c. Collated with the inscription in Bath Abbey. See Commentary
29 was] seem'd *inscription*

Yet in such Charities she pass'd the Day,　　　　　30
'Twas wond'rous how she found an Hour to Pray.
A Soul so calm, it knew not Ebbs or Flows,
Which Passion cou'd but curl; not discompose.
A Female Softness, with a manly Mind:
A Daughter duteous, and a Sister kind:　　　　　35
In Sickness patient; and in Death resign'd.

CYMON AND IPHIGENIA,
FROM BOCCACE

Poeta loquitur,

OLD as I am, for Ladies Love unfit,
The Pow'r of Beauty I remember yet,
Which once inflam'd my Soul, and still inspires my Wit.
If Love be Folly, the severe Divine
Has felt that Folly, tho' he censures mine;　　　　5
Pollutes the Pleasures of a chast Embrace,
Acts what I write, and propagates in Grace
With riotous Excess, a Priestly Race:
Suppose him free, and that I forge th' Offence,
He shew'd the way, perverting first my Sense:　　10
In Malice witty, and with Venom fraught,
He makes me speak the Things I never thought.
Compute the Gains of his ungovern'd Zeal;
Ill sutes his Cloth the Praise of Railing well!
The World will think that what we loosly write,　　15
Tho' now arraign'd, he read with some delight;
Because he seems to chew the Cud again,
When his broad Comment makes the Text too plain:
And teaches more in one explaining Page,
Than all the double Meanings of the Stage.　　20
　　What needs he Paraphrase on what we mean?
We were at worst but Wanton; he's Obscene.
I, nor my Fellows, nor my Self excuse;
But Love's the Subject of the Comick Muse:
Nor can we write without it, nor would you　　25
A Tale of only dry Instruction view;

Nor Love is always of a vicious Kind,
But oft to virtuous Acts inflames the Mind.
Awakes the sleepy Vigour of the Soul,
And, brushing o'er, adds Motion to the Pool.   30
Love, studious how to please, improves our Parts,
With polish'd Manners, and adorns with Arts.
Love first invented Verse, and form'd the Rhime,
The Motion measur'd, harmoniz'd the Chime;
To lib'ral Acts inlarg'd the narrow-Soul'd: 35
Soften'd the Fierce, and made the Coward Bold:
The World when wast, he Peopled with increase,
And warring Nations reconcil'd in Peace.
Ormond, the first, and all the Fair may find
In this one Legend to their Fame design'd,   40
When Beauty fires the Blood, how Love exalts the Mind.

In that sweet Isle, where *Venus* keeps her Court,
And ev'ry Grace, and all the Loves resort;
Where either Sex is form'd of softer Earth,
And takes the bent of Pleasure from their Birth;   45
There liv'd a *Cyprian* Lord, above the rest,
Wise, Wealthy, with a num'rous Issue blest.
 But as no Gift of Fortune is sincere,
Was only wanting in a worthy Heir:
His eldest Born a goodly Youth to view   50
Excell'd the rest in Shape, and outward Shew;
Fair, Tall, his Limbs with due Proportion join'd,
But of a heavy, dull, degenerate Mind.
His Soul bely'd the Features of his Face;
Beauty was there, but Beauty in disgrace.   55
A clownish Mien, a Voice with rustick sound,
And stupid Eyes, that ever lov'd the Ground.
He look'd like Nature's Error; as the Mind
And Body were not of a Piece design'd,
But made for two, and by mistake in one were join'd. 60
 The ruling Rod, the Father's forming Care,
Were exercis'd in vain, on Wit's despair;
The more inform'd the less he understood,
And deeper sunk by flound'ring in the Mud.
Now scorn'd of all, and grown the publick Shame,   65

The People from *Galesus* chang'd his Name,
And *Cymon* call'd, which signifies a Brute;
So well his Name did with his Nature sute.
　His Father, when he found his Labour lost,
And Care employ'd, that answer'd not the Cost, 　　70
Chose an ungrateful Object to remove,
And loath'd to see what Nature made him love;
So to his Country-Farm the Fool confin'd:
Rude Work well suted with a rustick Mind.
Thus to the Wilds the sturdy *Cymon* went, 　　75
A Squire among the Swains, and pleas'd with Banishment.
His Corn, and Cattle, were his only Care,
And his supreme Delight a Country-Fair.
　It happen'd on a Summers Holiday,
That to the Greenwood-shade he took his way; 　80
For *Cymon* shun'd the Church, and us'd not much to Pray.
His Quarter-Staff, which he cou'd ne'er forsake,
Hung half before, and half behind his Back.
He trudg'd along unknowing what he sought,
And whistled as he went, for want of Thought. 　　85
　By Chance conducted, or by Thirst constrain'd,
The deep Recesses of the Grove he gain'd;
Where in a Plain, defended by the Wood,
Crept through the matted Grass a Chrystal Flood,
By which an Alablaster Fountain stood: 　　90
And on the Margin of the Fount was laid
(Attended by her Slaves) a sleeping Maid.
Like *Dian*, and her Nymphs, when tir'd with Sport,
To rest by cool *Eurotas* they resort:
The Dame herself the Goddess well express'd, 　　95
Not more distinguish'd by her Purple Vest,
Than by the charming Features of her Face,
And ev'n in Slumber a superiour Grace:
Her comely Limbs compos'd with decent Care,
Her Body shaded with a slight Cymarr; 　　100
Her Bosom to the view was only bare:
Where two beginning Paps were scarcely spy'd,
For yet their Places were but signify'd:

The fanning Wind upon her Bosom blows, }
To meet the fanning Wind the Bosom rose; } 105
The fanning Wind, and purling Streams continue her repose.}
 The Fool of Nature, stood with stupid Eyes
And gaping Mouth, that testify'd Surprize,
Fix'd on her Face, nor cou'd remove his Sight,
New as he was to Love, and Novice in Delight: 110
Long mute he stood, and leaning on his Staff,
His Wonder witness'd with an Ideot laugh;
Then would have spoke, but by his glimmering Sense
First found his want of Words, and fear'd Offence:
Doubted for what he was he should be known,   115
By his Clown-Accent, and his Country-Tone.
 Through the rude Chaos thus the running Light
Shot the first Ray that pierc'd the Native Night:
Then Day and Darkness in the Mass were mix'd,
Till gather'd in a Globe, the Beams were fix'd: 120
Last shon the Sun who radiant in his Sphere
Illumin'd Heav'n, and Earth, and rowl'd around the Year.
So Reason in this Brutal Soul began:
Love made him first suspect he was a Man;
Love made him doubt his broad barbarian Sound,   125
By Love his want of Words, and Wit he found:
That sense of want prepar'd the future way
To Knowledge, and disclos'd the promise of a Day.
 What not his Father's Care, nor Tutor's Art
Cou'd plant with Pains in his unpolish'd Heart,   13o
The best Instructor Love at once inspir'd,
As barren Grounds to Fruitfulness are fir'd:
Love taught him Shame, and Shame with Love at Strife
Soon taught the sweet Civilities of Life;
His gross material Soul at once could find   13ǀ
Somewhat in her excelling all her Kind:
Exciting a Desire till then unknown,
Somewhat unfound, or found in her alone.
This made the first Impression in his Mind,
Above, but just above the Brutal Kind.   14ǀ
For Beasts can like, but not distinguish too,
Nor their own liking by reflection know;
Nor why they like or this, or t'other Face,

Or judge of this or that peculiar Grace,
But love in gross, and stupidly admire;   145
As Flies allur'd by Light, approach the Fire.
Thus our Man-Beast advancing by degrees
First likes the whole, then sep'rates what he sees;
On sev'ral Parts a sev'ral Praise bestows,
The ruby Lips, the well-proportion'd Nose,   150
The snowy Skin, the Raven-glossy Hair,
The dimpled Cheek, the Forehead rising fair,
And ev'n in Sleep it self a smiling Air.
From thence his Eyes descending view'd the rest,
Her plump round Arms, white Hands, and heaving Breast. 155
Long on the last he dwelt, though ev'ry part
A pointed Arrow sped to pierce his Heart.
   Thus in a trice a Judge of Beauty grown,
(A Judge erected from a Country-Clown)
He long'd to see her Eyes in Slumber hid;   160
And wish'd his own cou'd pierce within the Lid:
He wou'd have wak'd her, but restrain'd his Thought,
And Love new-born the first good Manners taught.
An awful Fear his ardent Wish withstood,
Nor durst disturb the Goddess of the Wood;   165
For such she seem'd by her celestial Face,
Excelling all the rest of human Race:
And Things divine by common Sense he knew,
Must be devoutly seen at distant view:
So checking his Desire, with trembling Heart   170
Gazing he stood, nor would, nor could depart;
Fix'd as a Pilgrim wilder'd in his way,
Who dares not stir by Night for fear to stray,
But stands with awful Eyes to watch the dawn of Day.
   At length awaking, *Iphigene* the Fair   175
(So was the Beauty call'd who caus'd his Care)
Unclos'd her Eyes, and double Day reveal'd,
While those of all her Slaves in Sleep were seal'd.
   The slavering Cudden prop'd upon his Staff,
Stood ready gaping with a grinning Laugh,   180
To welcome her awake, nor durst begin
To speak, but wisely kept the Fool within.

   Cymon and Iphigenia. 148 then] than *F*

Then she; What make you *Cymon* here alone?
(For *Cymon*'s Name was round the Country known
Because descended of a noble Race,   185
And for a Soul ill sorted with his Face.)
   But still the Sot stood silent with Surprize,
With fix'd regard on her new open'd Eyes,
And in his Breast receiv'd th' invenom'd Dart,
A tickling Pain that pleas'd amid the Smart.   190
But conscious of her Form, with quick distrust
She saw his sparkling Eyes, and fear'd his brutal Lust:
This to prevent she wak'd her sleepy Crew,
And rising hasty took a short Adieu.
   Then *Cymon* first his rustick Voice essay'd,   195
With proffer'd Service to the parting Maid
To see her safe; his Hand she long deny'd,
But took at length, asham'd of such a Guide.
So *Cymon* led her home, and leaving there
No more wou'd to his Country Clowns repair,   200
But sought his Father's House with better Mind,
Refusing in the Farm to be confin'd.
   The Father wonder'd at the Son's return,
And knew not whether to rejoice or mourn;
But doubtfully receiv'd, expecting still   205
To learn the secret Causes of his alter'd Will.
Nor was he long delay'd; the first Request
He made, was, like his Brothers to be dress'd,
And, as his Birth requir'd, above the rest.
   With ease his Sute was granted by his Syre,   210
Distinguishing his Heir by rich Attire:
His Body thus adorn'd, he next design'd
With lib'ral Arts to cultivate his Mind:
He sought a Tutor of his own accord,
And study'd Lessons he before abhorr'd.   215
   Thus the Man-Child advanc'd, and learn'd so fast,
That in short time his Equals he surpass'd:
His brutal Manners from his Breast exil'd,
His Mien he fashion'd, and his Tongue he fil'd;
In ev'ry Exercise of all admir'd,   220
He seem'd, nor only seem'd, but was inspir'd:
Inspir'd by Love, whose Business is to please;

He Rode, he Fenc'd, he mov'd with graceful Ease,
More fam'd for Sense, for courtly Carriage more,
Than for his brutal Folly known before.   225
    What then of alter'd *Cymon* shall we say,
But that the Fire which choak'd in Ashes lay,
A Load too heavy for his Soul to move,
Was upward blown below, and brush'd away by Love?
Love made an active Progress through his Mind,   230
The dusky Parts he clear'd, the gross refin'd;
The drowsy wak'd; and as he went impress'd
The Maker's Image on the human Beast.
Thus was the Man amended by Desire,
And tho' he lov'd perhaps with too much Fire,   235
His Father all his Faults with Reason scan'd,
And lik'd an error of the better Hand;
Excus'd th' excess of Passion in his Mind,
By Flames too fierce, perhaps too much refin'd:
So *Cymon*, since his Sire indulg'd his Will,   240
Impetuous lov'd, and would be *Cymon* still;
Galesus he disown'd, and chose to bear
The Name of Fool confirm'd, and Bishop'd by the Fair.
    To *Cipseus* by his Friends his Sute he mov'd,
Cipseus the Father of the Fair he lov'd: 245
But he was pre-ingag'd by former Ties,
While *Cymon* was endeav'ring to be wise:
And *Iphigene* oblig'd by former Vows,
Had giv'n her Faith to wed a Foreign Spouse:
Her Sire and She to *Rhodian Pasimond*,   250
Tho' both repenting, were by Promise bound,
Nor could retract; and thus, as Fate decreed,
Tho' better lov'd, he spoke too late to speed.
    The Doom was past, the Ship already sent,
Did all his tardy Diligence prevent: 255
Sigh'd to herself the fair unhappy Maid,
While stormy *Cymon* thus in secret said:
The time is come for *Iphigene* to find
The Miracle she wrought upon my Mind:
Her Charms have made me Man, her ravish'd Love   260
In rank shall place me with the Bless'd above.
For mine by Love, by Force she shall be mine,

Or Death, if Force should fail, shall finish my Design.
    Resolv'd he said: And rigg'd with speedy Care
A Vessel strong, and well equipp'd for War.   265
The secret Ship with chosen Friends he stor'd;
And bent to die, or conquer, went aboard.
Ambush'd he lay behind the *Cyprian* Shore,
Waiting the Sail that all his Wishes bore;
Nor long expected, for the following Tide   270
Sent out the hostile Ship and beauteous Bride.
    To *Rhodes* the Rival Bark directly steer'd,
When *Cymon* sudden at her Back appear'd,
And stop'd her Flight: Then standing on his Prow
In haughty Terms he thus defy'd the Foe,   275
Or strike your Sails at Summons, or prepare
To prove the last Extremities of War.
Thus warn'd, the *Rhodians* for the Fight provide;
Already were the Vessels Side by Side,
These obstinate to save, and those to seize the Bride.   280
But *Cymon* soon his crooked Grapples cast,
Which with tenacious hold his Foes embrac'd,
And arm'd with Sword and Shield, amid the Press he pass'd.
Fierce was the Fight, but hast'ning to his Prey,
By force the furious Lover freed his way: 285
Himself alone dispers'd the *Rhodian* Crew,
The Weak disdain'd, the Valiant overthrew;
Cheap Conquest for his following Friends remain'd,
He reap'd the Field, and they but only glean'd.
    His Victory confess'd, the Foes retreat,   290
And cast their Weapons at the Victor's Feet.
Whom thus he chear'd: O *Rhodian* Youth, I fought
For Love alone, nor other Booty sought;
Your Lives are safe; your Vessel I resign,
Yours be your own, restoring what is mine: 295
In *Iphigene* I claim my rightful Due,
Rob'd by my Rival, and detain'd by you:
Your *Pasimond* a lawless Bargain drove,
The Parent could not sell the Daughters Love;
Or if he cou'd, my Love disdains the Laws,   300
And like a King by Conquest gains his Cause:

290 confess'd,] confess'd F

Where Arms take place, all other Pleas are vain,
Love taught me Force, and Force shall Love maintain.
You, what by Strength you could not keep, release,
And at an easy Ransom buy your Peace.   305
   Fear on the conquer'd Side soon sign'd th' Accord,
And *Iphigene* to *Cymon* was restor'd:
While to his Arms the blushing Bride he took,
To seeming Sadness she compos'd her Look;
As if by Force subjected to his Will,   310
Tho' pleas'd, dissembling, and a Woman still.
And, for she wept, he wip'd her falling Tears,
And pray'd her to dismiss her empty Fears;
For yours I am, he said, and have deserv'd
Your Love much better whom so long I serv'd,   315
Than he to whom your formal Father ty'd
Your Vows; and sold a Slave, not sent a Bride.
Thus while he spoke he seiz'd the willing Prey,
As *Paris* bore the *Spartan* Spouse away:
Faintly she scream'd, and ev'n her Eyes confess'd   320
She rather would be thought, than was Distress'd.
   Who now exults but *Cymon* in his Mind,   ⎫
Vain hopes, and empty Joys of human Kind,   ⎬
Proud of the present, to the future blind!   ⎭
Secure of Fate while *Cymon* plows the Sea,   325
And steers to *Candy* with his conquer'd Prey,
Scarce the third Glass of measur'd Hours was run,
When like a fiery Meteor sunk the Sun;
The Promise of a Storm; the shifting Gales
Forsake by Fits, and fill the flagging Sails: 330
Hoarse Murmurs of the Main from far were heard,
And Night came on, not by degrees prepar'd,
But all at once; at once the Winds arise,
The Thunders roul, the forky Lightning flies:
In vain the Master issues out Commands,   335
In vain the trembling Sailors ply their Hands:
The Tempest unforeseen prevents their Care,
And from the first they labour in despair.
The giddy Ship betwixt the Winds and Tides

308 took,] took; F   326 Prey,] Prey. F

Forc'd back and forwards, in a Circle rides,   340
Stun'd with the diff'rent Blows; then shoots amain
Till counterbuff'd she stops, and sleeps again.
Not more aghast the proud Archangel fell,
Plung'd from the height of Heav'n to deepest Hell,
Than stood the Lover of his Love possess'd,   345
Now curs'd the more, the more he had been bless'd;
More anxious for her Danger than his own,
Death he defies; but would be lost alone.
     Sad *Iphigene* to Womanish Complaints
Adds pious Pray'rs, and wearies all the Saints;   350
Ev'n if she could, her Love she would repent,
But since she cannot, dreads the Punishment:
Her forfeit Faith, and *Pasimond* betray'd,
Are ever present, and her Crime upbraid.
She blames herself, nor blames her Lover less,   355
Augments her Anger as her Fears increase;
From her own Back the Burden would remove,
And lays the Load on his ungovern'd Love,
Which interposing durst in Heav'n's despight
Invade, and violate another's Right: 360
The Pow'rs incens'd awhile deferr'd his Pain,
And made him Master of his Vows in vain:
But soon they punish'd his presumptuous Pride;
That for his daring Enterprize she dy'd,
Who rather not resisted, than comply'd.   365
     Then impotent of Mind, with alter'd Sense,
She hugg'd th' Offender, and forgave th' Offence,
Sex to the last: Mean time with Sails declin'd
The wand'ring Vessel drove before the Wind:
Toss'd, and retoss'd, aloft, and then alow;   370
Nor Port they seek, nor certain Course they know,
But ev'ry moment wait the coming Blow.
Thus blindly driv'n, by breaking Day they view'd
The Land before 'em, and their Fears renew'd;
The Land was welcome, but the Tempest bore   375
The threaten'd Ship against a rocky Shore.
     A winding Bay was near; to this they bent,

And just escap'd; their Force already spent:
Secure from Storms and panting from the Sea,
The Land unknown at leisure they survey;   380
And saw (but soon their sickly Sight withdrew)
The rising Tow'rs of *Rhodes* at distant view;
And curs'd the hostile Shoar of *Pasimond*,
Sav'd from the Seas, and shipwreck'd on the Ground.
  The frighted Sailors try'd their Strength in vain   385
To turn the Stern, and tempt the stormy Main;
But the stiff Wind withstood the lab'ring Oar,
And forc'd them forward on the fatal Shoar!
The crooked Keel now bites the *Rhodian* Strand,
And the Ship moor'd, constrains the Crew to land: 390
Yet still they might be safe because unknown,
But as ill Fortune seldom comes alone,
The Vessel they dismiss'd was driv'n before,
Already shelter'd on their Native Shoar;
Known each, they know: But each with change of Chear; 395
The vanquish'd side exults; the Victors fear,
Not them but theirs; made Pris'ners e'er they Fight,
Despairing Conquest, and depriv'd of Flight.
  The Country rings around with loud Alarms,
And raw in Fields the rude Militia swarms;   400
Mouths without Hands; maintain'd at vast Expence,
In Peace a Charge, in War a weak Defence:
Stout once a Month they march a blust'ring Band,
And ever, but in times of Need, at hand:
This was the Morn when issuing on the Guard,   405
Drawn up in Rank and File they stood prepar'd
Of seeming Arms to make a short essay,
Then hasten to be Drunk, the Business of the Day.
  The Cowards would have fled, but that they knew
Themselves so many, and their Foes so few;   410
But crowding on, the last the first impel;
Till overborn with weight the *Cyprians* fell.
Cymon inslav'd, who first the War begun,
And *Iphigene* once more is lost and won.
  Deep in a Dungeon was the Captive cast,   415
Depriv'd of Day, and held in Fetters fast:

  396 fear,] fear; *F*   397 theirs;] theirs, *F*

His Life was only spar'd at their Request,
Whom taken he so nobly had releas'd:
But *Iphigenia* was the Ladies Care,
Each in their turn address'd to treat the Fair;   } 42
While *Pasimond* and his, the Nuptial Feast prepare.

   Her secret Soul to *Cymon* was inclin'd,
But she must suffer what her Fates assign'd;
So passive is the Church of Womankind.
What worse to *Cymon* could his Fortune deal,   42
Rowl'd to the lowest Spoke of all her Wheel?
It rested to dismiss the downward weight,
Or raise him upward to his former height;
The latter pleas'd; and Love (concern'd the most)   43
Prepar'd th' amends, for what by Love he lost.

   The Sire of *Pasimond* had left a Son,
Though younger, yet for Courage early known,
Ormisda call'd; to whom by Promise ty'd,
A *Rhodian* Beauty was the destin'd Bride:
Cassandra was her Name, above the rest   4
Renown'd for Birth, with Fortune amply bless'd.
Lysymachus who rul'd the *Rhodian* State,
Was then by choice their annual Magistrate:
He lov'd *Cassandra* too with equal Fire,
But Fortune had not favour'd his Desire;   4
Cross'd by her Friends, by her not disapprov'd,
Nor yet preferr'd, or like *Ormisda* lov'd:
So stood th' Affair: Some little Hope remain'd,
That should his Rival chance to lose, he gain'd.

   Mean time young *Pasimond* his Marriage press'd,   4
Ordain'd the Nuptial Day, prepar'd the Feast;
And frugally resolv'd (the Charge to shun,
Which would be double should he wed alone)
To join his Brother's Bridal with his own.

   Lysymachus oppress'd with mortal Grief   4
Receiv'd the News, and study'd quick Relief:
The fatal Day approach'd: If Force were us'd,
The Magistrate his publick Trust abus'd;
To Justice, liable as Law requir'd;
For when his Office ceas'd, his Pow'r expir'd:
While Pow'r remain'd, the Means were in his Hand

By Force to seize, and then forsake the Land:
Betwixt Extreams he knew not how to move,
A Slave to Fame, but more a Slave to Love:
Restraining others, yet himself not free,   460
Made impotent by Pow'r, debas'd by Dignity!
Both Sides he weigh'd: But after much Debate,
The Man prevail'd above the Magistrate.

Love never fails to master what he finds,
But works a diff'rent way in diff'rent Minds,   465
The Fool enlightens, and the Wise he blinds.
This Youth proposing to possess, and scape,
Began in Murder, to conclude in Rape:
Unprais'd by me, tho' Heav'n sometime may bless
An impious Act with undeserv'd Success: 470
The Great, it seems, are priviledg'd alone
To punish all Injustice but their own.
But here I stop, not daring to proceed,
Yet blush to flatter an unrighteous Deed:
For Crimes are but permitted, not decreed.   475
Resolv'd on Force, his Wit the Pretor bent,
To find the Means that might secure th' event;
Not long he labour'd, for his lucky Thought
In Captive *Cymon* found the Friend he sought;
Th' Example pleas'd: The Cause and Crime the same;   480
An injur'd Lover, and a ravish'd Dame.
How much he durst he knew by what he dar'd,
The less he had to lose, the less he car'd
To menage loathsom Life when Love was the Reward.
This ponder'd well, and fix'd on his Intent,   485
In depth of Night he for the Pris'ner sent;
In secret sent, the publick View to shun,
Then with a sober Smile he thus begun.
The Pow'rs above who bounteously bestow
Their Gifts and Graces on Mankind below,   490
Yet prove our Merit first, nor blindly give
To such as are not worthy to receive:
For Valour and for Virtue they provide
Their due Reward, but first they must be try'd:
These fruitful Seeds within your Mind they sow'd;   495

493 provide] provide, F

'Twas yours t' improve the Talent they bestow'd:
They gave you to be born of noble Kind,
They gave you Love to lighten up your Mind,
And purge the grosser Parts; they gave you Care
To please, and Courage to deserve the Fair.   50
    Thus far they try'd you, and by Proof they found
The Grain intrusted in a grateful Ground:
But still the great Experiment remain'd,
They suffer'd you to lose the Prize you gain'd;
That you might learn the Gift was theirs alone: 50
And when restor'd, to them the Blessing own.
Restor'd it soon will be; the Means prepar'd,
The Difficulty smooth'd, the Danger shar'd:
Be but your self, the Care to me resign,
Then *Iphigene* is yours, *Cassandra* mine.   51
Your Rival *Pasimond* pursues your Life,
Impatient to revenge his ravish'd Wife,
But yet not his; to Morrow is behind,
And Love our Fortunes in one Band has join'd:
Two Brothers are our Foes; *Ormisda* mine,   51
As much declar'd, as *Pasimond* is thine:
To Morrow must their common Vows be ty'd;
With Love to Friend and Fortune for our Guide,
Let both resolve to die, or each redeem a Bride.
    Right I have none, nor hast thou much to plead;   5.
'Tis Force when done must justify the Deed:
Our Task perform'd we next prepare for Flight;
And let the Losers talk in vain of Right:
We with the Fair will sail before the Wind,
If they are griev'd, I leave the Laws behind.   5:
Speak thy Resolves; if now thy Courage droop,
Despair in Prison, and abandon Hope;
But if thou dar'st in Arms thy Love regain,
(For Liberty without thy Love were vain:)
Then second my Design to seize the Prey,   5
Or lead to second Rape, for well thou know'st the way.
    Said *Cymon* overjoy'd, do Thou propose
The Means to Fight, and only shew the Foes;
For from the first, when Love had fir'd my Mind,
Resolv'd I left the Care of Life behind.   5

To this the bold *Lysymachus* reply'd,
Let Heav'n be neuter, and the Sword decide:
The Spousals are prepar'd, already play
The Minstrels, and provoke the tardy Day:
By this the Brides are wak'd, their Grooms are dress'd;   540
All *Rhodes* is summon'd to the Nuptial Feast,
All but my self the sole unbidden Guest.
Unbidden though I am, I will be there,
And, join'd by thee, intend to joy the Fair.
    Now hear the rest; when Day resigns the Light,   545
And chearful Torches guild the jolly Night;
Be ready at my Call, my chosen few
With Arms administer'd shall aid thy Crew.
Then entring unexpected will we seize
Our destin'd Prey, from Men dissolv'd in ease;   550
By Wine disabled, unprepar'd for Fight;
And hast'ning to the Seas suborn our Flight:
The Seas are ours, for I command the Fort,
A Ship well man'd, expects us in the Port:
If they, or if their Friends the Prize contest,   555
Death shall attend the Man who dares resist.
    It pleas'd! The Pris'ner to his Hold retir'd,
His Troop with equal Emulation fir'd,
All fix'd to Fight, and all their wonted Work requir'd.
    The Sun arose; the Streets were throng'd around,   560
The Palace open'd, and the Posts were crown'd:
The double Bridegroom at the Door attends
Th' expected Spouse, and entertains the Friends:
They meet, they lead to Church; the Priests invoke
The Pow'rs, and feed the Flames with fragrant Smoke: 565
This done they Feast, and at the close of Night
By kindled Torches vary their Delight,
These lead the lively Dance, and those the brimming Bowls invite.
    Now at th' appointed Place and Hour assign'd,
With Souls resolv'd the Ravishers were join'd: 570
Three Bands are form'd: The first is sent before
To favour the Retreat, and guard the Shore:
The second at the Palace-gate is plac'd,
And up the lofty Stairs ascend the last:

562 attends] attends, F

A peaceful Troop they seem with shining Vests,   575
But Coats of Male beneath secure their Breasts.
    Dauntless they enter, *Cymon* at their Head,
And find the Feast renew'd, the Table spread:
Sweet Voices mix'd with instrumental Sounds
Ascend the vaulted Roof, the vaulted Roof rebounds.   580
When like the Harpies rushing through the Hall
The suddain Troop appears, the Tables fall,
Their smoaking Load is on the Pavement thrown;
Each Ravisher prepares to seize his own:
The Brides invaded with a rude Embrace   585
Shreek out for Aid, Confusion fills the Place:
Quick to redeem the Prey their plighted Lords
Advance, the Palace gleams with shining Swords.
    But late is all Defence, and Succour vain;
The Rape is made, the Ravishers remain: 590
Two sturdy Slaves were only sent before
To bear the purchas'd Prize in Safety to the Shore.
The Troop retires, the Lovers close the rear,
With forward Faces not confessing Fear:
Backward they move, but scorn their Pace to mend,   595
Then seek the Stairs, and with slow hast descend.
    Fierce *Pasimond* their passage to prevent,
Thrust full on *Cymon*'s Back in his descent,
The Blade return'd unbath'd, and to the Handle bent:
Stout *Cymon* soon remounts, and cleft in two   600
His Rival's Head with one descending Blow:
And as the next in rank *Ormisda* stood,
He turn'd the Point: The Sword inur'd to Blood,
Bor'd his unguarded Breast, which pour'd a purple Flood.
    With vow'd Revenge the gath'ring Crowd pursues,   60
The Ravishers turn Head, the Fight renews;
The Hall is heap'd with Corps; the sprinkled Gore
Besmears the Walls, and floats the Marble Floor.
Dispers'd at length the drunken Squadron flies,
The Victors to their Vessel bear the Prize;   61
And hear behind loud Groans, and lamentable Cries.

      589 Defence,] Defence; F   vain;] vain, F

The Crew with merry Shouts their Anchors weigh
Then ply their Oars, and brush the buxom *Sea*,
While Troops of gather'd *Rhodians* croud the Key.
What should the People do, when left alone?   615
The Governor, and Government are gone.
The publick Wealth to Foreign Parts convey'd;
Some Troops disbanded, and the rest unpaid.
Rhodes is the Soveraign of the Sea no more;
Their Ships unrigg'd, and spent their Naval Store;   620
They neither could defend, nor can pursue,
But grind their Teeth, and cast a helpless view:
In vain with Darts a distant War they try,
Short, and more short the missive Weapons fly.
Mean while the Ravishers their Crimes enjoy,   625
And flying Sails, and sweeping Oars employ;
The Cliffs of *Rhodes* in little space are lost,
Jove's Isle they seek; nor *Jove* denies his Coast.
    In safety landed on the *Candian* Shore,
With generous Wines their Spirits they restore;   630
There *Cymon* with his *Rhodian* Friend resides,
Both Court, and Wed at once the willing Brides.
A War ensues, the *Cretans* own their Cause,
Stiff to defend their hospitable Laws:
Both Parties lose by turns; and neither wins,   635
'Till Peace propounded by a Truce begins.
The Kindred of the Slain forgive the Deed,
But a short Exile must for Show precede;
The Term expir'd, from *Candia* they remove;
And happy each at Home, enjoys his Love.   640

622 grind] grin'd F

PROLOGUE, EPILOGUE, SONG and SECULAR MASQUE from
THE PILGRIM

PROLOGUE

How wretched is the Fate of those who write!
Brought muzled to the Stage, for fear they bite.
Where, like *Tom Dove*, they stand the Common Foe;
Lugg'd by the *Critique*, Baited by the *Beau*.
Yet worse, their Brother *Poets* Damn the Play,   5
And Roar the loudest, tho' they never Pay.
The Fops are proud of Scandal, for they cry,
At every lewd, low Character,—That's I.
He who writes Letters to himself, wou'd Swear
The World forgot him, if he was not there.   10
What shou'd a Poet do? 'Tis hard for One
To pleasure all the Fools that wou'd be shown:
And yet not Two in Ten will pass the Town.
Most Coxcombs are not of the Laughing kind;
More goes to make a Fop, than Fops can find.   15
 Quack *Maurus*, tho' he never took Degrees
In either of our Universities;
Yet to be shown by some kind Wit he looks,
Because he plai'd the fool and writ Three Books.
But if he wou'd be worth a Poet's Pen,   20
He must be more a Fool, and write again:
For all the former Fustian stuff he wrote,
Was Dead-born Doggrel, or is quite forgot;
His Man of *Uz*, stript of his *Hebrew* Robe,
Is just the Proverb, and *As poor as* Job.   25

Prologue, &c. Text from The Pilgrim, A Comedy: . . . Likewise A Prologue, Epilogue, Dialogue and Masque, Written by the late Great Poet Mr. Dryden, just before his Death, being the last of his Works, *1700, collated with* The Comedies, Tragedies, and Operas . . . with a Secular Masque, *1701*
 Prologue. Heading *Prologue to the Masque 1701*   18 shown *1701*: shown; *1700*

One wou'd have thought he cou'd no lower Jog;
But *Arthur* was a Level, *Job's* a Bog.
There, tho' he crept, yet still he kept in sight;
But here, he flounders in, and sinks down right.
Had he prepar'd us, and been dull by Rule,   30
Tobit had first been turn'd to Ridicule:
But our bold *Britton*, without Fear or Awe,
O're-leaps at once, the whole *Apocrypha*;
Invades the *Psalms* with Rhymes, and leaves no room
For any Vandal *Hopkins* yet to come.   35
    But what if, after all, this Godly Geer,
Is not so Senceless as it wou'd appear?
Our Mountebank has laid a deeper Train,
His Cant, like *Merry Andrew*'s Noble Vein,
Cat-Call's the Sects, to draw 'em in for gain.   40
At leisure Hours, in Epique Song he deals,
Writes to the rumbling of his Coaches Wheels,
Prescribes in hast, and seldom kills by Rule,
But rides Triumphant between Stool and Stool.
    Well, let him go; 'tis yet too early day,   45
To get himself a Place in Farce or Play.
We know not by what Name we should Arraign him,
For no one Category can contain him;
A Pedant, Canting Preacher, and a Quack,
Are Load enough to break one Asses Back: 50
At last, grown wanton, he presum'd to write,
Traduc'd Two Kings, their kindness to requite;
One made the Doctor, and one dubb'd the Knight.

EPILOGUE

PERHAPS the Parson stretch'd a point too far,
When with our *Theatres* he wag'd a War.
He tells you, That this very Moral Age
Receiv'd the first Infection from the Stage.

26 lower *1701*: longer *1700*   29 flounders *1701*: founders *1700*. *See Commentary*
40 for gain *1701*: again *1700*

But sure, a banisht Court, with Lewdness fraught,   5
The Seeds of open Vice returning brought.
Thus Lodg'd, (as Vice by great Example thrives)
It first debauch'd the Daughters and the Wives.
London, a fruitful Soil, yet never bore
So plentiful a Crop of Horns before.   10
The *Poets*, who must live by Courts or starve,
Were proud, so good a Government to serve;
And mixing with Buffoons and Pimps profain,
Tainted the Stage, for some small Snip of Gain.
For they, like *Harlots* under *Bawds* profest,   15
Took all th' ungodly pains, and got the least.
Thus did the thriving Malady prevail,
The Court, it's Head, the *Poets* but the Tail.
The Sin was of our Native growth, 'tis true;
The Scandall of the Sin was wholly new.   20
Misses there were, but modestly conceal'd;
White-hall the naked *Venus* first reveal'd.
Who standing, as at *Cyprus*, in her Shrine,
The Strumpet was ador'd with Rites Divine.
E're this, if Saints had any Secret Motion,   25
'Twas Chamber Practice all, and Close Devotion.
I pass the Peccadillo's of their time;
Nothing but open Lewdness was a Crime.
A *Monarch*'s Blood was venial to the Nation,
Compar'd with one foul Act of Fornication.   30
Now, they wou'd Silence us, and shut the Door
That let in all the barefac'd Vice before.
As for reforming us, which some pretend,   ⎫
That work in *England* is without an end;   ⎬
Well we may change, but we shall never mend. ⎭   3
Yet, if you can but bear the present Stage,
We hope much better of the coming Age.
What wou'd you say, if we shou'd first begin ⎫
To Stop the Trade of Love, behind the Scene: ⎬
Where *Actresses* make bold with maried Men? ⎭   4
For while abroad so prodigal the *Dolt* is,
Poor Spouse at home as ragged as a Colt is.
In short, we'll grow as Moral as we can,
Save here and there a Woman or a Man:

But neither you, nor we, with all our pains,   } 45
Can make clean work; there will be some Remains,
While you have still your *Oats*, and we our *Hains*.

SONG of a *Scholar* and his *Mistress*,

who being Cross'd by their Friends,

fell Mad for one another;

and now first meet in *Bedlam*

Musick within.

The Lovers enter at Opposite Doors, each held by a Keeper.

Phillis.	LOOK, look, I see—I see my Love appear:
	'Tis he—'Tis he alone;
	For, like him, there is none:
	'Tis the dear, dear Man, 'tis thee, Dear.
Amyntas.	Hark! the Winds War; 5
	The foamy Waves roar;
	I see a Ship afar,
	Tossing and Tossing, and making to the Shoar:
	But what's that I View,
	So Radiant of Hue, 10
	St. *Hermo, St. Hermo,* that sits upon the Sails?
	Ah! No, no, no.
	St. *Hermo,* Never, never shone so bright;
	'Tis *Phillis,* only *Phillis,* can shoot so fair a Light:
	'Tis *Phillis,* 'tis *Phillis,* that saves the Ship alone, 15
	For all the Winds are hush'd, and the Storm is over-blown.
Phillis.	Let me go, let me run, let me fly to his Arms.
Amyntas.	If all the Fates combine,
	And all the Furies join,
	I'll force my way to *Phillis,* and break through the Charms. 20

Here they break from their Keepers; run to each other, and embrace.

Phillis.	Shall I Marry the Man I love?
	And shall I conclude my Pains?
	Now blest be the Powers above,

Song. 20 Charms] Charm *1700*

25

I feel the Blood bound in my Veins;
With a lively Leap it began to move,
And the Vapours leave my Brains.

Amyntas. Body join'd to Body, and Heart join'd to Heart,
To make sure of the Cure;
Go call the Man in Black, to mumble o're his part.

Phillis. But suppose he should stay— 30

Amyntas. At worst if he delay;
'Tis a Work must be done;
We'll borrow but a Day,
And the better the sooner begun.

CHORUS of Both.

At worst if he delay, &c.

They run out together hand in hand.

THE SECULAR MASQUE

Enter Janus.

Janus. CHRONOS, *Chronos*, mend thy Pace,
An hundred times the rowling Sun
Around the Radiant Belt has run
In his revolving Race.
Behold, behold, the Goal in sight, 5
Spread thy Fans, and wing thy flight.

Enter Chronos, *with a Scythe in his hand, and a great Globe on his Back, which*
he sets down at his entrance.

Chronos. Weary, weary of my weight,
Let me, let me drop my Freight,
And leave the World behind.
I could not bear 10
Another Year
The Load of Human-Kind.

Enter Momus *Laughing.*

Momus. Ha! ha! ha! Ha! ha! ha! well hast thou done,
To lay down thy Pack,
And lighten thy Back,
The World was a Fool, e'er since it begun,

	And since neither *Janus*, nor *Chronos*, nor I,	
	Can hinder the Crimes,	
	Or mend the Bad Times,	
	'Tis better to Laugh than to Cry.	20
Cho. of all 3.	*'Tis better to Laugh than to Cry.*	
Janus.	Since *Momus* comes to laugh below,	
	Old Time begin the Show,	
	That he may see, in every Scene,	
	What Changes in this Age have been,	25
Chronos.	Then Goddess of the Silver Bow begin.	

Horns, or Hunting-Musique within.

Enter Diana.

Diana.	With Horns and with Hounds I waken the Day,	
	And hye to my Woodland walks away;	
	I tuck up my Robe, and am buskin'd soon,	
	And tye to my Forehead a wexing Moon.	30
	I course the fleet Stagg, unkennel the Fox,	
	And chase the wild Goats or'e summets of Rocks,	
	With shouting and hooting we pierce thro' the Sky;	
	And Eccho turns Hunter, and doubles the Cry.	
Cho. of all.	*With shouting and hooting, we pierce through the Skie,*	35
	And Eccho turns Hunter, and doubles the Cry.	
Janus.	Then our Age was in it's Prime,	
Chronos.	Free from Rage.	
Diana.	————And free from Crime.	
Momus.	A very Merry, Dancing, Drinking,	
	Laughing, Quaffing, and unthinking Time.	40
Cho. of all.	*Then our Age was in it's Prime,*	
	Free from Rage, and free from Crime,	
	A very Merry, Dancing, Drinking,	
	Laughing, Quaffing, and unthinking Time.	

Dance of Diana's *Attendants.*

Enter Mars.

Mars.	Inspire the Vocal Brass, Inspire;	45
	The World is past its Infant Age:	
	Arms and Honour,	
	Arms and Honour,	

The Secular Masque. 27 *Day, 1701:* Day. *1700*

Set the Martial Mind on Fire,
And kindle Manly Rage.　　　　　　　　　　50
Mars has lookt the Sky to Red;
And Peace, the Lazy Good, is fled.
Plenty, Peace, and Pleasure fly;
　　The Sprightly Green
In *Woodland*-Walks, no more is seen;　　　55
The Sprightly Green, has drunk the *Tyrian* Dye.

Cho. of all.　*Plenty, Peace,* &c.

Mars.　Sound the Trumpet, Beat the Drum,
Through all the World around;
Sound a Reveille, Sound, Sound,　　　　　60
　　The Warrior God is come.

Cho. of all.　*Sound the Trumpet,* &c.

Momus.　Thy Sword within the Scabbard keep,
　　And let Mankind agree;
Better the World were fast asleep,　　　　65
　　Than kept awake by Thee.
The Fools are only thinner,
　　With all our Cost and Care;
But neither side a winner,
　　For Things are as they were.　　　　　70

Cho. of all.　*The Fools are only,* &c.

Enter Venus.

Venus.　Calms appear, when Storms are past;
Love will have his Hour at last:
Nature is my kindly Care;
Mars destroys, and I repair;　　　　　　75
Take me, take me, while you may,
Venus comes not ev'ry Day.

Cho. of all.　*Take her, take her,* &c.

Chronos.　The World was then so light,
I scarcely felt the Weight;　　　　　　　80
Joy rul'd the Day, and Love the Night.
But since the Queen of Pleasure left the Ground,
　　I faint, I lag,
　　And feebly drag
The pond'rous Orb around.　　　　　　　85

Momus.　All, all, of a piece throughout;

Pointing ⎫ to *Diana.* ⎭	Thy Chase had a Beast in View;
to *Mars.*	Thy Wars brought nothing about;
to *Venus.*	Thy Lovers were all untrue.
Janus.	'Tis well an Old Age is out, 90
Chro[*nos*].	And time to begin a New.
Cho. of all.	*All, all, of a piece throughout;*
	Thy Chase had a Beast in View;
	Thy Wars brought nothing about;
	Thy Lovers were all untrue. 95
	'Tis well an Old Age is out,
	And time to begin a New.

Dance of Huntsmen, Nymphs, Warriours and Lovers.

The Fair Stranger

HAPPY and free, securely blest,
  No Beauty cou'd disturb my Rest;
My Amorous Heart was in Despair
To find a new Victorious Fair.

'Till you descending on our Plains,   5
With Forrain Force renew my Chains.
Where now you rule without Controul,
The mighty Soveraign of my Soul.

Your Smiles have more of Conquering Charms,
Than all your Native Countries Arms;   10
Their Troops we can expel with Ease
Who vanquish only when we please.

But in your Eyes, oh! there's the spell;
Who can see them, and not Rebell?
You make us Captives by your stay,   15
Yet kill us if you go away.

The Fair Stranger. Text from |A New Collection of Poems on Several Occasions,
1701, collated with Tixall Poetry, *1813* (*TP*). *See Commentary*
   Heading in TP Witty Mr. Henningam's Song   3 was in Despair] no conquering faire *TP*   4 To ... Fair.] Had power to wound with new despaire, *TP*
6 renew] renew'd *TP*   9 Smiles] looks *TP*   11 Their] Your *TP*   12 Who]
They *TP*   when] while *TP*   13 spell;] spell *1701*   13–16 *TP has*
                              But all the force that in us lies,
                              Yeilds no defence against your eyes.
                              They make us languish whilst in sight,
                              But absent, we must perish quite.

[*Lines on* Tonson]

[Now the Assembly to adjourn prepar'd,
When *Bibliopolo* from behind appear'd,
As well describ'd by th' old Satyrick Bard:]
With leering Looks, Bullfac'd, and Freckled fair,
With two left Legs, and Judas-colour'd Hair,
With Frowzy Pores, that taint the ambient Air.

Lines on Tonson. Text from Faction Display'd. A Poem, *1704. The version in Powys's letter (see Commentary) runs:*

With leering look, bull faced and freckled fair,
With frowsy pores poisoning the ambient air,
With two left leggs and Judas coloured hair.

POEMS FROM
POETICAL MISCELLANIES:
THE FIFTH PART
(1704)

ON THE DEATH OF *AMYNTAS*:
A Pastoral ELEGY

'TWAS on a Joyless and a Gloomy Morn,
   Wet was the Grass, and hung with Pearls the Thorn;
When *Damon,* who design'd to pass the Day
With Hounds and Horns, and chase the flying Prey,
Rose early from his Bed; but soon he found   5
The Welkin pitch'd with sullen Clouds around,
An Eastern Wind, and Dew upon the Ground.
Thus while he stood, and sighing did survey
The Fields, and curs'd th' ill Omens of the Day,
He saw *Menalcas* come with heavy pace;   10
Wet were his Eyes, and chearless was his Face:
He wrung his Hands, distracted with his Care,
And sent his Voice before him from afar.
Return, he cry'd, return unhappy Swain,
The spungy Clouds are fill'd with gath'ring Rain;   15
The Promise of the Day not only cross'd,
But ev'n the Spring, the Spring it self is lost.
Amyntas,—Oh! he cou'd not speak the rest,
Nor needed, for presaging *Damon* guess'd.
Equal with Heav'n young *Damon* lov'd the Boy;   20
The boast of Nature, both his Parents Joy.
His graceful Form revolving in his Mind;
So great a Genius, and a Soul so kind,
Gave sad assurance that his Fears were true;
Too well the Envy of the Gods he knew: 25
For when their Gifts too lavishly are plac'd,
Soon they repent, and will not make them last.
For, sure, it was too bountiful a Dole,

The Mother's Features, and the Father's Soul.
Then thus he cry'd, The Morn bespoke the News,   30
The Morning did her chearful Light diffuse;
But see how suddenly she chang'd her Face,
And brought on Clouds and Rains, the Day's disgrace;
Just such, *Amyntas*, was thy promis'd Race!
What Charms adorn'd thy Youth where Nature smil'd,   35
And more than Man was giv'n us in a Child.
His Infancy was ripe: a Soul sublime
In Years so tender that prevented time:
Heav'n gave him all at once; then snatch'd away,
E're Mortals all his Beauties cou'd survey,
Just like the Flow'r that buds and withers in a day.   40

MENALCAS

The Mother Lovely, tho' with Grief opprest,
Reclin'd his dying Head upon her Breast.
The mournful Family stood all around;
One Groan was heard, one Universal Sound: 45
All were in Floods of Tears and endless Sorrow drown'd.
So dire a Sadness sate on ev'ry Look,
Ev'n Death repented he had giv'n the Stroke.
He griev'd his fatal Work had been ordain'd,
But promis'd length of Life to those who yet remain'd.   50
The Mother's and her Eldest Daughter's Grace,
It seems had brib'd him to prolong their space:
The Father bore it with undaunted Soul,
Like one who durst his Destiny controul:
Yet with becoming Grief he bore his part,   55
Resign'd his Son, but not resign'd his Heart.
Patient as *Job*; and may he live to see,
Like him, a new increasing Family:

DAMON

Such is my Wish, and such my Prophesie.
For yet, my Friend, the Beauteous Mold remains,   60
Long may she exercise her fruitful Pains:
But, ah! with better hap, and bring a Race
More lasting, and endu'd with equal Grace:

On the Death of Amyntas. 40 survey,] survey. *1704*

Equal she may, but farther none can go;
For he was all that was exact below.   65

MENALCAS

Damon, behold, yon breaking Purple Cloud;
Hear'st thou not Hymns and Songs Divinely loud?
There mounts *Amyntas*; the young Cherubs play
About their Godlike Mate, and Sing him on his way.
He cleaves the liquid Air, behold he Flies,   70
And every Moment gains upon the Skies;
The new come Guest admires th' Ætherial State,
The *Saphyr* Portal, and the *Golden* Gate;
And now admitted in the shining Throng,
He shows the Passport which he brought along;   75
His Passport is his Innocence and Grace,
Well known to all the Natives of the Place.
Now Sing yee joyful Angels, and admire
Your Brother's Voice that comes to mend your Quire:
Sing you, while endless Tears our Eyes bestow;   80
For like *Amyntas* none is left below.

OVID'S AMOURS. BOOK I. ELEGY I

FOR mighty Wars I thought to Tune my Lute,
And make my Measures to my Subject sute.
Six Feet for ev'ry Verse the Muse design'd,
But *Cupid*, Laughing, when he saw my Mind
From ev'ry Second Verse a Foot purloin'd.   5
Who gave Thee, Boy, this Arbitrary sway,
On Subjects not thy own, Commands to lay,
Who *Phœbus* only and his Laws obey?
'Tis more absur'd, than if the *Queen of Love*
Shou'd in *Minerva's* Arms to Battel move;   10
Or Manly *Pallas* from that Queen shou'd take
Her Torch, and o're the dying Lover shake.
In Fields as well may *Cynthia* sow the Corn,
Or *Ceres* wind in Woods the Bugle Horn.
As well may *Phœbus* quit the trembling String,   15
For Sword and Shield; and *Mars* may learn to Sing.

Already thy Dominions are too large;
Be not ambitious of a Foreign Charge.
If thou wilt Reign o're all, and ev'ry where,
The God of Musick for his Harp may fear.   20
Thus when with soaring Wings I seek Renown,
Thou pluck'st my Pinnions, and I flutter down.
Cou'd I on such mean Thoughts my Muse employ,
I want a Mistress, or a blooming Boy.
Thus I complain'd; his Bow the Stripling bent,   25
And chose an Arrow fit for his Intent.
The Shaft his purpose fatally pursues;
Now Poet there's a Subject for thy Muse.
He said, (too well, alas, he knows his Trade,)
For in my Breast a Mortal Wound he made.   30
Far hence ye proud *Hexameters* remove,
My Verse is pac'd, and travell'd into Love.
With Myrtle Wreaths my thoughtful Brows inclose,
While in unequal Verse I Sing my Woes.

OVID'S AMOURS. BOOK I. ELEGY IV

To his Mistress, whose Husband is invited to a Feast with them. The Poet
instructs her how to behave her self in his Company.

YOUR Husband will be with us at the Treat;
    May that be the last Supper he shall Eat.
And am poor I, a Guest invited there,
Only to see, while he may touch the Fair?
To see you Kiss and Hug your nauseous Lord,   5
While his leud Hand descends below the Board?
Now wonder not that *Hippodamia*'s Charms,
At such a sight, the Centaurs urg'd to Arms:
That in a rage, they threw their Cups aside,
Assail'd the Bridegroom, and wou'd force the Bride.   10
I am not half a Horse, (I wish I were:)
Yet hardly can from you my Hands forbear.
Take, then, my Counsel; which, observ'd, may be
Of some Importance both to you and me.
Be sure to come before your Man be there,   15
There's nothing can be done, but come howe're.

Sit next him, (that belongs to Decency;)
But tread upon my Foot in passing by.
Read in my Looks what silently they speak,
And slily, with your Eyes, your Answer make.   20
My lifted Eye-brow shall declare my Pain,
My Right-Hand to his fellow shall complain.
And on the Back a Letter shall design;
Besides a Note that shall be Writ in Wine.
When e're you think upon our last Embrace,   25
With your Fore-finger gently touch your Face.
If any Word of mine offend my Dear,
Pull, with your Hand, the Velvet of your Ear.
If you are pleas'd with what I do or say,
Handle your Rings, or with your Fingers play.   30
As Suppliants use at Altars, hold the Boord
When e're you wish the Devil may take your Lord.
When he fills for you, never touch the Cup;
But bid th' officious Cuckold drink it up.
The Waiter on those Services employ;   35
Drink you, and I will snatch it from the Boy:
Watching the part where your sweet Mouth has been,
And thence, with eager Lips, will suck it in.
If he, with Clownish Manners thinks it fit
To taste, and offers you the nasty Bit,   40
Reject his greasy Kindness, and restore
Th' unsav'ry Morsel he had chew'd before.
Nor let his Arms embrace your Neck, nor rest
Your tender Cheek upon his hairy Brest.
Let not his Hand within your Bosom stray,   45
And rudely with your pretty Bubbies play.
But, above all, let him no Kiss receive;
That's an Offence I never can forgive.
Do not, O do not that sweet Mouth resign,
Lest I rise up in Arms; and cry 'Tis mine.   50
I shall thrust in betwixt, and void of Fear
The manifest Adult'rer will appear.
These things are plain to sight, but more I doubt
What you conceal beneath your Petticoat.
Take not his Leg between your tender Thighs,   55
Nor, with your Hand, provoke my Foe to rise.

How many Love-Inventions I deplore,
Which I, my self, have practis'd all before?
How oft have I been forc'd the Robe to lift
In Company; to make a homely shift   60
For a bare Bout, ill huddled o're in hast,
While o're my Side the Fair her Mantle cast.
You to your Husband shall not be so kind;
But, lest you shou'd, your Mantle leave behind.
Encourage him to Tope, but Kiss him not,   65
Nor mix one drop of Water in his Pot.
If he be Fuddled well, and Snores apace,
Then we may take Advice from Time and Place.
When all depart, while Complements are loud,
Be sure to mix among the thickest Crowd: 70
There I will be, and there we cannot miss,
Perhaps to Grubble, or at least to Kiss.
Alas, what length of Labour I employ,
Just to secure a short and transient Joy!
For Night must part us; and when Night is come,   75
Tuck'd underneath his Arms he leads you Home.
He locks you in, I follow to the Door,
His Fortune envy, and my own deplore.
He kisses you, he more than kisses too;
Th' outrageous Cuckold thinks it all his due.   80
But, add not to his Joy, by your Consent;
And let it not be giv'n, but only lent:
Return no Kiss, nor move in any sort;
Make it a dull, and a malignant Sport.
Had I my Wish, he shou'd no Pleasure take,   85
But slubber o're your Business for my sake.
And what e're Fortune shall this Night befal,
Coakes me to morrow, by foreswearing all.

ON THE DEATH of A Very Young
Gentleman

HE who cou'd view the Book of Destiny,
And read whatever there was writ of thee,
O *Charming Youth*, in the first op'ning Page,

So many Graces in so green an Age,
Such Wit, such Modesty, such strength of Mind,   5
A Soul at once so manly, and so kind:
Wou'd wonder, when he turn'd the Volume o're,
And after some few Leaves shou'd find no more.
Nought but a blank remain, a dead void space,
A step of Life that promis'd such a Race: 10
We must not, dare not think that Heav'n began
A Child, and cou'd not finish him a Man:
Reflecting what a mighty Store was laid
Of rich Materials, and a Model made:
The Cost already furnish'd; so bestow'd,   15
As more was never to one Soul allow'd;
Yet after this profusion spent in vain,
Nothing but mould'ring Ashes to remain.
I guess not, lest I split upon the Shelf,
Yet durst I guess Heav'n kept it for himself;   20
And giving us the use did soon recal,
E're we cou'd spare the mighty Principal.
    Thus then he disappear'd, was rarify'd,
For 'tis improper Speech to say he dy'd:
He was exhal'd: His great Creator drew   25
His Spirit, as the Sun the Morning Dew.
'Tis Sin produces Death; and he had none
But the Taint *Adam* left on ev'ry Son.
He added not, he was so pure, so good,
'Twas but th' Original forfeit of his Blood: 30
And that so little, that the River ran
More clear than the corrupted Fount began.
Nothing remain'd of the first muddy Clay,
The length of Course had wash'd it in the way.
So deep, and yet so clear, we might behold   35
The Gravel bottom, and that bottom Gold.
    As such we lov'd, admir'd, almost ador'd,
Gave all the Tribute Mortals cou'd afford.
Perhaps we gave so much, the Pow'rs above
Grew angry at our superstitious Love: 40
For when we more than Human Homage pay,
The charming Cause is justly snatch'd away.

Thus was the Crime not his, but ours alone,
And yet we murmur that he went so soon;
Though Miracles are short and rarely shown.   45

Hear then, yee mournful Parents, and divide
That Love in many which in one was ty'd.
That individual Blessing is no more,
But multiply'd in your remaining Store.
The Flame's dispers'd, but does not all expire,   50
The Sparkles blaze, though not the Globe of Fire.
Love him by Parts, in all your num'rous Race,
And from those Parts form one collected Grace;
Then, when you have refin'd to that degree,
Imagine all in one, and think that one is He.   55

THE LADY's SONG

I

A QUIRE of bright Beauties in Spring did appear,
    To chuse a *May*-Lady to govern the Year:
All the Nymphs were in White, and the Shepherds in Green,
The Garland was giv'n, and *Phillis* was Queen:
But *Phillis* refus'd it, and sighing did say,   5
I'll not wear a Garland while *Pan* is away.

II

While *Pan*, and fair *Syrinx*, are fled from our Shore,
The Graces are banish'd, and Love is no more:
The soft God of Pleasure that warm'd our Desires,
Has broken his Bow, and extinguish'd his Fires;   1
And vows that himself, and his Mother, will mourn,
'Till *Pan* and fair *Syrinx* in Triumph return.

III

Forbear your Addresses, and Court us no more,
For we will perform what the Deity swore:
But if you dare think of deserving our Charms,
Away with your Sheephooks, and take to your Arms;
Then Lawrels and Myrtles your Brows shall adorn,
When *Pan*, and his Son, and fair *Syrinx*, return.

Upon Young Mr. *Rogers* of
GLOCESTERSHIRE

O F gentle Blood, his Parents only Treasure,
Their lasting Sorrow, and their vanish'd Pleasure,
Adorn'd with Features, Virtues, Wit and Grace,
A large Provision for so short a Race;
More mod'rate Gifts might have prolong'd his Date,   5
Too early fitted for a better State;
But, knowing Heav'n his Home, to shun Delay,
He leap'd o'er Age, and took the shortest Way.

A SONG

I

F AIR, sweet and young, receive a Prize
Reserv'd for your Victorious Eyes:
From Crowds, whom at your Feet you see,
O pity, and distinguish me;
As I from thousand Beauties more   5
Distinguish you, and only you adore.

II

Your Face for Conquest was design'd,
Your ev'ry Motion charms my Mind;
Angels, when you your Silence break,
Forget their Hymns to hear you speak;   10
But when at once they hear and view,
Are loath to mount, and long to stay with you.

III

No Graces can your Form improve,
But all are lost unless you love;
While that sweet Passion you disdain,   15
Your Veil and Beauty are in vain.
In pity then prevent my Fate,
For after dying all Reprives too late.

SONG

H IGH State and Honours to others impart,
But give me your Heart:
That Treasure, that Treasure alone
   I beg for my own.
So gentle a Love, so fervent a Fire   5
   My Soul does inspire.
That Treasure, that Treasure alone
   I beg for my own.

Your Love let me crave,
   Give me in Possessing   10
   So matchless a Blessing,
That Empire is all I wou'd have.

      Love's my Petition,
      All my Ambition;
      If e'er you discover   15
      So faithful a Lover,
      So real a Flame,
      I'll die, I'll die,
      So give up my Game.

(1777)

UPON THE DEATH OF THE VISCOUNT DUNDEE

Epitaphium in Vice-Comitem Dundee

ULTIME Scotorum, potuit, quo sospite Solo,
Libertas patriæ salva fuisse tuæ.
Te moriente novos accepit Scotia Cives,
Accepitq; novos te moriente Deos:
Illa nequit superesse tibi, tu non potes illi, 5
Ergo Calidoniæ nomen inane vale.
Tuq; vale nostræ Gentis fortissime Ductor,
Optime Scotorum, atq; ultime Grahme vale.

English'd by Mr. Dryden

O Last and best of *Scots*! who didst maintain
Thy Country's Freedom from a Foreign Reign;
New People fill the Land now thou art gone,
New Gods the Temples, and new Kings the Throne.
Scotland and thou did each in other live, 5
Thou wouldst not her, nor could she thee survive;
Farewel! who living didst support the State,
And couldst not fall but with thy Country's Fate.

Upon the Death, &c. Text from Poems on Affairs of State . . . III, *1704, collated with the version in* Poetical Miscellanies: The Fifth Part, *1704. The* Epitaphium *is not printed in* Poet. Misc. 5 *nequit superesse tibi*] tibi superesse negat *Scott's version* 8 *Optime*] Ultime *Scott's version* O Last and best, &c. 5 thou] Thee *Poet. Misc.* 6 Thou wouldst not] Nor wou'dst thou *Poet. Misc.* 7 Farewel! who living didst] Farewel, who dying did *Poet. Misc.*

OVID's ART OF LOVE

BOOK I. TRANSLATED

IN *Cupid*'s School, whoe'er wou'd take Degree,
Must learn his Rudiments, by reading me.
Seamen with sailing Arts their Vessels move;
Art guides the Chariot; Art instructs to Love.
Of Ships and Chariots others know the Rule;   5
But I am Master in Love's mighty School.
Cupid indeed is obstinate and wild,
A stubborn God; but yet the God's a Child:
Easie to govern in his tender Age,
Like fierce *Achilles* in his Pupillage.   10
That Heroe, born for Conquest, trembling stood
Before the Centaur, and receiv'd the Rod.
As *Chyron* mollify'd his cruel Mind
With Art; and taught his Warlike Hands to wind
The Silver Strings of his melodious Lyre: 15
So Love's fair Goddess does my Soul inspire
To teach her softer Arts; to sooth the Mind,
And smooth the rugged Breasts of Human Kind.
    Yet *Cupid* and *Achilles*, each with Scorn
And Rage were fill'd; and both were Goddess-Born.   20
The Bull reclaim'd and yok'd, the Burden draws:
The Horse receives the Bit within his Jaws.
And stubborn Love shall bend beneath my Sway,
Tho strugling oft he strives to disobey.
He shakes his Torch, he wounds me with his Darts;   25
But vain his Force, and vainer are his Arts.
The more he burns my Soul, or wounds my Sight,
The more he teaches to revenge the Spight.
    I boast no Aid the *Delphian* God affords,
Nor Auspice from the flight of chattering Birds;   30
Nor *Clio*, nor her Sisters have I seen,
As *Hesiod* saw them on the shady Green:
Experience makes my Work a Truth so try'd,
You may believe; and *Venus* be my Guide.

Ovid's Art of Love. Book I. Text from the edition of 1709 collated with Poetical Miscellanies: The Fifth Part, *1704. See Commentary*

Far hence you Vestals be, who bind your Hair;   35
And Wives, who Gowns below your Ankles wear.
I sing the Brothels loose and unconfin'd,
Th' unpunishable Pleasures of the Kind;
Which all a-like, for Love, or Mony find.

You, who in *Cupid*'s Rolls inscribe your Name,   40
First seek an Object worthy of your Flame;
Then strive with Art, your Lady's Mind to gain:
And last, provide your Love may long remain.
On these three Precepts all my Work shall move:
These are the Rules and Principles of Love.   45

Before your Youth with Marriage is opprest,
Make choice of one who suits your Humour best:
And such a Damsel drops not from the Sky;
She must be sought for with a curious Eye.

The wary Angler, in the winding Brook,   50
Knows what the Fish, and where to bait his Hook.
The Fowler and the Hunts-man know by Name,
The certain Haunts, and Harbour of their Game.
So must the Lover beat the likeliest Grounds;
Th' Assemblies where his Quarry most abounds.   55
Nor shall my Novice wander far astray;
These Rules shall put him in the ready Way.
Thou shalt not sail around the Continent,
As far as *Perseus*, or as *Paris* went:
For *Rome* alone affords thee such a Store;   60
As all the World can hardly shew thee more.
The Face of Heav'n with fewer Stars is crown'd,
Than Beauties in the *Roman* Sphere are found.

Whether thy Love is bent on blooming Youth,
On dawning Sweetness, in unartful Truth;   65
Or courts the juicy Joys of riper Growth;
Here mayst thou find thy full Desires in both.
Or if Autumnal Beauties please thy Sight
(An Age that knows to give, and take Delight;)
Millions of Matrons of the graver Sort,   70
In common Prudence, will not balk the Sport.

In Summer Heats thou needst but only go
To *Pompey*'s cool and shady *Portico*;

52 *indented in* 09

Or Concord's Fane; or that Proud Edifice,
Whose Turrets near the bawdy Suburb rise: 75
Or to that other *Portico*, where stands
The cruel Father, urging his Commands;
And fifty Daughters wait the Time of Rest,
To plunge their Ponyards in the Bridegroom's Breast.
Or *Venus* Temple; where, on Annual Nights,   80
They mourn *Adonis* with *Assyrian* Rites.
Nor shun the *Jewish* Walk, where the foul Drove,
On Sabbaths, rest from every thing but Love.
Nor *Isis* Temple; for that sacred Whore
Makes others, what to *Jove* she was before.   85
And if the Hall it self be not bely'd,
Even there the Cause of Love is often try'd.
Near it at least, or in the Palace Yard;
From whence the noisy Combatants are heard.
The crafty Counsellors, in formal Gown,   90
There gain another's Cause, but lose their own.
There Eloquence is nonplust in the Sute;
And Lawyers, who had Words at Will, are mute.
Venus, from her adjoyning Temple, smiles,
To see them caught in their litigious Wiles.   95
Grave Senators lead home the Youthful Dame;
Returning Clients, when they Patrons came.
But above all, the Play-House is the Place;
There's Choice of Quarry in that narrow Chace.
There take thy Stand, and sharply looking out,   ⎞   10
Soon mayst thou find a Mistress in the Rout;   ⎬
For Length of Time, or for a single Bout.   ⎠
The Theatres are Berries for the Fair:
Like Ants on Mole-hills, thither they repair:
Like Bees to Hives, so numerously they throng,   10
It may be said, they to that Place belong.
Thither they swarm, who have the publick Voice:
There choose, if Plenty not distracts thy Choice.
To see, and to be seen, in Heaps they run;
Some to undo, and some to be undone.   1

     From *Romulus* the Rise of Plays began,
To his new Subjects a commodious Man;
Who, his unmarried Soldiers to supply,

Took care the Common-Wealth should multiply:
Providing *Sabine* Women for his Braves,   115
Like a true King, to get a Race of Slaves.
His Play-House, not of *Parian* Marble made,
Nor was it spread with purple Sayls for Shade.
The Stage with Rushes, or with Leaves they strow'd:
No Scenes in Prospect, no machining God.   120
On Rows of homely Turf they sate to see,
Crown'd with the Wreaths of every common Tree.
There, while they sit in rustick Majesty,
Each Lover had his Mistriss in his Eye;
And whom he saw most suiting to his Mind,   125
For Joys of matrimonial Rape design'd.
Scarce cou'd they wait the *Plaudit* in their Haste;
But e're the Dances and the Song were past,
The Monarch gave the Signal from his Throne;
And rising, bad his merry Men fall on.   130
The Martial Crew, like Soldiers ready prest,
Just at the Word (the Word too was the Best)
With joyful Cries each other animate,
Some choose, and some at Hazzard seize their Mate.
As Doves from Eagles, or from Wolves the Lambs,   135
So from their lawless Lovers fly the Dames.
Their Fear was one, but not one Face of Fear;
Some rend the lovely Tresses of their Hair:
Some shreik, and some are struck with dumb Despair.
Her absent Mother, one invokes in vain;   140
One stands amaz'd, not daring to complain;
The nimbler trust their Feet, the slow remain.
But nought availing, all are Captives led,
Trembling and Blushing, to the Genial Bed.
She who too long resisted, or deny'd,   145
The lusty Lover made by Force a Bride;
And with superiour Strength, compell'd her to his Side.
Then sooth'd her thus:—My Soul's far better Part,
Cease weeping, nor afflict thy tender Heart:
For what thy Father to thy Mother was,   150
That Faith to thee, that solemn Vow I pass!
   Thus *Romulus* became so popular;

148 thus: *04*: thus! *09*   149 nor] not *04*

This was the Way to thrive in Peace and War;
To pay his Army, and fresh Whores to bring:
Who wou'd not fight for such a gracious King!   155
    Thus Love in Theaters did first improve;
And Theaters are still the Scene of Love.
Nor shun the Chariots, and the Courser's Race;
The *Circus* is no inconvenient Place.
No need is there of talking on the Hand;   160
Nor Nods, nor Signs, which Lovers understand.
But boldly next the fair your Seat provide;
Close as you can to hers; and Side by Side.
Pleas'd or unpleas'd, no matter; crowding sit;
For so the Laws of publick Shows permit.   165
Then find Occasion to begin Discourse;
Enquire whose Chariot this, and whose that Horse?
To whatsoever Side she is inclin'd,
Suit all your Inclinations to her Mind:
Like what she likes, from thence your Court begin;   170
And whom she favours, wish that he may win.
But when the Statues of the Deities,
In Chariots roll'd, appear before the Prize;
When *Venus* comes, with deep Devotion rise.
If Dust be on her Lap, or Grains of Sand;   175
Brush both away with your officious Hand.
If none be there, yet brush that nothing thence;
And still to touch her Lap make some Pretence.
Touch any thing of hers; and if her Train
Sweep on the Ground, let it not sweep in vain;   180
But gently take it up, and wipe it clean:
And while you wipe it, with observing Eyes,
Who knows but you may see her naked Thighs!
Observe who sits behind her; and beware,
Lest his incroaching Knee shou'd press the Fair.   185
Light Service takes light Minds: For some can tell
Of Favours won, by laying Cushions well:
By Fanning Faces, some their Fortune meet;
And some by laying Footstools for their Feet.
These Overtures of Love the *Circus* gives;   190
Nor at the Sword-play less the Lover thrives:

182 wipe it,] wipe, it 09

For there the Son of *Venus* fights his Prize;
And deepest Wounds are oft receiv'd from Eyes.
One, while the Crowd their Acclamations make;
Or while he Betts, and puts his Ring to Stake,   195
Is struck from far, and feels the flying Dart;
And of the Spectacle is made a Part.
   Cæsar wou'd represent a Naval Fight,
For his own Honour, and for *Rome*'s Delight.
From either Sea the Youths and Maidens come;   200
And all the World was then contain'd in *Rome*!
In this vast Concourse, in this Choice of Game;
What *Roman* Heart but felt a foreign Flame?
Once more our Prince prepares to make us glad;
And the remaining East to *Rome* will add.   205
Rejoice you *Roman* Souldiers in your Urn,
Your Ensigns from the *Parthians* shall return;
And the slain *Crassi* shall no longer mourn.
A Youth is sent those Trophies to demand;
And bears his Father's Thunder in his Hand: 210
Doubt not th' Imperial Boy in Wars unseen,
In Childhood all of *Cæsar*'s Race are Men.
Celestial Seeds shoot out before their Day,
Prevent their Years, and brook no dull Delay.
Thus Infant *Hercules* the Snakes did press;   215
And in his Cradle did his Sire confess.
Bacchus a Boy, yet like a Hero fought;
And early Spoils from conquer'd *India* brought.
Thus you your Father's Troops shall lead to Fight;
And thus shall vanquish in your Father's Right.   220
These Rudiments you to your Lineage owe;
Born to increase your Titles as you grow.
Brethren you had, Revenge your Brethren slain;
You have a Father, and his Rights maintain.
Arm'd by your Country's Parent, and your own,   225
Redeem your Country, and restore his Throne.
Your Enemies assert an impious Cause;
You fight both for divine and humane Laws.
Already in their Cause they are o'ercome;
Subject them too, by Force of Arms, to *Rome*.   230

206 Urn] Urns *09*

Great Father *Mars* with greater *Cæsar* joyn;
To give a prosperous *Omen* to your Line:
One of you is, and one shall be divine.
I prophecy you shall, you shall o'ercome;
My Verse shall bring you back in Triumph Home.   235
Speak in my Verse, exhort to loud Alarms:
O were my Numbers equal to your Arms!
Then will I sing the *Parthians* Overthrow:
Their Shot averse sent from a flying Bow.
The *Parthians*, who already flying fight;   240
Already give an *Omen* of their Flight.
O when will come the Day, by Heaven design'd,
When thou the best and fairest of Mankind,
Drawn by white Horses shalt in Triumph ride,
With conquer'd Slaves attending on thy Side;   245
Slaves, that no longer can be safe in Flight;
O glorious Object, O surprizing Sight,
O Day of Publick Joy; too good to end in Night!
On such a Day, if thou, and next to thee,
Some Beauty sits the Spectacle to see: 250
If she enquire the Names of conquer'd Kings,
Of Mountains, Rivers, and their hidden Springs;
Answer to all thou knowest; and if need be,
Of things unknown seem to speak knowingly:
This is *Euphrates*, crown'd with Reeds; and there   255
Flows the swift *Tigris*, with his Sea-green Hair.
Invent new Names of things unknown before;
Call this *Armenia*; that the *Caspian* Shore:
Call this a *Mede*, and that a *Parthian* Youth;
Talk probably; no Matter for the Truth.   260

    In Feasts, as at our Shows, new Means abound;
More Pleasure there, than that of Wine is found.
The *Paphian* Goddess there her Ambush lays;
And Love betwixt the Horns of *Bacchus* plays:
Desires encrease at ev'ry swilling Draught;   265
Brisk Vapours add new Vigour to the Thought.
There *Cupid's* purple Wings no Flight afford;
But wet with Wine, he flutters on the Board.
He shakes his Pinnions, but he cannot move;

237 Arms!] Arms. *09*

Fix'd he remains, and turns a Maudlin Love.   270
Wine warms the Blood, and makes the Spirits flow;
Care flies, and Wrinkles from the Forehead go:
Exalts the Poor, Invigorates the Weak;
Gives Mirth and Laughter, and a Rosy Cheek.
Bold Truths it speaks; and spoken, dares maintain: 275
And brings our old Simplicity again.
Love sparkles in the Cup, and fills it higher:
Wine feeds the Flames, and Fuel adds to Fire.
But choose no Mistress in thy drunken Fit;
Wine gilds too much their Beauties and their Wit.   280
Nor trust thy Judgment when the Tapers dance;
But sober, and by Day, thy Sute advance.
By Day-Light *Paris* judg'd the beauteous Three;
And for the fairest, did the Prize decree.
Night is a Cheat, and all Deformities   285
Are hid, or lessen'd in her dark Disguise.
The Sun's fair Light each Error will confess,
In Face, in Shape, in Jewels, and in Dress.
    Why name I ev'ry Place where Youths abound?
'Tis Loss of Time; and a too fruitful Ground.   290
The *Bajan* Baths, where Ships at Anchor ride,
And wholesome Streams from Sulphur Fountains glide:
Where wounded Youths are by Experience taught,
The Waters are less healthful than they thought.
Or *Dian*'s Fane, which near the Suburb lies;   295
Where Priests, for their Promotion, fight a Prize.
That Maiden Goddess is Love's mortal Foe,
And much from her his Subjects undergo.
    Thus far the sportful Muse, with Myrtle bound,
Has sung where lovely Lasses may be found.   300
Now let me sing, how she who wounds your Mind,
With Art, may be to cure your Wounds inclin'd.
Young Nobles, to my Laws Attention lend:
And all you Vulgar of my School, attend.
    First then believe, all Women may be won;   305
Attempt with Confidence, the Work is done.
The Grashopper shall first forbear to sing,
In Summer Season, or the Birds in Spring;
Than Women can resist your flattering Skill:

Ev'n She will yield, who swears she never will.   31

To Secret Pleasure both the Sexes move:

But Women most, who most dissemble Love.

'Twere best for us, if they wou'd first declare;

Avow their Passion, and submit to Prayer.

The Cow by lowing, tells the Bull her Flame: 31

The neighing Mare invites her Stallion to the Game.

Man is more temp'rate in his Lust than they;

And more than Women, can his Passion sway.

Biblis, we know, did first her Love declare;

And had Recourse to Death in her Despair.   32

Her Brother She; her Father *Myrrha* sought;

And lov'd; but lov'd not as a Daughter ought.

Now from a Tree she stills her odorous Tears;

Which yet the Name of her who shed 'em bears.

    In *Ida*'s shady Vale a Bull appear'd;   32

White as the Snow, the fairest of the Herd;

A Beauty Spot of black there only rose,

Betwixt his equal Horns and ample Brows:

The Love and Wish of all the *Cretan* Cows.

The Queen beheld him as his Head he rear'd;   33

And envy'd ev'ry Leap he gave the Herd.

A Secret Fire she nourish'd in her Breast;

And hated ev'ry Heifer he caress'd.

A Story known, and known for true, I tell;

Nor *Crete*, though lying, can the Truth conceal.   33

She cut him Grass; (so much can Love command)

She strok'd, she fed him with her Royal Hand:

Was pleas'd in Pastures with the Herd to rome;

And *Minos* by the Bull was overcome.

    Cease Queen, with Gemms, t' adorn thy beauteous Brows; 34

The Monarch of thy Heart no Jewel knows.

Nor in thy Glass compose thy Looks and Eyes;

Secure from all thy Charms thy Lover lies:

Yet trust thy Mirrour when it tells thee true;

Thou art no Heifer to allure his View.   34

Soon woud'st thou quit thy Royal Diadem

To thy fair Rivals; to be horn'd like them.

If *Minos* please, no Lover seek to find;

If not, at least seek one of humane Kind.

The wretched Queen the *Cretan* Court forsakes;   350
In Woods and Wilds, her Habitation makes:
She curses ev'ry beauteous Cow she sees;
Ah, why dost thou my Lord and Master please!
And think'st, ungrateful Creature as thou art,
With frisking awkardly, to gain his Heart.   355
She said; and straight commands, with frowning Look,
To put her, undeserving, to the Yoke.
Or feigns some holy Rites of Sacrifice;
And sees her Rival's Death with joyful Eyes:
Then, when the Bloody Priest has done his Part;   360
Pleas'd, in her Hand she holds the beating Heart:
Nor from a scornful Taunt can scarce refrain;
Go Fool, and strive to please my Love again.
   Now she wou'd be *Europa*—*Io*, now;
(One bore a Bull; and one was made a Cow.)   365
Yet she at last her Brutal Bliss obtain'd;
And in a woodden Cow the Bull sustain'd:
Fill'd with his Seed, accomplish'd her Desire;
Till, by his Form, the Son betray'd the Sire.
   If *Atreus* Wife to Incest had not run;   370
(But ah, how hard it is to love but one!)
His Coursers *Phœbus* had not driv'n away,
To shun that Sight, and interrupt the Day.
Thy Daughter, *Nisus*, pull'd thy purple Hair;
And barking Sea-Dogs yet her Bowels tear.   375
At Sea and Land *Atrides* sav'd his Life;
Yet fell a Prey to his adult'rous Wife.
Who knows not what Revenge *Medea* sought,
When the slain Offspring bore the Father's Fault?
Thus *Phœnix* did a Woman's Love bewail: 380
And thus *Hippolitus* by *Phædra* fell.
These Crimes revengeful Matrons did commit;
Hotter their Lust, and sharper is their Wit.
Doubt not from them an easie Victory:
Scarce of a thousand Dames will one deny.   385
All Women are content that Men shou'd woe:
She who complains, and She who will not do.
Rest then secure, whate'er thy Luck may prove,
Not to be hated for declaring Love:

And yet how can'st thou miss, since Woman-kind   390
Is frail and vain; and still to Change inclin'd.
Old Husbands, and stale Gallants they despise;
And more another's than their own, they prize.
A larger Crop adorns our Neighbour's Field,
More Milk his Kine from swelling Udders yield.   395
   First gain the Maid: By her thou shalt be sure
A free Access, and easie to procure:
Who knows, what to her Office does belong,
Is in the Secret, and can hold her Tongue.
Bribe her with Gifts, with Promises, and Pray'rs;   400
For her good Word goes far in Love Affairs.
The Time and fit Occasion leave to her,
When she most aptly can thy Sute prefer.
The Time for Maids to fire their Lady's Blood,
Is when they find her in a merry Mood.   405
When all things at her Wish and Pleasure move;
Her Heart is open then, and free to Love.
Then Mirth and Wantonness to Lust betray,
And smooth the Passage to the Lover's Way.
Troy stood the Siege, when fill'd with anxious Care: 410
One merry Fit concluded all the War.
   If some fair Rival vex her jealous Mind;
Offer thy Service to revenge in Kind.
Instruct the Damsel, while she combs her Hair,
To raise the Choler of that injur'd Fair: 41
And sighing, make her Mistress understand,
She has the Means of Vengeance in her Hand.
Then, naming thee, thy humble Suit prefer;
And swear thou languishest and dy'st for her.
Then let her lose no Time, but push at all;   42
For Women soon are rais'd, and soon they fall.
Give their first Fury Leisure to relent,
They melt like Ice, and suddenly repent.
   T' enjoy the Maid, will that thy Suit advance?
'Tis a hard Question, and a doubtful Chance.   42
One Maid corrupted, bawds the better for 't;
Another for her self wou'd keep the Sport.
Thy Bus'ness may be farther'd or delay'd,
But by my Counsel, let alone the Maid:

Ev'n tho she shou'd consent to do the Feat;   430
The Profit's little, and the Danger great.
I will not lead thee through a rugged Road;
But where the Way lies open, safe, and broad.
Yet if thou find'st her very much thy Friend;
And her good Face her Diligence commend: 435
Let the fair Mistress have thy first Embrace,
And let the Maid come after in her Place.
   But this I will advise, and mark my Words,
For 'tis the best Advice my Skill affords:
If needs thou with the Damsel wilt begin;   440
Before th' Attempt is made, make sure to win:
For then the Secret better will be kept;
And she can tell no Tales when once she's dipt.
'Tis for the Fowlers Interest to beware,
The Bird intangled, shou'd not scape the Snare.   445
The Fish once prick'd, avoids the bearded Hook;
And spoils the Sport of all the neighb'ring Brook.
But if the Wench be thine, she makes thy Way;
And for thy Sake, her Mistress will betray;
Tell all she knows, and all she hears her say.   450
Keep well the Counsel of thy faithful Spy:
So shalt thou learn whene'er she treads awry.
   All things the Stations of their Seasons keep:
And certain Times there are to sow and reap.
Ploughmen and Sailors for the Season stay,   455
One to plough Land, and one to plough the Sea:
So shou'd the Lover wait the lucky Day.
Then stop thy Suit; it hurts not thy Design:
But think another Hour she may be thine.
And when she celebrates her Birth at home,   460
Or when she views the publick Shows of *Rome*:
Know all thy Visits then are troublesome.
Defer thy Work, and put not then to Sea,
For that's a boding, and a stormy Day.
Else take thy Time, and when thou canst, begin   465
To break a *Jewish* Sabbath, think no Sin:
Nor ev'n on superstitious Days abstain:
Not when the *Romans* were at *Allia* slain.
Ill Omens in her Frowns are understood;

When She's in humour, ev'ry Day is good.   470
But than her Birth-day seldom comes a worse;
When Bribes and Presents must be sent of course;
And that's a bloody Day, that costs thy Purse.
Be stanch; yet Parsimony will be vain:
The craving Sex will still the Lover drain.   475
No Skill can shift 'em off, nor Art remove;
They will be Begging when they know we Love.
The Merchant comes upon th' appointed Day,
Who shall before thy Face, his Wares display.
To chuse for her she craves thy kind Advice;   480
Then begs again, to bargain for the Price:
But when she has her Purchase in her Eye,
She hugs thee close, and kisses thee to buy.
'Tis what I want, and 'tis a Pennorth too;
In many years I will not trouble you.   485
If you complain you have no ready Coin;
No matter, 'tis but Writing of a Line;
A little Bill, not to be paid at Sight;
(Now curse the Time when thou wert taught to Write.)
She keeps her Birth-day; you must send the Chear;   490
And she'll be Born a hundred times a year.
With daily Lies she dribs thee into Cost;
That Ear-ring dropt a Stone, that Ring is lost:
They often borrow what they never pay;
What e'er you lend her think it thrown away.   495
Had I ten Mouths and Tongues to tell each Art,
All wou'd be weary'd e'er I told a Part.

   By Letters, not by Words, thy Love begin;
And Foord the dangerous Passage with thy Pen.
If to her Heart thou aim'st to find the way,   500
Extreamly Flatter, and extreamly Pray.
Priam by Pray'rs did *Hector*'s Body gain;
Nor is an Angry God invok'd in vain.
With promis'd Gifts her easy Mind bewitch;
For ev'n the Poor in promise may be Rich.   505
Vain Hopes a while her Appetite will stay;
'Tis a deceitful, but commodious way.
Who gives is Mad; but make her still believe
'Twill come, and that's the cheapest way to give.

Ev'n barren Lands fair promises afford;   510
But the lean Harvest cheats the starving Lord.
Buy not thy first Enjoyment; lest it prove
Of bad example to thy future Love:
But get it *gratis*; and she'll give thee more,
For fear of losing what she gave before.   515
The losing Gamester shakes the Box in vain,
And Bleeds, and loses on, in hopes to gain.
   Write then, and in thy Letter, as I said,
Let her with mighty Promises be fed.
Cydippe by a Letter was betray'd,   520
Writ on an Apple to th' unwary Maid.
She read her self into a Marriage Vow;
(And ev'ry Cheat in Love the Gods allow.)
Learn Eloquence, ye noble Youth of *Rome*;
It will not only at the Bar o'ercome: 525
Sweet words, the People and the Senate move;
But the chief end of Eloquence, is Love.
But in thy Letter hide thy moving Arts;
Affect not to be thought a Man of Parts.
None but vain Fools to simple Women Preach;   530
A learned Letter oft has made a Breach.
In a familiar Style your Thoughts convey;
And Write such things, as Present you wou'd say.
Such words as from the Heart may seem to move:
'Tis Wit enough, to make her think you Love.   535
If Seal'd she sends it back, and will not read;
Yet hope, in time, the business may succeed.
In time the Steer will to the Yoke submit;
In time the restiff Horse will bear the Bit.
Ev'n the hard Plough-share, use will wear away;   540
And stubborn Steel in length of time decay.
Water is soft, and Marble hard; and yet
We see, soft Water through hard Marble Eat.
Though late, yet *Troy* at length in Flames expir'd;
And ten years more, *Penelope* had tir'd.   545
Perhaps, thy Lines unanswer'd she retain'd;
No matter; there's a Point already gain'd:
For she who Reads, in time will Answer too;
Things must be left, by just degrees to grow.

Perhaps she Writes, but Answers with disdain;   550
And sharply bids you not to Write again:
What she requires, she fears you shou'd accord;
The Jilt wou'd not be taken at her word.
    Mean time, if she be carried in her Chair,
Approach; but do not seem to know she's there.   555
Speak softly, to delude the Standers by;
Or, if aloud, then speak ambiguously.
If Santring in the *Portico* she Walk,
Move slowly too; for that's a time for talk:
And sometimes follow, sometimes be her guide;   560
But when the Croud permits, go side by side.
Nor in the *Play-House* let her sit alone:
For she's the *Play-House* and the *Play* in one.
There thou may'st ogle, or by signs advance
Thy suit, and seem to touch her Hand by chance.   56
Admire the Dancer who her liking gains,
And pity in the *Play* the Lover's pains;
For her sweet sake the loss of time despise;
Sit while she sits, and when she rises rise.
But dress not like a Fop: nor curle your Hair,   57
Nor with a Pumice make your Body bare.
Leave those effeminate and useless toys
To *Eunuchs*, who can give no solid joys.
Neglect becomes a Man: This *Theseus* found;
Uncurl'd, uncomb'd, the Nymph his Wishes Crown'd.   57
The rough *Hippolitus*, was *Phædra's* care;
And *Venus* thought the rude *Adonis* fair.
Be not too Finical; but yet be clean;
And wear well fashion'd Cloaths, like other Men.
Let not your Teeth be yellow, or be foul;   5
Nor in wide Shoes your Feet too loosly roul.
Of a black Muzzel, and long Beard beware;
And let a skilful Barber cut your Hair.
Your Nailes be pick'd from filth, and even par'd;
Nor let your nasty Nostrils bud with Beard.   5
Cure your unsav'ry Breath; gargle your Throat;
And free your Arm-pits from the Ram and Goat.
Dress not, in short, too little, or too much:
And be not wholly *French*, nor wholly *Dutch*.

Now *Bacchus* calls me to his jolly Rites: 590
Who wou'd not follow, when a God invites?
He helps the Poet, and his Pen inspires;
Kind and indulgent to his former Fires.
    Fair *Ariadne* wander'd on the shore
Forsaken now; and *Theseus* loves no more: 595
Loose was her Gown, dishevel'd was her Hair;
Her Bosom naked, and her Feet were bare:
Exclaiming, in the Waters brink she stood;
Her briny Tears augment the briny Flood.
She shreik'd, and wept, and both became her Face;   600
No posture cou'd that Heav'nly form disgrace.
She beat her Breast: The Traytor's gone, said she,
What shall become of poor forsaken me?
What shall become—she had not time for more,
The sounding Cymbals ratled on the Shore.   605
She swoons for fear, she falls upon the Ground;
No vital heat was in her body found.
The *Mimallonian* Dames about her stood;
And scudding *Satyrs* ran before their God.
Silenus on his Ass did next appear;   610
And held upon the Mane (the God was clear)
The drunken *Syre* pursues; the Dames retire;
Sometimes the drunken Dames pursue the drunken *Syre*.
At last he topples over on the Plain;
The *Satyrs* laugh, and bid him rise again.   615
And now the God of Wine came driving on,
High on his Chariot by swift *Tygers* drawn.
Her Colour, Voice and Sense forsook the fair;   ⎫
Thrice did her trembling Feet for flight prepare,   ⎬
And thrice affrighted did her flight forbear.   ⎭ 620
She shook, like leaves of Corn, when Tempests blow;
Or slender Reeds that in the Marshes grow.
To whom the God—Compose thy fearful Mind;
In me a truer Husband thou shalt find.
With Heav'n I will endow thee; and thy Star,   ⎫ 625
Shall with propitious Light be seen afar: ⎬
And guide on Seas, the doubtful Mariner.   ⎭
He said; and from his Chariot leaping light,

595 loves] Loves *04 09*   605 on *04*: in *09*   628 light, *04*: light; *09*

Lest the grim *Tygers* shou'd the Nymph affright,
His brawny Arms around her wast he threw;   630
(For Gods, what ere they will, with ease can do:)
And swiftly bore her thence; th' attending throng
Shout at the Sight, and sing the *Nuptial* song.
Now in full bowls her Sorrow she may steep:
The Bridegroom's Liquor lays the Bride asleep.   635

But thou, when flowing Cups in Triumph ride,
And the lov'd Nymph is seated by thy side;
Invoke the God, and all the mighty Powers;
That Wine may not defraud thy Genial hours.
Then in ambiguous Words thy suit prefer;   640
Which she may know were all addrest to her.
In liquid purple Letters write her Name:
Which she may read, and reading find thy Flame.
Then may your Eyes confess your mutual Fires;
(For Eyes have Tongues, and glances tell desires.)   64
When ere she Drinks, be first to take the Cup;
And where she laid her Lips, the Blessing sup.
When she to Carving does her Hand advance;
Put out thy own, and touch it as by chance.
Thy service ev'n her Husband must attend: 65
(A Husband is a most convenient Friend.)
Seat the fool Cuckold in the highest place;
And with thy Garland his dull Temples grace.
Whether below, or equal in degree,
Let him be Lord of all the Company;   65
And what he says, be seconded by Thee.
'Tis common to deceive through friendships Name:
But common though it be, 'tis still to blame.
Thus Factors frequently their Trust betray;
And to themselves their Masters gains convey.   66
Drink to a certain Pitch, and then give o're;
Thy Tongue and Feet may stumble, drinking more.
Of drunken Quarrels in her sight, beware;
Pot Valour only serves to fright the Fair.
Eurytion justly fell, by Wine opprest,   66
For his rude Riot, at a Wedding-Feast.
Sing, if you have a Voice: and shew your Parts

632 thence; *04*: thence, *09*

In Dancing, if endu'd with Dancing Arts.
Do any thing within your power, to please;
Nay, ev'n affect a seeming Drunkenness: 670
Clip every word; and if by chance you speak
Too home; or if too broad a Jest you break;
In your excuse the Company will joyn,
And lay the Fault upon the Force of Wine.
True Drunkenness is subject to offend;   675
But when 'tis feign'd, 'tis oft a Lover's Friend.
Then safely you may praise her beauteous Face;
And call him Happy, who is in her grace.
Her Husband thinks himself the Man design'd;
But curse the Cuckold in your secret Mind.   680
When all are risen, and prepare to go;
Mix with the Croud, and tread upon her Toe.
This is the proper time to make thy Court;
For now she's in the Vein, and fit for Sport.
Lay Bashfulness, that rustick Virtue, by;   685
To manly Confidence thy Thoughts apply.
On Fortune's Foretop timely fix thy hold;
Now speak and speed, for *Venus* loves the bold.
No Rules of Rhetorick here I need afford:
Only begin, and trust the following word;   690
It will be Witty of its own accord.

    Act well the Lover, let thy Speech abound
In dying words, that represent thy Wound.
Distrust not her belief; she will be mov'd.
All Women think they merit to be lov'd.   695

    Sometimes a Man begins to Love in Jest;
And after, feels the Torments he profest.
For your own sakes be pitiful ye Fair;
For a feign'd Passion, may a true prepare.
By Flatteries we prevail on Woman-kind;   700
As hollow Banks by Streams are undermin'd.
Tell her, her Face is Fair, her Eyes are Sweet:
Her Taper Fingers praise, and little Feet.
Such Praises ev'n the Chast are pleas'd to hear;
Both Maids and Matrons hold their Beauty dear.   795

    Once naked *Pallas* with *Jove's* Queen appear'd;
And still they grieve that *Venus* was prefer'd.

Praise the proud Peacock, and he spreads his Train:
Be silent, and he pulls it in again.
Pleas'd is the Courser in his rapid Race;   710
Applaud his Running, and he mends his pace.
But largely promise, and devoutly swear;
And, if need be, call ev'ry God to hear.
Jove sits above, forgiving with a Smile,
The Perjuries that easy Maids beguile.   715
He Swore to *Juno* by the *Stygian* Lake:
Forsworn, he dares not an Example make;
Or punish Falshood, for his own dear sake.
'Tis for our Int'rest that the Gods shou'd be;
Let us believe 'em: I believe they see;   720
And both reward, and punish equally;
Not that they live above, like lazy Drones,
Or Kings below, supine upon their Thrones:
Lead then your Lives as present in their sight;
Be Just in Dealings, and defend the right;   72
By Fraud betray not, nor Oppress by Might.
But 'tis a Venial Sin to Cheat the Fair;
All Men have Liberty of Conscience there.
On cheating Nymphs a Cheat is well design'd,
'Tis a prophane, and a deceitful Kind.   73
   'Tis said, that *Ægypt* for nine Years was dry,
Nor *Nile* did Floods, nor Heav'n did Rain supply.
A Foreigner at length inform'd the King,
That slaughter'd Guests would kindly Moisture bring.
The King reply'd, On thee the Lot shall fall,   73
Be thou, my Guest, the Sacrifice for all.
Thus *Phalaris*, *Perillus* taught to low,
And made him season first the brazen Cow.
A rightful Doom, the Laws of Nature cry,
'Tis, the Artificers of Death should die.   74
Thus justly Women suffer by Deceit;
Their Practice authorises us to cheat.
Beg her, with Tears, thy warm Desires to grant;
For Tears will pierce a Heart of Adamant.
If Tears will not be squeez'd, then rub your Eye,   7
Or noint the Lids, and seem at least to cry.

719 Gods] God's *o9*   721 equally;] equally. *o9*

Kiss, if you can: Resistance if she make,
And will not give you Kisses, let her take.
Fie, fie, you naughty Man, are Words of Course;
She struggles, but to be subdu'd by Force.   750
Kiss only soft, I charge you, and beware,
With your hard Bristles, not to brush the Fair.
He who has gain'd a Kiss, and gains no more,
Deserves to lose the Bliss he got before.
If once she kiss, her Meaning is exprest;   755
There wants but little Pushing for the rest.
Which if thou dost not gain, by Strength or Art,
The Name of Clown then sutes with thy Desert.
'Tis downright Dulness, and a shameful Part.
Perhaps she calls it Force; but if she 'scape,   760
She will not thank you for th' omitted Rape.
The Sex is cunning to conceal their Fires,
They would be forc'd, ev'n to their own Desires.
They seem t' accuse you, with a down-cast Sight,
But in their Souls confess you did them right.   765
Who might be forc'd, and yet untouch'd depart,
Thank with their Tongues, but curse you with their Heart.
Fair *Phœbe* and her Sister did prefer,
To their dull Mates, the noble Ravisher.
   What *Deidamia* did, in Days of Yore,   770
The Tale is old, but worth the telling o'er.
   When *Venus* had the golden Apple gain'd,
And the just Judge fair *Hellen* had obtain'd;
When she with Triumph was at *Troy* receiv'd,
The *Trojans* joyful, while the *Grecians* griev'd: 775
They vow'd Revenge of violated Laws,
And *Greece* was arming in the Cuckold's Cause;
Achilles, by his Mother warn'd from War,
Disguis'd his Sex, and lurk'd among the Fair.
What means *Eacides* to spin and sow?   780
With Spear, and Sword, in Field thy Valour show!
And leaving this, the Nobler *Pallas* know.
Why dost thou in that Hand the Distaff wield,
Which is more worthy to sustain a Shield?
Or with that other draw the woolly Twine,   785

773 obtain'd;] obtain'd. *og*   775 griev'd:] griev'd. *og*   779 Fair.] Fair; *og*

The same the Fates for *Hector*'s Thread assign?
Brandish thy Fauchion in thy pow'rful Hand,
Which can alone the pond'rous Lance command.
In the same Room by chance the Royal Maid
Was lodg'd, and, by his seeming Sex betray'd,   790
Close to her Side the Youthful Heroe laid.
I know not how his Courtship he began;
But, to her Cost, she found it was a Man.
'Tis thought she struggl'd, but withal 'tis thought,
Her Wish was to be conquer'd, when she fought.   795
For when disclos'd, and hast'ning to the Field,
He laid his Distaff down, and took the Shield,
With Tears her humble Suit she did prefer;
And thought to stay the grateful Ravisher.
She sighs, she sobs, she begs him not to part;   800
And now 'tis Nature, what before was Art.
She strives by Force her Lover to detain,
And wishes to be ravish'd once again.
This is the Sex; they will not first begin,
But when compell'd, are pleas'd to suffer Sin.   805
Is there, who thinks that Women first should woo;
Lay by thy Self-Conceit, thou foolish Beau.
Begin, and save their Modesty the Shame;
'Tis well for thee, if they receive thy Flame.
'Tis decent for a Man to speak his Mind;   810
They but expect th' Occasion to be kind.
Ask, that thou may'st enjoy; she waits for this:
And on thy first Advance depends thy Bliss.
Ev'n *Jove* himself was forc'd to sue for Love:
None of the Nymphs did first sollicit *Jove*.   815
But if you find your Pray'rs encrease her Pride,
Strike Sail awhile, and wait another Tide.
They fly when we pursue, but make Delay;
And when they see you slacken, they will stay.
Sometimes it profits to conceal your End;   820
Name not your self her Lover, but her Friend.
How many skittish Girls have thus been caught?
He prov'd a Lover, who a Friend was thought.
Sailors by Sun and Wind are swarthy made;

A tann'd Complexion best becomes their Trade.   825
'Tis a Disgrace to Ploughmen to be fair;
Bluff Cheeks they have, and weather-beaten Hair.
Th' ambitious Youth, who seeks an Olive Crown,
Is Sun-burnt, with his daily Toil, and brown;
But if the Lover hopes to be in Grace,   830
Wan be his Looks, and meager be his Face.
That Colour, from the Fair, Compassion draws;
She thinks you sick, and thinks her self the Cause.
Orion wander'd in the Woods for Love,
His Paleness did the Nymphs to Pity move;   835
His ghastly Visage argu'd hidden Love.
Nor fail a Night-Cap, in full Health, to wear;
Neglect thy Dress, and discompose thy Hair.
All things are decent, that in Love avail.
Read long by Night, and study to be pale.   840
Forsake your Food, refuse your needful Rest;
Be miserable, that you may be blest.

    Shall I complain, or shall I warn you most?
Faith, Truth and Friendship, in the World are lost;
A little and an empty Name they boast.   845
Trust not thy Friend, much less thy Mistress praise;
If he believe, thou may'st a Rival raise.
'Tis true, *Patroclus*, by no Lust miss-led,
Sought not to stain his dear Companion's Bed.
Nor *Pylades Hermione* embrac'd;   850
Ev'n *Phædra* to *Perithous* still was chaste.
But hope not thou, in this vile Age, to find
Those rare Examples of a faithful Mind.
The Sea shall sooner with sweet Hony flow;
Or, from the Furzes, Pears and Apples grow.   855
We Sin with Gust, we love by Fraud to gain;
And find a Pleasure in our Fellows Pain.
From Rival Foes you may the Fair defend:
But would you ward the Blow, beware your Friend.
Beware your Brother, and your next of Kin;   860
But from your Bosom Friend your Care begin.

    Here I had ended, but Experience finds,
That sundry Women are of sundry Minds;
With various Crochets fill'd, and hard to please,

They therefore must be caught by various Ways.   865
All things are not produc'd in any Soil,
This Ground for Wine is proper, that for Oil.
So 'tis in Men, but more in Women-Kind:
Diff'rent in Face, in Manners, and in Mind.
But wise Men shift their Sails with ev'ry Wind: 870
As changeful *Proteus* vary'd oft his Shape,
And did in sundry Forms and Figures 'scape;
A running Stream, a standing Tree became,
A roaring Lyon, or a bleating Lamb.
Some Fish with Harpons, some with Darts are struck,   875
Some drawn with Nets, some hang upon the Hook:
So turn thy self; and, imitating them,
Try sev'ral Tricks, and change thy Stratagem.
One Rule will not, for diff'rent Ages, hold;
The Jades grow cunning, as they grow more old.   880
Then talk not Bawdy to the bashful Maid;
Bug Words will make her Innocence afraid.
Nor to an ign'rant Girl of Learning speak;
She thinks you conjure, when you talk in *Greek*.
And hence 'tis often seen, the Simple shun   885
The Learn'd, and into vile Embraces run.
    Part of my Task is done, and part to do:
But here 'tis time to rest my self, and you.

EPITAPH *on the Monument of*
the Marquis of Winchester

HE who in impious Times untainted stood,
    And midst Rebellion durst be just and good;
Whose Arms asserted, and whose Sufferings more
Confirm'd the Cause for which he fought before,
Rests here, rewarded by an Heavenly Prince,   5
For what his Earthly could not recompence.
Pray (Reader) that such Times no more appear,
Or, if they happen, learn true Honour here.

Epitaph. Text from 'Lintott's Miscellany', Miscellaneous Poems and Translations. By Several Hands, *1712, collated with the inscription on the monument at Englefield, Berkshire* 1 untainted *inscription*: undaunted *12*

Ark of thy Age's Faith and Loyalty,
Which (to preserve them) Heav'n confin'd in thee,   10
Few Subjects could a King like thine deserve,
And fewer such a King so well cou'd serve.
Blest King, blest Subject, whose exalted State
By Sufferings rose, and gave the Law to Fate.
Such Souls are rare; but mighty Patterns given   15
To Earth, were meant for Ornaments to Heaven.

Epitaph on Mrs. Margaret Paston
of Barningham *in* Norfolk

So fair, so young, so innocent, so sweet;
So ripe a Judgment, and so rare a Wit,
Require at least an Age, in One to meet.
In her they met; but long they cou'd not stay,
'Twas Gold too fine to fix without Allay: 5
Heav'ns Image was in her so well exprest,
Her very Sight upbraided all the rest.
Too justly ravish'd from an Age like this;
Now *she* is gone, the World is of a Piece.

ÆSACUS *transform'd into a Cormorant*

THESE some old Man sees wanton in the Air,
And praises the unhappy constant Pair.
Then to his Friend the long-neck'd Corm'rant shows,
The former Tale reviving others Woes:
That sable Bird, he cries, which cuts the Flood   5
With slender Legs, was once of Royal Blood;
His Ancestors from mighty *Tros* proceed,
The brave *Laomedon* and *Ganymede*,
(Whose Beauty tempted *Jove* to steal the Boy)
And *Priam*, hapless Prince! who fell with *Troy*.   10
Himself was *Hector*'s Brother, and (had Fate
But giv'n his hopeful Youth a longer Date)

Epitaph. Text from 'Lintott's Miscellany', *1712*
Æsacus transform'd. Text from Ovid's Metamorphoses, *1717. See Commentary*

Perhaps had rival'd warlike *Hector*'s Worth,
Tho' on the Mother's Side of meaner Birth;
Fair *Alyxothoe*, a Country Maid,   15
Bare *Æsacus* by stealth in *Ida*'s Shade.
He fled the noisy Town and pompous Court,
Lov'd the lone Hills and simple rural Sport,
And seldom to the City would resort.
Yet he no rustick Clownishness profest,   20
Nor was soft Love a Stranger to his Breast:
The Youth had long the Nymph *Hesperie* woo'd,
Oft thro' the Thicket or the Mead pursu'd:
Her haply on her Father's Bank he spy'd,
While fearless she her silver Tresses dry'd;   25
Away she fled: Not Stags with half such Speed,
Before the prowling Wolf, scud o'er the Mead;
Not Ducks, when they the safer Flood forsake,
Pursu'd by Hawks, so swift regain the Lake.
As fast he follow'd in the hot Career;   30
Desire the Lover wing'd, the Virgin Fear.
A Snake unseen now pierc'd her heedless Foot;
Quick thro' the Veins the venom'd Juices shoot:
She fell, and 'scap'd by Death his fierce Pursuit.
Her lifeless Body, frighted, he embrac'd,   35
And cry'd, Not this I dreaded, but thy Haste:
O had my Love been less, or less thy Fear!
The Victory, thus bought, is far too dear.
Accursed Snake! Yet I more curs'd than he!
He gave the Wound; the Cause was giv'n by me.   40
Yet none shall say that unreveng'd you dy'd.
He spoke; then climb'd a Cliff's o'er-hanging Side,
And, resolute, leap'd on the foaming Tide.
Tethys receiv'd him gently on the Wave;
The Death he sought deny'd, and Feathers gave.   45
Debarr'd the surest Remedy of Grief,
And forc'd to live, he curst th' unask'd Relief.
Then on his airy Pinions upward flies,
And at a second Fall successless tries;
The downy Plume a quick Descent denies.   50
Enrag'd, he often dives beneath the Wave,
And there in vain expects to find a Grave.

His ceaseless Sorrow for th' unhappy Maid,
Meager'd his Look, and on his Spirits prey'd.
Still near the sounding Deep he lives; his Name   55
From frequent Diving and Emerging came.

[*Lines to Mrs* Creed]

So much religion in *your* name doth dwell,
Your soul must needs with piety excell.
Thus names, like   pictures drawn of old,
Their owners' nature and their story told.—
Your name but half expresses; for in you   5
Belief and practice do together go.
My prayers shall be, while this short life endures,
These may go hand in hand, with you and yours;
Till faith hereafter is in vision drown'd,
And practice is with endless glory crown'd.   10

[*Epitaph on* Erasmus Lawton]

STAY Stranger Stay and drop one Tear
She allways weeps that layd him Here
And will do, till her race is Run
His Father's fifth, her only Son.

Lines to Mrs Creed. Text from Malone, I. i. 341–2. See Commentary
Epitaph. Text from the mural tablet in the church of Great Catworth, Huntingdonshire

ON THE MARRIAGE OF
THE FAIR AND VERTUOUS LADY,
MRS ANASTASIA STAFFORD,
WITH THAT TRULY WORTHY AND
PIOUS GENT.
GEORGE HOLMAN, ESQ.
A PINDARIQUE ODE

I

WHEN nature, in our northern hemisphere,
Had shortned day-light, and deform'd the year;
 When the departing sun
 Was to our adverse tropique run;
And fair St Lucy, with the borrow'd light,   5
Of moon and stars, had lengthen'd night:
What more then summer's day slipt in by chance,
 To beautify the calendar?
What made a spring, in midst of winter to advance,
And the cold seasons leap into a youthfull dance, 10
 To rouse the drooping year?
Was this by miracle, or did they rise
By the bright beams of Anastasia's eyes?
 To light our frozen clime,
And, happily for us, mistook their time?   15
'Twas so, and 'twas imported in her name;
From her, their glorious resurrection came,
 And she renewed their perisht flame.
 The God of nature did the same:
His birth the depth of winter did adorn,   20
And she, to marriage then, her second birth was born.
 Her pious family, in every state,
 Their great Redeemer well can imitate.
They have a right in heaven, an early place;
The beauteous bride is of a martyr's race: 25

On the Marriage, &c. Text from Tixall Poetry; with Notes and Illustrations by
Arthur Clifford, Esq., *1813. See Commentary*

And he above, with joy looks down,
I see, I see him blaze with his immortall crown.
    He, on her nuptials, does his beams dispense,
    Blessing the day with better influence;
He looks from heaven with joy, and gives her joy from thence.   30

II

Now, let the reasonable beast, call'd man;
    Let those, who never truly scan
        The effects of sacred Providence,
But measure all by the grosse rules of sence;
Let those look up and steer their sight,   35
        By the great Stafford's light.
The God that suffered him to suffer here,
Rewards his race, and blesses them below,
Their father's innocence and truth to show;
To show he holds the blood of martyrs dear: 40
He crowned the father with a deathless diadem;
    And all the days from him he took,
He numbred out in his eternal book:
And said, let these be safely kept for them,
The long descendants of that hallow'd stem.   45
    To drye the mournfull widow's tears,
    Let all those dayes be turn'd to years,
        And all those years be whiten'd too:
Still some new blessing let 'em bring,
To those who from my martyr spring;   50
    Still let them bloom, and still bestow
Some new content upon his race below.
        Let their first revolution
        Bestow a bride upon his darling son,
And crown those nuptials with a swift increase,   55
        Such as the emptied ark did blesse:
Then, as the storms are more allay'd,
        And waves decay'd,
Send out the beauteous blooming maid:
And let that virgin dove bring to her house again,   60
An olive branch of peace, in triumph o'er the main.
    For whom, ye heavens! have ye reserv'd this joy?
        Let us behold the man you chose;

How well you can your cares employ,
And to what armes your maid dispose: 65
Your maid, whom you have chang'd, but cannot lose:
Chang'd as the morn into the day,
As virgin snow that melts away,
And, by its kindly moisture, makes new flowers to grow.
See then, a bridegroom worthy such a bride! 70
Never was happy pair so fitly tied;
Never were virtues more allied;
United in a most auspicious hour—
A martyr's daughter weds a confessor!
When innocence and truth became a crime, 75
By voluntary banishment,
He left our sacrilegious clime,
And to a forrain country went;
Or rather, there, by Providence was sent:
For Providence designed him to reside, 80
Where he, from his abundant stock,
Might nourish God's afflicted flock,
And, as his steward, for their wants provide.
A troop of exiles on his bounty fed,
They sought, and found with him their daily bread; 85
As the large troop increast, the larger table spread.
The cruse ne're emptied, nor the store
Decreas'd the more;
For God supplied him still to give, who gave in God's own stead.
Thus, when the raging dearth 90
Afflicted all the Egyptian earth;
When scanty Nile no more his bounty dealt,
And Jacob, even in Canaan, famine felt;
God sent a Joseph out before;
His father and his brethren to restore: 9
Their sacks were filled with corn, with generous wine
Their soules refresht, their ebbing store,
Still when they came, supply'd with more,
And doubl'd was their corn:
Joseph himself by giving, greater grew, 1
And from his loins a double tribe increast the chosen crew.

COMMENTARY

Upon the death of the Lord Hastings

(Page 1)

This poem first appeared in *Lachrymæ Musarum; The Tears of the Muses: Exprest in Elegies; Written By divers persons of Nobility and Worth, Upon the death of the most hopefull, Henry Lord Hastings, Onely Sonn of the Right Honourable Ferdinando Earl of Huntingdon Heir-generall of the high born Prince George Duke of Clarence, Brother to King Edward the fourth*, 1649. Page 76 has the note 'Here was the end of the Book intended to have been; and so was it Printed, before these following Papers were written or sent in.' Of the eight postscript elegies, five were by Dryden and other *alumni* of Westminster. Dryden must have seen the original contributions, since he draws on them.

Henry Lord Hastings was born on 16 January 1630 and died of smallpox on 24 June 1649, the eve of the day arranged for his marriage with the daughter of the king's physician, Sir Theodore Turquet de Mayerne (see ll. 95–96).

15–20. *Rare Linguist*, &c. Cf. Joseph Joynes's elegy in the same volume, ll. 46–58:

> Unless we justly make a doubt, wheth'r He
> At Eighteen could in full possession be
> (Without a Miracle) of all Tongues; one
> Whereof to purchase asks an Age alone.
> Him in's own Language might have heard indite,
> The Swarthy *Arab*, or the *Elamite*:
> What *Athens* heard, or *Solyma*, or *Rome*
> Of old, that from his tongue did flowing come. . . .

27–28. *His Body was an Orb*, &c. Cf. *Heroique Stanza's*, ll. 17–20, note; *Astræa Redux*, ll. 298–9; *Absalom and Achitophel*, ll. 838–9; *The Hind and the Panther*, iii. 19; and *Eleonora*, ll. 270–3.

38. *Celestial*, in contrast to other bodies which are set in the sublunar region and are corruptible.

42. *Astronomical*. Cf. *Eleonora*, ll. 263–5.

43. *Tycho*: Tycho Brahé (1546–1601), the Danish astronomer, who discovered a new star in the constellation of Cassiopeia in 1572.

49–50. *The Nations sin*: the execution of Charles I in January 1649. Cf. Denham's elegy in the same volume, ll. 19–32:

> . . . as the Leader of the Herd fell first
> A Sacrifice to quench the raging thirst
> Of inflam'd Vengeance for past Crimes: so none
> But this white fatted Youngling could atone,
> By his untimely Fate, that impious Stroke
> That sullied Earth, and did Heaven's pity choke.

63–64. *Or were these Gems*, &c. Cf. Carew, *Epitaph on the Lady S.*, ll. 5–10:

> Shee was a Cabinet
> Where all the choysest stones of price were set;
> . . . . . .
> Whose rare and hidden vertues, did expresse
> Her inward beauties, and minds fairer dresse.

81–84. *old three-legg'd gray-beards*, &c. Cf. Juvenal, *Sat.* x. 190 ff. In the Sphinx's riddle answered by Oedipus, man is the animal which walks on four legs in the morning, two at noon, and three—the third a staff—in the evening.

95–96. *Whose skilful Sire*, &c. Cf. Marvell's Elegy on Hastings, ll. 47–60 (*Poems*, ed. Margoliouth, p. 5).

99–100. Lovers whose procreation is spiritual rather than fleshly 'conceive and bear the things of the spirit . . . wisdom and all her sister virtues'; and their union is 'even more complete than that which comes of bringing children up, because they have created something lovelier and less mortal than human seed' (Plato, *Symposium*, 209).

106. *th' Irradiations which he cast.* Physiologists used 'irradiation' for 'the emission or emanation of any fluid, influence, principle, or virtue, from an active centre' (*OED*). Cf. Browne's use of the term in discussing generation: 'it seems not impossible, that impregnation may succeed from seminal spirits, and vaporous irradiations containing the active principle, without material and gross immissions'; 'the generation of bodies is not meerly effected as some conceive, of souls, that is, by Irradiation, or answerably unto the propagation of light, without its proper diminution . . .' (*Pseudodoxia Epidemica*, VII. xvi, III. ix).

To his friend the Authour, on his divine Epigrams

(Page 4)

Commendatory poems were also contributed to *Sion and Parnassus* by R. March and W. James, probably the Richard Marsh and William James who were King's Scholars with Dryden at Westminster School. Macdonald suggests that Hoddesdon too was a Westminster boy, though there is no record of him there.

11–16. *Young Eaglet*, &c. Pliny, X. iii. Cf. *Britannia Rediviva*, ll. 120–1; Spenser, *An Hymne of Heavenly Beautie*, ll. 138–9:

> . . . like the natiue brood of Eagles kynd,
> On that bright Sunne of glorie fixe thine eyes.

To Honor Dryden

(Page 5)

Honor Dryden (*c.* 1637–*c.* 1714) was the daughter of Sir John Dryden of Canons Ashby and sister to John Driden of Chesterton (see *Fables*, 'To my

Honour'd Kinsman'). Malone read the partly defaced date of this letter as 23 May 1655. No figures are now visible; but Dryden took his B.A. in January 1653/4, and there is no evidence that he continued in residence after that date. Malone probably misread 1653 as 1655.

40–45. *The Virgin Waxe*, &c. Cf. Spenser, *The Faerie Queene*, III. viii. 6:

> The same she tempred with fine Mercury,
> And virgin wex, that neuer yet was seald,
> And mingled them with perfect vermily,
> That like a liuely sanguine it seem'd to the eye.

Heroique Stanza's
(Page 6)

Cromwell died on 3 September and was buried on 10 November 1658. On 20 January 1659 Herringman entered in *SR* a book entitled *Three poems to the happy memory of the most renowned Oliver, late Lord Protector of this Commonwealth* by Marvell, Dryden, and Sprat. It was published as *Three Poems Upon the Death of his late Highnesse Oliver Lord Protector of England, Scotland, and Ireland. Written By Mr Edm. Waller. Mr Jo. Dryden. Mr Sprat, of Oxford. London, Printed by William Wilson*, 1659. Herringman probably withdrew for political reasons. Marvell's poem was not printed until 1681, and was replaced here by Waller's already published *Upon the Late Storme, And of the Death of His Highnesse Ensuing the same*. Dryden's poem was reprinted by some enemy in 1681 as *An Elegy on the Usurper O.C. By the Author of Absalom and Achitophel, published to shew the Loyalty and Integrity of the Poet*, and there were other reprints with the same malicious intention (Macdonald, pp. 5–6). A separate edition of *Heroique Stanza's* with the title *A Poem Upon the Death of His Late Highness, Oliver . . . 1659* has been regarded by previous editors as the first edition; but it seems to be a reprint issued by Tonson *c.* 1691 to complete made-up sets of Dryden's poems (see Macdonald, p. 7). On the choice of the quatrain for an elevated theme, see *Annus Mirabilis*, 'An account of the ensuing Poem', ll. 35–38.

1–4. *And now 'tis time*, &c. A reference to panegyrics written between Cromwell's burial on 10 November and the state funeral of 'Oliver lying in effigy' on 23 November. The Romans customarily liberated an eagle from an emperor's funeral pile; the bird carried his soul to heaven, and he was then enrolled among the Roman deities (Herodian, IV. ii).

17–20. The circle is Dryden's favourite symbol of perfection; see *Upon the death of the Lord Hastings*, ll. 27–28, note. Cf. Horace, *Sat.* II. vii. 83–88, 'sapiens . . . et in se ipso totus, teres, atque rotundus'; M. Antoninus, xi. 12 and xii. 3.

23–24. *And Warr's like mists*, &c. Cf. Donne, *Fifty Sermons*, xxxvi: 'Their light seems to be great out of the same reason, that a Torch in a misty night, seemeth greater than in a clear, because it hath kindled and inflamed much thicke and grosse Ayre round about it.'

27–28. *Nor was his Vertue poyson'd*, &c. Even when petitioned by Parliament on 31 March 1657 to assume the title of king, Cromwell answered that he was 'not able for such a trust and charge' (see Carlyle, *Letters and Speeches of Oliver Cromwell*, 1904, iii. 20–129).

31–32. Cromwell won the battle of Marston Moor in 1644, when he was 45, and died at the age of 59. Pompey reached the height of his fortunes with his return to Rome from the east in 61 B.C., when he was 45; he died at the hands of assassins in 48 B.C., in his fifty-ninth year. Just before his death he said to his wife: 'Thou hast hitherto been accustomed only to the Smiles of Fortune, which perhaps has deceived thee in This, that she has been constant to me beyond her usual custom' (*Plutarch's Lives*, 1727, v. 391).

41–48. *Our former Cheifs*, &c. The Earl of Manchester and other parliamentary leaders showed little inclination to follow up the victory of Marston Moor, and sought only to reform the old polity after an honourable peace. On 25 November 1644 Cromwell arraigned Manchester as always 'indisposed and backward to engagements, and the ending of the War by the sword', and on 9 December he declared: 'The important occasion now, is no less than To save a Nation, out of a bleeding, nay almost dying condition. . . . I do conceive if the Army be not put into another method, and the War more vigorously prosecuted, the People can bear the War no longer, and will enforce you to a dishonourable Peace' (*Letters and Speeches*, 1904, i. 182–7). *sticklers*: mediators.

Lines 47–48, which seem to refer only to Cromwell's vigorous prosecution of the war, were later taken by Dryden's calumniators to imply approval of Charles I's execution. So Robert Gould in *The Laureat. Jack Squabbs History* (1687; *POAS*, 1702, ii. 129):

> Nay, had our *Charles*, by Heav'ns severe Decree,
> Been found, and Murther'd in the Royal Tree,
> Ev'n thou hadst prais'd the Fact; his Father slain,
> Thou call'dst but gently breathing of a Vein:
> Impious and Villainous! to bless the blow ⎫
> That laid at once three lofty Nations low, ⎬
> And gave the Royal Cause a fatal Overthrow. ⎭

57–58. *His Palmes*, &c. 'It is proper for the Palme tree to mounte; the heauyer you loade it the higher it sprowteth' (Lyly, *Works*, ed. R. W. Bond, 1902, i. 191). The frontispiece of Εἰκὼν Βασιλική: *The Pourtraicture of His Sacred Majestie in his Solitudes and Sufferings*, 1649, represents Charles I kneeling, and two palms heavily weighted, with the motto *Crescit sub Pondere Virtus*. The figure had been applied earlier to Cromwell's achievements. Cf. Mew's 'Regnis minatur multa Regentium' in *Musarum Oxoniensium* ΕΛΑΙΟΦΟΡΙΑ, 1654 (*POAS*, 1702, ii. 2):

> Anglia, firma manens, triumphat.
> Vis nempe belli nulla, nec exteri
> Illam movebat, neve domestici:
> Sed pressa, palmæ par virenti,
> Ponderibus melius resurgit.

63–64. *Bolognia's Walls*, &c. It is said that during the siege of Bologna in 1512 a mine blew up part of the city wall on which was built a chapel dedicated to the Blessed Virgin. The chapel was lifted into the air by the explosion, but then fell so exactly into its original place that the breach was completely repaired (Guicciardini, *Storia d'Italia*, x).

65–68. Cf. Waller, *A Panegyrick to My Lord Protector*, ll. 81–98:

> A Race unconquer'd, by their Clime made bold,
> The *Caledonians* Arm'd with want and cold,
> Have by a fate indulgent to your fame,
> Been from all Ages kept for you to tame;
>
> .   .   .   .
>
> So kind *Dictators* made, when they came home,
> Their vanquisht Foes, Free Citizens of *Rome*;
> Like favour find the *Irish*. . . .

71. *Mine*: a variant spelling of *mien*.

72. *Love and Majesty together*. Cf. Marvell, *A Poem upon the Death of O.C.*, ll. 233–6:

> . . . he issu'd with that awfull state,
> It seem'd Mars broke through Janus' double gate;
> Yet always temper'd with an aire so mild,
> No April sunns that e'er so gently smil'd.

77. *Feretrian Jove*. When Romulus defeated the Cæninenses, he built a temple for Jove, 'giving that God a new Surname; *Jupiter Feretrius*, said he, I King *Romulus*, having been victorious, bring thee here the Arms of a King, and dedicate to thee a Temple . . . as a repository for rich Spoils, which all posterity, when they have slain Kings and Generals of their Enemies, in imitation of me, shall bring hither' (Livy, *Roman History*, 1686, I. x). Cf. *The Tenth Satyr of Juvenal*, l. 208.

85–88. 'His greatness at home was but a shadow of the glory he had abroad. It was hard to discover which feared him the most, France, Spain, or the Low Countries, where his friendship was current at the value he put on it. And as they did all sacrifice their honour and their interest to his pleasure, so there is nothing he could have demanded that either of them would have denied him' (Clarendon, *History*, xv. 152).

113–16. *He made us Freemen of the Continent*, &c. A reference to the auxiliary force of six thousand men sent by Cromwell in 1657 to support the French against the Spaniards, and to the cession of Dunkirk in 1658. Cf. Marvell, *A Poem upon the Death of O.C.*, ll. 172–4:

> Who once more joyn'd us to the Continent;
> Who planted *England* on the *Flandrick shoar*,
> And stretch'd *our frontire* to the *Indian Ore*.

120. *Alexander*: Alexander VII, Pope from 1655 to 1667.

121–4. *By his command*, &c. Dryden makes the best of the expedition sent to the West Indies under Penn and Venables in 1654. Venables landed in Hispaniola and marched through the jungle on San Domingo. The army 'was then set upon by ambuscadoes; fought miserably ill, the unruly persons of it, or would not fight at all; fled back to its ships a mass of miserable disorganic ruin; and "dying there at the rate of two-hundred a day," made for Jamaica' (Carlyle, in *Letters and Speeches*, ii. 466). The 'prize' was the Spanish bullion captured near Cadiz in 1656.

129–32. *Nor dy'd he*, &c. Cf. Waller, *Upon the Late Storme*, ll. 14–16:

> Our Dying Hero, from the Continent,
> Ravish'd whole Towns, and Forts from *Spaniards* reft,
> As his last Legacy to *Britain* left.

136. *like the Vestall*. The virgin Tarpeia treacherously let the Sabines into the citadel of Rome. According to one story, she asked for what they had on their left arms—their golden bracelets—and they heaped their bucklers upon her and killed her (Livy, *Hist*. I. xi).

137–40. *But first the Ocean*, &c. On 3 June 1658 a large whale came up the Thames; 'after a long Conflict it was killed with the harping yrons . . . & after a horrid grone it ran quite on shore & died' (Evelyn, *Diary*, where an elaborate description is given). On 30 August, while Cromwell lay dying, a great storm swept over England, 'that prognosticks that the great Leviathan of men, that Tempest and overthrow of Government, was now going to his own place' (Heath, *Flagellum*, 1663; see C. H. Firth, *NQ* VII. v. 404).

To my Honored Friend, Sr Robert Howard, On his Excellent Poems

(Page 13)

These lines first appeared in *Poems, viz. 1. A Panegyrick to the King. 2. Songs and Sonnets. 3. The Blind Lady, a Comedy. 4. The Fourth Book of Virgil. 5. Statius his Achilleis, with Annotations. 6. A Panegyrick to Generall Monck. By the Honorable Sr Robert Howard . . . London, Printed for Henry Herringman*, 1660. The book was advertised in *Mercurius Publicus*, 21–28 June 1660, a month after Charles II's entry into London. Dryden's verses were reprinted in *A Collection of Poems by Several Hands*, 1693.

Sir Robert Howard (1626–98) was a son of the Earl of Berkshire, and brother to Lady Elizabeth Howard whom Dryden married in 1663 (see *Annus Mirabilis*, 'An account of the ensuing Poem', ll. 1–8, notes, and Prologue . . . from *The Indian-Queen*, note). Howard's relations with Dryden seem to have been cordial throughout the years of their acquaintance, despite a literary dispute on the use of rhyme in drama, 1664–8 (see Macdonald, p. 93). At the

end of 'A Defence of an Essay of Dramatique Poesie', added to the second
edition of *The Indian Emperour*, 1668, Dryden closes the debate with these
remarks on Howard: 'I lay my Observation at his feet, as I do my Pen, which
I have often employ'd willingly in his deserved commendations, and now
most unwillingly against his Judgment. For his person and parts, I honour
them as much as any man living, and have had so many particular Obligations to him, that I should be very ungrateful, if I did not acknowledge them
to the World. . . . But as I was the last who took up Arms, I will be the first
to lay them down.' Howard, says Evelyn, was 'a Gent: pretending to all
manner of Arts & Sciences for which he had ben the subject of Comedy . . .
not ill-natur'd, but unsufferably boosting' (*Diary*, 16 February 1685). Shadwell
ridicules him in *The Sullen Lovers*, 1668, in the character of Sir Positive At-All
(see Pepys, *Diary*, 8 May 1668).

9–14. *Yet as when mighty Rivers*, &c. Cf. Denham, *Cooper's Hill*, 1655,
ll. 189–92:

> O could I flow like thee, and make thy stream
> My great example, as it is my theme!
> Though deep, yet clear, though gentle, yet not dull,
> Strong without rage, without ore-flowing full.

16. *Sampson's Riddle*: Judges xiv. 5–18.

69. *dress'd by Statius in too bold a look.* Cf. Epistle Dedicatory to *The Spanish
Fryar*, 1681: 'I remember some Verses of my own *Maximin* and *Almanzor*,
which cry, Vengeance upon me for their Extravagance, and which I wish
heartily in the same Fire with *Statius* and *Chapman*. . . . *Virgil* had all the
Majesty of a lawful Prince; and *Statius* only the blustring of a Tyrant.'

77–78. *Perspective*: an arrangement of mirrors which makes a designedly
distorted picture intelligible to the eye.

95–98. *With Monck you end*, &c. George Monk (1608–70), Cromwell's
commander-in-chief in Scotland, who marched south at the beginning of
1660 to assert 'the freedom and rights of three kingdoms from arbitrary and
tyrannical usurpations'. He gave no hint of an intention to restore the
monarchy, declaring 'all the while in the most solemn manner for a Commonwealth'; but he was instrumental in dissolving the Rump and calling a
new parliament, and in dispersing disaffected elements in the army 'with
great diligence and skill' so that 'the great turn was brought about without
the least tumult or bloodshed, which was beyond what any person could
have imagined' (cf. *Astræa Redux*, ll. 151–82). The service he did the royalist
cause 'was chiefly owing to the post he was in, and to the credit he had
gained: For as to the Restoration itself, the tide run so strong, that he only
went into it dexterously enough, to get much fame, and great rewards. . . . If
he had died soon after, he might have been more justly admired, because less
known, and seen only in one advantageous light: But he lived long enough to
make it known, how false a judgment men are apt to make upon outward

appearance' (Burnet, i. 83–89). Charles II made him Duke of Albemarle and gave him joint command of the fleet in 1666 (see *Annus Mirabilis*, ll. 185 ff. and notes).

Verginius Rufus, an officer of the Roman army in Gaul in A.D. 68, suppressed the rebellion of Vindex and resisted the repeated attempts of his soldiers to make him emperor. He is said to have composed for himself the epitaph which Dryden quotes (Pliny, *Epist.* vi. 10).

Astræa Redux. A Poem On the Happy Restoration and Return Of His Sacred Majesty Charles the Second
(Page 16)

Charles landed at Dover on 25 May 1660 and entered London four days later. *Astræa Redux* was published by Herringman within a few weeks: Thomason marked his copy 19 June; and the poem was advertised in *Mercurius Publicus*, 21–28 June. It was reprinted with *Annus Mirabilis*, *To His Sacred Majesty*, and *To My Lord Chancellor* in 1688.

By his choice of title and epigraph (Virgil, *Ecl.* iv. 6), Dryden implies two parallels: (i) between the ten years following the execution of Charles I and the Age of Iron in which Astræa, goddess of Justice, abandoned the earth:

> de duro est ultima ferro.
> protinus irrupit venae peioris in aevum
> omne nefas: fugere pudor, verumque fidesque:
>
> .   .   .   .   .   .
>
> iamque nocens ferrum, ferroque nocentius aurum
> prodierat: prodit bellum, quod pugnat utroque,
> sanguineaque manu crepitantia concutit arma.
>
> .   .   .   .   .   .
>
> victa iacet pietas: et virgo caede madentes
> ultima caelestum terras Astraea reliquit.

(Ovid, *Meta.* i. 127–9, 141–3, 149–50); (ii) between the Restoration and the return of the Age of Gold (see ll. 320–3, note). On the identification of the monarchy and Astræa see F. A. Yates, 'Queen Elizabeth as Astræa', *Journal of the Warburg and Courtauld Institutes*, x (1947), 27–82. The political context of this and other Restoration poems is described in H. T. Swedenberg, 'England's Joy: *Astræa Redux* in its Setting', *SP* 1 (1953), 30–44.

2. *a World divided from the rest*: Virgil, *Ecl.* i. 66, 'penitus toto divisos orbe Britannos'.

9–12. *Th' Ambitious Swede*, &c. Charles X of Sweden invaded Poland in 1655. In the following year the Danes declared war on him; and he abandoned the Polish campaign, which was proving difficult, to concentrate his strength against Denmark. In 1658 the Danes opened negotiations for peace and ceded large territories to Charles. He died in February 1660 while preparing an attack on Norway.

13–18. The Treaty of the Pyrenees in 1659 had brought to a temporary halt the long hostilities between France and Spain. Louis XIV married the Infanta Maria Theresa on 9 June 1660. See *Annus Mirabilis*, ll. 29–36, note.

35–36. *The Sacred Purple then*, &c. The episcopal purple and the scarlet of the peers. Apparently an inversion of the common notion that 'they that govern elephants never appear before them in white; and the masters of bulls keep from them all garments of blood and scarlet, as knowing that they will be impatient of civil usages and discipline, when their natures are provoked by their proper antipathies' (Jeremy Taylor, *Twenty-Five Sermons*, xvii, 'The Marriage Ring'; cf. Tilley, R59).

43–48. *The Rabble now*, &c. Cf. *Absalom and Achitophel*, ll. 55–56, and the First Part of *The Conquest of Granada*, I:

> *Almanzor.* Obey'd as Sovereign by thy Subjects be;
> But know, That I alone am King of me.
> I am as free as Nature first made Man, $\Big\}$
> 'Ere the base Laws of Servitude began,
> When wild in Woods the noble Savage ran.

With ll. 45–46 cf. Waller, *To the King, upon His Majesties happy Return*, ll. 19–21:

> *Great Britain*, like blind *Polipheme*, of late
> In a wild rage became the scorn and hate
> Of her proud Neighbours. . . .

59. *As Souls reach Heav'n*: e.g. Enoch and Elijah.

65. *laveering*: tacking.

67–70. The Roman emperor Galba, who followed Nero in A.D. 68, adopted the senator Piso as his successor instead of Otho, Nero's favourite. Otho had Galba and Piso assassinated; but his own position was made precarious by the revolt of Vitellius in Germany, and after a defeat at Brixellum he killed himself in despair. Otho was 'in privata vita mollis' (Eutropius, vii. 17).

74. *all at Worc'ster but the honour lost*: 'in imitation of the famous letter which Francis the First of France wrote to his mother after the battle of Pavia: "Madam, all is lost except our honour" ' (Scott).

75–88. The theme of this passage is common in poems on the Restoration. Cf. Waller, *To the King, upon His Majesties happy Return*, ll. 29–30, 41–44:

> Princes, that saw you, different passions prove,
> For now they dread the Object of their love:
>
> . . . .
>
> For, having view'd the persons and the things,
> The Councils, State and Strength of *Europe*'s Kings,
> You know your work; Ambition to restrain,
> And set them bounds, as Heav'n does to the Main.

In the 'Defence of the Epilogue' to The Second Part of *The Conquest of Granada*, Dryden returns to this theme from a different point of view: Charles's 'own mis-fortunes, and the Nations, afforded him an opportunity, which is rarely allow'd to Sovereign Princes, I mean of travelling, and being conversant in the most polish'd Courts of *Europe*: and, thereby, of cultivating a Spirit, which was form'd by Nature to receive the impressions of a gallant and generous education. At his Return, he found a Nation lost as much in Barbarism as in Rebellion. And as the excellency of his Nature forgave the one, so the excellency of his manners reform'd the other.' Cf. *To my Dear Friend Mr. Congreve*, ll. 1–10.

94. *the honour'd name of Counseller*: 'in nocte consilium.' Cf. Spenser, *The Faerie Queene*, I. i. 33: 'Vntroubled night they say giues counsell best.'

98–104. On the assassination of Henry III of France in 1589, Charles's maternal grandfather, Henry IV (1553–1610), became nominal king of France; but his Protestantism made him obnoxious to most of his subjects. The power of the Catholic League forced him to retire to the south to gather troops and money. He entered the Roman Church in 1593; and thereafter the most important cities in the kingdom moved to his side. The rest of his reign was marked by sound legislation and commercial prosperity.

117. *Rous'd by the lash of his own stubborn tail.* Cf. Waller, *To my Lord of Falkland*, ll. 37–40; *Batman uppon Bartholome, His Booke De Proprietatibus Rerum*, 1582, xviii. 65: 'By the tayle the boldnesse & heart of the Lyon is knowen . . . for when the Lion is wroth, first he beateth the Earthe with his Tayle, and afterwarde, as the wrath increaseth, he smiteth and beateth his owne backe' (Noyes).

121. *Portunus*: protector of harbours. Cf. *Fables*, 'To her Grace the Dutchess of Ormond', ll. 48–50, and Virgil, *Aen*. v. 241–3.

122. *A Lamb*, &c. Cf. Virgil, *Aen*. v. 772, 'tempestatibus agnam'.

125–8. *Yet as wise Artists*, &c. Cf. Preface to *Sylvæ*, ll. 413–14.

129–30. *So on us stole our blessed change*, &c. Cf. Cowley, *Davideis*, ii. 25: 'The manner *How* lies hid, th' *effect* we see.' 'The republicans went about as madmen, to rouse up their party; but their time was past. All were either as men amazed or asleep; they had neither the skill nor the courage to make any opposition. . . . Their union was broke, and their courage sank, without any visible reason for either; and a nation that had run on long in such a fierce opposition to the royal family was now turned as one man to call home the king' (Burnet-Airy, i. 158).

131–6. *Frosts that constrain the ground*, &c. Cf. *Annus Mirabilis*, ll. 1133–40.

144. *As Heav'n it self is took by violence.* Matt. xi. 12; cf. *The Character of that Glorious Martyred King, Charles I. . . . By W.P.*, 1660, 'seeming to take Heaven by a Holy violence, in the fervency of his Devotions'.

145. *Booth's forward Valour.* In the cavalier rising of 1659 Sir George Booth and Sir William Middleton seized Chester and 'ventured imprudently into the open field to face Lambert, by whom they were totally routed; so that the royal party in England never seemed to lie under such total depression, as when it was about to triumph over all opposition' (Scott).

151. *Monck.* See *To my Honored Friend, S*ʳ *Robert Howard*, ll. 95–98, note.

153–4. *The blessed Saints*, &c. Cf. *Annus Mirabilis*, ll. 61–64, and *Fables*, 'Palamon and Arcite', iii. 441–2.

155. *clues*: cords; ship's tackle.

167–8. *Through viewless Conduits*, &c. 'The animal spirits . . . are like a very subtle wind, or rather a very pure and vivid flame which, continually ascending in great abundance from the heart to the brain, thence penetrates through the nerves into the muscles, and gives motion to all the members' (Descartes, *Discourse on Method*, v; translated John Veitch).

181–2. Parliament was dissolved by Cromwell in 1653, and by Lambert in 1659.

187–90. *And as devouter Turks*, &c. Cf. *Purchas his Pilgrimage*, 1614, p. 294; Burton, III. iv. 1. 3; Butler, *Upon an Hypocritical Nonconformist*, xi. The story seems to originate in Ogier Ghiselin de Busbecq's *Itinera* (1581; Oxford, 1660): 'I saw an Old Man at *Constantinople*, who, after he had taken a Cup of Wine in his Hand to Drink, us'd first to make an hideous Noise. I asked his Friends, why he did so? They answer'd me, that, by this Outcry, he did as it were warn his Soul to retire into some secret corner of his Body, or else wholly to Emigrate, and pass out of it, that she might not be guilty of that Sin which he was about to commit, nor be defiled within the wine that he was to guzzle down' (English translation, 1694, p. 17).

193–4. *Like Zealous Missions*, &c. Cf. *The Hind and the Panther*, ii. 568–75 and note.

195–8. Salmoneus (Virgil, *Aen.* vi. 585–94) rode through Greece in a four-horse chariot,

> . . . divumque sibi poscebat honorem,
> demens, qui nimbos et non imitabile fulmen
> aere et cornipedum pulsu simularet equorum.

201–2. *Thus Sforza*, &c. Lodovico Sforza, *il Moro* (1451–1508), poisoned his nephew Giovanni Galeazzo and succeeded him as Duke of Milan. He was betrayed by his own mercenaries to Louis XII of France in 1500, and died a prisoner. 'He was one of the most restless and intriguing spirits that Italy, the mother of political genius, has ever produced' (Scott).

203. *Fogue*. Dryden 'had a vanity, unworthy of his abilities, to show, as may be suspected, the rank of the company with whom he lived, by the use of French words, which had then crept into conversation; such as *fraicheur* for *coolness*, *fougue* for *turbulence*, and a few more, none of which the language has incorporated or retained' (Johnson, i. 463–4).

205–6. *like Helots set*, &c. The Spartans dealt with their serfs 'very hardly; for it was a thing common to force them to drink to excess, and to lead them in that Condition into their publick Halls, that their Children might see what *a contemptible and beastly sight a drunken Man is:* they made them sing such Songs, and dance such Dances, as were uncomely and ridiculous' (*Plutarch's Lives*, 1727, i. 244).

219–20. Scheveling, now Scheveningen, a mile north-west of The Hague, was chosen by the king as the best place for embarkation. The day before he sailed for England, 'the shore was so full of people . . . as that it was as black (which otherwise is white sand), as every one could stand by another' (Pepys, *Diary*, 4 and 22 May 1660).

230–3. On the way over to Holland, tailors and painters had been at work 'cutting out some pieces of yellow cloth into the fashion of a crown and C.R. and put it upon a fine sheet, and that into the flag instead of the State's arms'. Before leaving Holland 'the King and the Duke altered the name of some of the ships, viz. the Nazeby into Charles; the Richard, James . . .' (Pepys, *Diary*, 13 and 23 May 1660).

235. *The Swift-sure groans*, &c. Cf. Virgil, *Aen.* vi. 412–13:

> . . . simul accipit alveo
> ingentem Aenean. gemuit sub pondere cumba. . . .

249. *submitted Fasces*. To answer false accusations against him during his consulship, Publius Valerius 'came into the Assembly with the *Fasces* down. That was a sight very grateful to the Multitude, to see the Ensigns of Government lowered in respect to them, and a confession thereby made, that the Majesty and the Power of the People was greater than that of the Consul' (Livy, *The Roman History . . . done into English*, 1686, p. 37).

253. *As you meet it, the Land approacheth you*. Cf. *Fables*, 'To her Grace the Dutchess of Ormond', ll. 51–52. 'I know not whether this fancy, however little be its value, was not borrowed. A French poet read to Malherbe some verses, in which he represents France as moving out of its place to receive the King. "Though this", said Malherbe, "was in my time, I do not remember it" ' (Johnson, i. 428).

262–5. *Thus when th' Almighty*, &c. Exod. xxxiii. 20–23, xxxiv. 5–7.

266–9. In the Declaration of Breda, 14 April 1660, Charles granted 'a free and general pardon' in order that 'the fear of punishment may not engage any . . . to a perseverance in guilt for the future, by opposing the quiet and happiness of their country in the restoration both of king, peers and people to their just, ancient and fundamental rights', and wished 'that all our subjects may enjoy what by law is theirs, by a full and entire administration of justice throughout the land, and by extending our mercy where it is wanted and deserved' (Browning, pp. 57–58). Cf. *Absalom and Achitophel*, l. 326, note, and *Threnodia Augustalis*, ll. 86–87.

284–7. 'This day came in his Majestie *Charles* the 2d to London. . . . This was also his Birthday, and with a Triumph of above 20000 horse & foote, brandishing their swords and shouting with unexpressable joy: The wayes straw'd with flowers, the bells ringing, the streetes hung with Tapissry, fountaines running with wine . . . Trumpets, Musick, & myriads of people flocking the streetes' (Evelyn, *Diary*, 29 May 1660).

288–91. *That Star*, &c. On the day of Charles's birth, 29 May 1630, a bright constellation was seen in the midday sky. 'To behold this babe Heaven seemed to open one more eye than usual ... from which most men presaged that the Prince should be of high undertakings and of no common glory among kings' (Gadbury, *The Nativity of King Charles*; Bryant, p. 4). To that star 'Dryden ascribes renewed force' (Christie). Cf. Cowley, *Ode. Upon His Majesties Restauration and Return*, ll. 20–23:

> Auspicious *Star* again arise,
> And take thy *Noon-tide Station* in the Skies,
> Again all *Heaven* prodigiously adorn;
> For lo! thy *Charles* again is *born*.

With Dryden's allusion to the star of Bethlehem, cf. Herrick, *Hesperides*, 'A Pastorall upon the birth of Prince *Charles*', ll. 19–24:

> And that his birth sho'd be more singular,
> At Noone of Day, was seene a silver Star,
> Bright as the Wise-mens Torch. . . .

292–3. *whiter*: more fortunate; cf. Horace, *Epist.* II. ii. 187–9. Dryden follows Virgil (*Ecl.* iv. 4–7) in associating 'Astræa redux' with a renewal of time:

> ultima Cumaei venit iam carminis aetas;
> magnus ab integro saeclorum nascitur ordo.
> iam redit et virgo, redeunt Saturnia regna,
> iam nova progenies caelo demittitur alto.

Cf. *Annus Mīrabilis*, ll. 69–72, *Absalom and Achitophel*, ll. 1028–9, and Cowley, *Ode. Upon His Majesties Restauration and Return*, ll. 255–7:

> Such are the *years* (Great *Charles*) which now we see
> Begin their *glorious March* with *Thee*:
> *Long* may their *March* to *Heaven*, and still *triumphant* be.

299. *boundless Circles*. Cf. *Upon the death of the Lord Hastings*, ll. 27–28, note.

310. *France that did an Exiles presence fear*. In the spring of 1654 Mazarin entered into negotiations with Cromwell, and Charles left Paris for Cologne in July. Under the treaty signed with Cromwell on 24 October 1655 France bound herself not to allow Charles, James, and seventeen royalists to reside in her territories.

316. *Edicts*: Charles's proclamation of 30 May 1660 against vicious, debauched, and profane persons (Firth).

320–3. Dryden recalls Anchises' prophecy (*Aen.* vi. 791 ff.) of the return of the Age of Gold with Augustus:

> hic vir, hic est, tibi quem promitti saepius audis,
> Augustus Caesar, divi genus, aurea condet
> saecula qui rursus Latio regnata per arva
> Saturno quondam. . . .

To His Sacred Maiesty, A Panegyrick On His Coronation

(Page 24)

Charles II was crowned on St. George's Day, Tuesday, 23 April 1661. Dryden's poem, one of many celebrating the occasion, was published by

Herringman in the same month. A second edition was included in *Complementum Fortunatarum Insularum. . . . With A Description of the Fortunate Islands. Written originally in French by P. D. C[ardonnel]*, 1662. The poem was reprinted with *Astræa Redux, To My Lord Chancellor*, and *Annus Mirabilis* in 1688.

17–20. Had Charles been crowned earlier than 25 March, the first day of 1661, two months of his exile (25 March–25 May 1660) would have been included in his coronation year.

23–24. *As Heav'n*, &c. Exod. xvi. 13–15.

26–32. *The Season*, &c. Cf. 'A Song of Welcome to King Charles', Jonson, viii. 416:

> . . . To Crowne the years, which you begin, great king,
> And you, with them, as Father of our Spring.

37–46. On 22 April Charles rode in state from the Tower to Whitehall with a 'magnificent Traine on horseback . . . thro the streetes, strew'd with flowers, houses hung with rich *Tapissry*, Windos & *Balconies* full of Ladies', and on the following day went by water to the Abbey to be crowned. See Evelyn, *Diary*.

56. *like Bees in their own sweetnesse drown'd*. 'Bees are causers of their own death . . . by excessiue deuouring of hony' (Holland, *The Historie of . . . Plinius Secundus*, 1601, xi. 19; see Tilley, B204).

57. *attone*: reduce to harmony.

81–84. In the Declaration of Breda Charles promised 'a liberty to tender consciences, and that no man shall be disquieted or called in question for differences of opinion in matter of religion which do not disturb the peace of the kingdom'; and he put forward a scheme of comprehension in the Worcester House Declaration, 25 October 1660. See Browning, pp. 359–60, 365–70. 'The quakers, anabaptists, and other inferior sects, applied, by petitions and humble addresses, to the king, to be permitted to worship God, according to their consciences. Thus, the whole modelling of ecclesiastical matters seemed to be in the hands of the king' (Scott).

102. *fraischeur*. See *Astræa Redux*, l. 203, note.

104. *Cæsars heart that rose above the waves*. 'The River *Anius* . . . was very rough, and so uneven and dangerous that the Pilot . . . ordered his Sailors to tack about. *Cæsar* upon This discovered himself, and taking the Pilot by the Hand, who was surprized to see Him there, said, *Go on boldly, my Friend, and fear nothing; thou carriest* Cæsar *and His Fortune along with thee*' (*Plutarch's Lives*, 1727, vi. 171).

107–8. *In stately Frigats*, &c. 'He understood navigation well: But above all he knew the architecture of ships so perfectly, that in that respect he was exact rather more than became a Prince' (Burnet, i. 94). 'The great and almost only Pleasure of Mind he seemed addicted to, was Shipping and Sea Affairs; which seemed to be so much his Talent both for Knowledge, as well as Inclination, that a War of that kind was rather an Entertainment, than any

Disturbance to his Thoughts' (Sheffield, *A Short Character of King Charles II*). Cf. *Annus Mirabilis*, l. 54.

111–16. *Beyond your Court,* &c. Charles set about improving St. James's Park, which had been neglected during the interregnum. He had a canal made through the park (Pepys, *Diary*, 16 September and 11 October 1660) and stocked it with wild fowl. A few years later Evelyn marvelled at the varieties of deer and 'ordinary & extraordinary Wild foule, breeding about the Decoy' (*Diary*, 9 February 1665). Cf. Waller, *On St. James's Park, as lately improved by His Majesty*.

127–8. *Two Kingdomes wait your doom,* &c. Spain was anxious to gain a diplomatic advantage by arranging a suitable marriage for Charles; and Portugal, which had been fighting for twenty years to throw off Spanish domination, was offering Catherine of Braganza as a bride. Charles's probable choice was 'the talk of the town' in the early months of 1661 (Pepys, *Diary*, 14 and 28 February). On 8 May he announced to Parliament his intention of marrying Catherine 'with full consideration of the good of my subjects in general, as of myself'.

129–32. Four triumphal arches were erected in London for the Coronation. One in Leadenhall Street carried a representation of Charles with 'Usurpation flying before him': 'Behind the said Figure of *Charles* II. in a large Table is deciphered the ROYAL OAK bearing Crowns, and Scepters, instead of Acorns; amongst the Leaves, in a Label, MIRATURQUE NOVAS FRONDES ET NON SUA POMA

> —————————Leaves unknown
> Admiring, and strange Apples not her own.

As designing its Reward for the Shelter afforded His Majesty after the Fight at *Worcester*: an expression of *Virgil*'s, speaking of the Advancement of Fruits by the Art of Graffing' (Ogilby, *The Relation of His Majestie's Entertainment Passing through the City of London to His Coronation*, 1661).

To My Lord Chancellor, Presented on New-years-day
(Page 28)

This poem was first published by Herringman in 1662, and was reprinted with *Astræa Redux*, *To His Sacred Majesty*, and *Annus Mirabilis* in 1688.

Edward Hyde (1609–74) became at the time of the Long Parliament 'a considerable man. . . . He went over to the court party when the war was like to break out, and was much in the late king's councils and confidence during the war. . . . The late king recommended him to this king, as the person on whose advices he wished him to rely most, and he was about the king all the while that he was beyond sea . . . he had nothing so much before his eyes as the king's service and doated on him beyond expression . . . he was a man that knew England well, and was lawyer good enough to be an able chancellor, and was certainly a very incorrupt man' (Burnet-Foxcroft, pp. 53–54). Hyde was created Baron at the Restoration, and Earl of Clarendon in 1661. He was Chancellor from 1658 until his impeachment by Parliament in 1667, and died in exile. His daughter Anne married the Duke of York in February 1661. In a letter unaddressed but reasonably taken to have been written to Hyde's son Lawrence in 1683, Dryden says 'on some occasions, perhaps not known to you, [I] have not been unserviceable to the memory and reputation of My Lord your father' (Ward, p. 21), but no service other than that of this poem is known.

5. *The Muses . . . your early courtship boast.* 'Whilst He was only a Student of the Law, and stood at Gaze, and irresolute what Course of Life to take, his chief Acquaintance were *Ben. Johnson, John Selden, Charles Cotton, John Vaughan,* Sir *Kenelm Digby, Thomas May,* and *Thomas Carew.* . . . Among these Persons Mr. *Hyde's* usual Time of Conversation was spent, till He grew more retired to his more serious Studies, and never discontinued his Acquaintance with any of them' (*Life. . . . Written by Himself,* 1759, i. 30, 36). He contributed commendatory verses to Davenant's *Albovine* (1629).

14. *those,* the cardinals.

45–48. *In you his sleep still wakes,* &c. Cf. *Annus Mirabilis,* ll. 1010–12.

53–54. *And like young David,* &c. 1 Sam. xvii. 38–39.

111–18. 'You direct the course of England among the nations, as God turns the earth on its axis and rolls it in its orbit among the other planets, so smoothly that it seems to be at rest.' Copernicus, *De Revolutionibus Orbis,* i. 8.

119–20. Clarendon 'fell under the hatred of most of the cavaliers upon two accounts. The one was the act of indemnity which cut off all their hopes of repairing themselves of the estates of those that had been in the rebellion. . . . The other thing was that, there being an infinite number of pretenders to employments and rewards for their services and sufferings, so that the king could only satisfy some few of them, he upon that, to stand between the king and the displeasure which those disappointments had given, spoke slightly of many of them and took it upon him that their petitions were not granted' (Burnet-Foxcroft, p. 55).

139–46. Cf. Denham, *Cooper's Hill,* 1655, ll. 39–46: Windsor has

> . . . such an easie and unforc't ascent,
> That no stupendious precipice denies
> Access, no horror turns away our eyes:
> But such a Rise, as doth at once invite
> A pleasure, and a reverence from the sight.

151. *it shall without a weight increase.* Cf. *Heroique Stanza's,* ll. 57–58, note.

155. *weightlesse,* as the lighter elements of fire and air move upwards; *immortal,* having its centre in the king and (beyond the king) in God.

(1823)

To My Honour'd Friend, Dr Charleton

(Page 32)

Dryden and Howard contributed commendatory poems to *Chorea Gigantum, or, The most Famous Antiquity of Great-Britain, Vulgarly called Stone-Heng, Standing on Salisbury Plain, Restored to the Danes; By Walter Charleton, D^r in Physic, and Physician in Ordinary to His Majesty*, 1663. Charleton's dedication is dated 27 April 1662, and the imprimatur 11 September 1662. A copy in the Folger Library is inscribed by the author 'For my Learned & obliging Friend, Mr. John Driden'. A second edition was published with Inigo Jones's *The Most Noble Antiquity of Great Britain* (1655) in 1725. Charleton proposed Dryden for membership of the Royal Society, to which he was admitted a Fellow on 26 November 1662. Charleton's dedication indicates that his interest in Stonehenge had been stimulated by Charles II, who discussed 'stupendious Antiquities' with him and Aubrey, and visited sites in their company (Aubrey, p. liv). Inigo Jones had argued in 1655 that Stonehenge was built by the Romans, not as a 'sepulchral monument' but as a temple dedicated to the god Coelus; Charleton believed that the Danes erected Stonehenge in the 'time of leisure and jollity' after their conquests in the south, 'as a place wherein to elect and inaugurate their supreme Commander, King of England' (p. 64). The problem exercised the antiquaries. Aubrey, despite his friendship with Charleton, offered 'a clear evidence these monuments were Pagan Temples; which was not made-out before' and suggested 'with humble submission to better judgements . . . that they were Temples of the Druids' (Aubrey MS. 14, ff. 25ᵛ–26; Aubrey, p. lv).

21–22. 'Is it not evident', asks Crites in *Of Dramatique Poesie, An Essay*, 'in these last hundred years (when the Study of Philosophy has been the business of all the *Virtuosi* in *Christendome*) that almost a New Nature has been reveal'd to us? that more errours of the School have been detected, more useful Experiments in Philosophy have been made, more Noble Secrets in Opticks, Medicine, Anatomy, Astronomy, discover'd, than in all those credulous and doting Ages from *Aristotle* to us?' (Ker, i. 36–37).

25. *Gilbert*: William Gilbert (1540–1603), physician to Elizabeth and James I, and founder of the modern science of magnetism. His chief work is *De Magnete, Magneticisque Corporibus, et de magno magnete tellure, Physiologia nova, plurimis & argumentis, & experimentis, demonstrata*, 1600.

27–28. *And noble Boyle*, &c. Robert Boyle (1627–91), experimental chemist, natural philosopher, and theologian, had by 1663 published a number of scientific treatises including *Physiological Essays* and *The Sceptical Chymist* (1661); his brother was Roger Boyle (1621–79), Earl of Orrery, politician and poet, to whom Dryden dedicated *The Rival Ladies* (1664).

31. *Harvey*: William Harvey (1578–1657), 'Dr. of Physique and Chirurgery, Inventor of the Circulation of the Bloud', who told Aubrey that when his

Exercitatio Anatomica de Motu Cordis et Sanguinis in Animalibus appeared (1628)
"'twas beleeved by the vulgar that he was crack-brained; and all the Physitians
were against his Opinion'; but 'in about 20 or 30 yeares time, it was recieved
in all the Universities in the world' (Aubrey, p. 131).

32. *Ent*: Sir George Ent (1604–89), an original Fellow of the Royal Society
and President of the College of Physicians 1670–5 and 1682–4. He defended
Harvey in *Apologia pro Circuitione Sanguinis* (1641).

Prologue To the Rival-Ladies

(Page 34)

The Rival Ladies. A Tragi-Comedy was first performed at the Theatre Royal,
Bridges Street, *c.* May 1664 (see Pepys, *Diary*, 4 August) and published by
Herringman that summer (*SR*, 27 June). No epilogue was printed with the
play. In Bodl. MS. Ash. 36, 37, f. 267, a good transcript of the Prologue in a
contemporary hand is immediately followed by an 'Epilogue by the Doctor'
in the same hand:

> 'Tis true, what as a iest our Poet meant,
> His little witt was in ye Prologue spent:
> None left t' excuse my part; unless you would
> Forbeare to damne it till t'were understood.
> T'would go ill wth us, should you give o^r play
> Halfe y^{ese} hard words y^{at} I gave you to day.

[f. 268] The Dcōrs man comes—& brings in an Urinall wth
> black water in it, & whispers ye Dcōr in his Eare.

> Whilst wee in vaine excuses wast our breath
> The Poet & his Muse are sick to death:
> Hees past my cure: as his condicon stands,
> I leave him in y^{ese} abler Doctors hands.

R. G. Ham argues for Dryden's authorship of this epilogue (*RES* xiii (1937),
76–80); but although it is probable that it was written for *The Rival Ladies*,
it is not necessarily Dryden's own. It was not included in any of the four
editions of the play published in his lifetime.

7–8. On the vogue of prologues and epilogues, see A. N. Wiley, *Rare Prologues and Epilogues 1642–1700*, 1940, pp. xxvi–xlv.

11. *Habits*: costumes other than the contemporary dress used in comedy
(see Nicoll, pp. 49–51). *Dances*, often performed by foreign artists and little
related to the play, became a common stage entertainment in the 1660's.
'Scenes, Habits, Dancing . . . take more with Spectators, than the best
Dramatick Wit' (Edward Howard, Preface to *The Six Days Adventure*, 1671;
cf. Pepys, *Diary*, 5 August 1667). *Scenes*: see Prologue . . . from *The Indian-
Queen*, note. *Rhymes*. In the Dedication of *The Rival Ladies* Dryden defends his
'following the New way, I mean, of Writing Scenes in Verse: Though, to

Speak properly, 'tis not so much a new way amongst us, as an old way new reviv'd. . . . But supposing our Country-men had not receiv'd this Writing till of late! Shall we Oppose our selves to the most Polish'd and Civiliz'd Nations of *Europe*. . . .' See Nicoll, pp. 100–2.

12. *High Language often; I, and Sense, sometimes.* Cf. Epilogue to *The Indian Emperour*, ll. 5–8, and Epilogue to *The Rehearsal* (1672):

> . . . for ours, and for the Kingdoms peace,
> May this prodigious way of writing cease.
> Let's have, at least, once in our lives, a time
> When we may have some Reason, not all Rhyme:
> We have these ten years felt its Influence;
> Pray let this prove a year of Prose and Sence.

14. *They blow out Candles.* An effective device (e.g. in *An Evening's Love*, v) which was overworked on the Restoration stage. It is ridiculed in the inset play in Shadwell's *A True Widow*, 1679, IV.

15–16. *And for Surprize*, &c. Cf. *The Rehearsal*, II. v. Two bands of soldiers 'all kill one another', and Bayes (Dryden) cries: 'Hold, hold. Now here's an odd surprise: all these dead men you shall see rise up presently, at a certain Note that I have made, in *Effaut flat*, and fall a Dancing. Do you hear, dead men? [*The music plays his Note, and the dead men rise; but cannot get in order.*]'

Prologue, Epilogue and Songs from The Indian-Queen, A Tragedy

(Page 35)

Sir Robert Howard and Dryden collaborated in writing *The Indian-Queen*, the first heroic play presented in London (Macdonald, pp. 88–89; Nicoll, pp. 106–7). Pepys saw 'the streete full of coaches at the new play' at the Theatre Royal on 27 January 1664. It was first published in *Four New Plays . . . Written by the Honourable Robert Howard*, 1665. A second edition, *Five New Plays*, appeared in 1692. In the 'Connexion of the *Indian Emperour*, to the *Indian Queen*', printed before *The Indian Emperour* (1667), Dryden says only that 'part of [the earlier] Poem was writ by me'. His contribution was not acknowledged in the early editions, and none of the pieces printed here can be certainly attributed to him, or to him alone. His part is discussed by J. H. Smith in *SP* li (1954), 54–74. On Dryden and Howard, see *To my Honored Friend, Sʳ Robert Howard*, note.

The Indian-Queen was splendidly produced, 'so beautified with rich Scenes as the like had never ben seene here, or happly (except rarely any where else) on a mercenarie *Theater*' (Evelyn, *Diary*, 5 February 1664). There is an oblique tribute to the memorable costumes in Aphra Behn's *Oroonoko*, 1688 (*Works*, 1915, v. 130). An operatic version, with music by Henry and Daniel Purcell, was produced in 1695 (see Macdonald, pp. 89–90; Day, p. 141).

Prologue. A dramatic prologue of this kind, presented from the main stage, was unusual. Cf. Prologue to *Wit without Money*, note.

11–13. *By ancient Prophesies,* &c. Cf. the High Priest in *The Indian Emperour*, I. ii:

> Old Prophecies foretel our fall at hand,
> When Bearded Men in floating Castles Land.

Songs. I. Act III. Ismeron, a magician in the service of the Indian Queen, calls up spirits from the realm of Sleep. On the popularity of this song, see Day, pp. 141–2.

11. *Dun*: toad.

II. Act III. Ismeron invokes

> You Spirits that inhabit the Air,
> With all your powerful Charms of Musick try
> To bring her Soul back to its Harmony.

III. Act v. Sung by a priest in the Temple of the Sun.

Prologue, Epilogue and Songs from The Indian Emperour, or, The Conquest of Mexico by the Spaniards

(Page 38)

The Indian Emperour . . . Being the Sequel of the Indian Queen was first performed at the Theatre Royal in the spring of 1665 (Macdonald, p. 92) and became one of Dryden's most popular plays. It was first published by Herringman in 1667, with an Epistle Dedicatory to the Duchess of Monmouth dated 12 October. In 'A Defence of an Essay of Dramatique Poesie', printed with the second edition (1668), Dryden says 'The former Edition . . . being full of faults which had escaped the Printer, I have been willing to overlook this second with more care: . . . by that little I have done, the Press is freed from some gross errors.'

Prologue. 5–6. *The Scenes are old,* &c. Scenes and costumes were carried over from *The Indian-Queen* (see Nicoll, pp. 36–37, 81 note).

6–7. The allusion in the lines which were omitted after the first edition is clearly to an animal prologue, though the vogue of such novelties, ranging from parrots to elephants, seems not to have developed till later. The comedian Haynes scored a hit by speaking the epilogue to Scott's *The Unhappy Kindness* from the back of an ass in the 1690's (Wiley, pp. 199–203).

Epilogue. 6. *lofty sound, and humble sence.* Cf. Prologue to *The Rival-Ladies*, l. 12, note.

Songs. I: Act II, Sc. i. II: Act IV, Sc. iii. Day (pp. 7–8) reproduces Pelham Humphrey's setting from *Choice Ayres, Songs, & Dialogues*, 1675.

Annus Mirabilis: The Year of Wonders, 1666. An Historical Poem

(Page 42)

Annus Mirabilis was licensed on 22 November 1666, and published by Herringman early in 1667 (Pepys bought a copy on 2 February). Some changes were made while the book was passing through the press (see ll. 267, 417–20 and notes); and despite Dryden's reliance on Howard to see his work into print, a lengthy errata list had to be provided. The 1668 edition was probably pirated (see Macdonald, pp. 14–15). The 1688 edition, which includes *Astræa Redux, To His Sacred Majesty* and *To My Lord Chancellor*, is valuable chiefly for its improved punctuation. In a note 'To the Readers' in 67 Dryden says he corrected only the grossest of the printer's errors, 'not such as by false stops have confounded the sense, but such as by mistaken words have corrupted it'; and he may have been responsible for some of the improvements in *88*. But most of the variants in *88* are degenerations or are due to carelessness. The epigraphs are from Pliny, *Epist.* x. 33, and *Aen.* ii. 363.

The title and theme of the poem seem to have been suggested by a series of seditious pamphlets, *Mirabilis Annus, the Year of Prodigies* (1661), and *Mirabilis Annus Secundus; or, The Second Year of Prodigies* (1662; in two parts). These contain accounts of apparitions and prodigies promising 'judgments', in the form of national disasters, on an iniquitous king and government. Dryden turns popular attention away from such prophecies, and from the numerous prophecies of a great fire which had been fulfilled in 1666, towards England's naval successes and future prosperity. The poem was designed 'to show that the disasters were but momentary interruptions in the path to wealth and glory, and that they had served to draw the King and his people together in the bonds of mutual suffering and affection' (E. N. Hooker, 'The Purpose of *Annus Mirabilis*', *HLQ* x (1946), 49–67). Dryden steers a cautious course through the events of 1665–6. He avoids the Plague; he ignores the widespread conviction that the Fire was the issue of a foreign plot; and he represents the naval war as a consistently heroic enterprise. His treatment of the war in accordance with the demands of the 'Historique and Panegyrique', and in the interests of policy, is discussed in detail in James Kinsley, 'The "Three Glorious Victories" in *Annus Mirabilis*', *RES*, N.S., vii (1956), 30–37.

'Virgil', says Dryden, 'has been my Master in this Poem: I have followed him every where.' His sustained personification of the Fire has Virgilian precedent, and serves indirectly to emphasize its accidental origin and its irresistible progress as the instrument, not of foreign enemies, but of Providence. For his numerous similes drawn from nature he had the examples of Virgil, and of Waller in *Instructions to a Painter, For the Drawing of the Posture and Progress of His Majesties Forces at Sea . . . June 3, 1665*. His most direct reminiscences and imitations of Virgil are these: l. 54, *Aen.* vii. 706–7; ll. 59–

60, *G*. iv. 394–5; l. 72, *Aen*. vi. 796; ll. 183–4, *G*. iv. 287–94; l. 201, *Aen*. vi. 724; l. 228, *Aen*. viii. 691–2; ll. 243–4, *Aen*. iv. 441–6; ll. 263–4, *Aen*. i. 393–6; l. 272, *Aen*. vi. 270; l. 292, *Aen*. i. 209; l. 384, *Aen*. ix. 791–8; ll. 425–32, *G*. iv. 511–15; ll. 435–6, *Aen*. ii. 726–8; ll. 437–40, *G*. i. 373–8; ll. 445–8, *Aen*. ii. 304–8; ll. 491–2, *G*. iii. 423–4; ll. 573–80, *G*. iv. 158–69 and *Aen*. i. 430–6; ll. 621–4, *G*. i. 136; l. 639, *Aen*. vi. 796; l. 701, *Aen*. v. 302; l. 731, *Aen*. i. 536; l. 736, *Aen*. i. 145–6; ll. 757–60, *Aen*. xii. 666–8 and v. 231; l. 870, *G*. iii. 565 and *Aen*. ii. 758; l. 877, *G*. iv. 263; l. 922, *Aen*. ii. 312; l. 938, *Aen*. ii. 706; ll. 973–4, *G*. iii. 468–9; l. 1069, see note; l. 1162, *G*. i. 488.

An account of the ensuing Poem, &c. On Sir Robert Howard, see *To my Honored Friend . . . On his Excellent Poems*, note. Dryden retired to Charlton near Malmesbury, the seat of Howard's father, in 1665 'when the violence of the last Plague had driven me from the Town', and seems to have remained there till the end of 1666. At Charlton he wrote *Annus Mirabilis*, *Of Dramatick Poesie, An Essay*, and probably *Secret Love*, which is doubtless the play referred to here (l. 5).

3. *You have . . . been careful of my Fortune*: probably a reference to Howard's good offices in the matter of a patent granted to Dryden's wife in 1662. None of the money had been paid by June 1666; but a letter written by the Drydens to the Chancellor of the Exchequer on 14 August shows Howard's assistance in arranging payment (Ward, p. 6 and notes).

10–11. *a most just and necessary War*. See stanzas 1–14. On 2 February 1664 Pepys met 'a merchant . . . of great observation and repute' who 'discoursed well of the good effects in some kind of a Dutch warr and conquest (which I did not consider before, but the contrary), that is, the trade of the world is too little for us two, therefore one must down'.

33. *those who rank Lucan*, &c. Cf. Davenant, Preface to *Gondibert*, 1651, p. 3: '*Lucan*, who chose to write the greatest actions that ever were allowed to be true . . . did not observe that such an enterprize rather beseem'd an Historian, than a Poet: for wise Poets think it more worthy to seek out truth in the Passions, than to record the truth of Actions.'

39. *The learned Languages*, &c. Cf. Milton, *Paradise Lost*, note on 'The Verse' (1668).

52–53. *the variety of Female Rhymes*. Cf. Preface to *Albion and Albanius*: 'Female, or double Rhime . . . is not natural to our Tongue, because it consists too much of Monosyllables, and those too, most commonly clogg'd with Consonants.'

56. *the Alarique, the Pucelle*: Georges de Scudéry, *Alaric, ou Rome vaincüe*, 1654; Jean Chapelain, *La Pucelle, ou la France délivrée*, 1656.

57–58. *Alexandrins . . . by Chapman*. 'Dryden has misnamed the verse of Chapman's *Iliads*; not Alexandrine but Septenarian' (Ker).

60–61. *my Stanza . . . defended in the Preface to Gondibert*: 'I believ'd it would be more pleasant to the Reader, in a Work of length, to give this respite or pause, between every *Stanza* (having endeavour'd that each should contain a period) than to run him out of breath with continu'd *Couplets*. Nor doth alternate Rhyme by any lowliness of cadence, make the sound less Heroick, but rather adapt it to a plain and stately composing of Musick' (*Gondibert: An Heroick Poem*, 1651, p. 18).

69. *those who . . . keep in general terms, would hide a fallacy.* Cf. the proverbs 'Dolor versatur in generalibus' and 'Fraus latet in generalibus'; *The Hind and the Panther*, ii. 79.

71–72. *Descriptas servare*, &c. Horace, *De Arte Poetica*, ll. 86–87.

73–77. *if I had little knowledge of the Sea*, &c. For criticism of Dryden's use of technical terms, see *The Spectator*, No. 297, and Johnson, i. 433. But it is one aspect of his persistent experimentation with language, doubtless encouraged by the philological interest of the Royal Society, and a corollary to his conception of the learned and richly endowed poet. Cf. Dedication of *The Satires of Juvenalis*, ll. 566–79; *The Second Book of the Georgics*, note; Dedication of the *Æneis*, ll. 2220–28.

86. *Omnia sponte suâ*, &c. 'The line seems like one from a schoolboy's exercise, compounded of Virgil's *Georgics*, ii. 460 and *Eclogues*, iv. 39 and Ovid's *Metamorphoses*, i. 416–17 and *Fasti*, iv. 370' (Noyes).

99, 104. *wit writing . . . Wit written.* 'The *school-distinction* which Dryden has in his mind is that of *Natura naturans* and *Natura naturata*. So in the case of Wit he distinguishes between Wit the faculty and Wit the product' (Ker).

100–4. *the faculty of imagination*, &c. Cf. Davenant, Preface to *Gondibert*, 1651, pp. 19–20: '*Wit* is the laborious, and the lucky resultances of Thought. . . . *Wit* is not onely the luck and labour, but also the dexteritie of thought, rounding the world, like the Sun, with unimaginable motion; and bringing swiftly home to the memorie, universal surveys.' With the metaphor of the spaniel cf. Hobbes, *Leviathan*, i. 3: 'Sometimes a man knows a place determinate, within the compasse whereof he is to seek; and then his thoughts run . . . as a Spaniel ranges the field, till he find a sent.' Dryden had already written of imagination as 'an High-ranging Spaniel' in the Dedication of *The Rival Ladies*, 1664.

107–8. *'Tis not the jerk or sting of an Epigram.* Cf. 'Of Heroique Playes. *An Essay*' prefixed to *The Conquest of Granada*, 1672: '*Lucan* . . . follow'd too much the Truth of History . . . and too often offer'd at somewhat which had more of the Sting of an Epigram, than of the Dignity and State of an Heroick Poem'; Dedication of *The Satires of Juvenalis*, ll. 2192–6, note.

113–19. *the first happiness of the Poet's imagination*, &c. Here Dryden develops his earlier account of Fancy, working with 'a confus'd Mass of Thoughts, tumbling over one another in the Dark' and 'moving the Sleeping Images of things towards the Light, there to be distinguish'd, and then either chosen or rejected by the Judgment' (Dedication of *The Rival Ladies*, 1664). See Preface to *Sylvae*, ll. 113–15, note. Dryden's analysis is discussed by T. S. Eliot in 'The Age of Dryden', *The Use of Poetry and the Use of Criticism*, 1933.

115. *deriving*: canalising.

120–1. *Ovid images . . . the movements and affections of the mind.* Cf. Preface to *Ovid's Epistles*, ll. 14–16; Dedication of the *Æneis*, ll. 1065–75; and Preface to *Fables*, ll. 269 ff.

144. *Totamque infusa*, &c. *Aen.* vi. 726–7.

147. *lumenque juventæ*, &c. *Aen.* i. 590–3.

152. *the Divinest part of all his writings.* Cf. Preface to *Sylvæ*, l. 190; *The First Book of the Georgics*, note; Montaigne, 'ses Georgiques, que j'estime le plus accomply ouvrage de la poësie' (*Essais*, ii. 10).

157. *Materiam superabat opus. Meta.* ii. 5.

163–4. *Dixeris egregie*, &c. *De Arte Poetica*, ll. 47–48.

175. *some words which I have innovated.* Cf. Dedication of the *Æneis*, ll. 2166–86, and *Æneis*, ix. 1095, note.

179–80. *Et nova*, &c. *De Arte Poetica*, ll. 52–53.

193–4. *deformed, as in that of a Lazar.* Cf. Preface to *Tyrannick Love*, 1670: 'If, with much pains and some success, I have drawn a deform'd Piece, there is as much of Art, and as near an imitation of Nature, in a *Lazare*, as in a *Venus.*'

198–9. *Stantes in curribus Æmiliani. Sat.* viii. 3.

200. *Spirantia mollius æra. Aen.* vi. 847.

204. *humi serpere.* Horace, *De Arte Poetica*, l. 28.

206. *Nunc non erat his locus. De Arte Poetica*, l. 19. Cf. Dryden's strictures on Donne, Dedication of *The Satires of Juvenalis*, ll. 112–17, and note.

214–15. *I wrong the Publick to detain you longer.* Cf. Horace, *Epist.* ii. i. 3–4.

218. *Nec sunt*, &c. *Epist.* vii. 28.

Verses to her Highness the Dutchess. It is clear from Dryden's references to these lines 'that they had been in circulation in manuscript, and the criticism to which they had been subjected was probably the verbal criticism of coffee-houses, &c.' (Macdonald). Since there were rumours of a rebellion in the north, the duke was sent into Yorkshire in August 1665, after his return from sea. He and the duchess made a triumphal progress through the Midlands and were loyally received at York, where they spent seven weeks. See *Hatton Correspondence*, 1878, i. 47.

52–57. *So when the new-born Phœnix*, &c. Cf. *Threnodia Augustalis*, ll. 364–71.

Annus Mirabilis. 1–4. *In thriving Arts*, &c. 'This afternoon Sir Thomas Chamberlin came to the office to me, and showed me several letters from the East Indys, showing the height that the Dutch are come to there, showing scorn to all the English . . . saying, that whatever their masters do or say at home, they will do what they list, and will be masters of all the world there; and have so proclaimed themselves Soveraigne of all the South Seas' (Pepys, *Diary*, 15 February 1664).

10. *In Eastern Quarries*, &c. Cf. The Second Part of *The Conquest of Granada*, III. i: 'Bright as young Diamonds in their Infant Dew.'

17–18. *Thus mighty in her Ships,* &c. Virgil, *Aen.* i. 13–14, 'Karthago . . . dives opum studiisque asperrima belli'. Cf. Epilogue to *Amboyna,* l. 19, note.

20. *our second Punick War.* The first Dutch war was fought under Cromwell in 1653–4.

29–36. Louis XIV's marriage with Maria Theresa in 1660 seemed to promise peace and dynastic union between France and Spain (cf. *Astræa Redux,* ll. 13–18). When hostilities broke out between England and Holland in 1663–4, some of Charles II's ministers hoped for an alliance with Spain; but France used her influence to keep Spain neutral, since it was in Louis's interest that England and Holland should weaken one another. When Philip IV of Spain died towards the end of 1665, leaving his throne to his infant son, Louis invaded the Spanish Netherlands, claiming them for Maria Theresa.

45–46. On 2 June 1664 Charles wrote to his sister Henriette-Anne: 'I never saw so great an appetite to war as is, in both this town and country, especially in the Parliament men, who, I am confident, would pawn their estates to maintain a war. But all this shall not govern me, for I will look merely [to] what is just and best for the honour and good of England, and will be very steady in what I resolve' (*Letters, Speeches and Declarations,* ed. Bryant, p. 159).

54. *He in himself did whole Armado's bring.* See *To His Sacred Maiesty,* ll. 107–8, note.

61–64. Rear-Admiral Tyddeman was out in late November 1664 capturing Dutch prizes; the main fleet, under the Duke of York, sailed from Spithead on 27 December. Two comets were seen, in November and December 1664 (Pepys, *Diary,* 15 December et seq.). Comets were usually taken to be bad omens (cf. ll. 1161–4). With ll. 61–62 cf. *Astræa Redux,* ll. 153–4; *Fables,* 'Palamon and Arcite', iii. 441–2; Sylvester, *Du Bartas His Divine Weekes and Workes,* I. i, God 'Spred Heav'ns blew Curtains & those Lamps . . . burnisht'.

65. *Exhalations,* produced from vapours drawn up by the sun: the traditional view. Cf. *Absalom and Achitophel,* ll. 636–7; Epilogue to *The Unhappy Favourite,* ll. 12–13; Shakespeare, *Romeo and Juliet,* III. v. 13, 'Yond light . . . is some Meteor that the Sun exhales'.

69–72. *Or one,* &c. See *Astræa Redux,* ll. 288–93, notes.

73–92. On 30 May 1665 James sailed in command of a fleet of 109 warships, and joined battle with a Dutch fleet of slightly superior strength off Lowestoft on 3 June. The English forced the Dutch to retire, but failed to follow up their victory. On Dryden's treatment of the engagement, see James Kinsley, 'The "Three Glorious Victories" in *Annus Mirabilis*', *RES,* N.S., vii (1956), 30–37.

81–84. *Lawson amongst the formost,* &c. Cf. Ovid, *Meta.* xii. 67–69:

> . . . et Hectorea primus fataliter hasta,
> Protesilae, cadis: commissaque proelia magno
> stant Danais: fortisque animae nece cognitus Hector.

91–92. *So reverently,* &c. Cf. *Secret Love* (1668), III. i:

> . . . as, when it thunders,
> Men reverently quit the open Air,
> Because the angry Gods are then abroad.

93–124. De Ruyter's fleet, returning from Guinea, managed to avoid interception. Diplomatic arrangements were made with the King of Denmark for an English force to attack the Dutch East India fleet as it lay in Bergen harbour, but the plan misfired. Dryden deals discreetly with a shameful episode; see Kinsley, art. cit. Cf. Johnson, i. 432.

113–16. *Amidst whole heaps of Spices*, &c. Cf. Waller, *Of a War with Spain, and a Fight at Sea*, ll. 83–84:

> Spices and Gums about them melting fry,
> And *Phœnix*-like, in that rich Nest they die.

125–40. These lines, as Dryden hints, are based on Petronius, *Sat.* 115: 'Who knows, I cry'd out, but this Wretch's Wife, in some part of the World, secure at home, may expect his coming; or perhaps a Son, ignorant of the fatal Storm, may wait the wisht arrival of his Father. . . . These are our great designs! . . . After this, let Mortals flatter themselves with Golden Dreams. . . . If we rightly consider it, in this Sea of Life we may be Shipwrackt every where' (translated Burnaby, 1694). Cf. Waller, *Of . . . a Fight at Sea*, ll. 51–60.

145–8. In return for subsidies, Bernhard von Galen, Bishop of Münster, agreed to invade Holland and gave his promise 'fide sincera et Germanica' to Temple, the English ambassador. He overran the province of Overyssel; but after France entered the war he came to terms with the Dutch, 'we having not supplied him with the money promised him; . . . our King and Court are displeased much at it' (Pepys, *Diary*, 7 and 22 April 1666). Tacitus, *Ann.* xiii. 54.

169–72. In fulfilment of his treaty with Holland, Louis XIV declared war in January 1666. 'Yesterday come out the King's Declaration of War against the French, but with such mild invitations of both them and the Dutch to come over hither with promise of their protection, that every body wonders at it' (Pepys, *Diary*, 11 February 1666). Lines 171–2 refer to 1 Kings iii. 16–28.

181. *The doubled charge.* On 15 October 1665 Parliament voted Charles an additional one and a quarter million pounds 'upon his Majestys representation of necessity of further supplyes in reference to the Dutch warre and probability of the French imbracing their interest' (Marvell, *Letters*, ed. Margoliouth, p. 39; Pepys, *Diary*, 15 October 1665). Two and a half million pounds had been voted a year before, 'the House being hot' to support the king (Pepys, *Diary*, 25 November 1664).

183–4. *So glad Egyptians*, &c. Cf. Virgil, *Georgics*, iv. 287–94; *The Medall*, ll. 168–74; *The Hind and the Panther*, i. 311–13, note.

185–8. Prince Rupert and the Duke of Albemarle (see *To my Honored Friend, Sʳ Robert Howard*, ll. 95–98, note) were placed in joint command of a fleet of eighty warships, which they joined on 29 May 1666. See Pepys, *Diary*, 23 April 1666. With ll. 187–8 cf. *To His Sacred Maiesty*, l. 104, note.

196–7. Dryden links some of his stanzas by repeating a rhyme: cf. ll. 296–7, 524–5, 576–7, 1024–5, and 1116–17.

197–200. Albemarle had played a leading part in the victory over the Dutch in 1653. In ll. 199–200 Dryden recalls Herodotus' story (iv. 3–4) of how the Scythians suppressed a slave rising by brandishing horse-whips instead of spears. The slaves, struck with astonishment, forgot to fight and fled.

204. *Examina infantium*, &c. *Panegyricus*, xxvi.

213–16. On 29 May it was rumoured that the French fleet was at the mouth of the Channel, and Rupert was detached with twenty ships to meet them. When news reached Charles that the Dutch were at sea, he ordered Rupert to rejoin Albemarle; but Albemarle had been engaging the Dutch for three days before Rupert reached him (see ll. 417 ff.). De Ruyter, with some ninety ships, anchored midway between Dunkirk and the North Foreland on 1 June, and Albemarle sailed to the attack with what remained of his fleet, against the judgement of many of his officers (Pepys, *Diary*, 11 June and 4 July 1666).

225. Naval tactics of the time are described in Ogg, i. 267–8.

235–6. *Such port the Elephant bears*, &c. See Pliny, *Nat. Hist.* viii. 29. The story is repeated in Sylvester's *Du Bartas*, I. vi.

239–40. *Deep in their hulls*, &c. Cf. Waller, *Of a War with Spain, and a Fight at Sea*, ll. 47–48:

> Through yielding Planks the angry Bullets flie,
> And of one wound hundreds together die.

241–68. Albemarle so engaged the Dutch fleet that only part of it came into action; and then, despite punishment, he foolhardily engaged the fresh remainder. The duke lost his breeches 'to his Skin' (*London Gazette*, 4–7 June). Berkeley's ship and others were cut off; and Berkeley, after heroic resistance, was shot in the throat and retired to his cabin to die. He was 'the most absolute of all the King's favourites. . . . And it was thought, if he had outlived the lewdness of that time, and come to a more sedate course of life, he would have put the King on great and noble designs' (Burnet, i. 99–100). The earlier reading of l. 267, '*Berkley* alone, not making equal way', is not an inaccurate description of the circumstances; but the later version is less ambiguous. *Lost Creüsa*: Virgil, *Aen.* ii. 736–40.

291. *a Father of the War*. Cf. Davenant, *Gondibert*, I. v. 4, 'The Father of those Fights we *Lombards* fought'.

313–16. The story of the swordfish attacking the whale is traditional: e.g. Donne, *The Progresse of the Soule*, xxxvi. I know no instance of an attack from within the whale.

326. *Chace-guns*: armament set in the bows or stern of the ship.

330. *fiery Cacus*: Virgil, *Aen.* viii. 190 ff.

344. *flies at check, and clips it*: turns aside from her quarry for a baser prey, and flies rapidly down the wind.

353–80. Dryden makes the best of the conduct of this battle, covering bad leadership with a shroud of panegyric. Both Albemarle and the officers under his command were harshly criticized. See Pepys, *Diary*, 10 and 24 June 1666, 4 April 1667; and Kinsley, art. cit.

391. *Nec trucibus*, &c. *Silvae*, v. iv. 5–6.

417–20. Rupert joined the retreating Albemarle on the afternoon of 3 June, and revived English hopes of a victory. The earlier version of ll. 419–20 was probably dropped on account of its blasphemy. But cf. ll. 453–4.

449–60. Some of Albemarle's ships struck the Galloper shoal some hours after Rupert came in sight, through 'pure dismaying and fear . . . and . . . it was a miracle they were not all lost' (Pepys, *Diary*, 4 July 1666). De Ruyter sent a squadron out to lure Rupert into the same trap, but he was not deceived.

476. *brings night back*, &c. Cf. Waller, *Of a War with Spain, and a Fight at Sea*, l. 44: 'And with their smoaky Cannons banish day.'

481–548. On Dryden's discreet handling of the battle of 4 June, which Pepys reckoned 'a great overthrow', see Kinsley, art. cit.

521–8. *So have I seen*, &c. Cf. Ovid, *Meta*. i. 533–8.

536. *Quos opimus fallere*, &c. *Od.*, IV. iv. 51–52.

545–6. *Though, as when Fiends*, &c. Mark iii. 11.

549. *Return'd, he with the Fleet resolv'd to stay*. In the satirical 'Directions to a Painter. By Sir *John Denham*' (*POAS*, 1702, pp. 42–43), the Duchess of Albemarle cries:

> Fall to thy Work there *George*, as I do here;
> Cherish the Valiant up, Cowards casheir:
> See that the Men have Pay, and Beef, and Beer.
>
> .   .   .   .
>
> What's that I see! ah, 'tis my *George* agen!
> It seems they in sev'n Weeks have rigged him then,
> The curious Heav'ns with Lightning him surrounds,
> To view him, and his Name in *Thunder* sounds.

565–600. There were discussions on 'the haste requisite to be made in getting the fleete out again' a few days after the four-day battle; and a new fleet was 'in all points ready to sayle, but for the carrying of the two or three new ships', a month later (Pepys, *Diary*, 9 June and 13 July 1666).

582. *Okum*: loose fibre drawn from old rope and used for caulking seams.

587. *paid o'r*: the nautical term for coating with pitch.

590. *sear-cloth*: wrap up. Cere-cloth was a waxed material used for waterproofing or as a winding-sheet. 'The body of the Marquess of *Dorset* seemed sound and handsomely cereclothed, that after seventy eight years was found uncorrupted' (Browne, *Hydriotaphia*, iii).

595. *big-corned*: of a large granulation. See Henshaw's history of making gunpowder printed in Sprat's *History of the Royal Society*, 1667, pp. 282–3.

601–2. *The goodly London*, &c. The *London*, a warship of 64 guns, blew up suddenly in the Nore on 7 March 1665; and three days later it was rumoured that 'the aldermen and several companies will build the king a ship to be

called the London' (Pepys, *Diary*, 8 March 1665; *CSP Dom.* 1664/5, p. 247).
Commissioner Taylor built the new ship on a different plan 'in hopes of
mending the Old London, built by him. "For," says he, "he finds that God
hath put him into the right. . . ." "And," says the King, "I am sure it must
be God put him in, for no art of his owne ever could have done it" ' (Pepys,
Diary, 21 April 1666). The new ship was fired by the Dutch in the Medway
in June 1667.

604. *on her shadow rides in floating gold.* Cf. Fairfax's translation of Tasso,
Godfrey of Bulloigne, xvi. 4:

> The Waters burnt about their Vessels good,
> Such Flames the Gold therein enchased threw.

639. *the Year*: the sun's annual course. Cf. *Threnodia Augustalis*, l. 353;
Britannia Rediviva, l. 306.

645–8. *The Ebbs of Tydes*, &c. 'Surely the Philosophy of flux and reflux was
very imperfect of old among the Greeks and Latins. . . . Nor can we affirm our
knowledg is at the height, who have now the Theory of the Ocean and narrow
Seas beside. While we refer it unto the Moon, we give some satisfaction for
the Ocean, but no general salve for Creeks, and Seas which know no floud;
nor resolve why it flows three or four feet at *Venice* . . . yet scarce at all at
Ancona' (Browne, *Pseudodoxia Epidemica*, vii. 13). Tidal problems exercised the
Royal Society from its early days. John Wallis's paper on a universal theory
of tides was printed in the Society's *Transactions* on 6 August 1666; cf. A.
Robertson, *Life of Sir Robert Moray*, 1922, p. 164.

653–4. *our Globe last verge*: the horizon, where (according to the old
astronomy) the terrestrial and celestial spheres meet. Cf. *To My Lord
Chancellor*, ll. 31–36.

657–64. Dryden was admitted a Fellow of the Royal Society on 26 November 1662 (cf. *To My Honour'd Friend, Dr Charleton*). The 'Apostrophe' here is
apologetical. The Society was already subject to two kinds of criticism. It
was accused by some of encouraging free-thinking—a charge answered in
Sprat's *History of the Royal Society*, 1667—and by others of unpractical and
pedantic virtuosity. Cf. Cowley's address *To the Royal Society*, ll. 148–55:

> Mischief and true Dishonour fall on those
> Who would to laughter or to scorn expose
> So Virtuous and so Noble a Design,
> So Human for its Use, for Knowledge so Divine.
> The things which these proud men despise, and call
> > Impertinent, and vain, and small,
> Those smallest things of Nature let me know,
> Rather than all their greatest Actions Doe.

669–80. News reached London on 29 June that 'the Dutch fleete, 130 sail,
are come upon the French coast', and on 3 July they were seen off Harwich.
The English fleet sailed sixteen days later (Pepys, *Diary*, 29 June, 3 and
19 July 1666).

681–700. In the new fleet, Sir Thomas Allin commanded the White Squadron; Sir Robert Holmes was rear-admiral in the Red Squadron, under Rupert and Albemarle; and Sir Edward Spragge was vice-admiral in the Blue Squadron, under Sir Jeremy Smith. 'The *Plimouth* Squadron' was Smith's fleet which went out to the Straits in December 1665 and caused Pepys much anxiety (*Diary*, 10 January and 11 February 1666). When France declared war in January 1666 her fleet was divided, part on the west coast and part at Toulon; and Smith's presence in the Straits prevented these forces from joining. Allin was sent out to the Mediterranean in August 1664 to provide convoy for English ships; and on 29 December his squadron of nine ships attacked a fleet of some thirty Dutch merchantmen homeward bound from Smyrna, and so precipitated the formal opening of war (A. W. Tedder, *The Navy of the Restoration*, 1916, pp. 91–97). Holmes led a small expedition to the Guinea Coast early in 1661 to carry out the Duke of York's design 'to dig for gold ore'; and led a larger expedition out in 1664, returning with great wealth (Pepys, *Diary*, 3 October 1660 and 10 December 1664). Spragge was knighted for gallant conduct in the battle of 3 June 1665 (see *To Mr Lee, on his Alexander*, ll. 31–32, note). Harman, rear-admiral of the Blue Squadron in the flagship *Henry*, was attacked by three fireships in succession in the battle of 1 June. The first was repelled; the second set the *Henry*'s sails on fire; the third was sunk; and Harman then killed the Dutch admiral with a broadside (see Tedder, op. cit., pp. 158–9). Sir Fretcheville Hollis, son of a royalist officer, lost an arm in the battle of 3 June 1665, and served as rear-admiral with Holmes in the attack on the Smyrna fleet (1672). Sir William Penn 'called him a conceited, idle, prating, lying fellow'; Sir William Batten's opinion is unprintable; and Pepys thought little of him (*Diary*, 14, 17, and 25 June 1667): but he was a courageous and enterprising sailor.

691–2. When the Roman senators admired some figs which Cato the Censor dropped in the Senate, 'he told them, *that the Country where that fine fruit grew was but three Days Sail from* Rome' (*Plutarch's Lives*, 1727, iii. 368). Cf. Epilogue to *Amboyna*, l. 19, note.

713–80. Battle was joined on 25 July. The Dutch van and centre retired to the coast, and on the next evening anchored off Flushing, covered from attack by shoals. They were joined on 27 July by the rear squadron, which Sir Jeremy Smith had been engaging. Dryden places the retreat before the main battle in order to emphasize Dutch cowardice and cunning, and to present the main action in a favourable light. In fact, the engagement ended in anticlimax (see Kinsley, art. cit.).

740. *draw their Curtains in the dead of night*. Cf. Shakespeare, *2 Henry IV*, I. i. 70–73:

> Even such a man, so faint, so spiritlesse,
> So dull, so dead in looke, so woe-be-gone,
> Drew *Priams* Curtaine, in the dead of night,
> And would have told him, Halfe his Troy was burn'd.

765–8. *Their batter'd Admiral*, &c. De Ruyter was in fact irate at the retreat of his captains and the cowardice of the men on his own ship (Tedder, op. cit., p. 175).

775–6. *As Varro*, &c. When Varro reached Rome after his flight from Cannae 'full of Infamy and Shame', the Senate 'commended him before the People, for that he did not despair of the safety of the Commonwealth after so great a Loss, but was come to take the Government into his hands' (*Plutarch's Lives*, 1727, ii. 242–3).

780. *dar'd*: fascinated. *Hobby: Falco subbuteo*, a small falcon used in hunting larks. Cf. Lovelace, *Poems*, ed. C. H. Wilkinson, notes to pp. 145, 175.

803–4. *Find him disowning*, &c. Henry IV of France and William the Silent, 'instructed in sound policy by their translation to the blessed, would, the one disown the war against Henry III into which he was compelled to enter to vindicate his right of succession . . . and the other detest the Dutch naval power, although the only means which could secure his country's independence' (Scott).

805–32. After the battle of 25 July the English fleet sailed up the coast of Holland, taking ships. On 8 August Holmes was detached with a small squadron to attack a Dutch fleet off Vlie Island. He destroyed about 150 ships and sacked Terschelling, 'burning the houses . . . as bonfires for his good success at sea' (Tedder, op. cit., pp. 176–7; *London Gazette*, 13–16 August 1666).

825–8. *Some English Wool*, &c. English wool, being finer than that of Holland, France, and Germany, was greatly in demand and smuggled abroad in defiance of a prohibition of export; and the French re-exported goods made from this wool to England. See Ogg, i. 71–72.

829. *rummage*: a nautical term; to scrutinize and sort the contents of a ship's hold.

845–8. *Yet, London*, &c. Cf. Prologue to *Wit without Money*, ll. 20–24. *Quum mare*, &c.: adapted from *Meta*. i. 257–8.

857–60. *Such was the rise of this prodigious fire*, &c. On the morning of 2 September 1666 fire broke out in the shop of the king's baker in Pudding Lane, off Thames Street and a little north-east of London Bridge. By night it had burned along the river almost to Queen Hythe, and into the city as far as Cannon Street. On the second day it moved some five hundred yards farther west along the Thames, east as far as Tower Street, and northwards beyond Cornhill and the Exchange. On the third day it reached its height, sweeping north and west to the city walls and liberties, destroying Cheapside, the Guildhall, and St. Paul's; and subsided on the fourth day. See W. G. Bell, *The Great Fire of London*, 1923.

863. *All was the nights*, &c. Varro's 'omnia noctis erant, placida composta quiete', quoted by Seneca, *Controversiae*, VII. i. 27.

869–72. *Then, in some close-pent room*, &c. Cf. *Fables*, 'Of the Pythagorean Philosophy', ll. 330–3.

881. *Hæc arte tractabat,* &c. Terence, *Heautontimorumenos,* ll. 366–7.

889–92. *The Ghosts of Traitors,* &c. London Bridge lay in the path of the flames on the first night; and the gate tower and houses at the northern end of the bridge were destroyed. The heads of traitors were impaled above the Southwark gate tower. The 'Fanatick Spectres' are the fifth-monarchy men executed in 1661, and other insurgents executed in 1662.

893–6. *Our Guardian Angel,* &c. See Dedication of *The Satires of Juvenalis,* ll. 516–79, note.

914–16. *Some run for Buckets,* &c. Leather buckets and ladders were kept in the city churches. The usual method of getting water for fire-fighting was to cut the wooden pipes, though some water-cocks had been set up. The 'Engines' were brass hand syringes. See Bell, op. cit., pp. 34–36, and illustrations.

917. *from the East, a Belgian wind.* A strong north-east wind blew across London throughout the days of the fire, driving the flames and scattering live flakes among the timber roofs.

926. *the fate of Simoeis.* The river Xanthus, calling on his tributary Simois for assistance, attempted to drown Achilles and was attacked by Hephaestus in flame (*Iliad,* xxi. 305 ff.).

944. *The Lombard Banquers and the Change.* The fire burnt throughout the second day among the houses of bankers and merchants in and around Lombard Street; and in the afternoon crossed Cornhill and destroyed Gresham's Royal Exchange all but its tower.

947–8. *But the main body,* &c. On the second day the western arm of the fire moved along the river towards the Fleet Ditch, and during the night houses were being pulled down in Whitefriars to arrest its progress.

949. *and with the day the King.* Cf. *Fables,* 'Palamon and Arcite', iii. 190.

953. *thick harbingers of smoke.* The curtain of smoke which spread over London is described with awe by observers (Bell, op. cit., p. 67). Evelyn records, with a probable exaggeration excusable in the author of *Fumifugium,* that on 3 September the clouds of smoke 'were dismall, & reached upon computation neere 50 miles in length: Thus I left it this afternoone burning, a resemblance of Sodome, or the last day'.

957–72. *More then his Guards,* &c. 'It is not indeede imaginable how extraordinary the vigilance & activity of the King & Duke was, even labouring in person, & being present, to command, order, reward, and encourage Workemen; by which he shewed his affection to his people, & gained theirs' (Evelyn, *Diary,* 6 September 1666; see Bell, op. cit., pp. 113–15, 313–14).

977–88. *The powder blows up all,* &c. Early suggestions by 'some stout Seamen' to arrest the fire by blowing up houses in its path were resisted by 'tenacious & avaritious Men, Aldermen &c.'; but the king put this plan into action (Evelyn, *Diary,* 5 September; Bell, op. cit., p. 114). It was effective in places; but in crowded areas the flames crossed the gap over pieces of debris, and the wind remained their strongest ally.

995–1008. Many were 'either forced to give one part to carry away the rest or to leave all to the fire. . . . The flight from it gave opportunity for miscarriage of thousands of pounds worth of goods, and to many thefts.' Exorbitant charges were made for carting and carrying (Waterhous, *A Short Narrative of the Fire*, 1667; Bell, op. cit., p. 78).

1011–12. *His Beams*, &c. Cf. *To My Lord Chancellor*, ll. 45–48.

1022. *require*: seek again.

1029–40. Citizens fleeing from the fire gathered in camps outside the walls, chiefly in the open spaces of Moorfields '& severall miles in Circle, Some under tents, others under miserable Hutts and Hovells, without a rag, or any necessary utinsils, bed or board, who from delicatnesse, riches & easy accomodations in stately & well furnishd houses, were now reduc'd to extreamest misery & poverty' (Evelyn, *Diary*, 5 September). Charles rode out to Moorfields, told the people that their calamity was 'immediate from the hand of God', and pledged himself to take care of them (Bell, op. cit., p. 318).

1045–60. *O God, said he*, &c. Cf. David's prayer in the pestilence, 1 Chron. xxi. 12–17.

1064. *And shrink*, &c. Cf. Cowley, 'The 34. Chapter of the Prophet *Isaiah*', iii: 'The wide-stretcht *Scrowl* of Heaven . . . Shall crackle, and the parts together shrink|Like *Parchment* in a fire.'

1066. *spotted deaths*: the plague of 1665.

1069. *frequent funerals*: numerous corpses; imitating Virgil, *Aen.* ii. 364–5, 'plurima perque vias sternuntur inertia . . . corpora'. Cf. *The First Satyr of Juvenal*, l. 109.

1097–1104. Laud's plan for the restoration of St. Paul's was frustrated by the civil war, and the funds he had raised were seized. The larger part of the cathedral was put to profane uses during the interregnum (cf. King's elegy on Charles I, Saintsbury, iii. 259–60; Harold Jenkins, *Edward Benlowes*, 1952, pp. 258–9). The fire destroyed the building a week after Evelyn served on a committee to make plans for restoration (*Diary*, 27 August 1666). The prophecy of Nostradamus concerning the fire (see introductory note) contains these lines:

> La grand peste de cité maritime
> Ne cessera que mort ne soit vengée
> Du juste sang par pris damné sans crime,
> De la grand dame par faincte n'outragée.

The 'Poet's Song' is Waller's poem *Upon His Majesty's Repairing of Paul's* (*c.* 1635).

1120. *give on*: assault.

1133–40. *As when sharp frosts*, &c. Cf. *Astræa Redux*, ll. 131–6.

1141–4. Two proclamations issued on 5 September provided for emergency supplies of bread, the king 'in his princely compassion and very tender care, taking into consideration the distressed condition of many of his good subjects'. Cf. Bell, op. cit., pp. 172–3.

1157–60. *Not with more constancy,* &c. Ezra i–iii.

1165–6. A 'trine' is the 'aspect' or relative position of two planets which are 120° (a third part of the zodiac) apart. The trine is a benign 'aspect', because the rays of the two planets fall obliquely and yield to one another. In malignant 'aspects' the rays of the two planets collide. Cf. *To the Pious Memory Of Mrs Anne Killigrew,* ll. 41–43; *Britannia Rediviva,* l. 327; *Fables,* 'Palamon and Arcite', iii. 389. Dryden adds the favourable circumstance of Jove in ascension.

1169. *Chymick*: alchemic, transmuting.

1173–6. Wren, the king's deputy surveyor, laid a plan for the rebuilding of London before the king and council on 10 September; Evelyn submitted 'a Plot for a new Citty' on 13 September; and there were other planners. Legislative measures were promptly taken, both to deal with the social problems created by the fire, and to start rebuilding (Bell, op. cit., pp. 230–74).

1177. *August.* ' "Augusta" is known as the name of London only in the fourth century. The authorities for it are Ammianus Marcellinus, xxvii. 8. 6 . . . and xxviii. 3. 1 . . ., and two coins struck at the London mint in the reign of Valentinian' (Nichol Smith).

Prologue and Song from Secret-Love, or The Maiden-Queen
(Page 106)

Secret-Love, or The Maiden-Queen was probably written at Charlton in 1665 or 1666 (see *Annus Mirabilis,* 'An account of the ensuing Poem', ll. 1–8 and notes. It was first performed at the Theatre Royal early in 1667: Pepys writes of it on 2 March 1667 as 'a new play of Dryden's, mightily commended for the regularity of it, and the strain and wit; and . . . there is a comical part done by Nell [Gwyn], which is Florimell, that I never can hope ever to see the like done again'. A copy of the first edition, published by Herringman, was bought 'newly printed' by Pepys on 18 January 1668. The epilogue was anonymously 'Written by a Person of Honour'. See Poems from *Covent Garden Drolery,* Prologue and Epilogue to *Secret-Love,* note.

Prologue. 3. *Th' exactest Rules.* In the Preface Dryden writes: 'For what else concerns this Play, I would tell the Reader that it is regular, according to the strictest of Dramatick Laws, but that it is a commendation which many of our Poets now despise, and a Beauty which our common Audiences do not easily discern. Neither do I value my self upon it, because with all that symmetry of parts, it may want an air and spirit . . . to set it off.' Cf. Epilogue to *Aureng-Zebe,* ll. 1–10.

7. *dead colours*: the preparatory layers of colour in a painting. Cf. Preface to *Fables*, l. 112.

10–15. *Plays are like Towns*, &c. 'Voyla Lecteur, ce que i'auois à vous dire: mais quelque deffence que i'aye employée ie sçay qu'il est des ouurages de cette nature, comme d'une Place de guerre: où quelque soin qu'ait apporté l'Ingenieur a la fortifier, il se trouue tousiours quelque Endroit foible, ou il n'a point songé, & par ou l'on attaque. Mais cela ne me surprenda point . . .' (Scudéry, Preface to *Ibrahim, ou l'Illustre Bassa*, 1641, translated by Henry Cogan, 1652).

54–58. *Throw boldly*, &c. A sustained metaphor from gaming. *Sets*, challenges by putting down a stake; *lay*, wager; *nick*, beat with a winning cast; *on Tick*, on credit.

Song. Act IV, Sc. ii. The song the Queen 'made of *Philocles*, and call'd it *Secret-Love*'. For transcripts and reprints see Day, p. 143.

8. *silently like dew on Roses*. Cf. Herrick, *Hesperides*, 'To Musique, to becalme his Fever'.

Prologue, Epilogue and Songs from Sʳ Martin Mar-all, or The Feign'd Innocence: A Comedy

(Page 109)

Sir Martin Mar-all was first performed by the Duke's company at Lincoln's Inn Fields in August 1667. Dryden was under contract to the King's players, but this was 'a play made by my Lord Duke of Newcastle, but, as everybody says, corrected by Dryden' (Pepys, *Diary*, 16 August 1667; see also 1 January 1668). 'Sir *Martin Marral*, The Duke of *New-Castle*, giving Mr. *Dryden* a bare Translation of it, out of a Comedy of the Famous *French* Poet *Monseur Moleire* [*L'Étourdi, ou, Les Contretemps*]: He Adapted the Part purposely for the Mouth of Mr. *Nokes*, and curiously Polishing the whole' (Downes, p. 28). The play was entered in *SR* on 24 June 1668 as Newcastle's, and published by Herringman that year. Dryden's name did not appear on the title-page until the fourth edition, 1691. On the make-up of the first edition, where Prologue and Epilogue are printed at the beginning of the play, see Macdonald, pp. 98–99, and Osborn, *MP* xxxix (1941), 82–83.

Prologue. 2. *Regalios*: choice entertainments or repasts.

10. *Woodcocks*: proverbially foolish birds (Tilley, W746). The word was applied to simpletons.

Epilogue. 13. *Lilly*: William Lilly (1602–81), astrologer and author of almanacs and books of prophecy. Cf. Epilogue to *The Unhappy Favourite*, ll. 12–15.

Songs. I: Act IV. On music and reprints, see Day, p. 143. II: Act V, sung by

Warner for Sir Martin. This song is adapted from Voiture's *L'Amour sou
sa loy*; the French text (*Œuvres*, 1652, ii. 61–63) is given in Day, pp. 144–5.

Prologues and Epilogues to The Wild Gallant: A Comedy
(Page 111)

The Wild Gallant was first performed at the Theatre Royal in Vere Street
on 5 February 1663 (Prologue, l. 14; Evelyn, *Diary*, 5 February). The greater
part of the town condemned it, says Dryden in the Preface: 'Yet it was
receiv'd at Court; and was more than once the Divertisement of His Majesty,
by His own Command. . . . It was the first attempt I made in *Dramatick
Poetry*.' See *To the Lady Castlemain*, note. The play was revived in 1667 and
first published by Herringman in 1669 (*SR*, 7 August 1667; *TC*, 19 May 1669).
There are two editions of 1669, conveniently distinguished by the title-page
spellings '*THEATER*', '*Herringman*' (Macdonald, 72 a) and '*THEATRE*',
'*Heringman*' (Macdonald, 72 b). Macdonald's argument for the priority of 72 a
has been disputed; conclusive evidence for the priority of 72 b, on which the
present text is based, is offered by Fredson Bowers in *The Library*, 5th ser., v
(1951), 51–54. In the 1669 editions, the two Prologues introduce the play and
the two Epilogues conclude it. The original Prologue is omitted in the third
and fourth editions.

    Prologue . . . first Acted. 11. *Scheme*, or 'Figure' (l. 13), a horoscope showing
the disposition of the planets and signs of the zodiac in the twelve 'houses' of
the heavens.

    14. *half an hour after three after Noon*: the time at which the first and testing
performance would end. In the 1660's the playhouses usually opened in the
early afternoon: 'there I took them up, it being almost twelve o'clock, or a
little more, and carried them to the King's playhouse, where the doors were
not then open; but presently they did open; and we in, and find many people
already come in, by private ways, into the pit' (Pepys, *Diary*, 18 May 1668).

    19. *Mathematicians*: astrologers.

    22–30. *First Jupiter*, &c. The lord of the ascendant is the planet within the
'house' of the 'ascendant' or degree of the ecliptic which at a given moment
is rising above the eastern horizon. This degree is the point of departure for a
horoscope. Jupiter is a beneficent planet, to which are assigned Sagittarius as
a solar 'mansion' or 'apartment' (l. 26) and Pisces as a lunar mansion (Ptolemy,
Tetrabiblos, I. v, xvii). Jupiter is here in the cadent twelfth 'house' of the
heavens, called κακὸς δαίμων, 'near grim *Saturn*' the maleficent planet
(Ptolemy, III. x, I. v). The sign Capricorn, the solar mansion of Saturn, is the
'depression' (ταπείνωμα) of Jupiter (Ptolemy, I. xvii, xix). The proximity of
Saturn counteracts the favourable influence of Jupiter in his mansion Sagittarius (ll. 25–30).

31–34. *Ptolomy the Learned says*, &c. The fifth 'house' signifies various forms of prosperity and speculative enterprises such as games and plays. Venus, the lady of that 'house', promotes the arts (Ptolemy, IV. iv). *Peregrine*: situated in an indifferent sign, which neither prejudices nor exalts her influence.

35–36. Perhaps a reference to the revival of Davenant's opera *The Siege of Rhodes* by the rival company in 1661, 'having new Scenes and Decorations, being the first that e're were Introduc'd in *England*. . . . It continu'd Acting 12 Days without Interruption with great Applause' (Downes, pp. 20–21). Cf. Prologue to *The Rival-Ladies*, l. 11, note.

38–40. Jupiter, 'the lord of *Spain*' (Ptolemy, II. iii), is at present in the twelfth 'house', the house of enemies and afflictions. The '*Spanish* Plot' is Sir Samuel Tuke's *The Adventures of Five Hours*, an adaptation of Antonio Coello's *Los Empeños de Seis Horas*, first performed at Lincoln's Inn Fields on 8 January 1663 (Pepys). The play, 'being Cloath'd so Excellently Fine in proper Habits, and Acted so justly well . . . took Successively 13 Days altogether, no other Play Intervening' (Downes, pp. 22–23). Evelyn credits it with a run of 'some weekes every day, & twas believed would be worth the Comedians 4 or 5000 pounds' (*Diary*, 8 January 1663). It was therefore a threat to the success of *The Wild Gallant*. Cf. Epilogue to *The Tempest*, ll. 4–6, and Wildblood in *An Evening's Love*, V: 'I hate your *Spanish* Honour, ever since it spoil'd our *English* Plays, with Faces about and t'other side.'

52. *mistakes*: in the 'deep Intrigue' of Tuke's play.

Prologue . . . Reviv'd. 8. *Whetstones Park*: 'A Lane betwixt *Holborn* and *Lincoln's-Inn-Fields*, fam'd for a Nest of Wenches, now de-park'd' (*Dict. Canting Crew, c.* 1695). Cf. *Miscellany Poems* (1684), '*Ovid's . . . Elegy the Nineteenth*', ll. 31–32; Pepys, *Diary*, 16 November 1668.

10–12. *He grows to break Glass-Windows*, &c. Cf. Prologue to *All for Love*, l. 22, note; Prologue to *The Spanish Fryar*, l. 39; Rochester, *The Maim'd Debauchee*, ll. 33–36:

> I'le tell of Whores attacqu'd their Lords at home,
> Bawds Quarters beaten up, and Fortress won:
> Windows demolish'd, Watches overcome,
> And handsom Ills by my contrivance done.

Epilogue . . . Reviv'd. 11–12. *like Turkes*, &c. Cf. Montaigne, *Essais*, I. xlviii: 'Pour verifier combien les armees turquesques se conduisent et maintiennent à meilleure raison que les nostres, ils disent qu'oultre ce que les soldats ne boivent que de l'eau, et ne mangent que riz et de la chair salee mise en pouldre . . .'. *Regallio's*: choice fare.

38. *writ of ease*: certificate of discharge from employment. Cf. Epilogue to *All for Love*, l. 19; Tuke, Prologue to *The Adventures of Five Hours*, ll. 23–26:

> But if through his ill Conduct, or hard Fate,
> This Foreign plot (like that of Eighty Eight)
> Should suffer Shipwrack in your Narrow Seas,
> You'll give your modern Poet his Writ of Ease.

44. *Vests.* On 7 October 1666 Charles 'declared his resolution of setting a new fashion for clothes' (Pepys, *Diary*, 8 October). An account of the new costume—a knee-length vest and surcoat—is given by Evelyn, who recalls that 'I had some time before indeede presented an Invectique against . . . our so much affecting the french fashion, to his Majestie in which I tooke occasion to describe the Comelinesse & usefullnesse of the Persian clothing in the very same manner, his Majestie clad himselfe; This Pamphlet I intituled *Tyrannus* or the mode [1661]' (*Diary*, 18 October 1666). 'A general Humour, in opposition to *France*, had made us throw off their Fashion, and put on Vests, that we might look more like a distinct People, and not be under the servility of imitation . . . it was thought that one of the Instructions Madam brought along with her [1670] was to laugh us out of these Vests' (Halifax, *Works*, ed. Raleigh, p. 90). The French fashion was resumed after 1670. See E. S. de Beer, 'King Charles II's own Fashion', *Journal of the Warburg Institute*, ii (1939), 105–15.

Prologue and Epilogue to The Tempest, or The Enchanted Island. A Comedy

(Page 116)

The Tempest was first performed at Lincoln's Inn Fields on 7 November 1667 by the Duke's company before a 'house mighty full; the King and Court there' (Pepys), and first published by Herringman in 1670 (*SR*, 8 January 1670; Dryden's Preface is dated 1 December 1669). An operatic version was performed in April 1674 and published as the second edition in the same year. For discussions of the authorship of the opera see Macdonald, pp. 102–3, and Nicoll, p. 430.

Sir William Davenant, says Dryden in the Preface, 'did me the honour to join me with him in the alteration' of the play: 'It was originally *Shakespear*'s: a Poet for whom he had particularly a high veneration, and whom he first taught me to admire'. Davenant 'design'd the Counterpart to *Shakespear*'s Plot, namely, that of a Man who had never seen a Woman; that by this means those two Characters of Innocence and Love might the more illustrate and commend each other'. The new character was Hippolito, probably referred to in the Prologue, ll. 29–38.

Prologue. 6. To Fletcher Wit, to labouring Johnson Art. Cf. *Of Dramatick Poesie, An Essay*, 1668: 'As for Comedy, Repartee is one of its chiefest Graces; the greatest pleasure of the Audience is a chase of Wit kept up on both sides, and swiftly manag'd. And this our Fore-Fathers, if not we, have had in *Fletcher*'s Plays, to a much higher degree of perfection than the French Poets can arrive at'; 'I think [Jonson] the most Learned and judicious Writer which any Theater ever had. . . . Wit and Language, and Humour also in some measure, we had before him; but something of Art was wanting to the *Drama* till he came' (Ker, i. 72 and 81–82).

11. *This did his Love . . . digest.* Cf. Preface to *Troilus and Cressida*, 1679: '*Shakespear* writ better betwixt Man and Man; *Fletcher*, betwixt Man and Woman: . . . Yet *Shakespear* taught *Fletcher* to write Love; and *Juliet*, and *Desdemona*, are Originals. 'Tis true, the Scholar had the softer Soul; but the Master had the kinder' (Ker, i. 227–8).

Epilogue. 4–6. A reference to adaptations and imitations of French and Spanish drama (see Nicoll, pp. 186–93). Cf. Prologue to *The Wild Gallant* 'as it was first Acted', ll. 38–40, note.

9. *King Richard's.* Shakespeare, *Richard III*, v. iii.

Prologue, Epilogue and Songs from Tyrannick Love, or The Royal Martyr. A Tragedy

(Page 118)

Tyrannick Love was first performed at the Theatre Royal at the end of June 1669 (Hotson, pp. 250–3), and first published by Herringman in 1670.

Prologue. 14–15. In a final paragraph added to the Preface in the second edition of the play, Dryden says: 'For the little Criticks, who pleas'd themselves with thinking they have found a flaw in that line of the Prologue, (*And he who servilely creeps after Sense, is safe*, &c.) as if I Patronized my own Nonsense, I may reasonably suppose they have never read *Horace, Serpit humi tutus*, &c. are his words: He who creeps after plain, dull, common Sense, is safe from committing Absurdities, but can never reach any height, or excellence of Wit; and sure I could not mean that any excellence were to be found in Nonsense.'

24–25. *They then*, &c. Cf. Preface: 'the great Censors of Wit and Poetry, either produce nothing of their own, or what is more ridiculous than any thing they reprehend. Much of ill Nature, and a very little Judgment, go far in finding the mistakes of Writers.'

Epilogue. Spoken by Mrs. Ellen, Nell Gwyn (1650–87). She became Charles II's mistress in 1668, 'the indiscreetest and wildest creature that ever was in a Court', and 'continued to the end of the King's life in great favour. . . . She acted all persons in so lively a manner, and was such a constant diversion to the King, that even a new mistriss could not drive her away' (Burnet, i. 263). The Epilogue is in character: Pepys speaks of her poor acting in a serious part as Cydaria in *The Indian Emperour* (*Diary*, 22 August 1667; cf. 26 December), and praises her performance as Florimel (see Prologue to *Secret-Love*, note). There is an illustration of this Epilogue in Buckingham's *Works*, 1715. Cf. Epilogue to *Piso's Conspiracy, A Tragedy*, 1676 (Macdonald):

It is a trick of late grown much in vogue,
When all are kill'd, to raise an epilogue.

20. *Easter-Term, in Tart and Cheese-cake time.* Cf. Millisent in *Sir Martin Mar-all*, I: 'I came up, Madam, as we Country-Gentlewomen use, at an *Easter*-Term, to the destruction of Tarts and Cheese-cakes, to see a New Play, buy a new Gown, take a Turn in the Park, and so down again to sleep with my Fore-fathers.'

Songs. I: Act IV, Sc. i. Parodied in *The Rehearsal*, V. i, where the two kings of Brentford 'descend in the Clouds, singing, in white garments; and three Fidlers sitting before them, in green'. 'Now', says Bayes, 'because the two Right Kings descend from above, I make 'em sing to the Tune and Stile of our modern Spirits.' Day (pp. 19–20) reproduces the anonymous setting of this song dated 8 June 1681 (BM Add. MS. 19759, ff. 29ᵛ–30). On Purcell's music for this and Song III, composed for a revival *c.* 1695, and on reprints, see Day, pp. 147–8. 13. *Gelly*: 'applied to the alga *Nostoc*, which appears as a jelly-like mass on dry soil after rain, and was supposed to be the remains of a fallen star' (*OED*). Cf. Dryden and Lee, *Oedipus*, II:

The shooting Stars end all in purple Jellies;
And Chaos is at hand.

II, III: Act IV, Sc. i. The songs are separated in the play by the comment of Placidius:

Some pleasing Objects do her Mind employ;
For on her Face I read a wandring Joy.

Prologue, Epilogue and Songs from An Evening's Love, or The Mock-Astrologer
(Page 122)

An Evening's Love was first performed at the Theatre Royal on 12 June 1668 (*LC* 5/139, p. 130), and published by Herringman in 1671. Two editions appeared that year; on the priority of the text followed here (Macdonald 75 a) see Macdonald, pp. 106–7. I have not seen a copy of the third edition, 1675.

Prologue. 2–10. *Like a young Bridegroom*, &c. Cf. *Examen Poeticum*, Prologue, 'Gallants, a bashful Poet . . .', ll. 1–10. The Prologue sets the tone of the play, which Evelyn thought 'very prophane, so as it afflicted me to see how the stage was degenerated & poluted by the licentious times' (*Diary*, 19 June 1668).

33. *but thrice a year.* When Dryden left the king's company in 1677 the actors presented a petition which opens: 'Whereas, upon Mʳ Drydens binding himselfe to write 3 Playes a yeare, Hee the said Mʳ Dryden was admitted & continued as a Sharer in the Kings Playhouse for divers yeares; and received for his Share & a quarter, 3 or 4 hundred pounds, Comunibus annis, but

though he received the monyes, we received not the Playes, not one in a yeare' (Nicoll, p. 329).

Epilogue. 3. *Judgement,* critic. Cf. Prologue to *Secret-Love,* l. 45.
10–16. *he stole th' Astrologer,* &c. Cf. Preface to the play: 'I am tax'd with stealing all my Plays. . . . 'Tis true, that where ever I have lik'd any story in a Romance, Novel, or foreign Play, I have made no difficulty, nor ever shall, to take the foundation of it, to build it up, and to make it proper for the *English* Stage. And I will be so vain to say it has lost nothing in my hands: . . . I need go no farther than this Play: It was first *Spanish,* and call'd *El Astrologo fingido*; then made *French* by the younger *Corneille* [*Le Feint Astrologue*]: and is now translated into *English.*' On theatre critics see Nicoll, pp. 14–16.

Songs. I: Act II. Sung by Wildblood to Jacintha to 'encourage one another to a breach by the dangers of possession'. II: Act II, 'a song *al' Angloise*'. In *Marriage A-la-Mode* (1673), III. i, the song is given dubious advertisement by Doralice, who reports its popularity in the country. Day (p. 25) reproduces Alphonso Marsh the elder's setting from *Choice Songs and Ayres for One Voyce,* 1673; for reprints see Day, p. 149. III: Act IV. Sung by Beatrix to attract Wildblood to Jacintha. For Marsh's setting, and reprints, see Day, pp. 27 and 149–50. IV: Act V. Sung by Wildblood and Jacintha 'for a frolick . . . and let the Company be judge who sings worst'. For reprints, see Day, p. 150.

Prologues, Epilogues and Songs from The Conquest of Granada by the Spaniards: In Two Parts
(Page 128)

The first part of *The Conquest of Granada* was first performed at the Theatre Royal in December 1670, and the second part in January 1671 (*HMC Rutland,* Rpt. xii, Appendix v, p. 22). On 9 February 1671 Evelyn records a performance at Whitehall of this 'famous Play . . . two days acted successively' with 'very glorious scenes & perspectives, the worke of Mr. *Streeter*' the king's Serjeant Painter. The play was first published by Herringman in 1672 (*SR,* 25 February 1671; *TC,* 7 February 1672).

Prologue to the First Part. On Nell Gwyn see Epilogue to *Tyrannick Love,* note. In her 'broad-brim'd hat, and wastbelt' she ridicules a comic device popular at the rival theatre. The Prologue to Aphra Behn's *The Amorous Prince* (performed by the Duke's players *c.* May 1671) refers to those of the audience

> Who love the comick Hat, the Jig and Dance
> Things that are fitted to their Ignorance.

The joke seems to have originated in an incident recorded by Downes, p. 29. The Duke's company were 'Commanded to *Dover,* in *May* 1670. The King with all his Court, meeting his Sister, the Dutchess of *Orleans,* there. . . . The

French Court wearing then Excessive short Lac'd Coats . . . with Broad wast Belts; Mr. *Nokes* having at that time one shorter than the *French* Fashion, to Act Sir *Arthur Addle* in; the Duke of *Monmouth* gave Mr. *Nokes* his Sword and Belt . . . to Ape the *French*: That Mr. *Nokes* lookt more like a Drest up Ape, than a Sir *Arthur*: Which upon his first Entrance on the Stage, put the King and Court to an Excessive Laughter; at which the *French* look'd very Shaggrin.' Cf. Epilogue to *The Wild Gallant Reviv'd*, l. 44, note.

7. *Nokes*: James Nokes (d. 1696), the leading comedian of the Duke's company. 'He scarce ever made his first Entrance in a Play, but he was received with an involuntary Applause, not of Hands only . . . but by a General Laughter, which the very Sight of him provoked, and Nature cou'd not resist . . . the Moment he spoke, the settled Seriousness of his Features was utterly discharg'd, and a dry, drolling, or laughing Levity took such full Possession of him, that I can only refer the Idea of him to your Imagination. . . . *This was an* Actor' (Cibber, pp. 120–2). See Leo Hughes, *A Century of English Farce*, 1956, pp. 160–4.

19. The other comedian was Edward Angel (d. 1673). Just before his death he played Haunce in Mrs. Behn's *The Dutch Lover* and, says the author in her Epistle, 'spoke but little of what I intended for him, but supplied it with a great deal of idle stuff, which I was wholly unacquainted with . . . so that Jack-pudding ever us'd to do: which though I knew before, I gave him yet the Part, because I knew him so acceptable to most o' th' lighter Periwigs about the Town'.

38–39. *French farce . . . is sent abroad, &c.* On the acclimatization of farce in England, and the influence of French comedy, see Nicoll, pp. 252–6. Cf. *Miscellany Poems*, 1684: Epilogue, 'No poor *Dutch* Peasant . . .', ll. 1–10, Prologue to *Arviragus Reviv'd*, ll. 5–22, and *Prologue spoken at the Opening of the New House*, ll. 38–48.

Epilogue. Transcripts of this piece and the Prologue to the Second Part are included in Sir William Haward's MS. book (Bodl. MS. Don. b. 8, pp. 248–9); see also Prologue and Epilogue to *Amboyna*, and Epilogue to *The Man of Mode*, notes. These transcripts have no authority, but they have every appearance of being derived from good copy—possibly from the actors themselves. Attention was first drawn to them by G. Thorn-Drury, *RES* i (1925), 324–30.

Charles Hart (d. 1683), to whom Haward's MS. gives this Epilogue, was one of the finest actors of the day. He acted Alexander in Lee's *The Rival Queens* (1677) 'with such Grandeur and Agreeable Majesty, That one of the Court was pleas'd to Honour him with this Commendation; That *Hart* might Teach any King on Earth how to Comport himself: He was no less Inferior in Comedy' (Downes, p. 16).

19. *When forty comes.* Dryden was now in his fortieth year.

23–24, 35–36. These lines, marked 'not spoke' by Haward, may have been thought too apologetic.

25. *this years delay.* Dryden's previous play, *Tyrannick Love*, had been presented eighteen months before, in June 1669.

31–32. Nell Gwyn had been absent with the 'sickness' to which Dryden refers: her son by Charles II, the future Duke of St. Albans, was born on 8 May 1670. The indiscretion of the reference may account for its being 'not spoke' (Haward); and it is possible that Haward's 'nine whole Moneths *were* lost', which makes the allusion more specific, is the original version.

Songs. The versions in *Westminster-Drollery* (1671) are collated here since they are earlier than those in the first edition of the play.

I: Act III. In the first edition this song is printed after the Epilogue, with the note 'Misplac'd. Sung at the dance, or *Zambra* in the third *Act*'. For Banister's setting in *Choice Songs and Ayres for One Voyce*, 1673, and reprints, see Day, pp. 31, 150–1.

22–28. *dye*: a common *double entendre*. Cf. Songs from *Marriage A-la-Mode*, II; Epilogue to *Cleomenes*, ll. 1–10.

II: Act IV, Sc. ii. For Alphonso Marsh's setting in *Choice Songs and Ayres for One Voyce*, 1673, and reprints, see Day, pp. 33, 151.

Prologue to the Second Part. Michael Mohun (d. 1684), to whom Haward's MS. gives this Prologue, was 'Eminent for *Volpone* . . . *Mithridates*, &c. An Eminent Poet seeing him Act this last, vented suddenly this Saying: *Oh Mohun, Mohun! Thou little Man of Mettle, if I should Write a* 100 *Plays, I'd Write a Part for thy Mouth*' (Downes, p. 17).

10. The Haward MS. adds four lines. These may be a reference to the Buckingham circle (see Macdonald, pp. 193–5); *The Rehearsal* was got ready for the stage in 1671. Dryden had detractors at court about this time: in the Dedication of *Marriage A-la-Mode* to Rochester in 1673 he says 'In my little Experience of a Court (which I confess I desire not to improve) I have found . . . Few Men there have that Assurance of a Friend, as not to be made ridiculous by him, when they are absent. There are a middling sort of Courtiers, who become happy by their want of Wit; but they supply that Want by an excess of Malice to those who have it.'

13. *Vizard Masque*: the mask was worn by ladies of fashion after the Restoration (see Pepys, *Diary*, 12 June 1663). Four years later it was less certainly a mask of modesty (ibid., 18 February 1667). In Etherege's *She wou'd if she cou'd* (1668), II. i, Courtall says that masks 'were pretty toys, invented, first, meerly for the good of us poor Lovers to deceive the jealous, and to blind the malicious; but the proper use is so wickedly perverted, that it makes all honest men hate the fashion mortally'. In *The Kind Keeper* (1680), IV. i, Aldo pacifies two squabbling whores with 'At the Playhouses, she shall ply the Boxes, because she has the better Face; and you shall have the Pit, because you can prattle best out of a *Vizor-Mask*'. Cf. Prologue to *Marriage A-la-Mode*, ll. 3–4, Epilogue *To the King and Queen*, ll. 11–20, Prologue to *The History of Bacon in Virginia*, ll. 6–9, and Epilogue to *Love Triumphant*, l. 15.

15–16. *Perks up*, &c. The combing of the wig in public was a common foppish habit. Cf. *Covent Garden Drolery* (1672), 'Prologue', p. 33:

> He who comes hither with design to hiss,
> And with a bum revers'd, to whisper Miss,
> To comb a Perriwig, or to shew gay cloathes,
> Or to vent Antique nonscense with new oathes,
> Our Poet welcomes as the Muses friend;
> For hee'l by irony each Play commend.

Gallants who 'like neither the Play nor the Women . . . seldom stay any longer than the combing of their Perriwigs, or a whisper or two with a Friend' (Etherege, *She wou'd if she cou'd*, 1668, I. ii). The white wig did not supplant the periwig till the first decade of the eighteenth century, but it became a mark of fashion in the 1670's. So Goldingham in Shadwell's *The Miser*, 1672, I: 'Handsomly, foolishly; to what end are these multitudes of Ribbands, this Flaxen Mop of Whores Hair, and this *Flanders* Lace upon the Shirt; I warrant this habit cost thirty Pound.'

19–20. On noise in the theatre, see Nicoll, pp. 15–19.

Epilogue to the Second Part. The first three editions of the play conclude with a 'Defence of the Epilogue. Or, *An Essay on the* Dramatique Poetry *of the last Age*', written, says Dryden, because 'I have so farr ingag'd my self in a bold *Epilogue* to this Play, wherein I have somewhat tax'd the former writing. . . . It is therefore my part to make it clear, that the Language, Wit, and Conversation of our Age are improv'd and refin'd above the last; and then it will not be difficult to inferr, that our Playes have receiv'd some part of those advantages.' Cf. Rochester, *An Allusion to Horace* (*c.* 1675), ll. 81–86.

3–6. 'Humour was [Jonson's] proper Sphere, and in that he delighted most to represent Mechanick people' (*Of Dramatick Poesie, an Essay*). 'In these low Characters of Vice and Folly, lay the excellency of that inimitable Writer. . . . The last and greatest advantage of our writing proceeds from conversation. In the Age, wherein those Poets liv'd, there was less of gallantry than in ours: neither did they keep the best company of theirs' (*Defence of the Epilogue*). Cobb is a water-bearer in Jonson's *Every Man in his Humour*, his 'version of the official clown, adapted to the circumstances and atmosphere of his bourgeois stage' (Jonson, i. 354). Otter is 'a land, and sea-Captaine' in *Epicoene, or The Silent Woman*: '*Tom Otters* bull, beare, and horse is knowne all ouer *England*, in *rerum natura*' (III. i). On the popularity of these two plays after the Restoration, see Jonson, ix. 169 and 209–14. 'Gentlemen will now be entertain'd with the follies of each other: and though they allow *Cob* and *Tib* to speak properly, yet they are not much pleas'd with their Tankard, or with their Raggs: And, surely, their conversation can be no jest to them on the *Theatre*, when they would avoid it on the street' (*Defence of the Epilogue*). Cf. *Mac Flecknoe*, introductory note.

7. *their love was mean.* Jonson is not 'a perfect pattern of imitation; except it be in humour: for Love, which is the foundation of all *Comedies* in other Languages, is scarcely mention'd in any of his Playes' (*Defence of the Epilogue*).

Song, In two Parts. Act IV. For a setting in *Choice Songs and Ayres for One Voyce,* 1673, and reprints, see Day, pp. 37 and 151–2.

A Song

(Page 136)

On the sequence of the miscellanies in which this song first appeared see Macdonald, p. 78. *New Court-Songs, and Poems,* from which the present text is taken, was compiled by Robert Veel (1648–*c.* 1674), who left Oxford without a degree, 'went to the great City, lived after the manner of Poets in a debauch'd way, and wrote partly for the use of his idle and vain Companions, but more to gain Money to carry on the Trade of Folly, these frivolous matters following, *viz.* New Court Songs and Poems . . .' (Wood, *Ath. Ox.* ii. 537).

The attribution of the song to Dryden, first made by Malone (I. i. 102–4), is based on two passages in the third edition of *The Rehearsal* (1675). In II. i, Bayes says: 'If I am to write familiar things, as Sonnets to *Armida,* and the like, I make use of Stew'd Prunes only; but, when I have a grand design in hand, I ever take Physic, and let blood.' In III. i, he speaks of 'my last new Song. . . . 'Tis to the Tune of Farewel, fair *Armida,* on Seas, and in battels, in Bullets, and all that'; there follows a parody of ll. 9–16. The attribution has been questioned, particularly by Thorn-Drury (ed. *Covent Garden Drollery,* 1928, pp. 126–9), but the parody in *The Rehearsal* is good if not conclusive evidence in its favour. Day (pp. 152–5) adds these points: (i) *Covent Garden Drolery* (pp. 39–40) contains a partial parody of this song beginning 'Farewel, dear *Revechia,* my joy and my grief', where Revechia is almost certainly Dryden's mistress Anne Reeves (see Macdonald, p. 96); (ii) in *Choice Songs and Ayres for One Voyce* (1673) and *Choice Ayres, Songs, & Dialogues* (1675) the song follows two pieces indisputably Dryden's, and is set by Robert Smith who collaborated with Dryden on other occasions.

In *A Key to The Rehearsal,* included in Buckingham's *Miscellaneous Works* (1704–5), the parody of this song is described as 'the latter part of a Song made by Mr. Bayes on the Death of Captain *Digby,* Son of George Earl of *Bristol,* who was a passionate Admirer of the Dutchess *Dowager* of Richmond, call'd by the Author *Armida*: he lost his Life in a Sea fight against the *Dutch,* on the 28th of May, 1672'.

Poems from Covent Garden Drolery
(Page 138)

The miscellany in which these poems appeared was first published as *Covent Garden Drolery, or A Colection, Of all the Choice Songs, Poems, Prologues, and Epilogues, (Sung and Spoken at Courts and Theaters) never in Print before. Written by the refined'st Witts of the Age. And Collected by R. B. Servant to His Majesty. Printed for James Magnes . . . 1672.* A later issue (*TC*, 21 November) corrects some errors, and gives the compiler as 'A. B.', who is tentatively identified by Thorn-Drury as Aphra Behn. There followed, also in 1672, 'The Second Impression, with *Additions*'. See Prologue to *Iulius Cæsar*, note.

Prologue and Epilogue to Secret-Love, *Spoken by the Women*
(Page 138)

These two poems were first attributed to Dryden by Scott, on the grounds of his 'connection both with the play, and with Mrs. Reeves, who spoke the epilogue'; and a transcript of both poems in BM Eg. MS. 2623, ff. 43–44, is endorsed 'Dryden' in a contemporary hand different from that of the copyist. The performance of *Secret-Love* by the women, of which there is no other record, must have been given (*a*) while the King's company was acting at Lincoln's Inn Fields after the fire at the Theatre Royal on 25 January 1672 (see Nicoll, p. 322; cf. *infra*, Prologue to *Wit without Money; Miscellany Poems*, 1684, Prologue to *Arviragus Reviv'd* and Prologue for the Women); and (*b*) after 4 July 1672, the date of the first performance of Ravenscroft's *The Citizen turn'd Gentleman* (Epilogue, l. 30).

Prologue. Mrs. Boutell 'generally acted the *young Innocent Lady* whom all the heroes are mad in love with; she was a Favourite of the Town' (see *Covent Garden Drolery*, ed. Summers, 1927, pp. 89–96).

9. *the sweet on 't*: the advantage of it.

Epilogue. Anne Reeves was probably Dryden's mistress about this time (see *A Song*, 'Farewel, fair *Armida*', note; Macdonald, p. 96, note).

1–4. *What think you Sirs, &c.* Cf. the Prologue to *Don Sebastian* 'Sent to the Authour by an unknown hand, and propos'd to be spoken by Mrs. *Monford* drest like an Officer', ll. 19–21:

> For want of Petty-coat I've put on buff,
> To try what may be got by lying rough:
> How think you Sirs, is it not well enough.

4. *cock*: swagger. Cf. Southerne, *The Loyal Brother* (1682), v. i: '. . . but now I'm charg'd with bottle Ale. . . . I'l strut, and cock, and talk as big, as wind, and froth can make me' (Gardner).

22. *our Legs are no ill sight.* Cf. Pepys's appreciation of an actress in men's clothes, *Diary*, 28 October 1661.

30. *Mamamouchi*: a reference to Ravenscroft's *The Citizen turn'd Gentleman.* See Prologue to *The Assignation*, ll. 30–37, notes.

The Prologue to Witt without Money: being the first Play acted after the Fire
(Page 140)

The Theatre Royal in Bridges-street was completely destroyed by fire on 25 January 1672. On 26 February following, the King's company resumed at the old theatre in Lincoln's Inn Fields which the Duke's company had left for Dorset Garden (see Prologue and Epilogue, *supra*, note). Their first play at Lincoln's Inn Fields was Beaumont and Fletcher's *Wit without Money*. Transcripts of this Prologue are contained in Bodl. MS. Eng. Poet. e. 4, p. 175, and BM MS. Sloane 4455, f. 26ᵛ. The second of these has a descriptive note: '. . . Feb. 26, 1671. The Curtaine being drawne up all the Actors were discover'd on the stage in Melancholick postures & Moone [Mohun] advancing before the rest speaks as follows, addressing himself chiefly to ye King then pʳsent.' Cf. the presentation of the Prologue to *The Indian-Queen*.

20. *our new-built City rises higher.* Cf. *Annus Mirabilis*, ll. 845–8.

29–30. In Bodl. MS. Eng. Poet. e. 4 these lines have a marginal note, 'To the King.'

Prologue to Albumazar
(Page 141)

Thomas Tomkis's *Albumazar* was first acted on 9 March 1614 at Trinity College, Cambridge, to celebrate a visit of James I. On 22 February 1668 Pepys saw it revived at the Duke's playhouse, 'this the second time of acting. It is said to have been the ground of B. Jonson's "Alchymist".' Jonson's play was performed in 1610, and cannot contain debts to Tomkis; but Dryden was apparently not the first to make this insinuation. The motto of the quarto edition of *The Alchemist* (1612) was replaced in the 1616 folio by '—*petere inde coronam,* | *Vnde priùs nulli velarint tempora Musæ*', a change 'probably occasioned by the appearance, in the interim, of T. Tomkis's *Albumazar*. . . . The only point of contact between the plays is that there is an astrologer in both' (Jonson, ii. 95–96, note).

The Prologue, which was not printed with the play, is ascribed to Dryden in *Miscellany Poems*. A transcript in Bodl. MS. Eng. Poet. e. 4 (pp. 172–3; endorsed 'J. D.') gives, apart from some trivial differences, the revised version in *Miscellany Poems*.

10. *He lik'd the Fashion well, who wore the Cloaths.* Jonson was 'a learned Plagiary of [the Ancients]; you track him every where in their Snow . . . you will pardon me therefore if I presume he lov'd their fashion when he wore their cloaths' (*Of Dramatick Poesie, An Essay*, 1668; Ker, i. 43).

13–14. *Like an unrighteous Conquerer he raigns*, &c. 'He invades Authours like a Monarch, and what would be theft in other Poets, is onely Victory in him' (ibid. i. 82).

15–18. Probably a reference to Sir Robert Howard's *The Duke of Lerma*, first performed a few days earlier at the Theatre Royal (Pepys, *Diary*, 20 February 1668). A. Harbage argues that this play is an alteration of a lost play by Ford (*MLR* xxxv (1940), 297–304). Cf. Dryden's ironical remarks on Howard's alteration in the 'Defence of an Essay of Dramatique Poesie' (Ker, i. 111–12).

25. *Country Tom*: the nickname given to a highwayman of the time (Thorn-Drury).

30. *make love to 'em, the Ægyptian, way.* In ancient Egypt the corpses of ladies of wealth and beauty were not given over to the embalmers until four days had elapsed to prevent sexual abuse (Herodotus, ii. 89; Burton, III. ii. I. 2).

38. *Jack Pudding*: a clown assisting a mountebank.

Prologue to Iulius Cæsar
(Page 142)

This Prologue was ascribed to Dryden in 1854 by Bolton Corney (*NQ* I. ix. 95–96), who drew attention to resemblances between the criticism of Shakespeare and Jonson here and that in *Of Dramatick Poesie, An Essay*. Christie and Noyes were disposed to accept the poem as Dryden's on the general evidence of style; and in support Thorn-Drury (ed. *Covent Garden Drollery*, 1928, pp. 120–3) cited a number of parallels from poems which are indisputably Dryden's. More significant than incidental echoes of other poems, or the commonplace contrast of the artless Shakespeare and the learned Jonson, is the criticism of Jonson's low comedy in ll. 31–35; cf. Epilogue to The Second Part of *The Conquest of Granada*, ll. 3–6, note. But 'though portions are clearly in Dryden's manner, the evidence for attributing the whole prologue to him is far from conclusive' (D. Nichol Smith, *Shakespeare Criticism*, 1916, p. 27).

Prologue, Epilogue and Songs from Marriage A-la-Mode. A Comedy
(Page 144)

The date of the first performance of *Marriage A-la-Mode* is not known. Dedicating the play to Rochester in 1673, Dryden reminds him that 'your Lordship . . . commended it to the view of His Majesty, then at *Windsor*, and by his Approbation of it in Writing, made way for its kind reception on the *Theatre*'. This service was probably done during Charles's stay at Windsor from late May till July 1671; and it is likely that the King's players would prepare for performance in the autumn following. But the Prologue refers to service in the war declared on Holland on 17 March 1672. There may have been delays in production, or the Prologue as we now have it may not have been written for the first performances. It is likely that the play was acted before June 1672, since the song 'Whil'st *Alexis* lay prest' was printed in *Westminster-Drollery* (advertised in *TC*, 24 June). See Nicoll, pp. 404–5; Macdonald, p. 110. The play was first published by Herringman in 1673.

The Prologue and Epilogue were first printed in *Covent Garden Drolery*, 1672—possibly from theatre copy, or from a shorthand version made in the theatre (cf. Prologue and Epilogue *spoken at Mithridates King of Pontus*, introductory note). Some readings are suspiciously more obvious than those in the first edition of the play—Prologue, ll. 4, 7, 29, 36, and Epilogue, ll. 7–8; and others may be the result of faulty hearing in the theatre—Prologue, l. 16, and Epilogue, ll. 13, 17, 18.

Prologue. On Hart, to whom *Covent Garden Drolery* gives the Prologue, see Epilogue to the First Part of *The Conquest of Granada*, note. He played Palamede in *Marriage A-la-Mode*.

3. *Fop-corner*: part of the pit frequented by dandies. See Prologue to the Second Part of *The Conquest of Granada*, ll. 13, 15–16, notes.

13. *powerful Guinnee cannot be withstood*. Cf. Horace, *Od.* III. xvi. 1–8; Tilley, L406. Fidelia in Lacy's *Sir Hercules Buffoon*, 1684, p. 4, says: 'Prithee consider, Sister, Virtue cannot maintain thee; and when once 'tis known a handsom Woman is in want, then as the Poet worthily says, the powerful Guiney cannot be withstood' (Macdonald).

16. *grinning Honour*. Cf. Falstaff in *1 Henry IV*, v. iii. 59–61: 'I like not such grinning honour as Sir *Walter* hath: Giue mee life, which if I can saue, so: if not, honour comes vnlook'd for, and ther's an end.'

22. *manages her last Half-crown with care*. A half-crown was the price of admission to the pit, and a whore's charge (cf. Prologue to *The Mistakes*, l. 22, and Epilogue to *Cleomenes*, ll. 35–36). In *A Satire, which the King took out of his Pocket*, attributed to Rochester, Nell Gwyn is described as first a fish-seller and

> Then . . . by Madam *Ross* expos'd to Town;
> I mean to those who would give *Half-a-Crown*.

Both meanings are intended here; the 'poor pensive Punk' decides not to spend her latest gain profitlessly in admission to an empty theatre.

24–27. A reference to the new rival theatre in Dorset Garden which attracted the citizens. Cf. Wycherley, Prologue 'to the City' and Epilogue to *The Gentleman Dancing-Master*, 1673: *Miscellany Poems*, 1684; Prologue to *Arviragus reviv'd*, l. 2, note; and 'Prologue for the Women', ll. 22–23.

28–37. *cutting Moorcraft*: the swaggering citizen. Cf. *Sylvæ*, 'From Horace, *Epod. 2d.*', ll. 96–102. Morecraft is a usurer turned gallant in Fletcher's *The Scornful Lady*, frequently revived after the Restoration; but it is improbable that Dryden refers to a revival at Dorset Garden since the play was the property of the King's company. Thorn-Drury (ed. *Covent Garden Drollery*, 1928) suggests that about 1672 the citizens patronized 'entertainments in the nature of masquerades . . . at which a prominent feature had been a retiring-room provided with a couch', and quotes 'The Prologue to *The Widdow*' (*London Drollery*, 1673, p. 11):

> But you this Winter find out other ways
> To kill your selves, and to destroy our Plays,
> You meet in Masquerade to pass your time
> Without the help of Reason or of Rime
>
> .   .   .   .   .   .
>
> For Courting still your selves, you seem to say
> That you Heaven Love, you have more wit than they,
> And that one Sceen o' th' Couch, is worth a Play.

But although this explains 'cutting *Moorcraft* . . . in Masquerade', it is possible that Dryden's ll. 32–37 refer simply to tiring-room facilities at Dorset Garden. Cf. Epilogue *To the King and Queen*, ll. 35–36, note.

Epilogue. On Mohun, to whom *Covent Garden Drolery* gives the Epilogue, see Prologue to the Second Part of *The Conquest of Granada*, note. Mohun played Rhodophil, husband of Doralice, in *Marriage A-la-Mode*.

3–6. *Not with dull Morals*, &c. Phlegmatic melancholy 'stirres up dull Symptomes, and a kinde of stupiditie, or impassionate hurt': its victims 'are sleepy, saith *Savonarola*, dull, slow, cold, blockish, ass-like, *Asininam melancholiam*, *Melancthon* calls it' (Burton, I. iii. 1. 3). Dryden jibes at the opening lines of Tuke's *The Adventures of Five Hours*, 1671 (see Prologue to *The Wild Gallant* 'as it was first Acted', ll. 38–40, note):

> How happy are the Men of easie Phlegm,
> Born on the Confines of Indifference;
> Holding from Nature, the securest Tenure,
> The Peaceful Empire o'r themselves. . . .

11–12. In Act V, the amours of Palamede with Rhodophil's wife Doralice, and of Rhodophil with Palamede's lady Melantha, are discovered. Palamede suggests 'a Blessed Community betwixt us four . . . Wife and Husband for the standing Dish, and Mistriss and Gallant for the Desert'; but it is finally resolved to 'make a firm League, not to invade each others Propriety'.

32. *I humbly cast my self upon the City.* The cuckold citizen is a conventional target in Restoration comedy. Cf. Prologue to *Cæsar Borgia*, ll. 9–10; *Miscellany Poems* (1684), 'Ovid's . . . *Elegy the Nineteenth*', l. 45.

Songs. I: Act I, sung by Doralice and Beliza. For Robert Smith's setting in *Choice Songs and Ayres for One Voyce*, 1673, and reprints, see Day, pp. 41 and 155.

II: Act IV, Sc. iii. For Nicholas Staggins's setting in *Choice Songs and Ayres*, and reprints, see Day, pp. 43 and 156.

11. *die*: a common *double entendre*. Cf. Songs from the First Part of *The Conquest of Granada*, I, ll. 22–28; Epilogue to *Cleomenes*, ll. 1–10.

Prologue, Epilogue and Song from The Assignation: or, Love in a Nunnery

(Page 148)

The Assignation was first performed by the King's company at the old Duke's theatre in Lincoln's Inn Fields in October 1672, and was first published by Herringman in 1673 (*TC*, 16 June, with *Marriage A-la-Mode*), with a dedication to Sedley.

Prologue. 24. *Th' unnatural strain'd Buffoon*: the gross 'humorous' character of farce. See Leo Hughes, *A Century of English Farce*, 1956, pp. 132–3.

30. *Mamamouchi.* Edward Ravenscroft's *The Citizen turn'd Gentleman: A Comedy* was performed on 4 July 1672 at Dorset Garden, and published in that year. It 'was look upon by the Criticks for a Foolish Play; yet it continu'd *Acting* 9 Days with a full House. . . . Mr. *Nokes* in performing the *Mamamouchi* pleas'd the King and Court, next *Sir Martin* [*Mar-all*], above all Plays' (Downes, p. 32).

34–37. In Ravenscroft's play, v, Jorden is invested as a Mamamouchi or Paladin to the accompaniment of 'Hula baba la chou' and other gibberish. In Act IV he exclaims: 'I am beholden to you for telling me, for I could ne'er have thought that *Marababa sahem*, should signifie, Ah how much in love am I! Ah this Turkish is a most admirable Language.' Ravenscroft replied to Dryden's ridicule in the Prologue to *The Careless Lovers*, 1673 (see Macdonald, pp. 204–5).

45. *Haynes*: Joseph Haines (1648–1701), at one time Sir Joseph Williamson's Latin secretary. Pepys saw him on 7 March 1668 at the Theatre Royal, 'only lately come thither from the Nursery, an understanding fellow, but yet, they say, hath spent £1,000 a-year before he come thither'. Haines played Benito in *The Assignation*, and was celebrated in prologues and epilogues (see Wiley, pp. 195–6, 335). Cf. Epilogue to *Henry the Second*, l. 20, note. Haines's reputation as a comedian is discussed by Leo Hughes, *A Century of English Farce*, 1956, pp. 166–9.

Epilogue. 3. *Coleman-Street*, running south from Moorgate. The reference is to the citizens.

21. *behind our Scenes*, i.e. in the tiring-room. See Epilogue *To the King and Queen*, l. 35, note.

Song and Dance. Act III, Sc. ii. For Robert Smith's setting in *Choice Songs and Ayres for One Voyce*, 1673, and reprints, see Day, pp. 45 and 156–7.

Prologue, Epilogue and Songs from Amboyna: A Tragedy
(Page 150)

Amboyna was first published by Herringman in 1673 (*SR*, 26 June; *TC*, 24 November). The date of the first performance at Lincoln's Inn Fields is unknown. C. E. Ward (*PMLA* li (1936), 786–92) argues for a date in 1672: (i) a prologue printed in *Westminster Drollery* and *Covent Garden Drolery* (1672) speaks of critics who 'dislocate' the scenes of a play with more art 'Then in *Amboyna* they the limbs of men'; (ii) a puppet-show, 'The Dutch Cruelties at Amboyna', was running at a Charing Cross booth in November 1672 (*CSP Dom. 1672–3*, p. 148); (iii) the play would be more effective as propaganda in 1672 than in 1673. But (i) the Amboyna massacre of 1623 was a familiar and often-revived story (see Summers, iii. 345); (ii) the puppet-show need not have been dependent on Dryden's play; (iii) anti-Dutch propaganda was as necessary in 1673 as at the beginning of hostilities in March 1672. In the spring of 1673 commercial jealousy of the Dutch was yielding to hatred of the French. 'Concern for Protestantism was intensified by our war against a state where the Protestants were in a majority, especially as we were joined by a Catholic ally', and the government seems to have sponsored propaganda to incite hatred of Holland (see Ogg, i. 371–2). Dryden's play is a significant piece of propaganda, commissioned by the government and, he says in the Dedication, 'contriv'd and written in a Month'; and it is unlikely that much time was lost in getting into print what had been successful support of the king's policy on the stage.

Haward's transcripts of the Prologue and Epilogue (see Epilogue to the First Part of *The Conquest of Granada*, note) may be based on theatre copy. They are more emphatic than the printed version (Prologue, ll. 9, 13–14, and additional couplet after l. 16) but plainly inferior. The copyist has avoided difficulties in Prologue, ll. 21, 33, and Epilogue, l. 5. On the concoction of these two poems in *POAS*, see Macdonald, p. 320.

Prologue. 18–22. *They have no more Religion*, &c. Cf. *The Hind and the Panther*, ii. 568–75, note.

27. *Their Pictures and Inscriptions.* 'The war being thus resolved on, some pretences were in the next place to be sought out to excuse it. . . . Some medals were complained of, that seemed dishonourable to the King; as also some pictures: And, tho' these were not made by publick order, yet a great noise was raised about them' (Burnet, i. 305). Cf. Shaftesbury's reference in the Commons on 5 February 1673 to 'the personal indignities, by pictures and medals and other public affronts, his Majesty hath received from the States' (Browning, p. 854).

Epilogue. 1. *A Poet*: Tyrtaeus, the Greek elegiac poet, who was contemptuously presented to the Spartans when they asked Athens for a general, and subsequently inspired them to victory over the Messenians with martial songs.

18. *two Kings Touch*: the alliance of Charles II and Louis XIV.

19. *As Cato, &c.* See *Annus Mirabilis*, ll. 691–2, note. The comparison of Holland with Carthage was a commonplace. Cf. *Annus Mirabilis*, ll. 17–20 and notes; *The Character of Holland* (attributed to Marvell), ll. 141–2; and Shaftesbury's speech on 5 February 1673: 'But you judged aright, that at any rate *delenda est Carthago*; that government is to be brought down. And therefore the king may well say to you, it is your war' (Browning, p. 854).

Epithalamium. Act III. For Robert Smith's setting from *Choice Songs and Ayres for One Voyce*, 1673, and reprints, see Day, pp. 47 and 157.

The Sea Fight. Act III. The song is followed by Harman Junior's taunt: 'See the Insolence of these *English*; they cannot do a brave Action in an Age, but presently they must put it into Metre, to upbraid us with their Benefits.'

To the Lady Castlemain, upon Her incouraging his first Play
(Page 154)

Barbara Villiers (1640–1709) was daughter and heir to the second Viscount Grandison, who died of wounds at Edgehill in 1642 (see ll. 23–24). She married Roger Palmer, created Earl of Castlemaine in 1661; became Charles II's mistress soon after; and was created Duchess of Cleveland in 1670. Her service to Dryden was the promotion of *The Wild Gallant* at court (see Prologues and Epilogues to the play, note). The earliest and fullest version of Dryden's lines was printed in *A New Collection of Poems and Songs. . . . Collected by John Bulteel*, 1674 (one issue has a cancel title-page, *Melpomene: or, The Muses Delight*, 1678). The version included in *Examen Poeticum* has every appearance of being Dryden's revision: the omitted ll. 37–38 and 55–58 might have drawn ridicule on him in the altered circumstances of 1693. The transcript in Bodl. MS. Eng. Poet. e. 4 (pp. 173–4) agrees with 93 against 74 at many points without being derived from 93, and indicates an original different from 74.

9–10. *Once Cato's Vertue, &c.* Lucan, *Pharsalia*, i. 128, 'victrix causa deis placuit sed victa Catoni'.

Prologue and Epilogue to Aureng-Zebe: A Tragedy
(Page 156)

Aureng-Zebe was first performed at the Theatre Royal, Drury Lane, in November 1675 (LC 5/141, p. 359 and LC 5/142, p. 52) and published by

Herringman in the following year (advertised in the *London Gazette*, 17–21 February 1676).

Prologue. 8. *Grows weary of his long-lov'd Mistris, Rhyme*. This was Dryden's last rhymed heroic play. Cf. Prologue to *All for Love*, l. 7, note.

13–24. *a secret shame*, &c. Cf. the Epistle Dedicatory: 'I desire to be no longer the *Sysiphus* of the Stage; to rowl up a Stone with endless Labour (which, to follow the Proverb, *Gathers no Moss*) and which is perpetually falling down again; I never thought my self very fit for an Employment, where many of my Predecessors have excell'd me in all kinds; and some of my Contemporaries, even in my own partial Judgment, have out-done me in *Comedy*. Some little hopes I have yet remaining . . . that I may make the World some part of amends, for many ill Plays, by an Heroick Poem.' Cf. Dedication of *The Satires of Juvenalis*, ll. 614 ff.

37. *our Neighbours*: the Duke's company at Dorset Garden.

Epilogue. 1–10. *A Pretty task . . . to please by Rule*, &c. Cf. Prologue to *Secret-Love*, l. 3, note.

15. *No Song! no Dance! no Show!* See Prologue to *The Rival-Ladies*, l. 11, note.

18. *like the French, abhors our Target-fight*. Between Acts I and II in *Aureng-Zebe* 'A Warlike Tune is plaid, shooting off Guns, and shouts of Soldiers are heard as in an Assault'. In *Of Dramatick Poesie, An Essay* Lisideius defends the French avoidance of 'tumult' on the stage. Dryden earlier admits his 'frequent use of Drums and Trumpets, and . . . Representations of Battels' in 'Of Heroique Playes. An Essay' (printed with *The Conquest of Granada*), and is represented in *The Rehearsal* (IV. i) as having designed 'a Conquest, that cannot possibly, I gad, be acted in less than a whole week: and I'l speak a bold word, it shall Drum, Trumpet, Shout, and Battel, I gad with any the most warlike Tragœdy we have, either ancient or modern'.

21. *Silk-weavers*, i.e. enemies to France. The English silk industry could not at this time compete with the French (see Clark, p. 48; Ogg, i. 67).

22–25. Prize-fighting with broad-swords went on at the Bear-garden on Bankside. Cf. Pepys, *Diary*, 9 September 1667 and 12 April 1669.

Epilogue to The Man of Mode

(Page 158)

Sir George Etherege's *The Man of Mode, or, Sr Fopling Flutter. A Comedy* was first performed by the Duke's company at Dorset Garden on 11 March 1676 (LC 5/142, p. 82) and published by Herringman in July (advertised in the *London Gazette*, 3–6 July). See *To Sir George Etherege*, note. Transcripts of the Epilogue are included in BM MSS. Sloane 203, f. 95r and Sloane 1458, f. 23r (see W. Thorp, *RES* ix (1933), 198–9), and in Bodl. MS. Don. b. 8, pp. 558–9 (Haward; cf. Epilogue to The First Part of *The Conquest of Granada*, note).

Sloane 1458 differs from the printed version in line arrangement: ll. 1–12, an additional couplet as supplied in the Haward MS. after l. 14, ll. 13–14, 17–20, 15–16, 21–22, 27–30, 23–24, 31–34.

7. *a Fool so nicely writ.* He is presented in the play (I. i) as 'the pattern of modern Foppery . . . a person indeed of great acquir'd Follies', with 'a Periwig more exactly Curl'd then a Ladies head newly dress'd for a Ball' and 'a pretty lisp' affected 'in imitation of the people of Quality of *France*'.

10. *I now.* 'I' is a common spelling of 'Ay'; 'vow' in 76 is clearly a printer's error for 'now'.

14. The additional couplet in Haward's MS. is a hit at Buckingham; see Epilogue to *All for Love*, l. 17, note. Brett-Smith takes it as 'obviously authentic, but . . . suppressed in the editions' (*Works of Etherege*, 1927, p. 294). The reason for such a suppression is not apparent.

15. *none Sir Fopling him, or him can call.* 'I remember very well, that upon the first acting this Comedy, it was generally believed to be an agreeable Representation of the Persons of Condition of both Sexes, both in Court and Town' (Dennis, ii. 248). See Brett-Smith, op. cit., pp. xxiv–xxv.

22. *the Toss*: a sudden throwing up of the head; *the new French Wallow*: 'a rolling walk or gait' (*OED*).

24. *Snake*: 'a long curl or tail attached to a wig' (*OED*).

28. *shog*: shake, jerk.

Prologue to Circe, A Tragedy

(Page 160)

Circe, the only play of Sir William Davenant's eldest son Charles (1656–1714), was first performed at Dorset Garden in May 1677 (see Nicoll, p. 400), and published by Tonson in the same year (licensed 18 June). Only the first ten lines are common to the version of the Prologue printed with the play and the 'Epilogue' printed in *Miscellany Poems*, 1684. Editors have generally regarded 'An Epilogue' as a revision of the 1677 Prologue; but it seems more likely that it is an epilogue written for some other young poet, with ten dramatically effective lines carried over from the Prologue to *Circe*. The figure of the green, virgin poet was a favourite with Dryden in these contributed pieces (cf. Epilogues to *Tamerlane the Great* and *The Loyal Brother*, and *Examen Poeticum*, Prologue, 'Gallants, a bashful Poet . . .').

(B) *An Epilogue.* 15. A reference to Sir Robert Stapylton's comedy, *The Slighted Maid*, 1663. Cf. Ker, ii. 145.

16–17. 'This opinion seems to be solely founded on the inferiority oɪ "Pericles", to the other plays of Shakespeare' (Scott).

19. *All Hawthorns do not bloom on Christmas-day.* The Glastonbury thorn, sprung from the staff of Joseph of Arimathea, is said to bloom on Christmas Day. Cf. Browne, *Pseudodoxia Epidemica*, II. vi. 4.

21. *burnish*: grow fat.

24. *stew'd*. Editors have proposed emendation to 'sterv'd', or 'rude'. But the sense 'laboured', 'sweated', fits the context well.

To Mr. Lee, on his Alexander
(Page 161)

Nathaniel Lee (1649?–92), who may have been like Dryden a Westminster boy, and was like Dryden at Trinity College, Cambridge, contributed verses to *The State of Innocence* in 1677. To this Dryden refers in ll. 3–6. Dryden collaborated with Lee in *Oedipus* (1679) and *The Duke of Guise* (1683), and contributed prologues or epilogues to Lee's *Mithridates King of Pontus* (1678), *Cæsar Borgia* (1680), *Sophonisba* (1681), and *Constantine the Great* (1684). *The Rival Queens, or The Death of Alexander the Great* was first performed at the Theatre Royal on 17 March 1677 (Nicoll, p. 419), and published by Magnes and Bentley in the same year with Dryden's verses and a prologue by Sir Carr Scrope.

8. *Bessus, and the Brothers of the Sword.* In Beaumont and Fletcher's *A King and No King* (IV. iii, v. iii) Bessus and two 'gentlemen o' th' sword' expound bravery as 'suffering and contemning' in 'a cudgell'd body', and after they have all been kicked by Bacurius conclude:

> *2 Sw.* Captain, we must request
>   Your hand now to our honours.
> *Bes.*   Yes, marry, shall ye;
>   And then let all the world come, we are valiant
>   To ourselves, and there's an end.
> *1 Sw.* Nay then, we must be valiant. Oh, my ribs! . . .

12. *By-ends*: selfish purposes. Bunyan's By-ends claims as his kindred 'almost the whole Town; and in particular, my Lord *Turn-about*, my Lord *Time-server*, my Lord *Fair-speech*. . . . Also Mr. *Smooth-man*, Mr. *Facing-both-ways*, Mr. *Any-thing*' (*The Pilgrim's Progress*, ed. Venables, 1925, p. 92).

31–32. Sir Edward Spragge (see *Annus Mirabilis*, ll. 681–700, note) destroyed a pirate force in the bay of Bugia in 1671, despite defensive fire from land forts and a boom drawn across the entrance of the bay. He was drowned in a battle with the Dutch on 11 August 1673.

Epilogue to Mithridates King of Pontus. A Tragedy
(Page 163)

Lee's *Mithridates* was first performed at Drury Lane in February 1678 and published by Magnes and Bentley in the same year (licensed 28 March). Dryden also provided a Prologue and Epilogue for the revival of 1681 (see *infra*, p. 1874).

21. *sophisticated*: adulterated. Cf. *To Dr Charleton*, l. 6.

24. *the old Half-crown way*. See Prologue to *Marriage A-la-Mode*, l. 22, note.

Prologue and Epilogue to All for Love: or, The World well Lost. A Tragedy
(Page 164)

All for Love, the last play Dryden wrote for the King's company, was first performed at the Theatre Royal in December 1677 (see Macdonald, p. 117) and published by Herringman in the spring following (advertised in the *London Gazette*, 21–25 March 1678).

Prologue to Anthony and Cleopatra. 7. *unarm'd; without his Rhyme*. In his Preface Dryden says: 'In my Stile I have profess'd to imitate the Divine *Shakespear*; which that I might perform more freely, I have disincumber'd my self from Rhyme. Not that I condemn my former way, but that this is more proper to my present purpose.' But see Prologue to *Aureng-Zebe*, l. 8 and note.

15. *Tonyes*. 'Tony' is a particular application of 'Antony': 'a silly Fellow, or Ninny' (*Dict. Canting Crew, c.* 1695). Cf. Prologue, &c., to *The Kind Keeper*, note.

22. *Hectors*: swashbucklers. 'I have seen danger in my life time. . . . I knew the Hectors, and before them the *Muns* and the *Titire Tu's*, they were brave fellows indeed; in those days a man could not go from the *Rose Tavern* to the *Piazza* once, but he must venture his life twice' (Shadwell, *The Scowrers*, 1691, I). Cf. Luttrell, iii. 2: 'On Sunday night last 3 hectors came out of a tavern in Holborn, with their swords drawn, and began to break windows, &c., which a watchman observing, desired them to desist; but one of them . . . run him thro'.' See Prologue to *The Wild Gallant Reviv'd*, ll. 10–12, note.

Epilogue. 17. *Mr. Bays*, representing Dryden, the chief butt of *The Rehearsal* (1672). Cf. Epilogue to *The Man of Mode*, l. 14, note; *To Sir George Etherege*, ll. 74–77; and Dedication of *The Satires of Juvenalis*, l. 172. In *The Vindication of the Duke of Guise* (1683) Dryden says: 'Much less am I concern'd at the noble name of *Bayes*: that's a *Brat* so like his own Father, that he cannot be mistaken for any other body: they might as reasonably have call'd *Tom Sternhold, Virgil*, and the resemblance would have held as well.'

19. *Writ of Ease*. See Epilogue to *The Wild Gallant Reviv'd*, l. 38, note.

Prologue to A True Widow. A Comedy
(Page 166)

Shadwell's *A True Widow* was published in 1679 by Benjamin Tooke, with an Epistle Dedicatory to Sedley dated 16 February 1678/9. The date of the first performance is uncertain. In Act I Lump, 'a methodical Blockhead, as regular as a Clock', announces with a glance at his journal that 'Upon the one and twentieth of *March*, I shall fifty years hence, dine with Mr. *Ananias Felt*'. This passage seems to date the first performance, and has some support in the topical allusion in the Prologue, ll. 13–14. But Shadwell speaks in the Dedication of the ill success of his play partly 'through the Calamity of the Time, which made People not care for Diversions', and the Epilogue refers to 'troubled Times, like these'—more probably to the exposure of the Popish Plot in August 1678 (see *Absalom and Achitophel*, ll. 108–9, note) and the excitement over Papists and Exclusion towards the end of the year, than to the political crisis of the spring. Dryden's Prologue was reprinted in 1690; see Prologue and Epilogue to *The History of Bacon in Virginia*, note.

9. *His Cruse ne'r fails*. 1 Kings xvii. 8–16.

13–14. In February 1678 the Commons voted supplies for a French war, but added a prohibition of all imports from France which, in loss of customs revenue, offset the war grant (Marvell, *Letters*, ed. Margoliouth, pp. 207–8; Clark, p. 87).

20. *Muss*: a game in which small objects are thrown down to be scrambled for. Cf. Shakespeare, *Antony and Cleopatra*, III. xiii. 91.

Prologue, Epilogue and Songs from Oedipus: A Tragedy
(Page 167)

Oedipus, by Dryden and Lee (see *To Mr. Lee, on his Alexander*, note), was first performed by the Duke's company at Dorset Garden late in 1678, and published by Bentley and Magnes in 1679 (licensed 3 January and advertised in the *London Gazette*, 10–13 March). This was the second of Dryden's plays performed by the Duke's players (the first was *The Kind Keeper*), and the occasion of a petition presented by the King's company: '. . . Mr Dryden has now jointly with Mr Lee . . . Written a Play call'd Adipus, and given it to the Dukes Company, contrary to his said agreemᵗ, his promise, and all gratitude and to the great prejudice, and almost undoing of the Company, They being the onely Poets remaining to us' (see Nicoll, p. 329).

The Prologue and Epilogue may safely be ascribed to Dryden. In *The Vindication of the Duke of Guise*, 1683 (p. 42), he replies to an accusation '*that I the said* Bays, *wou'd falsly and felloniously, have robb'd* Nat. Lee, *of his share in the Reputation of* Oedipus: Now I am *Culprit*; I writ the first and third Acts . . . and drew the *Scenary* of the *whole Play*'. The second and third songs are therefore probably Dryden's; the first song has at least something of his manner.

Prologue. 1–6. *When Athens*, &c. Cf. Rymer, *The Tragedies of the Last Age Consider'd*, 1678 (licensed 17 July 1677), p. 14: 'And now it was that . . . *Socrates* set up for *Morality*, and all the buz in *Athens* was now about vertue and good life. *Camerades* with him, and Confederates in his worthy design, were our *Sophocles* and *Euripides*.'

7–12. *Then, Oedipus, &c.* Cf. Preface to the play: '. . . both the *Prologue* and *Epilogue* inform'd you, that *Oedipus* was the most celebrated Piece of all Antiquity. That *Sophocles*, not only the greatest Wit, but one of the greatest Men in *Athens*, made it for the Stage, at the Publick Cost; and that it had the Reputation of being his Master-piece.'

25–26. *though at Mons you won, &c.* On 17 August 1678 'the Prince of Orange . . . marched to the attack of the French army, which blockaded Mons, and lay secured by the most formidable entrenchments. . . . The English and Scottish regiments, under the gallant earl of Ossory, had their full share in the glory of the day. . . . The enterprize . . . though successful, was needless as well as desperate, and merited Dryden's oblique censure' (Scott).

36. *The first Play bury'd since the Wollen Act.* An act of 1678 (30 Car. II, cap. iii) required burial shrouds to be made only of wool, as a means of promoting the industry (Ogg, i. 72).

Epilogue. 5–6. The weaknesses of Seneca's *Oedipus* and Corneille's *Oedipe* are discussed in the Preface to the play. 'The *French-man* followed a wrong Scent; and the *Roman* was absolutely at cold Hunting.'

19–20. *As some strong Churle, &c.* Cromwell is said to have removed the Black Prince's sword from its scabbard over the tomb in Canterbury Cathedral (cf. William Gostling, *Walk in . . . the City of Canterbury*, 1774 edition, p. 159).

32. *Charm! Song! and Show!* Cf. Prologue to *The Rival-Ladies*, l. 11, note.

34. *burning of a Pope.* See Prologue to *The Loyal Brother*, ll. 18–40, note.

Songs. I. *Song to Apollo*: Act II. Tiresias asks Manto to 'charm this God, this Fury in my Bosom . . . with pow'rful strains'.

II: Act III. These lines are printed as dialogue between Tiresias and the priests, but are clearly a chant if not a sung lyric. The sacrifice concludes in thunder and lightning, 'then groaning below the Stage'. The infernal gods are given the additional offering of Song III.

III: Act III. A stage direction follows: 'The Ghost of *Lajus* rises arm'd in his Chariot, as he was slain. And behind his Chariot sit the three who were murder'd with him.' Purcell set this song for a revival in 1692 (Day, p. 158). 43–44. *Demogorgon's name, at which Ghosts quake.* Cf. Spenser, *The Faerie Queene*, I. I. xxxvii:

> Great *Gorgon*, Prince of darknesse and dead night,
> At which *Cocytus* quakes, and *Styx* is put to flight.

Prologue, Epilogue and Song from Troilus and Cressida, or, Truth Found too Late. A Tragedy

(Page 172)

Troilus and Cressida was first performed at Dorset Garden in the spring of 1679 and published by Tonson later that year (*SR*, 14 April; *TC*, November).

On the edition of *c*. 1692 (dated 1679) see Macdonald, p. 121. Dryden's association with Tonson begins with the publication of this play.

Prologue. Thomas Betterton (? 1635–1710), who played Troilus and spoke the Prologue, was the leading actor in the company. '*Betterton* is the Centre to which all my Observations upon Action tend. . . . I never heard a Line in Tragedy come from *Betterton*, wherein my Judgment, my Ear, and my Imagination, were not fully satisfy'd. . . . Had it been practicable to have ty'd down the clattering Hands of all the ill judges who were commonly the Majority of an Audience, to what amazing Perfection might the *English* Theatre have arrived, with so just an Actor as *Betterton* at the Head of it' (Cibber, pp. 92–93). See R. W. Lowe, *Thomas Betterton*, 1891.

17–32. *Now, where are the Successours to my name*, &c. Cf. Prologue to *The Kind Keeper*, ll. 1–10.

27–29. *The fulsome clench*, &c. Cf. the criticism in *Of Dramatick Poesie, An Essay* (Ker, i. 31–33), of the poet who 'does . . . perpetually pay us with Clenches upon Words and a certain clownish kind of Raillery . . . the envy of a great Person, who is Lord in the Art of Quibling'; Dedication of *The Satires of Juvenalis*, ll. 2192–6 and note.

38–40. *How Trojan valour*, &c. Cf. Dedication of the *Æneis*, ll. 518–22.

Epilogue. Thersites was played by 'Roaring Mad *Cave*' Underhill, 'a correct, and natural Comedian' who again showed 'all that true perverse Spirit, that is commonly seen in much Wit, and Ill-nature' as Sir Sampson in *Love for Love* (Cibber, pp. 128–9).

7. *a keeping Pit.* Cf. Prologue to *All for Love*, l. 15, and Prologue, &c., to *The Kind Keeper*, note.

24. *wit in Spain.* Cf. *An Evening's Love* (1671), I. ii: 'I perceive the Women understand little of discourse; their Gallants do not use them to it: they get upon their Gennits, and prance before their Ladies Windows. . . . And this Horse-play they call making love.'

26. *John Lilbourn* (1614?–57), at his trial for sedition in 1649, appealed to the jury as judges of the law whose verdict the court judges were 'no more but cyphers to pronounce' (*DNB*).

Song. Act III, Sc. ii: sung by hired musicians, at Pandarus's command, to the sleeping Troilus and Cressida. For Thomas Farmer's setting in *Choice Ayres and Songs*, 1681, see Day, p. 55.

Prologue, Epilogue and Songs from The Kind Keeper; or, Mr. Limberham: A Comedy

(Page 174)

The Kind Keeper was first performed at Dorset Garden on 11 March 1678 (LC 5/145, p. 120), the first of Dryden's plays to be given by the Duke's company (see Prologue, &c., to *Oedipus*, note). In the Epistle Dedicatory Dryden says the play was printed 'in my Absence from the Town, this Summer'; but he speaks of its publication 'at so unseasonable a time, when the Great Plot of the Nation, like one of *Pharaoh*'s Lean Kine, has devour'd its younger Brethren of the Stage', and that cannot have been earlier than the autumn (see *Absalom and Achitophel*, ll. 108–9, note). The play 'was intended for an honest *Satyr* against our crying sin of *Keeping* [a mistress]; how it would have succeeded, I can but guess, for it was permitted to be acted only thrice. The Crime for which it suffer'd, was . . . that it express'd too much of the Vice which it decry'd.' See Macdonald, pp. 121–2, 250; Prologue to *Cæsar Borgia*, ll. 7–10.

Prologue. 1–10. *True Wit has seen its best days*, &c. Cf. Prologue to *Troilus and Cressida*, ll. 17–32.

2. *dipt in Show*: immersed in debt by expensive theatrical productions. Cf. Prologue to *The Rival-Ladies*, ll. 11–12, notes; Epilogue to *The Indian-Queen*; and the MS. Prologue to the operatic version of *The Tempest* (Shadwell, *Works*, ed. Summers, ii. 196). 'This sensual Supply of Sight and Sound, coming in to the Assistance of the weaker Party, it was no Wonder they should grow too hard for Sense and simple Nature. . . . Of which Encroachment upon Wit, several good Prologues in those Days frequently complain'd' (Cibber, pp. 79–80).

3. *Sense in . . . Clouds was lost.* For illustrations of the use of clouds in elaborate productions, see Nicoll, pp. 44–49.

8–9. *our Machining Lumber*, &c. Cf. *Miscellany Poems* (1684), 'A Prologue spoken at the Opening of the New House', notes. Line 9 probably refers to Shadwell's *Psyche*, 1675, elaborately designed 'to entertain the Town with variety of Musick, curious Dancing, splendid Scenes and Machines' including settings for heaven and hell in Act v. Cf. *Mac Flecknoe*, ll. 53–54, note.

27–28. *But drive away that Swarm*, &c. Exod. x. 19.

Epilogue. The 'tame, foolish Keeper' Limberham is betrayed by his 'Termagant kept Mistress' Mrs. Tricksy, but marries her in the end 'to give good Example to all Christian Keepers'. Woodall is a rake: 'I have beheld a handsom Woman at a Play, I am fall'n in love with her, and have found her easie . . . and hither I am come to accomplish my design' (Act I). Cf. Prologue to *All for Love*, l. 15, and Epilogue to *Troilus and Cressida*, l. 7.

18. *Pugs like mine.* 'Pug' is Limberham's term of endearment for Mrs. Tricksy, but here he turns to its other sense: '*Saffrette* . . . a flirt, queane, gixie, pug, punke' (Cotgrave).

20. *Counters*: compters, debtors' prisons. *Padders*: footpads.

22. *A Smithfield Horse*, &c. Cf. Shakespeare, *2 Henry IV*, I. ii. 55, and Moryson, *Itinerary* (1617), III. i. 3: 'The Londoners pronounce woe to him, that buys a Horse in Smyth-field, that takes a Servant in Pauls Church, that marries a Wife out of Westminster' (Tilley, W276).

Songs. I: Act I, sung by Mrs. Tricksy and Judith. II: Act III.

Ovid's Epistles, Translated by Several Hands

(Page 178)

This volume was first published by Tonson in 1680 (advertised in February and March; Macdonald, p. 17) and 'with the Addition of a New *Epistle*' in 1681. The title-page epigraph is

> vel tibi composita cantetur epistola voce;
> ignotum hoc aliis ille novavit opus

(*De Arte Amandi*, iii. 345–6). Among the fourteen contributors were Dryden and Mulgrave, Tate, Mrs. Behn, Otway, Rymer, Settle, and Butler. For these and his other translations from Ovid, Dryden may have used the edition by Heinsius (1652) and certainly used Borchard Cnipping's variorum edition (Amsterdam, 1670) in which Heinsius's work was incorporated. See J. M. Bottkol, 'Dryden's Latin Scholarship', *MP* xl (1943), 241–55.

The Preface. 1–3. George Sandys's *Ovid's Metamorphosis Englished, Mythologiz'd and Represented in Figures* first appeared in 1626. Cf. Dedication of *Examen Poeticum*, ll. 227–38, and Preface to *Fables*, ll. 26–28.

14. *no man has ever treated the Passion of Love,* &c. Cf. *Annus Mirabilis*, 'An account of the ensuing Poem', ll. 120–38, Dedication of the *Æneis*, ll. 1065–75, and Preface to *Fables*, ll. 269 ff.

18. *a certain Epigram.* Martial, xi. 20.

22. *that Authours Life,* by Suetonius.

26–28. 'Tandem cum venisset in suspicionem Augusti, creditus sub nomine Corinnæ amasse Juliam, in exilium missus est' (Cnipping's *Ovid*, 1683 ed., i. *6ᵛ).

31–32. *his Petition to Isis: Amores*, II. xiii.

38. *Ovid himself complains,* in *Amores*, III. xii. 7–12.

42–46. *in those obscure Verses,* &c. *Tristia*, II. 103. 'De causa relegationis Ovidii multi multa scripsere; in quibus non deest, qui credat eum vidisse ejus [Augusti] incestum cum filia Julia' (Cnipping).

56. *Sine veste Dianam. Tristia*, II. 105.

58–60. *The first Verses,* &c. *Amores*, III. xii. 13–18.

67–68. *all his Poems bear the Character of a Court,* &c. Cf. Preface to *Fables*, ll. 219 ff.

73–74. *a particular Account of his own Life. Tristia*, IV. x. 43–54.

97. *Seneca's Censure.* M. Annaeus Seneca, *Controversiæ*, IX. v. 17.

119. *Purpureus,* &c. *De Arte Poetica*, ll. 15–16.

128. *Heinsius has Judg'd,* in his introductory note to *Heroides*, where the epigraph of *Ovid's Epistles, Translated* is quoted.

134. *in his Art of Love,* i. 713.

140. *Quam celer,* &c. *Amores*, II. xviii. 27–28.

142–4. *Propertius,* iv. 3; cited in Heinsius's note to *Heroides*.

150–1. *he has Romaniz'd his Grecian Dames too much.* But cf. Preface to *Sylvæ*, ll. 31–32; Dedication of *The Satires of Juvenalis*, ll. 2694 ff.; and Dedication of the *Æneis*, ll. 2007–9.

167. *Horace . . . translated by Ben. Johnson.* Jonson's version, first printed 1640, was included in Alexander Brome's variorum *Poems of Horace*, 1666, 1671, 1680. Roscommon criticizes Jonson's literalism in the Preface to *Horace's Art of Poetry*, 1680. Cf. Johnson, *The Idler*, No. 69.

174–5. *to run division on the ground-work*: to execute a variation or descant of short notes based on a simpler passage of longer notes.

175. *Mr. Cowleys practice.* 'If a man should undertake to translate *Pindar* word for word, it would be thought that one *Mad man* had translated *another*. . . . I have in these two *Odes* of *Pindar*, taken, left out, and added what I please; nor make it so much my aim to let the Reader know precisely what he spoke, as what was his *way* and *manner* of speaking' (Cowley, Preface to *Pindarique Odes*, 1668).

177–312. With this discussion of the art of translation, cf. Preface to *Sylvæ*, ll. 20 ff.; Dedication of *Examen Poeticum*, ll. 216–38; and Dedication of the *Æneis*, ll. 1948 ff.

179. *Nec verbum*, &c. De *Arte Poetica*, ll. 133–4.

183–4. *the Expression of Sir John Denham.* Denham's verses were first printed in Fanshawe's *Il Pastor Fido; the Faithful Shepheard*, 1647. Dryden quotes ll. 15–16, 21–24.

197. *Atque ijdem*, &c. Heroid. vii. 8, translated below, '*Dido to Æneas*', l. 9.

211. *Brevis esse laboro*, &c. De *Arte Poetica*, ll. 25–26.

215. *Dic mihi*, &c. De *Arte Poetica*, ll. 141–2.

222–5. On Cowley see *supra*, l. 175, note. In the Preface to *The Destruction of Troy* (1656), a version of part of *Aeneid*, ii, Denham says: 'I conceive it a vulgar error in translating Poets, to affect being *Fidus Interpres*; let that care be with them who deal in matters of Fact, or matters of Faith: but whosoever aims at it in Poetry, as he attempts what is not required, so he shall never perform what he attempts; for it is not his business alone to translate Language into Language, but Poesie into Poesie.' Dryden quotes the next part of the Preface *infra*, ll. 259–62.

244–5. *A Genius so Elevated and unconfin'd as Mr. Cowley's.* Cf. Preface to *Sylvæ*, ll. 384 ff.; Dedication of *The Satires of Juvenalis*, ll. 2554–8; Dedication of the *Æneis*, ll. 2037 ff.; Preface to *Fables*, ll. 313 ff.; A. H. Nethercot, 'The Reputation of Abraham Cowley (1660–1800)', *PMLA* xxxviii (1923), 588–641.

267–71. *No man is capable*, &c. Cf. Preface to *Sylvæ*, ll. 63–74.

300. *Et quae*, &c. Horace, *De Arte Poetica*, ll. 149–50.

315. *That of Oenone to Paris*, by Aphra Behn. It is accompanied in the second edition by a version from John Cooper. See Prior, 'A Satire on the Modern Translators', *Dialogues*, ed. Waller, 1907, p. 49.

Canace to Macareus. Heroid. xi. The 'Argument' follows Cnipping. Lines 39–42 are added to Ovid.

Helen to Paris. Heroid. xvii. On Mulgrave see *Absalom and Achitophel*, l. 877, note.

Dido to Æneas. Heroid. vii. 115–16. *His Goddess Mother*, &c. A cryptic translation of Ovid, ll. 107–8:

> diva parens seniorque pater, pia sarcina nati,
> spem mihi mansuri rite dedere viri.

Prologue to Cæsar Borgia; Son of Pope Alexander the Sixth: A Tragedy
(Page 204)

Cæsar Borgia, by Nathaniel Lee (see *To Mr. Lee, on his Alexander*, note), was first performed at Dorset Garden in the autumn of 1679 and published by Bentley and Magnes in 1680.

7–8. *That fumbling Lecher*, &c. A recollection of the fate of *The Kind Keeper* (see Prologue, &c., to that play, note).

9–10. *Name but a Cuckold*, &c. Cf. Epilogue to *Marriage A-la-Mode*, l. 32. From Leaden Hall at the eastern end of Cornhill to Ludgate Hill in the west covers the City area. Ludgate Hill became an important trading centre after the Great Fire.

19. *The Bell that toll'd alone*, &c. I cannot identify these as specific references. But the miraculous ringing of bells is a familiar prodigy. Cf. Chaucer, *Troilus and Criseyde*, iii. 188–9,

> Withouten hond, me semeth that in towne,
> For this merveille, ich here ech belle sowne,

and F. N. Robinson's note on these lines. Stranded whales were often regarded as ominous: cf. *Heroique Stanza's*, ll. 137–40, note.

22. *One Theatre there is*, &c. The Court of Requests was held by the Lord Privy Seal for the relief of persons petitioning the king. Cf. North, p. 225: 'It was observable of *Oates*, that . . . he never failed to give his attendance in the Court of Requests and the Lobbies, to solicite hard in all Points, under deliberation, that might terminate in the Prejudice of the Church, Crown, or of any Gentlemen of the Loyal or Church of *England* Party.'

41–42. *But mark their Feasts*, &c. See Prologue to *The Loyal Brother*, ll. 18–40, note.

Prologue to The Loyal General, A Tragedy
(Page 205)

The Loyal General, by Nahum Tate (see *The Second Part of Absalom and Achitophel*, note), was first performed at Dorset Garden at the end of 1679 and published by Henry Bonwicke in 1680.

1–7. *If yet there be a few*, &c. Cf. Shadwell, Prologue to *The Woman-Captain* (performed *c*. September 1679):

> For News he now walks gravely up and down,
> And every Fop's a Politician grown,
> Instead of ――――
> Pox here's no Company, let's to *White-hall*,
> Or to the Park, or where is there a Ball?
> What News! ha' ye been at *Westminster* to day?
> How move the *French*? what do the great Ones say?
>
> .   .   .   .
>
> Each Coffee-house is fill'd with subtle folk,
> Who wisely talk, and politickly smoke.

The shrove-tide Crew: merrymakers, particularly apprentices, whose traditional holiday it was.

10. *Dancing on the Rope*: a popular entertainment at Bartholomew Fair (see Epilogue *spoken at Mithridates King of Pontus*, ll. 9–13, note).

11. *the Devil and the Pope*. See Prologue to *The Loyal Brother*, ll. 18–40, note.

16–17. 'The poets rebel against sense and criticism, like the parliament, in 1641, against the king; and . . . the audience judge as ill as those, who, in 1648, condemned Charles to the block. The parallel between the political disputes in 1680, and 1681, and those which preceded the great civil war, was fashionable among the Tories. A Whig author . . . complains [1680], "It hath been all the clamour of late, *forty-one, forty-one* is now coming to be acted over again" ' (Scott).

22–25. *Weak Stomacks with a long Disease*, &c. Cf. Prologue to *Albion and Albanius*, ll. 11–18, and Shadwell, Epilogue to *The Woman-Captain*:

> Good sence, like solid Meat to sickly Men,
> As soon as swallowed, is thrown up agen;
>
> .   .   .   .
>
> Remembring how you used that last he writ, ⎫
> He made this Low, so to your Level fit; ⎪
> Plenty of Noise, and scarcity of Wit― ⎬
> The Devil's in you all, if this don't hit. ⎭

Prologue and Songs from The Spanish Fryar or, The Double Discovery

(Page 206)

The Spanish Fryar was first performed at Dorset Garden on 8 March 1680 (LC 5/145, p. 120) and published by Tonson in 1681 (advertised in the *True Protestant Mercury*, 9–12 March). Some political allusions were omitted in the second edition (licensed 30 March 1686), and Prologue, ll. 12–13, were dropped (it was in January 1686 that Dryden and his family were said to be attending Mass; see *The Hind and the Panther*, introductory note). James II prohibited the play on 8 December 1686 (Nicoll, p. 10). See further L. I.

Bredvold, 'Political Aspects of Dryden's *Amboyna* and *The Spanish Fryar*', University of Michigan Publications, viii (1932), 119–32. The Epilogue was contributed 'By a Friend of the Author's', Robert Wolseley.

Prologue. 9. *like brass mony once a year in Spain.* Probably a reference to the chronic instability of the copper *vellon*, which provoked much discussion of economic reform in seventeenth-century Spain. See E. J. Hamilton, *American Treasure and the Price Revolution in Spain 1501–1650*, 1934, pp. 73–103 and 211–21.

11. The Tories 'styled the adversary *Birmingham* Protestants, alluding to false Groats counterfeited at that Place. This held a considerable Time; but the word was not fluent enough for hasty Repartee; and, after diverse Changes, the Lot fell upon *Whig*' (North, p. 321). Cf. *Absalom and Achitophel*, 'To the Reader', ll. 8–9; *Heraclitus Ridens*, No. 29, 16 August 1681: 'a *true* blue right *Bromidgham Whig*, is a certain kind of Antimonarchical Animal . . . the greatest Grievance of the Nation . . . the Enemy of Peace, the Bellows of Sedition, the Forge of Lies, Calumnies, and Detraction . . .'.

21. *notcht Prentices whole Sermons write.* Notcht: with closely cropped hair. Prentices commonly took notes of the sermon for their masters. Cf. Mrs. Marwood in Congreve, *The Way of the World*, 1700, v: 'What, and have your Name prostituted in a publick Court; . . . And then to have my young Revellers of the *Temple* take Notes, like Prentices at a *Conventicle.* . . .'

26. *Mum*: a beer originally brewed in Brunswick.

39. *Scowring the Watch.* Cf. Prologue to *The Wild Gallant Reviv'd*, ll. 10–12, note; Prologue to *All for Love*, l. 22, note.

40. *Tilting in the Pit.* On violent quarrels in the theatres see Summers, *The Restoration Theatre*, pp. 77–81, and Nicoll, pp. 17–19. Cf. Epilogue *To the King and Queen*, ll. 29–34.

43–45. Assaults and assassinations were not uncommon; but Dryden probably alludes to the attack on himself in Rose Alley on 18 December 1679 (see Macdonald, p. 218; *Absalom and Achitophel*, l. 877, note).

46. *the new found Pois'ning Trick of France.* The *Chambre Ardente* had condemned the Marquise de Brinvilliers for poisoning four of her family in 1676, and Catherine Deshayes, La Voisin, had been executed in February 1680. Cf. Prologue to *The Duke of Guise*, l. 15.

Songs. I: Act I. II: Act v, sung to the queen as 'the Song which poor *Olympia* made | When false *Bireno* left her' (see *Orlando Furioso*, x). The original music by Captain Pack is in BM Add. MS. 19759, f. 20ᵛ (Day, p. 59). For reprints see Day, p. 160, and Macdonald, p. 123.

Epilogue to Tamerlane the Great. A Tragedy

(Page 209)

Charles Saunders had been, like Dryden, a King's Scholar at Westminster, and was elected to Trinity College, Cambridge, in 1680. *Tamerlane the Great,* apparently his only play, was first performed at Drury Lane in the spring of 1681 and published by Bentley and Magnes soon after (*TC*, May 1681). Saunders says in his Preface that he did not venture to send the play 'forth into the World, until it had past the Censures of some (I may say) the greatest part of the Witty and Judicious Men of the Town; untill it had receiv'd some Rules for Correction from Mr. *Dryden* himself, who also was pleas'd to Grace it with an Epilogue, to which it ows no small part of its success'. See also *The Epilogue Spoken to the King . . . at Oxford*, note.

3. *A Woman Wit*: Mrs. Aphra Behn, who by early 1681 had written a dozen plays.

7. *Thus Cowley Blossom'd soon*. On the precocity of Cowley, who published *Poetical Blossomes* (1633) when he was 15, see Johnson, i. 3–4. With 'extraordinary hopes', says Sprat in his account of Cowley, 'he was remov'd to *Trinity* Colledge in *Cambridge*, where by the progress and continuance of his Wit, it appear'd that . . . it was both early-ripe and lasting'.

The Epilogue Spoken to the King at the opening the Play-House at Oxford on Saturday last. Being March the Nineteenth 1681

(Page 210)

There are two 1681 versions of this poem: (i) a single half-sheet with no imprint, the only known copy of which was found in Christ Church Library by W. G. Hiscock ('A Dryden Epilogue', *TLS*, 5 March 1931); (ii) a single half-sheet with the imprint '*LONDON*, Printed for *Rich. Royston*'. It was reprinted in *The Works of Tom Brown*, 1708, iii. 96, with the reading 'And you both Audience and Actors are' in l. 8. The Christ Church edition has the best claim to authority. It may have been printed at Oxford by L. Lichfield, jun. (see Mr. Hiscock's type facsimile, 1932) just after the occasion of the Epilogue, and is a better text than Royston's. The poem was written for a special performance of *Tamerlane the Great* (see *supra*, note), the first play presented at Oxford during the king's stay (*True Protestant Mercury*, 19–23 March 1681). Charles arrived on Monday, 14 March, and opened the critical Oxford Parliament on the following Monday. On Dryden's Prologues at Oxford see Macdonald, pp. 137–9.

2. *Species*: reflected images.

The Prologue at Oxford, 1680

(Page 211)

Sophonisba (see *To Mr. Lee, on his Alexander*, note) was first performed at Drury Lane in April 1675 and published in 1676. Dryden's prologue, first printed with the second edition of the play (*TC*, May 1681) was apparently spoken at an Oxford revival in 1680. It has usually been assumed that the text printed in *Miscellany Poems* (1684) is a revised version, elaborating the satiric references to the Popish Plot. But ll. 21–24 are quite inappropriate to *Sophonisba*; and it is probable that the version in *Miscellany Poems* was written for an Oxford performance of Settle's *The Female Prelate: being The History of the Life and Death of Pope Joan* (performed at Drury Lane in the autumn of 1679 and published in 1680), later adapted—not altogether satisfactorily— to introduce *Sophonisba*. The date 1680 in *Miscellany Poems* is a little difficult; it is unlikely that both plays and both versions of the Prologue were given at Oxford in the same 'Act'.

1–6. *Thespis*, &c. Horace, *De Arte Poetica*, ll. 275–80.

8. *Tossing Poets in a Tennis-Court*. Tennis courts were regularly used for dramatic performances at Oxford at this time (see Macdonald, p. 139; Sybil Rosenfeld in *RES* xix (1943), 366–75).

18. *The Oxford Bells*: a short poem printed in *Wit and Drollery* (1682) and elsewhere, and attributed to Henry Aldrich (1648–1710), later Dean of Christ Church.

22. *Pope Joan*: the mythical female occupant of the papal chair as John VIII. See Döllinger, *Papstfabeln des Mittelalters*, 1863.

25. *Swarez*: the Jesuit author of *Defensio Fidei Catholicæ adversus Anglicanæ Sectæ Errores* (1613), which had been answered from Oxford by a former Jesuit Andrew Sall in *The True Catholic and Apostolic Faith maintain'd* (1676).

Prologue and Epilogue spoken at Mithridates King of Pontus
(Page 212)

Lee's *Mithridates*, for which Dryden had written an epilogue in 1678, was revived at Drury Lane in the autumn of 1681 (the *Impartial Protestant Mercury*, 28 October). The Prologue and Epilogue were published on a single half-sheet, printed on both sides, by J. Sturton. Luttrell's copy, now in the Huntington Library, is dated 13 February 1681/2. He ascribes both poems to Dryden. The Ashley Library copy is also marked 'J. Dryden' (Macdonald, p. 141).

The printed text is not wholly satisfactory, and Luttrell made a number of marginal alterations to his copy. J. H. Smith ('Dryden's Prologue and Epilogue to *Mithridates*, Revived', *PMLA* lxviii (1953), 251–67) argues that since most of these changes are 'demonstrably better' than the printed version, and Luttrell did not habitually improve texts in this way, he must have believed that his alterations brought Sturton's text closer to what Dryden wrote. Mr. Smith suggests that Sturton printed from a shorthand version taken in the theatre, and that Luttrell was given access by his friend Tonson to 'a MS. on which Dryden had made some revisions' for a miscellany. But although Luttrell's corrections must have been made from a copy (either broadside or manuscript) which he believed to be more authoritative than Sturton's, that copy was not necessarily Dryden's; and Luttrell, once embarked on the correction of a bad text, is not above suspicion of having introduced alterations of his own. Some of his marginalia seem the work of an improver other than the author, toning expressions down (Prologue, l. 12; Epilogue, ll. 21, 30), changing to a more obvious or commonplace word (Prologue, ll. 6, 32; Epilogue, ll. 3, 15), avoiding an effective alliteration for an easier phrase (Prologue, l. 18), and unnecessarily altering rhythm (Prologue, ll. 21 and 41). But some of his changes must clearly be accepted: Epilogue, ll. 6 (correcting what is probably a slip in reading ll. 5–8), 14 (see note), 17 (restoring a less obvious and—in the context—more appropriate word), 22, 23 (Sturton has followed with the conventional 'Servant', upsetting the metre), and l. 40.

Prologue. 1–3. *After a four Months Fast*, &c. Cf. Prologue to *The Loyal General*, ll. 22–25 and note.

4. *As honest . . . as an Addresse*. At this time 'address' was commonly applied to a Tory paper presented to the king; the Whig equivalent was a 'petition'. Cf. *Absalom and Achitophel*, ll. 981–8; Prologue to *The Loyal Brother*, l. 7, note; and Epilogue to *Constantine the Great*, l. 8: D'Urfey, Prologue to *The Royallist* (1682): the Tory

> . . . loves his Prince and Country at his Heart;
> *Addresses* loves, to all Mankind is civil;
> But hates *Petitions* as he hates the Devil.

10–12. *the fruitful Bath*, &c. After Queen Catherine began visiting Bath and Tunbridge in the hope of curing her sterility, the spas became fashionable. Tunbridge 'is, at the season, the general rendezvous of all the gay and handsome of both sexes'; 'here is . . . no want of amorous intrigues' (Grammont, p. 320). 'Well may [the waters] be called *les eaux de scandale*, for they nearly ruined the good name of the maids and of the ladies . . . who were there without their husbands' (de Cominges; see Jusserand, *A French Ambassador at the Court of Charles II*, pp. 89–90). Cf. *Poetical Miscellanies: The Fifth Part* (1704), 'Upon Four New Physicians Repairing to *Tunbridge* Wells' (p. 305).

16. *grabble*: grope, fondle.

17. *Brothers of the Switch*: professional jockeys, who had followed the king back from Newmarket in October.

19. *Devil's Ditch*: an obstacle on the Newmarket course (J. H. Smith).

26–30. *The Plot's removed*, &c. Oates moved from Whitehall to the City in August 1681 (see *Absalom and Achitophel*, l. 632, note) and was said to have taken lodgings with a Quaker in Lombard Street. 'Since the *Salamanca* Dr's removal into the City, the *Whigs* are so generous in their Supplies, that Pigs, Geese, and Capons fly in at his Windows . . . nay, his Magick is so great, that it hath attracted two Infants in their Swadling-Cloaths to lie at his Door. . . . The one will be Christen'd *Titus*, and the other *Oates*' (the *Loyal Protestant Mercury*, 10 and 20 September; Lane, pp. 278–9).

37. *Irish Cattle.* The act against importing Irish cattle (1666) had been renewed, apparently not without protest, in 1681. Dryden's reference is to Irish informers (see *Absalom and Achitophel*, l. 1012, note, and *The Medall*, 'Epistle to the Whigs', l. 129, note).

41. *Jack Ketch*: the hangman.

Epilogue. Cardell Goodman was, by the end of 1681, the principal actor in the King's company, but he ruined himself with debauchery and crime. Elizabeth Cox played Indamora in *Aureng-Zebe* (1675), but seems to have left the stage soon afterwards, and her return celebrated in this Epilogue was not lasting. Goodman's opening lines reflect the sorry condition of the King's players, who gave up their struggle in April 1682 and signed articles of union with the Duke's company.

7. *Would Salamancha was a little nigher.* See *Absalom and Achitophel*, ll. 657–9, note.

9–13. *Have you not seen*, &c. These were popular entertainments at Bartholomew Fair. *Andrew*, a buffoon: cf. *Miscellany Poems* (1684), Epilogue, 'No Poor *Dutch* Peasant . . .', l. 11, note; Prologue to *Cleomenes*, ll. 11–12. *Was clean run off the Score*: had exceeded his credit with the onlookers. Jacob Hall was a celebrated rope-dancer, 'a mighty strong man' whose performance was 'a thing worth seeing, and mightily followed' (Pepys, *Diary*, 29 August and 21 September 1668).

14. *perk't up.* Sturton's reading is an error. Cf. Prologue to The Second Part of *The Conquest of Granada*, l. 15, a courtly version of the animal interest displayed at Bartholomew Fair.

22. *Nump's i'th' Stocks.* In Jonson's *Bartholomew Fair*, v. iv, Cokes derides Humphrey Waspe, who has been punished in the stocks, with 'O *Numps*, i' the Stocks, *Numps*?' Mrs. Cox is a 'numps', a foolish woman, in returning to a collapsing company.

23. Noyes defends the metre of Sturton's line, quoting *An Evening's Love*, III: 'Madam me no Madam, but learn to retrench your words; and say Mam; as Yes Mam, and No Mam . . . Madam! 'tis a year in pronouncing.' But there Dryden distinguishes the contracted form in spelling; and in ll. 28–29 below he rhymes 'Madam' with 'Fathom'.

31. *some Mental Reservation.* Cf. *Heraclitus Ridens*, No. 23, 5 July 1681: 'Nay, if those who call themselves *the true Protestants*, come to preach up Perjury, and teach Men to go to the Devil by the Art of Evasions, Reservations, and putting Interpretations upon Oaths contrary to the literal Sense and Meaning of the Lawgivers, the Devil and the Jesuits may e'en take a Nap, or go hang themselves for want of Employment.'

38. *When Grey-Beards Govern'd*: in 1676, when the company was controlled

by Mohun, Hart, and other old actors, excluded by Goodman and his associates in 1680. See Nicoll, pp. 325, 365–6.

Absalom and Achitophel. A Poem
(Page 215)

On 28 March 1681 Charles II dissolved the Oxford Parliament and threw the Whig opposition into disorder. On 8 April he made a successful appeal to the country by ordering the publication of *His Majesties Declaration To all His Loving Subjects Touching the Causes and Reasons That moved Him to Dissolve the Two last Parliaments.* 'The angry party . . . threatened bloody answers' (see Bryant, pp. 316–18). One of these, *A Letter from a Person of Quality to his Friend,* was answered for the Tories in *His Majesties Declaration Defended: In a Letter to a Friend,* published by 22 June 1681 (*The Observator*) and apparently written by Dryden (see R. G. Ham, 'Dryden as Historiographer-Royal', *RES* xi (1935), 284–98). An important move in the Tory counter-attack was the indictment of the Whig leader Shaftesbury, who was committed to the Tower on a charge of high treason on 2 July and tried on 24 November (see *The Medall,* introductory note). *Absalom and Achitophel,* said to have been undertaken at Charles's own request (see Macdonald, pp. 19 and 323), was in the making during these months of the king's triumph; and it was published by Tonson in mid-November, probably with the design of prejudicing Shaftesbury's trial. Luttrell dated his copy '17th. Novemb. Ex dono Amici Jacobi Tonson. An excellent poem agt ye Duke of Monmouth, Earl of Shaftsbury & that party & in vindication of the King & his friends.' Its effectiveness is indicated both by its running into at least three London editions within four months, and by the number of replies it provoked (Macdonald, pp. 223 ff.).

The application of the story of David, Absalom, and Achitophel to current politics was no novelty. The name Achitophel was used by the Puritans to mark Charles I's political advisers; and the royalists also adapted the story to their own needs. In Henry King's elegy on Charles I, for example, Charles is compared with 'the best of Judah's Kings', and the poet curses the 'mountebanks of State' who have destroyed the people's loyalty 'by Absolon's foul wile' (Saintsbury, iii. 255–67). At the Restoration, many preachers and poets emphasized the obvious parallel between the fortunes of David and those of Charles II (see R. F. Jones, 'The Originality of *Absalom and Achitophel*', *MLN* xlvi (1931), 211–18; cf. *Astræa Redux,* ll. 79–82). As late as 1677 Lee, in complimentary verses on *The State of Innocence,* urged Dryden:

> The troubles of Majestick *CHARLES* set down.
> Not *David* vanquish'd more to reach a Crown.
> Praise Him, as *Cowly* did that *Hebrew* King,
> Thy Theam's as great, do thou as greatly sing.

The growth of the Whig opposition in the 1670's, and the use which the

Whigs made of the Popish Plot and Monmouth 'the Protestant Duke' in the cause of Exclusion, increased the potentialities of the story of David and Absalom as political allegory. The most significant examples are these: (i) *A Letter to His Grace the Duke of Monmouth, this 15th of July, 1680. By a true Lover of his Person and the Peace of this Kingdom,* which describes Shaftesbury's party as 'they that set on Absalom to steal away the hearts of the people from the king' (*Somers Tracts,* viii. 216–19); (ii) D'Urfey's *The Progress of Honesty* (Luttrell's copy is dated 11 October 1680), describing the rebellion against Titus the Second—some of Shaftesbury's followers are given Old Testament names and Shaftesbury himself is 'Hophni', 'Achitophel', or 'chief Advocate for Hell' (see Ian Jack, *Augustan Satire,* 1952, pp. 55–56); and (iii) *Absalom's Conspiracy: Or, The Tragedy of Treason* (1680), a prose half-sheet elaborating the Biblical story as 'a Tragedy, whose Antiquity and Truth do equally recommend it as an Example to all Posterity, and a Caution to all Mankind, to take Care how they imbark in ambitious and unlawful Designs; and ... a particular Caveat to all young Men, to beware of such Counsellors, as the old *Achitophel,* lest, while they are tempted with the Hopes of a Crown, they hasten on their own Destiny, and come to an untimely End' (*Harl. Misc.* vii. 499–500). In addition, Dryden had an example of Biblical allegory in heroic verse, mixing narrative, speeches, and 'characters', in John Caryll's *Naboth's Vinyard: Or, The Innocent Traytor: Copied from the Original of Holy Scripture* (1679).

Many copies of early editions of *Absalom and Achitophel* have identifications of *dramatis personae*—some wildly conjectural—written in the margins; but the first complete key was printed in *The First Part of Miscellany Poems,* 1716. On other keys see Macdonald, pp. 26 and 225–6.

The editions collated here correspond to the items in Macdonald as follows: *A,* Macdonald 12 a; *B,* 12 d; *C,* 12 e i and 12 e ii; *D,* 12 f; *E,* 12 g; *F,* 12 h; *G,* 42 a; *H,* 42 b; *I,* 14 b. Bibliographically, *B* is the second London edition. The type has been partly reset, and the text of ll. 1–522 (sheets B, D, and E) differs considerably from *A* in accidentals, in addition to the variants given here; but for the remainder of the poem *A* and *B* are identical, except that *B* has 'cou'd' for 'coud' (l. 845). Commendatory verses by Lee and Duke first appear in some copies of *B* (see Macdonald, pp. 22–23). *C,* which exists in two states (cf. ll. 9 and 530), is the true second edition 'Augmented and Revised': new lines have been added (180–91 and 957–60) and there are numerous secondary changes. A full collation confirms Macdonald's note that *C, D,* and *E* are closely related and 'must have followed one another very quickly, probably continuously'. A number of common secondary variants place *G, H,* and *I* in a single derivative group. There are two undated Dublin editions, the first apparently set up from *A;* and two Latin translations were published in 1682.

The epigraph is from Horace, *De Arte Poetica,* ll. 361–2.

To the Reader. 4. *Whig and Tory.* 'Whiggamore', later shortened to 'Whigg', was first applied to the Scottish insurgents of 1648 and 1666; and so, in 1679, to the Exclusionists who opposed the succession of the Catholic Duke of York. 'Tory' (Irish *tóraidhe*, a pursuer) was first applied to the dispossessed Irish who plundered the English settlers; later, to any Irish Catholic or royalist in arms; and so, in 1679, to members of the court party who opposed Exclusion. See Burnet, i. 43 and 499.

8–9. *Anti-Bromingham*: Tory. See Prologue to *The Spanish Fryar*, l. 11, note.

11–23. *For there's a sweetness in good Verse*, &c. Cf. Dedication of *The Satires of Juvenalis*, ll. 2116–17, note. With ll. 19–21 cf. Preface to *Religio Laici*, ll. 329–30.

26. *Common-wealths-men.* See *Absalom and Achitophel*, l. 82, note.

52–53. *to hope with Origen*, &c. Origen shows hesitation over the ultimate fate of the evil spirits, though some of his adversaries are said to have accused him of teaching 'diabolum esse salvandum' (Charles Bigg, *The Christian Platonists of Alexandria*, 1913, p. 278). Cf. Browne, *Religio Medici*, i. 7: '[My second error] was that of *Origen*, that God would not persist in his vengeance for ever, but after a definite time of his wrath hee would release the damned soules from torture.' References to Shaftesbury as a rebellious *diabolus* are common. In *Animadversions to the Men of Shaftesbury* (1675) he is 'Mephistopheles, the Faery Fiend that haunts both Houses' (Brown, p. 239). In *The Badger In The Fox Trap, Or A Satyr Upon Satyrs* (Luttrell's copy is dated 8 July 1681) he is said to be called 'Achitophel', 'old Machiavel', and 'Devil'. Cf. *infra*, ll. 373–4; *The Spanish Fryar* (1681), v. ii:

> Raymond. What Treason is it to redeem my King,
> And to reform the State?
> Torrismond. That's a stale Cheat,
> The primitive Rebel, *Lucifer*, first us'd it,
> And was the first Reformer of the Skies.

60. *Ense rescindendum.* Ovid, *Meta.* i. 191.

Absalom and Achitophel. 1–6. *In pious times*, &c. Cf. Donne, *Elegies*, xvii. 38–49:

> How happy were our Syres in ancient times,
> Who held plurality of loves no crime!
> With them it was accounted charity
> To stirre up race of all indifferently . . .

7. *Israel's Monarch, after Heaven's own heart*: Charles II. 1 Sam. xiii. 13–14.

11. *Michal*: Catherine of Braganza, Princess of Portugal (1638–1705), who married Charles II in 1662. 2 Sam. vi. 23.

15. *like slaves*: a sly inversion of the common belief that Charles 'is at the command of any woman like a slave, though he be the best man to the Queene in the world . . . but yet cannot command himself in the presence of a woman he likes' (Pepys, *Diary*, 27 July 1667). Cf. l. 710, note.

17–18. *none So Beautifull, so brave as Absolon.* 2 Sam. xiv. 25. James Scott (1649–85) was the son of Charles II and Lucy Walter or Barlow, 'a Welsh woman of no good fame' (Clarendon). He was created Duke of Monmouth in

1663; and on his marriage that year with Anne, Countess of Buccleuch, he received the additional titles of Duke of Buccleuch and Earl of Dalkeith. He served at sea 1664–6, and won a reputation as a soldier fighting with the French in Holland 1672–3. In the Scottish campaign of 1679 he commanded the king's forces with great personal bravery. 'His figure and the exterior graces of his person were such, that nature perhaps never formed anything more complete. . . . He had a wonderful genius for every sort of exercise, an engaging aspect, and an air of grandeur; in a word, he possessed every personal advantage; but then he was greatly deficient in mental accomplishments. He had no sentiments but such as others inspired him with. . . . All the gay and beautiful of the fair sex were at his devotion. He was particularly beloved by the king; but the universal terror of husbands and lovers' (Grammont, p. 354). Cf. Evelyn, *Diary*, 15 July 1685.

30. *Paradise was open'd in his face.* Cf. Dante, *Paradiso*, xviii. 21, 'Che non pur ne' miei occhi è Paradiso'; Chaucer, *Troilus and Criseyde*, v. 817, 'Paradis stood formed in hire yën'.

34. *Annabel:* Anne, Countess of Buccleuch (1651–1732), a lady of great beauty and 'certainly one of the wisest & craftiest of her sex' (Evelyn, *Diary*, 16 March 1673). Dryden wrote of her in *The Vindication of the Duke of Guise* (1683), as 'the Patroness of my poor unworthy Poetry'. He dedicated *The Indian Emperour* to her in 1667; and in the Dedication of *King Arthur* (1691) he says that she read the play in manuscript and commended it to the queen.

39. *Amnon's Murther.* 2 Sam. xiii. Dryden probably refers to the vicious though not homicidal attack on Sir John Coventry in December 1670, at Monmouth's instigation. See James Kinsley, 'Historical Allusions in *Absalom and Achitophel*', *RES*, N.S., vi (1955), 291–2.

45. *The Jews:* the English.

51–52. *These Adam-wits*, &c. Cf. Milton, *Paradise Lost*, ix. 342–56, xii. 82–90:

> . . . yet know withall,
> Since thy original lapse, true Libertie
> Is lost, which alwayes with right Reason dwells
> Twinnd, and from her hath no dividual being:
> Reason in man obscur'd, or not obeyd,
> Immediatly inordinate desires
> And upstart Passions catch the Government
> From Reason, and to servitude reduce
> Man till then free.

55–56. *They led their wild desires*, &c. Cf. *Astræa Redux*, ll. 43–48, note. In the Epistle Dedicatory to *All for Love* (1678) Dryden expresses 'a loathing to that specious Name of a Republick; That mock-appearance of a Liberty, where all who have not part in the Government, are Slaves. . . . 'Twas indeed the Policy of [the Devil], when himself was fallen from the Station of Glory, to seduce Mankind into the same Rebellion with him, by telling him, he might yet be freer than he was: that is, More free than his Nature would allow. . . .

We have already all the Liberty which Free-born Subjects can enjoy; and all beyond it is but License.'

57–58. *Saul . . . Ishbosheth*: Oliver and Richard Cromwell. 2 Sam. iii–iv.

59. *Hebron*: Scotland. Charles was crowned king of Scots on 1 January 1651, and king of England on 23 April 1661. 2 Sam. v. 1–5.

72. *dishonest*: shameful. Cf. *Æneis*, vi. 668, note.

82. *The Good old Cause reviv'd*. There was a widespread belief that the Whig extremists were working for the restoration of a commonwealth. In 1675 Lord Digby, son of the Earl of Bristol, quarrelled with Shaftesbury and accused him of being 'against the King, and for seditions and factions, and for a commonwealth'. In 1679 Shaftesbury said in Charles's presence that if he were assured of a Protestant succession and might 'enjoy the known rights and liberties of the subjects, he would rather be under kingly government, but if he could not be satisfied of that he declared he was for a Commonwealth' (Brown, pp. 231–2; *HMC Ormonde*, N.S., v. 136). Cf. *The Medall*, l. 317, note.

86. *Jebusites*: Roman Catholics. Joshua xv. 63.

87. *And their's the Native right*. An imitation of the Virgilian hemistich, defended by Cowley as 'a thing that looks so naturally and gracefully' (*Davideis*, i, note 14). But see Dedication of the *Æneis*, ll. 2049–87.

99. *Priests of all Religions are the same*. Cf. *The Hind and the Panther*, iii. 197–8, note.

108–9. *From hence began that Plot*, &c. In August 1678 Ezereel Tonge, rector of St. Michael's, Wood Street, a man 'full of projects and notions' and a fanatical anti-Jesuit, contrived an audience with the king. He carried a narrative of Jesuit conspiracy against Charles, the government, and the Protestant faith. Tonge passed responsibility for his information to his confederate Titus Oates (see ll. 632–81, notes), who appeared before the Privy Council at the end of September with a greatly elaborated account of the Plot. When Parliament assembled on 21 October, committees were appointed to search for evidence and examine witnesses; and the correspondence of Coleman, the Duchess of York's secretary, seemed to confirm Oates's revelations (see Preface to *Religio Laici*, ll. 164–5, note). The Commons resolved that 'there has been and still is a damnable and hellish plot, contrived and carried on by Popish recusants, for the assassinating and murdering the king, and for subverting the government and rooting out and destroying the Protestant religion' (*Journals of the House of Commons*, ix. 530). Between the execution of Coleman on 3 December 1678 and that of Archbishop Plunket on 1 July 1681, more than thirty persons were condemned for complicity in the Plot. In conversations with Burnet in December 1678, Charles agreed 'that the greatest part of the evidence was a contrivance. But he suspected, some had set on *Oates*, and instructed him: And he named the Earl of *Shaftsbury*' (Burnet, i. 437). Cf. ll. 208–13. 'As to the Time, the Faction had the Ascendant of the Government, and the Multitude bore down all before them like a Torrent;

The Witnesses led the Rabble; the Plot-Managers led the Witnesses; and the Devil himself led the Leaders: For they were to pass to their Ends thorough Subornation, Perjury, Hypocrisy, Sacrilege, and Treason' (L'Estrange, *A Brief History*, 1687; Lane, p. 229).

116–17. *Succeeding times*, &c. Cf. *The Hind and the Panther*, iii. 718–22.

118–21. *Th' Egyptian Rites*, &c. Cf. Juvenal, *Sat.* xv. 1–13:

> Quis nescit, Volusi Bithynice, qualia demens
> Aegyptos portenta colat? . . .

Egypt is Catholic France (cf. ll. 281–6). Jibes at Catholic beliefs were common during trials for the Plot: at the trial of the Jesuits in December 1678, Chief Justice Scroggs declared 'They eat their God, they kill their King, and saint the Murtherer' (Pollock, pp. 359–60). Dryden later defended the doctrine of the Real Presence in *The Hind and the Panther*, i. 78–149.

130–1. According to the original revelations of Tonge and Oates, several attempts to shoot Charles had been made by a Benedictine lay brother, Thomas Pickering, and a layman, John Grove. They were brought to trial on 17 December 1678 and condemned to death.

136–41. *as when raging Fevers boyl the Blood*, &c. Cf. *supra*, 'To the Reader', ll. 61–64; *infra*, ll. 809–10 and 923–6.

150. *the false Achitophel*. Anthony Ashley Cooper (1621–83) fought on the royalist side in the Civil War; became one of Cromwell's council of state; and was associated with the invitation to Charles II in 1660. 'Sir Ant: Cooper', wrote Mordaunt to Charles on that occasion, 'is shifting againe and would be well understood of the Generall, but he is too full of trickes' (Brown, p. 96). He was created Baron Ashley in 1661, and became a member of Charles's Cabal in 1670. In 1672 he was made Earl of Shaftesbury and Lord Chancellor. He conducted himself in that office with dignity and—particularly in his judicial functions and in reforming the chancery—with marked success (ll. 186–93). Dismissed in 1673, he moved into opposition; and by 1676 he was established as leader of the 'country party' with a policy of anti-Popery, toleration, the checking of arbitrary government, and the destruction of the French alliance. Cf. Dryden's biographical sketch in *The Medall*, ll. 26–90. He had 'a wonderful faculty in speaking to a popular assembly', and 'a particular talent to make others trust to his judgment, and depend on it: And he brought over so many to a submission to his opinion, that I never knew any man equal to him in the art of governing parties, and of making himself the head of them. . . . He had a wonderful faculty at opposing, and running things down; but had not the like force in building up. . . . His strength lay in the knowledge of *England*, and of all the considerable men in it. He understood well the size of their understandings, and their tempers: And he knew how to apply himself to them so dextrously, that, tho' by his changing sides so often it was very visible how little he was to be depended on, yet he was to the last much trusted by all the discontented party. He was not ashamed to

reckon up the many turns he had made: And he valued himself on the doing it at the properest season, and in the best manner' (Burnet, i. 96–97).

156–8. *Fretted*: ravaged, consumed (cf. Spenser, *The Faerie Queene*, II. ii. 34). *Inform'd*: pervaded, vitalized; cf. Milton, *Paradise Lost*, iii. 593–4:

> Not all parts like, but all alike informd
> With radiant light, as glowing Iron with fire.

The imagery of Dryden's lines is common. Cf. Carew, *Maria Wentworth*, ll. 1–6, and the second *Epitaph on the Lady Mary Villers*, ll. 1–4:

> The purest Soule that e're was sent
> Into a clayie tenement
> Inform'd this dust, but the weake mold
> Could the great guest no longer hold.

In *An Essay upon Satyr* attributed to the Earl of Mulgrave (in circulation 1679; *POAS*, 1702, pp. 181–2), Shaftesbury is described as 'our little *Matchiavel*',

> (That nimblest Creature of the busie kind)
> His Limbs are cripled, and his Body shakes,
> Yet his hard Mind, which all this bustle makes,
> No pity of its poor Companion takes.

> 'Twere Crime in any man but him alone,
> To use a Body so, though 'tis one's own.

163–4. *Great Wits*, &c. Cf. Seneca, *De Tranq. Animi*, xvii. 10, 'nullum magnum ingenium sine mixtura dementiae fuit', following Aristotle, *Problemata*, xxx. 1.

170–1. *that unfeather'd, two Leg'd thing, a Son*, &c. An application of the definition of man, 'a two-legged unfeathered animal', attributed to Plato (Diogenes Laertius, vi. 40). Shaftesbury's son Anthony was born on 16 January 1652, two weeks before Shaftesbury joined the Long Parliament committee for legal reform.

172. *born a shapeless Lump*, &c. Cf. *The Hind and the Panther*, i. 35–36.

175–7. In 1668 England formed the Triple Alliance with Holland and Sweden; but in May 1670 Charles signed the secret Treaty of Dover with Louis XIV. Louis was to provide subsidies for Charles, and Charles undertook to declare himself a Catholic when circumstances permitted, and to join with France against the Dutch. In August he negotiated a secret Anglo-French *traité simulé*, a covering move in which Shaftesbury, Lauderdale, and Buckingham were the dupes. (See Ogg, i. 342–50.) When the war began in 1672 Charles had to try to conciliate public feeling: the country favoured attacks on the mercantile and naval power of Holland, but this enthusiasm was tempered by fear of France, and suspicion grew that the war was a camouflage for arbitrary designs and popery. Shaftesbury shares responsibility with the rest of the Cabal for joining England in the third Dutch war—which Dryden had favoured (see Prologue and Epilogue to *Amboyna*, note)—but hardly for fitting Israel to the foreign yoke of France.

179. *Usurp'd a Patriott's All-attoning Name.* 'Having lost his Honour with his Prince, and Reputation with the best of Men, he cringes, and creeps, and sneaks, to the lowest and basest of the People, to procure himself, among them, an empty, vain-glorious, and undeserved Name, the *Patriot* of his Country' ('The Character of a Disbanded Courtier' (1681), *Harl. Misc.* i. 357). Cf. *infra*, ll. 965–8; Dedication of the *Æneis*, ll. 399–400.

180–91. These lines were added in the second edition. Noyes suggests that since 'their absence occasions an abrupt and awkward transition' they may have been in Dryden's original manuscript 'but omitted, in order to deepen the satire on Shaftesbury', in the first edition; and that l. 179 was then altered 'partially to bridge the gap caused by their omission' (see also the bibliographical discussion in Macdonald, p. 21). Lines 180–91 may indeed have been omitted by mistake in the first printing. But (i) the alteration of l. 179 has no relevance here: Dryden seems merely to have improved the first word and corrected the third. (ii) The transition from l. 179 to l. 192 in the first edition is not 'abrupt and awkward'. In Dryden's view, Shaftesbury went into opposition as a 'patriot' to counteract the impression made by his activities in the Cabal and to serve his own ambition (ll. 175–9), not being content simply to continue his service as Chancellor (ll. 192–3). Lines 180–5 are merely a rhetorical elaboration of ll. 178–9, and ll. 186–91 an explanatory elaboration of ll. 192–3. The effect of the satire is enhanced by the additional lines (see Ian Jack, *Augustan Satire*, 1952, pp. 68–69, note).

188. *Abbethdin*: 'father of the court of justice', one of the two presiding judges of the Jewish civil court. E. S. de Beer suggests that Dryden took the name from Godwin's *Moses and Aaron: Civil and Ecclesiastical Rites, Used by the Ancient Hebrews*, 1625 (*RES* xvii (1941), 303); but the title survived in large Jewish communities in seventeenth-century Europe, notably in Poland.

194–5. *had the rankness of the Soyl been freed From Cockle.* Cf. *Threnodia Augustalis*, ll. 354–5, and Shakespeare, *Coriolanus*, III. i. 67–70: in soothing 'the mutable ranke-sented Meynie'

> we nourish 'gainst our Senate
> The Cockle of Rebellion, Insolence, Sedition,
> Which we our selues haue plowed for, sow'd, and scatter'd,
> By mingling them with vs, the honor'd Number.

196–7. 'David would have sung his praises instead of writing a psalm, and so Heaven would have had one immortal song the less' (Nichol Smith). H. Hammond (*RES*, N.S., v (1954), 60–62) suggests that l. 197 is a specific reference to Psalm cix, which some commentators in the seventeenth century interpreted as 'a direful prediction of Gods judgments' on Absalom and Achitophel.

198–9. *But wilde Ambition*, &c. Macaulay ('Sir William Temple', 1838) quotes a couplet under the portrait of Mustapha I in Knolles's *Historie of the Turkes* (1621, p. 1370):

Greatnesse, on Goodnesse loues to slide, not stand,
And leaues for Fortunes ice, Vertues firm land.

204. *manifest of Crimes*. A latinism. Cf. Sallust, *Bellum Iugurthinum*, xxxv. 8,
'Iugurtha manifestus tanti sceleris' (Christie); *Fables*, 'Palamon and Arcite',
ii. 623.

206. *Held up the Buckler of the Peoples Cause*. Cf. the Epistle Dedicatory to *All
for Love* (1678): 'He who has often chang'd his Party, and always has made
his Interest the Rule of it, gives little Evidence of his Sincerity for the Publick
Good: 'Tis manifest he changes but for himself, and takes the People for
Tools to work his Fortune.'

208. *The wish'd occasion of the Plot he takes*. Shaftesbury, already the leader of
a party committed to the defence of Protestantism, became the chief parliamentary investigator of the Plot. The Whigs patronized Oates and undoubtedly encouraged him in his revelations (see Pollock, pp. 226–9).
Shaftesbury made efforts to spread the Plot to Ireland; and is said to have
remarked: 'I will not say who started the Game, but I am sure I had the full
Hunting of it.' 'I find nothing of his Lordship's Midwifery in the bringing
forth that Discovery; for that seemed left to a lower Order. But it is more than
probable, he was behind the Curtain, and in the Depths of the Contrivance,
and, after the chief Throws were over, he was the Dry-Nurse. . . . A certain
Lord, of his Confidence in Parliament, once asked him what he intended to
do with the Plot, which was so full of Nonsense, as would scarce go down
with *tantum-non* Ideots; what then could he propose by pressing the Belief of
it upon men of Common Sense, and especially in Parliament? Its no Matter,
said he, the more Nonsensical the better; if we cannot bring them to swallow
worse Nonsense than that, we shall never do any Good with them' (North,
p. 95).

216–19. *Prime*: the beginning of a cycle, was confusedly applied to the
'golden number', the number of any year in the lunar cycle of nineteen years
(*OED*). This cycle was accommodated in the Hebrew Calendar. Dryden
refers to English demands for a change of government at intervals of about
nineteen years: the Long Parliament, the Restoration, and the troubles of
1679–81.

220–7. The Exclusionists encouraged the belief that Monmouth was legitimate and the rightful heir to the throne. As early as 1668 Buckingham and
Arlington intrigued to have him declared legitimate; another attempt was
proposed in 1673, when the Commons protested against York's marriage
with Mary of Modena; and rumours of Charles's marriage with Monmouth's
mother were encouraged by the Whigs in the face of a formal denial
by the king on 6 January 1679 (given in D'Oyley, p. 129). Monmouth
was hailed as 'ye great confessor for ye protestant religion' (*Hatton
Correspondence*, i. 194). The author of *A Letter to his Grace the Duke of
Monmouth* (*supra*, introductory note) warned him of 'a sort of Men who have

made it their Business of late to advance you higher than the Wisdom and Favour of the King has made you. We do say they are your Enemies, and seek after your Ruine.' Cf. *The Medall*, l. 317, note.

225. *still depending on the Crowd*. In 1679 a Whig pamphleteer, advocating Monmouth as heir in *An Appeal from the Country to the City*, reminded his readers that 'the old rule is, *He who hath the worst title ever makes the best King*, as being constrained by a gracious Government to supply what he wants in Title: that instead of *God and my right*, his motto may be *God and my people*' (D'Oyley, p. 153).

227. *Drawn to the dregs of a Democracy*. A reminiscence of a couplet in Needham's contribution to *Lachrymæ Musarum* (see *Upon the Death of the Lord Hastings*, note):

> It is decreed, we must be drain'd (I see)
> Down to the dregs of a *Democracie*.

Cf. *The Hind and the Panther*, i. 211.

230–1. *Auspicious Prince*, &c. Cf. *Astræa Redux*, ll. 288–91, note. Dryden may have known that Shaftesbury and Monmouth shared an interest in astrology. Shaftesbury 'had the dotage of Astrology in him to a high degree: He told me, that a *Dutch* doctor had from the stars foretold him the whole series of his life' (Burnet, i. 96). In Monmouth's pocket-book (BM MS. Egerton 1527) is a planetary wheel, dated 1680, with a favourable prediction for 1681 (see D'Oyley, p. 164).

239. *The Young-mens Vision, and the Old mens Dream*. Joel ii. 28.

252. *Heav'n, has to all allotted*, &c. Cf. Shakespeare, *Julius Cæsar*, IV. iii. 217 ff.: There is a Tide in the affayres of men', &c.

264. *Gath*: Brussels. I Sam. xxvii. 1–4.

268–9. *Behold him setting in his Western Skies*, &c. Cf. Shakespeare, *Richard II*, II. iv. 18–24; *Fables*, 'Sigismonda and Guiscardo', ll. 337–8; *Aureng-Zebe* (1676), I:

> *Solyman.* [He] Wishes each Minute he could unbeget
> Those Rebel-Sons, who dare t' usurp his Seat:
> To sway his Empire, with unequal Skill,
> And mount a Throne, which none but he can fill.
> *Arimant.* Oh! had he still that Character maintain'd,
> Of Valour, which in blooming Youth he gain'd,
> He promis'd in his East a Glorious Race;
> Now sunk from his Meridian, sets apace.

270. *Jordan's Sand*: Dover beach. 2 Sam. xix. 9–15. Cf. *Astræa Redux*, ll. 276–9.

273–4. Shaftesbury draws a parallel between Charles, with what the Whigs regarded as his desire for arbitrary power, and Lucifer: 'How art thou fallen from heaven, O Lucifer, son of the morning! . . . For thou hast said in thine heart, I will ascend into heaven, I will exalt my throne above the stars of God'

(Isa. xiv. 12–13). The parallel is ironic, in view of Dryden's portrayal of Achitophel as tempter and aspirant.

281–8. *If Pharaoh's doubtfull Succour*, &c. See *supra*, ll. 175–7, note.

299–302. *And Nobler is a limited Command*, &c. See *supra*, ll. 220–7, notes. 'It was one of Shaftesbury's principal advantages, to have chosen, for the ostensible head of his party, a candidate, whose right, had he ever attained the crown, must have fluctuated betwixt an elective and hereditary title' (Scott).

303. *What cannot Praise effect in Mighty Minds.* Cf. the First Part of *The Conquest of Granada*, II:

> *Abdalla.* Would he were ours!
> I'll try to gild th' injustice of his Cause;
> And court his Valour with a vast applause.
> *Zulema.* The Bold are but the instruments o' th' Wise:
> They undertake the Dangers we Advise.
> And while our Fabrick with their pains we raise,
> We take the Profit, and pay them with Praise.

310. *Too full of Angells Metal in his Frame.* The common double quibble on (i) 'angel' and the coin 'angel-noble' (cf. Shakespeare, *The Merry Wives of Windsor*, I. iii. 50) and (ii) 'metal' and 'mettle' (cf. *Measure for Measure*, I. i. 47–49).

318. *Mankinds Delight.* Titus, says Suetonius, viii (i), was 'amor atque deliciae generis humani'.

326. *Enclin'd to Mercy, and averse from Blood.* Charles's policy of letting the law and the crisis take their course during the trials for the Plot did not suppress his natural inclination: 'Let the blood lie on them that condemn them', he said when confronted with a death warrant, 'for God knows I sign with tears in my eyes' (Bryant, pp. 280 and 290). Cf. *Astræa Redux*, ll. 266–9, note; *Threnodia Augustalis*, ll. 86–87; and Shakespeare, *The Merchant of Venice*, IV. i. 193–6: Mercy

> is enthroned in the hearts of Kings,
> It is an attribute to God himselfe;
> And earthly power doth then shew likest Gods
> When mercie seasons Iustice.

329–30. *What could he gain*, &c. In his speech to the Oxford Parliament on 20 March 1681 Charles said: 'I, who will never use arbitrary government myself, am resolved not to suffer it in others. . . . It is as much my interest, and it shall be as much my care as yours, to preserve the liberty of the subject; because the Crown can never be safe when that is in danger. And I would have you likewise be convinced, that neither your liberties nor properties can subsist long, when the just rights and prerogatives of the Crown are invaded, or the honour of the government brought low and into disreputation' (*Letters, Speeches and Declarations*, ed. Bryant, 1935, pp. 317–18).

334. *The Dog-star heats their Brains.* The dog-star Sirius was thought to

cause great heat on the earth (cf. Virgil, *Georgics*, ii. 353). Cf. Pope, *Epistle to Dr. Arbuthnot*, ll. 3–6:

> The Dog-star rages! nay, 'tis past a doubt,
> All Bedlam, or Parnassus, is let out:
> Fire in each eye, and papers in each hand,
> They rave, recite, and madden round the land.

353. *His Brother . . . Opprest with Vulgar Spight.* Oates's revelations intensified popular suspicion of the Catholic Duke of York. Although Oates had cleared James of complicity in the Plot, the discovery of Coleman's correspondence (see Preface to *Religio Laici*, ll. 164–5, note) provoked attacks on him in Parliament. In November 1678 Charles was addressed to remove him from his counsels and person; and on 27 April 1679 the Commons resolved 'that the Duke of York being a Papist and the hopes of his coming such to the Crown hath given the greatest countenance and encouragement to the present conspiracies and designs of the Papists against the Crown and the Protestant religion'. As opposition to James hardened into Whig demands for his exclusion from the succession, Charles kept him out of the country as much as possible: he was exiled in Brussels March–September 1679, and spent November 1679–February 1680 and October 1680–March 1682 in Scotland. In giving a eulogy on James to Monmouth, Dryden tactfully ignores the hostility that had developed between uncle and nephew in the later 1670's.

In the Dedication of *The State of Innocence* (1677) to the Duchess of York, Dryden praises James as a prince 'whose Conduct, Courage, and Success in War, whose Fidelity to his Royal Brother, whose Love for his Countrey, whose Constancy to his Friends, whose Bounty to his Servants, whose Justice to Merit, whose Inviolable Truth, and whose Magnanimity in all his Actions, seem to have been rewarded by Heaven, by the Gift of You'. Cf. *The Duke of Guise*, v. i ('I know my Brother's Nature, 'tis Sincere . . .'); *Threnodia Augustalis*, ll. 429–90; Epilogue to *Albion and Albanius*; and *The Hind and the Panther*, iii. 906–14, note.

363–72. *Yet oh that Fate*, &c. Absalom is related to the heroes in Dryden's poetic drama by (i) the disparity between his birth and his aspirations— cf. Torrismond in *The Spanish Fryar* (1681), II. i:

> Good Heav'ns, why gave you me a Monarch's Soul,
> And crusted it with base Plebeian Clay!
> Why gave you me Desires of such extent,
> And such a Span to grasp 'em? Sure my Lot,
> By some o'er-hasty Angel was misplac'd
> In Fate's eternal Volume!

—and (ii) a nobility of character which, in driving him to realize unlawful ambition, amounts to a sublime fault leaving 'room for punishment on the one side, and pity on the other' (see Ker, i. 210–11). Cf. Indamora on Morat (*Aureng-Zebe*, v):

> How you confound desires of Good and Ill!
> For true Renown is still with Virtue join'd,
> But lust of Pow'r lets loose the unbridl'd Mind.
> Yours is a Soul irregularly Great,
> Which wanting Temper, yet abounds with Heat: }
> So strong, yet so unequal Pulses beat.
> As Sun which does through Vapours dimly shine:
> What pity 'tis you are not all Divine;

and Ventidius on Antony (*All for Love*, I):

> Virtue's his Path; but sometimes 'tis too narrow
> For his vast Soul; and then he starts out wide,
> And bounds into a Vice that bears him far
> From his first course, and plunges him in Ills.

390. *Sanhedrin*: Parliament; the supreme court and legislative council of the Jews. Cf. Epilogue to *The Unhappy Favourite*, l. 8, note.

417-18. 'The allusion is to the Republic, who acknowledged God alone for their king, but were dispossessed by Cromwell' (Scott).

431-2. An adaptation of the proverb 'Sike as the shepheards, sike bene her sheepe' (Spenser, *The Shepheardes Calender*, 'September', l. 141).

438. *a Legacy of Barren Land*. Probably a reference to the Border estates of Monmouth's wife.

439-40. *th' old Harp, &c.* Charles II, like David, was a lover of music (see Bryant, pp. 108-9). From Flanders he brought a guitar, which was entrusted to Pepys and caused him much trouble on the journey from Dover to London (*Diary*, 8 June 1660). What remains of Charles's poetry is as undistinguished as Achitophel implies.

445-52. *Though now his mighty Soul, &c.* Cf. *Fables*, 'Sigismonda and Guiscardo', ll. 240-4.

453. *The Prostrate Vulgar, passes o'r, and Spares.* Cf. Pliny, *Nat. Hist.* viii. 19, 'leoni tantum ex feris clementia in supplices; prostratis parcit . . .'; *The Hind and the Panther*, iii. 267-72. In January 1681 James had been compared in the Commons to 'a lion in the lobby' (see Turner, p. 201).

458. *Self-defence is Natures Eldest Law.* 'The Right of Nature . . . is the Liberty each man hath, to use his own power, as he will himselfe, for the preservation of his own Nature; that is to say, of his own Life' (Hobbes, *Leviathan*, I. xiv).

472. *Like womens Leachery, to seem Constrain'd.* Proverbial: cf. Shakespeare, *The Two Gentlemen of Verona*, I. ii. 53-54,

> Since Maides, in modesty, say no, to that,
> Which they would have the profferer construe, I;

Fables, 'Cymon and Iphigenia', ll. 308-11, 320-1.

486. *'Tis Juster to Lament him, than Accuse.* Cf. ll. 363-72, note, and 957-68.

512. *Not only hating David, but the King.* 'The conflict had been, and was still

with many, a conflict of political theories, and not merely a question of persons' (Hugh Walker). Cf. *The Second Part of Absalom and Achitophel*, l. 906.

513. *The Solymæan Rout*: the London rabble. Solyma or Hierosolyma, Jerusalem.

517. *Ethnick*: of the Gentiles (τὰ ἔθνη), i.e. the Jebusites or Catholics.

519. *Levites . . . pul'd before From th' Ark*: the dissenting ministers deprived of their benefices by the Act of Uniformity, 1662. 2 Chron. xi. 14–15.

525–6. *For who so fit for Reign*, &c. Cf. *The Character of a Fanatick: By a Person of Quality*, 1675: 'In short, this little Horn takes a Mouth to himself, speaking mighty Things, and his Language is, *Overturn, Overturn, Overturn*. And now he makes his Doctrine suitable to his Text, and owns above-board, that Dominion is founded in Grace, not Nature: That the Goods of this World are properly the Elects: That himself and his Hyperdolins are the only *Israelites*, and all the rest *Egyptians*' (*Harl. Misc.* vii. 597; cf. Ogg, ii. 610–11).

536. *Ador'd their fathers God, and Property.* 'The whigs were not the socially-ineligible fanatics caricatured by their opponents, since they included a considerable proportion of both the landed nobility and the landed gentry, as well as many city merchants and rich Dissenters. From these constituent elements can be deduced two of their fundamental principles—sanctity of private property and religious toleration' (Ogg, ii. 611).

544. *Zimri*: George Villiers (1628–87), second Duke of Buckingham. He had been a close friend of Charles II in boyhood and exile, and after the fall of Clarendon in 1667 he became the king's chief minister and adviser (see Pepys, *Diary*, 27 November 1667). He was impeached in 1674, chiefly for breaking the Triple Alliance (*supra*, ll. 175–7, note). 'Upon the breaking out of *Oates*'s Plot, he . . . did side with the Faction, and endeavoured with other discontented Lords to take all opportunities to vex and cross the King' (Wood, *Ath. Ox.* ii. 804). 'He had a great liveliness of wit, and a peculiar faculty of turning all things into ridicule: . . . he was drawn into chymistry: And for some years he thought he was very near the finding the philosopher's stone. . . . He had no principles of religion, vertue, or friendship. Pleasure, frolick, or extravagant diversion was all that he laid to heart. He was true to nothing, for he was not true to himself. He had no steadiness nor conduct. . . . He could never fix his thoughts, nor govern his estate, tho' then the greatest in *England*' (Burnet, i. 100). Buckingham ridiculed Dryden in *The Rehearsal* (performed 1671). In 1673 Dryden, writing to Rochester, derided Buckingham's military ambitions: 'Tis a strange quality in a man to love idlenesse so well as to destroy his Estate by it; and yet at the same time to pursue so violently the most toilesome, and most unpleasant part of businesse. These observations would easily run into lampoon, if I had not forsworn that dangerous part of wit' (Ward, pp. 9–10). See Epilogue to *All for Love*, l. 17, note; Dedication of *The Satires of Juvenalis*, ll. 2142–50.

The choice of the name Zimri may imply a parallel between Buckingham, the lover of the Countess of Shrewsbury and slayer of her husband in 1668, and Zimri the noble paramour of Cozbi the Midianite (Num. xxv); cf. *Absalon's IX Worthies* (1682):

> T' enjoy his *Cosbi*, He her Husband kill'd;
> The rest oth' story waits to be fulfill'd.

In a political context Dryden is more probably recalling Zimri, servant of Elah and captain of half his chariots, who conspired against him (1 Kings xvi. 8–20). 'Had Zimri peace, who slew his master?' (2 Kings ix. 31). See J. Q. Wolf, *MLN* xlvii (1932), 97–99; cf. King's *Elegy* (Saintsbury, iii. 267).

548–52. *Was every thing by starts,* &c. Cf. Juvenal, *Sat.* iii. 74–77; Butler, 'A Duke of Bucks': 'He is as inconstant as the Moon, which he lives under. . . . His Mind entertains all Things very freely, that come and go; but, like Guests and Strangers they are not welcome, if they stay long—This lays him open to all Cheats, Quacks, and Impostors. . . . His Ears are perpetually drilled with a Fiddlestick. He endures Pleasures with less Patience, than other Men do their Pains' (*Genuine Remains*, 1759, ii. 74–75).

568. *He left not Faction, but of that was left.* Cf. La Rochefoucauld, *Portrait du Cardinale de Retz*: 'il quitte la cour, où il ne peut s'attacher, et il s'éloigne du monde, qui s'éloigne de lui' (F. B. Kaye, *MLN* xxxix (1924), 251).

574. *well hung Balaam and cold Caleb.* Balaam is probably Theophilus Hastings (1650–1701), seventh Earl of Huntingdon, who repented of his adherence to Shaftesbury and was received back into royal favour in 1681 (cf. 2 Peter ii. 15–16, Num. xxiii. 11). *Well hung*: probably a *double entendre*— fluent (cf. Num. xxii. 5–6) and licentious (Rev. ii. 14). Caleb is probably Arthur Capel (1632–83), Earl of Essex. On these identifications see James Kinsley, 'Historical Allusions in *Absalom and Achitophel*', *RES*, N.S., vi (1955), 292–4, and correspondence, ibid. vii.

575. *Canting Nadab*: William, Lord Howard of Escrick (1626–94), formerly a sectary and preacher (see Ogg, ii. 642–3). 'He was a man of a pleasant conversation: But he railed so indecently both at the King and the Clergy, that I was very uneasy in his company' (Burnet, i. 503–4). *Porridge*—hotch-potch—was applied by dissenters to the Anglican services and prayer book (cf. Pepys, *Diary*, 24 August 1662, and Wheatley's note). In March 1681 Edward Fitzharris, an Irish informer for the court, was charged with framing a libel on the king, and accused Howard of being the author (Burnet, i. 497 ff.). Howard was committed to the Tower, and is said there to have taken the sacrament according to the Book of Common Prayer, using lamb's wool (a hot ale mixed with the pulp of roasted apples) for wine. Cf. *Absalon's IX Worthies* (1682):

> Then Prophane *Nadab*, that hates all Sacred things,
> And on that score abominateth Kings,
> With *Mahomet* Wine he damneth; with intent
> T' erect his Paschal-Lambs-Wool-Sacrament.

Howard's pseudonym is appropriate: Nadab was a son of Aaron the Levite

(Exod. vi. 23; cf. *supra*, l. 519, note), and 'offered strange fire before the Lord, which he commanded them not' (Lev. x. 1).

581. *Bull-fac'd Jonas*: Sir William Jones (1631–82), Attorney-General and director of prosecutions for the Plot until November 1679, and thereafter a vigorous Exclusionist. See Burnet, i. 395–6. His legal skill made him valuable to the Whigs; he was probably concerned in the drafting of parliamentary bills, and is said to have had a hand in *A Just and Modest Vindication of the Proceedings of the Two Last Parliaments*, an answer to *His Majesties Declaration* (Burnet–Airy, ii. 289 and note).

585. *Shimei*: Slingsby Bethel (1617–97), elected one of London's two Whig sheriffs in 1680. He had been a republican from the first, and in 1660 was employed by 'the most eminent persons' to raise troops against Monk (Ludlow's *Memoirs*, ed. Firth, ii. 251–2). 'He was a sullen and wilful man; and turned from the ordinary way of a Sheriff's living into the extream of sordidness, which was very unacceptable to the body of the citizens, and proved a great prejudice to the party.' His election was contrived by the Whigs to pack the juries with party men. 'It was said, that the King would not have common justice done him hereafter against any of them, how guilty soever. The setting up *Bethel* gave a great colour to this jealousy; for it was said, he had expressed his approving the late King's death in very indecent terms' (Burnet, i. 480). See 2 Sam. xvi. 5–14. Cf. Epilogue to *The Loyal Brother*, ll. 14–17; *The Medall*, 'Epistle to the Whigs', l. 89; Preface to *Religio Laici*, ll. 289–91; *The Hind and the Panther*, iii. 306–8.

595. *Vare*: a staff carried as a symbol of office (Sp. *vara*).

598. *The Sons of Belial had a glorious Time.* 'The Sons of Belial' connotes drunkenness and immorality (Judges xix. 22–25; cf. Milton, *Paradise Lost*, i. 500–5), but Dryden's primary reference is to rebellion: see Deut. xiii. 13, and 2 Sam. xx. 1–2; G. W. Whiting, *Milton's Literary Milieu*, 1939, pp. 222–31. H. T. Cunningham (*TLS*, 10 June 1939) suggests that the familiar pun on 'Balliol/Belial' had been applied to the Whigs at the time of the Oxford Parliament, when Balliol accommodated the Whig leaders.

617. *Rechabite*. See Jer. xxxv.

632. *Corah*: Titus Oates (1649–1705), the chief witness of the Popish Plot. He was the son of a Norfolk weaver turned Anabaptist preacher and 'dipper'. Sent down from Cambridge in 1669, he took orders; was turned out of his living in 1673; and two years later, confronted with a charge of perjury, went to sea as a naval chaplain. In 1677 he became Protestant chaplain in the Duke of Norfolk's household, and was received into the Roman Church in the same year. He was sent to the English College at Valladolid and expelled after a few months; and a second attempt to educate him for the priesthood at St. Omers proved no more successful. Oates returned with ignominy to London in June 1678, out of favour with the Jesuits; and by August his experience in Catholic institutions had been manipulated with the help of the maniacal

Tonge to fill out the narrative of the Plot. See *supra*, ll. 108–9, note; *The Second Part of Absalom and Achitophel*, l. 48, note. By mid-1681 Oates's credit as the saviour of the nation, and his terrible power as a witness, were in decline. At the trial of Stephen College 'the Protestant Joiner' for high treason in August 1681, Oates had exposed himself as a creature of the Whigs; he is said to have been castigated by the Attorney-General for attempting to justify 'so notorious a traitor'; and by early September he had been forced to leave his Whitehall lodgings for a place in the City (see Prologue *spoken at Mithridates King of Pontus*, ll. 26–30, note). Dryden's satire struck him at the crisis of his fortunes. Num. xvi.

633. *thou Monumental Brass.* Num. xxi. 6–9. Dryden may also be recalling the Old Testament application of 'brass' to 'a people impudent in sin': e.g. 'They are all grievous revolters, walking with slanders: they are brass and iron; they are all corrupters' (Jer. vi. 28).

636–7. *yet Comets rise*, &c. Cf. *Annus Mirabilis*, l. 65, note.

641. *Enobles all his Bloud.* Oates became embarrassed by his mean birth, 'and would needs be descended from some Ancient and worshipful Stock. . . . Heralds were sent for, to make out his Pedigree, and give him a Blazon. . . . And it was engraved on his Table and other Plate; for he was rich, set up for a solemn Housekeeper, and lived up to his Quality' (North, p. 223; see Lane, pp. 167–8).

642–3. Acts vi. 9–15.

645. *His Tribe were Godalmightys Gentlemen.* See Num. xvi. 8–9; cf. *supra*, ll. 519–22.

646–9. *Sunk were his Eyes*, &c. The Jesuit John Warner gives the fullest account of Oates's appearance and manner: 'Mentis in eo summa stupiditas, lingua balbutiens, sermo e trivio, vox stridula et cautillans, plorantis quam loquentis similior. Memoria fallax, prius dicta nunquam fideliter reddens, frons contracta, oculi parvi et in occiput retracti, facies plana, in medio, lancis sive disci instar, compressa, prominentibus hic inde genis rubicundis nasus, os in ipso vultus centro, mentum reliquam faciem prope totam aequans, caput vix corporis trunco extans, in pectus declive, reliqua corporis hisce respondentia, monstro quam homini similiora' (Pollock, pp. 7–8, note).

647. The conduct of Oates accords with traditional accounts of the choleric man, who has sharp wits and a lively memory, and is 'a greete entremyttre'; 'he louyth hasty wengeaunce' (*Secreta Secretorum*, EETS, p. 220). Choleric persons 'are bold and impudent, and of a . . . hair-brain disposition, apt to quarrell and think of such things . . . furious, impatient in discourse, stiff, irrefragable and prodigious in their tenents; and if they be moved, most violent, outragious, ready to disgrace, provoke any, to kill themselves & others; *Arnoldus* adds, stark mad by fits' (Burton, I. iii. 1. 3).

649. *A Church Vermilion, and a Moses's Face.* Corah has the red face of the luxurious priest of comedy: cf. *The Spanish Fryar* (1681), II. ii, where Father

Dominic is introduced as 'a huge fat religious Gentleman' with 'Gills . . . as rosie as a Turkey-Cock'. But Dryden ironically interprets his brightness as the illumination of the prophet, and compares the revealer of the Plot with Moses, whose face shone when he came down from Sinai with the tables of testimony (Exod. xxxiv. 29).

654. *Some future Truths are mingled in his Book.* Cf. *supra*, l. 114, and Evelyn, *Diary*, 18 July 1679: 'I do looke on *Oates* as a vaine, insolent man, puff'd up, with the favour of the Commons, for having discovered something realy true; as more especialy detecting the dangerous intrigue of Coleman, proved out of his owne letters: & of a generall designe, which the *Jesuited* party of the Papists, ever had, & still have to ruine the Church of England.'

657–9. *The Spirit caught him up*, &c. Cf. Epilogue *spoken at Mithridates King of Pontus*, ll. 5–7; *Religio Laici*, l. 406. Oates claimed that during his time at Valladolid, he journed to Salamanca and there 'was admitted Doctor of Divinity'. The Salamanca authorities strenuously denied this claim, and Castlemaine commented: 'If his Learning promoted him, (and you must re- member, That Doctors at Salamanca do defend in the open Schools, a whole Course of Divinity against every body that will oppose them) let any Man that knows Oates, judge of his Doctorship by it' (Lane, p. 57).

668–71. *Were I my self in witness Corahs place*, &c. It had become apparent that personal malice underlay many of Oates's accusations. He involved in the Plot members of the Society of Jesus who had dealt hardly with him in 1677–8. In 1679 he was charged with sodomy by his former servant John Lane; and although the jury returned a verdict of *ignoramus*, Oates exacted a full penalty by indicting Lane on a charge of hindering the exposure of the Plot. He bore a grudge against Pickering (see *supra*, ll. 130–1, note). He unsuccessfully charged a fellow student, Adam Elliott, with being a Jesuit, and later swore new information against him. Justice Bickley was victimized for commenting on the contradictions in Oates's evidence. (Lane, pp. 216–17, 224–6, 236–7, 247–8.)

672–3. *His Zeal . . . made him his Prince despise*, &c. Oates made no direct charges against Charles; but he took full advantage of the privileges which Charles was forced to give him at Whitehall, accused the queen of high treason and provoked the Commons to ask for her removal from the palace, and charged her physician, Sir George Wakeman, with complicity in a plot to poison Charles with her approval (Lane, pp. 139–41, 202–12). Cf. *The Second Part of Absalom and Achitophel*, ll. 51–68.

676. *Agag's murther.* Agag is traditionally identified as Sir Edmund Berry Godfrey, a London magistrate who was found dead on 17 October 1678 and was said to have been murdered by Papists. See J. D. Carr, *The Murder of Sir Edmund Godfrey*, 1936. The most likely identification is with Lord Stafford, who was imprisoned on Oates's accusations in October 1678 and condemned on Oates's evidence in December 1680: see James Kinsley, 'Historical Allu-

sions in *Absalom and Achitophel*, *RES*, N.S., vi (1955), 294–6, and correspondence, ibid. vii. (1 Sam. xv).

700. *Behold a Banisht man.* In September 1679 Monmouth was 'turned out of all command and banisht ye 3 Kingdoms. . . . This news . . . like gunpowder set on fire, did in an instant run over ye whole city to ye generall amazement of all people. All ye phanaticks and malecontents cry up ye Duke of Monmouth as ye great confessor for ye protestant religion. . . . His Ma^{ty} is resolved he shall goe . . . for ye Ld Shaf. and y^t party did put ye D of M upon solliciting their concerns and countenancing their designs' (*Hatton Correspondence*, 1878, i. 194–5). Monmouth returned from Holland in November without Charles's leave and was greeted with public acclamation (ibid. 203–5); but the king refused to see him, and he retired to his friends in the City.

705. *Ægypt and Tyrus*: France and Holland. Cf. Ezek. xxvii. 32–34, xxvi. 2.

710. *Bathsheba*: Louise-Renée de Kéroualle (1649–1734), a Breton maid of honour to Charles's sister, who became his mistress in 1671 and was made Duchess of Portsmouth two years later. 'She studied to please and observe him in every thing: So that he pass'd away the rest of his life in a great fondness for her. He kept her at a vast charge. And she . . . gained of him every thing she desired. She stuck firm to the *French* interest, and was its chief support'; and her influence with Charles 'exposed him to much contempt and distrust' (Burnet, i. 337–8). Cf. *Britannia and Rawleigh* (Marvell, *Poems*, ed. Margoliouth, p. 187), ll. 117–22:

> But his fair soul, transform'd by that French Dame,
> Had lost all sense of Honour, Justice, fame;
> Like a Tame spinster in 's seraglio sits,
> Beseig'd by 's whores, Buffoones, and Bastard Chitts;
> Luld in security, rouling in lust,
> Resigns his Crown to Angell Carwells trust.

729–30. On 26 July 1680 Monmouth set out from London 'attended with several of the gentry and nobility, towards the Bath', and from there made a triumphal progress through Somerset and North Devon to Exeter. He returned to London in September, and set out for Oxford, where 'the University took no notice of him' but 'Alderman Wright with a crew cried out "God save him and the Protestant religion" and he was entertained by the city' (D'Oyley, pp. 168–73; Ogg, ii. 645; Wood, *Life and Times*, ed. Clark, ii. 496). 2 Sam. xv. 1–6.

738. *Wise Issachar*: Thomas Thynne (1648–82) of Longleat in Wiltshire, known as 'the Protestant Squire', and a generous supporter of Monmouth. Gen. xlix. 14–15. See James Kinsley, 'Historical Allusions in *Absalom and Achitophel*', *RES*, N.S., vi (1955), 296–7.

750. *Indanger'd by a Brother and a Wife.* York was not touched in the original depositions of Tonge and Oates, and Oates undertook to exonerate him from complicity in the Coleman affair. But on 29 September 1679 Oates told Warcup that 'Lord Shaftesbury would dally no longer; he would impeach the

duke, against whome he had witnesses to prove high treason' (Warcup's Journal, in *EHR* xl (1925), 244). Oates thereafter abused the duke publicly (see Lane, p. 253). 'He over-shot himself most Damnably too, in the Bus'ness of the Duke of York. . . . He goes and Acquits him of the Plot. . . . And then when he would have given all the Shoes in his Shop afterward to have made a Traytor of him, the Basket was already Pinn'd, and there was no getting of him into 't'; but by August 1680 Oates and his confederates felt secure enough to implicate York in a plot against the king's life (L'Estrange, *Observator*, 58; Lane, pp. 129, 245). On the queen, see *supra*, ll. 672–3, note.

759–810. In this consideration of the main political issue, Dryden judiciously provides a link between his exposure of Whig personalities and designs and his presentation of the king's friends and the king's own case. The discussion falls into four parts. (i) He admits the dangers of the absolutism against which the Whigs claimed to be fighting (ll. 759–64), turning away from the extreme Hobbesian view that however miserable the subjects of a tyrant may be, the greatest evil of all is civil war (*Leviathan*, ii. 18). (ii) But (ll. 765–76), even if there is justice in the common view of kingship as based on a covenant between ruler and people and not on divine right, that covenant is continuous, and cannot be 'resumed' or contracted out of by altering the succession (see Achitophel's argument, ll. 409–18; cf. *Threnodia Augustalis*, ll. 311–22). So Hobbes: 'They that are subjects to a Monarch, cannot without his leave cast off Monarchy . . . nor transferre their Person from him that beareth it, to another Man, or other Assembly of men: for they are bound, every man to every man, to Own, and be reputed Author, of all that he that already is their Soveraigne, shall do, and judge fit to be done'; and 'it is necessary for the conservation of the peace of men, that as there was order taken for an Artificiall Man, so there be order also taken, for an Artificiall Eternity of life . . . which men call the Right of *Succession*. There is no perfect forme of Government, where the disposing of the Succession is not in the present Soveraign' (*Leviathan*, ii. 18 and 19). Dryden passes (iii) to the cognate problems of the limitation of the royal prerogative and the growth of popular power (ll. 777–94); and concludes (iv) with arguments against resisting the ruler to the destruction of the common-weal (ll. 795–810). He tactfully concedes the right to 'Patch the Flaws', but the view he expressed in 1678 in the Epistle Dedicatory to *All for Love*, and probably still held, is less moderate: 'Neither is it enough for them to Answer, that they only intend a Reformation of the Government, but not the Subversion of it: On such pretences all Insurrections have been founded; 'Tis striking at the Root of Power, which is Obedience. Every Remonstrance of private Men, has the Seed of Treason in it.'

786. *flowing to the mark, runs faster out*: fluctuates like the tides. 'The higher the tide and consequently the greater the distance between high and low water-mark (the interval of time between tides remaining the same), the

more rapid is the fall of the water at the ebb.' The next lines refer 'to another effect of the moon, mistress, in the opinion of the time, alike of madness and of the tides' (Verrall, *Lectures on Dryden*, 1914, p. 87).

794. *Natures state; where all have Right to all.* 'It is manifest, that during the time men live without a common Power to keep them all in awe, they are in that condition which is called Warre. . . . To this warre of every man against every man, this also is consequent; that nothing can be Unjust . . . that there be no Propriety, no Dominion, no *Mine* and *Thine* distinct; but onely that to be every mans, that he can get; and for so long, as he can keep it. And thus much for the ill condition, which man by meer Nature is actually placed in' (Hobbes, *Leviathan*, i. 13).

800. *Innovation: novae res*, revolution. Cf. Shakespeare, *1 Henry IV*, v. i. 74–78.

804. *touch our Ark*. See 1 Kings viii. 9, and 1 Chron. xiii.

817. *Barzillai*: James Butler (1610–88), twelfth Earl and first Duke of Ormonde, and Lord Lieutenant of Ireland for Charles I and Charles II (ll. 819–20). He committed his whole fortune in the royalist cause, and later followed Charles II into exile. He 'possessed the confidence and esteem of his master: the greatness of his services, the splendour of his merit and his birth, and the fortune he had abandoned in adhering to the fate of his prince, rendered him worthy of it' (Grammont, p. 105). During his Lord Lieutenancy, 1677–82, Ormonde came in for persistent criticism from the Whigs, but he resisted all attempts to remove him from his post. On 14 April 1680 he wrote to Coventry: 'Methinks the Crown and Monarchy and my bountiful master are too apparently threatened for a man that pretends to honour and gratitude to make a voluntary resignation. . . . I have a little stomach left yet that rises at the thought of giving some men their will just when they would have it of me' (*HMC Ormonde*, N.S., v. 304). 2 Sam. xix. 31–39.

825. *The Court he practis'd*: a Gallicism, *pratiquer le grand monde*. Ormonde was 'a man every way fitted for a Court: Of a graceful appearance, a lively wit, and a cheerful temper: A man of great expence, decent even in his vices, for he always kept up the form of religion' (Burnet, i. 95).

826–8. *larger was his Heart*, &c. In 1669 Sheldon, Archbishop of Canterbury, commended Ormonde as his successor in the Chancellorship of Oxford: 'a person . . . who, besides the eminency of his birth and dignities, hath made himself more illustrious by his virtues and merits . . . and . . . by his love of letters and learned men' (Wood, *Life and Times*, ed. Clark, ii. 166). Dryden dedicated *Plutarch's Lives* (1683) to Ormonde with a fine prose panegyric. Cf. Dedication of *Fables*, introductory note.

831. *His Eldest Hope*: Thomas, Earl of Ossory (1634–80). He distinguished himself in the naval wars of 1665–7 and 1672–4, and against the French in 1677–8 (ll. 841–3; cf. Prologue to *Oedipus*, ll. 25–26, note). 'O unhapy *England*! in this illustrious persons losse', wrote Evelyn at his death; 'he deserved all that a sincere friend, a brave Souldier, a Virtuous Courtier, a Loyal Subject,

an honest man, a bountifull Master, & good Christian could merit of his Prince & Country' (*Diary*, 26 July 1680). Dryden wrote to Ormonde in 1683: 'Never was one soul more fully interfused into another's breast. . . . Were not priority of time and nature in the case, it might have been doubted which of you had been most excellent; but Heaven snatched away the copy, to make the original more precious. . . . Three nations had a general concernment in his death, but I had one so very particular, that all my hopes are almost dead with him; and I have lost so much, that I am past the danger of a second shipwreck. But he sleeps with an unenvied commendation; and has left your Grace the sad legacy of all those glories which he derived from you' (Dedication of *Plutarch's Lives*; Malone, ii. 338–41). See letters to Ormonde on the death of Ossory, *HMC Ormonde*, O.S., i. 30, and N.S., v. 357 ff.

832–4. *By me*, &c. Cf. Virgil, *Aen.* v. 49–50:

> iamque dies, nisi fallor, adest, quem semper acerbum,
> semper honoratum (sic di voluistis) habebo.

Unequal Fates: 'fata iniqua' (*Aen.* ii. 257, x. 380).

838–9. *Oh Narrow Circle*, &c. Cf. *Upon the death of the Lord Hastings*, ll. 27–28, and note.

844–5. *Oh Ancient Honour*, &c. Cf. Virgil, *Aen.* vi. 878–80:

> heu pietas, heu prisca fides invictaque bello
> dextera! non illi se quisquam impune tulisset
> obvius armato. . . .

858–9. *Herse*: the structure erected over a bier, adorned with banners and devices, and carrying epitaphs from friends. Cf. Cowley, *On the Death of Mr William Harvey*, viii:

> Hence now, my *Muse*, thou canst not me delight;
>   Be this my latest verse
>   With which I now adorn his *Herse*,
> And this my *Grief*, without *thy* help shall write.

864. *Zadock the Priest*: William Sancroft (1617–93), appointed Dean of St. Paul's in 1664 and Archbishop of Canterbury in 1678. His candidature for the archbishopric, says Wood, was preferred by the Duke of York to that of the Bishop of London, who 'shewed himself an enimy to [the] papists at the Councell board' (*Life and Times*, ed. Clark, ii. 397). Sancroft was nominated 'when the B^p of London wase ye sole candidate. . . . But, if ye B^p of London misses it, he hath gained this great fame: y^t he wase judged most worthy in ye vogue of ye greatest of ye King's protestant subjects' (*Hatton Correspondence*, i. 156–7). Sancroft was 'a man of solemn deportment . . . had put on a monastick strictness, and lived abstracted from company. These things, together with his living unmarried, and his being fixed in the old maxims of high loyalty, and a superstitious valuing of little things, made the Court conclude, that he was a man, who might be entirely gained to serve all their

ends; or, at least, that he would be an unactive speculative man, and give them little opposition' (Burnet, i. 392).

866. *the Sagan of Jerusalem*: Henry Compton (1632–1713), youngest son of the Earl of Northampton, and Bishop of London since 1675. *Sagan*, the Jewish high priest's deputy. Compton 'was a great patron of the Converts from Popery' and made 'many complaints to the King, and often in Council, of the insolence of the Papists'; 'a weak man, willful, and strangely wedded to a party. He was a property to Lord *Danby*, and was turned by him as he pleased. The Duke hated him. But Lord *Danby* persuaded both the King and him, that, as his heat did no great hurt to any person, so the giving way to it helped to lay the jealousies of the Church party' (Burnet, i. 392).

868. *Him of the Western dome*: John Dolben (1625–86), who fought on the royalist side and was wounded at Marston Moor and York; became Dean of Westminster in 1662; and held that office *in commendam* with the bishopric of Rochester from 1666 till he was made Archbishop of York in 1683. He was 'a man of more spirit than discretion, and an excellent preacher, but of a free conversation, which laid him open to much censure in a vitious Court' (Burnet, i. 590). His pulpit manner was 'most passionat & pathetic' (Evelyn, *Diary*, 28 March 1673 and 30 January 1680). Lines 870–1 refer to the boys of Westminster School; cf. Acts iii. 25.

877. *Sharp judging Adriel*: John Sheffield (1648–1721), third Earl of Mulgrave and later Marquis of Normanby; soldier, courtier, orator, and poet. In the Epistle Dedicatory to *Aureng-Zebe* (1676) Dryden acknowledges Sheffield's friendship and 'the care you have taken of my Fortune; which you have rescu'd, not onely from the Power of others, but from my worst of Enemies, my own Modesty and Laziness'. Sheffield had shown interest in Dryden's design for a heroic poem (see Dedication of *The Satires of Juvenalis*, ll. 614 ff.) and had laid both that and the draft of *Aureng-Zebe* before the king. Dennis, dedicating *The Advancement and Reformation of Modern Poetry* to Sheffield in 1701, praises his continued patronage of Dryden: ''Tis known to all the observing World, that you generously began to espouse him, when he was more than half oppress'd, by a very formidable Party [including Buckingham and Rochester] in the Court of King *Charles* II. . . . Your Lordship, in Consideration of that rising Merit, cherish'd his Person, notwithstanding his pretended Frailties; and . . . cherish'd the Man on purpose, to make him instrumental in advancing the Art' (Dennis, i. 198). Cf. Dedication of the *Æneis*, ll. 209–48.

Dryden was widely suspected of having a hand in Sheffield's *Essay upon Satyr*: he 'was sett on in Covent Garden in the evening [18 December 1679] by three fellowes, who beat him very severely . . .: 'tis thought to be done by order of the dutchesse of Portsmouth, she being abused in a late libell called an Essay upon satyr of which Mr. Dryden is suspected to be the author' (Luttrell, i. 30). See the articles on this episode by J. H. Wilson and V. de S. Pinto, *RES* xv (1939), 294–301, and xvi (1940), 177–8.

880–1. When Charles deprived Monmouth of his places in 1679, Sheffield got the Lord Lieutenancy of the East Riding.

882. *Jotham*: George Savile (1633–95), first Baron Savile, Viscount (1668) and Marquis (1682) of Halifax. 'He was a man of a great and ready wit; full of life, and very pleasant; much turned to satyr. . . . And he was endless in consultations: For when after much discourse a point was settled, if he could find a new jest, to make even that which was suggested by himself seem ridiculous, he could not hold, but would study to raise the credit of his wit, tho' it made others call his judgment in question' (Burnet, i. 267–8; cf. Evelyn, *Diary*, 27 September 1662). In the Dedication of *King Arthur* (1691) to Halifax, Dryden praises Charles II as 'an exact Knower of Mankind . . . his secret Thoughts were communicated but to few; and those selected of that sort, who were *Amici omnium Horarum*, able to advise him in a serious Consult . . . and afterwards capable of entertaining him with pleasant Discourse, as well as profitable. In this Maturest part of his Age . . . he confined himself to a small Number of Bosom Friends; amongst whom, the World is much mistaken, if your Lordship was not first.' Halifax worked with Shaftesbury's party 1674–9, and took part in the impeachment of Danby; but in January 1680 he retired to the country to 'plant carrots and cucumbers'. On his return in September he was reputed anxious 'to hear all sides and then choose wisely' on the issue of Exclusion. When the Exclusion Bill was carried to the Lords on 18 November '*Essex* and *Shaftsbury* argued most for it: And the Earl of *Halifax* was the champion on the other side: He gained great honour in the debate; and had a visible superiority to Lord *Shaftsbury* in the opinion of the whole House. . . . The Commons were inflamed when they saw the fate of their bill: They voted an address to the King to remove Lord *Halifax* from his counsels and presence for ever' (Burnet, i. 482). See H. C. Foxcroft, *A Character of the Trimmer*, 1946, pp. 95, 106–26. Jotham protested eloquently against the attempt of the men of Shechem to prefer the usurper Abimilech (Judges ix. 1–21).

888. *Hushai the friend of David*: Laurence Hyde (1642–1711), Clarendon's second son, created Earl of Rochester in 1682. He was first lord of the Treasury 1679–85 and, as plenipotentiary, negotiated the Anglo-Dutch alliance of 1678. He was thought 'the smoothest man in the Court. . . . He has high notions of Government, and thinks it must be maintained with great severity. . . . He passes for a sincere man, and seems to have too much heat to be false' (Burnet, i. 258). Dryden owed him 'particular Obligations' (see Ward, pp. 20–22, and Preface to *Sylvæ*, ll. 380–2); and to him he dedicated *The Duke of Guise* (1683) and *Cleomenes* (1692). In the latter he writes: 'I shall be proud to hold my Dependance on you in Chief, as I do part of my small Fortune in *Wiltshire*. Your Goodness has not been wanting to me, during the Reign of my two Masters. And even from a bare Treasury, my Success has been contrary to that of Mr. *Cowley*; and *Gideon*'s Fleece has then been

moisten'd, when all the Ground has been dry about it.' 2 Sam. xvi. 16–19, 1 Chron. xxvii. 33.

899. *Amiel*: Edward Seymour (1633–1708), Speaker of the House of Commons 1673–8. 'He was a man of great birth, being the elder branch of the *Seimour* family. . . . He knew the House, and every man in it so well, that by looking about he could tell the fate of any question. So, if any thing was put, when the Court party was not well gathered together, he would have held the House from doing any thing, by a wilful mistaking or mistating the question' (Burnet, i. 382–3). 1 Chron. xxvi. 4–8.

910–11. The comparison is with Phaeton (Ovid, *Meta.* ii. 1–324). Cf. Henry King, *An Elegy upon the most incomparable King Charles the First* (Saintsbury, iii. 262), ll. 309–18:

> Whilst blind Ambition by successes fed
> Hath You beyond the bound of subjects led
> . . . .
> Needs must you with unskilful Phaeton
> Aspire to guide the chariot of the Sun,
> Though your ill-govern'd height with lightning be
> Thrown headlong from his burning axle-tree.

920. *plume*: pluck, despoil; a hawking term.

939-1025. Pope had a story that 'King Charles obliged Dryden to put his Oxford speech into verse, and to insert it towards the close of his *Absalom and Achitophel*' (Spence, *Anecdotes*, 1820, pp. 171–2; cf. Malone, 1. i. 154–5). Mr. Godfrey Davies has argued (*HLQ* x (1946), 69–82) that Dryden's chief debt here is to *His Majesties Declaration* (see *supra*, introductory note). Dryden was commissioned in the summer of 1681 to satirize the Whigs as a preliminary to their prosecution; but 'Charles knew that . . . [the] moderates had been won over by the promises of constitutional government and gentle rule in the *Declaration*. What more natural than to revive those parts of it which claimed that the Whigs were trying to wreck the constitution and that the King was its true guardian? Accordingly, the conclusion is keyed to an older tune.' Davies's argument is convincing; but he exaggerates the 'defensive attitude' in David's speech and overlooks the just reasonableness attributed to the king and his policy throughout the poem.

944. *Th' Offenders question my Forgiving Right.* In a last effort to prevent the trial of Danby, which would have had unhappy consequences for him and the king, Charles granted him a pardon on 1 March 1679. When the Commons were informed of this by Charles on 22 March, they attacked the pardon and questioned his right to give it (A. Browning, *Thomas Osborne Earl of Danby*, 1944–51, i. 317, 322–3). When Stafford was condemned in December 1680 Charles commuted the penalty of hanging, drawing, and quartering to one of decapitation. The sheriffs disputed the validity of this, and asked the advice of the Commons on whether the king could dispense with any part

of the execution: 'If he can dispense with a part, why not with all?' (Pollock, pp. 369–70).

957–60. *But oh that yet he woud repent*, &c. Cf. *Prologue to His Royal Highness*, ll. 27–29.

965–8. *Gull'd with a Patriots name*, &c. Cf. *supra*, l. 179, note.

976. *their Own*: what is theirs to give.

979–80. *Without my Leave a future King to choose*, &c. Cf. *supra*, ll. 759–810, note, and *His Majesties Declaration*: 'We have reason to believe, by what passed in the last Parliament at Westminster, that if we could have been brought to give our consent to a bill of exclusion the intent was not to rest there but to pass further, and to attempt some other great and important changes even in present' (Browning, p. 186).

987. *Unsatiate as the barren Womb or Grave*: Prov. xxx. 15–16, 'four things say not, It is enough: The grave; and the barren womb: the earth . . . and the fire'.

995. *No groundless Clamours shall my Friends remove*. *His Majesties Declaration* refers to 'strange illegal votes declaring divers eminent persons to be enemies to the king and kingdom, without any order or process of law, any hearing of their defence, or any proof so much as offered against them' (Browning, p. 185). To Whig objections to this passage, Dryden replied in *His Majesties Declaration Defended* (p. 15): 'They who will have a thing done, and give no reason for it, assume to themselves a manifest Arbitrary Power. Now this Power cannot be in the Representatives, if it be not in the People: or if it be in them, the People is absolute.'

1006–9. Firth paraphrases: 'They, i.e. the factious party, demand law and shall have law. They are not content with my clemency, grace or mercy— which is as it were the hinder parts of law and may be seen with safety— but rashly demand to see the very face of law.' 'Grace' is explained by ll. 939– 44, 'Law' by ll. 991–1003. Cf. *Astræa Redux*, ll. 262–5, and *The Hind and the Panther*, iii. 1040–1.

1010–11. *By their own arts*, &c. Cf. Ovid, *De Arte Amandi*, i. 655–6:

> . . . neque enim lex aequior ulla,
> quam necis artifices arte perire sua.

1012. *Against themselves their Witnesses will Swear*. Dugdale, Turberville, and Haynes, informers against the Catholics in the heat of the Plot, gave evidence for the prosecution at the trial of College 'the Protestant Joiner' in August 1681; and when *Absalom and Achitophel* was appearing, Irish informers who had been in Shaftesbury's service were being prepared to witness against him (see Ogg, ii. 393, 596, 626–31).

1013. *Viper-like their Mother Plot they tear*. 'Now if it be so ordained that some must regularly perish by multiplication, and these be the fruits of fructifying in the Viper; it cannot be said that God did bless, but curse this Animal' (Browne, *Pseudodoxia Epidemica*, iii. 16). Cf. the fate of the offspring of Errour in Spenser, *The Faerie Queene*, I. i. 25–26.

1026–7. *Th'Almighty, nodding,* &c. Cf. Virgil, *Aen.* ix. 104–6.
1028–9. *a Series of new time began,* &c. See *Astræa Redux*, ll. 292–3, note.

Prologue and Epilogue to The Unhappy Favourite: or The Earl of Essex. A Tragedy

(Page 244)

John Banks's *The Unhappy Favourite* was first performed at Drury Lane
c. September 1681, and published by Bentley and Magnes in 1682 with
Dryden's special Prologue and Epilogue and also 'Prologue, Spoken by Major
Mohun, The First Four Dayes' and 'Prologue, Intended to be spoken, Written
by the Author'. There is a transcript of Dryden's Prologue in BM Add. MS.
5947, pp. 274–8.

Prologue. 1–8. *When first the Ark,* &c. Cf. *Fables*, 'To Her Grace the Dutchess
of Ormond', ll. 70–79.
13–34. *Tell me you Powers,* &c. Cf. *The Medall*, ll. 123–44.

Epilogue. 2. *Dop*: dip suddenly.
5. *Lott'ry Cavaliers.* A monopoly of lotteries was granted for six years after
the Restoration to 'Truly Loyal Indigent Commissioned Officers' as a reward
for their fidelity; but the beneficiaries complained that the commissioners had
defrauded them of the profits and that the Crown ignored their monopoly
(Ogg, i. 111–12, 163–4).
8. *the Three last ungiving Parliaments,* of March 1679, October 1680, and
March 1681. In *His Majesties Declaration* (see *Absalom and Achitophel*, introductory note) Charles spoke of parliamentary votes which 'instead of giving us
assistance to support our allies, or enable us to preserve Tangier, tended
rather to disable us from contributing towards either by our own revenue or
credit, not only exposing us to all dangers that might happen either at home
or abroad, but endeavouring to deprive us of the possibility of supporting the
government itself, and to reduce us to a more helpless condition than the
meanest of our subjects' (Browning, pp. 185–6). Cf. *The Second Part of
Absalom and Achitophel*, ll. 254–5 and 574–7.
13. *but a Vapour.* Cf. *Annus Mirabilis*, l. 65, note.
14. *our last Fire . . . Lilly.* See Prologue to *Wit without Money*, note; Epilogue
to *Sir Martin Mar-all*, l. 13, note.
15. *Third dayes*: dramatists' benefit performances. Cf. Epilogue to *The
Husband His own Cuckold*, l. 13, note.
21. *the Hatfield Maid.* An account of an apparition said to have appeared to
Elizabeth Freeman, the 'Maid of Hatfield', prophesying the poisoning of the
royal blood. See Richard Wilkinson, *A True and Perfect Relation of Elizabeth*

Freeman. . . . *Of a Strange and Wonderful Apparition which* . . . *commanded her to declare a Message to His Most Sacred Majesty*, 1680. In the Tory paper *Heraclitus Ridens* (No. 5, 1 March 1681) is a satirical roll of the company expected at the wedding of 'Mr. *Popular Fears*, and Mrs. *Joan Jealousie* . . . at *Sedition-Sellers-Hall*', including 'Mrs. *Apparition* of *Hatfield*, the Lady with the white Hand, who hath promised to bring along with her *Joan* of *Arc* . . . and *Bess Barton* the Holy Maid of *Kent*, who are to be Bride-Maids. . . . They will beget Apparitions with white Hands and red Hands, Visions, Revelations, true Protestant Intelligences, Mercuries, Speeches, and so on to the end of the Chapter.'

23. *Democritus his Wars with Heraclitus*: probably the broadsides *Democritus Ridens; or, Comus and Momus* (1681); *Heraclitus Ridens; or, A Discourse between Jest and Earnest*, a Tory paper (1681–2).

Prologue and Epilogue to The Loyal Brother or The Persian Prince. A Tragedy

(Page 246)

The Loyal Brother, the earliest play by the Irish dramatist Thomas Southerne (1660–1746), was first performed at Drury Lane in February 1682, and published by Cademan in the same year. Tonson's separate edition of the Prologue and Epilogue is a single half-sheet printed on both sides, undated; Luttrell's copy, now in the Huntington Library, is dated 7 February 1682. Neither poem is assigned to Dryden in the first edition of the play.

In his Dedication Southerne says: 'Nor durst I have attempted thus far into the World, had not the Laureats own Pen secur'd me, maintaining the out-works, while I lay safe intrencht within his Lines; and malice, ill nature, and censure were forc'd to grinn at a distance.' Dryden came to think well of Southerne; he asked him to finish *Cleomenes* in 1692, and wrote in 1693 of Southerne and Congreve as beloved friends (Ward, p. 60). See Prologue to *The Disappointment* and *To Mr. Southern*. In *A Comparison Between the Two Stages*, 1702 (p. 65), Sullen says that Dryden 'has publickly Panegyrick'd one Author with the *Old Batchelor*, another with the *Relapse*, and Mr. *Southern* very frequently and on all occasions; and yet I have seen him bite his Nails for Vexation that they came so near him'. Warburton records a story of Southerne's that Dryden charged him more for a prologue than had been customary, ' "which (said he) young man, is out of no disrespect to you, but the players have had my goods too cheap" ' (see also Johnson, i. 367; Macdonald, p. 154).

Prologue. 7. *The fawning Whigg Petitions to the King*. In the face of a proclamation of 12 December 1679 forbidding petitions against the prorogation or dissolution of Parliament, the Commons resolved that such petitioning was the inalienable right of the subject; and they expelled Wythens for having promoted an address to the king abhorring the petitions. 'Two names were thus introduced into political terminology—Petitioners and Abhorrers' (Ogg, ii. 602). Cf. Prologue *spoken at Mithridates King of Pontus*, l. 4, note.

13. *the Whigg wou'd fain pull down the Guards*. A bill providing for the disbandment of the militia was rejected by Charles on 30 November 1678 (Ogg, ii. 574; Bryant, pp. 278, 285).

18–40. The accession of Elizabeth of England was celebrated annually by the Whigs on 17 November. In 1679 the procession included a bellman crying all the way 'Remember Justice Godfrey', a dead body representing Godfrey, a Jesuit giving pardons to all who were willing to murder protestants, six Jesuits with bloody daggers, and the Pope 'in a lofty, glorious pageant' with his 'privy counsellor, the degraded Seraphim . . . oft times instructing him aloud to destroy his majesty, to force a protestant plot, and to fire the city again' (Scott, vi. 222–5; Ogg, ii. 595–6). In 1681 the Pope's 'Primier Minister, that shared most of his Ear, was *il Signior Diavolo*, a nimble little Fellow, in a proper Dress, that had a strange Dexterity in climbing and winding about the Chair from one of the Pope's Ears to the other. . . . These stately Figures were planted in a Demilune about an huge Fire' and 'one after another, added to encrease the Flames: All which was perform'd with fitting *Salvos* of the Rabble echoed from the [Green Ribbon] Club, which made a proper Music to so pompous a Sacrifice' (North, pp. 577–8). Cf. Epilogue to *Oedipus*, l. 34; Prologue to *Cæsar Borgia*, ll. 41–42; Prologue to *The Loyal General*, l. 11; Preface to *Religio Laici*, l. 287; *The Hind and the Panther*, iii. 10–11.

22. *Dribs*: dribbles, weeps.

50. *an Act*: the Conventicle Act of 1670, prohibiting nonconformist religious meetings of five or more persons (Browning, pp. 384–6).

Epilogue. 'Impudent Sarah' Cooke (d. 1688) was celebrated for her skill in this type of verse. See Aphra Behn's *Works*, ed. Summers, vi. 436–7; Wiley, p. 333.

15. *An honest Jury*. See *Absalom and Achitophel*, l. 585, note.

21. *The leaden farthing*: the token 'issued by tradesmen in place of copper money, which, though not a legal tender of payment, continued to be current by the credit of the individual whose name they bore' (Scott).

25. *Pention-Parliament*: the name given by the Whigs to the Restoration Parliament, which sat till 1679.

26. *City-Clubs*. Cf. *The Second Part of Absalom and Achitophel*, ll. 524–33 and note.

40. *true Protestants*. An allusion to (i) Huguenot refugees, and (ii) the Whig assumption of the title of true protestant (cf. Prologue to *The Spanish Fryar*, l. 11, note).

The Medall. A Satyre against Sedition

(Page 250)

After more than four months in the Tower, Shaftesbury was indicted on a charge of high treason at the Old Bailey on 24 November 1681. The jury returned the bill marked 'Ignoramus'; and until Charles called the Lord Mayor to account three days later, the London rabble celebrated the Whig victory with bonfires, 'insolence and riot' (Ogg, ii. 628–30; *HMC Ormonde*, N.S., vi. 236–42). A medal was struck by George Bower, who prepared the medals for the king's restoration and marriage and was appointed embosser in ordinary to the Mint in 1664. The obverse of this medal carries a bust of Shaftesbury with the inscription 'Antonio Comiti de Shaftesbury'; the reverse bears a view of London Bridge and the Tower, with the sun breaking through a cloud, and the inscriptions 'Lætamvr' and '24 Nov. 1681'. See E. Hawkins, *Medallic Illustrations of the History of Great Britain*, 1885, i. 583, No. 259. The medal became a Whig badge; cf. *A Panegyrick on their Royal Highnesses*, 1682:

> Nearest their hearts, where late their *Georges* hung,
> The pale-fac't Medall with its Silver tongue
> Was plac't, whilst every Wearer still exprest
> His Joy to harbour there so fam'd a Guest.

Dryden's poem, which is said to have been suggested by Charles and rewarded with 'a present of a hundred broad pieces' (Macdonald, p. 26), was published by Tonson on or just before 16 March 1682. There were at least three issues of the first edition: (i) without the Latin lines at the end, and presumably the earliest; (ii) with the Latin lines, which are printed in subsequent editions; and (iii) with the Latin lines, the couplets ll. 179–80 and 181–2 transposed, and variant readings in ll. 174 and 182. The Edinburgh and Dublin editions of 1682 are reprints with slight differences in accidentals; the Edinburgh edition lacks ll. 323–4. The epigraph is from Virgil, *Aen*. vi. 588–9. The 'Epistle To the Whigs' is followed by commendatory poems from Nahum Tate and T. Adams. For Whig replies to *The Medall*, see Macdonald, pp. 228–33.

Epistle To the Whigs. 8–9. *many a poor Polander*, &c. It was a common Tory joke that Shaftesbury aspired to the throne of Poland in 1675, when Sobieski was elected. Otway ends the Prologue to *Venice Preserv'd* (1682) with:

> Oh *Poland! Poland!* had it been thy lot,
> T' have heard in time of this *Venetian-Plot*;
> Thou surely chosen hadst, one King from thence,
> And honour'd them, as thou hast *England* since.

In Aphra Behn's *The City-Heiress* (March 1682) Sir Timothy Treat-all, 'an old seditious Knight, that keeps open House for Commonwealths-men and true blue Protestants' and strongly resembles Shaftesbury, is 'prick'd down' and has his head measured for the crown of Poland. Cf. Macdonald, p. 223.

13. *B.*: George Bower. Cf. *The Medall*, ll. 18–21.

20. *No-protestant Plot*: a Whig tract in three parts (1681–2) by Robert Ferguson (see *The Second Part of Absalom and Achitophel*, l. 320, note). 'Tho' no Name is put to this, yet the general Report was that the Earl of *Shaftsbury* was the Author, or at least found Materials for it, and that his Servant who put it into the Printer's hands, was committed to Prison' (Wood, *Ath. Ox.* ii. 726).

24. *Scanderbeg*: George Castriota *alias* Iskander Beg (*c.* 1404–67), an Albanian who deserted the Turkish service and fought for his country's independence. 'The Turkes hauing gotten the towne of *Lissa*, did with a vehement and earnest desire search out the bodie of *Scanderbeg*: . . . ioyfull was he that could get or cary away any peece of his bodie were it neuer so litle: and those that had any part thereof, caused the same most religiously to be set and curiously enchased, some in siluer, some in golde, bearing it about them vpon some part of their bodies as a thing most holy, diuine and fatall . . . being fully perswaded, that all such as did beare those reliques about them, should enioy the like fortune, felicitie and priuiledge during their liues which *Scanderbeg* . . . had vsed and enioyed all his life time' (*The Historie of George Castriot. . . . Newly translated out of French*, 1596, p. 496).

31. *any Association of men.* In November 1680 the Lords, seeking 'expedients to prevent or restrain a Popish successor', considered a proposition 'for an Act of Association like that in Queen Elizabeth's time' (*HMC Ormonde*, N.S., v. 488–91). This was probably the origin of a draft paper, outlining a Protestant association against popery, mercenary armies, and York's succession, which was found in Shaftesbury's lodging and used as evidence at his trial. After his acquittal 'the Court did declaim with open mouth against these Juries. . . . And upon this a new set of addresses went round the Kingdom, in which they expressed their abhorrence of that association found in Lord *Shaftsbury*'s cabinet; and complained, that Justice was denied the King' (Burnet, i. 508–9). In the Epistle to the Tories before *The Medal of John Bayes: A Satyr* (May 1682) the Whig author describes the 'Association' as 'dropt out of the Clouds, entred into, and subscribed by no body, and seen by no one of our Party that ever we could hear of, (and we believe, by none of yours, but those that contrived the putting it into the Earls Closet)'. Cf. Prologue *To the King and Queen*, ll. 4–5.

46–47. *you have not right to petition in a Crowd.* In 1661 Parliament passed an act against tumultuous petitioning (13 Car. II, c. 5), making it illegal to obtain more than twenty signatures, or for more than ten persons to present a petition to Parliament.

54–56. *the third part,* &c. *The Third Part of No Protestant Plot: with Observations on the Proceedings. . . . Against the E. of Shaftesbury*, 1682; *An Account of the*

Growth of Popery, and Arbitrary Government in England, 1677, by Andrew Marvell, who died on or before 16 August 1678.

58. *the holy League.* See *Astræa Redux,* ll. 98–104, note; Prologue, &c. to *The Duke of Guise,* note.

63. *the instigations of Theodore Beza.* Theodore de Bèze (1519–1605) was Calvin's chief coadjutor and, after 1564, leader of the Genevan church. 'That *Beza* has been charged by the *Papists* for having instigated *Poltrotius Meræus* to Assassinate the Duke of *Guise,* is readily acknowledged; but withal, we know how usual, and how meritorious a thing it is with them, to brand Protestants with whatsoever they can suppose will render them odious' (*The Medal of John Bayes,* 'Epistle to the Tories').

63. *a Hugonot Minister.* In the Postscript to his translation of Maimbourg's *History of the League* (1684) Dryden draws a parallel between the political ideas of the Jesuits (see Preface to *Religio Laici,* ll. 173 ff., notes) and those of the Calvinists Buchanan, Knox, and Goodman: '. . . That when magistrates cease to do their duties, God gives the sword into the people's hands: evil princes ought to be deposed by inferior magistrates; and a private man, having an inward call, may kill a tyrant' (Malone, ii. 449–50). Cf. *The Medall,* ll. 201–4. On the Protestant monarchomachs, see P. J. Shirley, *Richard Hooker and Contemporary Political Ideas,* 1949, pp. 135–59.

82. *a parallel.* 'Another vote . . . was for an association, copied from that in Queen *Elizabeth*'s time, for the revenging the King's death upon all Papists, if he should happen to be killed. The precedent of that time was a specious colour: But this difference was assigned between the two cases: Queen *Elizabeth* was in no danger but from Papists. . . . But now, it was said, there were many Republicans still in the Nation [who] might by this means be encouraged to attempt on the King's life, presuming that both the suspicions and revenges of it would be cast upon the Duke and the Papists. Great use was made of this to possess all people, that this association was intended to destroy the King, instead of preserving him' (Burnet, i. 485–6).

89. *your own Jury.* See *Absalom and Achitophel,* l. 585, note.

93. *the same Pens.* For replies to *Absalom and Achitophel,* see Macdonald, pp. 223–31.

104–6. *Some of you have been driven to this Bay already,* &c. At the time of the publication of *The Medall,* the most conspicuous example of turning Dryden's own lines upon him had been *Azaria and Hushai,* written probably by Samuel Pordage (Luttrell's copy is marked 17 January 1682). Settle continued the parodies in *Absalom Senior* (Luttrell's copy is dated 6 April). 'The Non-conformist Parson' is Christopher Nesse, a London Calvinist minister and supposed author of *A Whip for the Fools Back, Who Styles Honorable Marriage A Curs'd Confinement, In his Profane Poem of Absalom and Achitophel* (1681) and *A Key . . . To open the Mystery & Iniquity of the Poem call'd, Absalom & Achitophel* (Luttrell's copy is dated 13 January 1682).

129. *Irish Witnesses.* See *Absalom and Achitophel*, l. 1012, note. After Shaftesbury's trial the witnesses left in guarded coaches, 'and it was but necessary, for a rabble of above six hundred men followed them very tumultuously, and with very ill language' (*HMC Ormonde*, N.S., vi. 237). The Whigs attempted to discredit these turncoat informers: 'Their *Notorious Adventures*, their *Swearing*, *Counter-Swearing*, *Quarrels* amongst themselves, *Suborning* and being *Suborn'd*, Endeavours to *drop* the Popish Plot, and *Sham* another upon *Protestants*, &c. are become the Common themes of every Table-talk, and the Subject matter of *Play-House Drolls*' (*The Irish Evidence Convicted by their Own Oaths*, 1682).

The Medall. 14. *Shrieval voice.* See *Absalom and Achitophel*, l. 585, note.

24. *his ever-changing Will.* See *Absalom and Achitophel*, l. 150, note.

31. *A Vermin, wriggling in th' Usurper's Ear.* 'Earwig' was a common metaphor for a whisperer or parasite (*OED*).

37. *His open lewdness.* Shaftesbury 'was not behind hand with the Court in the modest pleasures of the time' (North, p. 60). Charles hailed him in the year of his chancellorship as 'the greatest whoremaster in England', to which he replied, 'Of a subject, Sire' (Brown, p. 214). The Tories made the most of the libertinism of Shaftesbury and his following. 'Some of them are *Atheists*, some *Sectaries*, yet *ALL True Protestants*. *Most* of them love all *Whores*, but her of *Babylon* . . . 'tis no matter how a man lives; he is a *Saint* by *Infection* . . . his *wickedness* is no more than *frailty*' (Dryden, *The Vindication: or, the Parallel*, 1683; Malone, ii. 103). Cf. Epilogue to *Constantine the Great*, ll. 38–45.

41. *interlope*: trade without a licence. Cf. Prologue to *Amphitryon*, l. 17.

60. *gears*: draught harness.

62. *like white Witches, mischievously good.* The white witch used her craft to counteract the malignity of the black witch. Cf. Jonson, *The Sad Shepherd*, I. vi. 62; *The Spectator*, No. 131: 'The Country People . . . hearing of the Visit that I made to *Moll. White*, will needs have it that Sir ROGER has brought down a Cunning Man with him, to cure the old Woman, and free the Country from her Charms. So that the Character which I go under . . . is what they here call a *White Witch.*'

65. *our Triple hold.* See *Absalom and Achitophel*, ll. 175–7, note.

77–80. *When his just Sovereign*, &c. To conciliate public opinion on the Dutch war Charles issued a Declaration of Indulgence on 15 March 1672. The Commons, suspicious of his motives, questioned the legality of the Declaration and Charles's 'power in ecclesiastics'. The defence of the king's prerogative in ecclesiastical affairs was particularly Shaftesbury's concern (see Brown, pp. 196, 207–10). The Commons were insistent on the withdrawal of the Declaration, and Charles was forced to consent. He undertook to support a Test Bill (cf. *The Hind and the Panther*, ii. 30–35, note), and Shaftesbury worked to moderate its effects on dissenters. His activities in this connexion, and the belief that he was opposed to Charles's French alliance, earned him popularity as a Protestant champion in the spring and summer of 1673; and by the end of the year he had moved into opposition.

82–87. *He preaches to the Crowd,* &c. Cf. *Absalom and Achitophel,* ll. 220–7, note, 289–92, 409–16, 979–80, note.

88. *Int'rest never lyes.* Cf. *Absalom and Achitophel,* ll. 206, note, 501–4.

91–100. *Almighty Crowd,* &c. Cf. Montaigne's discourse on 'la tourbe, mère d'ignorance, d'injustice, et d'inconstance' (*Essais,* ii. 16) and Browne, *Pseudo-doxia Epidemica,* i. 3, 'Of . . . the erroneous disposition of the People'.

94. *Thou leapst,* &c. Cf. Preface to *Ovid's Epistles,* ll. 240–4; *Heraclitus Ridens,* No. 16 (17 May 1681), '*Pindarick,* which is the Poet's Latitudinarian way of Liberty of Conscience in Verse.'

95–98. *Athens, no doubt,* &c. Socrates was executed for impiety (399 B.C.) and Phocion on a charge of treason (317 B.C.). On each occasion the Athenians repented, and punished the accusers of the condemned man. After the death of Phocion, 'they decreed him a Statue of Brass, and his Bones to be buried honourably at the publick Charge. . . . These Proceedings against *Phocion* made the *Grecians* reflect upon the Fate of *Socrates*; their Cases were exactly parallel, and Both proved the Shame and Punishment of the *Athenians*' (*Plutarch's Lives,* 1727, vi. 290–1).

123–30. *Too happy England,* &c. Cf. *Absalom and Achitophel,* ll. 51–56, notes, 383–4; Prologue to *The Unhappy Favourite,* ll. 13–34.

131. *We loath our Manna, and we long for Quails.* Num. xi.

145–6. 'The Relation of *Lucillius,* and now become common, concerning *Crassus* the grand-father of *Marcus* the wealthy *Roman,* that he never laughed but once in all his life, and that was at an Ass eating thistles . . . an indifferent and unridiculous object' (Browne, *Pseudodoxia Epidemica,* vii. 16; Lucilius, *Reliquiæ,* ed. Marx, i. 89, 1299, and ii. 412). Cf. Cleveland, *To Prince Rupert,* ll. 50–52 (Saintsbury, iii. 63). *Mumbling*: chewing softly.

156–66. *They rack ev'n Scripture,* &c. Cf. Preface to *Religio Laici,* ll. 152–4; *Religio Laici,* ll. 398–426; *The Hind and the Panther,* i. 452–96, ii. 105–36.

168–74. *thou too fruitfull Nile,* &c. Cf. *Annus Mirabilis,* ll. 183–4, note.

181–2. The *Head* is Sir John Moore, a royalist merchant and 'a flexible and faint hearted man' (Burnet, i. 528), who was elected Lord Mayor of London at Michaelmas 1681. His *gouty Hands* are the Whig Sheriffs Pilkington and Shute, elected in June 1681. See *The Second Part of Absalom and Achitophel,* ll. 1131–8, note.

191. *In Gospel phrase their Chapmen they betray.* Cf. Earle, *Microcosmographie,* 'A Shop-keeper' (32): 'His Conscience was a thing, that would haue layde vpon his hands, and he was forc't to put it off: and makes great vse of honestie to professe vpon. . . . He neuer speakes so truely, as when hee sayes hee would vse you as his Brother, for hee would abvse his brother; and in his Shop, thinkes it lawfull. His Religion is much in the nature of his Customers, and

indeed the Pander to it; and by a misinterpreted sense of Scripture makes a gaine of his Godlinesse.'

201–4. *Whether the plotting Jesuite*, &c. See *supra*, 'Epistle To the Whigs', l. 63, note (2).

205–8. *their Trait'rous Combination*: the Association; see *supra*, 'Epistle To the Whigs', l. 31, note. *Treason*: cf. Harington, *Epigrams* (1633), iv, No. 5.

213. *scan*: assess. Cf. Prologue to *The Duke of Guise*, l. 45; Pope, *An Essay on Man*, ii. 1, 'Know then thyself, presume not God to scan.'

217–18. *when the Heir*, &c. Matt. xxi. 33–39.

228–9. *Perhaps not wholly to melt down the King*, &c. Cf. *Absalom and Achitophel*, ll. 65–66 and 226–7. Until the reign of Charles II, English coins were minted by clipping the metal with shears and hammering by hand. Since the rims were not marked, clipping the coin became an easy and common fraud. A mill which produced exactly circular coins with inscribed edges was introduced in 1663 (see the description in Pepys, *Diary*, 19 May); but for some time hammered and milled coins were current together (cf. Prologue to *King Arthur*, l. 3; Epilogue to *The Husband His own Cuckold*, l. 32, note; Dedication of the *Æneis*, l. 2113 and note). The practice of fraudulent clipping is described by Macaulay, *History of England*, chap. xxi. A coin clipped within the 'ring', i.e., the circle round the sovereign's head, was not legal tender; cf. Shakespeare, *Hamlet*, II. ii. 443, 'Pray God your voice like a peece of vncurrant Gold be not crack'd within the ring.'

252–5. *And though the Clymate*, &c. 'Our Government is like our Climate, there are Winds which are sometimes loud and unquiet, and yet with all the Trouble they give us, we owe great part of our Health unto them, they clear the Air, which else would be like a standing Pool. . . . There may be fresh Gales of asserting Liberty, without turning into such storms of Hurricane, as that the State should run any hazard of being Cast away by them' (Halifax, *Works*, ed. Raleigh, p. 63). Burton considers a 'bad clime' one of the causes of 'discontents, common grievances . . . wars, rebellions, seditions, mutinies, contentions' in the body politic, and discusses the effects of 'air' on temperament ('Democritus Junior to the Reader'; I. ii. 2. 5; II. ii. 3). For seventeenth-century notions of the effects of climate, see Dennis, i. 436–7.

263. *Religion thou hast none*. To Shaftesbury is attributed the remark that 'men of sense are really but of one religion', but 'men of sense never tell it'. 'He was as to religion a Deist at best' (Burnet–Airy, i. 172 and note). Cf. Evelyn, *Diary*, 13 July 1683, and *Heraclitus Ridens*, No. 37, 11 October 1681: 'There is no body swears against my L. *Shaftsbury* . . . for being a Protestant, or being publickly engaged against Popery; I never heard that he was accused for being of any Religion.'

270. *Stumm*: must used to renew vapid wine.

272. *the formidable Cripple*. Shaftesbury had a suppurating wound, the consequence of an operation for a cyst of the liver in 1668, which troubled him

throughout his life (see Brown, p. 185 and note). Allusions to this infirmity are numerous. In *Albion and Albanius,* III, the pedestal of Fame bears the figure of 'a Man with a long, lean, pale Face, with Fiends Wings, and Snakes twisted round his Body: He is incompass'd by several Phanatical Rebellious Heads, who suck Poison from him, which runs out of a Tap in his Side'. Cf. *Absalom and Achitophel,* ll. 156–8, note.

297. *The various Venoms on each other prey.* Cf. *Absalom and Achitophel,* ll. 1012–15, notes; *The Hind and the Panther,* iii. 1277–88.

311. *surly*: masterful, imperious. Cf. Shakespeare, *Twelfth Night,* II. v. 164, 'Be opposite with a kinsman, surly with seruants.'

317. *thrust out Collatine that bore their Name.* Lucius Tarquinius Collatinus and Brutus drove the Tarquins from Rome and were made first consuls. But Collatine was abominated because he was himself a Tarquin, and was forced into exile. A like fate, says Dryden, threatens the Stuart Monmouth. He had made a similar point in *His Majesties Declaration Defended,* 1681 (pp. 12–13): '. . . the Protestant Successor himself, if he be not wholly governed by the prevailing party, will first be declared no Protestant; and next, no Successor. . . . for all the bustle . . . concerning the Duke of *M.* proceeds from a Commonwealth Principle.' Cf. *Absalom and Achitophel,* ll. 82, 220–7, notes; *Heraclitus Ridens,* No. 71, 6 June 1682: '. . . if his Majesty, whom God preserve, had miscarried, they might have set up a popular Something, like *Oliver's Richard* the Fourth, who should have serv'd for a Property till they had dress'd up their Democratical Designs; and then all had been out, down with the Image, and *Hey boys up go we.*'

323–4. *Pudet hæc opprobria,* &c. Ovid, *Meta.* i. 758–9.

Prologue To His Royal Highness, Upon His first appearance at the Duke's Theatre since his Return from Scotland

(Page 262)

James Duke of York returned from his second stay in Scotland in March 1682, and arrived in London on 8 April (see *Absalom and Achitophel,* l. 353, note). The *Observator* of 27 April advertises 'Mʳ Drydens Prologue; *And* Mr. Otways Epilogue *to* Venice Preserv'd, *Spoken by* Mr. Smith, *and* Mr. Betterton, *upon his* Royal Highness *the* Duke of Yorks *Coming to the* Theatre. *Recommended to All Men of Sense and Loyalty*'. Both poems were separately published, in single half-sheets; there were two issues of the Prologue. Luttrell's copy (now in the Huntington Library) is dated 21 April, and the Ashley Library copy a day earlier. Otway's *Venice Preserv'd, or, A Plot Discover'd. A Tragedy* had an obvious topical significance, and contains a caricature of Shaftesbury as Antonio, 'a fine Speaker in the Senate'. On Otway's relations with Dryden see Macdonald, pp. 211–12. He is given a place with Dryden in the Whig *The*

Tory-Poets: A Satyr (1682), where his political prologues and plays are derided.

William Smith (d. 1695) was one of the finest actors of the day, and a man 'zealously attach'd to the Interest' of James (see Downes, pp. 166–8). He seems to have been one of the most popular speakers of prologues (see Wiley, pp. 341–2).

14–17. *Still we are throng'd so full,* &c. Cf. *The Second Part of Absalom and Achitophel,* ll. 825–8, note.

20–25. Job i, xlii. Cf. *Examen Poeticum,* 'The First Book of Ovid's Metamorphoses', ll. 227–8, note.

27–29. *Kings can forgive,* &c. Cf. *Absalom and Achitophel,* ll. 326, note, 957–60.

Prologue To The Dutchess, On Her Return from Scotland
(Page 263)

The Duke of York returned to Edinburgh in May 1682 to escort his duchess to London (see *The Second Part of Absalom and Achitophel,* ll. 1065–1102, note). They reached Whitehall on 27 May, and 'at night were ringing of bells, and bonefires in several places, and other publick expressions of joy' (Luttrell, i. 189). As before (see *supra*), Dryden and Otway wrote a special Prologue and Epilogue for *Venice Preserv'd* to mark the occasion, and both poems were separately published in single half-sheets. Luttrell's copy of the Prologue (now in the Huntington Library) is marked 'At ye Dukes theater at Venice preserv'd &c Acted 31 May 1682'. Dryden's lines were reprinted without alteration in *Examen Poeticum.* Scott (ix. 402) lists other poems celebrating the return of the duke and duchess.

Dryden had already paid tribute to the duchess's beauty in the Dedication of *The State of Innocence* (1677): 'You render Mankind insensible to other Beauties; and have destroy'd the Empire of Love, in a Court which was the Seat of his Dominion. You have subverted (may I dare to accuse you of it) even our Fundamental Laws, and reign absolute over the Hearts of a stubborn and free-born People, tenacious almost to Madness of their Liberty.' Even the prejudiced Burnet joins in the praise (Burnet–Airy, ii. 50 and note). Cf. *To the Pious Memory of Mrs Anne Killigrew,* ll. 134–41; *Britannia Rediviva,* ll. 304–14.

24–25. *Like Joseph's Dream,* &c. Gen. xli.

26–46. *For Her,* &c. Cf. *Fables,* 'To Her Grace the Dutchess of Ormond', ll. 80–95.

Mac Flecknoe
(Page 265)

The first edition of *Mac Flecknoe* was 'Printed for D. Green, 1682'. Green is otherwise known only as the publisher of *Satyr to his Muse* (1682), 'A Whiggish thing ag^t ye Tories, abusing Dryden most severly' (Luttrell); and his *Mac Flecknoe* has no authority. There is good evidence that the poem was written in 1678, and circulated in manuscript between that date and 1682. A transcript of part of it in Oldham's hand (Bodl. MS. Rawl. Poet. 123, f. 232) is dated 'A° 1678' (see P. L. Babington in *MLR* xiii (1918), 25–34, and G. Thorn-Drury, ibid. 276–81); and there are numerous instances of borrowing by other poets from *Mac Flecknoe* before 1682 (see Thorn-Drury and others in *RES* i (1925), 187–90; xi (1935), 74–78; xviii (1942), 322–3, and M. Van Doren, *The Poetry of John Dryden*, 1931, pp. 281–90). From collation of the printed editions and seven manuscript versions, G. B. Evans suggests that *1682* may 'be treated as simply another manuscript transcript which happened to escape into print' (*Harvard Library Bulletin*, vii (1953), 32–54). V. A. Dearing attempts to explain manuscript variants as mainly 'resulting from authorial revisions' (*SB* vii (1955), 85–102). The authoritative text is that in *Miscellany Poems* (1684; *SR*, 4 February), reprinted with *Absalom and Achitophel* and *The Medall*, without significant change, in 1692.

The occasion of this satire on Shadwell is unknown. For ten years he and Dryden had been engaged in a critical dispute on rhyme, wit, humour, and other issues. In *Of Dramatick Poesie, an Essay* (1668) Dryden praised Jonson as a learned and judicious writer, but added, 'One cannot say he wanted wit, but rather that he was frugal of it.' In the Preface to *An Evening's Love* (1671) he replied to 'some ingenious Men, for whom I have a particular esteem', who resented his criticism of Jonson: 'they confound the notion of what is witty, with what is pleasant. That *Ben. Johnson*'s Plays were pleasant, he must want reason who denies. But that pleasantness was not properly Wit, or the sharpness of Conceit. . . . I would have more of the *Urbana, venusta, salsa, faceta*, and the rest which *Quintilian* reckons up as the Ornaments of Wit; and these are extremely wanting in *Ben. Johnson*.' Shadwell spoke with unqualified admiration of Jonson in the Preface to *The Sullen Lovers* (1668), and defended Jonson's wit in the Preface to *The Humorists* (1671). Dryden returned to a close criticism in the *Defence of the Epilogue* (1672). Shadwell, in his view, showed no understanding of true 'wit', and indeed no just appreciation of Jonson. 'I am made a Detractor from my Predecessors, whom I confess to have been my Masters in the Art. . . . I will be no more mistaken for my good meaning: I know I honour *Ben Johnson* more than my little Critiques, because without Vanity I may own, I understand him better' (Dedication of *The Assignation*, 1673). This controversy is the basis of *Mac Flecknoe*: Shadwell is portrayed as a literary dunce. D. M. McKeithan argues that the dispute culminated in Shadwell's praise of *The Rehearsal*—an insult to Dryden—in the Dedication of *The History of Timon of Athens* to Buckingham in 1678, and provoked the attack in *Mac Flecknoe* (*PMLA* xlvii (1932), 766–71). But Dryden had been carrying on a critical battle for ten years without any display of personal animosity towards his opponent; and it is more likely that some personal quarrel occasioned this poem. Dryden later claimed, with some justification, that he had seldom resorted to lampoon (Dedication of *The Satires of Juvenalis*, ll. 1776–88).

3. *Fleckno*. Richard Flecknoe (d. 1678?), dramatist and poetaster, had praised Dryden clumsily in *Epigrams of All Sorts* (1670), and seems to have been chosen as Shadwell's poetical parent less from personal antipathy than as a poet 'as Famous as any in his Age, for indifferent Metre' (Langbaine). In the Dedication of *The Kind Keeper* (1680) Dryden points out 'how natural the connection of thought is betwixt a bad Poet and *Fleckno*'. J. H. Smith suggests (*PQ* xxxiii (1954), 338–41) that Dryden may have taken offence at a general criticism of dramatists in the Prologue to *Emilia* (1672), a revision of Flecknoe's *Erminia* (1661). Macdonald suggests (p. 191) that lines in 'Former Playes and Poets vindicated' (Flecknoe's *Epigrams*, 1671) may be a rebuke to Dryden for his judgement on Jonson; if so, the link between Shadwell and Flecknoe is a little strengthened.

15–24. *Sh—* alone, &c. Cf. the repetition of the name of Abdon in Cowley, *Davideis*, iv (1680 edition, p. 139).

21–24. *Some Beams of Wit*, &c. A reminiscence of *Davideis*, i (1680, pp. 5–6):

> There is a place deep wondrous deep below,
> Which genuine *Night* and *Horrour* does o'reflow;
>
> .   .   .   .
>
> Here no dear glimpse of the *Suns* lovely face,
> Strikes through the *Solid* darkness of the place;
> No dawning *Morn* does her kind reds display;
> One slight weak beam would here be thought the *Day*.

29. *Heywood and Shirley*: Thomas Heywood (*c.* 1574–1641) and James Shirley (1596–1666), dramatists; cf. *infra*, ll. 100–3. In *The Tory-Poets: A Satyr* (1682; Luttrell's copy dated 4 September), traditionally ascribed to Shadwell, an attempt is made to return this satiric shot:

> *Shadwell* and *Settle* are both Fools to *Bays*,
> They have no bawdy Prologues to their Plays;
>
> .   .   .   .
>
> Alas! says *Bays*, what are your Wits to me ?
> *Chapman*'s a sad dul Rogue at *Comedy*;
> *Shirley*'s an Ass to write at such a rate
> But I excel the whole Triumverate.

32–34. *sent before but to prepare thy way*, &c. Matt. iii. 3–4. Flecknoe and Shadwell are ironically represented as prophets, priests, and kings of Dulness: cf. *infra*, ll. 118–19, 214–17.

33. *Norwich Drugget*: a coarse fabric of wool or wool and linen. Shadwell was a Norfolk man. A writer to *The Gentleman's Magazine*, xv (1745), 99—doubtless assisted in his recollection by *Mac Flecknoe*—remembered 'plain *John Dryden* . . . in one uniform cloathing of *Norwich* drugget'.

35. *My warbling Lute*. In *Fleckno, an English Priest at Rome* Marvell describes Flecknoe's 'hideous verse' and his attempts 't' allure me with his Lute' (*Poems*, ed. Margoliouth, pp. 83–84; see Margoliouth's note). Shadwell

claims, in the Preface to *Psyche: A Tragedy* (1675), to have 'some little know-ledge' of music, 'having been bred, for many years of my Youth, to some performance in it'. In D'Urfey's *Sir Barnaby Whigg* (1681), III. ii, Sir Barnaby, a caricature of Shadwell, sings 'Though I fall a damn'd Poet, I'le mount a Musician'. Tom Brown's Giusippe Hanesio sends an account of an infernal merry-making to his friends at Will's coffee-house: 'Tom Shadwell, who still keeps up his musical talent in these gloomy territories, began the entertain-ment with thrumming upon an old broken theorbo, and merry Sir John Falstaff sung to him' (*Letters from the Dead to the Living*, ed. Hayward, 1927, p. 334).

37–50. *that glorious day*, &c. There are in these lines echoes of Waller, *Of the Danger His Majesty (being Prince) Escaped in the Road at Saint Anderes*. With ll. 38, 39–40, 43, 45–46, and 49, cf. Waller:

On the smooth back of Silver *Thames* to ride	(62)
These mighty Peers plac'd in the gilded Barge, Proud with the burden of so brave a charge	(39–40)
While to his Harp Divine *Arion* sings The Loves, and Conquests, of our *Albion* Kings	(11–12)
Healths to both Kings, attended with the roar Of Cannons eccho'd from th' affrighted shoar	(7–8)
With the sweet sound of this harmonious lay About the Keel delighted Dolphins play.	(33–34)

42. *in Epsom Blankets tost*: the fate of Sir Samuel Hearty, a coxcomb 'that, by the help of humorous, nonsensical By-Words, takes himself to be a Wit', in Shadwell's *The Virtuoso* (1676), II.

47–48. *Pissing-Ally . . . A—— Hall*. *A New View of London* (1708) has these entries (i. 64): '*Pissing alley*, a broad and large passage between *Friday str.* and *Bread str.*' and '*Pissing alley*, a passage from the *Strand* into *Hollywell str.*'. Dryden may be referring to either alley. The first, like other places in the poem, was in the City; the second was nearer the Thames and Shadwell's music. Aston Hall has not been identified.

50. This and other 'low' lines in the poem are mentioned in Pope's note on *The Dunciad*, ii. 75.

53–54. *Psyche*: Shadwell's 'long expected Opera . . . came forth in all her Ornaments; new Scenes, new Machines, new Cloaths, new *French* Dances' at Dorset Garden in February 1675 (Downes, p. 35). It had been long in preparation. On 22 August 1673 James Vernon wrote to Williamson that the Duke's company was planning an opera 'and great machines. They will have dansers out of France, and St. André comes over with them, who is to have a pension of the King, and a patent of master of the compositions for ballets' (*Letters to Sir Joseph Williamson at Cologne*, 1874, i. 180–1). St. André, whom Shadwell in the Preface calls 'the most famous Master of *France*', was said to have been brought over by Monmouth, to whom *Psyche* is dedicated (*A Com-*

parison Between the Two Stages, 1702, p. 48). He danced in Crowne's *Calisto* in 1675. Cf. Prologue to *The Kind Keeper,* ll. 8–9, note.

57–59. *Singleton forswore,* &c. John Singleton (d. 1686) was one of the king's musicians, who were often employed in the theatre. In 1677 he was one of the petitioners in 'his Ma^ts Band of Violins ag^t Mr Charles Killigrew Master of the Reuells for dismissing them their attendance at the play house' (Nicoll, p. 62, note). In Shadwell's *Bury-Fair* (1689), the '*Thetford* Musick . . . the best Musick in *England*' are said to 'Sing *Charon, Oh gentle Charon,* and *Come my Daphne,* better than *Singleton* . . . did' (III. i). Villerius is a character in Davenant's *Siege of Rhodes. . . . The Story sung in Recitative Musick* (1656). The combination of 'the Lute and Sword' had been ridiculed in *The Rehearsal,* v, where Bayes introduces two persons wearing armour and carrying lutes, to 'play the battel in *Recitativo*', in parody of Villerius and Solyman in *The Siege of Rhodes.*

61. *the hopefull boy*: the massive 36-year-old Shadwell. Cf. Cowley, *Davideis,* ii, note 28, on 'The innocent *Boy* his cruel burthen bore'. Some make David 10, others as old as 33. 'Some of the *Jews* 36. none of which are contrary to the *Hebrew* use of the word *Boy*; for so all young men are termed.'

64–65. *Augusta . . . much to fears inclin'd. Augusta,* 'The old name of *London*' (see *Annus Mirabilis,* l. 1177). The 'fears' are of Popish intrigue. Cf. Prologue to Crowne's *Calisto* (1675), ll. 42–45:

> Do you not see *Augusta*, Rich and Fair,
> (Though to her Lap, I all my Treasure bear)
> Will for no comfort stay her Tears ?
> *Augusta* is inclin'd to fears.

On Dryden's satire on the City and its values in this poem, see Rachel Trickett in *RES,* N.S., viii (1957), 318.

72–73. *Where their vast Courts,* &c. Parodying Cowley, *Davideis,* i (1680, p. 5):

> Where their vast *Court* the *Mother-Waters* keep,
> And undisturb'd by *Moons* in silence sleep.

In 'The Author's Apology for Heroick Poetry' before *The State of Innocence* (1677), Dryden quotes Cowley's lines and adds: 'How easie 'tis to turn into ridicule the best Descriptions, when once a Man is in the humour of laughing till he wheezes at his own dull Jest! But an Image which is strongly and beautifully set before the Eyes of the *Reader,* will still be Poetry when the merry Fit is over; and last when the other is forgotten.'

74. *a Nursery.* A number of 'nurseries' for the training of young actors were established in London in the years following the Restoration. That referred to here was erected by Lady Davenant in 1671 (see Hotson, pp. 190–4).

76–77. *Where unfledg'd Actors,* &c. Parodying Cowley, *Davideis,* i (1680, p. 5):

> Beneath the Dens where *unfletcht Tempests* lye,
> And infant *Winds* their tender *Voices* try. . . .

78. *little Maximins the Gods defy*. Maximin is the ranting tyrant of Rome in *Tyrannick Love* (1670). Dryden repented of Maximin's extravagances 'amongst my Sins': 'All I can say for those Passages . . . is, that I knew they were bad enough to please, even when I writ them' (Epistle Dedicatory to *The Spanish Fryar*, 1681).

81. *Simkin*. 'The Humours of Simpkin' is a droll in Kirkman's collection *The Wits, or Sport upon Sport*, 1672, 'humours and pieces of Plays, which passing under the Name of a merry conceited Fellow, called *Bottom the Weaver*, *Simpleton the Smith*, *John Swabber*, or some such title, were only allowed us, and that by stealth too, and under pretence of Rope-dancing, or the like' when the theatres were closed after the Civil War (Kirkman, 'To the Readers'). There may have been other 'Simkin' pieces which have not survived; 'Simkin' is a simpleton (*OED*). Timothy in Shadwell's *The Miser* (1672) rejoices in '*Simkin* in the Chest' and other 'Pretty harmless Drolls' (III. iii).

82. *this Monument of vanisht minds*: a phrase from Davenant's *Gondibert*, II. v. 36, describing a repository of books, 'Th' assembled souls of all that Men held wise'; and here adapted to satire by a 'turn' on 'vanisht'.

83. *Clinches*. See Prologue to *Troilus and Cressida*, ll. 27–29, note.

84. *Panton*: apparently another character in a farce. Derrick's statement that Panton was 'a famous punster' seems only a fanciful deduction from 'waging harmless War with words'.

91–93. Allusions to Shadwell's early plays. In the Preface to *Ibrahim* (1677) Settle refers to 'the humbler and modester days' of *The Humorists* (1671), *The Miser* (1672), and *The Hypocrite* (otherwise unknown), 'three as silly Plays as a Man would wish to see'. The printing of 'Hypocrites' in roman type in *82* and *84* suggests that the jibe had become obscure; cf. l. 122. Raymond and Bruce are gentlemen of wit in *The Humorists* and *The Virtuoso* (1676) respectively.

94. *Empress Fame*. Cf. Virgil, *Aen.* iv. 173 ff.

101. *Martyrs of Pies*. Cf. *Of Dramatick Poesie, An Essay* (1668): 'he is the very *Withers* of the City: they have bought more Editions of his Works then would serve to lay under all their Pies at the Lord Mayor's *Christmass*.'

102. *Ogleby*: John Ogilby (1600–76), a Scot of great energy and versatility and 'an excellent and prudentiall Witt', dancing master, Master of the Revels in Ireland and founder of the Dublin theatre, printer, translator, and cartographer (see Aubrey, pp. 219–21; W. S. Clark, *The Early Irish Stage*, 1955, pp. 27–72). He translated Virgil in 1649, the *Iliad* in 1660, and the *Odyssey* in 1665. Dryden derides him again in the Prefaces to *Sylvæ* (l. 46) and *Fables* (l. 672); but he deserves honour for his cartography (see H. G. Fordham in *The Library*, 4th ser., vi (1925), 157–78). In the list of 'His Majesties Servants in Ordinary' in Chamberlayne's *Angliae Notitia*, 1674 (p. 192) 'One *Cosmographer*, John Ogilby Esq;' immediately precedes 'One *Poet Laureat*, John Dryden Esq:'.

105. *H[erringman]*: Dryden's publisher until 1678, and the publisher of all Shadwell's plays from *Epsom-Wells* (1673) to *Timon of Athens* (1678). The reason for Dryden's break with him is not known.

108–11. *our young Ascanius*, &c. Virgil's 'magnae spes altera Romae' (*Aen.* xii. 168). Dryden parodies *Aen.* ii. 682–4:

> ecce levis summo de vertice visus Iuli
> fundere lumen apex, tactuque innoxia mollis
> lambere flamma comas et circum tempora pasci.

112. *As Hannibal*, &c. Livy, *Hist.* xxi. 1.

120–1. *In his sinister hand*, &c. When the sovereign leaves the Abbey after coronation, the orb is in the left hand and the sceptre in the right. On Shadwell's love of 'potent Ale' see *The Second Part of Absalom and Achitophel*, l. 459, note.

122. *Love's Kingdom*: 'A Pastoral Trage-Comedy' by Flecknoe, 1664.

126. *Poppies*. This ornament has three significances: the poppy is soporific (e.g. *Aen.* iv. 486), parching and sterilizing (*Georgics*, i. 78), and aphrodisiac but not fertilizing (see Browne, *Pseudodoxia Epidemica*, vii. 7).

129–31. The owl signifies apparent wisdom disguising real stupidity. For the story of Romulus's vultures, see Plutarch's *Life*.

134–8. Dryden parodies (i) the classical representations of Jupiter (cf. *Aen.* x. 113–15), (ii) Virgil's description of the frenzied Sibyl (*Aen.* vi. 46–51, 77–82), and probably (iii) Cowley's account of the anointing of Saul in *Davideis*, iv (1680, p. 131): Samuel

> tells the mighty *Fate* to him assign'd,
> And with great rules fill'd his *capacious mind*.
> Then takes the sacred *Vial*, and does shed
> A *Crown* of mystique drops around his head.

144. *all the people cry'd Amen*. Cf. Neh. viii. 6.
147–8. *Success let others teach*, &c. Cf. Virgil, *Aen.* xii. 435–6:

> disce puer virtutem ex me verumque laborem,
> fortunam ex aliis.

149. *Let Virtuoso's in five years be Writ*. Rochester called Shadwell 'hasty' in *An Allusion to Horace The 10th Satyr of the 1st Book* (*c.* 1675), and was rebuked by Dryden in the Preface to *All for Love* (1678). In the Prologue to *The Virtuoso* (1676) Shadwell declares that 'Wit, like *China*, should long buri'd lie', and hits at 'Drudges of the Stage' who 'must be bound to scribble twice a year' (on Dryden's contract see Nicoll, pp. 328–9). The suggestion that *The Virtuoso* was five years in the making is probably a deliberate misreading of Shadwell's reference in his Dedication to 'the *Humorists*, written five Years since'.

151. *gentle George*: the common nickname for Sir George Etherege (cf. Rochester, *A Session of the Poets*, 1676–7, ll. 16–18). The allusions in the following lines are to characters in Etherege's plays: Dorimant, Mrs. Loveit and

Fopling in *The Man of Mode*, Cully in *The Comical Revenge*, and Cockwood in *She wou'd if she cou'd.*

163–4. *let no alien S—dl—y interpose, &c.* Sedley wrote a poor prologue for Shadwell's *Epsom-Wells* (1673). In a note on two lines in his own 'Prologue to the King and Queen' Shadwell replies to the rumour spread by 'some impotent and envious Scriblers, and some industrious Enemies of mine' that Sedley also helped with the text of the play. But Sedley gave *A True Widow* (1679; see Dryden's Prologue, note) the benefit of his 'Correction and Alteration'; and, says Shadwell in his Dedication, 'I heartily wish, you had given your self the trouble, to have review'd all my Plays, as they came incorrectly and in hast from my hands'.

166. *do not labour to be dull.* Cf. Shadwell's Prologue to *Timon of Athens*, ll. 20–21:

> Some Scriblers will Wit their whole bus'ness make,
> For labour'd dullness grievous pains will take.

168. *Sir Formal's oratory.* Sir Formal Trifle is 'the greatest Master of Tropes and Figures: The most *Ciceronian* Coxcomb: the noblest Orator breathing' in *The Virtuoso*: 'he never speaks without Flowers of Rhetorick'.

170. *thy Northern Dedications.* Of his nine plays produced by 1678, five were dedicated to the Duke or Duchess of Newcastle. In *The Vindication: or The Parallel* (1683) Dryden declares that 'even this their celebrated Writer, knows no more of *Style* and *English*, than the *Northern Dedicator*. As if *Dulness* and *Clumsiness* were fatal to the *Name* of *TOM!*'

173–4. *Let Father Fleckno, &c.* Cf. Virgil, *Aen.* iii. 342–3:

> ecquid in antiquam virtutem animosque viriles
> et pater Aeneas et avunculus excitat Hector ?

178. *rail at Arts he did not understand.* A direct hit on *The Virtuoso*.

179–80. *Prince Nicander. . . . Psyche's humble strain.* Nicander pursues Psyche with 'Industrious Love' and high rhetoric. Shadwell says in the Prologue (ll. 12–14):

> You must not here expect exalted Thought,
> Nor lofty Verse, nor Scenes with labor wrought:
> His Subject's humble, and his Verse is so.

181. To 'sell bargains' commonly meant to overreach, make a fool of. Dryden's use has the special meaning of prurient exchanges in conversation. Cf. Prologue to *The Prophetess*, l. 47, and Pope, *Of the Art of Sinking in Poetry*, xii. 3: 'But the principal branch of the *Alamode* is the PRURIENT. . . . It consists wholly of metaphors drawn from . . . the very Bathos of the human body, . . . and *selling of Bargains*, and *double Entendre*.' Dryden echoes Sir Samuel Hearty in *The Virtuoso*, II: 'Prethee, *Longvil*, hold thy peace, with a whipstitch, your nose in my breech, I know what I have to do mun' (1676, p. 20; cf. pp. 23, 74, and 86). 'Whip stitch, your Nose in my Breech, and such Linkboy phrases' (Settle, Preface to *Ibrahim*, 1677).

182. *Promis'd a Play,* &c. 'I have endeavour'd, in this Play, at Humour, Wit, and Satyr, which are . . . the life of a Comedy. Four of the Humors are entirely new; and (without vanity) I may say, I ne'er produc'd a Comedy that had not some natural Humour in it not represented before, nor I hope never shall. Nor do I count those Humours which a great many do, that is to say, such as consist in using one or two By words . . . nor in the affectation of some *French* words, which several Plays have shown us [e.g. Dryden's *Marriage A-la-Mode*, 1673]. I say nothing of impossible, unnatural Farce Fools, which some intend for Comical, who think it the easiest thing in the World to write a Comedy' (Dedication of *The Virtuoso*).

184. *As thou whole Eth'ridg dost transfuse.* There were some exchanges on plagiarism between Shadwell (Preface to *The Sullen Lovers*, 1668) and Dryden (Preface to *An Evening's Love*, 1671). Dryden's accusation here is unfair. There are similarities of situation in *Epsom-Wells* and Etherege's *She wou'd if she cou'd*, and no more.

185–6. *so transfus'd as Oyl,* &c. 'That *Oyl* mixt with any other liquor, still gets uppermost, is perhaps one of the chiefest *Significancies* in the *Ceremony* of *Anointing Kings* and *Priests*' (Cowley, *Davideis*, iv, note 28; a comment on the lines quoted *supra,* ll. 134–8, note).

187–8. *This is thy Province,* &c. Cf. *supra,* l. 182, note; Prologue *To the King and Queen,* l. 33.

189–92. *This is that boasted Byas of thy mind,* &c. Parodying Shadwell's definition in the Epilogue to *The Humorists,* ll. 15–18:

> A Humor is the Byas of the Mind,
> By which with violence 'tis one way inclin'd:
> It makes our Actions lean on one side still,
> And in all Changes that way bends the will.

194. *likeness*: that is, to Jonson. *Tympany*: 'A kind of obstructed flatulence that swells the body like a drum' (Johnson).

195–6. *A Tun of Man,* &c. Cf. Shakespeare, *1 Henry IV,* II. iv. 440, 'a Tunne of Man is thy Companion'. *Kilderkin*: the fourth part of a tun.

202. *It does but touch thy Irish pen, and dyes.* 'One contrary hath another, and poyson is not without a poyson unto it self' (Browne, *Pseudodoxia Epidemica,* vii. 17). Shadwell protested against Dryden's 'giving me the *Irish* name of *Mack,* when he knows I never saw *Ireland* till I was three and twenty years old, and was there but four Months' (Dedication of *The Tenth Satyr of Juvenal,* 1687).

204–8. Anagrams and acrostics were rejected as false wit by Cowley in 1656 (*Miscellanies,* 'Of Wit', 6); but they still needed castigation in 1711 (*The Spectator,* Nos. 61–63). Poems in shapes were a common form of 'gentle dulness' in the seventeenth century; but 'wings . . . and Altars' may be specific references to George Herbert's 'Easter Wings' and 'The Altar' in *The Temple,* 1633.

212–13. In *The Virtuoso*, III, Bruce and Longvil, 'Gentlemen of wit and sense', dispose of the rhetorical amorist Sir Formal through a trap-door in the very midst of a flight of eloquence.

215–17. *Born upwards*, &c. Cf. 2 Kings ii. 9–13: 'And Elisha said, I pray thee, let a double portion of thy spirit be upon me ... and Elijah went up by a whirlwind into heaven. And Elisha saw it, and he cried, My father, my father. ... He took up also the mantle of Elijah that fell from him, and went back.' Flecknoe's mantle, however, is returned from below.

The Second Part of Absalom and Achitophel. A Poem
(Page 272)

This sequel, which carries Dryden's account of the political crisis on to September 1682, was published by Tonson early in November (Luttrell dated his copy 10 November) and reprinted in a corrected and somewhat altered form before the end of the year. On the three issues of the first edition see Macdonald, p. 32. The epigraph is from Virgil, *Ecl.* vi. 9–10.

The greater part of the poem is the work of the Irish dramatist Nahum Tate (1652–1715). Dryden's friendship with Tate seems to date from the end of 1679, when he wrote a prologue for *The Loyal General* and invited Tate to contribute to the translation of Ovid's Epistles. Tate qualified for further patronage by writing complimentary verses on *Absalom and Achitophel* (printed in the third edition, 1682) and *The Medall*, and he may have collaborated with Dryden after 1682. An anonymous satirist wrote some years later of 'University Men, & ... Country Gentlemen, who ... enter'd themselves Journeymen Rhymers under Bays & Tate' (Macdonald, p. 67, note).

According to a note in *The First Part of Miscellany Poems*, 1716, Dryden's performance in *Absalom and Achitophel* 'was applauded by every one; and several Persons pressing him to write a Second Part, he, upon declining it himself, spoke to Mr. Tate to write one, and gave him his Advice in the Direction of it; and [ll. 310–509] ... were intirely Mr. Dryden's Compositions, besides some Touches in other places.' Dryden, says Scott, 'has obviously contributed much to the poem at large. ... Much of the character of Corah [ll. 79–102], for example, is unquestionably Dryden's; so probably is that of Arod, and the verses generally descriptive of the Green-ribbon Club [ll. 522–55]. ... Such pungent satire is easily distinguished from the smooth insipid flow of other parts, in which Dryden's corrections probably left nothing for censure, and which Tate was unable to qualify with any thing entitled to praise.' It is unlikely that Dryden contributed much to the drafting of the poem or to the selection of characters. Tate tried to repeat the pattern of *Absalom and Achitophel*—the dialogues of Absalom and his seducer, the portraits of the king's enemies and friends, and David's own speech—but his work falls far short of Dryden's in formal excellence. His political sentiment is too often mere rhetorical variation on Dryden's. Of his Hebrew names, moreover, some appear to have been chosen at random and none is applied with Dryden's subtlety and wit.

48. *pamper'd Corah . . . advanc't to Court.* Following his depositions on the Popish Plot (see *Absalom and Achitophel*, ll. 108–9, 632, notes) Oates was given special favour and protection. 'He was now in his trine Exaltation. . . . He had Lodgings in Whitehall, and 1200. *l. per Annum* pension. . . . He put on an Episcopal Garb (except the Lawn Sleeves), Silk Gown and Cassock, great Hat, Sattin Hat-band and Rose, long Scarf, and was called, or most blasphemously called himself, The Saviour of the Nation. Whoever he pointed at, was taken up and committed; so that many People got out of his Way, as from a Blast, and glad they could prove their two last Years Conversation. The very Breath of him was pestilential' (North, p. 205).

51. *the Charge.* See *Absalom and Achitophel*, ll. 11, 672–3, notes.

69–72. Allusions to the Plague (1665), the Fire of London (1666), and the Dutch wars (1665–7 and 1672–4).

77–78. *Trust was no more, &c.* 'Whatsoever therefore is consequent to a time of Warre . . . is consequent to the time, wherein men live without other security, than what their own strength, and their own invention shall furnish them withall. In such condition, there is no place for Industry . . . no Navigation . . . no commodious Building . . . no Knowledge of the face of the Earth; no account of Time; no Arts; no Letters; no Society; and which is worst of all, continuall feare, and danger of violent death; And the life of man, solitary, poore, nasty, brutish, and short' (Hobbes, *Leviathan*, i. 13).

107. *the Good Old Cause.* See *Absalom and Achitophel*, l. 82, note.

109–12. *These raise the Plot, &c.* See *Absalom and Achitophel*, ll. 208, 353, notes.

146. *His Soul's anointed Temple may invade.* Cf. Shakespeare, *Macbeth*, II. iii. 68–70:

> Most sacrilegious Murther hath broke ope
> The Lords anoynted Temple, and stole thence
> The Life o' th' Building.

152–6. *Those very Arms, &c.* See *The Medall*, l. 317, note.

165–70. *The Crowns true Heir, &c.* Cf. *Absalom and Achitophel*, ll. 441–6.

175–8. *Your trivial Faults, &c.* See *Absalom and Achitophel*, l. 700, note.

190–5. *Did you for this, &c.* See *Absalom and Achitophel*, ll. 729–30, note.

203. *my Removal.* When Charles formed a new privy council after the fall of Danby in 1679, he summoned a number of members from the Country Party and appointed Shaftesbury Lord President; but Shaftesbury, who was openly backing Monmouth in the Exclusion debates, proved difficult and was dismissed in the autumn of the same year (Brown, pp. 258–64).

208–9. *Who private Interest never yet persu'd, &c.* Cf. *Absalom and Achitophel*, ll. 179, 206, notes.

216. *at your instance quasht each penal Law.* See *The Medall*, ll. 77–80, note.

220-5. *Ev'n Property*, &c. See *Absalom and Achitophel*, l. 536, note. In 1672 Clifford submitted to Charles a proposal for suspending payment of the assignations on crown loans, in order to build a fund for equipping a new fleet against the Dutch. Shaftesbury opposed the scheme; but he was blamed for the stop, and accused of avoiding his share in the bankers' loss by withdrawing his own money beforehand (Brown, pp. 194-5, 258).

226. *the tripple Cov'nant broke.* See *Absalom and Achitophel*, ll. 175-7, note; *The Medall*, ll. 65-68.

237. *the King a Slave in Trust.* See *Absalom and Achitophel*, ll. 409-18, 759-810, note.

254-5. *Who with Exclusive Bills*, &c. Cf. Epilogue to *The Unhappy Favourite*, l. 8, note.

269. *Till Peace it self*, &c. Cf. *Absalom and Achitophel*, l. 752.

270. *Associations.* See *The Medall*, 'Epistle to the Whigs', ll. 31, 82, notes.

280. *Extorting Ishban*: Sir Robert Clayton (1629-1707), a zealous Whig who had been Lord Mayor in 1679. A scrivener by profession, he became 'so prodigiously rich & opulent, that he was reckoned one of the welthiest Citizens: . . . some believ'd him gilty of hard-dealing . . . but I never saw any ill by him, considering the trade he was off' (Evelyn, *Diary*, 18 November 1679; cf. 26 September 1672 and 12 October 1677). Clayton's hankering after a peerage (ll. 294-7) is ridiculed in *The Last Will and Testament of the Charter of London*, 1683 (*Somers Tracts*, viii. 392-4).

298. *Railing Rabsheka*: Sir Thomas Player (d. 1686), Chamberlain of the City, to whom *The Last Will and Testament of the Charter of London* bequeaths 'all the mannor of Moorfields, with all the wenches and bawdy houses thereunto belonging . . . to enjoy and occupy all from the bawd to the whore downward, at 19s. in the pound cheaper than any other person'. It was said in September 1679 that Player 'termed yᵉ Duke an enemy to [yᵉ] city' and 'did likewise presse that, during yᵉ Dukes stay in England, a stronger guard of yᵉ militia might be upon yᵉ watch every night' (*Hatton Correspondence*, i. 194-5). He is said to have observed, during a crisis of the Plot, 'I do not know, but, the next morning, we may all rise with our throats cut' (Scott). 2 Kings xviii. 17-xix. 4.

320. *that false Hebronite*: Robert Ferguson of Inverurie (d. 1714), 'the Plotter'. He went into England some time before the Restoration and had a living in Kent. Ejected by the Act of Uniformity in 1662, he busied himself as a theological writer and nonconformist preacher; and by 1679 he had attached himself to Shaftesbury's party. '*Ferguson* was a hot and a bold man, whose spirit was naturally turned to plotting: He was always unquiet, and setting people on to some mischief. . . . He had the management of a secret press, and of a purse that maintained it: And he gave about most of the pamphlets writ of that side: And with some he past for the author of them' (Burnet, i. 542). He is credited with *An Appeal from the Country to the City* (see

Absalom and Achitophel, l. 225, note); and in a catalogue of 'Papers which I do heartily repent the having been the author of' (1712) he includes *No Protestant Plot* (see *The Medall*, 'Epistle to the Whigs', l. 20, note). While Dryden and Tate were preparing their poem for the press, Ferguson was apparently negotiating schemes of rebellion and assassination which culminated in the Rye House Plot of 1683. See James Ferguson, *Robert Ferguson the Plotter*, 1887, pp. 39–109, 385. Dryden alludes in ll. 324–7 to a nonconformist school at Islington superintended by Ferguson.

330. *Phaleg*: James Forbes, a Scottish 'gentleman of parts, virtue, and prudence' whom the Duke of Ormonde appointed travelling tutor to the Earl of Derby, husband of his granddaughter. Forbes was ill-used by his obstinate and ruffianly charge, and Ormonde recalled him. But there seems no warrant for the calumny in ll. 338–41, for Forbes was considered some years after as a possible tutor for Ormonde's grandson (1678; see *HMC Ormonde*, N.S., iv. 220–1, 243–4).

336–7. *that buzzing Insect*, &c. See La Fontaine, *Fables*, vii. 9 (1678).

338–9. *Can dry Bones Live?* Ezek. xxxvii. 3.

353. *Ben-Jochanan*: Samuel Johnson (1649–1703), chaplain to the Whig leader Russell. He attempted to refute the doctrine of passive obedience (see *The Hind and the Panther*, iii. 134–43, note) in *Julian the Apostate: Being a Short Account of his Life; the Sense of the Primitive Christians about his Succession; and their Behaviour towards him: Together with a Comparison of Popery and Paganism* (1682). Northleigh's *The Triumph of our Monarchy*, to which Dryden contributed complimentary verses, contains 'Remarks' on Johnson's book. He was imprisoned, whipped, and degraded from the priesthood for his views; but Charles Hatton noted in 1695 that 'Julian Johnson . . . is noe wayes modish in changing his opinion, but firmly adheres to his darling doctrine of ye power of ye people over kings' (*Hatton Correspondence*, ii. 213).

384–5. *did the Drunken Patriarch*, &c. Gen. ix. 18–27.

392. *thy hot Father*: St. Gregory Nazianzenus, whose invective against Julian is used by Johnson.

396. *Balack*: Gilbert Burnet (see *The Hind and the Panther*, iii. 310-19, 1121, notes). Out of favour at court in 1675, says Burnet, 'I applied my self to my studies, and my function, being then settled preacher at the Rolls, and soon after Lecturer of St. *Clements*. I lived many years under the protection of Sir *Harbottle Grimstone*, Master of the Rolls, who continued steady in his favour to me, tho' the King sent Secretary *Williamson* to desire him to dismiss me' (i. 380).

403. *David's Psalms translated*: the metrical psalter of Thomas Sternhold and John Hopkins (completed 1562), which was superseded by the version of Nahum Tate and Nicholas Brady in 1696. In the Preface to *Ibrahim* (1677), Settle abuses Shadwell 'our *Hopkin Rhimer*'. Cf. *Religio Laici*, l. 456.

405. *lame Mephibosheth the Wisard's Son*: Samuel Pordage (1633–91?), son of

a Berkshire 'physician and astrologer' who was deprived of his living in 1654 on a charge of (*inter alia*) conversation with evil spirits (*State Trials*, 1742, ii. 217–59). 'Limping Pordege' was probably the author of *Azaria and Hushai* (see *The Medall*, 'Epistle to the Whigs', ll. 104–6, note) and *The Medal Revers'd. A Satyre against Persecution*, both of which appeared early in 1682 (Macdonald, pp. 226–9). 2 Sam. iv. 4.

407. *rotten Uzza* cannot be certainly identified. The Key of 1716 gives 'J. H.', whom editors have taken to be the obscure Jack Hall ridiculed in Mulgrave's *Essay upon Satyr* (l. 229). Tonson's discreet use of initials suggests that 'J. H.' was still alive in 1716. Dryden may be striking at John How (1657–1722), a Shaftesbury man with a reputation as an amorist and lampooner, and 'the most rancorous and unprincipled of Whigs' (Macaulay). The name Uzza certainly indicates a bold extremist (1 Chron. xiii. 7–11; cf. *Absalom and Achitophel*, ll. 804–8).

412. *Doeg*: Elkanah Settle (1648–1724), author of *The Empress of Morocco. A Tragedy* (1673), which had been acted first at court and later at Dorset Garden. 'Mr. *Settle* began to grow Insolent, as any one may see who reads the *Epistle Dedicatory*. . . . Mr. *Dryden*, Mr. *Shadwell*, and Mr. *Crown* began to grow Jealous; and They Three in Confederacy' wrote *Notes and Observations on The Empress of Morocco* (1674). Settle replied in *Notes and Observations . . . Revised* (1674) and, 'according to the Opinion which the Town had then of the Matter . . . had by much the better of them all. In short, Mr. *Settle* was then a formidable Rival to Mr. *Dryden*' (Dennis, ii. 118, *Remarks upon Mr. Pope's . . . Homer*, 1717). R. G. Ham argued (*MP* xxv (1928), 409–16) that the feud was continued by Settle in *A Session of the Poets* (ascribed to Rochester; see Macdonald, p. 221) and in *Azaria and Hushai* and *The Medal Revers'd* (*supra*, l. 405, note); but there was sufficient provocation for the portrait of Doeg in Settle's next unquestioned poem *Absalom Senior: or, Achitophel Transpros'd*, which contains a coarse attack on Dryden (Luttrell's copy is dated 6 April 1682).

Settle began as a court poet, passed into the pay of Shaftesbury, and in his *Narrative* (1683) shook hands 'with that troublesom Companion Whiggism' only to turn again into Whig service in 1688. The name of the Edomite traitor Doeg ('fearful, uneasy'; 1 Sam. xxii) accords with what is known of his character.

415–17. *Through Sense and Non-sense*, &c. Cf. *Notes and Observations on The Empress of Morocco*, Preface and Postscript: 'In short, he's an Animal of a most deplor'd understanding without Reading & Conversation: his being is in a twilight of Sence, and some glimmering of thought, which he can never fashion either into Wit or English. . . . He would perswade us he is a kind of Phanatick in Poetry, and has a light within him; and writes by an inspiration which (like that of the Heathen Prophets) a man must have no sense of his own when he receives.'

419–20. *Faggotted his Notions*, &c. Cf. Flecknoe, *Enigmaticall Characters* (1658), p. 77: a schoolboy's learning is 'all *capping* verses, and *Faggotting Poets* looser lines, which fall from him as disorderly as Faggott-sticks, when the band is broak' (Malone). Settle is said in *Notes and Observations* (p. 2) to write 'by chance, is resolv'd upon the Rhime before hand, and for the rest of the Verse has a Lottery of words by him, and draws them that come next, let them make sense or non-sense when they come together he matters not what'.

429–30. *For Almonds he'll cry Whore*, &c. Cf. Shakespeare, *Troilus and Cressida*, v. ii. 193–5: '*Patroclus* will give me any thing for the intelligence of this whore: the Parrot will not doe more for an Almond, then he for a commodious drab.' In *A Character of the True Blue Protestant Poet* (April 1682) is an account of how Otway, 'a Man of the Sword as well as the Pen, finding himself most coarsly dealt withal', challenged Settle to a duel. Settle 'presently took *Pen, Ink,* and *Paper* out of his Pocket' and 'writ these following words, (viz.) *I confess I Writ the* Session of the Poets, *and am very sorry fo't and am the Son of a Whore* for doing it; Witness my hand E. S.' (see Macdonald, pp. 239–40). In Settle's *Absalom Senior* Absalom is the Duke of York.

437–40. *The Woman*, &c. See 'The four Legg'd Elder; or a Relation of a Horrible Dog and an Elders Maid' in *Rump: or an Exact Collection of the Choycest Poems and Songs relating to the Late Times* (1662), i. 350.

444. *to write Verse with him is to Transprose.* An allusion to *Absalom Senior: or, Achitophel Transpros'd*, which recalls the satire on Dryden in *The Rehearsal*, I. i:

> *Bayes.* Why, Sir, my first Rule is the Rule of Transversion, or *Regula Duplex*: changing Verse into Prose, or Prose into Verse. . . . I take a Book in my hand . . . if there be any Wit in 't, as there is no Book but has some, I Transverse it. . . .
> *Johnson.* Methinks, Mr. *Bayes*, that putting Verse into Prose should be call'd Transprosing.
> *Bayes.* By my troth, Sir, 'tis a very good Notion, and hereafter it shall be so.

446. *Who makes Heaven's gate*, &c. *Absalom Senior* opens:

> In gloomy times, when priestcraft bore the sway,
> And made heav'ns gate a lock to their own key. . . . .

451. *In Fire-works give him leave to vent his spight.* Settle was responsible for Whig celebrations (see Prologue to *The Loyal Brother*, ll. 18–40, note). Cf. *Heraclitus Ridens* (No. 50, 10 January 1681): 'I know a lusty Fellow, that would not willingly be thought Valiant, who has an indifferent Hand at making of Crackers, Serpents, Rockets, and the other Play-things, that are proper on the Fifth of *November*; and has for such his Skill received Applause and Victuals from the munificent Gentlemen about *Temple Bar* . . . he forsooth is design'd *Poet Laureat* too . . . his Squibs and his Poems have much what the same Fortune; they crack and bounce, and the Boys and Girls laugh at 'em.'

454. *to be Master of a Puppet-show.* Possibly a reference to the Whig popeburnings. But Dryden may also have known of Settle's association with the

actress Elizabeth Leigh, with whom he contracted in 1681 'to write or compose a certain Interlude or Stage Play'. Elizabeth Leigh was the daughter of a Mrs. Mynn who kept booths at Bartholomew Fair and Southwark Fair; and later, at least, Settle was writing drolls for Mrs. Mynn (Hotson, pp. 274–6). In *The Vindication: or The Parallel* (1683) Dryden jibes at the Whigs, who 'must take up with *Settle*, and such as they can get: *Bartholomew-Fair Writers* . . . : there's a famine of Wit amongst them, they are forc'd to give unconscionable rates, and after all to have only Carrion for their money' (see Malone, ii. 132–3).

459. *Og*: Thomas Shadwell (see *Mac Flecknoe*, introductory note), who had become a party writer for the Whigs. *The Medal of John Bayes: A Satyr against Folly and Knavery* (May 1682), a scurrilous attack on Dryden's life and politics, may have been by Shadwell, and there is evidence that he was generally supposed to be the author (Macdonald, pp. 232–3). That Dryden thought Shadwell had abused him in print, and that he considered the magnificent contempt of ll. 457–509 the most satisfactory sort of retaliation, is indicated in *The Vindication: or the Parallel*, 1683: '*Og* may write against the King if he pleases, so long as he *Drinks* for him; and his *Writings* will never do the Government so much *harm*, as his *Drinking* does it *good*: for true Subjects, will not be much perverted by his *Libels*; but the Wine *Duties* rise considerably by his *Claret*. He has often call'd me an *Atheist* in Print, I would believe more charitably of him; and that he only goes the *broad way*, because the other is too *narrow* for him. He may see by this, I do not delight to meddle with his course of *Life*, and his *Immoralities*, though I have a long *Bead-roll* of them. I have hitherto contented my self with the *Ridiculous* part of him, which is enough in all conscience to employ one man: even without the story of his late fall at the *Old Devil*, where he *broke no Ribbs*, because the hardness of the *Stairs* cou'd reach *no Bones*; . . . but to leave him, who is not worth any further consideration, now I have done laughing at him, Wou'd every man knew his own Tallent, and that they who are only born for *drinking*, wou'd let both *Poetry* and *Prose* alone' (see Malone, ii. 106–8).

464–5. *matter . . . batter*. See Dedication of *The Satires of Juvenalis*, l. 2464, note.

506–7. *But of King David's Foes*, &c. Cf. 2 Sam. xviii. 32.

524–33. A description of Shaftesbury's Green-Ribbon Club, which met at the King's Head Tavern near Temple Bar, and took its name from 'the Signal of *a Green Ribbon*, agreed to be worn in their Hats in the Days of *Street Engagements*' (North, p. 572).

535. *Industrious AROD*: Sir William Waller (d. 1699), son of the Cromwellian general, and a justice of the peace for Middlesex. He was 'a great Inquisitor of Priests and Jesuits, and Gutter (as the Term was for Stripping) of Popish Chapels. In which he proceeded with that scandalous Rigor, as to bring forth the Pictures, and other Furniture of great Value, and burn them

publicly; which gave Occasion to suspect, and some said positively, that, under this Pretence, he kept good Things for himself' (North, p. 277).

549. *False Gehazi.* 2 Kings v. 20–27.

551–5. Apparently a reference to Waller's parliamentary manœuvring. He was deprived of the dignity of 'Zaken' (elder, magistrate) in the spring of 1680; 'haveing taken one Higgie out of the Gatehouse, where he was committed for treason by order of the councill, and kept him drinking all night in a tavern, his majestie has turn'd him out of commission of peace' (Luttrell, i. 39).

574–7. *Who for their own Defence,* &c. See Epilogue to *The Unhappy Favourite,* l. 8, note.

592. *His Absence David does with Tears advise.* See *Absalom and Achitophel,* l. 353, note. Charles wrote to James on 28 February 1679: 'As I am truly sorry for the cause of our separation, you may also assure yourself that I shall never wish your absence to continue longer than is absolutely necessary for your good and my service. . . . You may easily believe that it is not without a great deal of pain I write you this, being more touched with the constant friendship you have had for me than with anything else in the world' (*Letters, Speeches and Declarations,* ed. Bryant, 1935, pp. 304–5).

689. *our Brib'd Jews.* Louis XIV, 'engaged in sterilizing all political activity against himself, knew that parliament might well prove too strong for the English king; so he turned his attention to the Country party with presents of money and assurances that if they helped him in parliament he would not attack their liberties or religion' (Ogg, ii. 551; cf. Brown, p. 249).

793. *From Hebron now,* &c. See *Prologue To His Royal Highness,* note.

811. *Jothran*: George Legge (*c.* 1648–91), created Earl of Dartmouth in December 1682; son of the royalist colonel William Legge, and 'a greate favorite of the Dukes, an active & understanding Gent in sea affaires' (Evelyn, *Diary,* 4 June 1683).

819. *Benaiah*: Colonel Edward Sackville, who had distinguished himself at Tangier, and incurred the enmity of Oates in 1679 for declaring in Parliament 'That they were Sons of Whores, who said there was a Plot, and that he was a lying Rogue that said it. Whereupon the Colonel was immediately sent to the Tower, and order'd to be expelled the House' (Echard; Lane, p. 175). 2 Sam. xxiii. 20–23.

825–8. 'A marginal note on Luttrell's copy points out the Earl of Anglesea as particularly concerned in this sarcasm' (Scott). Anglesey was certainly of Presbyterian inclination, and a friend of Monmouth's. Cf. *Prologue To His Royal Highness,* ll. 14–17.

906. *David not their Grievance, but the King.* Cf. *Absalom and Achitophel,* l. 512, note.

913–30. *Who now an envious Festival enstalls,* &c. When the Duke of York was invited to dine with the Artillery Company on 21 April 1682 the Whigs

organized a dinner in opposition to mark their thankfulness for deliverance
from Papist designs. Tickets were issued at a guinea each. On 19 April
Charles prohibited the meeting 'as an insolent attempt, in manifest derogation of his right, and of dangerous consequence . . . tending to sedition, and
raising distinctions and confederacies among his subjects'. This disappointment 'was of great disadvantage to the Whigs. It made them ridiculous;
which is more fatal to a political party than any other misfortune' (Scott).
Cf. Otway's Prologue to Aphra Behn's *The City-Heiress* (1682), ll. 35–42:
Oates

> lately drew in many a Guest,
> To part with zealous Guiney for—no Feast.
> Who, but the most incorrigible Fops,
> For ever doom'd in dismal Cells, call'd Shops,
> To cheat and damn themselves to get their Livings,
> Wou'd lay sweet Money out in Sham-Thanksgivings ?
> Sham-Plots you may have paid for o'er and o'er;
> But who e'er paid for a Sham-Treat before ?

938. *Lawrell'd Asaph*: Dryden. Asaph was chief of those appointed by David
'to record, and to thank and praise the Lord'. 1 Chron. xvi. 4–5.

941. *Bezaliel*: Henry Somerset (1629–1700), Marquis of Worcester and
(1682) Duke of Beaufort, Lord President of the Council of Wales (ll. 943–6;
Num. xxiv. 21). On the patriarchal life of Beaufort at Badminton, see
North's account (Ogg, i. 63–64). He was a strong opponent of Exclusion: in
1680 Shaftesbury's party attacked the duke's supporters and desired 'bouldly
My Lord Halifax, the Marques of Worcester . . . might be removed from all
places, and his Majestys presence, for haveing councell'd him' against Exclusion (Clarke, i. 652; cf. Burnet, i. 484). In 1682 Beaufort was conspicuously
active in the king's campaign against the borough charters (Ogg, ii. 635–9).
Exod. xxxi. 1–3.

967. *Brave Abdael*: Christopher, Duke of Albemarle (1653–88), son of
General Monk (see *To My Honored Friend, Sʳ Robert Howard*, ll. 95–98, note).
The 'Prophets School' is Cambridge, of which Albemarle was Chancellor. He
was given command of the king's Guards when Monmouth was deprived
in 1679.

985. *Eliab*: Henry Bennet, Earl of Arlington (1618–85), who went into
exile with Charles II and returned in 1660 to be one of his ablest ministers.
He resigned his secretaryship of state in 1674 and became Lord Chamberlain.
See Evelyn, *Diary*, 10 Sept. 1677. Eliab was David's brother (1 Sam. xvi–xvii).

991–1002. *one mild Heiress . . . Othniel's Bride*, &c. On 1 August 1672 Evelyn
attended the marriage of Lord Arlington's only daughter Isabella (c. 1667–
1723), 'a Sweete Child, if ever there was any', to the Duke of Grafton, the
king's natural son by the Duchess of Cleveland. 'The Duke of Grafton was
bred to the sea. After Monmouth had taken . . . popular courses . . . the king
endeavoured to set Grafton, though inferior in all personal accomplishments,

in opposition to him, in the hearts of the people' (Scott). For the name Othniel see Joshua xv. 17.

1003. *Helon*: Louis de Duras (1640?–1709), a nephew of Marshal Turenne. He became an English subject after the Restoration, and succeeded to the title of Earl of Feversham on the death of his father-in-law in 1677. He held positions of trust in the royal household; and when the dying Charles agreed to receive the last rites in secret from a Roman priest, Duras was one of the two Protestant noblemen York trusted sufficiently to allow them to remain with the king (Burnet, i. 607).

1013. *Amri*: Heneage Finch (1621–82), Earl of Nottingham, Solicitor-General (1670), and Shaftesbury's successor as Lord Keeper (1673) and Lord Chancellor (1675–82). 'He was a man of probity, and well versed in the laws. He was long much admired for his eloquence: But it was laboured and affected: And he saw it as much despised before he died. . . . He was an incorrupt Judge' (Burnet, i. 365).

1025. *Sheva*: Roger L'Estrange (1616–1704), who distinguished himself in the royalist cause in 1644, and was appointed licenser of the press in 1663. A prolific journalist and pamphleteer, L'Estrange was one of the most dangerous opponents of Oates and Shaftesbury: 'a man who had lived in all the late times, and was furnished with many passages, and an unexhausted copiousness in writing' (Burnet, i. 461). 'Appearing first against the Dissenters, in severall Tractates, [he] had now for some yeares turn'd his style against those whom . . . they called Whiggs & Trimmers; under the title of *Observator*, which came out 3 or 4 days every weeke' (Evelyn, *Diary*, 7 May 1685). The *Observator* ran from 13 April 1681 till 9 March 1687. See George Kitchin, *Sir Roger L'Estrange*, 1913. Sheva 'was scribe . . . about David' (2 Sam. xx. 25).

1050. *How tender of th' offending Young man's Fame*. See *Absalom and Achitophel*, 'To the Reader', ll. 32–46.

1065–1102. York, who had returned to London from Edinburgh in March 1682, set out again on 3 May 'to fetch the Dutchess bigg with child out of Scotland; he chose to go by sea in the GLOCESTER frigat with several smaller vessels to attend him, which, thorough the unskilfulness or treachery of Captain Ayres the Pilot (who was try'd and condemn'd afterwards) was lost, and the Duke himself in great danger of being so too. . . . Most of the persons of quality and His Royal Highnesse's Servants got off.' Those who were abandoned through 'the timorousness of the boatmen . . . (thō ready to be swalloud up) gave a great huzza assoon as they saw his Royal Highness in safety, to the no less honour to the English Seamen for their intrepiditie and zeal, than the Duke's for haveing gain'd so great an esteem amongst them' (Clarke, i. 730–1).

1100. *Urania*: Venus, the Duchess of York.

1131–8. *Ziloah*: Sir John Moore (see *The Medall*, ll. 181–2, note). Ziph and Shimei are the Whig sheriffs Cornish and Bethel (see *Absalom and Achitophel*,

l. 585, note); the 'viler Pair', their successors Pilkington and Shute. In July 1682, largely through Moore's resolution, the Tory party scored a victory in the election of Dudley North and Peter Rich as sheriffs (Burnet, i. 528–30; Ogg, ii. 636–7).

Religio Laici or A Laymans Faith. A Poem
(Page 302)

Religio Laici was published on or just before 28 November 1682 (the date on Luttrell's copy), with commendatory poems, one anonymous and one by Thomas Creech. Of the three issues of the first edition, the second contains a few variants, and the third differs from the second only in the title-page. The second edition of 1682 is probably a reprint hurriedly prepared to meet demand for the poem (see Macdonald, p. 35). A third edition appeared in 1683, with an additional commendatory poem by Roscommon. The epigraph is from Manilius, *Astron.* iii. 39.

The occasion of the poem was the publication of Henry Dickinson's translation (1682) of Simon's *Histoire Critique du Vieux Testament*—a history of the Hebrew text, illustrating the unreliability of the manuscripts and reviewing translations, which was first published in 1678, suppressed, and republished at Amsterdam in 1680. Tonson accepted Dickinson's translation; but he refused to publish it, since Dickinson would not guarantee that it was harmless to 'sound doctrine and good manners'. The copies were passed to Walter Davies; but Dickinson later persuaded Tonson to take back unsold copies, since no offence had been given by publication. The first issue describes the translation as 'By a Person of Quality', and bears Davies's imprint; the second, with Tonson's imprint, gives the translator's initials on the title-page. See C. E. Ward, '*Religio Laici* and Father Simon's *History*', *MLN* lxi (1946), 407–12.

Simon's book caused a stir among orthodox Anglicans. Evelyn wrote to Dr. Fell, Bishop of Oxford, on 19 March 1682: 'It cannot but be evident to your Reverend Lordship, to how great danger and fatal consequences the *Histoire Critique* . . . now lately translated (tho' but ill translated) into English, exposes not onely the Protestant & whole Reformed Churches abroad, but . . . the Church of England at home, which with them acknowledge the Holy Scriptures alone to be the Canon and Rule of Faith; but which this bold man not onely labours to unsettle, but destroy. . . . Whether he be realy a *Papist*, *Socinian*, or meerely a *Theist*, or something of all three, is not easy to discover; but this is evident—as for the Holy Scriptures, one may make what one will of them for him. He tells the world we can establish no Doctrine or Principles upon them, and then, are not we of the Reform'd Religion in a blessed condition. For the love of God, let our Universities, my Lord, no longer remaine thus silent' (*Diary and Correspondence*, 1871, pp. 677–8).

'From many minute particulars', says Scott, 'I think it almost decisive, that Dryden, when he wrote the *"Religio Laici"*, was sceptical concerning revealed religion. . . . His view of the doctrines of Christianity, and of its evidence, were such as could not legitimately found him in the conclusions he draws in favour of the Church of England; and accordingly, in adopting them, he evidently stretches his complaisance towards the national religion, while perhaps in his heart he was even then disposed to think there was no middle course between natural religion and the church of Rome. . . . [He did not] except in outward profession, abandon the church of England for that of Rome, but was converted to the Catholic faith from a state of infidelity, or rather of Pyrrhonism' (i. 307–15). Dryden's scepticism, and his consistent intellectual advance from the explicit anti-rationalism of *Religio Laici* to the defence of fideism and authority in *The Hind and the Panther*, are discussed in L. I. Bredvold, *The Intellectual Milieu of John Dryden*, 1934. Cf. E. N. Hooker, 'Dryden and the Atoms of Epicurus', *ELH* xxiv (1957), 177–90.

The Preface. 1. *so bold a Title.* The form of the title was not indeed uncommon. There is a possible model in Herbert of Cherbury's *De Religione Laici* (1645); and Sir Thomas Browne's *Religio Medici* (1642) and Sir George Mackenzie's *Religio Stoici* (1665) have also been suggested.

17. *the Sword of Goliah.* 1 Sam. xxi. 9. Cf. *The Hind and the Panther*, ii. 599–600.

28–29. *a judicious and learned Friend.* D. Nichol Smith has suggested (*John Dryden*, 1950, pp. 88–89) that Dryden refers here to Tillotson, who became Dean of St. Paul's in 1680. I owe the following note to Dr. John Mackay: 'Tillotson's consistent opposition to Rome would justify the description given, and there is a general resemblance between the argument of *Religio Laici* and that of *The Rule of Faith* (1666). There is however a difficulty in that the judicious and learned friend advised Dryden to omit from his poem the passage on the Athanasian Creed; but the view there stated is very like that which Tillotson later expressed to Burnet, when he said of the same Creed, "I wish we were well rid of it" (Letter of 23 October 1694, Bodl. Add. MS. D. 23. f. 62).'

63–65. *the light of Nature* . . . *which St. Paul concludes to be the Rule of the Heathens.* Rom. ii. 14–15.

69–74. *our Modern Philosophers,* &c. Dryden's immediate reference is to deism. The points enumerated in ll. 72–74 are essentially those set out in Herbert of Cherbury's *De Veritate* (1624) and *De Religione Laici* (1645) as 'catholic truths' which must be thought not 'a Fide aliqua sive Traditione neutiquam pendere: Sed in Mente humana a Deo descriptas': 'scilicet 1. *Esse aliquod Supremum Numen.* 2. *Numen illud coli debere.* 3. *Virtutem cum pietate conjunctam optimam esse rationem Cultus Divini.* 4. *Resipiscendum esse a peccatis.* 5. *Dari Præmium vel Pœnam post hanc vitam transactam*' (*De Religione Laici*, ed. H. R. Hutcheson, 1944, p. 128). Dryden returns to these 'truths' in the poem, ll. 42 ff. But not only the deists 'too much exalted the faculties of our Souls'.

To brand the Cambridge Platonists as mere prophets of reason triumphant is unfair; but Whichcote, who lectured at Cambridge in Dryden's time, was rebuked for having 'cried up reason'; and More's Christianity 'rational throughout', and Culverwel's defence of reason, laid them open to uninformed criticism. See J. Tulloch, *Rational Theology in England*, 1874, ii; E. Cassirer, *The Platonic Renaissance in England*, 1953, pp. 38–41.

75–77. *unatainable by our Discourse . . . without the benefit of Divine Illumination.* Cf. Dryden's Life of Lucian (1696?; printed in *The Works of Lucian*, 1711): 'We have indeed the highest probabilities for our revealed religion; arguments which will preponderate with a reasonable man, upon a long and careful disquisition; but I have always been of opinion, that we can demonstrate nothing, because the subject-matter is not capable of a demonstration. It is the particular grace of God, that any man believes the mysteries of our faith' (Scott, xviii. 63).

82–83. *some Principle of motion.* Cf. Hobbes: 'The causes of universal things (of those, at least, that have any cause) are manifest of themselves . . . for they have all but one universal cause, which is motion. For the variety of all figures arises out of the variety of those motions by which they are made; and motion cannot be understood to have any other cause besides motion' (*Works*, ed. W. Molesworth, 1839–45, i. 69).

128. *in opposition to the Socinians.* On the growth of Socinian opinions and writings, especially after 1640, see H. J. McLachlan, *Socinianism in Seventeenth Century England*, 1951, chapters x–xvii.

152–3. *detorted. . . . Texts of Scripture*, &c. See *The Medall*, ll. 156–66, note.

164–5. *Mr Colemans Letters . . . are the best Evidence.* Edward Coleman, secretary to the Duchess of York, corresponded with Louis XIV's Jesuit confessor la Chaise and others on the means of advancing the cause of the duke and the Catholic faith, 'the conversion of three kingdoms, and by that means perhaps the subduing of a pestilent heresy'. His letters were taken in the early stages of inquiry into the Popish Plot; and although they did not relate to Oates's fabricated 'Plot', Oates had accused Coleman and the letters were widely regarded as confirmation. Coleman was executed in December 1678. See *Absalom and Achitophel*, ll. 108–9, note.

173–80. *the practice of Jesuited Papists*, &c. The Jesuits were looked on as the unscrupulous exponents of the lawfulness of resisting the temporal power, and even of regicide, in the interests of the Church. For the views of some of the continental Jesuits named by Dryden see T. Griesinger, *The Jesuits*, 1903, pp. 507–11, and F. J. Shirley, *Richard Hooker and Contemporary Political Ideas*, 1949, chapter viii. The English Jesuit Edmund Campion (1540–81) undertook a missionary journey to England in 1580 and was hanged for plotting the death of the queen; and Robert Parsons (1546–1610), who accompanied Campion, escaped to the Continent and under the name of Doleman published *A Conference about the Succession to the Crown of England* (1594), setting out the claims of the Infanta and upholding the Church's right over kings. Cf. *The Medall*, 'Epistle To the Whigs', ll. 63–66, notes.

195. *Bellarmine . . . in his Apology, &c. Apologia . . . pro responsione sua ad librum Jacobi Magnæ Britanniæ Regis*, 1610. 'The *Dominium directum* is the right of seignory competent to a feudal superior, in opposition to the *Dominium utile*, or actual possession of the lands which is held by the vassal' (Scott).

205. *declare their Innocency in this Plot*. Responsibility for the Popish Plot was thrown upon the Jesuits, not only by Protestants but by some Catholics. The prosecutions increased the number of moderate Catholics who favoured the oath of allegiance. See Pollock, pp. 196–204.

210. *their Father Cres*: Hugh Paulinus Serenus Cressy (*c.* 1605–74), Benedictine apologist and chaplain to Catherine of Braganza. 'One of his Adversaries tells us, that *Cressy was an Author grave and sober, whose Reason was very keen and sharp, and that he was the* Coriphæus *of the* Roman *Party*: which is true' (Wood, *Ath. Ox.* ii. 530).

222–3. *this present Pope has condemn'd the Doctrine of King-killing*. Innocent XI condemned a number of doubtful propositions in 1679, but by decrees of the Holy Office and not '*ex Cathedra . . .* or in open consistory'. There seems not to have been any explicit condemnation of the doctrine of tyrannicide. Dryden implies that he had his information at second hand.

237. *let my Lord Herbert's History . . . inform you*. 'For, as the Scriptures began then commonly to be read, so out of the literal sense thereof, the manner of those times was, promiscuously to draw arguments, for whatsoever in matter of state or otherwise was to be done. . . . As the people did not sufficiently separate the more clear and necessary parts thereof from the obscure and accessory; and as again taking the several authors to be equally inspired, they did equally apply themselves to all; they fell into many dangerous opinions. . . . While few men agreeing on the same interpretation of the harder places, vexed each other's conscience, appropriating to themselves the gift of the Spirit' (*The Life and Reign of King Henry the Eighth*, 1649; 1872 edition, pp. 469–70).

255–6. *the Works of our venerable Hooker, &c. Of the Lawes of Ecclesiasticall Politie*, 1593. Gauden's Life (1662) was superseded by Walton's in 1665. George Cranmer's 'Letter unto Mr. Richard Hooker' (1598) was printed with Hooker's work, and is Dryden's source for what follows. Cranmer relates the initial 'small difference about Cap and Surplice', the '*Admonitions . . .* directed to the Parliament', 'in defence of them, Volumes . . . published in English, and in Latin', 'Devices . . . set on foot to erect the Practice of the Discipline without Authority', the Martin Marprelate writings, and the consequence that 'the railing Spirit did not only not further, but extreamly disgrace and prejudice the Cause' (1682 edition, p. 30).

263–4. *the Marvel of those times, &c.* Perhaps a reference to Andrew Marvell, as Whig pamphleteer (cf. *The Medall*, 'Epistle To the Whigs', ll. 55–56, note).

H. M. Margoliouth suggests that this is a retaliation for Marvell's rough treatment of Dryden in 'On Mr. Milton's Paradise Lost', 1674 (*Poems and Letters of Marvell*, 1927, i. 260–1).

271–2. *the Doctoral Degree of Wit*. Cf. *Absalom and Achitophel*, ll. 657–9, note.

274. *grin'd at it with a pious smile*. Cf. *The Hind and the Panther*, i. 29–30. 'The court writers at this period were anxious to fix upon the presbyterians and the non-conformists in general, the anti-monarchical principles of the fanatics, who brought Charles I. to the scaffold' (Scott).

284. *Hacket and Coppinger*. On 16 July 1591 two fanatics, Edmund Coppinger and Henry Arthington, proclaimed William Hacket in the London streets as the representative of Christ, come to divide the good from the bad, establish the Gospel, and hold sway over the kings of Europe. Hacket was taken, tortured, and executed on 28 July; Coppinger died in prison; and Arthington was spared to repent. See F. Paget, *Introduction to the Fifth Book of Hooker's Treatise*, 1907, Appendix VI. The story, with the 'Preaching out of a Pease-Cart', is referred to in Cranmer's 'Letter' (*supra*, ll. 255–6, note).

287. *they celebrate Queen Elizabeth's Birth-night*. See Prologue to *The Loyal Brother*, ll. 18–40, note.

290. *a Fanatique Lord Mayor and two Sheriffs of their Party*. See *Absalom and Achitophel*, l. 585, note; *The Second Part of Absalom and Achitophel*, ll. 1131–8.

294–7. *There is in every one*, &c. Of the *Lawes of Ecclesiasticall Politie*, Preface, conclusion of section 8.

305. *Meimbourg in his History*. Louis Maimbourg, *Histoire du Calvinisme*, 1682. Cf. Preface to *Sylvæ*, l. 3, note.

329–30. *I . . . tell them they are spar'd*. Cf. *Absalom and Achitophel*, 'To the Reader', ll. 19–21.

Religio Laici. 1–11. *Dim, as the borrow'd beams*, &c. Cf. Virgil, *Aen*. vi. 270–1, 'quale per incertam lunam sub luce maligna', &c. The whole passage closely resembles Donne's *ΒΙΑΘΑΝΑΤΟΣ*, 'The Third Part of the Law of God', I. i: 'That light which issues from the Moone, doth best represent and expresse that which in our selves we call the light of Nature; for as that in the Moone is permanent and ever there, and yet it is unequall, various, pale, and languishing, So is our light of Nature changeable. . . . And then those Artificiall Lights, which our selves make for our use and service here, as Fires, Tapers, and such, resemble the light of Reason. . . . But because of these two kindes of light, the first is too weake, and the other false . . . we have therefore the Sunne, which is the Fountaine and Treasure of all created light, for an Embleme of that third best light of our understanding, which is the Word of God.'

18. *interfering*: colliding.

39–40. *How can the less*, &c. Cf. *The Hind and the Panther*, i. 104–5.

42. *The Deist thinks he stands on firmer ground*. See *supra*, Preface, ll. 69–74, note.

43. ἔυρεκα: properly εὕρηκα. Spelling and metre show that Dryden's

pronunciation of Greek words was based on accent and not quantity. Cf. Jonson, ix. 486.

69. *Reason saw not, till Faith sprung the Light*. Cf. Matt. iv. 16, 'to them which sat in the region and shadow of death light is sprung up'; *supra*, Preface, ll. 75–77, note.

76–77. *Has thou a Wit so deep*, &c. Cf. Job xi. 7–8, 'Canst thou by searching find out God?', &c.; *Tyrannick Love* (1670), IV. i:

> Thus with short Plummets Heav'ns deep Will we sound,
> That vast Abyss where Humane Wit is drown'd!
> In our small Skiff we must not Launch too far;
> We here but Coasters, not Discoverers are.

80. *Those Gyant Wits, in happyer Ages born*. Virgil, *Aen*. vi. 649, 'magnanimi heroes, nati melioribus annis'.

193. *Sons*: pleonastic genitive.

199–205. *more the great Apostle has exprest*, &c. Rom. ii. 14–15.

211. *Rubrick-Martyrs*: contained in the calendar of saints.

213. *Th' Egyptian Bishop*: Athanasius.

241. *Junius, and Tremellius*: Emanuel Tremellius (1510–80) and Franciscus Junius (1545–1602), joint translators of the Bible into Latin. Cf. Dedication of the *Æneis*, l. 1349.

257. *Cou'd not but find the weakness of the New*. Cf. Evelyn's letter quoted above, introductory note.

291. *like Esdras*, &c. 2 Esdras xiv.

297–300. *And that the Scriptures*, &c. Cf. *The Hind and the Panther*, ii. 100–10.

334–47. 'Lest therefore the name of Tradition should be offensive to any, considering how far by some it hath been, and is abused, we mean by Traditions, Ordinances made in the Prime of Christian Religion, established with that Authority which Christ hath left to his Church for matters indifferent' (Hooker, *Of the Lawes of Ecclesiasticall Politie*, v. lxv). Cf. *The Hind and the Panther*, ii. 168–71, note.

339. *best Authority's next Rules*. Scott and other editors read 'best authorities, next rules'. But the phrase may be interpreted as it stands: 'the rules of the best authority (the Fathers), being nearest (next) in time from the original texts'.

346. *provoke*: appeal, especially to a higher ecclesiastical tribunal.

391. *Their Estate*. Cf. *The Hind and the Panther*, ii. 384.

406. *The Spirit gave the Doctoral Degree*. Cf. *Absalom and Achitophel*, ll. 657–9, note.

412. *No measure ta'n from Knowledge, all from GRACE*. Cf. Hooker, *Of the Lawes of Ecclesiasticall Politie*, III. viii: 'An opinion hath spread it self very far in the World; as if the way to be ripe in Faith, were to be raw in Wit and Judgement; as if Reason were an enemy unto Religion, childish simplicity the

Mother of Ghostly and Divine Wisdom.' The 'Apostle teacheth . . . that Nature hath need of Grace, whereunto I hope we are not opposite, by holding, that Grace hath use of Nature'.

417–20. *While Crouds unlearn'd*, &c. Cf. Butler, *Hudibras*, III. ii. 7–12:

> So, e'r the Storm of War broke out,
> Religion spawn'd a various Rout,
> Of Petulant Capricious Sects,
> The Maggots of Corrupted Texts,
> That first run all Religion down,
> And every Swarm its own.

431–2. *Faith is not built*, &c. Cf. *Tyrannick Love* (1670), IV. i:

> Faith's necessary Rules are plain and few;
> We many, and those needless Rules pursue:
> Faith from our Hearts, into our Heads we drive;
> And make Religion all Contemplative.

453–6. *And this unpolish'd, rugged Verse, I chose*, &c. Cf. *supra*, Preface, ll. 343–55. But l. 456 is an unnecessary jibe: 'This . . . is a composition of great excellence in its kind, in which the familiar is very properly diversified with the solemn, and the grave with the humorous; . . . nor will it be easy to find another example equally happy of this middle kind of writing, which, though prosaick in some parts, rises to high poetry in others' (Johnson, i. 442). *Sternhold*: see *The Second Part of Absalom and Achitophel*, l. 403, note.

Prologue and Epilogue To The King and Queen, At The Opening of Their Theatre

(Page 323)

On 4 May 1682 articles of union were signed between the King's players and the Duke's players, thereafter known as the King's company (see Nicoll, pp. 329–32). The new company began acting on 16 November, which is the date on Luttrell's copy of Dryden's *Prologue* (now in the Huntington Library). The reprint of these poems in *Miscellany Poems* (1702) is headed 'A Prologue to the King and Queen upon the Union of the two Companies'. On prologues written to mark events in theatre history, see Wiley, pp. 135–41. Betterton (see Prologue to *Troilus and Cressida*, note) was the leading actor in the new company. He and Smith (see *Prologue To His Royal Highness*, note) frequently took prologue and epilogue together (Wiley, pp. 59–60). 'Batterton' is a common contemporary spelling.

Prologue. 4–5. *How Pensilvania's Air*, &c. The Quaker William Penn, a substantial creditor of Charles, was granted the charter of Pennsylvania in March 1681 and sailed out in late August 1682. Shaftesbury was one of the eight proprietors to whom Charles granted a charter of lands in Carolina in 1663. *Associators*: see *The Medall*, 'Epistle To the Whigs', ll. 31, 82, notes.

13. *The Factious Natives.* On the disputes which marked the last days of the old King's company see Nicoll, pp. 326–30.

23. *catch a Tartar*: 'in stead of catching, to be catcht in a Trap' (*Dict. Canting Crew, c.* 1695); Tilley, T73.

24. *Charter.* On Charles's campaign in 1682–3 against the borough charters, particularly that of the Whig stronghold, the City of London, see Ogg, ii. 634–9. Cf. Prologue to *The Duke of Guise,* ll. 41–42.

26. *call'd to Twelve*: invited to participate.

33. *dull fat Fool*: Shadwell. Cf. *Mac Flecknoe,* ll. 187–92, notes; *The Second Part of Absalom and Achitophel,* l. 459, note.

42. *Whigg Sheriffs.* See *The Second Part of Absalom and Achitophel,* ll. 1131–8, note.

Epilogue. 5. *Pratlers in the Pit.* Cf. *Miscellany Poems* (1684), Epilogue, 'Though what our Prologue said . . .', ll. 7–24; Nicoll, pp. 15–19.

11. *Vizard Masque.* See Prologue to The Second Part of *The Conquest of Granada,* l. 13, note.

12. *the mid Gallery.* Cf. Prologue to *The Disappointment,* ll. 57–64.

24. *Tom Dove*: a well-known bear exhibited at the Bear Garden (see Evelyn, *Diary,* 16 June 1670, and note); and perhaps named after the entertainer in Deloney's *Thomas of Reading* (1623) who inspired the song 'Welcome to towne, Tom Dove, Tom Dove'.

26. *their unpaying Masters.* 'Gentlemen apparently could enter without payment for a single act, or could rely on credit if they had not sufficient money to pay the door-keeper' (Nicoll, p. 12). Cf. Pepys, *Diary,* 7 January 1668, and Wheatley's note.

29–34. *Next, in the Play-house,* &c. See Prologue to *The Spanish Fryar,* l. 40, note.

35. *our Scene-room.* The tiring-room was a favourite resort of gallants and citizens, who seem to have paid for the privilege of entry. Cf. Epilogues to *The Assignation* (ll. 20–21), *Henry the Second* (ll. 21–34), *The Pilgrim* (ll. 38–40); Wycherley, Epilogue to *The Gentleman Dancing-Master* (1673), ll. 24–29:

> You good men o' th' *Exchange,* on whom alone
> We must depend, when Sparks to Sea are gone;
> Into the Pit already you are come,
> 'Tis but a step more to our Tyring room;
> Where none of us but will be wondrous sweet
> Upon an able Love of *Lombard*-street.

Prologue, Epilogues and Song from The Duke of Guise. A Tragedy

(Page 326)

The Duke of Guise, by Dryden and Lee, was ready for the stage in July 1682; but it was banned on political grounds, finally approved by the king on

29 October, and first performed at the Theatre Royal in November. The queen attended a performance on 1 December (LC 5/145, p. 120; Nicoll, p. 349). Tonson's edition of *Prologue, To The Duke of Guise,* with the Epilogue and 'Another Epilogue Intended to have been Spoken to the Play, before it was forbidden, last Summer', was published about this time: Luttrell's copy, now in the Huntington Library, bears the dates '30 Nov' and '4 Dec 1682'. The play itself, without the second Epilogue, was first published early in 1683.

In *The Vindication: or The Parallel of The French Holy-League, and The English League and Covenant* . . ., written in the spring of 1683 in reply to attacks on the play (see Macdonald, pp. 241-3), Dryden says that this was his first 'essay' in drama. It was put aside on the advice of friends, and taken up by Lee and himself in 1682 'to make . . . a Parallel, betwixt the *Holy League* plotted by the House of *Guise* and its *Adherents,* with the *Covenant* plotted by the *Rebels* in the time of King *Charles* the First, and those of the *new Association,* which was the Spawn of the *old Covenant*'. On the 'Association' see *The Medall,* 'Epistle To The Whigs', ll. 31, 82, notes. An account of the delay in production is given by Macdonald, pp. 125-6.

On the actors William Smith and Sarah Cooke, see *Prologue To His Royal Highness* and Epilogue to *The Loyal Brother,* notes.

Prologue, To The Duke of Guise. 1-2. *The Holy League,* &c. See *Astræa Redux,* ll. 98-104, note; *The Medall,* 'Epistle To The Whigs', ll. 61-63. 'Our Cov'nant' is 'A solemn League and Covenant for Reformation and Defence of Religion', 1643 (Rushworth, *Historical Collections,* III. ii), of which the Whig 'Association' is the 'Spawn'.

3. *our hot-brain'd Sheriffs.* See *Absalom and Achitophel,* l. 585, note; *The Second Part of Absalom and Achitophel,* ll. 1131-8, note. During the elections of July 1682 the old sheriffs were committed to the Tower for rioting (Ogg, ii. 637).

6. *their godly Beggars:* Huguenots, who were seeking refuge in England even before the revocation of the Edict of Nantes (1685). See *The Hind and the Panther,* 'To the Reader', l. 30, note.

15. *their pois'ning way.* See Prologue to *The Spanish Fryar,* l. 46, note.

18-19. *your true Protestant . . . Flail.* In the heat of the Popish Plot citizens carried, for protection against Papist assailants, 'a certain Pocket Weapon, which, for its Design and Efficacy, had the Honour to be called a *Protestant Flail.* It was for Street and Croud-Work, and the Engine, lurking perdue in a Coat Pocket, might readily sally out to Execution; and so, by clearing a great Hall, or Piazza, or so, carry an Election by a choice way of polling, called knocking down' (North, *Examen,* pp. 572-3). For an illustration, see Lane, p. 240.

41. *Make London independant of the Crown.* See Prologue *To The King and Queen,* l. 24, note.

43. *Ignoramus Juries.* See *The Medall,* introductory note. In May 1682 'there

were two verdicts given by an Ignoramus Jury at Guildhall upon two indict-
ments against a couple of Whigs, that all the standers-by stood amazed to
see that, upon the fullest and clearest proofs imaginable, the jury brought
them in not guilty' (*HMC Graham of Netherby*, p. 352). Cf. *Heraclitus Ridens*,
No. 25, 19 July 1681: 'I am glad I was not born to be a King; for I find if my
Life had lain never so much at stake, *Ignoramus* would have been . . . far from
endeavouring to preserve it.'

45. *scan*: assess. Cf. *The Medall*, l. 213; Pope, *An Essay on Man*, ii. 1.

46. *what in Coffee-houses you began.* 'As to handing Treasonable Papers about
in Coffee Houses, *every body knows* it was the Original of the very thing call'd
a Coffee-House, and that it is the very Profession of a Coffee-Man to do so'
(Defoe, *Review*, 12 March 1713). Cf. Ogg, i. 101–2.

Epilogue. 3–5. *no one Man was meant*, &c. Dryden denies at length in *The
Vindication* that he intended any parallel of the Dukes of Guise and Monmouth: 'The *One* was manifestly the *Leader*, the *Other*, at the worst, is but
misled. The *Designs* of the *One* tended openly to *Usurpation*: those of the *Other*
may yet be interpreted more fairly; and I hope from the natural candour and
probity of his temper, that it will come to a perfect submission and reconcile-
ment at last. . . . The first words of the *Prologue* spake the *Play* to be a
Parallel; . . . it is not . . . a Parallel of the *Men*, but of the *Times*. A Parallel of the
Factions, and of the *Leaguers*.' *frank*: lavish.

12. *Se defendendo never was a Sin.* Cf. *Absalom and Achitophel*, l. 458, note.

23. *Trimmer*: a term applied at this time to moderates like Temple and
Halifax (see *Absalom and Achitophel*, l. 882, note). 'This innocent word
Trimmer signifieth no more than this,' says Halifax, 'That if Men are together
in a Boat, and one part of the Company would weigh it down on one side,
another would make it lean as much to the contrary; it happeneth there is a
third Opinion of those, who conceive it would do as well, if the Boat went
even; without endangering the Passengers' (*Works*, ed. Raleigh, p. 48). The
high Tory naturally suspected the Trimmer of Whiggish inclinations; in
The Character of a Whig (1700) there is a portrait of 'A Whig Trimmer, or a
Jack of all Sides'.

30. *Jack Ketch*: the public hangman.

34. *him that hung*, &c. Erasmus, who criticized Lutherans and Papists in
equal measure, and declined either to support or to oppose Luther. Cf. Congreve, *The Double-Dealer* (1694), IV: 'Hell has served you even as Heaven has
done, left you to your self.—You're in a kind of *Erasmus* Paradice. . . .'

Another Epilogue. 1. *Two Houses joyn'd.* See Prologue and Epilogue *To The
King and Queen*, note.

5. *Bilbo*: a sword noted for the temper of its blade. See Prologue to *The
Spanish Fryar*, l. 40, note.

8. *Marybone*: Marylebone Fields, frequently used as a duelling ground.
Cf. Evelyn, *Diary*, 20 December 1684.

14. *four Shillings*: the price of admission to the boxes. Cf. Shadwell, *The Sullen Lovers* (1668), II: 'At t'other house there's a rare Play, with a Jigg in 't ... but if there were nothing else in 't, you might have your four shillings out in Thunder and Lightning.'

26. *Ogling one another*. In the Epilogue to Shadwell's *The Lancashire Witches* (1682), 'ogling' is glossed in the margin as 'A foolish Word among the Canters for glancing'. Cf. *The Spectator*, No. 46, 23 April 1711. Ogling among men is remarked on in Shadwell's *The Virtuoso* (1676), II: young men are 'good for nothing but to roar and make a noise in a Playhouse. To be very brisk with pert Whores in Vizards. ... And when Whores are not there, they play Monkey-tricks with one another, while all sober men laugh at them.'

39. *Towzing*: amorous horse-play. Cf. *Sir Martin Mar-all* (1668), I: 'Why, Girl, he'll make fierce Love to you, but ... play the Innocent. ... And be sure when he has tows'd you, not to appear at Supper that Night, that you may fright him.'

A Song in the Fifth Act. At the banquet Malicorne calls for music, and 'a Song and Dance' follows. The song is printed with the music at the end of the play. For the music and reprints, see Day, pp. 62–63 and 161.

An Epigram of Agathias
(Page 331)

Tonson published the first volume of *Plutarchs Lives. Translated from the Greek by Several Hands* in the spring of 1683. The fifth and last volume appeared in 1686; there were other editions in 1688 and 1693. Dryden contributed the Dedication to the Duke of Ormonde (see *Absalom and Achitophel*, ll. 817, 831, notes) and a Life of Plutarch which concludes (pp. 127–8): 'The Epigram of *Agathias*, deserves also to be remember'd: This Author flourish'd about the year five hundred, in the Reign of the Emperour *Justinian*: The Verses are extant in the *Anthologia*, [xvi. 331], and with the Translation of them, I will conclude the praises of our Author; having first admonish'd you, that they are suppos'd to be written on a Statue erected by the *Romans* to his Memory.' The Greek text and translation follow.

The Art of Poetry, Written in French by The Sieur de Boileau, Made English
(Page 332)

Boileau's *L'Art poétique* appeared in 1674. This translation, first published anonymously by Bentley and Magnes in 1683, was reprinted by Tonson in *The Annual Miscellany: For the Year 1694* (1708) as 'Made *English* by Sir *William Soame*, Bart. And Revis'd and Alter'd, by Mr. *John Dryden*', with the following

Advertisement: 'This translation of Monsr. Boileau's *Art of Poetry* was made in the year 1680 by Sir William Soame of Suffolk, Bart. who being very intimately acquainted with Mr. Dryden, desired his Revival of it. I saw the Manuscript lye in Mr. Dryden's Hands for above Six Months, who made very considerable Alterations in it, particularly the beginning of the 4th Canto; and it being his Opinion that it would be better to apply the poem to English Writers, than keep to the French Names . . . that was entirely done by Mr. Dryden. . . .'

This practice was common: Oldham's version of Horace's *De Arte Poetica* (1681) introduced 'English names of Men, Places and Customs' as 'more agreeable to the relish of the present Age'. Dryden's 'application' is not consistently good. Appropriate substitutions are Waller (ll. 17, 131–42) for Malherbe, Duffett (l. 90) for the 'pitoyable auteur' d'Assoucy, 'empereur du burlesque', and Jonson (ll. 822–9) for Molière (iii. 393–400). Less satisfactory are Spenser (ll. 117–20) for Marot (i. 119–22), and Spenser, Cowley, Denham, Waller, and Dryden (ll. 1052–7) for Corneille, Racine, Benserade, and Segrais (iv. 196–202). Some replacements do not suit at all: e.g. Fairfax (ll. 115–16) for Villon (i. 117–18), Davenant (ll. 121–30) for Ronsard, and Chaucer (ll. 395–8) for Régnier (ii. 168–70). Dubartas (ll. 21–26) replaces Saint-Amant, author of *Moyse sauvé*, as better known in England through Sylvester's translation (see ll. 101–2, note).

55. *Halls*. Boileau has 'des *plafonds* les ronds et les ovales' (i. 55).

90. *the Mock-Tempest*: *The Mock Tempest, or, The Enchanted Castle* (1675), one of Duffett's Drury Lane travesties of popular successes at the Dorset Garden theatre.

96. *Butler*. See Dedication of *The Satires of Juvenalis*, ll. 2455 ff.

101–2. These lines are added to Boileau (i. 100) as illustration, and are taken with modification from *Dubartas his Second Weeke*, I. iv. 186–7. Dryden quotes the passage in the Dedication of *The Spanish Fryar* (1681) with the comment: 'an injudicious Poet who aims at Loftiness runs easily into the swelling puffie Style, because it looks like Greatness. I remember, when I was a Boy, I thought inimitable *Spencer* a mean Poet in comparison of *Sylvester's Dubartas*: and was rapt into an ecstasie when I read these Lines. . . . I am much deceived if this be not abominable Fustian.'

115. *Fairfax*. His *Godfrey of Bulloigne* (1600) places him *after* Spenser. Cf. Preface to *Fables*, ll. 28–33, note.

126. *Mock-Gondibert*. Two satires on Davenant's *Gondibert* (1651): *Certain Verses written by severall of the Authors Friends; to be reprinted with the Second Edition of Gondibert* (1653), and *The Incomparable Poem Gondibert, Vindicated* (1655).

131. *Waller came last*, &c. Cf. Ker, i. 7, and Dedication of *The Satires of Juvenalis*, ll. 366–9.

251. *Randal*: probably Thomas Randolph (1605–35). Scott objects that

Randolph's pastorals 'are rather ornate, and duly garnished with classical names'; but all Dryden needed was a pastoral poet.

268. Dryden and Soame take 'D'un ton un peu plus haut, mais pourtant sans audace' (ii. 38) with Pastoral; but Boileau opens his paragraph on Elegy with it.

366. *The Brittish Round*, &c. Boileau's 'Le rondeau, né gaulois, a la naïveté' (ii. 140). The footnote to Madrigal (l. 369) has obviously slipped out of place, and refers to the 'Round'.

418. *Mr. S——*: for the 'poète idiot' de Lignières (ii. 194). On Dryden's antipathy to Settle, see *The Second Part of Absalom and Achitophel*, l. 412, note.

428. *Logan*: replacing Nanteuil, 'fameux graveur' (ii. 204).

556. *Chapman, in Bussy D'Ambois took delight.* Cf. Dedication of *The Spanish Fryar* (1681): 'I have sometimes wonder'd, in the reading, what was become of those glaring Colours which amaz'd me in *Bussy Damboys* upon the Theatre: but when I had taken up what I suppos'd, a fallen Star, I found I had been cozen'd with a Jelly. . . . A dwarfish Thought, dress'd up in gigantick Words. . . . I have Indignation enough to burn a *D'amboys* annually to the Memory of *Johnson*.'

620–59. *In vain*, &c. Cf. Dedication of *The Satires of Juvenalis*, ll. 448–52, note.

650. *leaky Boat*: for 'fatale barque' (iii. 223). Cf. *The Fourth Book of the Georgics*, l. 735, note.

656. *old Janus with his front of Brass*: for 'la Guerre au front d'airain' (iii. 229). Janus Quirinus or Martialis presided over war.

669. The translators substitute the Frankish king Chilperic for Boileau's Childebrand (iii. 242), the hero of Carel de Sainte-Garde's epic (1666).

714. *his Story*: translating 'votre ouvrage' (iii. 287). Boileau returns to his critical advice in this line; the translators link it to the account of Virgil.

793. *Otter*: 'a land, and sea-Captaine' in Jonson's *Epicoene*. Cf. Epilogue to the Second Part of *The Conquest of Granada*, ll. 3–6, note.

828–9. *When in the Fox*, &c. In Jonson's *Volpone*, v. iv, Sir Politique Would-bee disguises himself as a tortoise to escape three merchants:

> Here, I' haue a place, sir, to put backe my leggs,
> (Please you to lay it on, sir) with this cap,
> And my blacke gloues, I'le lye, sir, like a tortoyse,
> Till they are gone.

857. *Jack Puddings*: mountebanks' assistants: Boileau's 'laquais' (iii. 428). Cf. Prologue to *Albumazar*, l. 38.

891. *Herringman*. See *Mac Flecknoe*, l. 105, note.

894. *The Counter-scuffle*: a burlesque on a quarrel in the counter-prison (included in *Miscellany Poems*, the Third Part, 1716, pp. 333–51):

> . . . And now let each one listen well,
> While I the famous Battel tell,
> In *Woodstreet-Counter* that befel. . . .

903. *Sh—ll*: Shadwell. See *Mac Flecknoe*, introductory note.

1072. *Patriots Forms*. Cf. *Absalom and Achitophel*, l. 179, note.

1077. *boutfeaus*: boutefeux, firebrands.

Epilogue to Constantine the Great

(Page 362)

Lee's *Constantine the Great: A Tragedy* seems to have been first performed at Drury Lane in November 1683. In his copy of the first edition of the play (1684) Malone wrote beneath the Prologue 'Published first in folio Nov. 12, 1683'; and Luttrell's copy of the authorized edition of the Epilogue (1684) is dated 14 November 1683 (Macdonald, p. 144; Wiley, p. 182).

The Prologue (by Otway) and the Epilogue by Dryden were first published, without any indication of authorship, as a single half-sheet 'Printed for C. Tebroc, 1683'. This has every appearance of being pirated, and may have been printed from an inaccurate and clumsily completed shorthand version taken in the theatre (see J. H. Smith, *PMLA* lxviii (1953), 257–8, note). Tonson's 'True Coppy' of the Epilogue, a single half-sheet printed on one side, appeared in the next year and gave the poem to Dryden. The first edition of the play (1684), published also by Tonson, gives substantially the same text as *A True Coppy*, but does not assign the Epilogue to Dryden.

Tebroc's edition describes the Epilogue as '*Spoken by Mrs. Cook*'; see Epilogue to *The Loyal Brother*, note.

4. *a true Protestant*. See Prologue to *The Spanish Fryar*, l. 11, note.

8. *every Trimmer turn'd Addressing Tory*. See Epilogue to *The Duke of Guise*, l. 23, note; Prologue *spoken at Mithridates King of Pontus*, l. 4, note.

10. Claus is elected king of the beggars in Beaumont and Fletcher's *The Beggars Bush*, II. i.

21–31. 'The severity of the Austrian government . . . towards those who dissented from the Roman Catholic faith, occasioned several insurrections. The most memorable was headed by Count Teckeli, who allied himself with the sultan, assumed the crown of Transylvania, as a vassal of the Porte, and joined, with a considerable force, the large army of Turks which besieged Vienna. . . . A similarity of situation and of interest induced the Whig party in England to look with a favourable eye upon this Hungarian insurgent' (Scott).

28. *nose*: confront.

32. *the last Plot*: the Rye House Plot to murder the king, which came to light in June 1683 (Ogg, ii. 647–50).

38–45. *The Original Trimmer*, &c. Probably Shaftesbury; see *The Medall*, l. 37, note. With ll. 40–45 cf. *The Hind and the Panther*, i. 377–87.

Poems from Miscellany Poems . . . By the most Eminent Hands (1684)

(Page 364)

On Tonson's Miscellanies, 1684–1727, see Macdonald, p. 67. The 1684 volume contains translations of Virgil's eclogues, some of Ovid's elegies and Horace's odes, and miscellaneous translations and original poems. Dryden's contributions, which include *Mac Flecknoe*, reprints of *Absalom and Achitophel*, *The Medall*, and four prologues and an epilogue, as well as versions of *Eclogues* iv and ix which he revised for the 1697 *Virgil*, run to more than a third of the book. Amongst the contributors were Creech, Roscommon, Sedley, and Tate.

Elegy the Nineteenth

(Page 364)

22. *Bulks*: stalls projecting from the fronts of shops, where the destitute might find a place to sleep. Cf. Johnson, ii. 398–9.

30. *The Watchman.* In place of 'dum servat Juno sinuatam cornibus Io' (l. 29), Dryden takes the reading of Heinsius: 'dum nimium servat custos Iunonius Io.'

31. *an easie Whetstone Whore.* See Prologue to *The Wild Gallant Reviv'd*, l. 8, note.

45. *The sneaking City Cuckold*: for 'stultus' (l. 46). See Epilogue to *Marriage A-la-Mode*, l. 32, note.

Amaryllis, Or the Third Idyllium of Theocritus, Paraphras'd

(Page 366)

There are correspondences of line and phrase between Dryden's versions of Theocritus here and in *Sylvæ*, and Creech's complete translation (1684). It is impossible to distinguish debtor and creditor.

48. *Kisses are but empty, when Compar'd*: i.e. with fuller pleasure. Cf. *Sylvæ*, 'Daphnis', ll. 5–6.

72. *lease*: glean.

76. *resty*: sluggish, inactive. The reference is to divination by turning a sieve held on a pair of shears: the sieve trembled when the significant name was mentioned.

Prologue, To the University of Oxon. Spoken by Mr. Hart, at the Acting of the Silent Woman
(Page 369)

On Dryden's addresses to the University, see Macdonald, pp. 137–9. Writing to Rochester in the early summer of 1673, Dryden refers to a prologue and epilogue 'which I made for our players when they went down to Oxford. I heare since they have succeeded; And by the event your Lordship will judge how easy 'tis to passe any thing upon an University; and how grosse flattery the learned will endure' (Ward, p. 10). These are the only two poems among Dryden's University addresses which can be assigned to 1673; and some of the allusions in them support this date. On Charles Hart, see Epilogue to The First Part of *The Conquest of Granada*, note. The popularity of *Epicoene, or The Silent Woman* on the Restoration stage is illustrated in Jonson, ix. 209–14.

32–33. *the Lucretian way,* &c. De Rerum Natura, ii. 1059–63.

40. *He owns no Crown,* &c. The Praetorian guards were instituted by Augustus as a personal defence. In time 'the firmest and best-established princes were obliged . . . to purchase their precarious faith by a liberal donative; which, since the elevation of Claudius, was exacted as a legal claim, on the accession of every new emperor' (Gibbon, *Decline and Fall*, v).

Epilogue, Spoken by the same
(Page 370)

1–2. *No poor Dutch Peasant,* &c. A reference to the destructive invasion of Holland by France in 1672.

7. *A French Troop.* Probably the company of French comedians who came over in December 1672 and left in May 1673 (Nicoll, p. 253). Cf. *infra*, Prologue to *Arviragus Reviv'd*, ll. 5–22; *A Prologue spoken at the Opening of the New House*, ll. 38–48.

11. *Th' Italian Merry-Andrews.* An Italian troupe led by Tiberio Fiorilli came over in April 1673. Evelyn records a performance at court, apparently by this company, on 29 May; and on 4 September Charles ordered 'vnto Scaramouchi and Harlekin vnto each of them a Medall & Chayne of Gold' (Nicoll, p. 250). Cf. Marvell, *Poems and Letters*, ed. Margoliouth, ii. 320.

22. *Machines.* On the development of scenery on the Restoration stage, see Nicoll, pp. 35–61. Cf. Prologue to *The Kind Keeper*, l. 2, note.

30. *Macbeth, the Simon Magus of the Town.* Davenant's operatic version of *Macbeth* was performed by the Duke's company in February 1673 'drest in all it's Finery, as new Cloath's, new Scenes, Machines, as flyings for the Witches; with all the Singing and Dancing in it' (Downes, p. 33). At this

time Dryden was writing for the rival King's company. Simon Magus 'before-time in the city used sorcery' (Acts viii. 9).

Prologue, to the University of Oxford, 1674. Spoken by Mr. Hart

(Page 372)

14. *The Sphere of Chrystal.* Cf. Spenser, *The Faerie Queene*, III. ii. 19:

> It vertue had, to shew in perfect sight,
> What euer thing was in the world contaynd,
> Betwixt the lowest earth and heauens hight,
> So that it to the looker appertaynd;
>
> .   .   .   .
>
> For thy it round and hollow shaped was,
> Like to the world it selfe, and seem'd a world of glas.

24. *Muses so severe are worshipt here.* Martial, *Epi.* IX. xi. 17, 'qui Musas colimus severiores'.

27. *see th' offended God, and dye.* Exod. xx. 19, xxxiii. 20.

Epilogue to Oxford. Spoken by Mrs. Marshal

(Page 373)

The first edition of *Miscellany Poems* contains two versions of the Epilogue (S7ʳ–S8ʳ and T2ʳ–T3ʳ). Only the first of these is reprinted in the second edition. The second version, which has every appearance of having been tidied up by a printer, was probably set up from a printed text accidentally included in the copy for the miscellany.

17. *Bathurst*: Ralph Bathurst (1620–1704), President of Trinity, Vice-Chancellor 1673–6, and an accomplished Latin poet.

Prologue to the University of Oxford

(Page 374)

The date of this poem is uncertain; but the probable date of the excursion of the '*Scotch* Rebels' to Edinburgh is during the residence of the Duke of York at Holyrood from November 1680 to March 1682 (see James Kinsley, 'A Dryden Play at Edinburgh', *SHR* xxxiii (1954), 129–32).

16. *a Copper-lace*: a piece of lace or embroidery, in which a copper thread was substituted for a gold one. *Drugget*: cf. *Mac Flecknoe*, l. 33, note.

19. *a plume for Indian Emperour.* William Tytler remembered having seen a play-bill advertising Dryden's *The Indian Emperour* (1667) in Edinburgh

during the duke's residence (*Transactions of the Society of Antiquaries of Scotland,* i (1792), 503).

27. *Teg*: the stock name for an Irishman (see J. O. Bartley, *Teague, Shenkin and Sawney,* 1954, pp. 102–4 and 105–10). Ormonde, the Chancellor of Oxford, brought an Irish company over in 1677, and there was a plan to bring them again in 1680 (Nicoll, pp. 306–7). But Irish companies cannot have been uncommon. There was one in Edinburgh in 1681 (Kinsley, art. cit.; *Register of the Privy Council of Scotland,* 3rd ser., vii (1915), 161–2.

30. *a second Massacre.* The first was in 1642 (Burnet, i. 41).

Prologue to the University of Oxford
(Page 375)

Attention was first drawn to the transcript of this poem (Bodl. MS. Eng. Poet. e. 4, f. 178, dated 1676) by R. G. Ham in *The London Mercury,* xxi (1930), 421. Although there were rumours in 1686–7 that Dryden was a candidate for the Wardenship of All Souls (Macdonald, p. 138), there is no evidence in this Prologue for Ham's suggestion that his 'ambitions in respect to [Oxford] were . . . clearly in mind by July, 1676'.

5–6. *and Trade in Ore,* &c. Cf. Vasquez in *The Indian Emperour* (1667), I. i:

> Methinks we walk in Dreams on Fairy Land,
> Where Golden Ore lies mixt with common Sand.

31–32. *Not in the suffragating Tribes,* &c. For a provincial community the first step towards Roman citizenship was the receipt of the *ius Latii,* which did not include the privilege of the *ius suffragii.* The poets, says Dryden, ask not for full membership of the University but merely for the advantages which association with Oxford confers on the provincial.

Prologue to Arviragus Reviv'd: Spoken by Mr. Hart
(Page 376)

Lodowick Carlell's *Arviragus and Philicia* (1639) and others of his plays 'were formerly acted at the Blackfryers' and were 'allowed of to his Ma^tes Servants at ye New Theatre' in 1668/9 (Nicoll, pp. 353–4). From the opening lines of the Prologue it is clear that the revival took place at Lincoln's Inn Fields after the burning of the Theatre Royal in 1672 (see Prologue to *Wit without Money,* note). It is referred to in *London Drollery: Or, The Wits Academy,* 1673 (Macdonald, p. 69). On Hart, see Epilogue to The First Part of *The Conquest of Granada,* note.

2. *Glorious Theatres and New.* The Duke's company began playing at their new theatre in Dorset Garden in November 1671 (Downes, p. 31). See Prologue to *Marriage A-la-Mode,* ll. 24–27, note.

6. *A Brisk French Troop.* See *supra, Epilogue* 'Spoken . . . at the Acting of the *Silent Woman*', l. 7, note.

7. *bloody Bills*: the play-bills of the French troupe, printed in red (see M. Summers, *The Restoration Theatre*, 1934, pp. 8–9).

Prologue for the Women, when they Acted at the Old Theatre in Lincolns-Inn-Fields

(Page 377)

On performances at Lincoln's Inn Fields, see Prologue and Epilogue to *Secret-Love*, 'Spoken by the Women', note.

9–10. *For much good Pastime*, &c. Cf. *The Sixth Satyr of Juvenal*, ll. 85–86.

13. *the hot Burgundian.* Burgundians were celebrated for desperate violence and skill in fencing. Cf. *Every Man in his Humour* (1616), IV. iv. 17, 'that rogue, that foist, that fencing *Burgullian*', and Simpson's note (Jonson, ix. 383).

14. *Vizard Masque.* See Prologue to The Second Part of *The Conquest of Granada*, l. 13, note.

23. *The Gaudy House with Scenes.* The new theatre in Dorset Garden spared no cost in providing astonishing scenic effects to attract the citizens. Cf. Prologue to *Marriage A-la-Mode*, ll. 24–27, and note.

A Prologue spoken at the Opening of the New House, Mar. 26. 1674

(Page 378)

The new Theatre Royal in Drury Lane designed by Wren was built at a cost of £4,000 to replace the old theatre burnt down in 1672. The King's company had been in financial difficulties for some time; and the cost of the new building, which had to be met in instalments from daily takings, was a heavy additional burden (Hotson, pp. 254–9; Nicoll, pp. 323–4). Dryden again ridicules the 'Gaudy House with Scenes' at Dorset Garden (see *supra, Prologue for the Women*, l. 23, note). In a manuscript Prologue to the operatic *Tempest* (1674) a reply is made to Dryden's criticism (*Works of Thomas Shadwell*, ed. Summers, ii. 196):

> Wee, as the ffathers of the Stage have said,
> To treat you here a vast expense have made;
> What they have gott from you in chests is laid,
> Or is for purchas'd Lands, or houses paid,
> You, in this house, all our estates may find,
> Wch for your pleasures wholly are design'd. . . .

27. *The dangling Knee-fringe, and the Bib-Cravat.* Decorative fringes on

breeches were popular in the late 1620's; the fashion was revived after 1660 and often carried to ludicrous extremes. Cravats developed in size and ornamental value through the later seventeenth century.

36. *Scenes, Machines, and empty Opera's reign.* There had been spasmodic attempts at drama with music just before the Restoration, and Charles II showed some interest in Italian opera. But there was little interest in native opera until the 1670's. Davenant's operatic version of *Macbeth* was performed at Dorset Garden in February 1673 (see *supra*, Epilogue 'Spoken . . . at the Acting of the *Silent Woman*', l. 30, note); and when the 'New House' opened the Duke's company was rehearsing the operatic *Tempest* (Nicoll, p. 430).

38. *Troops of famisht Frenchmen.* French comedians were in England in 1673 (see *supra*, Epilogue 'Spoken . . . at the Acting of the *Silent Woman*', l. 7, note); and French opera was given in 1673 and 1674 (Nicoll, p. 253).

53. *Machines and Tempests will destroy the new.* H. M. Hooker records a variant reading of this line, 'Tempests and Operas will destroy ye New', in Huntington Library MS. EL 8923 (*HLQ* vi (1943), 224–8). Dryden's reference may be either to the operatic *Tempest* then in preparation, or to 'the superfluity of thunder and lightning and flying effects in D'Avenant's *Macbeth*' (W. J. Lawrence, *The Elizabethan Playhouse*, 1912, p. 203).

Epilogue by the same Author
(Page 379)

8. *vallancy*: fringing the face. Cf. Shakespeare, *Hamlet*, II. ii. 428, 'Why, thy face is valanced since I saw thee last.'

19. *Midnight Scowrings.* See Prologue to *The Wild Gallant Reviv'd*, ll. 10–12, note; Prologue to *All for Love*, l. 22, note.

22. *by each others Swords to fall.* See Prologue to *The Spanish Fryar*, l. 40, note.

32. *three Boys in Buff.* Noyes suggests that the reference is to a droll, *The Three Merry Boyes*, or to the comic parts of Fletcher's *Rollo Duke of Normandy* on which the droll was based. The first is the more plausible alternative: Fletcher's play was popular in Dryden's day (see J. D. Jump's edition, 1948, pp. xxxi–xxxiv), and Lisideius speaks well of it (Ker, i. 60). *The Three Merry Boyes* is included in Kirkman's *The Wits, or, Sport upon Sport*, 1672 (ed . J. J. Elson, 1932).

33. *the Poets Heads.* Cf. D'Urfey, *Collin's Walk through London and Westminster*, 1690, Canto iv, 'Wednesdays Walk to the Play House', p. 149: at Dorset Garden

> He saw each Box with Beauty crown'd,
> And Pictures deck the Structure round;
> *Ben, Shakespear,* and the learned Rout,
> With Noses some, and some without.

Prologue and Epilogue to the Princess of Cleves

(Page 380)

Nathaniel Lee's *The Princess of Cleve* was performed at Dorset Garden in 1681 and published in 1689; Dryden's Prologue and Epilogue were not printed with the play. It seems likely, from the allusion in the Prologue to *Absalom and Achitophel*, that they were written for a performance in late 1681 or early 1682. The plot of the play concerns the passions of Nemours (Prologue, ll. 1–6) for the virtuous Princess of Cleves. The princess confesses her love for Nemours to her husband, who dies of grief. Thereafter, placing honour before love, she rejects Nemours and retires from court life (Epilogue, ll. 23–28).

Prologue. 19. *perjuria ridet Amantum.* Ovid, *De Arte Amandi,* i. 633.

34. *Renouncing*: in Dryden's day, 'revoking'; failing to follow suit though having the right card.

Epilogue intended to have been spoken by the Lady Henr. Mar. Wentworth when Calisto was acted at Court

(Page 383)

Calisto; or, The Chaste Nymph, a masque by John Crowne, was produced at court in the spring of 1675 and published, with Crowne's Prologue and Epilogue, later in the year (see E. Boswell, *The Restoration Court Stage*, 1932, pp. 177–227). This Epilogue was apparently first printed in *Miscellany Poems*, but was not assigned to Dryden until the third edition (1702). It closes the first section of the miscellany, stands apart from Dryden's other stage pieces, and may have been included as an afterthought. Gardner (pp. 341–5) questions the attribution of this epilogue to Dryden. He argues that (i) since Dryden, the poet laureate, had been passed over in favour of the insignificant Crowne —probably through Rochester's spite (cf. Macdonald, p. 210)—it is unlikely that he contributed an epilogue for the performance; (ii) parallels between this poem and the Epilogue printed with the play suggest that Crowne wrote both; (iii) the Epilogue in *Miscellany Poems* was the original one, but the 'undiplomatic' references to the Franco-Dutch war (ll. 21–28) made it advisable to rewrite it in the form printed with the play; (iv) Tonson ascribed the Epilogue to Dryden in 1702, after Dryden's death and 'about the time of Crowne's death', to enhance the value of his miscellany. But (i) Crowne admits in his address to the reader that writing *Calisto* was a trial to him, and acknowledges Dryden's superior claims; there is no reason why he should not have sought Dryden's help in providing a graceful epilogue. (ii) Crowne's own Epilogue resembles that in *Miscellany Poems* only in general terms, and the parallels do not prejudice Dryden's claims. (iii) Lines 21–28 are not undiplomatic; Charles would welcome the compliment (cf. Bryant, pp. 240–1). (iv) Crowne died in 1712. The question of authorship, however, remains open. The internal evidence is inconclusive; there is a clumsiness in the style of the poem which is not characteristic of Dryden, though ll. 19–28 are in his manner.

Lady Henrietta Maria Wentworth (1660–86), who played Jupiter, succeeded her father as Baroness Wentworth of Nettlestead in 1665 or 1667. She became Monmouth's mistress.

29. *Two glorious Nymphs*: the daughters of the Duke of York. Mary, aged 12, played Calisto; Anne, aged 10, played Nyphe.

Prologue To a New Play, Call'd, The Disappointment: Or, The Mother in Fashion
(Page 385)

Dryden contributed a prologue and an epilogue to Southerne's first play in 1682 (see Prologue to *The Loyal Brother*, note). His second play, *The Disappointment*, was first performed at Drury Lane in April 1684. The Prologue (without ascription) and Epilogue ('By Another Hand') were published separately as a single half-sheet printed on both sides (1684). In the first edition of the play (*TC*, June 1684) the Prologue is assigned to Dryden and the Epilogue to 'the Honourable John Stafford Esquire'. On Betterton, see Prologue to *Troilus and Cressida*, note.

38. *the High Dice, and the Low*: 'loaded dice, contrived some for high, and others for low throws' (Scott).

42. *Love behind our Scenes*. See Epilogue *To The King and Queen*, l. 35, note.

49–50. *Brings her in Triumph*, &c. Cf. *The Wild Gallant*, III: 'I'm glad with all my Heart this Minx is prevented of her design. . . . His old Father in the Country would have given him but little thank for 't, to see him bring down a fine-bred Woman, with a Lute, and a Dressing-Box, and a handful of Money to her Portion.'

51. *Scowring*. Cf. Prologue to *The Wild Gallant Reviv'd*, ll. 10–12, note; Prologue to *All for Love*, l. 22, note.

54. *rap and rend*: snatch, steal.

55–56. *But while abroad*, &c. Cf. Epilogue to *The Pilgrim*, ll. 41–42.

57–64. *Last, some there are*, &c. Cf. Epilogue *To The King and Queen*, ll. 11–12.

60. *grubble*: fondle.

To the Earl of Roscomon, on his Excellent Essay on Translated Verse
(Page 387)

Wentworth Dillon, fourth Earl of Roscommon (1633?–85), was born in Ireland during the lieutenancy of his uncle Strafford, was educated on the

Continent during the interregnum, and returned after the Restoration to a place of favour at court. 'And about this time, in imitation of those learned and polite assemblies, with which he had been acquainted abroad . . . he began to form a Society for the refining, and fixing the standard of our language; in which design his great friend Mr. *Dryden* was a principal assistant' (*The Works of Edmund Waller*, ed. Fenton, 1744, p. cxl). *An Essay on Translated Verse* was published by Tonson in 1684, with Dryden's poem, Latin verses by Dryden's son Charles, and others by Chetwood and Amherst. A second edition was being discussed in the autumn of 1684 (see l. 47, note) and appeared in 1685.

11–12. *barb'rous Nations*, &c. Cf. Ben Jonson, *The Vnder-wood*, xxix, 'A Fit of Rime against Rime'; Milton, *Paradise Lost*, 'The Verse'; and the summary of contemporary attitudes to rhyme in Dennis, i. 499–500. Roscommon refers to the 'barb'rous aid' of rhyme in *An Essay*; see Preface to *Sylvæ*, ll. 155–6, note.

15–23. Dryden's admiration for the Italian language is expressed at length in the Preface to *Albion and Albanius* (Ker, i. 273–4).

31. *an ESSAY*: 'a loose sally of the mind; an irregular indigested piece; not a regular and orderly composition' (Johnson, *Dictionary*).

36. *His own example*: translations of Virgil, *Ecl.* vi, and Horace, *Od.* i. 22 and iii. 6 (*Miscellany Poems*, 1684), and *De Arte Poetica* (1680; reprinted 1684).

47. Dryden wrote to Tonson in August or September 1684: 'For my Lord Roscomons Essay, I am of your opinion, that you shou'd reprint it, & that you may safely venture on a thousand more. In my verses before it, pray let the printer mend his errour, & let the line stand thus, That heer his Conque'ring Ancestors were nursd:—Charles his copy is all true' (Ward, pp. 22–23).

60. *an English Peer*. Mulgrave (see *Absalom and Achitophel*, l. 877, note) joined with Dryden in the version of 'Helen to Paris' in *Ovid's Epistles, Translated*.

72. *He both Minerva's*, &c. The earlier reading 'He' is preferable syntactically; 'Who' looks like a printer's alteration on the analogy of 'whom' in l. 68. Roscommon serves Minerva in her dual character of goddess of wisdom and the liberal arts, and goddess of war (cf. *Britannia Rediviva*, ll. 208–9).

73–74. *infus'd Titan*: Prometheus (see Ovid, *Meta.* i. 78–86). Dryden is following Juvenal, *Sat.* xiv. 33–35, which Stapylton translated (1673 edn.) as:

> Perhaps *one* youth, or *two*, untainted live,
> . . . . whose hearts *Tytan* may
> Have fram'd with more art, and of better clay.

To the Memory of Mr. Oldham
(Page 389)

John Oldham (1653–83) was an usher at Croydon school when his manuscript poems attracted the attention of Rochester. He then spent some years in Surrey as a tutor, and in 1681 'being out of all business and employ, he retired to the great City, set up for a Wit, and . . . at length being made known to that most generous and truly noble *William* Earl of *Kingston,* he was taken into his Patronage, lived with him in great respect at *Holme-Pierpont* in *Nottinghamshire,* where he made his last *Exit*' (Wood, *Ath. Ox.* ii. 751). His friendship with Dryden probably dated only from 1681. His *Remains* appeared in the year after his death (*TC,* November 1684) with memorial poems by Dryden, Flatman, Tate, D'Urfey, and others.

9. *Thus Nisus fell.* Virgil, *Aen.* v. 328. Oldham was twenty-two years younger than Dryden; but his *Satyrs Upon the Jesuits,* written in 1679, brought him earlier to the front as a satirist.

11–18. *O early ripe,* &c. Cf. Dryden's reflections on Persius, Dedication of *The Satires of Juvenalis,* ll. 1528–38.

22–25. *farewel thou young . . . Marcellus,* &c. See Virgil, *Aen.* vi. 854–86; *Æneis,* vi. 1221, note.

Poems from Sylvæ: or, The Second Part of Poetical Miscellanies

(Page 390)

Tonson published the second miscellany early in 1685 (advertised in *The Observator,* 1 January). Writing to Tonson from Northamptonshire in the previous autumn, Dryden says: 'Your opinion of the Miscellanyes is likewise mine: I will for once lay by the Religio Laici, till another time. But I must also add, that since we are to have nothing but new, I am resolvd we will have nothing but good, whomever we disoblige.' He promises 'four Odes of Horace, which I have already translated' and versions of Lucretius and Virgil; and although he reminds Tonson that 'my business heere is to unweary my selfe, after my studyes, not to drudge', he sent more verse for the miscellany than he at this time proposed (Ward, p. 23; see opening of the Preface). To this volume, which is made up almost entirely of translations, he contributed the Preface and almost half the poetry, including three translations of Virgil which he later revised for the complete version of 1697. See introductory note on the *Virgil.*

Preface. 3. *the History of the League.* A translation of Maimbourg's *Histoire de la Ligue,* undertaken at the king's command, and published in July 1684 (see Macdonald, p. 170).

13. *Roscomon's Essay.* See *To the Earl of Roscomon,* note.

21. *I have many times exceeded my Commission,* &c. Dryden's translation is consistently free. See Preface to *Ovid's Epistles,* ll. 177–312; Dedication of *Examen Poeticum,* ll. 216–38; Dedication of the *Æneis,* ll. 1948 ff.

31–32. *if he were living, and an Englishman,* &c. Cf. Preface to *Ovid's Epistles,* ll. 150–51; Dedication of *The Satires of Juvenalis*, ll. 2694 ff.; Dedication of the *Æneis*, ll. 2007–9.

41–42. *whose beauties I have been endeavouring all my Life to imitate.* Cf. *Annus Mirabilis*, 'An account of the ensuing Poem', ll. 167–72; Ker, ii. 148; Dedication of the *Æneis*, ll. 1867–69.

46. *our Ogleby's.* See *Mac Flecknoe*, l. 102, note.

52–54. *the knowledge of Men . . . both Sexes.* Cf. Boileau, *L'Art poétique*, iv. 121–4:

> Que les vers ne soient pas votre éternel emploi.
> Cultivez vos amis, soyez homme de foi:
> C'est peu d'être agréable et charmant dans un livre,
> Il faut savoir encore et converser et vivre.

In the Dedication of *Troilus and Cressida* (1679) Dryden laments 'how barbarously we yet write and speak', and remarks that the improvement of the French language 'was the employment of the whole Academy for many Years, for the perfect knowledge of a Tongue was never attain'd by any single Person. The Court, the College, and the Town must be joyn'd in it.' Cf. Johnson, i. 417–18.

63–74. *Thus it appears necessary*, &c. Cf. Preface to *Ovid's Epistles*, ll. 267–71.

81. *a late noble Painter*: probably Sir Peter Lely, who died in 1680.

106. *Symalæpha's.* Cf. Dedication of *Examen Poeticum*, ll. 249 ff.

113. *ambition, which is the vice of Lucan.* 'Ambition', pomp. Cf. Donne, *LXXX Sermons* (1640), p. 579, 'costly and expensive ambitions at Court, one worme or other shall devoure his riches'. In 'A Parallel of Poetry and Painting' Dryden says: 'bold metaphors . . . must be judiciously applied; for there is a difference betwixt daring and fool-hardiness. Lucan and Statius often ventured them too far; our Virgil never' (Ker, ii. 149).

113–15. *my definition of Poetical Wit . . . propriety of thoughts and words.* Dryden, at different times, uses 'wit' in three main senses: (i) the faculty which produces conceits and brilliance of style (Ker, i. 138–9); (ii) 'wit in a larger signification', a blend of fancy and judgement in creative writing (Ker, i. 172); (iii) propriety of thoughts and words. 'The Definition of Wit (which has been so often attempted, and ever unsuccessfully, by many Poets) is only this, That it is a Propriety of Thoughts and Words; or in other Terms, Thoughts and Words elegantly adapted to the Subject' (*The State of Innocence*, 1677, 'The Author's Apology for Heroick Poetry, and Poetick Licence'). This definition is elaborated in the Preface to *Albion and Albanius* (1685): 'Propriety of Thought is that Fancy which arises naturally from the Subject, or which the Poet adapts to it. Propriety of Words, is the cloathing of those Thoughts with such Expressions, as are naturally proper to them: and from both these, if they are judiciously perform'd, the delight of Poetry results.' This conception of 'wit' as the dominant element in composition, from the 'first Work' of fancy in 'moving the Sleeping Images of things towards the Light' to the final expression of the poet's thought in 'apt, significant and sounding words', is implicit in Dryden's earliest consideration of poetry (cf. *Annus Mirabilis*, 'An account of the ensuing Poem', ll. 113–19, note). In his Life of Lucian (written about 1696) he acknowledges that what he had thought to be his own definition of 'wit' as 'propriety of thoughts and words' is to be found in Aristotle (*Poet.* vi. 22; Malone, iii. 378).

121. *Hannibal Caro's in the Italian.* Dryden later became critical of this version of the *Aeneid* (1581); see Dedication of *The Satires of Juvenalis*, l. 393, and Dedication of the *Æneis*, l. 1790.

124. *Tasso tells us. Discorsi del poema eroico,* end of lib. ii.

155–6. *Roscomon justly observes,* at the end of *An Essay on Translated Verse* (1684):

> When in Triumphant State the *British* Muse,
> True to her self, shall barb'rous aid Refuse,
> And in the *Roman* Majesty appear,
> Which none know better, and none come so near.

166. *two particular Lines,* &c. Dryden made the correction in his translation of 1697 (*Æneis*, x. 1299–1300).

190. *more perfect in their kind, than even his Divine Æneids.* Cf. *Annus Mirabilis*, 'An account of the ensuing Poem', l. 152, note; *The First Book of the Georgics*, note.

203. *doubt of some eternal Truths*: 'have doubts in their favour, be unable to reject them peremptorily like Lucretius' (Ker).

278. *the Essay on Poetry*: by Sheffield, published anonymously in 1682. See *Absalom and Achitophel*, l. 877, note; Dedication of the *Æneis*, ll. 209–48; Johnson, ii. 175, 179.

281. *in his Ode concerning Wit*: Miscellanies, 'Of Wit', vi.

297. *one mistake*: 'Lucretius the Fourth Book', l. 26.

303. *Non ego,* &c. De *Arte Poetica,* ll. 351–3.

312–13. *the . . . Translatour of Lucretius*: Thomas Creech (1659–1700), Fellow of All Souls, whose complete translation (1683) earned the commendation of Tate, Otway, and Evelyn. See Macdonald, pp. 246–7.

336–9. *His Shepherds . . . Guarini.* Cf. Rapin, *De Carmine Pastorali* (translated in Creech's *Theocritus,* 1684): 'Therefore let *Pastoral* never venture upon a lofty subject, let it not recede one jot from its proper matter, but be employ'd about Rustick affairs: such as are mean and humble in themselves; and such are the affairs of Shepherds, especially their Loves'; ' *Tasso, Bonarellus, Guarinus, Marinus* . . . and most of the *Italians* grievously offend, for they make their *Shepherds* too polite, and elegant, and cloth them with all the neatness of the Town, and Complement of the Court'. Cf. *The Works of Virgil, infra,* 'To . . . Lord Clifford', ll. 85 ff.

348. *This was impossible for Virgil to imitate,* &c. Cf. Rapin, loc. cit: ''Tis certain that *Virgil* in his Bucolicks useth the same words which *Tully* did in the Forum or the Senate: and *Tityrus* beneath his shady Beech speaks as pure and

good Latin as *Augustus* in his Palace.' Dryden's discipleship of Virgil in his versions of Theocritus has unfortunate results.

352–4. *I direct*, &c. Cf. Dedication of the *Æneis*, ll. 2220–28, note.

361. *incomparably beyond Juvenals.* Contrast Dedication of *The Satires of Juvenalis*, l. 1828.

364–5. *As difficult as he makes it . . . to imitate Pindar. Od.* IV. ii.

374–5. *in Petronius is call'd Curiosa Felicitas*, &c. *Satyr.* 118; Horace, *Epist.* II. i. 166.

380–1. *the present Earl of Rochester.* See *Absalom and Achitophel*, l. 888, note.

385–6. *the happy Genius of Mr. Cowley.* See Preface to *Ovid's Epistles*, ll. 244–5, note.

391. *of more equal of Thoughts.* Editors emend to 'of more equal Thoughts'; but 'equal' was sometimes used substantively. Cf. Spenser, *The Faerie Queene*, v. ii. 34, 'all things to an equall to restore'.

399. *Miltons Paradice Lost*, &c. Cf. Dedication of *The Satires of Juvenalis*, ll. 370 ff.

413–14. *It must be done*, &c. Cf. *Astræa Redux*, ll. 125–8.

415–16. *quod nequeo dicere*, &c. Adapted from Juvenal, *Sat.* vii. 56.

422. *Fungar vice*, &c. Horace, *De Arte Poetica*, ll. 304–5.

425. *Some of them are too nearly related to me.* Unless Dryden was related to some of the anonymous contributors to *Sylvæ*, he refers merely to his son Charles's Latin verses 'Horti Arlingtoniani'.

Lucretius The beginning of the First Book
(Page 401)

1–25. *Delight of Humane kind.* &c. Dryden translates with reminiscences of Spenser's imitation of Lucretius (*The Faerie Queene*, IV. x. 44–46). Cf. *Fables*, 'Palamon and Arcite', iii. 129–44, note.

Translation of the Latter Part of the Third Book of Lucretius; Against the Fear of Death
(Page 405)

De Rerum Natura, iii. 830–1094; translated with occasional debts to Creech. With ll. 1–2, 76–77, 147–8, 162, compare Creech, iii. 809–10, 876–7, 945–6, 958.

211. *smoaks along the plain.* Dryden uses 'smoke' with connotations of foam, steam, and violent movement. Cf. *Æneis*, v. 185, vii. 909, ix. 516; *Fables*, 'Palamon and Arcite', ii. 474; Pope, *Odyssey*, iii. 613–15, 'the coursers . . . smok'd along the field'.

Lucretius The Fourth Book. Concerning the Nature of Love
(Page 413)

De Rerum Natura, iv. 1052–1287.

83. *the gather'd bag:* for 'collecta cupido' (l. 1115). Cf. Carew, *Poems* (1640), 'A Rapture', ll. 55–78:

> Then, as the empty Bee . . .
>
> . . . .
>
> So will I rifle all the sweets, that dwell
> In my delicious Paradise, and swell
> My bagge with honey, drawne forth by the power
> Of fervent kisses, from each spicie flower
>
> . . . .
>
> From the mixt masse, one soveraigne Balme derive,
> Then bring that great *Elixar* to thy hive.

106. *Point:* lace used as a kerchief; for 'anademata', hair-ribbons (l. 1129).

107–8. *French fashions,* &c. Modernizing Lucretius, iv. 1131–2. Cf. *supra,* Preface, ll. 31–32.

120. *ogling:* for 'iactare oculos' (l. 1139). See 'Another Epilogue' to *The Duke of Guise,* l. 26, note.

146. *make a Slattern of a Slut:* reducing Lucretius's contrast in 'immunda et fetida acosmos' (l. 1160) to a merely verbal distinction. Cf. the proverb 'a Slut's good enough to make Sloven's porridge' (Tilley, S553).

150. *two handed:* sturdy. Cf. *Dict. Canting Crew* (*c.* 1695), 'Strapping Lass, a swinging two-handed woman' (*OED*); *The First Satyr of Juvenal,* l. 30.

Horat. Ode 29. Book 3. Paraphras'd in Pindarique Verse
(Page 434)

See *supra,* Preface, l. 380; *Absalom and Achitophel,* l. 888, note.

40–41. *Thou, what befits,* &c. See *The Second Part of Absalom and Achitophel,* ll. 1131–8, note.

From Horace, Epod. 2d.
(Page 437)

78. *Heathpout:* 'heath-poult', the young heath-cock; Horace's 'Afra avis', guinea-fowl (l. 53).

96. *Morecraft.* See Prologue to *Marriage A-la-Mode,* ll. 28–37, note.

A New Song
(Page 440)

Ascribed to Dryden in the second edition of *Sylvæ*. An anonymous Latin translation was published in *The Gentleman's Journal*, September 1693, pp. 309–10. For reprints, see Day, p. 166.

Song
(Page 441)

Ascribed to Dryden in the second edition of *Sylvæ*. A musical setting by Robert King, with a somewhat different text, is reprinted by Day (p. 74) from *The Theater of Music*, 1685, i. 30. A setting by Henry Purcell (1686) is in BM Add. MS. 30382, ff. 36–37^v. For reprints, see Day, pp. 166–7.

Threnodia Augustalis: A Funeral-Pindarique Poem Sacred to the Happy Memory of King Charles II
(Page 442)

Charles II died on Friday 6 February 1685. Throughout the winter he 'looked better than he had done for many years' (Burnet, i. 606; cf. ll. 9–35). But on Monday, 2 February, he 'fell down all of a sudden in a fit like an apoplexy. . . . And the physicians did very much apprehend the return of another fit. . . . So they looked on him as a dead man' (Burnet). After two days of rigorous medical treatment, he was declared to be out of danger (ll. 110–29); and on Thursday 'he was very sensible of his condition . . . and spoke very freely and said many good things'. But a change occurred later in the day, and 'for near two hours the report was that his Majesty could not recover out of it, which made all persons of all ranks and degrees melt into tears and fall a-crying' (James Fraser; see Bryant, p. 366). 'In the forth day he grew so much wors that all those hopes vanished, and the Doctors declared they absolutely dispair'd of his life' (Clarke, i. 746; ll. 160–95). That night he received the last rites of the Roman church in private. 'The company was suffered to come in. And the King went thro' the agonies of death with a calm and a constancy, that amazed all who were about him, and knew how he had lived' (Burnet, i. 608; ll. 196–219). Bishop Ken 'presented the Duke of *Richmond*, Lady *Portsmouth*'s son, to be blessed by the King. Upon this some that were in the room cried out, the King was their common father. And upon that all kneeled down for his blessing, which he gave them' (Burnet; ll. 220–3). 'His Majesty express'd the greatest kindness and tenderness for the Duke that could possebly be conceiv'd, he owned in the most publick manner the sence he had of his Brotherly affection during the whole cours of his life, and . . . commended his great submission and constant obedience to all his commands, and asked him pardon alowd for the rigorous treatment he had so long exercised his patience with' (ll. 224–38, 257–68); 'and then his sences begining to fail him, (which had continued perfect till about an hour before his death) he expired betwixt eleaven and twelve a clock in fryday morning' (Clarke, i. 749).

Threnodia Augustalis was published by Tonson some weeks after Charles's death (advertised in *The Observator*, 14 March 1685). 'The Second Edition' was advertised on 25 March. An apparently unique copy in the Harvard Library is set in a smaller type than that of the edition usually taken as first (Macdonald 20 a) and 'The Second Edition' (Macdonald 20 b, which was printed from the same setting as 20 a and is merely a late state of that edition). The 'Harvard' edition was probably earlier than 20 a. It was unusual for books of this kind to appear first in a smaller type than that of later editions, but the explanation here may be haste in publication—a suggestion I owe to Dr. Herbert Davis. Dryden clearly took much trouble over the poem, and may have left little time for Tonson to get it out within a reasonable period after the king's death. The 'Harvard' edition, though typographically superior to 20 a, was evidently issued without careful proof-reading. It is less accurate than 20 a (see ll. 28, 105, 125, 232, 259, 347, 484); but it is related textually to 20 a rather than to the later 20 b (see ll. 126, 164, 288, 371, 494). The Dublin edition of 1685 follows 20 a except where noted in the apparatus.

Johnson criticized 'Augustalis' in the title as 'a term I am afraid neither authorized nor analogical' (i. 438 and note). Dryden's epigraph is from Virgil, *Aen*. ix. 446–7.

7. *Like Niobe we Marble grow*. Cf. Ovid, *Meta*. vi. 301–9.

28. *This Now becalm'd, and perishing the next*. Cf. *Eleonora*, ll. 305–8.

31–33. *with a mighty Flaw*, &c. *Flaw*: fissure. Cf. *Æneis*, ix. 970, and *All for Love*, v:

> Was it for me to prop
> The Ruins of a falling Majesty ?
> To place myself beneath the mighty flaw,
> Thus to be crush'd, and pounded into Atomes,
> By its o'erwhelming weight ?

With the image of the world's flaming wall cf. Lucretius, i. 73, 'flammantia moenia mundi'.

35. *Our Atlas fell indeed; But Hercules was near*. Hercules is said to have lightened the labour of Atlas by taking the weight of the heavens on his own shoulders. Ovid, *Heroides*, 'Deianira Herculi', l. 18: 'Hercule supposito sidera fulcit Atlas.'

36. *His Pious Brother*. See *Absalom and Achitophel*, l. 353, note.

70. *An Iron Slumber sat*, &c. Cf. Virgil, *Aen*. x. 745–6:

> olli dura quies oculos et ferreus urget
> somnus, in aeternam clauduntur lumina noctem.

86–87. *Mercy . . . . her Resemblance here below.* Cf. *Astræa Redux,* ll. 266–9, note; *Absalom and Achitophel,* l. 326, note.

100. *The first . . . Petitioners*: i.e. the first petitioners to mean well. See Prologue *spoken at Mithridates King of Pontus,* l. 4, note.

106–9. *His Death,* &c. The 'five Degrees' are the five days of the king's sickness. Hezekiah, 'sick unto death', reminded God 'how I have walked before thee in truth and with a perfect heart' and asked for a respite; and as a sign God 'brought the shadow ten degrees backward, by which it had gone down in the dial of Ahaz' (2 Kings xx. 1–11).

134. *Eagre.* Cf. Browne, *Pseudodoxia Epidemica,* vii. 13: 'From the peculiar disposition of the earth at the bottom, wherein quick excitations are made, may arise those Agars and impetuous flows in some aestuaries and Rivers, as is observable about *Trent* and *Humber* in England.'

150–1. *The Royal Soul,* &c. 'The vain *Heathen* had an opinion, that the Moon, when she was eclips'd, did labour, as if in an agonie, and suffer a kind of death by the Incantations of witches. . . . Besides, it was generally believ'd, that by such means the Moon might be brought down from Heaven, and so at such times they fear'd the loss of that heavenly light' (Holyday, *Juvenalis . . . Translated,* 1673, illustrating *Sat.* vi. 443).

153. *on liking.* 'To engage upon *liking,* (an image rather too familiar for the occasion,) is to take a temporary trial of a service, or business, with licence to quit it at pleasure' (Scott).

188. *Short*: Thomas Short (1635–85), Papist and Tory physician, who replaced the Whig Dr. Lower at court after the Popish Plot, 'struck in, carried all before him there, and got riches as he pleased' (Wood, *Ath. Ox.* ii. 858). Duke's version of Theocritus xi (*Miscellany Poems,* 1684, p. 253) praises Short

> Who both in Physick's sacred Art excell,
> And in Wit's Orb among the brightest shine,
> The Love of *Phœbus,* and the tunefull nine.

Short spoke of 'foul dealing' in the king's illness, and died soon after of 'a large draught of wormwood wine', poisoned, as it was supposed, for his free speaking (Burnet, i. 609). In the 1701 folio edition of Dryden's poems Tonson substituted '*Short* and *Hobbs*' for '*Short* himself', and 'He' in l. 187 is corrected to 'They' in the errata. Hobbs was Dryden's physician at least in the 1690's (see Postscript to the *Æneis,* l. 111); but he does not appear in the accounts of Charles II's death, and the alteration is probably Tonson's compliment.

236. *Nor want, nor Exile,* &c. Cf. *Absalom and Achitophel,* l. 353, note.

239–45. *That King,* &c. On his death-bed David charged Solomon to take vengeance on Joab and Shimei (1 Kings ii. 1–11). Lines 244–5 refer to Monmouth, then exiled in Holland. But William of Orange said that Charles had pardoned Monmouth: 'I know that in the bottom of his heart he has always some friendship for him, and that the King cannot be angry with him' (Dalrymple; D'Oyley, p. 254).

267. *Their best Camillus.* M. Furius Camillus, a Roman general and 'a most devout Person in point of Religion', went into exile rather than submit to an unjust fine. The parallel with the Duke of York is a close one. Camillus was 'the greatest Man both in War and Peace, before he was banished; more famous in his banishment; . . . being restored to his Country, he restored the Country to itself at the same time. For which reason he was afterward . . . lookt upon as worthy to be stiled the *Second Founder* of the City, after *Romulus*' (Livy, *The Roman History . . . done into English*, 1686, pp. 142, 149, 175).

288. *By the still Voice,* &c. 1 Kings xix. 12.

311–22. *Succession, of a long Descent,* &c. See *Absalom and Achitophel*, ll. 759–810, note.

323–6. When Shaftesbury urged Charles in the Oxford Parliament of 1681 to recognize Monmouth as his successor, the king replied: 'My lord, let there be no self-delusion. I will never yield, and I will not be intimidated. The older I grow the more steadfast I become, and I will not stain my reputation in the little time that perhaps remains for me to live' (Bryant, pp. 313–14).

353. *Out of the Solar walk and Heav'ns high way.* Cf. *Annus Mirabilis*, l. 639; *Britannia Rediviva*, l. 306.

354–5. *rank Geneva Weeds . . . and Cockle.* Cf. *Absalom and Achitophel*, ll. 194–5, note.

364–71. *As when the New-born Phœnix,* &c. Cf. *Annus Mirabilis*, 'Verses to Her Highness the Dutchess', ll. 52–57.

377. *Tho little was their Hire, and light their Gain.* Cf. *The Hind and the Panther*, iii. 247–50, note; Dedication of *The Satires of Juvenalis*, ll. 636–7, note.

388. *Thou Fabius of a sinking State.* Fabius Maximus 'outdid his Fathers, and equalized his Grandfathers great Actions. . . . Yet this same *Fabius* was reckoned cautious rather than eager; and as you may doubt, whether he were in his Nature more given to make delays, or that such delays were, in the War then in hand, very convenient to be made; so nothing is more certain than this, *That one man by his delays restored our Commonwealth*, as *Ennius* has it' (Livy, *The Roman History . . . done into English*, 1686, p. 559).

430. *A Prince, long exercis'd by Fate.* Virgil, *Aen.* iii. 182, 'nate, Iliacis exercite fatis'.

435–42. *False Heroes,* &c. Cf. *The Hind and the Panther*, i. 251–62.

465–9. Ancus Martius was fourth king of Rome and Numa's *grandson,* and led the Romans *against* the Latins. Like James II, he 'thought that the leisure and ease which *Numa* had, himself should hardly enjoy without some inconvenience: that his patience was tried, and being tried contemned' (Livy, *The Roman History*, 1686, p. 20).

Prologue and Epilogue to Albion and Albanius: An Opera

(Page 456)

Albion and Albanius was first presented at Dorset Garden on 6 June 1685 (Malone, I. i. 188), but 'the Nation being in a great Consternation' over Monmouth's landing on 11 June, 'it was perform'd but Six times' (Downes, p. 40). Contrary to usual practice, the dialogue was set throughout to music by the French composer Lewis Grabu (see Macdonald, pp. 127–8, note). The first edition was advertised in *The Observator*, 8 June 1685. The leaf carrying the Prologue and Epilogue was issued separately, and not all copies of the first edition contain it: Luttrell's copy (now at Yale) is marked '1ˢ 3 June', and the prologue and epilogue leaf is marked '1ᵈ 6 June, 1685' (Macdonald, pp. 128, 145; J. M. Osborn, *MP* xxxix (1941), 91 and 94). *Albion and Albanius* had been rehearsed before Charles II; but after the king's death on 6 February it was adapted to meet the new situation 'by the Addition of Twenty or Thirty Lines, in the Apotheosis of *Albion*', as satisfactorily 'as if there were a kind of Fatality, even in the most trivial things concerning the Succession' (Postscript). The accession of James II is celebrated in the Epilogue.

Prologue To the Opera. 3. *John Ketches*: hangmen.

6. *you brib'd like Oates.* The evidence is against the belief that Oates or his friends bribed the hangman to be lenient in administering the whipping to which he was sentenced in May 1685 (see Evelyn, *Diary*, 22 May 1685; Lane, pp. 320–1).

8. *beating Nut-trees, makes a larger Crop*: proverbial (Tilley, W644). Cf. Webster, *The White Devil*, v. i. 183: 'Why do you kick her? say—Do you thinke that she's like a walnut-tree? Must she be cudgel'd ere shee beare good fruite?'

11–18. *Satyre was once your Physick*, &c. Cf. Prologue to *The Loyal General*, ll. 22–25, note.

24. *The Wise Italians first invented show.* Cf. Preface to the opera: 'whosoever undertakes the Writing of an *Opera* . . . is obliged to imitate the Design of the *Italians*, who have not only invented, but brought to Perfection, this sort of Dramatick Musical Entertainment'.

37–40. *Each sings his part*, &c. French opera 'wonderfully favours the Genius of such a gay airy People. The Chorus . . . gives the Parterre frequent Opportunities of joining in Concert with the Stage. This Inclination of the Audience to sing along with the Actors, so prevails with them, that I have sometimes known the Performer on the Stage do no more in a Celebrated Song, than the Clerk of a Parish Church, who serves only to raise the Psalm, and is afterwards drowned in the Musick of the Congregation' (Addison, *The Spectator*, No. 29, 3 April 1711).

45. *help your Charter to restoring.* Cf. Prologue *To the King and Queen*, l. 24, note.

Epilogue To the Opera. 5–6. For other eulogies of James II, see *Absalom and Achitophel*, l. 353, note.

To my Friend Mr. J. Northleigh, Author of the Parallel. On his Triumph of the British Monarchy

(Page 459)

John Northleigh (1657–1705), lawyer, physician, and Tory pamphleteer, was the author of *The Parallel: or, The New Specious Association An Old Rebellious Covenant* (1682) and *The Triumph of our Monarchy, over the Plots and Principles of our Rebels and Republicans* (1685).

11. *under covert of his sev'n-fold shield.* Homer, *Iliad*, viii. 266–72. Cf. *To Sir Godfrey Kneller*, l. 78.

To the Pious Memory Of the Accomplisht Young Lady Mrs Anne Killigrew, Excellent in the two Sister-Arts of Poësie, and Painting

(Page 459)

Anne Killigrew (1660–85) was the daughter of Dr. Henry Killigrew, chaplain to Charles I and, after the Restoration, Almoner to the Duke of York and Master of the Savoy Hospital—appointments made in recognition of his suffering during the interregnum (cf. ll. 77–79). His tragedy *The Conspiracy* (1638), subsequently revised and published as *Palantus and Eudora* (1653), 'found the Approbation of the most excellent Persons which were in that time. *Ben Johnson* . . . gave a Testimony to this Piece, *even to be envied*' (Wood, *Ath. Ox.* ii. 1035; cf. ll. 23–28). Anne, says Wood, was 'a Grace for Beauty, and a Muse for Wit . . . most admirable in the Arts of Poetry and Painting. She was one of the Maids of Honour to the Dutchess of *York*; but dyed of the Small-Pox, to the unspeakable Reluctancy of her Relations . . . on the 16th Day of *June* 1685 . . . and was buried in the Chancel of St. *John Baptist*'s Chapel in the *Savoy* Hospital.' *Poems By Mrs Anne Killigrew* was published soon after, though the title-page bears the date 1686: the book was licensed on 30 September and advertised in *The Observator*, 2 November 1685. The frontispiece is an engraving after a self-portrait.

This, says Johnson (i. 439), 'is undoubtedly the noblest ode that our language ever has produced. The first part flows with a torrent of enthusiasm. "Fervet immensusque ruit."' See R. Wallerstein, *SP* xliv (1947), 519–28; E. M. W. Tillyard, *Five Poems. 1470–1870* (1948), pp. 49–65; James Kinsley, 'Dryden and the Art of Praise', *ES* xxxiv (1953), 57–64.

6–11. *Whether, adopted to some Neighbouring Star,* &c. 'Whether you are stellified among the wandering stars, or planets, or among the fixed stars beyond these in the firmament, or among the seraphim in the very presence of God.'

23. *Traduction.* 'Some hold that it is *ex traduce* . . . that one man begets another, body and soul: or as a candle from a candle, to be produced from the seed: otherwise, say they, a man begets but half a man, and is worse than a beast that begets both matter and form' (Burton, I. i. 2. ix).

29–33. *But if thy Præexisting Soul,* &c. 'The *Pythagorians,* defend *Metempsychosis,* and *Palingenesis,* that souls go from one body to another, *epotâ prius Lethes undâ* . . . as they were inclined in their lives, or participated in conditions. . . . *Plato* in *Timæo,* and in his *Phædon* (for ought I can perceive) differs not much from this opinion, that it was from God at first . . . and that it was put into the body for a punishment, and thence it goes into a beasts, or mans, as appears by his pleasant fiction *de sortitione animarum,* lib. 10 *de. Rep.,* and after 10000. years is to return into the former body again' (Burton, I, i. 2. ix).

41–43. *the Milder Planets did combine,* &c. Cf. *Annus Mirabilis,* ll. 1165–6, note.

50–51. *And if no clust'ring Swarm,* &c. A reference to the story of the bees settling on the lips of the infant Plato as a presage of his eloquence (Aelian, *Varia Historia,* x. 21).

56–65. *O Gracious God,* &c. Cf. Preface to *Fables,* l. 132, note.

82. Dryden probably alludes, not to Epictetus, but to Diogenes of Sinope, who lit a lamp in broad daylight and went about saying, 'I am looking for a man' (Diogenes Laertius, vi. 41).

103. *the Dumb-sister.* Cf. *To Sir Godfrey Kneller,* ll. 3–6, note.

130–3. *the Image of his Heart,* &c. See *Absalom and Achitophel,* l. 353, note.

134. *Our Phenix Queen.* Cf. *Prologue to the Dutchess,* note.

147–8. *To such Immod'rate Growth,* &c. Cf. Martial, *Epi.* VI. xxix. 7, 'immodicis brevis est aetas, et rara senectus', which is the epigraph of Anne Killigrew's *Poems.*

160–4. *O double Sacriledge,* &c. Cf. Cowley, 'On the Death of Mrs. Katherine Philips' (1678), ll. 11–19:

> Was't not enough, when thou, profane disease,
> Didst on this Glorious Temple seize ?
>
> .   .   .   .
> Was't not enough thus rudely to defile,
> But thou must quite destroy the goodly Pile ?
> And thy unbounded Sacriledge commit
> On th' inward Holiest Holy of her Wit ?

The parallel between Anne Killigrew and Katherine Philips is just: both were poets, both were notably virtuous, and both died untimely of smallpox. 'We might well', runs the Preface to *Poems by . . . The Matchless Orinda,* 'have call'd her the English Sappho, she of all the female poets of former Ages, being for her verses and her virtues both, the most highly to be valued. . . . And for her virtues, they as much surpass'd those of Sappho as the Theological do the Moral . . .' (Saintsbury, i. 492–3; cf. *supra,* ll. 29–33 and 77–87).

165. *her warlike brother:* Henry Killigrew (d. 1712), naval captain and later admiral. In 1686 he was in the Mediterranean on a campaign to suppress piracy, and did not return to England till 1689.

180. *the Valley of Jehosaphat.* Joel iii. 2.

To my Ingenious Friend, Mr. Henry Higden, Esq; On his Translation of the Tenth Satyr of Juvenal
(Page 465)

Henry Higden was a member of the Middle Temple and 'an agreeable and facetious companion . . . well known to all the sprightly and conversible part of the town' (see Brown's *Letters from the Dead to the Living*, ed. Hayward, 1927, p. 343). His version of Juvenal, *Sat.* xiii, appeared in 1686: *A Modern Essay on the Tenth Satyr of Juvenal* was licensed on 2 June 1686, but was not published till 1687. On Shadwell's unchivalrous treatment of Higden over this translation see Macdonald, p. 43, note; see also C. E. Ward, 'Dryden, Higden and Tonson', *RES* xiii (1937), 305–6. Higden made a calamitous excursion into drama with *The Wary Widdow* (1693), which was received 'with a barbarous variety of Noise and Tumult' and had to be closed after the third act because the players got drunk (Nicoll, pp. 16 and 18).

22. *your Author's Principle.* Juvenal, *Sat.* x. 346–66.

33. *I have Cur'd my Self.* Cf. Dedication of *The Satires of Juvenalis,* ll. 1776 ff.; *The Works of Virgil*, 'Postscript to the Reader', ll. 31–36.

The Hind and the Panther. A Poem, In Three Parts
(Page 467)

Dryden says in his address 'To the Reader' that this poem was written during the winter of 1686 and the following spring. On 12 January 1687 Tonson entered his caveat in *SR* 'that noe person enter the poem called the Hinde and ye Panther'. It was licensed on 11 April, entered in *SR* on 27 May, and probably published on that date. The epigraph is from Virgil, *Aen.* iii. 96 and i. 405.

Parts of *The Hind and the Panther* reflect the hopes which James and the Catholics entertained at his accession, that the Roman and Anglican churches might be reconciled (e.g. i. 327–30, iii. 670–9), and 'The First Part' contains violent satire on the nonconformists. By 1687, however, James had alienated the Anglicans: 'it was plain, all the services they had done him, both in opposing the Exclusion, and upon his first accession to the Crown, were forgot' (Burnet, i. 701). On 4 April 1687 he issued a Declaration of Indulgence to Catholics and Dissenters alike: 'We cannot but heartily wish, as it will easily be believed, that all the people of our dominions were members of the Catholic Church. Yet we humbly thank Almighty God it is, and hath of long time been, our constant sense and opinion . . . that conscience ought not to be constrained, nor people forced in matters of mere religion' (Browning, pp. 395–6). Dryden wrote or adapted his address to the reader to meet this shift in policy; and the poem itself bears the marks of adjustment. Scott suggests that the portrait of the Doves (iii. 946 ff.) is so much more virulent than that of the Anglican Panther, that it was written after the Declaration, 'when the king had decidedly turned his favour from the Established Church'; but Dryden seems to have thought hardly of clergy of any persuasion, and is no less critical of the Jesuits than of the Anglicans. Noyes argues that the references to the penal laws (ii. 268; iii. 380–1 and 633–4) preceded the Declaration, which suspended these laws; but the moderate Catholic party to which Dryden belonged (see iii. 419, note) regarded the suspension as a temporary respite from the threat of persecution (iii. 382–3). More likely additions in the light of the Declaration are iii. 811–12, 892–7, and 1233–55.

The date of Dryden's conversion to the Roman church is not known. Evelyn notes in his *Diary*, 19 January 1686, that 'Dryden the famous play-poet & his two sonns . . . were said to go to Masse; & such purchases were no greate losse to the Church'; but Tom Brown speaks of Dryden's 'Conversion in 1685' (*The Reasons of Mr Bays Changing His Religion*, 1688, p. 21). *The Hind and the Panther* is a logical sequel to *Religio Laici*: Dryden's 'assent to Catholicism was . . . in the nature of a retreat to an impregnable fortification when the more forward position had been proved untenable' (Bredvold, p. 128; see *Religio Laici*, introductory note).

On Dryden's choice of appropriate animals to represent churches and sects in his fable, see James Kinsley, 'Dryden's Bestiary', *RES*, N.S., iv (1953), 331–6.

Some changes were made in the text of the poem as the first edition was passing through the press (iii. 1147–54). Some states of the last leaf of this edition have no *Errata*; some have a 3-line and others a 4-line *Errata* slip. The Edinburgh and Dublin reprints of 1687 follow the early version of iii. 1147–54 and are incompletely corrected. The poem was twice republished in London in 1687. For the numerous satirical rejoinders, 1687–90, see Macdonald, pp. 253–63.

To the Reader. 30. *the Proceedings of a Foreign Prince*: Louis XIV's revocation of the Edict of Nantes in October 1685, and the subsequent persecution of the Huguenots. French Protestant refugees poured into England and, in spite of James II's unwillingness, received charitable relief. James deplored the use of 'booted missionaries' in France as 'impolitic and unchristian'; but the reports of the French ambassador Barillon reveal his private enthusiasm over Louis's measures 'to destroy heresy' (Turner, pp. 310–15). Cf. Prologue to *The Duke of Guise*, ll. 5–6.

33–34. *That he has restor'd God to his Empire over Conscience*. From the address of thanks offered by the London Presbyterians in April 1687 (Browning, pp. 397–8).

46. *Classical Ordination*: ordination by a presbytery. Cf. Butler, *Hudibras*, I. i. 836–8:

> . . . Bear-baiting may be made out
> In Gospel times, as lawful as is
> Provincial or Parochial Classis.

52. *Cyrus, a Heathen Prince, and a Foreigner*. Ezra i. 1–4.

66–73. *'Tis evident that some part*, &c. James II showed the curious Pepys 'two papers, containing about a quarter of a sheete on both sides, written in the late Kings owne hand, severall Arguments opposite to the Doctrine of the *Church of England*', and said that Charles 'both was, & died a *R: Cath:*' (Evelyn, *Diary*, 2 October 1685). In 1686 James ordered the publication of *Copies of Two Papers Written by the Late King Charles II. Together with a Copy of a Paper written by the late Dutchess of York*. The third paper is dated 20 August 1670, and sets out the duchess's reasons for her conversion to the Roman church. Stillingfleet, then Dean of St. Paul's, wrote *An Answer* to this publication; and the Catholics replied in *A Defence of the Papers . . . Against the Answer made to them*, of which the third part, dealing with the duchess's apologia, was by Dryden. Stillingfleet returned to the attack in *A Vindication of the Answer to some Late Papers Concerning the Unity and Authority of the Catholick Church* (imprimatur 10 January 1686/7), to which Dryden refers here. See also iii. 160–340, notes.

76. *some Original Treatise of Humility*. Dryden closes his defence of the duchess's paper by invoking Stillingfleet's charity and meekness, adding that 'he is such a stranger to that spirit, because among all the volumes of divinity written by the Protestants there is not one original treatise, at least that I have seen or heard of, which has handled distinctly, and by itself, that Christian virtue of humility' (Scott, xvii. 251). Stillingfleet replied that 'within a few years, (besides what hath been printed formerly,) such a book hath been published in London' (ibid. 277). Cf. iii. 212–16, note.

77–81. *the magnified Piece of Duncomb . . . Translated from the Spanish*. The Jesuit Alonso Rodriguez published *Exercicio de Perfecion i virtudes religiosas* at Seville in 1609. A translation of part of this work appeared as *A Treatise of Humilitie* by 'T. B.' in 1631. The book published in London 'within a few years', to which Stillingfleet refers, is probably *A Practical Discourse of Humility*, translated by W[illiam] A[llen], 1681. In the Preface to *The Hind and the Panther Transvers'd* (1687) Montague and Prior mark Dryden's reference to 'Duncomb' as a stupid error for 'Allen'. No translation by Duncomb has been identified; but it is possible that Dryden uses 'Piece of *Duncomb*' simply as a derogatory phrase, 'a wretched piece of writing'. Several persons of this name wrote controversial pamphlets.

84. *matter of Fact was the Principal Debate*. The duchess's paper, says Stillingfleet in *A Vindication*, 'chiefly relates to matter of fact'; but he is there concerned, not with its authenticity, but with what Dryden 'saith which reflects

on the honour of the church of England'. Dryden 'affects to consider the dispute as entirely limited to the authenticity of the paper, which it cannot be supposed Stillingfleet ever seriously intended to impeach' (Scott). Cf. iii. 310–19, note.

89–90. *Mrs. James*. Elinor James, widow of a London printer, was the author of *Mrs. James's Vindication of the Church of England* (1687) and a religious eccentric. She later spoke for the church's reputation against the scandalous Oates, who struck her 'in a violent and riotous manner' on the head (Lane, pp. 360–1).

91. *concerning the Poem as such*, &c. Dryden was artist as well as controversialist, and does not keep rigidly to the scheme outlined here. See the analysis in Johnson, i. 444–6.

The First Part
(Page 470)

1. *A Milk white Hind*: the Roman church; a symbol of prophetic wisdom, antiquity, and immortality. See Kinsley, art. cit.

8. *doom'd to death, though fated not to dy*. Montague and Prior asked 'are not *doom* and *fate*, much the same thing?' (*The Hind and the Panther Transvers'd*; Prior, *Dialogues*, ed. A. R. Waller, 1907, p. 9). 'It is obvious that the doom, or sentence, of an earthly tribunal is placed in opposition to the decree of Providence' (Scott).

14. *Caledonian*: 'Not *Scottish*, but taken generally for Britain, as *Hercynian wood* might be taken for Germany' (Saintsbury).

29. *Grin'd*: showed their teeth. Cf. Preface to *Religio Laici*, l. 274; Spenser, *The Faerie Queene*, vi. xii. 27:

> . . . Tygres, that did seeme to gren,
> And snar at all, that euer passed by.

35. *The bloudy Bear*: the Independents; symbolizing neglect of external forms, and destructiveness. See Kinsley, art. cit.

37. *the Quaking Hare*: the Quakers; symbolizing timidity, melancholy, and aversion to music and merriment. See Kinsley, art. cit.

39–42. *the Buffoon Ape*, &c. In *The Hind and the Panther Transvers'd* Bayes (Dryden) quotes ll. 39–42 and adds: 'That Gauls somewhere; I gad I can't leave it off, tho I were cudgel'd every day for it' (Prior, *Dialogues*, ed. Waller, p. 11). Scott deduces that the reference is personal, and suggests a hit at Sunderland, who 'made the step to Popery all of the sudden, without any previous instruction or conference: So that the change he made looked too like a man who, having no religion, took up one . . . to serve a turn' (Burnet, i. 756). But Montague and Prior may have read a personal allusion into Dryden's lines only with the intention of compromising him; he is not likely to have cast aspersions on the character of James's minister. The date of Sunderland's 'fatal Apostacy' is uncertain; see Evelyn, *Diary*, 20 August 1688 and note. The association of atheism and state-craft was not uncommon. Cf. *The Medall*, l. 263, note; Oldham, *Satyrs Upon the Jesuits* (1679), iii:

> Next for *Religion*, learn what's fit to take,
> How small a Dram do's the just Compound make,
> As much as is by th' Crafty *States-men* worn
> For Fashion only, or to serve a turn.

41. *the Lyon*: James II. Cf. *Absalom and Achitophel*, ll. 447 ff.

43. *the bristl'd Baptist Boar*. In Dryden's day the association of the Baptists with the violent Anabaptists of München was common. See Kinsley, art. cit.

53. *False Reynard*: the Socinians; symbolizing heresy and subtlety. See Kinsley, art. cit.

78–86. *my doubts are done*, &c. Dryden 'insists that the Protestant churches, which have consented to postpone human reason to faith, by acquiescing in the orthodox doctrine of the Trinity, are not entitled to appeal to the authority which they have waived, for arguments against the mystery of the real presence in the eucharist. This was a favourite mode of reasoning of the Catholics at the time. . . . The Protestant divines took a distinction; and . . . while they received the doctrine of the Trinity as an infinite mystery, far above their reason, they contended against that of transubstantiation as capable of being tried by human faculties, and as contradicted by an appeal to them' (Scott). Cf. Evelyn, *Diary*, 6 March 1687 and note.

95–99. *Impassible*: incapable of suffering injury. In natural philosophy 'penetration' is the occupation of the same space by two bodies at the same time. Dryden's example of divine penetration is drawn from John xx. 19. Cf. *Eleonora*, l. 252; Marvell, *Fleckno*, ll. 97 101; Jeremy Taylor, *The Real Presence*, xi. 32: 'There is only remaining that we account concerning Jesus's entering into the assembly of the apostles, "the doors being shut": To this I answer, that this infers not a penetration of bodies, or that two bodies can be in one place . . . because there are so many ways of affecting it without that impossibility. . . .'

105. *how can finite grasp infinity?* Cf. *Religio Laici*, ll. 36–41.

106–11. *'Tis urg'd again*, &c. Cf. *Religio Laici*, ll. 146–51.

150–2. Dryden returns to the Socinians, who were gaining ground in Poland. Cf. Burton, III. iv. 1. i: 'The Western Church . . . [is] so ecclipsed with several schisms, heresies and superstitions, that one knows not where to finde it . . . *Poland* is a receptacle of all Religions, where *Samosetans, Socinians, Photinians . . . Arrians, Anabaptists*, are to bee found.'

153. *th' insatiate Wolfe*: the Presbyterian, the enemy of the flock and persecutor of the church. See Kinsley, art. cit.

165. *pricks up his predestinating ears*. 'A Geneva cloak and band, with the hair close cropped, and covered with a sort of black scull-cap, was the discriminating attire of [Presbyterian] teachers. This last article of dress occasioned an unseemly projection of their ears, and procured . . . the nick-name of prick-eared fanatics' (Scott).

170–1. *Full many a year*, &c. The Anglo-Saxon king Edgar rooted 'Theeves and Robbers . . . almost out of the land, and wild Beasts of prey altogether; enjoining *Ludwall* King of *Wales* to pay the yearly tribute of 300 Wolves, which he did for two years together, till the third year no more were to be found, nor ever after' (Milton, *The History of Britain*, 1670, v). Cf. Spenser, *The Shepheardes Calender*, 'September', ll. 151–3 and gloss. Dryden probably refers to the story of the massacre by Ethelfrith of twelve hundred monks of Bangor, occasioned by the refusal of the British church to acknowledge the supremacy of Rome (Bede, *Hist. Eccles.* II. ii). In his translation of Bede (1565) the Catholic Thomas Stapleton describes the Welsh as a 'detestable host' of 'schismatics'.

177. *his innate antipathy to kings*. Wyclif's views were not anti-monarchical; but in the Preface to *Fables* (ll. 357–72) Dryden associates Chaucer with Wyclif and John of Gaunt, and speaks of him as 'a little dipt in the Rebellion of the Commons'.

182–9. *In Israel some believe him whelp'd*, &c. Peter Heylyn, in the Preface to *Aerius Redivivus; or, The History of the Presbyterians* (1670), says that some of them 'out of pure zeal unto the cause' claim descent from the Jewish Sanhedrin, and satirically suggests that Presbyterianism originated in the rebellion of Corah, Dathan, and Abiram against Moses and Aaron (Num. xvi).

189. *class*. See *supra*, 'To the Reader', l. 46, note.

211. *Drawn to the dreggs of a Democracy*. See *Absalom and Achitophel*, l. 227, note.

212–13. *As where in fields*, &c. Fairies 'dance on Heaths and Greens, as *Lavater* thinks with *Tritemius*, and as *Olaus Magnus* adds, leave that green circle, which we commonly find in plain fields, which others hold to proceed from a Meteor falling, or some accidental rankness of the ground, so Nature sports her self; they are sometimes seen by old women and children' (Burton, I. ii. I. 2).

222. *onely dogs for physick use*. 'The Dogge hauing surfetted, to procure his vomitte eateth grasse, and findeth remedy' (Lyly, *Works*, ed. R. W. Bond, i. 208).

229–32. *But as the Poisons*, &c. Cf. *Aureng-Zebe* (1676), iv:

> Could you shed Venom from your reverend Shade,
> Like Trees, beneath whose Arms 'tis death to sleep:

—a reference to the upas-tree of Java, the 'Hydra Tree of Death' (see Summers, iv. 497–8).

235–8. *From Celtique woods*, &c. An allusion to the persecution of the Huguenots; see *supra*, 'To the Reader', l. 30, note.

251–62. *One portion*, &c. Cf. *Threnodia Augustalis*, ll. 435–42.

274. *kneaded up with milk*. Cf. Shakespeare, *Macbeth*, I. v. 14–15, 'thy Nature . . . is too full o' th' Milke of humane kindnesse'. In such passages as the Song of Solomon, v. 1, 'milk' is commonly glossed as the graces of the godly.

284. *the blessed Pan:* 'Christ, the very God of all shepheards, which calleth himselfe the greate and good shepherd. . . . [Plutarch] sayth, that about the same time, that our Lord suffered his most bitter passion for the redemtion of man, certein passengers sayling from Italy to Cyprus . . . heard a voyce calling alowde . . . that the great Pan was dead; . . . I think it . . . meant of the death of Christ, the onely and very Pan, then suffering for his flock' (Spenser, *The Shepheardes Calender*, 'Maye', l. 54, gloss). Cf. Milton, *On the Morning of Christs Nativity*, ll. 85–92.

289–90. *Such mercy,* &c. In February 1687 James 'sent a Proclamation of indulgence to *Scotland* [and] repealed all the severe laws that were past in his Grandfather's name during his infancy: He with that took off all disabilities that were by any law laid on his Roman Catholick subjects, and . . . slackned all the laws made against the moderate Presbyterians. . . . It was strangely drawn, and liable to much just censure' (Burnet, i. 712–13).

298. *The common benefit of vital air.* Cf. Virgil, *Aen.* vii. 229–30.

311–13. *A slimy-born and sun-begotten Tribe,* &c. Cf. *Annus Mirabilis,* ll. 183–4, note; *All for Love* (1678), v:

> Th' original Villain sure no God created;
> He was a Bastard of the Sun, by *Nile*,
> Ap'd into Man; with all his Mother's Mud
> Crusted about his Soul.

'The dregs of the fanaticism of the last age fermented . . . into various sects of sullen enthusiasts, who distinguished themselves by different names. . . . In many cases they rejected all the usual aids of devotion, and, holding their meetings in the open air, and in solitary spots, nursed their fanaticism by separating themselves from the more rational part of mankind' (Scott).

318. *Souls that can scarce ferment their mass of clay.* Cf. *Absalom and Achitophel,* ll. 156–8, note.

319. *divisible:* material.

321–2. *Such souls as Shards produce,* &c. Cf. Pettie, *A Petite Pallace:* 'The humblebee flieth all day in the pleasant air, and thinketh much to alight even upon the sweet flowers, but at night taketh no scorn to lodge in a cow's foul shard' (1908, ii. 124).

327. *The Panther:* the Anglican church; symbolizing dangerous fascination and corrupt beauty. See Kinsley, art. cit.

339–40. *Though unpolluted yet,* &c. Cf. *Absalom and Achitophel,* l. 567; Juvenal, *Sat.* xiii. 209–10:

> nam scelus intra se tacitum qui cogitat ullum,
> facti crimen habet. cedo si conata peregit.

341–4. *If, as our dreaming Platonists report,* &c. Cf. Plato, *Symposium* 202D–E; Augustine, *De Civitate Dei,* VIII. xiv; Milton, *Paradise Lost,* iii. 460–5. In *King Arthur* (1691), ii, Philidel tells Merlin:

An Airy Shape, the tender'st of my kind,
The last seduc'd, and least deform'd of Hell;
Half white, and shuffl'd in the Crowd, I fell;
Desirous to repent, and loth to sin;
Awkward in Mischief, piteous of Mankind. . . .

Dryden later discusses the idea of intermediary spirits: Dedication of *The Satires of Juvenalis,* ll. 516–79, note.

351–6. *A Lyon old*: Henry VIII. Cf. *Fables,* 'The Cock and the Fox', ll. 55–66, note.

377–9. *The full fed Musulman,* &c. Cf. Epilogue to *Constantine the Great,* ll. 40–45.

386–7. *in this masquerade of mirth and love,* &c. Cf. Browne, *Pseudodoxia Epidemica,* I. v: 'How their faiths could decline so low, as to concede their generations in Heaven, to be made by the smell of a Citron, or that the felicity of their Paradise should consist in a Jubile of copulation, that is, a coition of one act prolonged unto fifty years.'

390. *Burnish'd*: fat.

417–29. *Her Novices are taught,* &c. See the Anglican Catechism.

430. *Her wild belief on ev'ry wave is tost.* James i. 6: 'He that wavereth is like a wave of the sea driven with the wind and tossed.'

432. *True to her King her principles are found.* At his accession, James declared to his Privy Council: 'I shall make it my endeavour to preserve this government in Church and State as it is now by law established. I know the principles of the Church of England are for monarchy and the members of it have shewed themselves good and loyal subjects, therefore I shall always take care to defend and support it' (Turner, p. 240; Evelyn, *Diary,* 6 February 1685). But by 1687 both the loyalty of the church, and James's unimaginative reliance on it, had been sorely tried.

442. *In death undaunted as an Indian wife.* Cf. *Aureng-Zebe* (1676), v:

'Tis the Procession of a Funeral Vow,
Which cruel Laws to *Indian* Wives allow,
When fatally their Virtue they approve;
Chearful in Flames, and Martyrs of their Love.

449. *Isgrim.* In *The Hind and the Panther Transvers'd* Bayes says: 'Take it from me . . . there is as good *Morality,* and as sound Precepts, in the *delectable History of Reynard the Fox,* as in any Book I know, except *Seneca.* Pray tell me where in any other Author could I have found so pretty a Name for a Wolf as *Isgrim*?' (Prior, *Dialogues,* ed. Waller, pp. 16–17).

460. *If she reform by Text.* Cf. *The Medall,* ll. 156–66, note.

497–506. Dryden argues that 'if the church of England would be reconciled to Rome, she should be gratified with a delegated portion of innate authority over the rival sectaries; instead of being obliged to depend upon the civil power for protection' (Scott).

537. *The ten-horn'd monster*, in Rev. xvii; commonly taken by the reformers to prefigure the Roman church.

539–41. *'twas offence*, &c. Cf. *supra*, ll. 78–86, note.

552. *Yet cou'd not howl, the Hind had seen him first.* A satiric inversion of the proverb, 'a man becomes hoarse or dumb, if a Wolf have the advantage first to eye him' (Browne, *Pseudodoxia Epidemica*, III. viii); see Tilley, W621.

563. *Her friend and fellow-suff'rer in the plot.* 'Although the Roman Catholic plot was made the pretence of persecuting the Papists . . . yet the high-flying party of the Church of England were also levelled at, and accused of being Tantivies, Papists in masquerade, &c.' (Scott). Cf. *Heraclitus Ridens*, No. 7, 15 March 1681.

The Second Part
(Page 485)

5. *sagacious*: having an acute sense of smell. Cf. *Fables*, 'The Cock and the Fox', l. 752; Milton, *Paradise Lost*, x. 279–81:

> So sented the grim Feature, and upturnd
> His Nostril wide into the murkie Air,
> Sagacious of his Quarrey from so farr.

7–8. Coleman's correspondence implicated the Duke of York in the Plot (see Preface to *Religio Laici*, ll. 164–5, note; Turner, pp. 144–51). The 'priestly calves' are the Jesuits who were brought to trial for alleged complicity and executed on 20 June 1679: Whitbread, Provincial of the English Jesuits; Fenwick, the London agent for the college at St. Omers; Ireland or Ironmonger, Procurator of the English province; and the Benedictine Pickering (Pollock, pp. 326 ff.).

30–35. *The Test*, &c. The Test Act of 1678 required every member of Parliament to take the oaths of allegiance and supremacy, and to subscribe to a declaration 'that in the sacrament of the Lord's Supper there is not any transubstantiation of the elements of bread and wine into the body and blood of Christ at or after the consecration thereof by any person whatsoever' (Browning, pp. 391–2).

34. *salvo*: dishonest solution.

67. *subterranean Rome*: the catacombs, described in Bosio's *Roma Sotterranea*, 1632. See Evelyn, *Diary*, 1 May 1645.

74–75. 'Many excellent questions appertain to this sense [of sight], discussed by Philosophers: as whether this sight be caused *intra mittendo, vel extra mittendo, &c.*, by receiving in the visible species, or sending of them out; which *Plato, Plutarch, Macrobius, Lactantius* and others dispute' (Burton, I. i. 2. 6). Browne upholds 'the principles of *Aristotle* . . . and others, who hold that sight is made by Reception, and not by extramission': the 'opinion of sight by extramission' is 'now sufficiently convicted from observations of the Dark Chamber' (*Pseudodoxia Epidemica*, III. vii).

79. *fallacies in Universals live.* See *Annus Mirabilis*, 'An account of the ensuing Poem', l. 69, note.

85–95. *some Doctours,* &c. Dryden is accommodating contemporary Gallicanism, and the controversy which developed over the Declaration of the French Assembly in 1682. The Assembly affirmed, *inter alia,* that the primacy of the Holy See is limited by General Councils and the bishops, whose assent alone can give final authority to papal decrees. Cf. Isaac Barrow, *A Treatise of the Pope's Supremacy* (1680), Introduction, xv: 'I know there are within the Roman communion great store of divines, who do contract the papal sovereignty within a much narrower compass . . .' (*Enchiridion Theologicum Anti-Romanum,* 1852, pp. 34–37). Scott notes that the moderate attitude expressed in ll. 80–84 was that of pamphlets circulated by James II's printing press at the time, 'whether because James really held the opinion of the . . . Gallican church, in this point, or that he thought the more moderate statement was most likely to be acceptable to new converts'.

100–10. *If any should in after times appear,* &c. Cf. *Religio Laici,* ll. 297–300, 356–69.

161. *Where Piles with piles, and eagles Eagles met.* Lucan, *Pharsalia,* i. 6–7:

> . . . infestisque obvia signis
> signa pares aquilas et pila minantia pilis.

168–71. *The Panther smil'd,* &c. Cf. John Cosin, 'A Letter to the Countess of Peterborough': 'If the Roman Catholics would make the essence of their Church (as we do ours) to consist in these following points, we are at accord with them. . . . 3. All the decrees of faith and doctrine set forth, as well in the first four General Councils, as in all other Councils, which those four approved and confirmed. . . . 4. The unanimous and general consent of the ancient Catholic Fathers and the universal Church of Christ in the interpretation of the Holy Scriptures, and the collection of all necessary matters of Faith from them' (*Works,* 1843–55, iv. 332–6). See *Religio Laici,* ll. 334–47, note.

227. *the ladder, and its omen too*: the gallows. Cf. Tilley, L27.

228. *The Panther's breath was ever fam'd for sweet.* Cf. Pliny, *Nat. Hist.* viii. 23; Lyly, 'the beautie whereof is . . . a delicate bayte with a deadly hooke, a sweete *Panther* with a deuouring paunch, a sower poyson in a siluer potte' (*Works,* ed. R. W. Bond, i. 202 and note).

230. *the blatant beast*: a monstrous figure of calumny in Spenser, *The Faerie Queene,* with some canine characteristics which justify Dryden's application of the name to the Wolf. It is a 'hellish Dog' (VI. vi. 12) which barks and bays 'with bitter rage and fell contention' (V. xii. 41), the offspring of Cerberus and Chimaera (VI. i. 7–8). Discussing the Beast, Warton points out that Luther and Calvin were often represented by continental painters as monsters 'expiring beneath the feet of triumphant popery' (*Observations on The Fairy Queen,* 1762, i. 221–2).

247. *set those toys traditions quite aside.* 'The authority of the Holy Scripture

. . . dependeth not on the testimony of any man or Church; but wholly upon God (who is truth itself) the author thereof. . . . Nothing is at any time to be added, whether by new revelations of the Spirit or traditions of men' (*Westminster Confession*, 1643, I, 'Of the Holy Scripture').

265–6. *like a Mule . . . never breed.* Hybrids, says Pliny, are observed 'non gignere in omni animalium genere; idcirco mulas non parere. est in annalibus nostris peperisse saepe, verum prodigii loco habitum' (*Nat. Hist.* viii. 69).

286. *For purging fires traditions must not fight.* Cf. Jeremy Taylor, *A Dissuasive from Popery*, I. i.: 'The doctrine of purgatory is the mother of indulgences. . . . But if the patent of indulgences be not from Christ and his apostles; if, upon this ground, the Primitive Church never built, the superstructures of Rome must fall.' 'How vainly the Church of Rome . . . infers the belief of purgatory, every man may satisfy himself, by seeing the writings of the fathers' (*Works*, 1839, x. 145, 148).

322–3. *Thus faith was,* &c. Cf. *Religio Laici*, ll. 270–5.

344–5. *what one Saint has said,* &c. 2 Peter iii. 16.

382. *the Hungary for which they fight.* Hungary, as a natural bulwark against Mohammedan incursion, was one of the territorial stakes in the long struggle between the Turks and the Austrians, who were recovering much of it in 1687.

384. *the fair estate.* Cf. *Religio Laici*, ll. 388–93.

398. *she whom ye seek am I.* John xviii. 5–6.

407–12. 'In a Polish Diet, where unanimity was necessary, the mode adopted of ensuring it was for the majority to hew to pieces the first individual who expressed his dissent by the fatal *veto*' (Scott). *Crown-gen'ral* is a translation of the Polish title which Sobieski held before his election to the throne in 1675.

416–17. *To church-decrees,* &c. Article XX.

419. *Curtana*: the pointless (*curtus*) sword carried in coronation processions as an emblem of mercy.

423. *hit the blots*: in backgammon, to 'throw a number which enables the player to take up an unguarded man, that is, one left single and alone on any point in his adversary's tables'; hence, to discover a failing (*OED*).

443. *play at hard-head*: fight by butting with the head. Cf. Dryden's *Troilus and Cressida* (1679), II. iii:

> Set 'em to prate, to boast their brutal strength,
> To vie their stupid Courage, till they quarrel,
> And play at hard-head with their empty Skuls.

454. *The Consubstantiating church*: the Lutherans. Cf. *supra*, ii. 141–2.

456. *The French reform'd, from preaching you restrain.* 'The Huguenot preachers, being Calvinists, had received classical, not episcopal ordination: hence, unless re-ordained, they were not admitted to preach in the established church of England' (Scott).

488. *Immunity from errours, you disown.* See, for example, Jeremy Taylor, *A Discourse of the Liberty of Prophesying*, v–ix (*Works*, 1839, viii). In the second of Charles II's papers (see 'To the Reader', ll. 66–73, note) the dilemma of the Anglicans is described as 'either they must say, that they are infallible, which they cannot pretend to, or confess, that what they decide in matters of conscience is no further to be followed, than as it agrees with every man's private judgment' (Scott, x. 190).

499–514. *So when of old*, &c. Cf. Milton, *Paradise Lost*, iii. 56–273.

518–19. *What from his Wardrobe*, &c. Revelation xxi. 2.

527. *Entire, one solid shining Diamond.* Cf. Spenser's description of Arthur's shield, *The Faerie Queene*, I. vii. 33:

> Not made of steele, nor of enduring bras,
> Such earthly mettals soone consumed bene:
> But all of Diamond perfect pure and cleene
> It framed was, one massie entire mould,
> Hewen out of Adamant rocke with engines keene,
> That point of speare it neuer percen could,
> Ne dint of direfull sword diuide the substance would.

535–7. *Still when the Gyant-brood invades*, &c. Ovid, *Meta.* i. 151–5; Virgil, *Georgics*, i. 281–3.

538–47. *like Ægyptian Sorcerers*, &c. Exod. viii, ix.

552–5. *The Gospel-sound diffus'd*, &c. Dryden was at work on his translation of Bouhours's Life of St. Francis Xavier, 'Apostle of the *Indies*, and of *Japan*', published in the summer of 1688.

568–75. The Dutch dominated European trade with Japan; and they were allowed to remain in the country during the persecution of the Christians, and after the expulsion of the Portuguese Jesuits in 1637–8, because of their cautious avoidance of religious issues. Gulliver met a 'malicious reprobate' Dutchman in the company of Japanese pirates, unwilling to intercede for fellow-Christians; and prudently pretending to be a Dutch merchant while at the Japanese court, he asked to be excused 'the ceremony imposed on my countrymen, of trampling upon the crucifix, because I had been thrown into [the] kingdom by my misfortunes, without any intention of trading' (*Gulliver's Travels*, III. i and xi). Cf. *Astræa Redux*, ll. 193–4; Prologue to *Amboyna*, ll. 18–22.

585. *Old heresies*: the doctrines of Wyclif, revived by the reformers.

599–600. *Those monumental arms*, &c. Cf. Shakespeare, *Troilus and Cressida*, III. iii. 150–3:

> Perseuerance, deere my Lord,
> Keepes honor bright, to haue done, is to hang
> Quite out of fashion, like a rustie male,
> In monumentall mockrie.

Goliah's sword, I Sam. xxi. 9; cf. Preface to *Religio Laici*, ll. 17–19.

603. *Old standard faith.* In forestry, a standard is a tree left standing when a coppice is cut down.

609. *digits*: twelve divisions of the diameter of the sun or moon, used to express the magnitude of an eclipse (*OED*).

630. *seav'n successive ages*. In the first edition Dryden apparently reckons from the coming of Augustine in 597 to the Reformation. The change from nine to seven in the second edition closes the era of faith with the Lollards. Seven has the secondary advantage of being the scriptural number of perfection.

646–8. *That pious Joseph*, &c. 'The English Benedictine monks executed a renunciation of the abbey lands, belonging to the order before the Reformation, in order to satisfy the minds of the possessors, and reconcile them to the re-establishment of the ancient religion, by guaranteeing the stability of their property' (Scott).

654–62. Scott suggests that '*James* his late nocturnal victory' is the defeat of Monmouth in the night engagements at Sedgemoor on 6 July 1685, and (without evidence) that the 'pleasing triumphs' were 'some extraordinary display of the aurora borealis' on that night.

705–13. *This peacefull Seat*, &c. Cf. Virgil, *Aen.* viii. 362–5:

> ut ventum ad sedes, 'haec' inquit 'limina victor
> Alcides subiit, haec illum regia cepit.
> aude, hospes, contemnere opes et te quoque dignum
> finge deo, rebusque veni non asper egenis.'

A hymn to Alcides precedes these lines (*Aen.* viii. 293–302): 'tu . . . invicte',

> te Stygii tremuere lacus, te ianitor Orci
> ossa super recubans antro semesa cruento. . . .

Dryden draws a fanciful parallel in ll. 709–10 between the 'victor Alcides' who, as the last and greatest of his labours, overcame Cerberus, and the victorius Christ who 'led Hell Captive maugre Hell'. Alcides, 'vera Iovis proles' and therefore nephew of Pluto, was 'of the Stygian race'. *Mighty Pan*, Christ: see i. 284, note.

The Third Part

(Page 503)

3. *Caledon*. See i. 14, note.

8–11. *And mother Hubbard*, &c. Spenser, *Mother Hubberds Tale*, ll. 949 ff.; the allusion is to Queen Elizabeth (see Prologue to *The Loyal Brother*, ll. 18–40, note).

18–19. *she cannot dye*, &c. Cf. i. 1–8; *Upon the death of the Lord Hastings*, ll. 27–28, note. *round eternity*: cf. Vaughan, *Silex Scintillans* (1655), 'The World':

> I saw Eternity the other night
> Like a great *Ring* of pure and endless light

> .   .   .   .   .   .

> One whisper'd thus,
> *This Ring the Bride-groome did for none provide*
> *But for his bride.*

25. *frequent Senate*: crowded Convocation. Cf. Milton, *Paradise Lost*, i. 792–7.

42. *Her faith unshaken to an exil'd Heir.* Scott explains this as a reference to the Anglican adherence to James's interests when he was sent to Brussels in March 1679 with 'the Bill of Exclusion against him . . . in dependence'. But Dryden probably refers to a later occasion. James was sent to Scotland on 20 October 1680, and some days later Parliament began to draft a new Exclusion Bill. This was carried to the Lords on 15 November and rejected by sixty-three votes to thirty, every bishop present voting against it (*HMC Ormonde*, N.S., v. 488–91, 496).

121–2. *Some German quarrel, or . . . some French.* A 'querelle d'Allemand' is 'a quarrell, or brable, entred into upon a sleight, or drunken, occasion' (Cotgrave). The French quarrel is probably Louis XIV's persecution of the Huguenots (see 'To the Reader', l. 30, note).

134–43. *thus her Passive character maintain'd,* &c. The old theory of divine right and the obedience of the subject had been thrust into prominence by the attempts at Exclusion. In 1681 the University of Cambridge addressed Charles II, declaring 'that it belongs not to subjects either to create or to censure, but to honour and obey their sovereign, who comes to be so by a fundamental hereditary right of succession, which no law, no fault or forfeiture can alter or diminish'. In 1683 Oxford published a *Judgement and Decree . . . Against Certain pernicious Books and Damnable Doctrines, Destructive to the Sacred Persons of Princes,* defending 'that most necessary doctrine which in a manner is the badge and character of the Church of England, of submitting to every ordinance for the Lord's sake; . . . this submission is to be clear, absolute, and without exception of any state or order of men'. See G. R. Cragg, *From Puritanism to the Age of Reason*, 1950, chap. viii.

149. *grandame gold*: 'old Hoarded Coin'. Cf. *The Wild Gallant*, IV, 'Frances has an 120 pieces of old Grandam and Aunt Gold left her'; Preface to *Fables*, l. 581.

159. *The wanton boyes wou'd piss upon your grave.* '[They] seek to get them a name by pissing against the holy waterstock (as the prouerb is) for there are a great number that wold be spoken of and renoumed for their naughty and wicked deeds' (Tomson, *Sermons of Calvin*, 1579; Tilley, N30).

160. *sons of Latitude.* 'Latitudinarian' was a term first applied to the Cambridge Platonists (Burnet, i. 186) and later to liberal Anglican theologians. Dryden charges the Latitudinarians with favouring nonconformity (cf. *infra*, ll. 187–90). A Latitudinarian 'believes the Way to Heaven is never the better for being strait, and if it could be made wider it would be much more convenient' (Butler, *Genuine Remains*, 1759, ii. 177). Stillingfleet, Tillotson, Burnet, and others had open minds on the possibility of comprehension; and Tillotson was criticized for 'his tender methods of treating with dissenters and his endeavours to unite all Protestants among themselves' (Birch, in Tillotson's *Works*, 1820, i. xxi). *A Defence of the Papers* (see *supra*, 'To the Reader', ll. 66–73, note) contains an attack on Stillingfleet and 'the juggling designs of his faction to draw in the nonconformists to their party' (Scott, xvii. 210).

168. *all that Scorpio claims.* Manilius, *Astron.* ii. 453–65:

> accipe diuisas hominis per sidera partes
> singulaque in propriis parentia membra figuris,
> in quis praecipuas toto de corpore uires
> exercent. . . .
> Libra regit clunes, et Scorpio inguine gaudet.

191–2. *Your Delphick Sword*, &c. Aristotle, *Polit.* i. 2.

193–4. *Some sons of mine*, &c. The 'Author and Supervisers' of *A Vindication of the Answer* (see *supra*, 'To the Reader, ll. 66–73, note). In his edition of this poem (1900) W. H. Williams suggested that the 'steeples' are three dignitaries 'such as Burnet, Stillingfleet, and Tillotson, whom Dryden supposed to be the authors of the three parts of the *Answer*', and that 'Argent' refers to 'their professed purity, in strong contrast with the *sable field* of their real motives'. This interpretation of 'Argent' and 'sable field' is convincing; but the three steeples are probably an emblem of bad eminence. Cf. ll. 229–32 *infra*, and the proverb versified in Cleveland's 'Elegy upon the Arch-bishop of Canterbury' (*Works*, 1687, p. 64):

> No Church-man can be Innocent and High,
> 'Tis height makes *Grantham* Steeple stand awry.

195. *Have sharply tax'd your converts.* In the *Defence* of the Duchess of York's paper, Dryden describes the Bishop of Winchester as 'that prelate of rich memory'. Stillingfleet replies with a personal jibe in the *Vindication*: 'Could nothing be said of him, then, but "that prelate of rich memory"? or, had he a mind to tell us he was no poet? or, that he was out of the temptation of changing his religion for bread?' (Scott, xvii. 220, 257). But it does not seem that Dryden gained financially from his conversion to Rome (L. I. Bredvold, 'Notes on Dryden's Pension', *MP* xxx (1933), 267–74). Cf. *infra*, ll. 221–6.

197–8. *Such who themselves of no religion are*, &c. In the *Vindication* Stillingfleet declares that 'if I thought there were no such thing in the world as true religion, and that *the priests of all religions are alike*' (*Absalom and Achitophel*, l. 99), 'I might have been as nimble a convert, and as early a defender of the royal papers, as any one of these champions. For why should not one who believes no religion, declare for any?' (Scott, x. 246). Finch, the Warden of All Souls, met Dryden in January 1687 and 'wished him much joy of his *new* religion. "Sir", said Dryden, "you are very much mistaken; my religion is the *old* religion." "Nay", replyed the other, "whatever it be in itself I am sure 'tis new for you for within these 3 days you had no religion at all" ' (*HMC, 12th Rpt.*, App., pt. vii, p. 202).

199–202. A versification of Stillingfleet's criticism of Dryden: 'If bold sayings and confident declarations, will do the business, he is never unprovided; but if you expect any reason from him, he begs your pardon; he finds how ill the character of a grim logician suits with his inclination' (Scott, xvii. 274).

203–11. *Thus our eighth Henry's marriage they defame*, &c. The immediate cause of the English Reformation, says Dryden in *A Defence,* was the Pope's refusal to grant Henry VIII a divorce: 'The king only knew whether it was conscience and love, or love alone, which moved him to sue for a divorce. But this we may say, that if conscience had any part in it, she had taken a long nap of almost twenty years together before she awakened, and perhaps had slept on till doomsday, if Anne Bolleyn, or some other fair lady, had not given her a jog' (Scott, xvii. 242). Stillingfleet answers this charge in the *Vindication,* quoting Henry's declaration 'in a solemn assembly . . . of the dissatisfaction of his conscience' (ibid., p. 265).

212–16. *With the same impudence,* &c. See 'To the Reader', l. 76, note. 'Suppose we had not such particular books', says Stillingfleet in the *Vindication,* 'we think the Holy Scripture gives the best rules and examples of humility of any book in the world' (Scott, xvii. 277).

247–50. *Unpitty'd Hudibrass,* &c. Samuel Butler (1612–80) 'printed a witty Poeme called *Hudibras,* which tooke extremely; so that the King and Lord Chancellor Hyde . . . promised him great matters, but to this day he haz got no Employment, only the King gave him 300 pounds' (Aubrey, p. 46). Cf. Oldham, 'A Satyr. *The Person of* Spencer *is brought in, Dissuading the Author from the Study of* Poetry':

> On *Butler* who can think without just Rage,
> The Glory and the Scandal of the Age ?
> Fair stood his hopes, when first he came to Town,
> Met every where with welcome of Renown.
>
> . . . .
>
> Of all his Gains by Verse he could not save
> Enough to purchase Flannel, and a Grave.

Writing to Rochester about 1683, Dryden says: 'I onely thinke I merite not to sterve . . . some small Employment wou'd render my condition easy. . . . Tis enough for one Age to have neglected Mr Cowley, and sterv'd Mr Buttler' (Ward, p. 21). Cf. *Threnodia Augustalis,* l. 377; Dedication of *The Satires of Juvenalis,* ll. 636–7.

256. *Imprimatur.* See 'To the Reader', ll. 66–73, note.

261–6. *she . . . suppress'd,* &c. Cf. Dedication of *The Satires of Juvenalis,* ll. 2129 ff.

267–72. *So when the gen'rous Lyon,* &c. Cf. *Absalom and Achitophel,* ll. 447–54.

308. *Shimei.* See *Absalom and Achitophel,* l. 585, note.

310–19. In *A Defence* Dryden castigated Stillingfleet for questioning the integrity of the duchess, 'and the truth of her plain relations, even so far as to blast, what in him lies, her blessed memory, with the imputation of forgery and deceit'; Stillingfleet replied that 'I do not in the least question the relation now given . . . of the passages concerning her; and therefore I have nothing more to say as to what relates to the person of the Duchess' (Scott, xvii. 209, 260). Cf. *supra,* 'To the Reader', l. 84, note.

Scott argues that 'he who councell'd him' is Burnet (Dryden always speaks of the pamphlets on the Papers as of multiple authorship), and interprets the 'score' which Burnet has paid as the satiric portrait of the Buzzard (*infra*, ll. 1141 ff.). But Dryden clearly refers to Burnet's fortunes in 1687. Out of favour at court, he went into voluntary exile in 1685 (Burnet, i. 628); and in 1686 he published an account of his continental tours 'to expose both Popery and Tyranny. The book was well received, and was much read: And it rais'd the King's displeasure very high' (ibid., p. 726). The Dutch refused to extradite Burnet to stand trial for high treason, and he was indicted in Scotland on 19 April 1687 and in England in June. Since *The Hind and the Panther* appeared in May, Dryden is referring in ll. 311–13 to a topical crisis in Burnet's fortune. See Burnet-Foxcroft, pp. 251–3. 'Permitted ills' are the pamphleteering which was Burnet's only weapon; and 'ev'ry Tyre' (broadside) refers to the *Tour* and 'some papers in single sheets . . . reflecting on the proceedings of *England* . . . which inflamed the King the more against me; for he believed they were written by me, as indeed most of them were' (Burnet, i. 726). A year later he was still regarded as a witty and dangerous pamphleteer (see Sybil Rosenfeld, 'The Second Letterbook of Sir George Etherege', *RES*, N.S., iii (1952), 22).

326–7. Dryden, says Stillingfleet in the *Vindication*, 'proceeds from immediate and original, to concomitant causes' of the Reformation; 'which, he saith, "were revenge, ambition, and covetousness". . . . However, he takes a leap from causes to effects; and here he tells us, "the immediate effects of this schism, were sacrilege, and a bloody persecution" ' (Scott, xvii. 274).

328–40. *Now last your sons*, &c. See 'To the Reader', ll. 76 and 77–81, notes.

344. *a saver*: in gaming, one who manages to avoid loss but without gain. Cf. *King Arthur*, ii:

> . . . As when the Lover, with the King is mixt,
> He puts the gain of *Britain* in a Scale,
> Which weighing with the loss of *Emmeline*,
> He thinks he's scarce a Saver.

419. *The Swallows fortune.* Scott suggested, on unsubstantiated evidence, that this fable (and particularly the 'common council', ll. 445 ff.) refers to a meeting of the leading Catholics at the Savoy under Father Petre's leadership. But Dryden's reference is probably quite general. 'Neither fanaticism nor ambition, neither resentment for past wrongs nor the intoxication produced by sudden good fortune, could prevent the most eminent Roman Catholics from perceiving that the prosperity which they at length enjoyed was only temporary, and, unless wisely used, might be fatal to them' (Macaulay, *History*, VI). The Panther prognosticates a fate for the Swallows which the moderate Catholics feared; and both Dryden's intellectual temper and his attitude to the Jesuit zealot Petre suggest that he belonged to the moderate party (see Bredvold, *The Intellectual Milieu of John Dryden*, 1934, pp. 180–3; *infra*, l. 461, note). The moderates, 'men of quiet or of fearful tempers', thought

that 'the Priests went too fast, and the King was too eager in pursuing every thing that was suggested by them' (Burnet, i. 672). Dryden wrote to Etherege on 16 February 1687: 'Oh that our Monarch wou'd encourage noble idleness by his own example, as he of blessed memory did before him; for my minde misgives me, that he will not much advance his affairs by Stirring' (Ward, p. 27).

434. *Endu'd with particles of soul divine.* Cf. Horace, *Sat.* ii. ii. 79, 'divinae particulam aurae'.

438. *time turn'd up the wrong side of the year.* Cf. Horace, *Sat.* i. i. 36, 'simul inversum contristat Aquarius annum'; *Examen Poeticum*, 'Song to a Fair, Young Lady', l. 4.

445–6. *Her sons . . . vote a flight.* The French ambassador Barillon, not often sensitive to public feeling, reported in the spring of 1686 that discontent was widespread (Turner, p. 364); and the Florentine minister Terriesi wrote about the same time that many Catholics were contemplating selling their property and taking refuge abroad (see Bredvold, op. cit., p. 176).

450–2. *But whether upward to the moon,* &c. 'Do they sleep in winter, like *Gesners* Alpine mice; or do they lie hid (as *Olaus* affirmes) *in the bottome of lakes and rivers,* spiritum continentes. . . . Or do they follow the Sun. . . . Or lie hid in the caves, rocks, and hollow trees, as most think, in deep *Tin-mines* or *Sea-cliffes* . . .? I conclude of them all . . . whence they come, whither they goe, *incompertum adhuc,* as yet we know not' (Burton, ii. ii. 3).

456. *a mackrel gale:* a fresh wind which ruffles the water and favours the catching of mackerel.

461. *the Martyn:* probably Edward Petre, the king's confessor; 'descended from a noble family, a man of no learning, nor any way famed for his vertue, but who made all up in boldness and zeal . . . the *Jesuit* of them all that seemed animated with the most courage. He had . . . suggested things, that shewed him a resolute and undertaking man' (Burnet, i. 672; cf. Burnet-Foxcroft, pp. 259–60). 'So furiously does the Jesuite drive, & even compell Princes to violent courses' (Evelyn, *Diary,* 17 January 1687). Petre was 'for a dignity design'd': James asked for a bishopric for him in October 1685; and it was widely rumoured that the archbishopric of York, vacant from April 1686 till November 1688, was intended for him (Turner, p. 305, note).

469. *the Swallow brought him in.* In 1686 James seems to have offered Petre a place in the privy council; Petre declined, but was given James's old lodgings in Whitehall, and charge of the new royal chapel (Turner, p. 305; *infra,* ll. 539–40).

475–6. *A Raven from a wither'd Oak,* &c. Virgil, *Ecl.* ix. 14–15 and i. 16–17 (with an additional line, 'saepe sinistra cava praedixit ab ilice cornix', in the Delphin edition). Dryden probably refers to Thomas Tenison of St. Martin's: '*Whitehall* lying within that parish, he stood as in the front of the battel all King *James's* reign; and maintained, as well as managed, that dangerous post

with great courage and much judgment, and was held in very high esteem'
(Burnet, i. 190). He became Archbishop of Canterbury in 1694.

490. *The mad Divineress:* Virgil's 'insana vates' (*Aen.* iii. 443).

493–4. *A Dame shou'd drown*, &c.: adapting the fable of Icarus, who flew too
near the sun and was drowned in 'caerulea . . . aqua: quae nomen traxit ab
illo' (Ovid, *Meta.* viii. 229–30). *Chelidonian:* χελιδών, the swallow.

515–16. *Till grosser atoms*, &c. Cf. *Fables*, 'The Cock and the Fox', ll. 325–41,
note.

538. *Of Ahaz dial, and of Joshuah's day.* 2 Kings xx. 8–11 (cf. *Threnodia
Augustalis*, ll. 106–9, note); Joshua x. 12–14 (cf. *Annus Mirabilis*, l. 472).

547–9. *Some Swifts*, &c. 'The Irish Catholics, with the sanguine Talbot at
their head' (Scott). The description fits the massive Richard Talbot, distinguished for the excessive zeal with which he applied himself to the Catholic
cause (Burnet, i. 681–2), and recently appointed Lord Deputy in Ireland, 'to
the astonishment of all sober men, & to the evident ruine of the Protestants in
that Kingdome' (Evelyn, *Diary*, 17 January 1687). Cf. the portrait in the anonymous *Advice to a Painter to draw the Duke by*, ll. 66–73 (Marvell's *Poems*, ed.
Margoliouth, p. 199):

> Now Talbott must by his great master stand,
> Laden with folly, flesh and Ill got land:
> He's of a size indeed to fill a porch,
> But nere can make a piller for a church;
> His sword is all his argument, and his book. . . .

The Gibeonites were cursed by Joshua (ix. 22–23): 'there shall none of you be
freed from being bondmen, and hewers of wood and drawers of water for the
house of my God'.

604. *birds met birds, and justled in the dark.* Cf. Dryden and Lee, *Oedipus* (1679),
IV:

> And for an universal rout of Nature
> Through all the inmost Chambers of the Sky,
> May there not be a glimpse, one Starry spark,
> But Gods meet Gods, and justle in the dark.

618–19. *the winds*, &c. Cf. Virgil, *Georgics*, i. 318.

633–4. *the laws provide*, &c. The act against Jesuits and seminarists (27
Elizabeth, c. 2) required all Roman priests to 'depart out of this realm of
England . . . so soon . . . as the wind, weather, and passage shall so serve'
(Henry Bettenson, *Documents of the Christian Church*, 1943, pp. 339–40). Any
who remained were liable to the penalty for high treason.

655. *an old fanatick Authour*: John ('Century') White, a Welsh puritan member of the Long Parliament, who was active in the ejection of the clergy, and
author of *The First Century of Scandalous Malignant Priests*, 1643. ''Tis said [he]
cried out, and condemned himself at his dying Hour for his undoing so many
guiltless Ministers . . . and at length died distracted' (Wood, *Ath. Oxon.* ii. 71).

689–91. *Curs'd be the wit*, &c. See 1 Kings xii. 6–11.

698. *The Test*: the acts of 1673 and 1678 (see *supra*, ii. 30–35, note). 'Though the Test-act was devised by a statesman whom they hated, and carried by a party whom they had opposed, the high-church clergy were not the less unwilling to part with it when they found the advantages which it gave them against the Papists in King James's reign.' (Scott).

718–22. *What more could you have done, &c.* See *Absalom and Achitophel*, l. 632, note; cf. *The Second Part of Absalom and Achitophel*, ll. 115–18. William Bedloe was an adventurer who had been in the household of the Catholic Lord Bellasis, met Oates at Valladolid in 1677, and thereafter gave evidence on the Plot in support of Oates. He died of a fever in August 1680, and was splendidly buried at Bristol as one who helped to save 'Three trembling Kingdoms from a Popish Grave' (Lane, p. 246).

727. *the Hag uncas'd.* Cf. Spenser, *The Faerie Queene*, I. viii. 46:

> So as she bad, that witch they disaraid,
> And robd of royall robes, and purple pall
>
> .   .   .   .
>
> Such as she was, their eyes might her behold,
> That her misshaped parts did them appall,
> A loathly, wrinckled hag, ill fauoured, old,
> Whose secret filth good manners biddeth not be told.

754–5. *As if 'twere Toby's rival to expell, &c.* Tobit viii. 1–3. Cf. Milton, *Paradise Lost*, iv. 167–70.

759. *the But and peace*: peace and its benefits. In the Dryden-Davenant *Tempest* (1670), Ventoso and Stephano offer to make peace with Trinculo on condition that the wine-butt is 'comprehended in the Treaty'. After deliberation (IV):

Ventoso. Duke *Trincalo*, we have consider'd.
Trinculo. Peace, or War?
Mustacho. Peace, and the Butt. . . .
Trinculo. You shall enjoy the benefits of Peace; and the first Fruits of it, amongst all civil Nations, is to be drunk for joy: . . . let old quarrels be drown'd in this draught.

Cf. Prologue to *The Mistakes*, l. 35.

809–12. Arguments for and against the toleration of nonconformists abound in the reigns of Charles II and James II (see G. R. Cragg, *From Puritanism to the Age of Reason*, 1950, chap. ix; *supra*, l. 160, note). Following the Declaration of Indulgence, some Anglican pamphleteers, including Halifax, urged dissenters to treat James's favour with suspicion (see H. C. Foxcroft, *A Character of the Trimmer*, 1946, pp. 236–7).

813. *th' associating name.* See *The Medall*, 'Epistle to the Whigs', l. 31, note.

823–4. *Immortal pow'rs . . . men below.* Cf. *Britannia Rediviva*, ll. 190–1; Homer, *Iliad*, i. 403–4; ii. 813–14; xx. 74.

856. *Wishing that happier Planet wou'd ascend*: looking to the accession of William of Orange.

876. *he protects your Friends opprest.* See 'To the Reader', l. 30, note.

906–14. *A Plain good Man:* James II. 'I go next to the duke; he has not the king's wit nor quickness, but that is made up by great application and industry. . . . He has naturally a candour and a justice in his temper very great, and is a firm friend, but a heavy enemy. . . . He understands business better than is generally believed, for though he is not a man of wit or fancy, yet he generally judges well when things are laid before him. . . . He is a prince of great courage and very serene in action, and naturally hates a coward' (Burnet's MS., *c.* 1683; Burnet-Foxcroft, pp. 50–51). Cf. *Absalom and Achitophel*, l. 353, note.

941. *rais'd the Fabrick where he pray'd.* James built a magnificent chapel at Whitehall, which was opened on Christmas Day, 1686, and dismantled at the Revolution. See the description by Evelyn, who went there 'to heare the Musique of the Italians' and came away 'not believing I should ever have lived to see such things in the K. of Englands palace, after it had pleas'd God to enlighten this nation' (*Diary*, 5 January 1687 and notes).

947. *cross the Proverb, and abound with Gall.* On the notion that pigeons have no gall, see Browne, *Pseudodoxia Epidemica*, III. iii.

950–1. With this attitude to the Anglican abandonment of the principle of celibacy, cf. i. 365–9, iii. 982–3, iii. 1064 and note. *Salt*: church endowments (*salarium*, salt-money). The pigeon's dung 'containeth very much Salt'; 'from the letter of the Scripture we may conclude it is no mild, but a fiery and furious animal, according to that of *Jeremy, Facta est terra in desolationem à facie iræ Columbæ*' (Browne, *Pseudodoxia Epidemica*, III. iii).

953. *bound by Promise.* Cf. *supra*, i. 432, note.

977. *rank, and breeding Melancholy Blood.* 'Though these be fair in feathers, pleasant in tast, and have a good out-side, like Hypocrites, white in plumes, and soft, their flesh is hard, black, unwholsome, dangerous, melancholy meat; *Gravant & putrefaciunt stomachum*' (Burton, I. ii. 2. 1).

1006. *The Bird that warn'd St. Peter.* Cf. Spenser, *The Faerie Queene*, v. vi. 27:

> What time the natiue Belman of the night,
> The bird, that warned *Peter* of his fall,
> First rings his siluer Bell. . . .

1017–33. *The World was fall'n*, &c. Cf. *supra*, i. 361–75. Lines 1032–3 parody Article XII of the Church of England.

1040–1. *For Vice*, &c. Cf. *Absalom and Achitophel*, ll. 1006–9, note.

1042–55. *An hideous Figure of their Foes they drew*, &c. See, for example, Oldham's *Satyrs upon the Jesuits* (1679), iii, '*Loyola*'s Will'.

1056. *Holland Emblem.* 'Emblems, like puns, being the wit of a heavy people, the Dutch seem to have been remarkable for them' (Scott). Cf. *The Hind and the Panther Transvers'd*: '*Bayes*: . . . I must needs say, at a *Fable* or an *Emblem*, I think no Man comes near me. . . . I was proffer'd a Pension to go into *Holland*,

and contrive their *Emblems*. But hang 'em they are dull Rogues, and would spoil my Invention' (Prior, *Dialogues*, ed. Waller, pp. 13–14).

1064. *the Birds of Venus*: symbolizing wantonness. Cf. Catullus, lxviii. 125–8:

> nec tantum niveo gavisast ulla columbo
>   conpar, quae multo dicitur inprobius
> oscula mordenti semper decerpere rostro,
>   quam quae praecipue multivolast mulier.

1067. *A Law*. See *supra*, ll. 633–4 note, 698 note, 728–33.

1093–4. *For those whom God*, &c. A common proverb: Jonson, *Catiline*, iii. 392–4; Shakespeare, *Antony and Cleopatra*, III. xiii. 111–15; Herbert, *Outlandish Proverbs* (1640), 688: 'When God will punish, hee will first take away the understanding.'

1098. *Such as the Meccan Prophet us'd*. A common medieval legend; cf. Langland, *Piers Plowman*, B. xv. 389–403; Massinger, *The Renegado*, IV. iii:

> He taught a Pigeon to feed in his Ear;
> Then made his credulous Followers believe
> It was an Angel, that instructed him
> In the framing of his *Alcoran*.

1121. *The noble Buzzard*: Gilbert Burnet (1643–1715), Scottish historian and pamphleteer, appointed Bishop of Salisbury after the Revolution. Burnet was a thorn in the flesh of James and the Catholics (see *supra*, ll. 310–19, note); and he had recently offended Dryden. A translation of Varillas's *Histoire des Révolutions . . . en matière de Religion* (1686) by Dryden was licensed on 29 April 1686, but was never published. In the same year, at Amsterdam, Burnet published *Reflections* on Varillas's book; Varillas wrote an *Answer*, to which Burnet responded with *A Defence of the Reflections* (published in August or September 1687). There Burnet suggests that his *Reflections* discredited Varillas and prevented Dryden from continuing the translation: 'as for his *Morals*, it is scarce possible for him to grow a *worse man* than he was. He has lately wreaked his Malice on me for spoiling his three moneths labour' (pp. 138–9). In *The Hind and the Panther Transvers'd* Bayes refers to Burnet's intrusion, and goes on: 'But I think I have my revenge on him sufficiently. . . . Don't you think this Fellow will hang himself?' (Prior, *Dialogues*, ed. Waller, p. 24).

1142. *A Son of Anach*. Num. xiii. 33.

1146. *A Prophet form'd, to make a female Proselyte*. 'There was a gentlewoman at the Hague originally of Scotch extraction but of a family long setled in Holland. . . . I was desired to visit her but declined it for I had no thoughts of marriage . . . yet seeing her accidentally I liked her conversation so well that ~~upon her invitation~~ I went to visit her and . . . came to like her so well and was so acceptable to her that we were married in May 1687' (Burnet's autobiography in Burnet-Foxcroft, p. 492). This courtship was known at Whitehall: James, 'understanding that I was like to have one of the best matches in the Hague . . ., he thought to have broke this by accusing me of high treason' (ibid., p. 251).

1154. *A fair Behaviour, and a fluent Tongue.* 'I first heard that famous & Excellent Preacher Dr. *Burnet* . . . on: 3 Coloss: 10: . . . with such a floud of Eloquence & fullnesse of matter as shew'd him to be a person of extraordinary parts' (Evelyn, *Diary*, 15 November 1674). 'When Burnet preached, part of his congregation *hummed* so loudly and so long that he sat down to enjoy it, and rubbed his face with his handkerchief' (Johnson, ii. 37).

1165–8. *The Hero, and the Tyrant change their style*, &c. When James was proceeding against Burnet early in 1687 (see *supra*, ll. 310–19, note) Burnet let it be known by letter from Holland that if 'a sentence should pass against me, I might be perhaps forced to justify my self, and to give an account of the share that I had in affairs these twenty years past: In which I might be led to mention some things, that I was afraid would displease the King: And therefore I should be sorry, if I were driven to it' (Burnet, i. 726–7). This letter was addressed to Middleton, one of the secretaries of state, with whom one of Dryden's sons was serving in 1687 (see Ward, p. 27).

1174. *A Greek*, &c. Virgil, *Aen.* ii. 49, 'timeo Danaos et dona ferentis'.

1179–82. In April 1675 Burnet disclosed both before a committee and in the House of Commons some remarks which Lauderdale had made privately to him. Burnet's first intention was to 'controul' his patron: 'I said to some, that Duke *Lauderdale* had gone so far in opening some wicked designs to me, that I perceived he could not be satisfied, unless I was undone. So I told what was mentioned before of the discourses that pass'd between him and me.' 'I was much blamed for what I had done. Some, to make it look the worse, added, that I had been his Chaplain, which was false; and that I had been much obliged to him, tho' I had never received any real obligation from him. . . . Yet the thing had an ill appearance, as the disclosing of what had pass'd in confidence' (Burnet, i. 373, 380).

1187. *scow'rs the streets.* See Prologue to *The Wild Gallant Reviv'd*, ll. 10–12, note.

1188. *runs an Indian muck.* The erroneous division of 'amuck' was not uncommon. Cf. Marvell, *The Rehearsal Transpros'd*, 1672, i. 59: 'like a raging Indian . . . he runs a mucke (as they call it there) stabbing every man he meets' (*OED*).

1233–55. *a Doom*: the Declaration of Indulgence. See *supra*, introductory note.

1258. *For Shiloh comes the Scepter to Remove.* Gen. xlix. 10.

1259–60. *Reduc'd . . . like Dyonysius to a private Rod.* 'Dionysius quidem tyrannus, Syracusis expulsus, Corinthi pueros docebat; usque eo imperio carere non poterat' (Cicero, *Tusc. Disp.* iii. 27).

1268. *Became the Smiths of their own Foolish Fate.* 'This wisdom the Romans did take much knowledge of: *Nam pol sapiens* (saith the comical poet) *fingit fortunam sibi*, and it grew to an adage, *Faber quisque fortunae propriae*' (Bacon, *Of the Advancement of Learning*, ed. A. W. Pollard, 1900, p. 354).

1277–88. *But each have sep'rate Int'rests*, &c. Cf. *Absalom and Achitophel*, ll. 1012–15, notes; *The Medall*, l. 297.

1278. *Two Czars*. Peter the Great and his brother Ivan were crowned joint rulers of Russia in 1682.

1283. *Bare benting times*. Bent: reedy grass. Cf. Ravenscroft, *Deuteromelia* (1609): 'The Pigion is neuer woe, till abenting she goe' (Tilley, P316).

1286. *the Tumultuous Colledge of the Bees*. Virgil, *Georgics*, iv. 66–87.

A Song for St Cecilia's Day, 1687
(Page 538)

In 1683 began a series of annual concerts, arranged by the stewards of a society of musicians to celebrate St. Cecilia's Day (22 November). The stewards were responsible for commissioning a poet and a composer to provide an ode for the occasion; the performance, with orchestra and chorus, usually took place at the Stationers' Hall. Dryden provided two odes—*A Song* in 1687 and *Alexander's Feast* in 1697. Among the librettists in other years were Oldham, Tate, and Shadwell. See W. H. Husk, *An Account of the Musical Celebrations of St. Cecilia's Day*, 1857. *A Song* was published by Dring in 1687 as a single half-sheet, the text printed in double column. The music was composed by 'that excellent & stupendious Artist' Giovanni Baptista Draghi, an Italian who may have come to England as one of Mary of Modena's musicians, and quickly rose to favour at court. He was organist of the queen's chapel from 1677 to 1684, and later music master to the Princess Anne. Cf. Evelyn, *Diary*, 25 July 1684; 28 January and 14 March 1685. An analysis of text and musical score for five-part chorus and string orchestra is given by Ernest Brennecke, 'Dryden's Odes and Draghi's Music', *PMLA* xlix (1934), 1–36.

1–2. *From Harmony . . . This universal Frame began.* A Platonic doctrine: cf. Job xxxviii. 1–7; Milton, 'On the Morning of Christ's Nativity', ll. 117 ff.; Katherine Philips, 'L'Accord du Bien' (Saintsbury, i. 563). Verrall points to correspondences between *A Song* and Milton's 'At a Solemn Musick' (*Lectures on Dryden*, 1914, pp. 183–5).

8. *Then cold, and hot,* &c. Cf. Milton, *Paradise Lost*, ii. 898 and iii. 708–15:

> I saw when at his Word the formless Mass,
> This Worlds material mould, came to a heap:
> Confusion heard his voice
>
> . . . .
>
> Swift to thir several Quarters hasted then
> The cumbrous Elements, Earth, Flood, Aire, Fire.

16. *What Passion cannot Musick raise and quell!* The doctrine of musical 'effect'.

See James Kinsley, 'Dryden and the *Encomium Musicae*', *RES*, N.S., iv (1953), 263–7.

17. *Juhal*: 'the father of all such as handle the harp and organ' (Gen. iv. 21).

53–54. *An Angel . . . Mistaking Earth for Heaven.* Cf. *Alexander's Feast*, ll. 161–70; Jonson, 'The Musicall strife' (*The Under-wood*, iii), ll. 21–24:

> O sing not you then, lest the best
> Of Angels should be driven
> To fall againe; at such a feast,
> Mistaking earth for heaven.

In medieval legend St. Cecilia is provided with a guardian angel (cf. Chaucer, *The Canterbury Tales*, VIII. 152 ff.), here metamorphosed into the spirit of harmony attracted to earth. The association of St. Cecilia with organ music seems to be a renaissance development of the legend.

61–63. *The Trumpet shall be heard*, &c. Isa. xxvii. 13; 1 Cor. xv. 52. Cf. Cowley, *Pindarique Odes*, 'The Resurrection', ii:

> Till all *gentle Notes* be drown'd
> In the *last Trumpets* dreadful sound;
> That to the *Spheres* themselves shall *silence* bring,
> Untune the *Universal String*.

Lines on Milton

(Page 540)

In 1680 Samuel Simmons, who published the first three editions of *Paradise Lost*, assigned his rights in the poem to Brabazon Aylmer; and they passed from Aylmer to Bently and Tonson. Tonson's edition of 1688, the first illustrated edition, is 'Adorn'd with Sculptures'. Dryden's epigram was engraved anonymously below Milton's portrait, and his name was attached to the reprint in *Miscellany Poems*, 1716.

'These lines were perhaps suggested by the distich written by Selvaggi in honour of the youthful poet, while he was at Rome, which Dryden has very happily amplified:

> "Græcia Mæonidem, jactet sibi Roma Maronem,
> "Anglia Miltonum jactat utrique parem." '

(Malone, I. i. 205.) Dryden's lines were translated into Latin by Cowper in 1780 (*Works*, ed. Southey, 1837, x. 237).

Britannia Rediviva: A Poem on the Birth of the Prince

(Page 541)

On 10 June 1688 the queen 'was hapely deliver'd of a Prince, and notwithstanding the malicious combination of those who design'd to aspers him, and were industriously absent, there were still more than sufficient in the roome to

testify the reality of his birth. . . . The birth of the Prince as it was an argument of the greatest joy to the King and Queen, and to all those who wished
them well; so it gaue the greatest agonys immaginable to the generality of
the Kingdom, but to none more, than the Prince of Orange' (Clarke, ii. 160–1;
cf. ll. 51–53 and 118–27). 'It became a distinguishing mark of a true Protestant,
to hold for spurious the birth of a prince, which took place in the presence
of more people than is either consistent with custom or decency' (Scott).
'Besides that so many of the King's Children were dead, (and they thought
this might haue the same fate) the Prince soon began to be so ill, the world
reported it, of him too'; and he 'was reduced to such extremity that his life
was dispair'd of'. The king 'as a last experiment consent'd that a Nurs should
be given him, which he immediately took too', and 'by degrees he gain'd
strength, and became a healthy child and likely for life' (Clarke, ii. 161–2).

   Britannia Rediviva was licensed on 19 June 1688 and published by Tonson in
folio (Malone's date, 23 June, was probably derived from Luttrell's copy).
A quarto edition followed from Edinburgh, 'Re-printed by Mr. P. B. Enginier,
Printer to the King's Most Excellent Majesty, for His Houshold, Chappel
and Colledge. 1688.' The London edition of *c.* 1691 (Macdonald, pp. 49–50)
is dated 1688. Dryden's epigraph is from Virgil, *Georgics,* i. 498–502, with
puerum substituted for *iuvenem. Perjuria*: false testimony given against
Catholics during prosecutions for the Plot.

   'Dryden, who knew how to assume every style that fitted the occasion,
writes here in the character of a devout and grateful Catholic, with much of
the *unction* which marks the hymns of the Roman Church. In English Poetry,
we have hardly another example of the peculiar tone which the invocation of
saints, and an enthusiastic faith in the mystic doctrines of the Catholic faith,
can give to poetry' (Scott).

   35–36. *Hail Son of Pray'rs, &c.* Cf. *Astræa Redux,* ll. 141–4.
   37–40. *late to thy Paternal Skyes retire, &c.* Cf. Horace, *Od.* i. ii. 43–49 (to
Augustus):

> filius Maiae, patiens vocari
>   Caesaris ultor;
> serus in caelum redeas diuque
> laetus intersis populo Quirini,
> neve te nostris vitiis iniquum
>   ocior aura
> tollat. . . .

   55–60. *when Alcides, &c.* See Theocritus, xxiv.
   78. *He sees his bleeding Church in Ruine lye.* Cf. *The Hind and the Panther,* i. 9–24.
   80–81. *the Sign, &c.* 'In one of the marches of Constantine, he is reported to
have seen with his own eyes the luminous trophy of the cross, placed above
the meridian sun, and inscribed with the following words: "By this, conquer."
. . . his astonishment was converted into faith by the vision of the ensuing
night. Christ appeared before his eyes; and displaying the same celestial sign

of the cross, he directed Constantine to frame a similar standard, and to march, with an assurance of victory, against Maxentius and all his enemies' (Gibbon, *Decline and Fall*, xx). Dryden treats James II's adoption of Romanism as a portent of Christian victory in the Turkish war on the Danube.

84. *another Sylvester*: Pope Innocent XI, on whose relations with James see Clark, p. 124, and Turner, pp. 325–8.

86. *Large of his Treasures*: Virgil, *Aen.* xi. 338, 'largus opum'.

89. *of the Brittish Line*. The birthplace of Constantine, 'as well as the condition of his mother Helena, have been the subject not only of literary but of national disputes. Notwithstanding the recent tradition, which assigns for her father a British king, we are obliged to confess, that Helena was the daughter of an innkeeper. . . . This tradition . . . was invented in the darkness of monasteries [and] has been defended by our antiquarians of the last age' (Gibbon, *Decline and Fall*, xiv).

91. *Whose Exile many sought*. See *Absalom and Achitophel*, l. 353, note.

94. *Moon-ey'd*: affected with intermittent blindness (attributed to the influence of the moon).

97. *that One Shipwrack on the Fatal Ore*. See *The Second Part of Absalom and Achitophel*, ll. 1065–1102, note. The Lemmon Ore is a sandbank in Yarmouth road.

121. *the true Eaglet safely dares the Sun*. Cf. *To his friend the Authour* (Hoddesdon), ll. 11–16.

154–6. The Great Plague and Fire. See *Annus Mirabilis*, ll. 857–60, note, 1066 ff.

157. *perjur'd Plots, the still impending Test*. Cf. *Absalom and Achitophel*, ll. 108–9, 208, 632, 672–3, notes; *The Medall*, 'Epistle to the Whigs', l. 129, note; *The Hind and the Panther*, ii. 30–35, iii. 698, notes.

165–6. *Enough of Early Saints*, &c. See *supra*, introductory note.

169–72. *Enough already*, &c. 'A very dry, cold easterly windy, backward Spring. . . . The weather was until now so cold & sharp, by an almost perpetual East wind, which had continued many moneths, that there was little appearance of any Spring; & yet the winter was very favourable as to frosts or Snow' (Evelyn, *Diary*, 15 and 29 April 1688).

176. *Araunah's threshing-floor*. The reference should be to 2 Sam. xxiv.

184. *Five Months to Discord and Debate were giv'n*. On James's attempts to concentrate power in the hands of Papist office-holders, his protracted campaign against Magdalen College, and the unsuccessful prosecution of the Anglican bishops who petitioned against the Second Declaration of Indulgence in May 1688, see Turner, pp. 334–44 and 395–405. 'Dryden, like other men of sense, probably began to foresee the consequences of so violent and general irritation; and expresses himself in moderate and soothing language, both as to the past and future' (Scott).

190–1. *Let Conscience*, &c. Cf. *The Hind and the Panther*, iii. 823–4 and note.

199–201. 'The name of the guardian deity of Rome was kept a profound secret, lest the enemies of the republic might lure him away; . . . the real name . . . of the city itself was wrapt in mystery and might never be uttered, not even in the sacred rites' (J. G. Frazer, *The Golden Bough*, 1922, 'Taboo', p. 391).

208–9. *As Joves Increase*, &c. Cf. *To the Earl of Roscomon*, l. 72, note.

231. *reprises*: not 'reprisals' (Noyes), but occasions, renewals of Fame's report.

237. *Earth's Gigantick brood by moments grow*. Not the *gigantes* themselves but the twins Otus and Ephialtes, fathered by Neptune on Iphimedia wife of the giant Aloeus (Homer, *Od.* xi. 305–20). Dryden exaggerates their growth; Homer says that they were nine fathoms tall at nine years old. The *gigantes* and the Aloidae are placed together in Virgil, *Aen.* vi. 580–4.

241–4. The centre of the earth 'may be full of winde, or a sulphureous innate fire, as our Meteorologists enform us, which sometimes breaking out, causeth those horrible Earth-quakes, which are so frequent in these dayes in *Japan, China*' (Burton, II. ii. 3). Cf. Browne, *Pseudodoxia Epidemica*, II. v. 5.

287. *Philistims*. Heb. *p'lishtīm*. Cf. the plural 'seraphims' in Isa. vi. 2. The collected edition of 1701 has '*Philistines*'.

304. *Propitious Queen*. Cf. *Prologue To the Dutchess*, note.

306. *Beyond the Sunny walks, and circling Year*. Cf. *Annus Mirabilis*, l. 639.

327. *Trine*: trinity, with a quibble on the astrological term (see *Annus Mirabilis*, ll. 1165–6, note).

329. *The Royal Sov'raign*: 'a glorious vessel of burden' built in 1637, 'being for burthen, defense, and ornament the richest that ever spread cloth before the Wind'; rebuilt *c.* 1659 and again *c.* 1685; and burnt at Chatham in 1696 (Evelyn, *Diary*, 19 July 1641; 2 February 1696).

333. *The Name of Great*, &c. For Dryden's other panegyrics on James see *Absalom and Achitophel*, l. 353, note.

335–44. 'Of all *Aristides*'s Virtues, the best known, and That by which he was most distinguished, was his Justice, as being of most constant Use, and of the greatest Extent. Thence . . . he acquired the most Royal and Divine Sirname, or Appellation of *Just*, a Title Kings and Tyrants were never fond of' (*Plutarch's Lives . . . Translated*, 1727, iii. 273).

The Prologue and Epilogue to the History of Bacon in Virginia

(Page 551)

Aphra Behn's *The Widdow Ranter or, The History of Bacon in Virginia. A Tragi-Comedy* was posthumously performed at Drury Lane towards the end of 1689. The Prologue and Epilogue, 'written by Mr. Dryden', were licensed and entered in *SR* on 20 November 1689; and the two pieces were published together by Tonson before the end of the year. In 1690 James Knapton published *The Widdow Ranter* with Dryden's Prologue to Shadwell's *A True Widow* (1679) and, for epilogue, a piece which had appeared in *Covent Garden Drolery* (1672) as 'Prologue to [Beaumont and Fletcher's] the double Marriage' and later served as Prologue to the 1693 edition of Mrs. Behn's *Abdelazer, or The Moor's Revenge* (1677). Tonson probably refused Knapton the right to print Dryden's Prologue and Epilogue, and Knapton utilized the Prologue to *A True Widow* (which he had just reissued or was about to reissue in 1689) and the old prologue to *The Double Marriage*. See R. G. Ham in *The London Mercury*, xxi (1930), 425–6; Wiley, pp. 278–82. Miss Wiley illustrates the practice of attaching old prologues to new plays.

Prologue. 3. *the Product of Virginian Ground*. The serious part of *The Widdow Ranter* is based on *Strange News from Virginia, being a full and true Account of the Life and death of Nathaniel Bacon Esq.*, 1677. Nathaniel Bacon (1642–76) emigrated to Virginia and won fame as a rebel and reformer.

7. *Vizard-Masks*. See Prologue to The Second Part of *The Conquest of Granada*, l. 13, note.

23. *Bug-words*: words that terrify or alarm. Cf. *infra*, Ovid's *Art of Love. Book* I, ll. 881–2; Duffett, *The Mock-Tempest* (1675), iii. 1: 'I say keep the Peace, do you not tremble to use such bug words, if any body should hear you it would bring a scandal on the house, and make 'em think us Whores.'

31. *Mundungus*: vile (tobacco). In the play (II. ii) the Widow Ranter describes Captain Dullman as 'a walking Chimney, ever smoaking with nasty Mundungus'.

41. An allusion to the victory of the men of Enniskillen at Newtown Butler on 9 August 1689 (see Clark, pp. 293–4).

Epilogue. 8. *crumpt*: crooked, curled.

9. *the Author's dead*. Aphra Behn died on 16 April 1689. Her play, says the author of the 1689 Dedication, 'had not that Success which it deserv'd, and was expected by her Friends; The main fault ought to lye on those who had the management of it'. Injudicious cuts were made, and many of the parts 'given to those whose Tallents and Genius's suited not our Author's Intention'.

Prologue and Epilogue to Don Sebastian, King of Portugal: A Tragedy

(Page 553)

Don Sebastian was first performed at Drury Lane on 4 December 1689, and published by Tonson soon after (advertised in the *London Gazette*, 2–6 January 1690, for publication 'on Thursday next'). This edition contains a second Prologue 'Sent to the Authour by an unknown hand'.

Prologue. 3–4. *So may cast Poets write,* &c. At the Revolution of 1688 Dryden lost his offices as Poet Laureate and Historiographer-Royal, and with them his pension. His misfortunes, he says in the Preface, 'have once more brought him, against his will, upon the Stage. While I continue in these bad circumstances, (and truly I see very little probability of coming out) I must be obliged to write; and if I may still hope for the same kind usage, I shall the less repent of that hard necessity.'

15. *Jove was alike,* &c. Virgil, *Aen.* x. 105–8.

41–44. At the Revolution an act was passed prohibiting any 'Papist or reputed Papist' from possessing a horse worth more than five pounds (1 Gul. & Mar., c. 15).

Epilogue. A dramatic commentary on the plot of the play, spoken by Antonio (Mountfort), a Portuguese slave of noble birth, and his lover Morayma (Mrs. Mountfort), the Mufti's daughter, who steals her father's jewel casket for Antonio's sake (l. 34). They refer here to the main plot, in which Sebastian and the captive Queen Almeyda are established in control of the kingdom, but are separated by the discovery that their love is incestuous. Sebastian becomes an anchorite, Almeyda a nun. In tragedy, Mountfort was 'the most affecting Lover'; and he had 'a particular Talent, in giving Life to *bons Mots* and *Repartees:* The Wit of the Poet seem'd always to come from him *extempore,* and sharpen'd into more Wit, from his brilliant manner of delivering it' (Cibber, p. 107). Mrs. Mountfort 'was Mistress of more variety of Humour, than I ever knew in any one Woman Actress. . . . She was so fond of Humour, in what low Part soever to be found, that she would make no scruple of defacing her fair Form, to come heartily into it. . . . But what found most Employment for her whole various Excellence at once, was the Part of *Melantha,* in *Marriage-Alamode*' (ibid., pp. 137–40).

25–28. *To copy their Example,* &c. So Sebastian in Act V:

> To have but one poor night of all our lives;
> It was indeed a glorious, guilty night:
> So happy, that, forgive me Heav'n, I wish
> With all its guilt, it were to come again. . . .

36. *thundring Votes of lives and fortune*: like the addresses presented to William of Orange at the Revolution.

Prologue to The Prophetess

(Page 556)

The Prophetess: or, The History of Dioclesian. Written by Francis Beaumont and John Fletcher. With Alterations and Additions, After the Manner of an Opera was first performed at Dorset Garden in May or early June 1690 and published by Tonson soon afterwards (advertised in the *London Gazette,* 12–16 June).

Langbaine (p. 214) says that the play was 'lately . . . reviv'd by Mr. *Dryden*'; but more weight may be given to Downes (p. 42): 'The *Prophetess*, or *Dio-clesian* an Opera, wrote by Mr. *Betterton*; being set out with Coastly Scenes, Machines and Cloaths: The Vocal and Instrumental Musick, done by Mr. *Purcel*; and Dances by Mr. *Priest*; it gratify'd the Expectation of Court and City; and got the Author a great Reputation.' It has been suggested that Dryden had a hand in the songs in *The Prophetess* (see Day, pp. 168–9), but there is no evidence that he contributed more than the Prologue. The music was so successful that Purcell, after some delay, published the full score in 1691. *The Vocal and Instrumental Musick of The Prophetess* has an Epistle Dedicatory signed by Purcell; but the original draft of the dedication (BM MS. Stowe 755, ff. 34–35) carries a note in a contemporary hand: 'This Epistle is the handwriting of John Dryden Esq . . . the first draught of an Epistle Dedicatory to some Opera's of Mr Purcell, and writ at his Request & for his use' (see R. G. Ham, in *PMLA* l (1935), 1065–75). On Dryden's relations with Purcell at this time, see J. A. Westrup, *Purcell*, 1937, pp. 67–73.

The Prologue was suppressed after the first night. A note accompanying a reprint in *The Muses Mercury: or The Monthly Miscellany*, 1707, pp. 3–5, says that Shadwell was 'the occasion of its being taken notice of by the Ministry'. He took the beginning of the piece to have 'a *double Meaning*, and that Meaning to reflect on the *Revolution*'; and 'told a Gentleman, *He would immediately put a stop to it. . . . Because while Mr.* Dryden *was Poet Laureat, he would never let any Play of his be Acted.*' The explanation is false, and Noyes describes this note as 'absolutely untrustworthy'. But the maligned Shadwell might well have made such an exaggerated charge; and the note was printed under the editorship of the Whig Oldmixon, who may have been less ill-informed than Noyes suggests. Even without the intervention of Shadwell, Dryden's sarcasms on William's Irish war would invite prohibition. 'It must be confess'd, that this Prologue had some familiar, metaphorical Sneers, at the Revolution itself; and as the Poetry of it was good, the Offence of it was less pardonable' (Cibber, p. 283).

The Prologue was reprinted in *Poems on Affairs of State* (1698), *The Muses Mercury*, and the 1708 edition of *The Annual Miscellany* for 1694. The text in *POAS* is an 'improved' and inferior text; most of its variants are also to be found in the transcripts in BM Add. MS. 28558 and Philipps MS. 8301. The text in *The Annual Miscellany*, published by Tonson, significantly shows almost no departure from that in *The Prophetess*. *The Muses Mercury* follows in part *The Prophetess* and in part the manuscripts and *POAS*, and was probably printed from another transcript. Transcripts of a prohibited piece are likely to have been numerous. Line 25 may have been in the spoken Prologue and discreetly omitted in the first edition.

3–5. *Prospective . . . Tube.* Synonyms for telescope.

16. *three Storys*: (i) from the feet to the gathered skirts—the first form of the

bustle, which came in about this time; (ii) the bust and shoulders; (iii) the gathering of the hair and the decorative wire-framed head-dress. For an account of the extravagant head-tiring of the 1680's and 1690's, see Iris Brooke, *English Costume of the Seventeenth Century*, 1950, pp. 78 and 86.

21. *New Honour calls you hence.* The Irish 'Patriot Parliament' held by James II in Dublin in 1689 recognized James as king, declared Ireland independent, and attainted adherents of William of Orange. William sent Schomberg over to Ulster and, urged on by an impatient Parliament, crossed himself on 24 June 1690. Dryden refers to the muster of William's army.

23. *Bilbo Blade*: a sword noted for its temper. Cf. Another Epilogue to *The Duke of Guise*, l. 5.

28. *Teague*: the Irish. See J. O. Bartley, *Teague, Shenkin and Sawney*, 1954, pp. 102–4 and 105–10.

34–35. The Irish, copper-collared, would be cheaper and less ornamental pages than the fashionable silver-collared negroes; one of whom is represented in Mignard's portrait of the Duchess of Portsmouth (1682) in the National Portrait Gallery.

47. *Selling facetious Bargains.* See *Mac Flecknoe*, l. 181, note.

48. *Dum-founding.* Illustrated in Shadwell, *Bury-Fair* (1689), III:

Sir Hum[phrey] *Dumfounds the Count with a smart rap on the Shoulders.*

Cou. Morbleu, vat is dat? Monsieur *Wildish*, did you hittè me?
Wild. Not I, Monsieur. [*Sir* Hum. *raps him again.*]
Cou. Nor you, my Lore?
Bell. Not I, Monsieur le Count.
Cou. Ventre bleu, is dere again! Sire, vat you mean by dat, to strike me between de Head and de Shouldere?

Prologue, Epilogue and Songs from Amphitryon; or, The Two Socia's. A Comedy
(Page 558)

Amphitryon was first performed, with music by Purcell, at Drury Lane in October 1690, and published by Tonson (advertised in the *London Gazette*, 30 October–3 November). The printed text is followed by the musical settings, with the sub-title 'The Songs in *Amphitryon*, with the Musick'. 'What has been wanting on my Part', says Dryden in the Dedication to Sir William Leveson Gower, 'has been abundantly supplied by the Excellent Composition of Mr. *Purcell*; in whose Person we have at length found an *English* Man, equal with the best abroad. At least my Opinion of him has been such, since . . . the Experience I have had of him, in the setting my three Songs for this *Amphitryon*: To all which, and particularly to the Composition of the *Pastoral Dialogue*, the numerous Quire of Fair Ladies gave so just an Applause on the Third Day.' See Prologue to *The Prophetess*, note; *An Ode, on the Death of Mr. Henry Purcell*.

Anne Bracegirdle (*c.* 1663–1748), the favourite of Congreve, was a popular 'prologue' in the 1690's (see Wiley, pp. 331–2). 'Never any Woman was in such general Favour of her Spectators, which, to the last Scene of her Dramatick Life, she maintain'd, by not being unguarded in her private Character. This Discretion contributed, not a little, to make her the *Cara*, the Darling of the Theatre; . . . the most eminent Authors always chose her for their favourite Character . . .' (Cibber, pp. 141–2). On Mrs. Mountfort, see Epilogue to *Don Sebastian*, note.

Prologue. 5. *What gain you, by not suffering him to teize ye?* Probably a reference to the prohibited Prologue to *The Prophetess.*

17. *Julian's interloping Trade*: trade without a licence. Cf. *The Medall*, l. 41. Robert Julian copied and distributed lampoons; in the anonymous *Exclamation Against Julian, Secretary to the Muses* (1679), he is addressed as

> Thou Common Shore of this Poetick Town,
> Where all our Excrements of Wit are thrown.

See further Macdonald, pp. 214–15.

20–21. *Jig . . . gig.* 'The verb seems literally to denote the action of some kind of *gig* or whipping-top of peculiar construction, having inside it a smaller *gig* of the same shape, which was thrown out by the effect of rapid rotation' (*OED*).

37. *Hence ye Prophane*: Virgil, *Aen.* vi. 258, 'procul, o procul este, profani'.

Songs. For the music of these songs see *The Works of Purcell*, ed. Alan Gray, 1906, xvi. 31–41, and Summers, vi. 221–30; for their later history see Day, pp. 169–71. I. *Song*: Act III.

II. *Mercury's Song to Phædra*: Act IV, accompanied by 'a fantastick Dance'.

III. *A Pastoral Dialogue*: Act IV. 'Come up, Gentle-folks, from below', says Phædra, 'and sing me a Pastoral Dialogue, where the Woman may have the better of the Man; as we always have in Love matters.'

Prologue to The Mistakes, or, The False Report: A Tragi-comedy
(Page 563)

The Mistakes, by Joseph Harris, was first performed at Drury Lane in December 1690, and published by Hindmarsh in 1691 (*TC*, February). Harris (*c.* 1650–*c.* 1715) was a seal-cutter turned actor and singer, 'a Comedian of no great Note; but by the Assistance of his Friends he Aim'd at being an Author' (see Macdonald, p. 162). Joseph Williams, by this time a leading actor, appropriately plays the central part in the Prologue; his 'Industry was not equal to his Capacity; for he lov'd his Bottle better than his Business' (Cibber, p. 162).

10. *that's as long as Cork.* Cork was taken by Marlborough on 28 September 1690 after a five-day siege.

22. *A Common Harlots price.* See Prologue to *Marriage A-la-Mode*, l. 22, note.

35. *Peace and the Butt.* See *The Hind and the Panther*, iii. 759, note.

Prologue, Epilogue and Songs from King Arthur: or, The British Worthy. A Dramatick Opera

(Page 564)

'This Poem', says Dryden in his Epistle Dedicatory to Halifax, 'was the last Piece of Service, which I had the Honour to do, for my Gracious Master, King *Charles* the Second.' The play was, however, first performed at Dorset Garden in May or June 1691, and published by Tonson about the same time (advertised in the *London Gazette*, 4–8 June). On the issues of the first edition see Macdonald, p. 133, and J. M. Osborn in *MP* xxxix (1941), 92: the early copies did not include the Prologue and Epilogue. The music is by Purcell (see Prologues to *The Prophetess* and *Amphitryon*, notes; *An Ode, on the Death of Mr. Henry Purcell*). Dryden says in the dedication that he has had to cramp his verses to accommodate Purcell's music: but 'I flatter my self with an Imagination, that a Judicious Audience will easily distinguish betwixt the Songs, wherein I have comply'd with him, and those in which I have followed the Rules of Poetry, in the Sound and Cadence of the Words'.

On Betterton, who spoke the Prologue and played Arthur, see Prologue to *Troilus and Cressida*, note; on Mrs. Bracegirdle, who spoke the Epilogue and played Emmeline, see Prologue and Epilogue to *Amphitryon*, note.

Prologue. 3. *Clipp'd Money.* See *The Medall*, ll. 228–9, note.

10–12. *Shovel-Board*: a game in which the players drive metal weights by hand from their respective ends of the board. A piece must be shoved (laid) across a line 4 feet from the starting-point, if the shot is to be reckoned; an over-violent shot throws the piece into the 'box' at the other end of the board.

32–37. Dryden alludes to the war with France (1689–97), in which the main land theatre was Flanders. Pietro Ottoboni, Pope Alexander VIII from 1689 till February 1691, maintained the privileges of the Holy See against France. His successor, Innocent XII, was not elected until 12 July 1691. When *King Arthur* was first presented, the disposition of the next Pope towards France 'was matter of anxious speculation to the politicians' (Scott).

48–49. *While thus*, &c. Cf. Epilogue to *Cleomenes*, ll. 19–20.

Epilogue. 17. *the kind Couch above in Bridges-Street.* Cf. Crowne, Epilogue to *Sir Courtly Nice*, 1685:

> Our *Bridges-Street* is grown a Strumpet Fair,
> Where higling Bawds do palm their rotten Ware. . . .

Songs. On reprints of these songs, see Day, pp. 172–8.

I: Act I, sung by Saxon priests. 'The Scene represents a place of Heathen Worship; The three Saxon Gods, *Woden*, *Thor*, and *Freya* placed on Pedestals. An Altar.'

18. *Tanfan:* an obscure Germanic deity. See Tacitus, *Annales*, i. 51.

II: Act I. With ll. 1–4 cf. *A Song for Sᵗ Cecilia's Day, 1687*, ll. 25–32.

III: Act II. A musical strife between the 'Airy Spirit' Philidel and Grimbald the 'fierce Fiend' of the Saxon magician Osmond, with their respective spirits; addressed to Arthur and his Britons who are pursuing the Saxon king Oswald.

IV: Act II. A musical interlude of song and dance by 'Kentish Lads and Lasses' for the entertainment of Emmeline.

V: Act III. Sung by Philidel, who restores Emmeline's sight with a vial given him by Merlin.

VI: Act III. Philidel summons the singers to Emmeline

> to Congratulate
> Your new-born Eyes; and tell you what you gain
> By sight restor'd, and viewing him you love.

VII: Act III. Later popular as the 'Frost Music' performed in the intervals of stage plays (Day, p. 174). Osmond changes the scene to Iceland to show the force of love and gain Emmeline.

VIII: Act IV. Cf. Spenser, *The Faerie Queene*, II. xii. 63–68, and the similar situation in Fairfax, *Godfrey of Bulloigne*, xv. 63:

> Put off those Arms and fear not *Mars* his rage,
> Your Sword, your Shield, your Helmet needless is:
> Then Consecrate them here to endless rest,
> You shall Love's Champion be, and Souldiers blest.

IX: Act IV. The temptation of 'Fantastick Fairy Joys', following the temptation of the Sirens in VIII.

X: Act V. 33. *Hovels*, granaries. XI: Act V.

To Sir George Etherege. Mr. D—— Answer
(Page 578)

Etherege went as James II's minister to Ratisbon in 1685. In January and April 1686 he sent two jocular verse epistles to Middleton, one of the secretaries of state, describing the insufficient but indispensable charms of the German ladies. To these Dryden, who was on friendly terms with Etherege, wrote his *Answer* (probably at Middleton's request) in the same metre and style. All three epistles are printed in the poetical miscellany published with *The History of Adolphus* (see Macdonald, p. 82).

1–4. In his second epistle Etherege complains that although he has moved two degrees south from London (lat. 51° 30′) to Ratisbon (lat. 49°), the beauties of the Danube do not accord with the warmer climate. Dryden's calculation is therefore not 'As Map informs'; he seems to have been misled by Etherege's statement that love and wine are 'brisker' in the sunshine, or by his reference to the 'Nymphs of gentle *Thames*' who 'warm me hither'. The date of Etherege's birth is unknown; but 1634–5 has been conjectured, partly on the evidence of l. 4 of Dryden's *Answer*.

10–12. *young in Loves Affairs of State*, &c. Cf. Etherege's first epistle, ll. 8–13: Ratisbon is an 'Idle sneaking Place' where

> . . . in a troublesome disguise,
> The Wife seems honest, the Husband wise,
> For Pleasure here has the same fate
> Which do's attend Affairs of State.

25. *Chop'd*: chapped, cracked.

28–29. *What Region*, &c. Cf. Virgil, *Aen.* i. 460, 'quae regio in terris nostri non plena laboris?'

30–31. *Triptolemus* drove over the earth in Ceres' chariot distributing corn (Ovid, *Meta.* v. 642–61).

45. *Rummers*: large drinking-cups (Du. *roemer*). Cf. Etherege's letter to Buckingham, 12 November 1686: 'The best Furniture of their Parlours (instead of innocent *China*) are tall overgrown Rummers, and they take more care to enlarge their Cellars than their patrimonial Estates. In short, Drinking is the Hereditary Sin of this Country' (*Works*, ed. H. F. B. Brett-Smith, 1927, p. lvii).

47. *Three holy Miter'd Hectors*: the archbishops of Mainz, Trèves, and Cologne, who with four temporal rulers made up the Electorate.

60. *'Tis the sour Sawce*, &c. Proverbial; see Tilley, M839.

65. *defi'd*: renounced (at baptism).

66–67. Etherege's last play was *The Man of Mode* (1676), for which Dryden had written the Epilogue. In a letter of 16 February 1687 Dryden hails him 'O thou immortal source of Idleness'; and Etherege replies: 'You have noe share in that noble Laziness of minde, wch all I write make out my just title to. . . . Tho' I have not been able formerly to forbear playing the fool in verse and prose I have now judgement enough to know how much I ventur'd, & am rather amaz'd at my good fortune, than vain upon a little success' (Ward, pp. 26, 28, 29). On 7 December 1685 Middleton had told Etherege that *The Man of Mode* was played at court 'with the usuall applause, and the King was pleas'd to tell me, that he expected you shou'd put on your Socks' (*Works*, ed. Brett-Smith, p. xlii).

73. *The Duke St. Aignan*: François de Beauvilliers (d. 1687), a favourite of Louis XIV and author of a tragi-comedy *Bradamante*.

75. *a Farce*: Buckingham's *Rehearsal*, begun about 1663–4 but not published till 1672 (see Macdonald, p. 194). Cf. Epilogue to *All for Love*, l. 17, note.

To Mr. Southern; on his Comedy, called the Wives Excuse
(Page 580)

The Wives Excuse: or, Cuckolds make Themselves. A Comedy was first performed at Drury Lane in December 1691 and published by Samuel Brisco in 1692 (*TC*, February). On Dryden's friendship with Southerne see Prologue and Epilogue to *The Loyal Brother*, note.

7–8. *Farce, in it self,* &c. Cf. Prologue to *The Loyal General*, ll. 22–25, note.

11–12. *But, let a Monster Muscovite,* &c. Cf. *To Mr. Granville*, ll. 21–22.

18. *Nokes.* See Prologue to the First Part of *The Conquest of Granada*, l. 7, note.

27. *one dead.* Etherege died in Paris early in 1691 (Luttrell, ii. 171).

Eleonora: A Panegyrical Poem Dedicated to the Memory of the Late Countess of Abingdon
(Page 582)

Eleonora was the eldest daughter of Sir Henry Lee of Ditchley in Oxfordshire, and wife of James Bertie, first Earl of Abingdon. She died on 31 May 1691. Dryden's poem was published by Tonson in the following spring (Luttrell's copy dated 7 March). The epigraph is *Aen.* vi. 128–31.

To the Right Honourable The Earl of Abingdon, &c. 3–6. *Ovid . . . excus'd the Faults of his Poetry,* &c. *Tristia*, I. i.

55–64. *Doctor Donn . . . acknowledges,* &c. 'My defence is, that my purpose was to say as well as I could: for since I never saw the Gentlewoman, I cannot be understood to have bound my self to have spoken just truths, but I would not be thought to have gone about to praise her, or any other in rime; except I took such a person, as might be capable of all I could say' (Donne, *Letters*, 1651, p. 239). Ben Jonson said to Drummond 'that Dones Anniversarie was profane and full of Blasphemies: that he told Mr Donne, if it had been written of yᵉ Virgin Marie it had been something, to which he answered that he described the Idea of a Woman and not as she was' (Jonson, i. 133). Cf. James Kinsley, 'Dryden and the Art of Praise', *ES* xxxiv (1953), 57–64.

80–82. In Phidias's representation of 'the Fight of the *Amazons* upon the Goddess's Shield; He had there express'd a kind of Figure or Resemblance of himself, like a bald old Man, holding aloft a great Stone with both Hands; and had put in a very fine Picture of *Pericles* fighting with an *Amazon*' (*Plutarch's Lives . . . Translated*, 1727, ii. 195).

Eleonora. 71–74. *So Pharaoh,* &c. Gen. xli.

79–82. *Perhaps a thousand other Worlds,* &c. On the 'new astronomy' in seventeenth-century poetry, see Marjorie Nicolson, *Science and Imagination*, 1956, pp. 30–57.

193–4. *Charity was not more fruitful*, &c. Lady Abingdon had six sons and three daughters. Spenser's Charissa (*The Faerie Queene*, I. x. 4, 30–31)

> to a louely fere
> Was lincked, and by him had many pledges dere.

197–200. *Anchises look'd not*, &c. Virgil, *Aen.* vi. 752–853.

252. *Though Bodies cannot, Souls can penetrate*. See *The Hind and the Panther*, i. 95–99, note.

263–5. *but short*, &c. Cf. *Upon the death of the Lord Hastings*, ll. 41–42.

272–3. *The Figure*, &c. See *Upon the death of the Lord Hastings*, ll. 27–28, note.

291–8. *Her fellow Saints*, &c. Cf. *Poetical Miscellanies: The Fifth Part*, 'On the Death of a Very Young Gentleman', ll. 1–8; Donne, *An Anatomie*, 'A Funerall Elegie', ll. 83–90:

> Hee which not knowing her said History,
> Should come to reade the booke of destiny,
>
> .   .   .   .
>
> And measuring future things, by things before,
> Should turne the leafe to reade, and reade no more,
> Would thinke that either destiny mistooke,
> Or that some leaves were torne out of the booke.

303–8. *So was she soon exhal'd*, &c. Cf. *Poetical Miscellanies: The Fifth Part*, 'On the Death of a Very Young Gentleman', ll. 23–26; *Threnodia Augustalis*, l. 28.

317–18. *No Pains she suffer'd*, &c. Cf. Donne, *Songs and Sonets*, 'A Valediction: forbidding Mourning', ll. 1–4:

> As virtuous men passe mildly away,
>   And whisper to their soules, to goe,
> Whilst some of their sad friends doe say,
>   The breath goes now, and some say, no. . . .

339. *the third Errand*. The others had been for Enoch (Gen. v. 24) and Elijah (2 Kings ii. 11).

Prologue, Epilogue and Song from Cleomenes, The Spartan Heroe. A Tragedy
(Page 595)

Cleomenes was for a few days prohibited on the ground that it reflected on the government; but, says Dryden in his Preface, the reasons 'were so ill founded, that my Lord Chamberlain no sooner took the pains to read it, but they vanish'd'. Rochester is thanked in the Epistle Dedicatory for representing the play to the queen 'as wholly Innocent of those Crimes, which were laid unjustly to its charge'. It was first performed at Drury Lane in April 1692, and published by Tonson about the same time (advertised in the *London Gazette*, 2–5 May). On Mountfort, who spoke the Prologue, see Epilogue to *Don Sebastian*, note; on Mrs. Bracegirdle, who spoke the Epilogue, see Prologue and Epilogue to *Amphitryon*, note.

Prologue. 1–10. On rowdyism in the theatre, see Nicoll, pp. 15–19.

11. *A Merry-Andrew, such a Mob will serve.* Cf. Prior, *Poems on Several Occasions,* ed. A. R. Waller, 1905, p. 133.

28. *dust a Stand:* toss off a drink. Cf. Shadwell, *Epsom-Wells,* 1673, 1; the country justice Clodpate says 'I had forgot, I have the rarest stand of Ale to drink out in the Afternoon, with three or four honest Country fellows; you shall be very welcom to it I fack, and we'l dust it away'.

31. *Farce Lovers.* In his Preface Dryden says 'the World is running mad after *Farce,* the Extremity of bad Poetry, or rather the Judgment that is fallen upon Dramatique Writing. Were I in the Humour, I have sufficient cause to expose it in its true Colours.' On the development of farce at this time see Nicoll, pp. 247–63; cf. Leo Hughes, 'Attitudes of some Restoration Dramatists toward Farce', *PQ* xix (1940), 268–87, and Prologue to *The Loyal General,* ll. 22–25, note.

38. *Fescu's:* pointers used in teaching children to read.

Epilogue. 4. *teach thee how to die*: an indecent quibble. Cf. Songs from the First Part of *The Conquest of Granada,* I, ll. 22–28; Songs from *Marriage A-la-Mode,* II.

19–20. *I give my Courage,* &c. Cf. Prologue to *King Arthur,* ll. 48–49.

22. *Mr. Fuller*: turncoat and informer, who was declared by the House of Commons on 24 February 1692 to be 'a notorious impostor, a cheat, and a false accuser, having scandalized their Majesties, abused this house, and falsely accused several persons of honour and quality' of complicity in a Jacobite plot.

32. *Wickham's Will.* One William Morell imposed on his landlord as 'a Worthy Gentleman near *Banbury,* viz. *Humphrey Wickham* of *Swakely* Esq.', bequeathed extravagant legacies to the landlord and others, and with this practical joke died on 3 January 1692. This imposture 'made a very amazing Noise in the Town'. See *The Notorious Impostor, Or the History of the Life of William Morell* (1692).

36. *Half-a-Crown*: the price of admission to the pit; here a bawdy quibble. See Prologue to *Marriage A-la-Mode,* l. 22, note.

Song: Act II, Sc. ii; set by Purcell. For reprints, see Day, p. 178.

Epilogue to Henry the Second, King of England; with The Death of Rosamond. A Tragedy

(Page 598)

Henry the Second was first performed at Drury Lane on 8 November 1692 and published by Tonson in 1693 (advertised in the *London Gazette,* 24–28 November 1692). The authorship is uncertain. The Epistle Dedicatory is signed by the actor William Mountfort; Gildon gives the play to John

Bancroft, a surgeon. See Nicoll, pp. 388–9; Macdonald, p. 163. On Mrs. Bracegirdle, see Prologue and Epilogue to *Amphitryon*, note.

1. *the sad Catastrophe*. In Stow's version o the legend, 'Rosamond the fayre daughter of Walter Lord Clifford, concubine to Henry II (poisoned by Queen Elianor as some thought) dyed at Woodstocke, where King Henry had made for her a house of wonderfull working, so that no man or woman might come to her but he that was instructed by the King . . . it was commonly said that lastly the queene came to her by a clue of thridde or silke, and so dealt with her that she lived not long after.'

20. *like Haynes, return to Mother-Church*. Joseph Haines the comedian (see Prologue to *The Assignation*, l. 45, note) became a Papist for a time and then recanted. For satirical comment on his conversions see Macdonald, pp. 260–1.

22. *Chappels of Ease behind our Scenes*. Chapels of ease were built for the convenience of parishioners living far from the parish church (cf. *The Hind and the Panther*, iii. 539–40). On tiring-room entertainment see Epilogue *To the King and Queen*, l. 35, note.

The Satires of Decimus Junius Juvenalis . . . Together with the Satires of Aulus Persius Flaccus
(Page 599)

In his address 'To the Reader' in *Examen Poeticum* (1693) Tonson says that he would have followed up the success of *Sylvæ* (1685) 'long before now', 'had I not almost ever since . . . been Solliciting the Translating of *Juvenal*, and *Persius*'. On 9 February 1691 he entered on the Stationers' Register '*the* 1st *ye* 6th & *the* 10th *Satyrs of* Juvenal. Translated . . . by Mr. John Dryden'; and in *The Gentleman's Journal* for February 1692 Motteux announced a translation of Juvenal and Persius 'by several hands', 'Mr. Dryden having done *four* Satyrs of the first and *two* of the last' (Malone, I. i. 220). A team of poets was assembled—Bowles, Congreve, Creech, Duke, Hervey, Power, Stepney, Tate, and Dryden's sons Charles and John—and Dryden 'distributed the work among us and gave it us to do' (Stepney to Leibniz, 8/18 March 1693; Macdonald, p. 53). Publication was delayed so that he could himself translate the whole of Persius (*The Gentleman's Journal*, May 1692); and the book was at last advertised in the *London Gazette* for 24–27 October 1692. The epigraph is from Juvenal, *Sat*. i. 85–86.

For his texts Dryden went to Isaac Casaubon's *Persius* (Paris, 1605) and the Delphin edition of Juvenal and Persius by Ludovicus Prateus (Paris, 1684). He also used the translation of Juvenal and Persius by Barten Holyday (1673) and Robert Stapylton's version of Juvenal (1644, 1647). Holyday's illustrations provided him with hints in interpretation.

To The Right Honourable Charles, Earl of Dorset. Charles Sackville, Lord Buckhurst (1638-1706), was created Earl of Middlesex in 1675 and succeeded to the title of Earl of Dorset in 1677. He was appointed Lord Chamberlain by William III in 1689. Despite the praise of Dryden, Prior, Addison, and others, his poems are merely 'the effusions of a man of wit' (Johnson); but he was an acknowledged arbiter of letters and a generous patron. His qualities 'distinguish'd Him in an Age of great Politeness, and at a Court abounding with Men of the finest Sense and Learning'. 'When, as Lord Chamberlain, He was obliged to take the King's Pension from Mr. *Dryden*, who had long before put Himself out of a Possibility of Receiving any Favor from the Court: my Lord allowed Him an Equivalent, out of his own Estate. However displeased with the Conduct of his old Acquaintance, He relieved his Necessities; and while He gave Him his Assistance in Private; in Public, He extenuated and pitied his Error' (Prior, Dedication of *Poems on Several Occasions*, 1718). Cf. Preface to *Fables*, l. 663, note.

7. *Titus Vespasian.* See *Absalom and Achitophel*, l. 318, note.

54. *An Essay: Of Dramatick Poesie* (1668, 1684; reprinted 1693). Cf. *To the Earl of Roscomon*, l. 31, note.

78. *the Competitours of Themistocles.* 'When the generals . . . distributed the ballots at the altar of Neptune, selecting the first and second out of all; thereupon every one gave his vote for himself, each thinking himself the most valiant; but with respect to the second place, the majority concurred in selecting Themistocles' (Herodotus, viii. 123).

80. *Longo, sed proximi Intervallo.* Virgil, *Aen.* v. 320.

91. *The best Good Man*, &c. Rochester, *An Allusion to Horace, The 10th Satyr of the 1st Book*, ll. 59–60. Cf. Burnet, i. 264: 'Lord *Dorset* was a generous good natured Man. . . . Never was so much ill nature in a pen as in his, joined with so much good nature as was in himself, even to excess; for he was against all punishing, even of malefactors. He was bountiful . . . And charitable to a fault.'

112–17. *He affects the Metaphysicks*, &c. Cf. *Ovid's Art of Love, Book I*, ll. 530–1; Urquhart, *The Jewel* (1652): '. . . young ladies, whose tender hearing, for the most part, being more taken with the insinuating harmony of a well-concerted period . . . than with the never-so-pithy a fancy of a learned subject . . . the sweetness of their disposition is more easily gained by undermining passion than storming reason' (J. Willcock, *Sir Thomas Urquhart*, 1899, pp. 174–5).

140–3. *Fame is in it self a real good*, &c. Cicero, *Tusc. Disp.* v. 16; Virgil, *Aen.* iv. 175; Epicurus, *Kyriai Doxai*, i (cf. Lucretius, *De Rerum Natura*, ii. 646–51).

170. *at Rovers*: at random. Cf. *Fables*, 'The First Book of Homer's Ilias', l. 77, note.

172. *I answer'd not the Rehearsall*, &c. See Epilogue to *All for Love*, l. 17, note; *Absalom and Achitophel*, l. 544, note.

216–18. *Clipt Poetry, and false Coyn.* See *The Medall*, ii. 228–9, note. Some issues of both guineas and shillings in the reign of Charles II bore, on the reverse side, four crowned shields in the form of a cross. At the centre of the guinea only were four sceptres, terminating respectively in the orb, thistle, fleur-de-lis, and harp.

257. *Martial says of him*: *Epi*. viii. 18, ll. 5–8.

319–22. *Tasso . . . confesses himself to have been too Lyrical*, &c. In *Lettere Poetiche* to Scipione Gonzaga, published with the first edition of *Discorsi* (1587). See Ker, ii. 278. In the Preface to *An Evening's Love* (1671) Dryden speaks of Tasso as 'the most excellent of modern Poets . . . whom I reverence next to *Virgil*'.

332. *Owen's Epigrams*. John Owen (*c*. 1560–1622) wrote eleven books of Latin epigrams (1606, 1607, 1612, and probably 1613), 'wherein an ingenious liberty of joking being by him used, was, and is now with some, especially Foreigners, not a little pleasing and delightful' (Wood, *Ath. Ox.* i. 471). 'Owen is a pure Pedantique Schoolmaster sweeping his living from the Posteriors of litle children, and hath no thinge good in him, his Epigrames being bare narrations' (Jonson, i. 138). Cf. Dedication of the *Æneis*, l. 1901.

332. *Fleckno*. See *Mac Flecknoe*, l. 3, note.

342. *their Saint Lewis*, &c. Pierre Le Moyne, *Saint Louys, ou la Sainte Couronne reconquise sur les infidèles* (1653); Jean Chapelain, *La Pucelle, ou la France délivrée* (1656); and Georges de Scudéry, *Alaric, ou Rome vaincüe* (1654). Cf. *Annus Mirabilis*, 'An Account of the ensuing Poem', l. 56; Dedication of the *Æneis*, ll. 282–6.

370. *As for Mr. Milton, whom we all admire*, &c. Cf. Preface to *Sylvæ*, ll. 399 ff.

374. *Mr. Rymer's Work*. Rymer ends his *Tragedies of the Last Age Consider'd* (1678) by promising Fleetwood Shepherd, to whom the book is addressed, that 'with the remaining *Tragedies* I shall also send you some reflections on that *Paradise lost* of *Miltons* which some are pleas'd to call a Poem, and assert *Rime* against the slender Sophistry wherewith he attacques it'. Dryden drafted a rejoinder to Rymer in his copy of the essay. His notes were published by Tonson in an edition of Beaumont and Fletcher (1711), and are reprinted in Johnson, i. 471–9. See Macdonald, p. 179.

382. *he imitated Spencer, as Spencer did Chawcer*. Cf. *infra*, ll. 2563–7; Preface to *Fables*, ll. 32–37.

385–92. *Obsolete Words*, &c. Here and later (*infra*, ll. 2558–65) Dryden modifies the view of Milton's diction he had taken in the Preface to *Sylvæ* (ll. 399 ff.). His attitude to archaism in his later years is more liberal than that of many of his contemporaries (cf. Preface to *Fables*, ll. 557–9). For a summary of Augustan criticism of Milton's diction, see Dennis, i. 429–30.

388. *the Rule of Horace. De Arte Poetica*, ll. 47–48.

393. *Hannibal Caro*. See Preface to *Sylvæ*, l. 121, note.

405. *as Sir William Davenant says*. Perhaps an inaccurate recollection of the Preface to *Gondibert* (1651, p. 21): 'Old men . . . think [wit] lies . . . in a kind of an alike tinkling of words; or else in a grave telling of wonderfull things. . . .'

448–52. *'Tis Objected,* &c. Boileau, *L'Art poétique,* 1674, iii. 193–236. Here Dryden opens his contribution to the current controversy on the use of Christian or pagan machinery in modern epic (a summary is given in Dennis, i. 460–2; cf. R. A. Sayce, *The French Biblical Epic,* 1955, pp. 12 ff., 162 ff.). Dryden worked out his own solution. As early as 1672 he had declared 'that neither *Homer, Virgil, Statius, Ariosto, Tasso,* nor our *English Spencer,* could have form'd their Poems half so beautiful, without those Gods and Spirits, and those Enthusiastick parts of Poetry, which compose the most Noble Parts of all their Writings. . . . An Heroick Poet is not tied to a bare Representation of what is true, or exceeding probable. . . . 'Tis enough that in all Ages and Religions, the greatest part of Mankind have believ'd the power of Magick; and that there are Spirits or Spectres which have appear'd. This, I say, is foundation enough for Poetry: And I dare further affirm, that the whole Doctrine of separated Beings . . . may be better explicated by Poets, than by Philosophers or Divines' ('Of Heroique Playes', prefixed to *The Conquest of Granada*).

462. *our Religion (says he) is depriv'd of . . . those Machines.* Virgil's 'Machines', wrote Dryden to Dennis early in 1694, will not 'be of any service to a Christian Poet. We see how ineffectually they have been try'd by Tasso, and by Ariosto. 'Tis using them too dully if we only make Devils of his Gods: As if, for example, I would raise a Storm, and make use of Æolus, with this only difference of calling him Prince of the Air. What invention of mine would there be in this?' (Ward, p. 71).

464–8. *Ariosto, Orlando Furioso,* xiv. 75–81; Tasso, *Gerusalemme Liberata,* ix.

516–79. *The perusing of one Chapter,* &c. Dan. x. 10 ff. The Platonic doctrine of intermediary spirits (e.g. *Symposium,* 202–3), as developed in neo-Platonic philosophy, became a commonplace in seventeenth-century thought. Ker quotes Henry More, *Defence of the Cabbala* (1662, p. 48); but interest in the nature and functions of tutelar spirits was not confined to the Cambridge Platonists. Cf. Burton, I. ii. 1. 2: 'They can produce miraculous alterations in the ayre, and most wonderful effects, conquer armies, give victories, help, further, hurt, cross and alter humane attempts and projects (*Dei permissu*) as they see good themselves'; Cowley, *Discourse by way of Vision*; Browne, *Religio Medici,* i. 31 and 33: 'I doe thinke that many mysteries ascribed to our owne inventions have beene the courteous revelations of Spirits . . . and therefore beleeve that those many prodigies and ominous prognostickes, which fore-run the ruines of States, Princes, and private persons, are the charitable premonitions of good Angels. . . . I am so farre from denying their existence, that I could easily beleeve, that not onely whole Countries, but particular persons, have their Tutelary, and Guardian Angels . . . and if not manifestly defin'd in Scripture, yet is it an opinion of a good and wholesome use in the course and actions of a mans life.' See also *The Second Satyr of Persius,* Explanatory Notes, 6.

569. *Virgil.* The reference is probably to *Aen.* vi, with its debts to Platonic conceptions of the state of the dead (see Cyril Bailey, *Religion in Virgil*, 1935, pp. 264–5).

604. *Satan appearing . . . to Uriel. Paradise Lost*, iii. 636–53, 689–90.

614–17. *And what I had intended to have put in practice*, &c. Cf. Prologue to *Aureng-Zebe*, ll. 13–24, note.

636–7. *my little Sallary ill paid.* Cf. *Threnodia Augustalis*, l. 377; *The Hind and the Panther*, iii. 247–50, note. Dryden wrote to Rochester about 1683 for help: 'I know not whether my Lord Sunderland has interceded with your Lordship, for half a yeare of my salary: But I have two other Advocates, my extreame wants, even almost to arresting, & my ill health. . . . Be pleasd to looke on me with an eye of compassion; some small Employment wou'd render my condition easy. The King is not unsatisfyed of me, the Duke has often promisd me his assistance; & Your Lordship is the Conduit through which their favours passe' (Ward, pp. 20–21).

669. *Ne, forte*, &c. Horace, *De Arte Poetica*, ll. 406–7.

687. *Curiosa felicitas.* Petronius, *Satyr.* 118.

699. *Ut sibi quivis*, &c. Horace, *De Arte Poetica*, ll. 240–2.

710. *Cœna dubia.* Terence, *Phormio*, II. ii. 28; Horace, *Sat.* II. ii. 77.

742. *The most Perfect Work of Poetry . . . is Tragedy. Poetics*, xxvi.

756. *the greatest Work of Human Nature.* Cf. Dedication of the *Æneis*, ll. 1 ff.

764. *the latter Forms a Hero, and a Prince.* Cf. Dedication of the *Æneis*, l. 331, note.

776. *Vida and Bossu*: Marco Girolamo Vida, *De Arte Poetica* (1527), which contains exalted praise of Virgil (especially i. 165–289 and iii. 554–92); René le Bossu, *Traité du Poëme épique* (1675). Bossu's systematic analysis of the epic seems to have been first brought to the notice of English critics by Dryden, who calls him 'the best of modern Critics' in the Preface to *Troilus and Cressida* (1679), and by Sheffield's praise in *An Essay upon Poetry* (1682). The book is one of Dryden's authorities in the Dedication of the *Æneis*. It was translated into English in 1695.

788. *Casaubon, Heinsius*, &c. Casaubon, *De Satyrica Graecorum Poesi et Romanorum Satira* (Paris, 1605), Dryden's chief critical source in this essay; Heinsius, 'De Satyra Horatiana', in his edition of Horace (Leyden, 1612); Rigaltius, 'De Satyra Juvenalis', in his edition of Juvenal (Paris, 1616); Dacier, preface to the satires in *Œuvres d'Horace* (1681–9), printed in Latin with the Delphin Horace, and translated into English in 1692; and the Delphin edition of Juvenal and Persius by Prateus (1684). Only Dryden's chief debts to these are noted below.

792. *Julius Scaliger, Poetices Libri Septem*, 1561.

828–918. Derived from Casaubon, op. cit. I. i.

935. *Libertasque recurrentes*, &c. Horace, *Epist.* II. i. 147–55.

944. *The Law of the Decemviri.* From a note in the Delphin edition of Horace, *Epist.* II. i.

953–67. *Thespis,* &c. Derived from Casaubon, op. cit. i. 3.

965. *the Cyclops.* A Latin version of the *Cyclops* was printed with Casaubon's treatise.

1000. *the Definition.* Casaubon, op. cit. i. 3, pp. 130–1.

1010. *They were so call'd, says Casaubon.* Casaubon does not derive 'silli' from 'Silenus'; but there is in the 1605 edition (p. 286) a misprint 'Silenorum Xenophanis' for 'Sillorum Xenophanis' which may have misled Dryden in careless reading. The alternative derivation is given on pp. 281–2 (ii. 3).

1048. *Quintilian says,* &c. Quintilian, *Inst. Orat.* X. i. 93; Horace, *Sat.* I. x. 66. Dryden here follows Dacier.

1056. *the derivation of Satyrus.* Scaliger, *Poet.* i. 12.

1064–8. *Casaubon judg'd better,* &c. Op. cit. ii. 4.

1079–81. *Virgil . . . in his Georgiques,* &c. ii. 194, 394.

1086. *tack'd Bills of Parliament.* A 'tack' was an appendix fixed, to ensure its passing, to a bill dealing with a different matter—particularly to a money bill, of which the Commons denied the Lords the right of amendment. See Evelyn, *Diary,* 10 April 1700, note.

1093. *Porphyrius*: an error for 'Porphyrio', correctly named by Casaubon (ii. 4).

1112–13. *Italian Farces of Harlequin, and Scaramucha.* Cf. *Miscellany Poems* (1684), Epilogue, 'No poor *Dutch* Peasant', l. 11, note.

1129–34. *Souldiers also,* &c. Derived from Heinsius, op. cit., p. 21.

1147. *says Livy*: vii. 2, quoted by Dacier.

1214. *Those Fables,* &c. Casaubon, op. cit. ii. 1 (p. 241); Valerius Maximus, II. iv. 4.

1216. *an old Commentator on Juvenal*: in a note on *Sat.* iii. 175, quoted by Casaubon, op. cit. ii. 1 (p. 242).

1264. *he himself believ'd,* &c. See *The Sixth Satyr of Persius,* Dryden's note 3.

1284. *Quid cum est,* &c. Horace, *Sat.* II. i. 62–63.

1306. *Dacier justly taxes Casaubon.* Noyes points out that Dryden here follows Dacier in a misinterpretation of Casaubon, who holds only that Lucilius and Ennius differed in subject-matter and 'non . . . in genere carminis' (ii. 3, pp. 273–4).

1336–42. *Dousa, the Son*: Franciscus, son of Janus Dousa, and editor of the fragments of Lucilius (1597). Dryden's apology is a translation of Dacier.

1350. *the Varronian Satire.* Dryden draws on Casaubon, op. cit. ii. 2 (pp. 256 ff.), and Dacier. Cf. Ian Jack, *Augustan Satire,* pp. 25 and 70–71.

1356. *Quintilian . . . adds,* &c. *Inst. Orat.* X. i. 95.

1373. *Tully . . . introduces Varro.* *Acad.* i. 2, quoted by Casaubon, op. cit. ii. 2 (pp. 258–9).

1414. *Petronius Arbiter . . . made compleat: Satyricon cum fragmentis Albae*

Graecae recuperatis anno 1688 (Cologne, 1691). The additions were forgeries by François Nodot.

1420. *the Mock Deification*: *Apocolocyntosis*, a skit written to please Nero, in prose and verse.

1422. *Barclay's Euphormio, and a Volume of German Authors. Euphormionis Lusinini Satyricon* (1603–7), a satirical romance by the continental Scot John Barclay (1582–1621). Dryden quotes from the *Satyricon* in the Dedication of *The Rival Ladies*. Ker suggests that the German book was the *Epistolae Obscurorum Virorum* (1515–17).

1423. *Charles Killigrew*, cousin of Anne Killigrew and Master of the Revels.

1438. *Medisance*. 'En François qui dit *satire*, dit *médisance*' (Dacier).

1479. *Sir Matthew Hales*. Sir Matthew Hale (1609–76), Lord Chief Justice (1671–6); 'the Pillar and *Basis* of Justice (who would not have done an unjust Act for any worldly Price or Motive), the Ornament of his Majesty's Government, and Honour of *England*' (Baxter; Wood, *Ath. Ox.* ii. 574). Evelyn, North, and Marvell spell his name 'Hales'.

1493–6. *Casaubon . . . Stelluti*: Casaubon's edition of Persius (Paris, 1605); Stelluti's, with Italian translation and commentary (Rome, 1630).

1510. *the purity of Latin being more corrupted, than in the time of Juvenal*. Dryden errs in placing Juvenal earlier than Persius; an error 'the more extraordinary, as [he] mentions, a little lower, the very emperors under whom these poets flourished' (Scott).

1516. *a Scotch Gentleman*: David Wedderburn (1580–1646), rector of Aberdeen Grammar School, grammarian and Latin poet. His edition of Persius was published by his brother at Amsterdam in 1664. See *Scottish Poetry: A Critical Survey*, ed. James Kinsley, 1955, pp. 94–95.

1528–38. *After all, he was a Young Man, &c.* Cf. *To the Memory of Mr. Oldham*, ll. 11–18.

1556. *what his Patron Casaubon can alledge*. An epitome of Casaubon's defence in the Prolegomena to his edition of Persius.

1588. *Cornutus*. See *The Fifth Satyr of Persius*, 'The Argument'.

1602. *Holyday*. See *supra*, introductory note.

1613. *Æschines. Ctes.* 167.

1681. *the present Bishop of Salisbury*: Gilbert Burnet. See *The Hind and the Panther*, iii. 1121, note. 'The Satyrical Poets, *Horace*, *Juvenal*, and *Persius*, may contribute wonderfully to give a Man a Detestation of Vice, and a Contempt of the common Methods of Mankind. . . . *Persius* his Second Satyr may well pass for one of the best Lectures in Divinity' (*A Discourse of the Pastoral Care*, 1692, p. 162).

1715–17. *Horace . . . such another. Sat.* I. vi. Dryden's witty friend is the dramatist Wycherley. His father refused him financial help, and he 'was suffer'd to languish Seven Years in a close Imprisonment, while the worthless Writers of Farce flourish'd; and that for an inconsiderable Debt, his Merit and

Fortune consider'd; and experienc'd all that Baseness in his Relations, Friends, and Acquaintance, against which the *Plain-Dealer* with so much Warmth inveigh'd' (Dennis, ii. 121). See *infra*, l. 1909, note.

1743. *Non nostrum*, &c. Virgil, *Ecl.* iii. 108.

1748. *He who says*, &c. Horace, *Od.* IV. ii. 1–4.

1828. *Juvenal is the more delightful Author.* Contrast Preface to *Sylvæ*, ll. 360–2.

1860. *Ne Sententiæ*, &c. *Satyr.* 118.

1872. *Omne vafer*, &c. Persius, *Sat.* i. 116–17.

1909. *my Friend the Plain Dealer.* Wycherley's comedy was acted in 1676 and published in 1677, when Dryden praised it as 'one of the most bold, most general, and most useful Satyrs which has ever been presented on the *English* Theater' ('Apology for Heroique Poetry', prefixed to *The State of Innocence*).

1917. *on Carpet Ground.* Cf. Preface to *Sylvæ*, l. 105.

1948. *Non tu*, &c. Virgil, *Ecl.* iii. 26–27.

1998. *Dion Cassius, Hist.* liv. 27.

2013. *In the first Book of his Annals*, lxxii. In this paragraph Dryden draws on the commentary in the Delphin edition of Tacitus.

2095–7. *Persius says*, &c. Persius, *Sat.* i. 114–15; Juvenal, *Sat.* i. 165–6.

2116–17. *the nicest and most delicate touches of Satire consist in fine Raillery.* Here Dryden sets out theoretically what had been a major principle in his own satires. He has moved far from the conventional claim of the satirist to write primarily for the castigation of error and vice, towards a view of the satirist's function as artistic rather than corrective. Cf. *Absalom and Achitophel*, 'To the Reader', ll. 11–23, 57; A. M. Clark, 'The Art of Satire', in *Studies in Literary Modes*, 1946.

2138. *Jack Ketche*: public hangman until just after Monmouth's execution in 1685. Cf. *Prologue Spoken at Mithridates King of Pontus*, l. 41; Epilogue to *The Duke of Guise*, l. 30; Prologue to *Albion and Albanius*, l. 3.

2144. *too witty to resent it as an injury.* The ascription of *Poetical Reflections on . . . Absalom and Achitophel* (1681) to a vengeful Duke of Buckingham is based on a statement by Wood, and is not on internal evidence convincing. See Macdonald, p. 224.

2160. *Ense rescindendum.* Ovid, *Meta.* i. 191.

2184–6. *Sarmentus and Cicerrus . . . Rupilius and Persius.* Horace, *Sat.* I. v. 52, I. vii. 1–2.

2192–6. *A miserable Clench . . . King Charles the Second.* Cf. Prologue to *Troilus and Cressida*, ll. 27–29, note; Dennis, ii. 383–4; 'I remember a Country School-master of my Acquaintance told me once, that he had been in Company with a Gentleman whom he looked upon to be the greatest *Paragrammatist* among the Moderns. . . . [He] had dined that day with Mr. *Swan*, the famous Punnster; and . . . told me that he generally talked in the *Paronomasia*, that he sometimes gave into the *Ploce*, but that in his humble Opinion he shined most in the *Antanaclasis*' (*The Spectator*, No. 61). For a specimen of Swan's wit, see

Ward, p. 137. On the survival of puns and other kinds of verbal wit in Restoration preaching, see W. Fraser Mitchell, *English Pulpit Oratory from Andrewes to Tillotson*, 1932, chaps. ix and x.

2234. *the Statues of the Sileni.* Plato, *Symposium*, 215.

2275–6. *the Words of Virgil.* Aen. v. 308–14.

2296. *nomen famâ*, &c. *Georgics*, iii. 47–48.

2301. *Mr. Maidwell*: Lewis Maidwell (1650–1715), schoolmaster and later the unsuccessful 'projector' of an academy; author of *An Essay upon the Necessity and Excellency of Education* (1705) and (with Nahum Tate) *Nova Grammatices Experimenta, or Some New Essays of a Natural and Artificial Grammar* (1707).

2325. *Heinsius,* in his edition of Horace (Leyden, 1612).

2349. *the Grande Sophos of Persius.* The phrase is Rigaltius's (*Juvenal*, 1616, a4ᵛ).

2355–6. *there was never such a fall,* &c. Dryden makes the same error in chronology in the Dedication of the *Georgics*, ll. 36–37.

2392. *Mascardi in his Discourse: Prose Volgari* (1630), 'Discorso . . . dell' Unità della Favola Drammatica' (Ker).

2456. *our Excellent Hudibras.* See *The Hind and the Panther*, iii. 247–50, note.

2464. *the double Rhyme.* Cf. *Annus Mirabilis*, 'An account of the ensuing Poem', ll. 52–53, note; Dennis, 'These Rhymes . . . seem to me to be as peculiarly becoming of a Jest, as a roguish Leer, or a comical tone of a Voice' (Preface to *Miscellanies in Verse and Prose*, 1693); Addison, *The Spectator*, Nos. 60 and 249.

2493–4. *Tassone and Boileau.* Alessandro Tassoni (1565–1635), *La Secchia Rapita* (1622; translated by Perrault, 1678); Boileau, *Le Lutrin* (1674–83).

2495. *Merlin Coccajus*: otherwise Teofilo Folengo (c. 1496–1554), *Poema Macaronicum de gestis . . . Baldi* (1517; translated into French as *Histoire maccaronique de Merlin Coccaie, prototype de Rabelais*, 1606).

2503. *Scarron*: Paul Scarron (1610–60), *Typhon, ou la Gigantomachie* (1644), and *Virgile travesti* (1648–59; imitated by Charles Cotton in *Scarronnides, or Virgile Travestie*, 1664). For Boileau's criticism of the burlesque style, see *L'Art poétique*, i. 79 ff.

2511–13. *Nec tibi,* &c. Aen. iv. 365–7. Boileau's lines are part of a passage in *Le Lutrin*, ii, which was omitted after the edition of 1682 (*Œuvres*, ed. Gidel, 1870–3, ii. 439–40, notes).

2525–30. *Admiranda tibi,* &c. *Georgics*, iv. 3–5, 208–9.

2541. *the Beautiful Turns of Words and Thoughts,* &c. A *locus classicus* for the Augustan movement from the metaphysical paradox and conceit towards less complex devices of antithesis and opposition (cf. Spingarn, i, pp. xlv–xlvi; G. Williamson, 'The Rhetorical Pattern of Neo-classical Wit', *MP* xxxiii (1935), 55–81). For a modified opinion of 'turns' see Dedication of the *Æneis*, ll. 1750 ff.; Preface to *Fables*, ll. 295 ff.

2545. *that Noble Wit of Scotland*: Sir George Mackenzie of Rosehaugh (1636–91), Lord Advocate, the 'Bluidy Advocate MacKenyie' of the Cameronian persecutions, 'who, for his worldly wit and wisdom, had been to the rest as a god' (Scott, *Redgauntlet*, xi); founder of the Advocates' Library in 1682, and a scholar and philosopher.

2554–8. *the Darling of my youth, &c.* See Preface to *Ovid's Epistles*, ll. 244–5, note; cf. *supra*, ll. 326–8.

2566. *his Master, Spencer.* Cf. *supra*, l. 382; Preface to *Fables*, ll. 32–37.

2572. *in his late ingenious Preface.* Walsh says nothing of Italian 'turns' in the Preface to *Letters and Poems Amorous and Gallant*, 1692; Dryden may be recalling a conversation with Walsh which arose from the Preface. Walsh, says Dennis, 'was a learned, candid, judicious Gentleman . . . a very indifferent Poet; but . . . a Man of a very good Understanding, in spight of his being a Beau' (i. 416). Surviving letters between Dryden and Walsh reveal Dryden as a painstaking preceptor and friend. Cf. *The Works of Virgil*, 'Postscript to the Reader', l. 87.

2580. *Heu quantum, &c. Meta.* xv. 88–90.

2585. *Tum jam nulla, &c.* Catullus, lxiv. 143–8.

2593. *Si nisi, &c. Heroid.* xv. 39–40.

2599. *Cùm subita, &c. Georgics,* iv. 488–9.

2604. *no English Prosodia.* Dryden's scattered observations on prosody are gathered and analysed by R. D. Jameson in *MP* xx (1923), 241–53. Cf. Dedication of the *Æneis*, ll. 1704–6.

2664. *Pulverulenta, &c.* Misquoted from *Aen.* viii. 596.

2694. *to make him speak that kind of English, &c.* Cf. Preface to *Ovid's Epistles*, ll. 150–1, note.

The First Satyr of Juvenal. (Page 670.) 30. *two handed*: sturdy. Cf. *Sylvæ*, 'Lucretius . . . Concerning the Nature of Love', l. 150, note.

62. *thrice Concocted Blood.* 'Sanguis . . . is here put *pro Semine. . . .* For in Nature the *Semen* is but a perfecter concoction and preparation of the Blood. Yet this, by that Preparation, is so much enspirited, that to lose one dram of *Semen*, weakens as much as the loss of 60 ounces of blood' (Holyday).

66. *the Vanquish'd Rhetorician Dyes.* Prateus and Holyday observe that an unsuccessful orator might be '(not drown'd, but) *ducked* over head and ears in the next River'; Dryden follows Stapylton.

72. *pill'd*: plundered, impoverished. Cf. Shakespeare, *Richard II*, ii. i. 247: 'The Commons hath he pil'd with greeuous taxes.'

87. 'Adulterers used to bequeath their whole Estates to their Adulteresses: which enormity *Domitian* endeavour'd to prevent by a Law, by which he made all such infamous Women incapable of Legacies; who did notwithstanding delude the Law, by making their own Husbands Pandars to their Lust, and so causing the Legacies to be given to Them' (Holyday).

109. *frequent on the Bier.* Cf. *Annus Mirabilis*, l. 1069, note.

122. *S——ll*: Shadwell. See *Mac Flecknoe*, introductory note; *The Second Part*

of *Absalom and Achitophel*, l. 459, note. Juvenal's victim (l. 80) is Cluvienus, 'ineptum versificatorem sui sæculi' (Prateus).

173–5. Dryden elaborates Juvenal's 'quæque salutato Crepitat concordia nido' (l. 116) from Prateus: 'Concordia, in cujus ædis fastigio aves nidificantes sonitum edunt & crepitant . . . & pullos quasi salutant. . . . Cornices intelligit Politian. . . . Alii tamen Ciconias significari volunt, quia pietas illis inest admirabilis . . . & quoniam Concordia Ciconiæ forma colebatur.'

177. *Vails*: perquisites.

The Third Satyr of Juvenal. (Page 679.) 14. *Padders*: footpads.

193. *Walls and very Floors.* Dryden translates 'aulam' (l. 112) in Prateus; modern editors read 'aviam'.

288. *by Tradition, is for Wit allow'd.* Added: cf. Dedication, *supra*, ll. 851–2.

395. *Shole*: crowd. Cf. Spenser, *The Shepheardes Calender*, 'Maye', l. 20: 'I sawe a shole of shepeheardes outgoe.'

440. *scouring.* Cf. Prologue to *The Spanish Fryar*, l. 39 and note.

The Sixth Satyr of Juvenal. (Page 694.) *Argument.* 22–24. *Sir C. S.*: Sir Charles Sedley. Dryden had decided to translate this satire himself by February 1691, when Tonson made his entry on *SR*. On 8/18 March 1693 Stepney wrote of the *Juvenal* to Leibniz: 'Mr Dryden . . . has reserved the sixth Satire for his own hand, and I can fully assure you, to his honour, that the original has lost none of its shamelessness through him' (Macdonald, p. 53).

Argument. 41. *Every Vice is a Loader.* The metaphor is from gaming: a 'loader' is a throw in which both dice show the same number. Cf. *Love Triumphant* (1694), IV. i: '*Dalinda.* . . . Am I the first frail Creature, that had the Misfortune of two Great Bellies . . . ? *Carlos.* Nay don't aggravate the Matter: consult your Note, and you'll find but one Bastard charg'd upon you; you see I was not for laying loaders.'

21. *or if a Sire the Sun.* Dryden's addition. See Lucretius, *De Rerum Natura*, v. 797–820.

85–86. *Many a fair Nymph*, &c. Cf. *Miscellany Poems* (1684), 'Prologue for the Women', ll. 9–10.

88. *The Park*, &c. Translating 'porticibus . . . spectacula' (ll. 60–61). Dryden's modernization is anticipated in Stapylton's heading: 'The *Roman* spring-garden. Play-houses.'

95–99. *A third is Charm'd*, &c. Translating '. . . subitum et miserabile longum| attendit Thymele; Thymele tunc rustica discit' (ll. 65–66). Holyday, following tradition in taking 'subitum' and 'miserabile' to 'implie mimical actions', translates '*The start* and *Well-a-day* | With long attention Thymele does note'; and Dryden brings this interpretation up to date. Apart from Davenant's isolated experiment, native English opera dates from the 1670's; and Purcell's main operatic work belongs to the years when the *Juvenal* was in preparation.

188. *Ropy*: sticky. Cf. *The Second Book of the Georgics*, l. 333.

349. *Plastron*: 'A Fencing-Master's quilted Breast-Leather, which serves for his Scholars to push at' (Phillips, *New World of Words*, 1706).

384. *Tiller*: till, a drawer or inner box in a cabinet. Cf. Herbert, *The Temple*, 'Confession':

> . . . within my heart I made
> Closets; and in them many a chest;
> And, like a master in my trade,
> In those chests, boxes; in each box, a till.

394. *Homo is a Common Name for all*: translating 'homo sum' (l. 284) with Prateus's interpretation: 'Sexus me fragilem et errori proximam facit: humana infirmitate lapsa sum.'

419. *Eringoes.* Dryden's addition. The root of the sea holly (*Eryngium maritimum*) was considered aphrodisiac. Cf. Shakespeare, *The Merry Wives of Windsor*, v. v. 20–23: 'let it thunder, to the tune of Greene-sleeues, haile kissing Comfits, and snow Eringoes: Let there come a tempest of prouocation. . . .'

634. *A pinch must, for the Mortal Sin, compound.* A neat modernization; Juvenal's lady takes the lash to her dresser (ll. 491–2).

746. *Twelve Houses, and their Lords*: the twelve astrological divisions of the heavens, and the planets exercising influence in each.

759. *Brachman*: translating 'Phryx augur et Indus' (l. 585), which Prateus glosses 'Brachmanes et Gymnosophista, seu Indorum Sapiens'.

808. *The Thund'rer*, &c. Dryden's translation of 'quam si fecisset Juno maritum | insanum' (ll. 619–20), and his note, are based on the illustration of the passage in Holyday (No. 74).

The Tenth Satyr of Juvenal. (Page 720.) 103. *hanging*: 'downcast', with the quibbling suggestion of 'hangable, born to be hanged'. Cf. Shakespeare, *Measure for Measure*, iv. ii. 35: 'A good fauor you haue, but that you haue a hanging look.' Shadwell's version of *Sat.* x (1687) has 'a hanging look' here.

180–5. *The Boy*, &c. A deliberate mistranslation of Juvenal, ll. 114–17, where the aspiring pupil has a 'custos angustae vernula capsae'. Dryden heightens the comedy by transferring the diminutiveness in 'vernula' and 'angustae capsae' to the boy himself.

191. *I, thy Consul sole, consol'd thy Doom.* Dryden carries over the jingle of 'O fortunatam natam me consule Romam' (l. 122) after Shadwell's example: 'When I thy Consul did consult for thee.'

236–42. Translating Juvenal, ll. 148–51:

> . . . hic est quem non capit Africa Mauro
> percussa oceano Niloque admota tepenti
> rursus ad Aethiopum populos aliosque elephantos.
> additur imperiis Hispania.

Dryden follows the Delphin editor in interpreting Ethiopia as 'pars Africæ

amplissima cis & ultra Æquatorem', divided by the Nile. The 'other Mountains' are 'ad Mauritaniam et Libyam Africæ Provincias, in quibus reperiuntur
elephanti', to the west of the Nile.

319. *Mumble*: chew toothlessly. Shadwell uses the same word.

375. *Hackney Jade*: prostitute. Cf. Stapylton, *Third Satyr of Juvenal*, l. 76:
'And hackney-wenches, that ith *Circus* stand.'

490. *Makes Colon suffer for the Peccant part.* A humorous personification of
'quosdam moechos et mugilis intrat' (l. 317); cf. *Musarum Deliciæ* (1656), 'To
a Friend upon a Journey to *Epsam* Well', l. 105. Adulterers 'dearly pay for
their pleasure, being by force, according to the nature of Jealousie, clyster'd
with a Mullet' (Holyday).

The Satires of Aulus Persius Flaccus
(Page 741)

These translations have a sub-title, and are introduced in complimentary
verses by Congreve. The epigraph is from Martial, *Epi.* iv. 29.

The First Satyr of Persius. 109–10. *thy Verse is wretched Rhyme*, &c. Cf. Chaucer,
The Canterbury Tales, vii. 930–1:

> Thy drasty rymyng is nat worth a toord!
> Thou doost noght elles but despendest tyme.

244. *King Midas.* Dryden follows Casaubon's 'auriculas asini Mida rex
habet' (l. 121) for 'auriculas asini quis non habet'. 'Reddimus autem Persio
suam scripturam: quam a Cornuto interpellatam Neronis metu . . .' (p. 153).

277–9. *Such, all the Morning*, &c. Translating 'his mane edictum, post
prandia Callirhoen do' (l. 134) with Casaubon's note: 'Studia eorum exponit,
quibus satirarum suarum lectione interdicebat: ait istos duo solum curasse:
forum, propter auaritiam: & lupanaria, amore voluptatis. . ... Callirhoes voce
heic . . . vniuersa voluptariorum studia, atq. occupationes συνεκδοχικῶς
intelliguntur' (pp. 167–8).

The Second Satyr of Persius. (Page 752.) 70. *she adds a length of Navel-string.*
Dryden's amplification (Persius, l. 37). On the widespread superstition that
the navel-string is bound up with prosperity, see J. G. Frazer, *The Golden
Bough*, 1922, I. i. 182–201.

Explanatory Notes, 6. Browne, *Religio Medici*, i. 31: see *supra*, Dedication,
ll. 516–79, note.

The Third Satyr of Persius. (Page 757.) *Argument.* 13–15. *The Title*, &c. Casaubon, op. cit., p. 229.

Argument. 18–21. *I remember*, &c. Dr. Richard Busby was master of Westminster School until his death in 1695; 'an encourager of vertuous and for-

ward Youth, of great Learning and Hospitality, and the chief Person that educated more Youths that were afterwards eminent in the Church and State, than any Master of his time'. In 1656 he 'published for the use of *Westminster* School the Satyrs of *Juvenal* and *Persius* . . . castrated of their bawdy expressions' (Wood, *Ath. Ox.* ii. 923). Dryden's *juvenilia* have not survived.

12. *why when!* Bewildered exclamations: 'verumne? itan?' (l. 7).

92–96. *Cog*: manipulate dishonestly; *Sice*: the number six on the dice; *Ames–Ace*: double ace, the lowest possible throw; *Bones*: dice.

104. *Medians in Trunk-Breeches*. Translating 'bracatis . . . Medis' (l. 53), on which Prateus comments: 'Per braccas certe peregrinam vestem potius et barbaram Persius videtur voluisse indicare, quam proprium Persis ac Medis indumentum.' Dryden tries to suggest something of this with 'Trunk-Breeches', the full hose fashionable in the early seventeenth century, but much out-moded by the 1690's.

126. *Conquest and Guibbons*: for 'Craterus' (l. 65). William Gibbons (1649–1738), Fellow of the College of Physicians (1692), was one of Dryden's medical attendants. Cf. *Virgil*, 'Postscript to the Reader', l. 111; *Fables*, 'To My Honour'd Kinsman', l. 82.

147. *Mother*: scum.

The Fourth Satyr of Persius. (Page 765). *Argument.* 6–7. *Lucan has not spar'd him. Pharsalia*, i. 33–38.

68. *Wimble*: gimlet; used for broaching a cask.

110–12. *When the pleas'd People*, &c. An amplification of 'egregium cum me vicinia dicat, | non credam?' (ll. 46–47), 'particularly aim'd at *Nero*'. Casaubon comments: 'Dum adhuc latebant flagitia Neronis, omnes illum laudabant' (p. 350).

120–3. *If thy lewd Lust*, &c. An amplification of 'si puteal multa cautus vibice flagellas' (l. 49) in the light of Casaubon's note: 'id est, si tanta est tua petulantia & lasciuia, vt nocturnus præmiator grasseris, cum obuiis rixam contrahens, & pudori matronarum illudens, nullum denique insolentiæ genus prætermittens. Hoc genere insignem primum se fecit Nero, cum foras erumperet illius probra . . .' (p. 354). Cf. Prologue to *All for Love*, l. 22, note.

127. *cobbled Rhymes*: '. . . munera cerdo' (l. 51). Dryden's commentators, and Holyday, take 'cerdo' not as a name for 'one of the rabble' (Conington), but as a cobbler. The metaphorical application is his own.

The Fifth Satyr of Persius. (Page 771.) *The Reverend Dr. Busby.* See *supra*, Argument to *The Third Satyr*, note.

80. *Doddard.* This word presents some difficulty. Dryden's usual spelling is 'dodder'd' (cf. Virgil's *Pastorals*, ix. 13; *Æneis*, ii. 702; *Fables*, 'Palamon and Arcite', iii. 905). Dr. C. T. Onions suggests that 'doddard' is probably 'dot(t)ard', a decayed trunk—a word which Dryden may have known in Northamptonshire—altered by association with 'dod', to lop, and subsequently

participialized to 'dodder'd'. Cf. the spellings 'haggar'd', 'hagger'd' in *The Hind and the Panther*, i. 166 and iii. 1116, and *The Fourth Book of the Georgics*, l. 370.

137. *As well he for an Ass a Harp might string*. Translating 'sambucam citius caloni aptaveris alto' (l. 95). Dryden's version is proverbial. 'Asinus ad liram, An asse at an harpe. A prouerbe applied vnto theym, whyche haue no iudgement in wysedome and learnyng' (Cooper, 1548; Tilley, A366). Cf. Chaucer, *Troilus and Criseyde*, i. 731–5.

147. *High-shoo'd*. Holyday's translation of 'peronatus', hide-booted (l. 102). High shoes were worn by rustics in the seventeenth century; 'high-shoed' was a synonym for 'boorish'.

175–6. *Virtue and Vice*, &c. Translating 'haereat in stultis brevis ut semuncia recti. | haec miscere nefas' (ll. 121–2). Dryden's note, and his translation, are based on Casaubon (p. 432).

214–17. Dryden brings Persius (ll. 146–8) thoroughly up to date. *Cubb'd*: cooped up; *Brown George*: coarse black bread used as a naval ration; *Swobbers*: deck-swabbers; *Boracchio*: a leather wine-bottle.

247. *draw you to her, with a single Hair*: proverbial. Cf. Howell, *Epistolæ Ho-Elianæ* (1655), ii. 4, 'Tis a powerful sex . . . they must needs be strong, when one hair of a woman can draw more than a hundred pair of Oxen'; Pope, *The Rape of the Lock*, ii. 27–28.

267. *curtail'd*: circumcised.

271. *Squintifego*: 'one that Squints very much' (*Dict. Canting Crew, c.* 1695): translating 'lusca', one-eyed (l. 186).

Explanatory Notes, 21. Sedley's play was *Bellamira, or The Mistress* (1687).

The Sixth Satyr of Persius. (Page 781.) 6. *The Beauties of the first Created Spring*. Dryden expands Casaubon's reading, 'primordia rerum' (l. 3), where modern editors read 'primordia vocum'.

186–7. *Then say*, &c. Cf. *supra*, Dedication, ll. 1600–4.

Poems from Examen Poeticum:
Being the Third Part of Miscellany Poems
(Page 790)

Examen Poeticum was published by Tonson in the summer of 1693 (*The Gentleman's Journal*, June, July). Dryden contributed the Dedication, and— in addition to five poems already published—new poems occupying a quarter of the miscellany. Tonson says in his address to the reader that the delay between *Sylvæ* (1685) and *Examen Poeticum* was due to 'Solliciting the Translating of *Juvenal*, and *Persius*'. He has been unable to publish all the 'many very Ingenious Copies' sent in; but would 'willingly try if there could be an Annual Miscellany, which I believe might be an useful diversion to the

Ingenious. By this means care would be taken to preserve ev'ry Choice Copy that appears; whereas I have known several Celebrated Pieces . . . utterly lost in three or four years time after they were written.' The epigraphs are from *Georgics*, iv. 100–1 and 157.

To The Right Honourable, My Lord Radcliffe. Edward Lord Radclyffe (1655–1705), heir to the Earl of Derwentwater, married Mary, daughter of Charles II and the actress Mary Davies, in 1687 (see *infra*, ll. 186–92). Dryden vainly expected financial help from him. Thanking Tonson on 30 August 1693 for personal services, he says: 'I am sure you thought My Lord Radclyffe wou'd have done something: I ghessd more truly, that he cou'd not; but I was too farr ingagd to desist; though I was tempted to it, by the melancholique prospect I had of it' (Ward, p. 58).

36–37. *the best Poet . . . said.* Dorset, 'To Mr Edward Howard on his incomparable, incomprehensible Poem.' On Dorset, see Dedication of *The Satires of Juvenalis*, introductory note.

46. *Zoili, and Momi.* Zoilus was a grammarian of Amphipolis, and a severe critic of Isocrates, Plato, and Homer; Momus was the god of pleasantry.

47. *he who endeavour'd to defame Virgil.* 'Est et adversus Æneida liber Carbilii Pictoris, titulo Æneido-mastix' (Donatus).

58–60. *Petronius . . . on Lucan. Satyr.* 118–24.

62–71. *Julius Scaliger: Poetices Libri Septem*, v. 3 (on Homer); vi. 5 ('Hypercriticus', on Claudian); vi. 6 (on Lucan).

82. *Horace took notice. Epist.* II. i. 88–89.

99–115. *another sort of Insects, &c.* Dryden refers particularly to Rymer's *A Short View of Tragedy: It's Original, Excellency, and Corruption, With Some Reflections on Shakespear, and other Practitioners for the Stage*, published towards the end of 1692. Dryden is 'seemingly Courted' in Rymer's suggestion that he should 'try his Pen' on the theme of Aeschylus's *Persæ* and '*Pit, Box,* and *Gallery*, far beyond any thing now in possession of the Stage, however wrought up by the unimitable *Shakespear*' (p. 17); but '*Pit, Box,* and *Gallery*' is a phrase from *The Rehearsal*, and there are other covert hits in Rymer's book. Dryden wrote to Dennis in March 1694: 'I reverence Mr. Rym—s Learning, but I detest his Ill Nature and his Arrogance. I indeed, and such as I, have reason to be afraid of him, but Shakespear has not' (Ward, p. 72). Cf. *To my Dear Friend Mr. Congreve*, ll. 41–48; Prologue to *Love Triumphant*, ll. 47–50. Soon after the publication of *Examen Poeticum*, Dryden heard 'That one of the Secretaryes, I suppose Trenchard had informd the Queen, that I had abusd her Government [ll. 16–21, *supra*] . . . & that thereupon, she had commanded her Historiographer Rymer, to fall upon my Playes; wᶜʰ he . . . is now doeing. I doubt not his malice . . . who you know has spoken slightly of me in his last Critique: & that gave me occasion to snarl againe' (Ward, pp. 58–59). But cf. Preface to *Fables*, ll. 72–76.

121. *the quantum mutatus.* In the Dedication of *A Short View* Rymer says

that three epics 'are reckon'd in the degree of Perfection: But amongst the Tragedies, only the *Oedipus* of *Sophocles*. That, by *Corneille*, and by others, of a Modern Cut, *quantum Mutatus!*' See Prologue and Epilogue to *Oedipus*, notes.

134. *arguing like Perault*, in *Parallèle des Anciens et des Modernes* (1688–97). The third volume, dealing with poetry, appeared in 1692.

139–40. *who beginning from a Chorus*, &c. *A Short View* opens: 'What Reformation may not we expect now, that in *France* they see the necessity of a *Chorus* to their Tragedies? . . . The *Chorus* was the root and original, and is certainly always the most necessary part of Tragedy.'

169. *Horace . . . commends Lucilius. Sat.* I. x.

216–38. *For my own part*, &c. See Preface to *Ovid's Epistles*, ll. 177–312, note.

218. *Mr. Chapman . . . professes. The Whole Works of Homer* (1616), 'Preface to the Reader': 'Alwaies conceiuing how pedanticall and absurd an affectation it is in the interpretation of any Author (much more of *Homer*) to turn him word for word, when (according to *Horace* and other best lawgiuers to translators) it is the part of euery knowing and iudiciall interpreter . . . sentences to weigh diligently, and to clothe and adorne them with words, and such a stile and forme of Oration, as are most apt for the language into which they are conuerted.' Cf. Spingarn, i, pp. xlviii–lviii.

228. *Sandys*. See Preface to *Ovid's Epistles*, ll. 1–3, note.

241. *the Dutch Commentatours*: Heinsius and Cnipping. See *Ovid's Epistles*, introductory note.

249. *Synalephas*. Cf. Preface to *Sylvæ*, ll. 106 ff.

250. *turns*. See Dedication of *The Satires of Juvenalis*, l. 2541, note.

280. *Musas colere severiores*. Martial, *Epi.* IX. xii. 17.

293. *one by Mr. Congreve*. Congreve contributed two pieces, '*Priam*'s Lamentation and Petition', and 'The Lamentations of *Hecuba*, *Andromache*, and *Helen*'.

331. *the irascible appetite, as our Philosophers call it*. 'Perturbations and passions, which trouble the phantasie . . . are commonly reduced into two inclinations, *Irascible*, and *Concupiscible*' (Burton, I. ii. 3. 3).

355. *Sir Samuel Tuke has said*: in the Prologue to *The Adventures of Five Hours* (see Prologue to *The Wild Gallant* 'as it was first Acted', ll. 38–40, note).

The First Book of Ovid's Metamorphoses. (Page 799.) From a complaining letter written by Tonson about the end of 1692 (Ward, pp. 49–52), it appears that he and Dryden originally agreed on translations of 'several Authours without naming Ovid' for fifty guineas. Dryden translated the first book of the *Metamorphoses* to the end of the story of Daphne, 'in yᵉ lattin 566, in yᵉ English 759', and unsuccessfully tried to sell this to a rival bookseller for twenty guineas. 'That', says Tonson, 'makes for 40 guyneas . . . 1518 lines; And all that I have for fifty guyneas are but 1446.' The protest was effectual: Dryden added almost 100 lines to his versions of Ovid, and the other new poems brought up his total contribution to the 1,900 lines Tonson thought he deserved.

82. *th' unwholsum year*: the annual harvest. Dryden's addition, imitating the Latin use of 'annus'. Cf. *Æneis*, ii. 409.

175. *rummaging*. See *Annus Mirabilis*, l. 829, note.

199. *Red Light'ning*: Ovid's 'fulmine' (l. 155). Cf. Milton, *Paradise Lost*, i. 174–5, the thunder 'Wingd with red Lightning and impetuous rage'.

227–8. *This Place . . . the Loovre of the Skie*: Ovid's 'haud timeam magni dixisse Palatia coeli' (l. 176). Sandys also modernizes to 'Heauen's *White-Hall*'. Cf. *Prologue To His Royal Highness*, l. 21.

411. *Insulting*: exulting. Cf. Dedication of *Amphitryon* (1690), 'the Nobility . . . are not apt to insult on the Misfortunes of their Country-men'.

418. *The Stag swims faster, than he ran before*: translating 'crura nec ablato prosunt velocia cervo' (l. 306). 'Ovid is not answerable for the speed of the stag's exertions in the water' (Scott); but Cnipping glosses 'ablato' as 'celeritate pedum subducto'.

507. *Gradual*: altar steps ('templi . . . gradus', l. 375). A nonce-use.

569. *crusted Creatures*: 'animalia' (l. 425). See *The Hind and the Panther*, i. 311, note.

575. *temper*: mixture ('temperiem', l. 430).

648. *Son*: grandson ('nepotes', l. 482).

681. *I follow not a Foe*, i.e. as a foe ('non insequor hostis', l. 504).

723–4. *turn*: a hare's change of direction, manœuvred by the dog. Cf. *Annus Mirabilis*, ll. 521–8.

855–6. *As she who knew*, &c. Dryden underlines 'timuitque Iovem et fuit anxia furti' (l. 623) from Cnipping's gloss: 'Ne Jupiter ad consuetudinem ejus rediret.'

1087. *Levè*, in the basic sense of rising from bed ('unde oritur', l. 774). The current sense was a reception; but cf. Congreve, *The Way of the World* (1700), IV: 'O, nothing is more alluring than a Levee from a Couch in some Confusion.'

The Fable of Iphis and Ianthe. (Page 828.) *Meta.* ix. 665–796.

14–16. *Besides when born*, &c. An explanatory elaboration of 'onerosior altera sors est' (l. 675).

38. *Crocodile*: translating 'serpens' (l. 693) after Cnipping.

196–9. *Her sparkling Eyes*, &c. An expansion of 'plusque vigoris adest, habuit quam femina' (l. 789). *Burnish*: increase in breadth.

207–9. *Venus and Juno*, &c. A clumsy arrangement of the three *dii coniugales*: 'cum Venus et Iuno sociosque Hymenaeus ad ignes | conveniunt' (ll. 795–6).

The Fable of Acis, Polyphemus, and Galatea. (Page 834.) *Meta.* xiii. 750–897.

19–22. *wilder far*, &c. A characteristic expansion of 'horrendus silvis, et visus ab hospite nullo | impune' (ll. 760–1).

31. *Simagres*: affected glances ('feros . . . vultus', l. 767). Cf. *The Kind Keeper* (1680), III. 1: 'By these languishing Eyes, and those *Simagres* of yours, we are given to understand, Sir, you have a Mistress in this Company.'

Song to a Fair, Young Lady. (Page 840.) For the musical setting attributed to John Blow, see Day, p. 103.

4. *Storms invert the Year.* Cf. *The Hind and the Panther*, iii. 438, note.

Prologue to the University of Oxford, 1681. (Page 841.) The occasion of this poem is uncertain, but the political allusions in ll. 11–20 confirm the date. See *The Epilogue Spoken to the King . . . at Oxford*, note; *Absalom and Achitophel*, l. 585, note. The Parliament of 1681 was held in Oxford, away from the influence of the London aldermen and mob.

1–2. *The fam'd Italian Muse*, &c. Cf. Drayton, *Nymphidia*, ll. 193–4:

> The *Thuskan* Poet doth aduance,
> The franticke *Paladine* of France.

The allusion is to Ariosto, *Orlando Furioso*, xxxiv. 82–86.

19–24. 'It would seem that the players had made an unsuccessful attempt to draw houses during the short sitting of that Parliament' (Scott). One of the Sibyls tried to sell nine books of her prophecies to Tarquin II. He jibbed at the price; and she departed, burned three of the books, and returned to ask the original price for the remainder. He again refused, and she burned three more. Tarquin was astonished into buying the last three.

27–30. *He, whose undaunted Muse*, &c. Noyes takes these lines as a reference to Dryden's political satires, and therefore regards the date 1681 as too early. But by 1681 he had sufficiently castigated 'the Vices of the Age' in the theatre.

Prologue. (Page 841.) The date and occasion of this poem are unknown. It has been suggested that since it resembles the Epilogue to *Tamerlane the Great* (q.v.) it may have been written for a performance of that play (Macdonald, p. 158). But the figure of the virgin poet is common; cf. Prologue to *Circe*, Epilogue to *The Loyal Brother*. E. S. de Beer cites a number of deserters' bills (see l. 15) between 1689 and 1693, and argues for dating the Prologue in these years (*NQ* clxxix (1940), 440–1).

17. *Mercury*: a general term for newspapers.

25. *the blue*: 'glossy blue', and therefore sound and worth plucking.

Veni Creator Spiritus, Translated in Paraphrase. (Page 843.) Translated from the hymn attributed to Hrabanus Maurus (S. Gaselee, *Oxford Book of Medieval Latin Verse*, No. 31). Bouhours, whose life of St. Francis Xavier Dryden had translated in 1688, recorded that this was the saint's favourite hymn (Scott, xvi. 473). Scott printed from manuscript sources two other translations which English Catholic tradition ascribed to Dryden (i. 342–5). It has been claimed that all the hymns in *The Primer, or, Office of the B. Virgin Mary, Revis'd: With a New and Approv'd Version of the Church-Hymns* (1706), which includes 'Veni Creator Spiritus' and the two other translations, were written by Dryden; but there is no evidence for the attribution of any but 'Veni Creator Spiritus'. See *Hymns attributed to John Dryden*, ed. G. R. Noyes and G. R. Potter, 1937.

Rondelay. (Page 844.) Day prints the musical setting from *Deliciae Musicae* (1695) by John Gilbert. For other reprints, see Day, p. 180.

An Epitaph on the Lady Whitmore. (Page 845.) Frances Brooke married (1665?) Sir Thomas Whitmore of Bridgenorth, who died in 1682; and Matthew Harvie of Twickenham, who died in 1693. She died in 1690, and her epitaph is inscribed on the base of Harvie's monument in the gallery of Twickenham church. There are no variants.

An Epitaph, on Sir Palmes Fairborne's Tomb in Westminster-Abby. (Page 845.) On 24 October 1680 Sir Palmes Fairborne rode outside the town of Tangier to observe the besieging Moorish army; and 'as he was walking under the walls, received a mortal wound, which the Spanish horse so bravely resented, that immediately, without command, they mounted and charged the Moors with that courage, that they killed many of them, with the loss of seven or eight of themselves'. Fairborne died on 27 October; and Colonel Sackville, now in command, rode out that day 'with 1500 foot and 300 horse, and fell upon the Moors with such bravery, that, notwithstanding the inequality of their number, and the stout resistance they made, they beat them out of the trenches . . . and gave them a total defeat; pursuing them a mile into the country, with a great slaughter' (*London Gazette*, Nos. 1567, 1569; Scott, xi. 156–7). The version of the Abbey epitaph printed in *Poetical Recreations . . . Part II.*, 1688 (pp. 6–7), is a careless and incomplete transcript.

The Last parting of Hector and Andromache. (Page 846.) *Iliad* vi. 369–502.

35. *Hippoplacus . . . in Thebe*: Homer's Θήβη Ὑποπλακίη (l. 397). Dryden takes Chapman's erroneous spelling, 'Hippoplace'.

To my Dear Friend Mr. Congreve, On His Comedy, call'd, The Double-Dealer

(Page 852)

William Congreve's first play, *The Old Batchelour*, was first performed in March 1693 (see *infra*, l. 55, note); and his second, *The Double-Dealer*, in November following (advertised in the *London Gazette*, 4–7 December). In August 1693 Dryden wrote to Tonson: 'I am Mr Congreve's true Lover & desire you to tell him, how kindly I take his often Remembrances of me: I wish him all prosperity; & hope I shall never loose his Affection' (Ward, p. 59). In December he forwarded a presentation copy of *The Double-Dealer* to Walsh, saying that the play 'is much censur'd by the greater part of the Town: and is defended onely by the best Judges, who, you know, are commonly the fewest. Yet it gets ground daily. . . . The women thinke he has exposd their Bitchery too much; & the Gentlemen, are offended with him;

for the discovery of their follyes. . . . My verses, which you will find before it, were written before the play was acted, but I neither alterd them nor do I alter my opinion of the play' (Ward, pp. 62–63). Congreve paid a fine tribute to Dryden's friendship in the Dedication of Dryden's *Dramatick Works* (1717; see Nichol Smith, pp. 1–3). 'The epistle is one of the most elegant and apparently heart-felt effusions of friendship, that our language boasts; and the progress of literature from the Restoration, is described as Dryden could alone describe it' (Scott).

7–10. *Like Janus,* &c. Janus was believed to have introduced agriculture and civilization into Italy (see Ovid, *Fasti,* i. 63 ff.). Cf. *Astræa Redux,* ll. 75–88, note.

14. *The second Temple,* built after the Exile (Ezra v, vi): 'Who is left among you that saw this house in her first glory? and how do ye see it now? is it not in your eyes in comparison of it as nothing?' (Haggai ii. 3).

15. *Vitruvius:* M. Vitruvius Pollio, Augustan architect and author of the only extant treatise of the ancient world on architecture.

20. *In easie Dialogue is Fletcher's Praise.* Cf. *Of Dramatick Poesie, An Essay:* 'As for Comedy, Repartee is one of its chiefest graces; the greatest pleasure of the Audience is a chase of wit kept up on both sides, and swiftly manag'd. And this our forefathers, if not we, have had in *Fletchers* Plays, to a much higher degree of perfection that the French Poets can, reasonably, hope to reach' (Ker, i. 72).

22–23. *Great Johnson,* &c. See *Mac Flecknoe,* introductory note.

29. *Courtship:* courtliness.

30. *Manly:* the hero of Wycherley's *The Plain Dealer,* 1677.

35–38. *Fabius might joy in Scipio,* &c. 'Had Scipio been as loveable as you, the envious Fabius would have rejoiced in his early fame and supported him, even though Fabius had in his own day been unsuccessful against Hannibal.' Fabius opposed Scipio's proposal to carry the war against Carthage into Africa: 'The common People thought that he envied the Fame of *Scipio,* and that he was afraid lest this young Conqueror should have the Glory . . . to end the War. . . . [He] too manifestly laid open his envious and morose Humour, when nothing (not done by himself) could please him' (*Plutarch's Lives,* 1727, ii. 252–4).

39–40. *Thus old Romano bow'd,* &c. An error: Giulio Romano was Raphael's pupil. Dryden probably confused him with Pietro Vanucci, whose school at Perugia the young Raphael entered, and with whom he collaborated as pupil.

41–48. At the Revolution, Dryden lost the offices of Poet Laureate and Historiographer-Royal to Shadwell ('*Tom* the first'). In 1692 Tate succeeded Shadwell as Laureate, and Rymer ('*Tom* the Second') became Historiographer. See Dedication of *Examen Poeticum,* ll. 99–115, note; cf. Prologue to *Love Triumphant,* ll. 47–50.

49. *my Patron:* the Earl of Dorset, who as Lord Chamberlain appointed the

Laureate and Historiographer. See Dedication of *The Satires of Juvenalis*, introductory note.

55. *Thy first attempt*. Southerne says that when Dryden read *The Old Batchelour* in manuscript, at the request of an acquaintance of Congreve's, he 'sayd he never saw such a first play in his life . . . the stuff was rich indeed, it wanted only the fashionable cutt of the town. To help that Mr. Dryden, Mr. Arthur Manwayring, and Mr. Southern red it with great care, and Mr. Dryden putt it in the order it was playd' (MS. 'Memoirs relating to Mr. Congreve'; Macdonald, p. 54).

63. *she*; *his* in l. 69. 'In all probability Dryden had written "Nature that once was prodigal before" (cf. "Nature" in the lines on Milton), but, on noticing that he had just used "native", hastily altered "Nature" to "Heaven" (a monosyllable) and inserted "but" for the sake of the metre' (Nichol Smith).

66–69. *Already I am worn*, &c. Cf. Prologue and Epilogue to *Love Triumphant*, note. Yalden, in an ode 'To Mr. *Congreve* . . . Occasion'd by his late Play' (*Examen Poeticum*, 1693, pp. 343–8), speaks of Congreve's choice to serve 'a *Barb'rous Age*, and an ungrateful *Muse*';

> Since *Dryden*'s self, to Wit's great Empire born,
>   Whose Genius and exalted Name,
>   Triumph with all the *Spoils* of *Wit* and *Fame*;
> Must midst the loud *Applause* his barren *Laurels* mourn.
>
>   .   .   .   .   .   .
>
>   In all his Wants Majestick still appears,
>   Charming the *Age* to which he owes his Cares,
> And cherishing that *Muse* whose *fatal Curse* he bears.

Prologue, Epilogue and Songs from Love Triumphant; or, Nature will Prevail. A Tragi-Comedy

(Page 854)

Love Triumphant was first performed in January 1694 at Drury Lane, and published by Tonson soon after (advertised in the *London Gazette*, 12–15 March). On 11 January Evelyn 'sup'd at Mr. Ed Sheldons where was Mr. Dryden the Poet, who now intending to Write no more Plays (intent upon the Translation of Virgil) read to us his Prologue & Epilogue to his last Valedictory Play, now shortly to be Acted' (*Diary*). On Betterton, who spoke the Prologue and played Alphonso, see Prologue to *Troilus and Cressida*, note; on Mrs. Mountfort, who played Dalinda and spoke the Epilogue (l. 7), see Epilogue to *Don Sebastian*, note.

Prologue. 24. *make the Ladies look they know not how*. Cf. Vanbrugh, *The Provok'd Wife* (1697), III. iii: '. . . my Glass and I cou'd never yet agree what Face I shou'd make when they come blurt out with a nasty thing in a Play: For all the Men presently look upon the Women, that's certain; so laugh we must not, tho' our Stays burst for 't; Because that's telling Truth, and owning we understand the Jest. . . . For my part I always take that Occasion to blow my Nose.'

43. *Roaring Boys.* Cf. Prologue to *Cleomenes*, ll. 1–10; Nicoll, pp. 15–19.

47–50. *Shakespear's Critique*: Rymer. See Dedication of *Examen Poeticum*, ll. 99–115, note; *To my Dear Friend Mr. Congreve*, ll. 41–48. Rymer's own experiment in heroic tragedy, *Edgar, or The English Monarch* (1678) was not successful: cf. Robert Gould's *The Play-House. A Satyr* (1685), in M. Summers, *The Restoration Theatre*, 1934, p. 309.

Epilogue. 6. *Sparks behind our Scenes.* See Epilogue *To the King and Queen*, l. 35, note.

15. *Masks and Misses*: whores. See Prologue to The Second Part of *The Conquest of Granada*, l. 13, note. Cf. Evelyn, *Diary*, 9 January 1662: 'the faire & famous Comœdian call'd *Roxalana* . . . [was] taken to be the E. of *Oxfords* Misse (as at this time they began to call lew'd women)'.

20–23. Sancho in the play is a colonel who marries Dalinda and accepts her bastard children (Act v). The scene is followed by Congreve's song, 'How Happy's the Husband, whose Wife has been try'd'.

Songs. Song of Jealousie: Act iii, Sc. i. *Song for a Girl*: Act v, Sc. i. Day (pp. 109, 111) gives John Eccles's settings from *Thesaurus Musicus* (1694) and *The Gentleman's Journal* (January–February 1694). With *Song of Jealousie*, ll. 24–25, cf. Milton, *Paradise Lost*, i. 62–63:

> . . . . yet from those flames
> No light, but rather darkness visible.

To Sir Godfrey Kneller
(Page 858)

Sir Godfrey Kneller (1646–1723) studied painting in Holland and Italy, and came to England in 1676. He rapidly gained popularity, and succeeded Lely as court painter in 1680. He painted Dryden about 1693, and it is probable that he suggested the translation of Du Fresnoy's *De Arte Graphica* which Dryden made in 1695.

This epistle, and a version of *Georgics* iii, which was revised for the complete *Virgil* in 1697, were Dryden's only contributions to *The Annual Miscellany: for the Year 1694. Being the Fourth Part of Miscellany Poems* (see Poems from *Examen Poeticum*, introductory note). There is no evidence that Dryden was responsible for the omissions from the reprint of 1701, and it is possible that the omission of ll. 115–23 and 164–5 was due to Kneller himself, who may have resented such qualified praise. 'Pope laid a wager that there was no flattery so gross but Kneller would swallow' (Johnson, iii. 265, notes). In the draft Dedication which Dryden wrote for Purcell (see Prologue to *The*

Prophetess, note) is a discussion of the parallel between painting, music, and poetry which is deleted in the manuscript and does not appear in the published version. R. G. Ham (*PMLA* l (1935), 1065–75) points out a number of correspondences between the ideas in the draft and those in *To Sir Godfrey Kneller* and the 'Parallel, Of *Poetry* and *Painting*' prefixed to Dryden's translation of Du Fresnoy.

3–6. *True she was dumb,* &c. Cf. *To the Pious Memory Of . . . Mrs Anne Killigrew*, l. 103, and the draft Dedication of *The Prophetess*: 'Painting . . . is a dumb Lady, whose charmes are onely to the eye: a Mute actour upon the stage, who can neither be heard nor read there, nor read afterwards.'

14–21. *Shadows are but privations,* &c. Cf. the draft Dedication: 'Yet let it allwayes be acknowledgd, that painting and Statuary can express both our actions & our passions: that if they neither speake nor move, they seem to do both: and if they impose on the eye, yet they deceive nobly: when they make shadows pass for substances, and even animate the brass & marble.'

22. *Prometheus.* See *To the Earl of Roscomon*, ll. 73–74, note.

47–50. *Till Goths,* &c. Cf. 'A Parallel, Of *Poetry* and *Painting*': 'The two arts . . . were both in a manner extinguished by the irruption of the barbarous nations, and both restored about the times of Leo the Tenth, Charles the Fifth, and Francis the First' (Ker, ii. 135).

54. *Bantam's Embassy*: at court in 1682. Evelyn, *Diary*, 20 June 1682.

78. *Teucer*. Homer, *Iliad*, viii. 266–72.

An Ode, on the Death of Mr. Henry Purcell; Late Servant to his Majesty, and Organist of the Chapel Royal, and of St. Peter's Westminster
(Page 863)

Purcell died on 21 November 1695 and was buried five days later at the foot of the organ in Westminster Abbey, where he had been organist since 1679, 'much lamented, being a very great Master of Musick' (see J. A. Westrup, *Purcell*, 1947, pp. 85–86). Dryden's ode was first published by Playford in 1696 'Sett to Musick by Dr. *Blow*', the text of the poem printed on the verso of the title-page and, with some differences, accompanying Blow's music. It was reprinted without the music among the prefatory poems in *Orpheus Britannicus*, 1698. See Prologue &c. from *Amphitryon*, introductory note.

Epilogue to The Husband His own Cuckold. A Comedy
(Page 864)

This play, by Dryden's second son John, was first performed late in 1695 or early in 1696. Dryden says in his Preface that 'it was sent me from *Italy* some years since . . . to try its fortune on the Stage', and that in the summer of 1695 the author, after 'my long delays of his expectation', took steps to have it performed under the patronage of Sir Robert Howard. 'If I am not partial, he has already shewn, that a Genius is not wanting to him. All that I can reasonably fear, is that the perpetual good success of ill Plays may make him endeavour to please by writing worse, and by accommodating himself to the wretched capacity and liking of the present Audience, from which, Heaven defend any of my Progeny.' On 26 May 1696 Dryden asked Tonson to make an offer for the play, 'that I may take the fairest Chapman, as I am bound to do, for his benefit' (Ward, p. 82); and Tonson published it that summer (advertised in the *London Gazette*, 9–13 July).

On 15 June 1694 Dryden made an agreement with Tonson for the translation of Virgil, undertaking not to engage meanwhile in any other work except the translation of Du Fresnoy, minor pieces, and 'the writing of the Prolouge Epilouge or songs' to *The Husband His own Cuckold*; and C. E. Ward reprints two songs from the play which 'seem . . . to have the authentic Dryden touch' (*RES* xiii (1937), 301–4). But the Epilogue is his only certain contribution. He appears to have had some part, however, in preparing the text for the stage: for he assured Tonson, in a letter which may be dated November 1695, that 'When my Sonns play is acted I intend to translate [from Virgil] again, if my health continue' (Ward, p. 79).

On Mrs. Bracegirdle, see Prologue and Epilogue to *Amphitryon*, note.

Epilogue. 13. *a Third Day*: the author's benefit performance. Cf. Epilogue to *The Unhappy Favourite*, l. 15. In his Dedication to Howard the younger Dryden speaks of those who assume 'the name of Poet, who never had any other call to that Art besides the hope of a third day'.

32. *Clipt Money*. See *The Medall*, ll. 228–9, note. Cf. Evelyn, *Diary*, 15 July 1694: 'Many Executed at London &c: for Clipping mony, which was now don to that intollerable degree, that there was hardly any mony stiring that was intrinsicaly worth above halfe the value, to such a strange exorbitance things were arived, beyond that any age can shew example.' A Proclamation of 19 December 1695 stopped the general circulation of clipped half-crowns and crowns.

The Works of Virgil: Containing His Pastorals, Georgics, and Æneis. Translated into English Verse

(Page 867)

Writing to Walsh on 12 December 1693, Dryden says: 'I have undertaken to translate all Virgil: & as an Essay, have already paraphrasd, the third Georgique, as an Example; it will be publishd in Tonsons next Miscellanyes [*The Annual Miscellany . . . 1694*]. . . . I propose to do it by subscription; haveing an hunderd & two Brass Cutts, with the Coats of Armes of the Subscriber to each Cutt.' The formal agreement with Tonson is dated 15 June 1694. By October 1695 Dryden had translated the seventh Aeneid—and expected fifty pounds from Tonson when the eighth was ready. Ten books were finished by the summer of 1696. The book was in the press by February 1697; it was advertised in the *London Gazette*, 24–28 June; and by September Dryden was rejoicing in its success 'beyond its desert or my Expectation. . . . the profits might have been more, but neither my conscience nor honour wou'd suffer me to take them'. In December he 'bestowd nine entire days' on revision, and returned his work with curses on the printer's head—he 'is a beast, and understands nothing I can say to him of correcting the press' (Ward, pp. 64, 77, 83, 85, 94, 97, 98).

Dryden's letters throw some light on the way in which the *Virgil* was prepared for the printer. The manuscript was 'transcribd in a legible hand' under Tonson's supervision, '& then sent back to me, for the last review. . . . I feare you can scarcely make any thing of my foul copy; but it is the best I have. . . . transcribe in very large paper; & leave a very large margin' (Ward, pp. 83, 84–85).

Dryden worked chiefly from Ruaeus's Delphin edition of Virgil (Paris, 1675). A comparison of his translation with this text shows him more faithful to his original than comparison with a modern edition suggests. He also made full use of Ruaeus's commentary and prose *interpretatio*, and of earlier translations of Virgil. For the Eclogues, he drew on Ogilby's complete *Virgil* (1654) and on the series of translations in *Miscellany Poems* (1684) to which he had himself contributed. For the *Georgics*, he used May, *Virgil's Georgicks Englished* (1628), and Ogilby; Lauderdale's *Virgil*, which was lent in manuscript (see Dedication of the *Æneis*, ll. 2189–2202, note); Cowley's 'Praise of a Country Life' in his essay *Of Agriculture*; and translations in Tonson's Miscellanies. See Helene M. Hooker, 'Dryden's Georgics and English Predecessors', *HLQ* ix (1946), 273–310. In the *Æneis* his heaviest debts are to Lauderdale and Ogilby; but he owed something also to Denham's 'The Destruction of Troy' and 'The Passion of Dido for Aeneas' (*Works*, ed. T. H. Banks, 1928, pp. 159–78 and 181–9), and to Stafford's 'Episode of the Death of Camilla' in *Sylvæ*. His commonest borrowings are rhyme-words, and occasional words and phrases; adaptations of complete lines and couplets are few.

The text is based on the edition of 1697, with the exception of *Pastorals* iv and ix, and *The Third Book of the Georgics*, which are revisions of poems contributed to Tonson's Miscellanies. Towards the end of 1696, Dryden sent Tonson 'the fourth & ninth Ecclogue . . . corrected in my wife's printed Miscellany' (Ward, p. 85). It has usually been assumed that he refers to his wife's copy of *Miscellany Poems* (1684), revised for the printer; but the Miscellany was reprinted in 1692, and collation shows that the copy he sent was probably of the reprint. The first version of *The Third Book of the Georgics* appeared in *The Annual Miscellany . . . 1694,* and a revised copy of this may have been sent to Tonson in the same way in 1696. It is notable that, in the second edition of the *Virgil,* Dryden reverts to many of the original readings of *1694.* The present text of those parts of the *Æneis* which first appeared in miscellanies (parts of books v, viii, ix, x) is based on *1697,* since so many alterations were made in these that they were probably set up from a fresh manuscript. Of Dryden's extensive commentary on his translation, only relevant passages are included in the following notes. See 'Postscript to the Reader', l. 117, note. The epigraph is *Aen.* ii. 724.

Virgil's Pastorals

(Page 869)

To The Right Honourable Hugh Lord Clifford. Hugh Clifford (1663–1730), second Baron Chudleigh, was the son of Thomas, Lord Clifford (1630–73), a member of the Cabal, Charles II's Lord Treasurer (1672), and Dryden's patron. A Roman Catholic, Thomas Clifford relinquished the Treasurership on account of the Test Act (1673), and Dryden celebrated his 'voluntary neglect of Honours' in the Dedication of *Amboyna.* He may have been concerned in Dryden's appointment as Poet Laureate; he was responsible for the repayment of a loan of £500 which Dryden made to the king in 1667 (C. E. Ward, in *RES* xiii (1937), 297–8). Cf. the Dedication of *The Assignation* (1673) to Sedley: '. . . I, who am the least amongst the Poets, have yet the fortune to be honour'd with the best Patron, and the best Friend: For . . . I can make my boast to have found a better *Mæcenas* in the Person of my Lord Treasurer *Clifford,* and a more Elegant *Tibullus* in that of Sir *Charles Sedley.*'

54. *young Manlius*: whose father, Manlius Torquatus, 'had the courage and heart to put [him] to death . . . because he had engaged one of the enemy, and obtained an honourable victory, without his previous permission' (Lemprière).

85. *the Boorish Dialect of Theocritus,* &c. Cf. Preface to *Sylvæ,* ll. 332 ff.

93. *Cherry-trees.* 'Cerasi ante victoriam Mithridaticam L. Luculli non fuere in Italia, ad urbis annum DCLXXX. is primum invexit e Ponto' (Pliny, *Nat. Hist.* xv. 30).

100. *the Piscatory Eclogues,* by Jacopo Sannazaro (1526), in which he is 'induced . . . to remove the scene from the fields to the sea, to substitute fishermen for shepherds, and derive his sentiments from the piscatory life, for which he has been censured' (Johnson, *The Rambler,* No. 36). See Dorothy Broughton, *The Works of William Diaper,* 1951, pp. xxviii–xl.

103. *Monsieur Fontinelle*: Bernard le Bovier de Fontenelle (1657–1757), who attempted the pastoral mode, and in his *Discours sur l'Églogue* roughly used Theocritus and Virgil. Knightly Chetwood contributed a Preface to Dryden's *Pastorals* 'With a short Defence of *Virgil,* Against some of the Reflections of Monsieur *Fontanelle*'.

107–8. *Si Pergama*, &c. *Aen.* ii. 291–2.

126–7. *Nec imbellem*, &c. Horace, *Od.* IV. iv. 31–32.

The First Pastoral. 25–26. *And the hoarse Raven*, &c.: translating 'saepe sinistra cava praedixit ab ilice cornix' (l. 18, Ruaeus).

The Second Pastoral. 30. Dryden elaborates 'Amphion Dircaeus in Actaeo Aracyntho' (l. 24). 'Aracynthum in Bœotiâ . . . prope Thebas, in mare prominentem . . .' (Ruaeus).

The Third Pastoral. 15. *crept the Hedges*: Dryden's amplification. Editors emend to 'cropt': but Menalcas cut only the vines; and the transitive use of 'creep' is not uncommon. Cf. Milton, *Paradise Lost*, vii. 523: 'every creeping thing that creeps the ground'.

97. *Phyllis*: Virgil's Galatea (l. 64). Dryden probably altered the second edition to accord with ll. 119–23.

The Fifth Pastoral. 5. Mopsus's opening, 'tu maior; tibi me est aequum parere, Menalca' (l. 4), is omitted here and worked in at l. 9, apparently to preserve the balance of the dialogue.

14. *dying Phillis*: 'Phyllidis ignis' (l. 10). 'Die' has an erotic significance in Restoration poetry: see Songs from the First Part of *The Conquest of Granada*, I. 22–28, note.

The Sixth Pastoral. 75–76. *Though lab'ring Yokes*, &c.: translating (ll. 49–51)

> at non tam turpis pecudum tamen ulla secuta
> concubitus, quamvis collo timuisset aratrum,
> et saepe in levi quaesisset cornua fronte.

In the 1697 version, Dryden has mistaken the subject of 'timuisset' and 'quaesisset'. 'Tho soft and white as flakes of falling Snow' may be an attempt to deal with 'ille latus niveum molli fultus hyacintho . . . ruminat' (l. 53), which is otherwise poorly rendered in ll. 78–79 *infra*.

The Seventh Pastoral. 29. *With all my Codrus*, &c. An obscure rendering of 'mihi carmen, quale meo Codro, concedite' (ll. 21–22).

97–100. *These Rhymes*, &c. *98* is a more successful attempt to expand the Latin (ll. 69–70),

> haec memini, et victum frustra contendere Thyrsim.
> ex illo Corydon Corydon est tempore nobis,

which Servius paraphrases '. . . ex illo tempore Corydon est nobis, habetur à nobis, victor nobilis supra omnes' (Ruaeus).

The Ninth Pastoral. 13. *dodder'd*. See *The Fifth Satyr of Persius*, l. 80, note.

Virgil's Georgics
(Page 912)

To The Right Honourable Philip Earl of Chesterfield, &c. Philip Stanhope (1633–1713), second Earl of Chesterfield, had been a notable figure in

Restoration court circles; but in loyalty to the Stuarts he declined office under William of Orange and retired to Bretby in Derbyshire. The *Georgics* is fittingly dedicated to the owner of a celebrated house and gardens (see *The Journeys of Celia Fiennes*, ed. C. Morris, 1947, pp. 170–3). Writing to Chesterfield on 17 February 1697, Dryden says that these poems 'are suitable to the retir'd life which you have chosen, and to your studies of Philosophy'. Chesterfield acknowledged the Dedication as an honour to 'a country Gentleman, who being in no post whereby he may merit such a favour, must value it the more, as proceeding from no other motive than your kindness'; and delighted in the compliment 'not out of vanity in having my inconsiderable name placed (by so great a man) in the front of one of his Works, but because it gives the World a testimony of his friendship to me. I confess that I have always esteem'd you the Homer of this Age. . . . But I do not pretend to offer the incence of praise, to him who is the best teacher of others how to give it' (Ward, pp. 86–87, 89).

3–4. *Quod optanti*, &c. *Aen.* ix. 6–7.

36–37. *he descended*, &c. Dryden makes the same error in chronology in the Dedication of *The Satires of Juvenalis*, ll. 2355–6.

47. *the Gleanings of that Ephraim . . . Abiezer*. Judges viii. 2.

51. *Jam Senior*, &c. *Aen.* vi. 304.

75. *A Prodigal Fire*. Chesterfield appears in Pepys as a deadly duellist and one of the licentious 'young Hectors' about the Duke of Monmouth (*Diary*, 17 January 1660 and 9 June 1667). 'A long residence in Italy had made him . . . jealous in his connection with women: he had been much hated by the king; because he had been much beloved by Lady Castlemaine' (Grammont, pp. 186–7).

82. *where the Principles are only Phlegm*. Of the five principles or elements of which all bodies were supposedly made up, three were active—spirit, oil, and salt—and two were passive—water (phlegm) and earth (*OED*).

97. *Dignum Laude*, &c. Horace, *Od.* IV. viii. 28.

104. *Digito monstrari*, &c. Persius, *Sat.* i. 28.

164. *Res non parta labore*, &c. Martial, *Epi.* X. xlvii. 3.

168. *Qui Zonam perdidit*. Horace, *Epist.* II. ii. 40.

191. *O Fortunatos nimiùm*, &c. *Georgics*, ii. 458–9.

205. *Et secura quies*, &c. *Georgics*, ii. 467.

The First Book of the Georgics. (Page 918.) 'The Poetry of this Book is more sublime than any part of *Virgil*, if I have any Taste. And if ever I have Copied his Majestick Stile 'tis here. The Compliment he makes *Augustus* almost in the beginning is ill imitated by his Successors *Lucan* and *Statius*. They Dedicated to Tyrants; and their Flatteries are gross and fulsome. *Virgil*'s Address is both more lofty and more just' (Dryden's note). Cf. *Annus Mirabilis*, 'An account of the ensuing Poem', l. 152 and note; Preface to *Sylvæ*, l. 190. Dryden wrote to Chesterfield in 1697: 'the Georgiques . . . are his Masterpiece in which he has not onely out done all other Poets, but himself. Accordingly I have labour'd and I may say I have cultivated the Georgiques with more care than any other part of him, and as I think my self with more success' (Ward, p. 86).

46. *seated near the Ballance*: Dryden's addition (l. 32), from Ruaeus's note: 'Veteres diu *Libram* signum ignoraverunt, medium inter *Virginem* et *Scorpium*: unde *Chelas*, id est, forfices et brachia Scorpii, dicit poëta post Virginem sequi.'

51–60. The sense requires a slightly altered punctuation. Lines 52–58 are parenthetical, and are bracketed in Ruaeus's text (ll. 36–39).

270. *Weevel*: *Weezel* 97, 98. Dryden was apparently following not the Latin text ('curculio', l. 186), but Ogilby's translation (1654) in which 'Weevels' is misprinted 'Weesels'.

308. *Argo*. Dryden adds this constellation from Ruaeus's note (l. 218). The misspelling '*Argos*' may de due to careless reading of Lauderdale's MS. which Dryden was following here. The printed text of Lauderdale's version (ll. 216–17) runs:

> Then when the *Bull* unlocks the opening Year,
> When backward *Argo*'s Star forsakes the Sphere.

337. *Abhor to dive beneath the Southern Sea*: '[Arctos] Oceani metuentes æquore tingi' (l. 246). Scott emends to 'northern sea'; but probably Dryden means that the Bears fear to fall south into the sea.

377. *red Thunder*: 'fulmine' (l. 283). See *Examen Poeticum*, 'The First Book of Ovid's Metamorphoses', l. 199, note.

499. *erected*: a latinism which suggestively combines the two senses of 'erectus'—'elevated', and 'anxious', 'intent'.

502. *The seeming Stars fall headlong*: 'stellas . . . videbis | praecipites caelo labi' (ll. 365–6). 'Seeming' is a concentration of Ruaeus's note: 'Consentiunt omnes nullam cœlo stellam labi, sed hoc è vulgi mente dictum esse, cui labi videtur.'

570. *the Crows exult, and frisking Lambs rejoice*: 'et laetae pecudes et ovantes gutture corvi' (l. 423).

656. *a sullen Sky*. There seems no good reason for the alteration in 98 of 'so serene a Sky' ('caelo . . . sereno', l. 487). Ruaeus emphasizes the significance of lightning in a clear sky.

The Second Book of the Georgics. (Page 936.) 'The Praises of *Italy*, (Translated by the Learned, and every way Excellent Mr. *Chetwood*) which are Printed in one of my[1] Miscellany Poems [1684], are the greatest Ornament of this Book. Wherein for want of sufficient skill in Gardening, Agriculture, *&c.* I may possibly be mistaken in some Terms . . .' (Dryden's note). Cf. *Annus Mirabilis*, 'An account of the ensuing Poem', ll. 73–77, note.

96. *thin-leav'd Arbute*: translating 'arbutus horrida' (l. 69) with Ruaeus's note: '*Horrida*, quia raris est foliis.'

[1] my *98*: the *97*

109–17. *In whose moist Womb*, &c. Dryden frequently humanizes crops and trees in the *Georgics* (cf. *infra*, ll. 165, 302, 408, 497–500). Such conceits were traditional: cf. Spenser, *The Faerie Queene*, II. xii. 53–54, 61; Saintsbury, ii. 312, ll. 46–48, and iii. 126–7.

146–7. *Nor must Bumastus*, &c.: translating '. . . tumidis Bumaste racemis' (l. 102) with Ruaeus's note: 'βουμαστὸς, vaccæ mammam magnitudine referens'.

209–10. *Nor pois'nous Aconite*, &c.: translating 'nec miseros fallunt aconita legentes' (l. 152). The qualification in l. 210 is based on Ruaeus: '*Aconita* . . . Nascuntur et in Italiâ, teste Servio: sed poëta arte utitur ut rem excuset: nam ea innuit non abesse, quia sunt omnibus nota, nec *fallunt legentes*.'

214. *stupend'ous*. The unstressed suffixes *-ous*, *-eous*, *-ious* were often confused in the seventeenth century. Cf. H. C. Wyld, *A History of Modern Colloquial English*, 1936, p. 281.

333. *rope around*: become viscid. Cf. *The Sixth Satyr of Juvenal*, l. 188; *The Third Book of the Georgics*, l. 759.

457. *Let me dare to sing*: 'crediderim' (l. 338). The 97 phrase 'so sweet Poets sing' is based on Ruaeus: 'Disceptatur, quo tempore mundus conditus sit: verno, an autumnali. . . . Poëtæ omnes pro vere stant.'

489. *sturdy Steers*. A revision made without reference to the Latin 'luctantes iuvencos' (l. 357), which is correctly translated in 97.

540. *honest*: comely ('honestum', l. 392).

576. *Nor when*. Dryden changes his construction at l. 582. 'But when' would make a better link with 'Yet still'.

The Third Book of the Georgics. (Page 957.) Virgil's attribution of personality to the animals appealed to Dryden's comic sense, and he elaborates wittily— e.g. in the language of love (ll. 194–203, 330–8) and in describing the education of the calf (ll. 259–80).

30. *Whorlbat*: whirl-bat, the conventional seventeenth-century translation of 'caestus', 'a certain game . . . among the ancients, wherein they whirled leaden plummets at one another' (see *OED*).

45–46. *Next him Niphates*, &c.: 'addam . . . pulsumque Niphaten' (l. 30). 'It has been objected to me, that I understood not this Passage of *Virgil*, because I call *Niphates* a River, which is a Mountain in *Armenia*. But the River arising from the same Mountain, is also called *Niphates*. And having spoken of *Nile* before, I might reasonably think, that *Virgil* rather meant to couple two Rivers, than a River and a Mountain' (Dryden's note).

171–2. In *98* Dryden restores the closer version of ll. 108–9:

> iamque humiles, iamque elati sublime videntur
> aëra per vacuum ferri atque adsurgere in auras.

224–5. 'The transition is obscure in *Virgil*. He began with Cows, then proceeds to treat of Horses: Now returns to Cows' (Dryden's note).

438. *boring*. Defined in this context in *OED* as advancing 'by gradual persistent motion' (cf. *Æneis*, iii. 660). But Dryden may also have had a more technical use in mind. '[With horsemen] a horse is said to boar or bore, when he shoots out his nose as high as he can' (Bailey, 1731; *OED*); and this sense obviously applies to mares in heat. Cf. *The Sixth Satyr of Juvenal*, l. 435.

487. *Camelots*. The usual sense of camlet was a rich fabric of wool and silk—in Spenser's river wedding, 'Medua' wears a glittering vesture 'like water Chamelot' (*The Faerie Queene*, IV. xi. 45). Cf. Pepys, *Diary*, 1 July 1660: a 'fine Camlett cloak, with gold buttons, and a silk suit'. But Dryden applies the word simply to a goatskin coat; and in the eighteenth century it generally referred to a fabric of goat hair.

625. *beamy*: antlered; apparently from the technical term 'beam', a stag's horn (cf. *Æneis*, i. 260, vii. 670, x. 1020). Dryden uses this word in two other senses: (i) bright (e.g. *Æneis*, viii. 825 and 901); (ii) massive, as a beam (e.g. *Æneis*, xii. 444, translating Virgil's 'teloque . . . trabali', l. 294). See Nowell Smith's letter in *TLS*, 17 July 1930.

683. *mother'd*: scummy. 'Mother' was the stock translation of 'amurca' (l. 448). Cf. *The Third Satyr of Persius*, l. 147.

759. *roapy*: sticky. Cf. *The Sixth Satyr of Juvenal*, l. 188.

The Fourth Book of the Georgics. (Page 979.) Dryden elaborates Virgil's account of the life of the hive in human terms. He multiplies such phrases as 'trading Citizens', 'raw Souldiers', 'reconcil'd Deserters' (ll. 20, 32, 91); he humorously applies the language of court and parliament to the society of the bees (e.g. ll. 92–95, 162, 308–10, 316); and he occasionally extends Virgil's description (e.g. ll. 276–7, 370–1, 374).

27. 'My most Ingenious Friend Sir *Henry Shere*, has observ'd through a Glass-Hive, that the Young Prince of the *Bees*, or Heir presumptive of the Crown, approaches the King's Apartment with great Reverence; and for three successive Mornings demands permission, to lead forth a Colony of that Years Bees. If his Petition be granted, which he seems to make by humble hummings; the Swarm arises under his Conduct. If the Answer be, *le Roy s'avisera* . . . the next Morning the Prince is found dead, before the Threshold of the Palace' (Dryden's note).

305. *Grandsires, Grandsons the long List contains*: 'avi numerantur avorum' (l. 209). Scott emends to 'grandsires' grandsires'; but Dryden may have been glancing at Lauderdale's 'Sons their Sires succeed', and his version takes in the five generations indicated in the Latin.

354. *Lizards*. For the 'Worms' of 97 Dryden may have intended to substitute 'Beetles' (Lauderdale's word, and the obvious translation of 'blattis', l. 243), and carelessly carried forward 'Lizards' from l. 352.

422. *burnish'd*: with the dead skin rubbed off.

477. 'The Poet here records the Names of Fifteen[1] River Nymphs. And

[1] Fifteen] Fifty *97 98*

for once I have Translated them all. But in the *Æneis* I thought not my self oblig'd to be so exact; for in naming many Men who were kill'd by Heroes, I have omitted some, which wou'd not sound in *English* Verse' (Dryden's note).

484. *softly*. Noyes remarks that Dryden's construction is confused; and Scott emends to 'lofty', destroying the pattern of contrasts in ll. 483–5. 'Softly' is possible as an archaic adjectival form: cf. Spenser, *The Faerie Queene*, VI. vii. 6, 'Ryding a softly pace with portance sad'.

591–2. In ll. 589–94 Dryden revised his tenses to accord with 'fiet enim subito sus horridus . . .' (l. 407). The adjustment of the rhyme here completes the revision.

660. 'The *Episode* of *Orpheus* and *Eurydice* begins here. And contains the only Machine which *Virgil* uses in the *Georgics*. I have observ'd in the Epistle before the *Æneis*, that our Author seldom employs Machines but to adorn his *Poem*: And that the Action which they seemingly perform, is really produc'd without them. Of this Nature is the Legend of the Bees restor'd by Miracle; when the Receipt which the Poet gives, wou'd do the Work without one . . .' (Dryden's note).

684. Normanby's translation of part of *Georgics* iv was published in *Miscellany Poems* (1684).

735. *the leaky Sculler*: 'cumba' (l. 506). In Dryden's *Juvenal*, Tate had translated *Sat*. ii. 151 as '*Charon* wafting Souls in leaky Boat'. Cf. Dryden and Soame, *The Art of Poetry*, l. 650, note.

The Dedication of the Æneis

(Page 1003)

To The Most Honourable John, Lord Marquess of Normanby, &c. See *Absalom and Achitophel*, l. 877, note.

24. *Bossu*. *Traité du Poème épique* (1675), ii. 8, 'Des fautes qui corrompent l'Unité de l'Action'. See Dedication of *The Satires of Juvenalis*, l. 776, note.

70. *Divinæ particulam Auræ*. Horace, *Sat*. II. ii. 79.

88. *Corneille*. *Troisième Discours*, 'Des Trois Unités'. See Ker, i. xxxvi–xlix.

105–9. *Chymical Medicines. . . . Galenical Decoctions*. The distinction is between the chemical or metallic medicines favoured by the Paracelsian, 'spagyric' or 'Hermetical' school, and the traditional vegetable remedies of the Galenists. The battle between the Galenists and the 'sooty empiricks' who followed Paracelsus reached its crisis in the mid-seventeenth century. Burton rejoiced in it, but did not take sides (II. v. 1. 3). Cf. Herbert of Cherbury, *Autobiography*, ed. Sidney Lee, p. 30; Henry Vaughan, *Works*, ed. L. C. Martin, ii. 549–50. By 1661 Robert Boyle was criticizing both schools in *The Sceptical Chymist* for unscientific absorption in dialectic. With Dryden's contrast cf. Shadwell, *Epsom-Wells* (1673), 1: 'We like subtle Chymists extract and refine our pleasure; while they like Fulsom Galenists take it in gross.'

153. *the Epick Poem is more for the Manners, &c.* Cf. Le Bossu, *Traité*, i. 2: 'L'Épopée est plus pour les mœurs & pour les habitudes que pour les passions. Celles-ci naissent tout à coup, & leur violence est de peu de durée; mais les habitudes sont plus tranquilles. . . . Donc l'action Epique ne pouvoit être renfermée en un jour, comme celle du Théâtre; il lui falloit un espace plus juste & plus long que celui de la Tragédie, qui est pour les passions.'

172–4. *A Subject, &c.* The allusion is doubtless to William III and the national debt (see Clark, pp. 169–70). Cf. Preface to *Fables*, l. 241.

184. *Tryphon*: Martial's bookseller (*Epi.* iv. 72, xiii. 3); here probably Tonson.

185. *Ruelle*: a bedroom where ladies of fashion received visitors of distinction; hence a reception of this kind (*OED*).

189. *the fine Woman ends, &c.* Horace, *De Arte Poetica*, ll. 3–4.

193. *Speciosa Miracula*. Ibid., l. 144.

209. *Your Essay of Poetry*, first published anonymously in 1682. Cf. Preface to *Sylvæ*, l. 278; Johnson, ii. 175, 179.

222. *a puny Councellor*: a 'puisné', junior counsellor.

252. *Dacier*: *La Poëtique d'Aristote, traduit . . . avec des remarques critiques* (Paris, 1692).

259. *Scaliger the Father, or Heinsius.* 'On the contrary, Scaliger in the Epistle before his *Poetice*, says: "Nam et Horatius Artem quum inscripsit adeo sine ulla docet arte ut Satyrae propius totum opus illud esse videatur" ' (Ker). On Heinsius, see Dedication of *The Satires of Juvenalis*, l. 788, note.

274. *the Jerusalem*: Tasso, *La Gerusalemme Liberata* (1581).

280. *Fortunam Priami, &c.* Horace, *De Arte Poetica*, l. 137; attributed by the commentators to Maevius, although it is not certain that Horace had any specific poet in mind.

282–6. Luigi Pulci, *Il Morgante Maggiore* (1483); Matteo Boiardo, *Orlando Innamorato* (1506); Ludovico Ariosto, *Orlando Furioso* (1516); Pierre Le Moyne, *Saint Louys* (1653); Georges de Scudéry, *Alaric, ou Rome vaincuë* (1654); Jean Chapelain, *La Pucelle, ou la France délivrée* (1656).

298. Dryden owes much on the theory of epic poetry to Jean Regnauld de Segrais's critical preface to his *Énéide* (1668).

304. *Volat irrevocabile verbum.* Horace, *Epist.* I. xviii. 71.

328. *Macrobius*: *Saturnalia*, v, vi.

329–30. *Tanneguy le Fèvre*: Tanaquillus Faber (1615–72), classical scholar and editor; *Valois*: probably Hadrianus Valesius (1607–92), author of *Valesiana, ou les Pensées critiques, historiques et morales . . . de Monsieur de Valois, Conseiller du Roi et Historiographe de France* (1694); *and another*: probably the Seigneur de St. Évremond (Ker). St. Évremond lived in England from 1662 to 1703 and enjoyed great popularity as a critic. His 'Character', prefixed to his

Miscellaneous Essays (1692), was begun by Chetwood and finished by Dryden. Dryden's rejoinder there to St. Évremond's strictures on the character of Aeneas is much milder than that in the present Dedication.

331. *the Moral of his Poem*. French critics emphasized the didactic function of heroic poetry, and read back into classical epic the allegorical and didactic significance of renaissance epic. Homer, says Le Bossu, devised the *Iliad* as a corrective to the dissensions of the Greek states, taking 'pour le fond de sa Fable, cette grande Vérité, Que la mésintelligence des Princes ruïne leurs propres Etats. *Je chante*, dit-il, *la colère d'Achille, si pernicieuse aux Grecs, & qui a fait périr tant de Héros*' (i. 8). So for Virgil, 'L'Empire des Romains étoit un nouvel établissement; c'étoit le changement d'une République, à laquelle les Sujets d'Auguste avoient toûjours été extrémement attachez, en une Monarchie qu'ils n'avoient pû souffrir jusqu'alors. . . . Il devoit instruire Auguste comme le Fondateur d'un grand Empire, & lui inspirer aussi-bien qu'à ses Successeurs, le même esprit & la même conduite qui avoit fait cet Empire si grand' (i. 11). Dryden elaborates these interpretations in what follows. Cf. Dedication of *The Satires of Juvenalis*, l. 764.

353. *Quicquid delirant*, &c. Horace, *Epist.* I. ii. 14.

391. *Stavo ben*, &c. I have been unable to trace this; but the sentiment is proverbial. Cf. Erasmus, *Adagia*, 173A, 'Ohe actum, ajunt, ne agas'; and Shakespeare, *Sonnets*, ciii:

> Were it not sinfull then striving to mend,
> To marre the subiect that before was well.

The epitaph is quoted in *The Spectator*, No. 25.

400. *Patriots for their own Interest*. Cf. *Absalom and Achitophel*, l. 179, note.

432. *Secretosque Pios*, &c. *Aen.* viii. 670. Cf. *Æneis*, vi. 1156, note.

446–53. *Montaigns Principles*, &c. Montaigne was speaking, not of himself, but of La Boétie: 'I know, that had it beene in his choyce, he would rather have beene borne at *Venice*, than at *Sarlac*; and good reason why: But he had another maxime deepely imprinted in his minde, which was, carefully to obey, and religiously to submit himselfe to the lawes, under which he was borne' (*Essais*, I. xxvii; Florio's translation).

481. *Bochartus*: Samuel Bochart (1599–1667), French theologian and philologist. Segrais (see *supra*, l. 298, note) quotes his 'Lettre . . . sur la question si Enée a jamais esté en Italie' (20 December 1663).

506–7. *Memmii . . . destroy'd Corinth*. Dryden is in error: Virgil mentions the Memmii (*Aen.* v. 117) and Lucretius dedicated his work to Memmius; but the destroyer of Corinth was L. Mummius.

511. *genus irritabile Vatum*. Horace, *Epist.* II. ii. 102.

513. *Animamque, in Vulnere ponit*. Adapted from *Georgics*, iv. 238.

518–19. *We . . . are of the same Humour*. Cf. Prologue to *Troilus and Cressida*, ll. 38–40.

526–7. 'En un mot, le Héros de Virgile devoit être comme Auguste, nouveau Monarque, Fondateur d'un Empire, Législateur, Pontife, & grand Capitaine' (Le Bossu, i. 11).

546. *Priamus*. On the 97 reading, '*Atis*', Dryden says in his 97 errata: 'my Memory betray'd me; for had I consulted *Virgil*, he calls not the Son of *Polites* by the name of *Atis*, but of *Priamus*. 'Tis true he mentions *Atis* immediately afterwards, on the account of the *Atian* Family, from which *Julius Cæsar* was descended by his Grandmother.' *Aen.* v. 563–9.

571. *Pater arma*, &c. *Aen.* xii. 192, 'socer arma', &c. William of Orange behaved otherwise.

582. *I know not*, &c. Le Bossu had taken notice: 'La premiere partie de cette Action est, le changement d'un Etat, celui d'un Roi, & celui d'un Soverain Pontife . . .' (ii. 7). Dennis (i. 136) had drawn attention to this 'admirable Observation of *Bossu*' in *Remarks on . . . Prince Arthur*, 1696.

586. *Sacra, suosque tibi*, &c. *Aen.* ii. 293.

593. *Horace writes an Ode*: III. iii. Dryden's traditional and literal interpretation of this poem is long out of fashion.

635. *the Dauphin's Virgil*: Ruaeus's edition, *argumentum* to the *Aeneid*.

667. *from Bossu*. *Traité*, iv. 5: 'Si un Héros Poëtique doit être honnête-homme.'

673–5. *Tasso . . . split his Heroe in two*. Cf. Spenser's Letter to Raleigh, *The Faerie Queene*, ed. J. C. Smith, ii. 485.

679. *from Segrais*: op. cit., pp. 37 ff.

714–24. *stetimus tela*, &c. *Aen.* xi. 282–92.

744. *Proxima quæque metit gladio*. *Aen.* x. 513.

750. *he was invulnerable without them*. 'Dryden had forgot, what he must certainly have known, that the fiction of Achilles being invulnerable, bears date long posterior to the days of Homer. In the Iliad he is actually wounded' (Scott).

765. *War-luck*. 'The Scots, about Dryden's time, had many superstitions concerning individuals, whom they supposed to be shot-proof, by virtue of a satanic charm. The famous Viscount of Dundee was supposed to be invulnerable to bullets of lead. . . . But the word *warlock*, or *warlough*, means a male sorcerer in general; and has not, as Dryden seems to suppose, any reference to this particular charm' (Scott).

804–12. *his wretched Criticks*, &c. Ker cites Perrault, *Parallèle des Anciens et des Modernes* (1692), p. 135. The censor who 'argues' Aeneas of cowardice is St. Évremond, who quotes *Aen.* i. 92–93 to the hero's disadvantage, and observes that '*Enée* sait craindre & pleurer sur tout ce qui le regarde. Il est vrai qu'il fait la même chose pour ses Amis; mais on doit moins l'attribuer à une Passion noble & genereuse, qu'à une Source inépuisable d'apprehensions & de pleurs, qui lui en fournit naturellement pour lui & pour les autres' ('Reflexions sur nos Traducteurs', 1673; translated in his *Miscellaneous Essays*,

1692, pp. 174–88). Dryden makes a brief reply to this criticism in his 'Character' of St. Évremond (see *supra*, ll. 329–30, note).

819. *Mr. Moyl*: Walter Moyle (1672–1721), a member of the Middle Temple and of the fraternity at Will's Coffee-house. Dryden acknowledges his help in the Preface to *De Arte Graphica* (1695), and praises his learning in the Life which he contributed to *The Works of Lucian* (1711; Dryden's contribution is said to have been written about 1696).

832–3. *Parce metu*, &c. *Aen.* i. 257–8.

842–9. *Aen.* x. 622–7, 632. Dryden quotes these passages in the wrong order.

854–7. *Trojae sub mœnibus altis*, &c. *Aen.* x. 469–72. 'Manent' is an error for 'vocant'.

860. *Sir Robert Howard.* See *To my Honored Friend, S*ᵣ *Robert Howard*, note; *Æneis*, x. 662, note.

881. *Segrais observes*: op. cit., pp. 38–40.

894–5. *Vultis & his mecum*, &c. *Aen.* i. 572–3.

905. *write booty*: set out the evidence falsely; a variant of the common phrase 'play booty'. Cf. *The Spectator*, No. 60: 'Or would not one be apt to believe that the Author played booty, and did not make his List of Rhymes till he had finished his Poem?'

906. *Doctor Cudworth*: Ralph Cudworth (1617–88), Master of Christ's College and leader of the Cambridge Platonists, who examines the arguments for atheism with prolix thoroughness, as a preliminary to a defence of theism, in *The True Intellectuall Systeme of the Universe* (1678; only the first part, on atheism, was completed). On the growth of the criticism to which Dryden refers, see L. P. Courtines, *Bayle's Relations with England and the English*, 1938, pp. 47 f.

929. *Fata obstant*, &c. *Aen.* iv. 440.

935–6. *Curam sub Corde*, &c. *Aen.* iv. 332, 395. The false contiguity is doubtless due to Dryden's habit of quoting from memory.

946. *his two Translators*: Robert and Antoine le Chevalier d'Agneaux, who translated Virgil in 1582 (Ker). Cf. *infra*, l. 1789.

1000. *Dares Phrygius.* An error for Dictys Cretensis, who describes the ambush of Hector by Achilles in *De Bello Troiano*, iii. 15 (Ker).

1020. *varium & mutabile semper femina. Aen.* iv. 569–70.

1032. *Notumq; furens quid femina possit. Aen.* v. 6.

1039. *as Sir Henry Wootton has defin'd.* Wotton, passing through Germany, was requested by Christopher Flecamore 'to write some sentence in his albo', and contributed 'a pleasant definition of an ambassador in these very words: *Legatus est vir bonus, peregre missus ad mentiendum reipublicae causa.* Which Sir Henry Wotton could have been content should have been thus Englished: "An ambassador is an honest man, sent to lie abroad for the good of his country." But the word for lie, being the hinge upon which the conceit was to turn, was not so expressed in Latin as would admit, in the hands of an enemy especially, so fair a construction as Sir Henry thought in English'; and the definition 'caused the king to express much wrath against him' (Walton, *Life of Wotton*).

1042–3. *One who imitates Bocaline. I Ragguagli di Parnaso* of Trajano Boccalini (1556–1613) was translated by Henry, Earl of Monmouth, as *Advertisements from Parnassus* (1656). I cannot trace this particular imitator. There were numerous 'assizes of the poets' in the seventeenth century; see Macdonald, pp. 221–2; R. Thomas, 'Trajano Boccalini's Influence', *Aberystwyth Studies*, iii (1922), 73–102.

1065–75. *Ovid takes it up after him*, &c. Cf. *Annus Mirabilis*, 'An account of the ensuing Poem', ll. 120–38; Preface to *Ovid's Epistles*, ll. 14–16; Preface to *Fables*, ll. 269 ff.

1082. *says Aristotle. Poetics*, xxv. 8.

1087. *splendid Miracles.* Horace, *De Arte Poetica*, l. 144, 'speciosa miracula'.

1094. *Tasso in one of his Discourses*: 'Dell' Arte Poetica.'

1116–17. *Nec pars ulla*, &c. A distortion of *Trist.* ii. 535–6.

1134. *pulchramq; Uxorius Urbem Extruis. Aen.* iv. 266–7.

1148–9. *Neque hæc in fædera veni. Aen.* iv. 337, 339.

1170. *strange.* Malone emends to 'strong', and Noyes concurs. But Scott reasonably suggests that '*strange* here seems to signify *alarming*, or *startling*'.

1187. *Quid prohibetis Aquas*, &c. Ovid, *Meta.* vi. 349.

1207. *Æneadum Genetrix*, the opening of *De Rerum Natura*.

1218. *that servile Imitator*, &c. Horace, *Epist.* I. xix. 19: 'o imitatores, servum pecus'.

1284. *another French Critick.* Probably St. Évremond, *Sur les Poëmes des Anciens* (1685): 'Quelquefois les comparaisons nous tirent des objets qui nous occupent le plus, par la vaine image d'un autre objet, qui fait mal à propos une diversion' (Ker).

1294–5. *Similitudes . . . are not for Tragedy.* Cf. Le Bossu, vi. 3: 'Les Comparaisons ne diminuent pas la passion dans ceux qui les écoutent; mais elles marquent dans ceux qui les disent quelques réfléxions, qui ordinairement ne tombent pas dans un esprit agité & inquiét. Ainsi, il est rare qu'elles soient naturelles & vrai-semblables dans la bouche d'une personne passionée.' In the Preface to *Troilus and Cressida* (1679) Dryden says that 'pointed Wit, and Sentences affected out of Season . . . are nothing of kin to the violence of Passion: no Man is at leisure to make Sentences and Similies, when his Soul is in Agony'.

1326–34. *Ac, veluti*, &c. *Aen.* i. 148–56.

1341. *Nunc, non erat hisce locus.* Horace, *De Arte Poetica*, l. 19.

1345. *Macrobius and Pontanus. Supra*, l. 328, note. Pontanus published an edition of Virgil in 1599.

1349. *Junius and Tremellius.* See *Religio Laici*, l. 241, note.

1358–9. *Bossu leaves it doubtful,* &c. *Traité,* iii. 12. In pondering the story of the Black Prince in Spain as a theme for a heroic poem, Dryden was attracted by 'the compass of Time, including only the Expedition of one Year' (Dedication of *The Satires of Juvenalis,* ll. 619–25). English neo-classical critics were not generally as much concerned as their French contemporaries with rigid unity of time.

1368. *Ronsard,* Preface to *La Franciade* (1572).

1388–90. Ruaeus summarizes Segrais's computation in his prefatory 'De Natura Æneidos' and in his note on *Aen.* i. 535.

1398. *Quinetiam Hyberno moliris sydere Classem. Aen.* iv. 309.

1432–5. *Aurora in roseis,* &c. *Aen.* vii. 26–27, 32–34.

1448. *Cum subito, assurgens fluctu nimbosus Orion. Aen.* i. 535.

1459. *Dum pelago desævit hyems, & aquosus Orion. Aen.* iv. 52.

1488–90. *Virgil, generally speaking,* &c. Cf. Le Bossu, v. 5: 'Virgile use de diverses maniéres où l'on peut reconnoître cette exclusion de nécessité. Quelquefois la chose qui est faite par un Dieu, sera nécessaire, mais elle pourra être faite par une personne mortelle. Enée devoit être instruit des avantures de Didon: mais il n'étoit pas nécessaire que Vénus se déguisât sous la forme d'une fille Tyrienne qui chasse en un bois. Une simple fille pouvoit l'instruire; & c'est comme il faut ordinairement interpréter ces déguisemens des Dieux en hommes. Ce sont des façons Poëtiques.'

1498–9. *O nimium Cælo,* &c. *Aen.* v. 870–1.

1503. *We who are better taught,* &c. See Dedication of *The Satires of Juvenalis,* ll. 448–579, notes.

1512. Tasso, *Gerusalemme Liberata,* xviii. 92–97.

1515. *the Episode of Camilla: Aen.* xi. 836 ff. Cf. Dryden's note on *Æneis,* x. 312.

1543. *Nec Deus intersit, nisi dignus vindice nodus,* l. 191.

1566–7. *Non me tua turbida,* &c. An inaccurate version of *Aen.* xii. 894–5.

1571. *Milton has borrow'd. Paradise Lost,* iv. 990–1015.

1577–9. *Jupiter ipse duas,* &c. *Aen.* xii. 725–7.

1581. *Damnabis tu quoque votis. Ecl.* v. 80.

1583. *the Text in Daniel:* v. 27.

1596. *Imparibus fatis,* &c. A composite line; cf. *Aen.* xii. 149, 218 (Noyes).

1620–2. *O soror,* &c. *Aen.* xii. 632–4.

1637. *Ornari,* &c. Manilius, *Astron.* iii. 39; the epigraph of *Religio Laici.*

1638. *Sermoni propiora.* Horace, *Sat.* I. iv. 42.

1650. *Cæsura:* here elision.

1673–4. *Who teaches himself,* &c. See Tilley, F490.

1687–9. *Si plura,* &c. *De Arte Poetica,* ll. 351–3.

1702. *Et succus pecori & lac subducitur Agnis. Ecl.* iii. 6.

1703. *nobis non licet, esse tam disertis.* Martial, *Epi.* IX. xii. 16.

1704–6. *I have long had by me,* &c. See Dedication of *The Satires of Juvenalis,* l. 2604, note.

1708. *Malherb first brought them into France.* An exaggerated claim. Noyes suggests that Dryden is working from Boileau, *L'Art poétique*, i. 131–2:

> Enfin Malherbe vint, et, le premier en France,
> Fit sentir dans les vers une juste cadence.

1712–13. *Dic quibus*, &c. *Ecl.* iii. 106–7.

1716. *the sweetness of these two Lines.* Denham, *Coopers Hill*, ll. 191–2. Dryden's comment provoked innumerable imitations and analyses (notably by Johnson and Monboddo) in the eighteenth century. See *The Poetical Works of Denham*, ed. T. H. Banks, 1928, pp. 333–50.

1738–9. *Formerly the French . . . had but five Feet.* 'Dryden probably judged hastily, from the decasyllabic verse of the *Franciade*, that the Alexandrine was not of long standing in French poetry' (Ker).

1739–41. *they found their Tongue too weak*, &c. Cf. Rymer, Preface to Rapin's *Reflections on Aristotle's Treatise of Poesie* (1674): 'The *French* now only use the long *Alexandrins*, and would make up in length what they want in strength and substance; yet are they too faint and languishing, and attain not that *numerosity* which the dignity of Heroick Verse requires, and which is ordinary in an *English* Verse of *ten* syllables.'

1750. *The turn on Thoughts and Words.* See Dedication of *The Satires of Juvenalis*, l. 2541, note.

1757. *Ignoscenda quidem*, &c. *Georgics* iv. 489.

1762. *Semivirumq; bovem, semibovemq; virum.* An inversion of *De Arte Amandi*, ii. 24. For the story of Ovid's 'darling Sin' see Seneca, *Controversiae*, ii. 2.

1765. *one of their own great Authors*, probably St. Évremond. See Ker, ii. 302–3.

1778–81. *Non fu si santo*, &c. Ariosto, *Orlando Furioso*, xxxiv. 25.

1789. *the two Brothers.* See *supra*, l. 946, note.

1790. *Hannibal Caro.* See Preface to *Sylvæ*, l. 121, note.

1793. *Le Clerc*: Jean Le Clerc (1657–1736), professor at Amsterdam and a voluminous writer in theology and classical scholarship; editor of the *Bibliothèque Universelle* (1686–93), in which there is an essay (ix; 1688) on Hebrew poetry (Ker).

1801–2. *Quarles, and Withers.* On the decline of the literary reputation of Francis Quarles (1592–1644), see A. H. Nethercot in *MP* xx (1923), 225–40. Dryden struck early at George Wither (1588–1667), a 'most profuse pourer forth of English Rhime': a bad poet is described in *Of Dramatick Poesie, An Essay* (1668) as 'the very *Withers* of the City: they have bought more Editions of his Works then would serve to lay under all their Pies at the Lord Mayor's *Christmass*'.

1808. *Doctor Morelli*: Henry Morelli, a member of the College of Physicians.

1818–25. *Sorti Pater æquus utrique. Aen.* x. 450. Dryden's interpretation is unconvincing. Pallas is replying to Turnus's 'cuperem ipse parens spectator adesset' (x. 443). Ruaeus paraphrases x. 450 'genitor *meus* paratus est utrique fortunæ'.

1831. *Sic ait; atq; oculos Rutulorum rejicit arvis. Aen.* x. 473.

1845–50. *Some of our Country-men*, &c. Sheffield's version of part of *Georgics*, iv, and Roscommon's version of *Ecl.* vi, in *Miscellany Poems* (1684); Denham's translations from *Aen.* ii and iv (there is also a manuscript version of *Aen.* ii–vi which seems to be Denham's; see *Poetical Works*, ed. T. H. Banks, 1928, p. 41); *The Passion of Dido for Æneas. . . . Translated* by Waller and Godolphin (1658); and Cowley's version of *Georgics*, ii. 458–540 in *Several Discourses* (1668).

1865. *in a former Dissertation*: 'A Parallel, Of Poetry and Painting' (Ker, ii. 147).

1873–5. *Segrais*. In his preface (pp. 2–4) Segrais distinguishes three classes of critics, who judge a work by words, 'belles pensées', or 'discours'. Dryden's three classes judge by quibbles and conceits, fustian, and the truly sublime.

1884–5. *who have not Land*, &c. Persons possessing freeholds to the value of 40*s.* a year were, until 1832, the only county voters. Cf. Browning, pp. 212–13.

1893. *the Mançanares at Madrid.* Bouhours, *Entretiens d'Ariste et d'Eugène*, ii: 'Pour moy je n'entends jamais ces mots et ces expressions de la langue Castillane, que je ne me souvienne du Mançanares. On diroit à entendre ce grand mot que la rivière de Madrid est le plus grand fleuve du monde: et cependant ce n'est qu'un petit ruisseau, qui est le plus souvent à sec; et qui, si nous en croyons un Poëte Castillan, ne mérite pas d'avoir un pont' (Ker).

1901. *Owen's Epigrams.* See Dedication of *The Satires of Juvenalis*, l. 332, note.

1904. *the vain Man.* Seneca, *Epist. Morales*, cxi. 3.

1913. *not being of God*, &c. A saying of Rochester's; cf. Preface to *Fables*, ll. 325–7.

1933. *Marini's Adone*: the long, vacuous, but richly decorated poem (1623) of Giovan Battista Marino (1569–1625).

1935. *Mobilitate viget, viresq; acquirit eundo. Aen.* iv. 175.

1946. *Nec dona moror. Aen.* v. 400.

1946. *Dampier has inform'd us*, &c. Captain *Dampier's Voyages*, ed. John Masefield, 1906, i. 176 and ii. 60.

1949. *not to Translate a Poet literally.* See Preface to *Ovid's Epistles*, ll. 177–312, note.

1959. *Manilius, made English.* Creech's translation of the *Astronomica* was first published in 1697.

1967. *Philarchus . . . taxes Balzac.* Jean Goulu de St. François, *Lettres de Phyllarque à Ariste où il est traicté de l'éloquence françoise*, I (1627), xxi (Ker).

1970–3. *Some things too I have omitted*, &c. Cf. Preface to *Sylvæ*, l. 21, note.

2007–9. *I have endeavour'd*, &c. Cf. Preface to *Sylvæ*, ll. 31–32, note.

2028. *the affected purity of the French*, &c. Cf. *supra*, ll. 1739–41, note; *To my Friend, the Author* (Motteux), l. 44.

2038. *our English Pindar*: Cowley. See Preface to *Ovid's Epistles*, ll. 175, 244–5, notes.

2040–2. *For through the Iniquity of the times*, &c. Cowley spent some ten years in France, as royalist agent and secretary to the exiled queen. 'Upon this wandring condition of the most vigorous part of his life, he was wont to reflect, as the cause of the long interruption of his Studies' (Sprat, 'Account' prefixed to Cowley's *Works*, 1668).

2045. *the Painter*, &c. In Sidney's *Arcadia*, II. xxv, a painter who 'was to counterfette the skirmishing betwene the *Centaures* and *Lapithes*, and had bene very desirous to see some notable wounds, to be able the more lively to expresse them', loses his hands at a stroke of Dorus's sword.

2055. *he frequently affects half Verses*, taking Virgil as sufficient authority 'especially in a thing that looks so naturally and gracefully. . . . There are some places in him, which I dare almost swear have been made up since his death by the putid officiousness of some Grammarians' (*Davideis*, I, note 14).

2068. *Quem tibi jam Trojâ. Aen.* iii. 340.

2076-7. *Misenum Æolidem*, &c. *Aen.* vi. 164-5. Virgil, says Donatus (xxxiv), completed his unfinished line during a reading of the passage by his scribe Eros.

2079-80. *reasons . . . in the Book of Painting.* 'A Parallel, Of *Poetry* and *Painting*' (Ker, ii. 150-1).

2090. *the Excuse of Boccace. Il Decameron*, 'Conclusione dell' autore'.

2113. *hammer'd Money for want of Mill'd.* See *The Medall*, ll. 228-9, note; Epilogue to *The Husband His own Cuckold*, l. 32, note. Dryden complains of adulteration of the coinage in 1695-6 (Ward, pp. 75, 82). Cf. Evelyn, *Diary*, 24 May, 11 June, and 16 August 1696.

2135. *Cupid*: an error for Ascanius (*Aen.* i. 691-4).

2146-9. *quisquis studet*, &c. Adapted from Horace, *Od.* IV. ii. 1-4.

2152-3. *Aude Hospes*, &c. *Aen.* viii. 364-5.

2158-9. *false Florimel made of Snow. The Faerie Queene*, V. iii. 22-24.

2166-7. *who shall hinder me to Import them.* Cf. *Annus Mirabilis*, 'An account of the ensuing Poem', l. 175; *Æneis*, ix. 1095, note.

2189-2202. *The late Earl of Lauderdail*, &c. Richard Maitland (1653-95), fourth Earl of Lauderdale, translated Virgil during his exile in Paris in the early 1690's. Lintott published it from the 'more Correct Copy', referred to by Dryden, early in the eighteenth century. Lauderdale drew upon Dryden's translations from Virgil in *Sylvæ*. It has been suggested (see Macdonald, pp. 323-4) that Dryden at first allowed him to incorporate these, but later, when his own translation was planned, requested him to provide for himself and so had to obtain his permission before accepting Tonson's proposals. But the obvious explanation is that Dryden hesitated to work in rivalry against Lauderdale.

2203. *Mr. Congreve.* See *To my Dear Friend Mr. Congreve*, note.

2208. *Two other Worthy Friends*: Addison, who contributed the Preface to the *Georgics*, and the prose arguments; and Knightly Chetwood, who contributed the Preface to the *Pastorals* (Ward, p. 98), and the Life of Virgil.

2214–15. *like Terence,* &c. Suetonius, Life of Terence.

2220–8. *why I Writ not always in the proper terms,* &c. On the evidence of this passage, Ker says (i. 286) that Dryden changed his mind about the propriety of 'terms of art' (see *Annus Mirabilis,* 'An account of the ensuing Poem', ll. 73–77, note). But technical terms abound in his work, not least in the *Virgil.* He 'Writ not *always*' technically, because he wrote for persons of quality; and in all his verse, when technicalities confronted him, he tried with varying success to maintain a balance between the proprieties of 'terms of art' and the requirements of a not too nicely knowing circle of readers. Cf. Preface to *Sylvæ,* ll. 352–4.

2229. *the Four Preliminary Lines:*

> Ille ego, qui quondam gracili modulatus avena
> carmen, et egressus silvis vicina coegi
> ut quamvis avido parerent arva colono,
> gratum opus agricolis, at nunc horrentia Martis
> arma virumque cano. . . .

2251–3. 'Nisus grammaticus audisse se a senioribus aiebat, Varium duorum librorum ordinem commutasse, et qui tunc secundus erat in tertium locum transtulisse, etiam primi libri correxisse principium, his versibus demptis: "Ille ego . . ." ' (Donatus, xlii).

2287. *A Sixth Pastoral,* &c. 'A *Pharmaceutria*' is probably one or both of the versions of *Ecl.* viii by Stafford and Chetwood in *Miscellany Poems* (1684); for the others, see *supra,* ll. 1845–50, note.

2294. *as Erichthonius,* &c. Ruaeus glosses *Georgics,* iii. 113: '. . . illum Atheniensium regem . . . anguipedem, qui, ut pedum deformitatem tegeret, dicitur currum fabricâsse'.

Virgil's Æneis

(Page 1064)

The First Book of the Æneis. **89.** *driving Soul:* imitating Lat. 'anima', air; wind (cf. *Aen.* viii. 403, 'ignes animaeque').

167. *bulg'd:* in the nautical sense, struck rock so violently as to damage the 'bilge', or ship's bottom. Ogilby's version has 'bilg'd'.

169. *Pictures.* A mistranslation of 'tabulae' (l. 119), planks. Dryden elsewhere translates 'tabula' correctly (e.g. *Æneis,* ix. 715): he seems to have carelessly followed Lauderdale here.

260. *beamy.* See *The Third Book of the Georgics,* l. 625, note.

579. *a thousand bleeding Hearts:* Dryden's addition, based on Ruaeus's note on l. 416: 'Tacitus I. 2 de sacris Paphiæ Veneris. . . . *Sanguinem aræ offundere vetitum, precibus et igne puro altaria adolentur.*'

898. *Jars of gen'rous Wne,* &c. Translating 'laetitiamque Dei' (l. 636) with Ruaeus's note: 'Vinum; lætitiam Dei, id est, Bacchi.'

980. *in order sate the rest*: 'stratoque super discumbitur ostro' (l. 700). 'This, I confess, is improperly Translated; and according to the Modern Fashion of sitting at Table. But the ancient Custom of lying on Beds, had not been understood by the Unlearn'd Reader' (Dryden's note).

The Second Book of the Æneis. (Page 1091.) 242. *as Calchas did ordain*: translating 'ita digerit omnia Calchas' (l. 182). 'Legunt aliqui *omina*' (Ruaeus).

318. *Four times he struck*: 'quater ipso in limine portae substitit' (ll. 242–3), translated 'three times it stuck' by Denham, whom Dryden follows at many places in this book (see *Denham's Poetical Works*, ed. T. H. Banks, 1928, pp. 161–78). 'Struck' may be a misprint; but it is possible that Dryden, paying little heed to the Latin and recollecting ll. 65–69 *supra*, where 'the clashing sound of Arms' is produced by the striking of a spear against the horse, misread Denham's 'stuck'. He does not elsewhere refer to the *horse* as 'he'.

343. *the Podalyrian Heroe*: Virgil's 'Machaon' (l. 263), 'Æsculapii filius, Podalirii frater' (Ruaeus).

409. *the yellow Year*: 'sata laeta' (l. 306). Dryden imitates Lat. 'annus', the produce of the year.

491. *frequent Funerals*: numerous corpses. Cf. *Annus Mirabilis*, l. 1069, note.

702. *Dodder'd*. See *The Fifth Satyr of Persius*, l. 80, note.

934. *shake*: 'excutere' (l. 686). Scott and Noyes emend to 'slake'.

The Third Book of the Æneis. (Page 1120.) 28. *Enos, nam'd from me*: 'Aeneadasque meo nomen de nomine fingo' (l. 18). Dryden follows Mela (*De Situ Orbis*, ii. 2, cited by Ruaeus) in confusing Aeneia with the Thracian Aenos (Eno).

526–7. *Tack to the Larboord, &c.* These lines are taken, with little alteration, from Lauderdale's translation (ll. 441–2). In the original, Aeneas's instructions are to make for the land and seas on the left and avoid the shores and waters on the right (ll. 412–13). So Dryden's technical language may be paraphrased thus: 'Tack to the left, out to sea and away from the Italian shore; veer southwest towards Sicily, keeping first the Straits of Messina and later the Sicilian coast on your right (star-board)'.

The Fourth Book of the Æneis. (Page 1144.) 196. *A flow'rd Cymarr*. See *Fables*, 'The Flower and the Leaf', ll. 341–3, note.

198. *a Golden Caul*: 'crines nodantur in aurum' (l. 138), which Ruaeus glosses 'in reticulum aurei contextûs implexi crines'. Dryden's use of 'caul' is archaistic, here and in *Fables*, 'Ceyx and Alcyone', l. 394. Cf. 'a skelliton, and, about the skull, an antient caul, which was a sort of cap or cornet that women wore formerly' (*OED*, 1697).

376. *the steerage of his Wings*: an imitation of the Virgilian 'remigium alarum' (*Aen.* vi. 19). Cf. *Fables*, 'Ceyx and Alcyone', l. 351.

496. *Delphian Oracle*: 'Gryneus Apollo' (l. 345). Dryden has misread a reference to Delos in Ruaeus's commentary.

631. *My Death shall glut the Hatred of his Brest*: 'quam mihi cum dederit, cumulatam morte remittam' (l. 436). Ruaeus annotates: 'Et sensus est: *Hoc beneficium moræ paulò longioris, hanc gratiam extremam cùm mihi contulerit; remittam illum, dimittam, sinam abire, et mortem meam quasi cumulum votis ejus adjiciam.* Estque hæc amantum locutio, qui perfidis amantibus munus conferre morte suâ existimant.' Dryden's version in 97 is taken verbatim from Lauderdale (l. 468).

855. Dryden does not translate 'infelix Dido, nunc te fata impia tangunt' (l. 596, Ruaeus). In his note to l. 944 *infra*, he says: 'I should have added a Note on that former Verse . . . Which in the Edition of *Heinsius* is thus Printed. *Nunc te facta impia tangunt?* The word *facta* instead of *fata*, is reasonably alter'd. For *Virgil* says afterwards, she dy'd not by Fate, nor by any deserv'd Death. *Nec Fato, meritâ nec morte peribat*, &c. When I Translated that Passage, I doubted of the Sense: And therefore omitted that *Hemystic*; *Nunc te fata impia tangunt*. . . .'

944–7. *and must I die*, &c. 'This is certainly the Sense of *Virgil*; on which I have paraphras'd, to make it plain. His Words are these;

> *Moriemur Inultæ?*
> *Sed Moriamur ait; sic, sic juvat ire sub Umbras.*

. . . Mr. *Cowley* . . . wou'd retrench the latter part of the Verse, and leave it a *Hemystic*. . . . That *Virgil* never intended to have left any *Hemystic*, I have prov'd already in the *Preface*. That this Verse was fill'd up by him, with these words, *sic, juvat ire sub Umbras*, is very probable; if we consider the weight of them. For this procedure of *Dido*, does not only contain, that *dira Execratio, quæ nullo expiatur Carmine* (as *Horace* observes in his *Canidia*) but besides that, *Virgil*, who is full of Allusions to History, under another Name, describes the *Decii*, devoting themselves to *Death* this way, though in a better Cause, in order to the Destruction of the Enemy. The Reader, who will take the pains to Consult *Livy*, in his accurate Description of those *Decii*, thus devoting themselves, will find a great resemblance betwixt these two Passages. . . . *Dido* only doubts whether she shou'd die before she had taken her Revenge, which she rather wish'd: But considering that this devoting her self was the most certain and infallible way of compassing her Vengeance, she thus exclaims;

> *Sic, sic juvat ire sub umbras:*
> *Hauriat hunc oculis ignem crudelis ab alto*
> *Dardanus, & nostræ secum ferat omina mortis*.' [ll. 660–2.]

(Dryden's note). On the allusion to Cowley, see Dedication of the *Æneis*, l. 2055, note.

The Fifth Book of the Æneis. (Page 1170.) 115–16. *Thus riding*, &c. An expansion of 'incendebat' (l. 88). Cf. *Fables*, 'The Flower and the Leaf', ll. 261–3; Spenser, *The Faerie Queene*, III. i. 5; 'His fomy steed, whose fierie feete did burne | The verdant grasse.'

373–475. Dryden contributed a version of this episode to *Sylvæ* (1685), here collated (*S*). See *The Works of Virgil*, introductory note.

404. *a Silver'd, studded Ax*: 'caelatamque argento . . . bipennem' (l. 307). Scott's emendation has the support of 'With Silver studded' in *Sylvæ*; but the later (and more difficult) reading of *97* and *98* seems to have been introduced in the light of Ruaeus's paraphrase, 'securim *tectam* cælato argento'.

782. *Which Troy, the Youths the Trojan Troop, they name.* A clumsy translation of 'Troiaque nunc pueri, Troianum dicitur agmen' (l. 602). 'Lusus ipse, quem vulgo pyrrhicham appellant, Troia vocatur' (Servius).

917. *wast*: the middle of the upper deck, between the quarter-deck and the forecastle. Cf. Sidney, *Arcadia*, II. xxiv. 5: 'already [the fire] did embrace and devoure from the sterne, to the wast of the Ship.'

The Sixth Book of the Æneis. (Page 1201.) 285. *glittering Shadow.* Cf. l. 297 *infra*; Spenser, *The Faerie Queene*, I. xi. 14 ('glaring lampes . . . that made a dreadfull shade') and I. i. 14:

> his glistring armor made
> A little glooming light, much like a shade.

416. *Eyes, like hollow Furnaces on Fire*: 'stant lumina flamma' (l. 300). Dryden's simile brings out the meaning of 'stant' through Ruaeus's gloss: 'oculi *pleni* sunt igne'.

461. *Amidst the Spirits Palinurus press'd.* Cf. *The Second Part of Absalom and Achitophel*, l. 310.

668. *Dishonest*: disgraceful, translating 'inhonesto vulnere' (l. 497). Cf. *Absalom and Achitophel*, l. 72.

733–4. *Lo to the secret Shadows*, &c.: 'discedam, explebo numerum reddarque tenebris' (l. 545). 'These two Verses in *English* seem very different from the *Latine* . . . Yet they are the Sense of *Virgil*; at least, according to the common Interpretation of this place: I will withdraw from your Company; retire to the Shades, and perform my Penance of a Thousand Years. But I must confess the Interpretation of those two words, *explebo numerum* is somewhat Violent, if it be thus understood, *minuam numerum*; that is, I will lessen your Company by my departure. For *Deiphobus* being a Ghost, can hardly be said to be of their Number. Perhaps the Poet means by *explebo numerum, absolvam sententiam*: As if *Deiphobus* reply'd to the *Sibil*, who was angry at his long Visit: I will only take my last leave of *Æneas*, my Kinsman and my Friend, with one hearty good-wish . . . and then leave you to prosecute your Voyage. That Wish is express'd in the words immediately following, *I Decus, I nostrum*, &c. . . . This Conjecture is new, and therefore left to the discretion of the Reader' (Dryden's note).

901–2. *Those who, to worth*, &c. A free translation of 'quique sui memores alios fecere merendo' (l. 664) for an age of patronage.

982. *and both the Radiant Lights*: 'lucentemque globum lunae Titaniaque astra' (l. 725). 'Here the Sun is not express'd, but the Moon only; though a less, and also a less radiant Light. Perhaps the Copies of *Virgil* are all false; and

that instead of *Titaniaque Astra*, he writ *Titanaque & Astra*; and according to those words I have made my *Translation*. 'Tis most certain, that the Sun ought not to be omitted . . .' (Dryden's note).

1156. *Great Cato*. 'There is no Question but *Virgil* here means *Cato* Major, or the *Censor*. But the Name of *Cato* being also mention'd in the Eighth *Æneid*, I doubt whether he means the same Man in both places. I have said in the Preface, that our Poet was of Republican Principles. . . . *Montaign* thinks this [in Book viii] was *Cato* the *Utican*, the great Enemy of Arbitrary Power, and a profess'd Foe to *Julius Cæsar*. *Ruæus* wou'd perswade us that *Virgil* meant the Censor. But why shou'd the Poet name *Cato* twice, if he intended the same person? Our Author is too frugal of his Words and Sense, to commit Tautologies in either . . .' (Dryden's note). Cf. Dedication of the *Æneis*, ll. 429 ff.

1221. *A new Marcellus shall arise in thee*: 'tu Marcellus eris' (l. 883). 'How unpoetically and baldly had this been translated; *Thou shalt* Marcellus *be!* Yet some of my Friends were of Opinion, that I mistook the Sense of *Virgil* . . .' (Dryden's note). He rejects the interpretations 'if you break through your hard Destiny, so as to be born, you shall be call'd *Marcellus*', and 'you shall be the same *Marcellus* by the Transmigration of his Soul'; and argues that much less than the required thousand years between death and transmigration had elapsed between the death of 'the first *Marcellus*' and the time of Virgil. 'By which 'tis plain, that *Virgil* cannot mean the same *Marcellus*; but one of his *Descendants*; Whom I call a new *Marcellus*; who so much resembled his Ancestor . . . that *Virgil* cries out, *quantum instar in ipso est!* which I have translated, *How like the former, and almost the same* [l. 1195].'

The Seventh Book of the Æneis. (Page 1233.) 90–91. *whose holy Hair*, &c.: 'sacra comam multosque metu servata per annos' (l. 60). Cf. Donne, *The Progresse of the Soule*, xvi; Benlowes, *Theophila*, XII. lxxii, 'full-hair'd trees', and XIII. ii, 'to barb the flow'ry tresses of the verdant plains'.

104–5. *From the same parts*, &c.: 'partes petere agmen easdem | partibus ex isdem' (ll. 69–70). 'Apes è Tyrrheni maris partibus venerant Laurentum, insederant lauri apicem: quo significabatur, exteros Tyrrheno mari venturos, victores futuros, summum imperium adepturos' (Ruaeus).

367. *One only Daughter*. 'This has seem'd to some an odd Passage: That a King shou'd offer his Daughter and Heir, to a Stranger Prince, and a wanderer, before he had seen him. . . . But these Criticks have not well consider'd the Simplicity of former times; when the Heroines almost courted the Marriage of illustrious Men. . . . Fathers, in those ancient Ages, considering Birth and Vertue, more than Fortune, in the placing of their Daughters. . . . The contrary of which being now practis'd, I dare not say in our Nation, but in *France*, has not a little darken'd the Lustre of their Nobility' (Dryden's note).

478. *wicker*: *OED*, citing this line and Jonson's 'the scritching Owle . . . flutters with her wicker wings' (*The Sad Shepherd*, I. v), suggests that the word describes 'various sinister creatures'. But it may signify no more than pliancy.

724. *The Clowns, a boist'rous, rude, ungovern'd Crew*: 'indomiti agricolae' (l. 521). See *Fables*, 'Cymon and Iphigenia', ll. 399–408, note.

839. *Carrhæ's bloody Plain*. The detail is added from Lauderdale, l. 604. Ruaeus mentions Crassus, who was killed near Carrhae while fighting the Parthians.

909. *smoaks*. See *Sylvæ*, 'Translation of . . . the Third Book of Lucretius', l. 211, note.

1010. *demi-Launces*: 'aclydes' (l. 730), 'vel exigua missilia . . . vel clavæ breves' (Ruaeus). The demi-lance, a short-shafted weapon, was outmoded by Dryden's time.

1111. *Caul*: 'fibula' (l. 815). See *Æneis*, iv. 198, note.

The Eighth Book of the Æneis. (Page 1262.) 36. *Species*: the sun's reflected rays.

234. *Treat*: a gratuitous entertainment or feast.

254. *indigested*: chaotic, confused.

473–4. *They view'd*, &c.: 'armenta videbant | Romanoque foro et lautis mugire Carinis' (ll. 360–1). Dryden draws out the satiric implications. Cf. Flatman, *Poems and Songs* (1686; Saintsbury, iii), 'The Review', vi.

484–538. Dryden contributed a version of this episode to *Sylvæ* (1685), here collated (*S*). See *The Works of Virgil*, introductory note.

825, 901. *beamy*. See *The Third Book of the Georgics*, l. 625, note.

923. *Fool as she was*. Dryden misses the point of Virgil's 'nefas' (l. 688; Ruaeus interprets 'proh scelus!'), which expresses the Roman revulsion at Antony's relations with a barbarian woman.

The Ninth Book of the Æneis. (Page 1288.) 219–600. Dryden contributed a version of this episode to *Sylvæ* (1685), here collated (*S*). See *The Works of Virgil*, introductory note.

515. *belay*: beleaguer, obstruct with armed men.

588. *bor'd*: thrust out of the course. A stable term; cf. *The Third Book of the Georgics*, l. 438, note.

853–4. 'The first of these Lines, is all of Monosyllables; and both Verses are very rough: But of choice; for it had been easie for me to have smooth'd them. But either my Ear deceives me, or they express the thing which I intended in their Sound: For the stress of a Bow which is drawn to the full extent, is express'd in the harshness of the first Verse, clogg'd not only with Monosyllables, but with Consonants; and these words, the tough *Eugh*, which conclude the second line, seem as forceful, as they are Unharmonious. *Homer* and *Virgil* are both frequent in their adapting Sounds to the thing they signifie . . .' (Dryden's note).

970. *Flaw*. Cf. *Threnodia Augustalis*, ll. 31–33, note.

1094. *rash'd*: slashed. Cf. Spenser, *The Faerie Queene*, v. iii. 8: 'Rashing off helmes, and ryuing plates a sonder.'

1095. *falsify'd*. 'When I read this *Æneid* to many of my Friends, in company together, most of them quarrel'd at the word falsify'd, as an Innovation in our Language. The fact is confess'd; for I remember not to have read it in any *English* Author; though perhaps it may be found in *Spencer's Fairy Queen*: But suppose it be not there: Why am I forbidden to borrow from the *Italian* (a polish'd Language) the word which is wanting in my Native Tongue? *Terence* has often Grecis'd: *Lucretius* has follow'd his Example; and pleaded for it; *sic quia me cogit patrii Sermonis Egestas. Virgil* has confirm'd it by his frequent practice. . . . I use the word falsifie in this place, to mean that the Shield of *Turnus* was not of Proof against the Spears and Javlins of the *Trojans*; which had pierc'd it through and through (as we say) in many places. . . . But I said I borrow'd the Word from the *Italian*: *Vide* Ariosto, *Cant.* 26 [124].

> *Ma si l'Usbergo d'Ambi era perfetto*
> *Che mai poter falsarlo in nessun Canto.*

Falsar cannot otherwise be turn'd, than by falsify'd; for his shield was falsed, is not *English* . . .' (Dryden's note). Cf. *Annus Mirabilis,* 'An account of the ensuing Poem', l. 175; Dedication of the *Æneis,* ll. 2166–86.

    The Tenth Book of the Æneis. (Page 1320.) 10. *Fate*: determination of the gods. Cf. *Æneis,* vii. 405.

    149–50. *So Winds,* &c. Virgil has 'ceu flamina prima | cum deprensa fremunt silvis' (ll. 97–98). Dryden takes his conceit from Cowley; see *Mac Flecknoe,* ll. 76–77, note.

    312. *A Choir of Nereids,* &c. 'These were transform'd from Ships to Sea-Nymphs: This is almost as violent a Machine, as the death of *Aruns* by a Goddess in the *Episode* of *Camilla.* But the Poet makes use of it with greater Art: For here it carries on the main Design. These new made Divinities, not only tell *Æneas* what had pass'd in his Camp . . . but warn him to provide for Battel the next day, and fore-tell him good success: So that this *Episodical* Machine is properly a part of the great Poem. . . . Whereas the Machine relating to *Camilla,* is only Ornamental' (Dryden's note). Cf. Dedication of the *Æneis,* ll. 1515 ff.

    417. *Stretcher*: 'a sort of staff fixed athwart the bottom of a boat, for the rower to place his feet against' (Falconer; *OED*).

    662. *Nor I, his mighty Sire, cou'd ward the Blow.* 'I have mention'd this Passage in my Preface to the *Æneis* [ll. 850–71]; to prove, that Fate was superiour to the Gods. . . . Sir *Robert Howard* has since, been pleas'd to send me the concurrent Testimony of *Ovid* [*Meta.* xv. 779–82, 807–17]. . . . *Jupiter* you see is only Library-Keeper, or *Custos Rotulorum* to the Fates' (Dryden's note).

    1015. *unconsummate Night*: 'infectos . . . hymenaeos' (l. 720).

    1020. *beamy.* See *The Third Book of the Georgics,* l. 625, note.

    1071–1313. Dryden contributed a version of this episode to *Sylvæ* (1685), here collated (*S*). See *The Works of Virgil,* introductory note.

    1299–1300. *Nor ask I Life,* &c. See Preface to *Sylvæ,* ll. 166 ff.

1312–13. This couplet, here an inexact translation, is repeated at the close of *Æneis*, xii, where 'disdainful Soul' renders 'vitaque . . . indignata'.

The Eleventh Book of the Æneis. (Page 1355.) 514. *a closs Caballer, and Tongue-valiant Lord*: 'consiliis habitus non futtilis auctor | seditione potens' (ll. 339–40). Dryden's up-to-date satiric version improves on Lauderdale's 'A great Caballer with the giddy Throng' (l. 389). *Tongue-valiant*: cf. *Fables*, 'The First Book of Homer's Ilias', l. 336; ibid., 'The Speeches of Ajax and Ulysses', l. 147; Milton, *Samson Agonistes*, l. 1181, 'Tongue-doughtie Giant'.

942. *drunk with Blood*: 'sanguine in alto' (l. 633). Cf. *Æneis*, ii. 792; and vii. 744, ix. 555, xi. 1176, xii. 563–4.

964. *exerted*: thrust forward: cf. *Sylvæ*, 'Lucretius the Fourth Book', l. 223; *Eleonora*, ll. 164–5; *The Second Book of the Georgics*, l. 596. Dryden's translation of 'unum exserta latus pugnæ' (l. 649) accommodates the related meaning of 'exserta' brought out in Ruaeus's paraphrase: '*nudata* secundùm *unam mammam* ad prælium'.

1184. *ranch'd*: tore; a dialectal nasalized form of 'rased'. Cf. Chapman, *Iliad*, v. 856, 'a javelin ranch'd the flesh'; *Fables*, 'Meleager and Atalanta', l. 140.

The Twelfth Book of the Æneis. (Page 1388.) 55–60. *With what Success*, &c. Translating, rather obscurely, ll. 32–33:

> ex illo qui me casus, quae, Turne, sequantur
> bella, vides, quantos primus patiare labores.

100–7. *At this*, &c. '*Virgil*, though in favour of his Heroe, he never tells us directly, that *Lavinia* preferr'd *Turnus* to *Æneas*, yet has insinuated this preference twice before [see *Æneis*, vii. 538–64; xi. 721–32]. . . . She not only sheds Tears but changes Colour. She had been bred up with *Turnus*, and *Æneas* was wholly a Stranger to her. *Turnus* in probability was her first Love; and favour'd by her Mother, who had the Ascendant over her Father. But I am much deceiv'd, if (besides what I have said) there be not a secret Satire against the Sex, which is lurking under this Description of *Virgil*, who seldom speaks well of Women. . . . This Fable of *Lavinia* includes a secret Moral; that Women in their choice of Husbands, prefer the younger of their Suitors to the Elder; are insensible of Merit, fond of Handsomness; and generally speaking, rather hurried away by their Appetite, than govern'd by their Reason' (Dryden's note).

162. *And meditates*, &c. A detail transferred from *The Third Book of the Georgics*, l. 361.

444. *beamy*. See *The Third Book of the Georgics*, l. 625, note.

540. *Butes*. Ruaeus has 'Buten'; modern editors read 'Asbyten' (l. 362).

563–4. *The Latian Fields are drunk*, &c. Dryden's addition to Virgil's l. 382. Cf. *Æneis*, xi. 942, note.

590. *solliciting the Dart*: a latinism; 'spicula dextra sollicitat' (ll. 403–4). Cf. Pope, *Iliad*, xiii. 749–50, 'good Agenor. . . . The spear sollicits'.

641. *beamy*. See *The Third Book of the Georgics*, l. 625, note.

790. *Cretheus*. 'Cisseus' is an error; Cisseus was already slaughtered (see *Æneis*, x. 442).

808. *Sea-born Messapus, with Atinas*. 'The Poet had said, in the preceding lines, that *Mnestheus*, *Seresthus*, and *Asylas*, led on the *Trojans*, the *Tuscans*, and the *Arcadians*: But none of the Printed Copies, which I have seen, mention any Leader of the *Rutulians* and *Latins*, but *Messapus* the Son of *Neptune*. *Ruæus* takes notice of this passage, and seems to wonder at it; but gives no Reason, why *Messapus* is alone without a Coadjutor. The four Verses of *Virgil* [548–51] run thus.

> *Totæ adeò conversæ acies, omnesque Latini*
> *Omnes Dardanidæ, Mnestheus, acerque Seresthus*
> *Et Messapus equum Domitor, & fortis Asylas,*
> *Tuscorumque Phalanx, Evandrique Arcadis alæ.*

I doubt not but the third Line was Originally thus, *Et Messapus equum domitor, & fortis Atinas:* For the two Names of *Asylas* and *Atinas* are so like, that one might easily be mistaken for the other by the Transcribers. And to fortify this Opinion, we find afterward, in the relation of *Sages* to *Turnus*, that *Atinas* is join'd with *Messapus* [ll. 661–2]' (Dryden's note).

1093. *beamy*. See *The Third Book of the Georgics*, l. 625, note.

1313. *the sickly Fancy*, &c.: 'in somnis' (l. 908). See *Fables*, 'The Cock and the Fox', ll. 325–41, note.

Postscript To the Reader. (Page 1424.) 24–29. *One is for raking in Chaucer*, &c. Cf. Preface to *Fables*, ll. 542–7.

37. *Cynthius Aurem vellit, & admonuit.* Virgil, *Ecl.* vi. 3–4.

50. *the Earls of Darby and of Peterborough*: William Stanley (1655?–1702), ninth Earl of Derby, a subscriber to the *Virgil*; and Charles Mordaunt (1658–1735), third Earl of Peterborough, a soldier-statesman and a leading supporter of William of Orange. Peterborough was 'the first of all the *English* Nobility that came over openly to see the Prince of *Orange*. . . . He was with the Prince in 1686: And then he pressed him to undertake the business of *England*: And he represented the matter as so easy, that this appeared too romantical to the Prince to build upon it' (Burnet, i. 762).

60. *Sir William Trumball* (1639–1716), ambassador, and a secretary of state 1695–7. He told Pope that Dryden's 'personal Qualities were as amiable as his poetical' (Pope, Letter to Wycherley, 26 December 1704); but there is little evidence of his friendship with Dryden. He was something of a man of letters (see *HMC Downshire*, i. 922–3).

65–66. *Extremum hunc Arethusa*, &c. Virgil, *Ecl.* x. 1, 3.

68. *Gilbert Dolben* (1658–1722), barrister and Member of Parliament for

Peterborough, and a friend of Trumbull's. On his father, see *Absalom and Achitophel*, l. 868, note.

71. *the Dolphins*, Ruaeus's edition. See *The Works of Virgil*, introductory note.

72. *Fabrini*: Giovanni Fabrini, author of an Italian translation and commentary on Virgil published at Venice in 1604 and 1623.

75. *Sir William Bowyer* (1639–1722), a Cambridge friend who entered Trinity College two years after Dryden. 'Nature has conspir'd with Art', says Dryden in his note to *The Second Book of the Georgics*, 'to make the Garden at *Denham-Court*, of Sir *William's* own Plantation, one of the most delicious Spots of Ground in *England*'; and he seems to have spent much time there. Cf. Ward, p. 92.

82. *the Earl of Exeter*: John Cecil (1648–1700), fifth Earl, and owner of Burghley House, near Stamford-Baron in Northamptonshire. See *The Journeys of Celia Fiennes*, ed. C. Morris, 1947, pp. 68–70.

87. *Will. Walsh*. See Dedication of *The Satires of Juvenalis*, l. 2572, note.

90. *the Duke of Shrewsbury*: Charles Talbot (1660–1718), twelfth Earl and only Duke of Shrewsbury, who was influential in the Revolution of 1688, and became an important member of William's administration. 'He seemed to be a man of great probity', with 'no ordinary measure of learning, a correct judgment, with a sweetness of temper that charmed all who knew him' (Burnet, i. 762–3).

101 8. '*Amor omnibus idem*: Or, the Force of *Love* in all *Creatures*' appeared in *Examen Poeticum* (1693), and Addison's version of *Georgics* iv in *The Annual Miscellany* (1694). On the other translations see Dedication of the *Æneis*, ll. 1845–50, note.

111. *Dr. Guibbons, and Dr. Hobbs*. See *The Third Satyr of Persius*, l. 126, note; *Threnodia Augustalis*, l. 188, note.

113. *the only one*, &c. Blackmore. See Preface to *Fables*, l. 663, note.

117. *the few Notes which follow*, &c. Writing to Tonson early in 1696, Dryden says: 'I am not sorry that you will not allow any thing towards the Notes; for to make them good, wou'd have cost me half a yeares time at least. Those I write shall be onely Marginall to help the unlearned, who understand not the poeticall Fables. The Prefaces, as I intend them, will be somewhat more learned' (Ward, pp. 80–81).

Alexander's Feast; Or The Power of Musique. An Ode, In Honour of St. Cecilia's Day
(Page 1428)

On 3 September 1697 Dryden told his sons in a letter: 'I am writing a Song for St Cecilia's feast, who you know is the Patroness of Musique. This is troublesome, & no way beneficiall: But I coud not deny the Stewards of the feast, who came in a body to me, to desire that kindness' (Ward, p. 93; see

A Song for St Cecilia's Day, 1687, note). There is an eighteenth-century story that Bolingbroke found Dryden one morning 'in an unusual agitation of spirits', having completed the ode at one sitting overnight; but Johnson's report that 'he spent a fortnight in composing and correcting' is more credible (Johnson, i. 388 and note). *Alexander's Feast* was performed on 22 November, with music (now lost) by Jeremiah Clarke, and published by Tonson. There were other performances in December (Day, p. 182). Dryden wrote to Tonson in December: 'I am glad to heare from all Hands, that my Ode is esteemd the best of all my poetry, by all the Town: I thought so my self when I writ it but being old, I mistrusted my own Judgment. I hope it has done you service, & will do more' (Ward, p. 98).

Dryden has combined the traditional story of Timotheus and Alexander with the amour of Alexander and Thais, to illustrate the doctrine of the complex psychological 'effect' of music. See James Kinsley, 'Dryden and the *Encomium Musicae*', *RES,* N.S., iv (1953), 263–7.

9. *Thais.* Dryden asked Tonson in a letter to 'remember in the Copy of Verses for St. Cecilia, to alter the name of Lais, wch is twice there, for Thais; those two Ladyes were Contemporaryes, wch caused that small mistake' (Ward, p. 96).

30. *Olympia:* Olympias, the mother of Alexander. She claimed that he was the son, not of Philip of Macedon, but of a supernatural serpent. This claim added weight to the belief in Alexander's divine origin, and he himself demanded worship as a god. Cf. *Fables,* 'To my Honour'd Kinsman', ll. 160–3, and 'The Cock and the Fox', ll. 659–60.

52. *honest:* glorious.

170. *She drew an Angel down.* See *A Song for St Cecilia's Day, 1687,* ll. 53–54, note.

To Mr. Granville, on his Excellent Tragedy, call'd Heroick Love

(Page 1433)

George Granville (1667–1735), created Lord Landsdowne in 1711, was a friend of Dryden and Pope. *Heroick Love: A Tragedy* was first performed at Lincoln's Inn Fields at the end of 1697, and published in the following year (advertised in the *London Gazette,* 17–21 February 1698).

In 1695 Betterton and many of the prominent actors seceded from the united company at Drury Lane (see Prologue and Epilogue *To the King and Queen,* note) and were granted a licence to reopen the old theatre in Lincoln's Inn Fields. On the subsequent rivalry between the theatres, see Nicoll, pp. 334–42. Dryden's allusions here to the 'war' provoked a reply by the Drury Lane actor George Powell, in the Preface to *The Fatal Discovery* (see Macdonald, p. 288).

5–6. *With less regret,* &c. 'Here I am afraid, he makes him but a course Compliment, when this great Wit, with his Treacherous Memory, forgets that he had given away his Lawrels upon Record no less then twice before, *viz.* once to Mr. *Congreve,* and another time to Mr. *Southern.* Pr'ithee, old *Oedipus,* expound this Mystery' (Preface to *The Fatal Discovery*). See *To Mr. Southern* and *To my Dear Friend, Mr. Congreve.*

21–22. *And in Despair,* &c. Cf. *To Mr. Southern,* ll. 11–12.

24. *Murd'ring Plays, which they miscal Reviving.* This, says Powell, is Dryden's 'most mortal Stroke at us'. ''Tis true, his more particular Pique against us, as he has declared himself, is in relation to our reviving his *Almanzor.*' Plays produced at Drury Lane in 1696–1701 are listed in Hotson, pp. 377–9, and Nicoll, pp. 337–8.

32. *Where thine,* &c. Cf. *The Hind and the Panther,* i. 77.

To my Friend, the Author [Peter Motteux]
(Page 1434)

Peter Anthony Motteux (1663–1718), a French Huguenot, settled in England in 1685. He edited *The Gentleman's Journal,* 1692–4 (see Macdonald, pp. 272–3), completed Urquhart's translation of Rabelais (1693–4), and published a translation of *Don Quixote* (1700–3). See R. N. Cunningham, *Peter Anthony Motteux,* 1933. *Beauty in Distress. A Tragedy,* his fifth play, was first performed *c.* April 1698 at Lincoln's Inn Fields and published in the following summer (advertised in the *London Gazette,* 16–20 June). Dryden's epistle is a contribution to the vindication of the stage against Collier (see Preface to *Fables,* l. 132, note; Epilogue to *The Pilgrim;* Dennis, i. 466–70).

19. *Rebellion,* &c. 'Rebellion is as the sin of witchcraft' (1 Sam. xv. 23).

44. *Their Tongue infeebled, is refin'd so much.* Cf. Dedication of the *Æneis,* ll. 1739–41, note, ll. 2026–9.

Fables Ancient and Modern; Translated into Verse, from Homer, Ovid, Boccace, & Chaucer; with Original Poems
(Page 1437)

On Candlemas Day, 1699, Dryden wrote to Mrs. Steward: 'In the mean time, betwixt my intervalls of physique and other remedies which I am useing for my gravell, I am still drudging on: always a Poet, and never a good one. I pass my time sometimes with Ovid, and sometimes with our old English poet, Chaucer; translating such stories as best please my fancy; and intend besides them to add somewhat of my own: so that it is not impossible, but ere the summer be pass'd, I may come down to you with a volume in my hand, like a dog out of the water, with a duck in his mouth' (Ward, p. 109); and on 20 March 1699 Tonson agreed to pay two hundred and fifty guineas 'in consideration of ten thousand verses . . . whereof seaven thousand five hundred verses, more or lesse, are allready in the said Jacob Tonson's possession' (Malone, I. i. 560). But in December 'my Book is printing, & my Bookseller makes no hast' (Ward, p. 130), and the *Fables* did not appear till March 1700. Dryden was delighted with its reception: 'The Ladies of the Town . . . like my last Book of Poems, better than any thing they have formerly seen of mine' (ibid., p. 135). The epigraph is *Aen.* v. 55–57.

To His Grace The Duke of Ormond. James Butler (1665–1745), second Duke, was the second son of Thomas, Earl of Ossory, and succeeded his grandfather as Duke of Ormonde in 1688. He conducted himself with distinction in the Netherlands campaigns, particularly at Landen in 1693 (see *HMC Ormonde*, N.S., viii, pp. vii–xxxiii). For Dryden's tributes to his family, see *Absalom and Achitophel*, ll. 817 ff. and notes.

52. *Poplicola*, Publius Valerius.

92. αἰδέομαι Τρῶας: *Iliad*, vi. 442, xxii. 105; Cicero, *ad Atticum*, ii. 5.

109. *Numen commune*, &c. Claudian, *De Raptu Proserpinae*, i. 89–91.

132. *The Ulysses of Ovid*: *Meta.* xiii. 291 ff.

149. *Spatiis exclusus iniquis*: *Georgics*, iv. 147.

173. *Non ignara mali miseris, succurrere disco*: *Aen.* i. 630.

176. *de meliore luto*: Juvenal, *Sat.* xiv. 35.

177–8. *Teucri pulcherrima proles*, &c. *Aen.* vi. 648–9.

202–3. *Ostendunt*, &c. *Aen.* vi. 869–70.

Preface. 7. *a certain Nobleman*: probably George Villiers, Duke of Buckingham (see *Absalom and Achitophel*, l. 544, note). He 'fell into a new way of expence in building, in that sort of architecture which Cicero calls, *Insanae substructiones*; and himself, when his friends dissuaded him from it, called it his folly' (Brian Fairfax; *The Rehearsal*, ed. Arber, 1902, p. 8). On his house at Cliveden, see Evelyn, *Diary*, 23 July 1679.

27. *Sandys*. See Preface to *Ovid's Epistles*, ll. 1–3, note.

28–33. Edward Fairfax's translation of Tasso, *Godfrey of Bulloigne, or The Recoverie of Jerusalem*, was first printed in 1600. He survived both Spenser and Queen Elizabeth by more than thirty years. On Waller's discipleship, cf. Fenton, *Works of Waller*, 1744 edn., p. xxx).

32. *Milton was the Poetical Son of Spencer*. Cf. Dedication of *The Satires of Juvenalis*, ll. 382, 2563–7.

34. *the Soul of Chaucer*. See the passage on 'Dan *Chaucer*, well of English vndefyled' in *The Faerie Queene*, IV. ii. 32–34:

> . . . through infusion sweete
> Of thine owne spirit, which doth in me surviue,
> I follow here the footing of thy feete.

Cf. *To the Pious Memory Of . . . Mrs Anne Killigrew*, ll. 23 ff.

58. *according to Mr. Hobbs*. *Leviathan*, I. iii, beginning 'By *Consequence*, or TRAYNE of Thoughts. . . .'

72–76. Rymer, *A Short View of Tragedy* (1693), p. 78: '*Chaucer* found an Herculean labour on his Hands; And did perform to Admiration. He seizes all Provencal, French or Latin that came in his way, gives them a new garb and livery, and mingles them amongst our English.' Cf. Dedication of *Examen Poeticum*, ll. 99–115, note.

112. *Dead-colouring*: a preparatory layer of colour. Cf. Prologue to *Secret-Love*, l. 7.

128. *Versus inopes rerum*, &c. *De Arte Poetica*, l. 322.

132. *a Religious Lawyer*: Jeremy Collier (1650–1726), a country clergyman who came up to London in 1685 and was appointed lecturer at Gray's Inn. In the controversy which followed his *Short View of the Immorality, and Profaneness of the English Stage; Together with the Sense of Antiquity upon this Argument* (1698), Dryden's part was slight; he recognized the general validity of Collier's charges. Cf. *infra*, ll. 704 ff.; *To the Pious Memory Of . . . Mrs Anne Killigrew*, ll. 56 ff.; *To My Friend, the Author* (Motteux); *infra*, 'Cymon and Iphigenia', ll. 1–41; Epilogue to *The Pilgrim*; Dennis, i. 466–70.

137–43. *my Intentions*, &c. In 1684 Dryden told Tonson that 'Homer shall sleep on for me'; but in 1699, encouraged by the reception of the *Virgil*, he was taking a different attitude: 'My thoughts at present are fixd on Homer: And by my translation of the first Iliad; I find him a Poet more according to my Genius than Virgil: and consequently hope I may do him more justice, in his fiery way of writeing. . . . Since 'tis for my Country's honour as well as for my own, that I am willing to undertake this task; I despair not of being encouragd in it' (Ward, pp. 23, 121).

170–4. *Mr. Hobbs*, &c. Hobbes (born 1588) translated the *Odyssey* in 1673–5 and the *Iliad* in 1676 (published together in 1677). His late experiments in poetry were perhaps more fortunate than his ventures in mathematics. He had 'long followed the Court, and passed there for a mathematical man, tho' he really knew little that way' (Burnet, i. 187; cf. Aubrey, pp. 150–1). For his controversy with the mathematicians, see G. C. Robertson, *Hobbes*, 1886, pp. 167 ff. The preface to his translations is a short treatise 'Concerning the Vertues of an Heroique poem'. The first virtue mentioned is 'contained in the choice of words', but Hobbes does not argue that it is more important than the others, or the first to be considered in criticism.

192–6. *Achilles . . . Æneas*. Horace, *De Arte Poetica*, l. 121; Virgil, *Aen.* v. 709.
202. *Longinus*: xii. 4–5.
219. *The Manners*, &c. Cf. Preface to *Ovid's Epistles*, ll. 66 ff.
222. *Philology*: the study of literature, polite learning.
228–36. *most of Chaucer's Stories*, &c. Doubt was not cast on Chaucer's indebtedness to *Il Decameron* until the nineteenth century. Dryden apparently missed Francis Thynne's observation (1598) that *The Knight's Tale* was taken 'out of the Thesayde of Bocas' (*Animadversions*, ed. F. J. Furnivall, 1875, p. 43). He derives his notion of the source of *Troilus and Criseyde* from Speght's

edition of Chaucer (1598; reprinted, with some change, in 1687). Speght, misled by Lydgate, refers to 'Troilus and Creseid called *Throphe* in the Lumbard tongue, translated; not verbatim, but the Argument thence taken and most cunningly amplified by Chaucer'.

241. *Kings . . . in Debt.* The allusion is doubtless to William III and the national debt (see Clark, pp. 169–70). Cf. Dedication of the *Æneis*, ll. 172–4.

276. *inopem me copia fecit. Meta.* iii. 466. Cf. *Annus Mirabilis*, 'An account of the ensuing Poem', ll. 120–1, note.

280–1. *John Littlewit,* &c. In *Bartholomew Fair,* I. 1, Littlewit enters saying: 'A pretty conceit, and worth the finding! I ha' such luck to spinne out these fine things still, and like a Silke-worme, out of my selfe' (Jonson, vi. 19).

295. *the Turn of Words.* See Dedication of *The Satires of Juvenalis,* l. 2541, note.

313. *One of our late great Poets*: Cowley. See Preface to *Ovid's Epistles,* ll. 244–5, note.

330. *Catullus.* A mistake for Martial, *Epi.* iii. 44.

332. *Tacitus: Orat.* xxi: 'verbis ornata et sententiis, auribus iudicum accommodata'.

337–47. Dryden refers to Speght, who, prompted perhaps by Thynne's strictures on his first edition (1598), added a note in the second (1602): 'And for his verses, although in divers places they may seeme to us to stand of unequall measures: yet a skilfull Reader, that can scan them in their nature, shall find it otherwise. And if a verse here and there fal out a sillable shorter or longer than another, I rather aret it to the negligence and rape of *Adam Scrivener,* that I may speake as *Chaucer* doth, than to any unconning or oversight in the Author.'

358. *dipt in the Rebellion of the Commons.* Usk's *Testament of Love* was regarded as Chaucer's until the nineteenth century, and from it is derived the story of Chaucer's political misdemeanours which Dryden takes over from Speght. 'It seemeth', says Speght, 'that he was in some trouble in the daies of King Richard the second, as it may appeare in the Testament of Love: where hee doth greatly complaine of his owne rashnesse in following the multitude, and of their hatred against him for bewraying their purpose.'

360. *was well with Henry the Fourth.* Chaucer survived Richard II by less than a year; but the annuity granted to him by Richard was renewed and increased by Henry IV.

370–2. *As for the Religion of our Poet,* &c. The *Plowman's Tale* was generally regarded as Chaucer's until Tyrwhitt rejected it in his edition of 1775. Speght introduces the *Tale* thus: 'A complaint against the pride and couetousnesse of the Cleargie: made no doubt by Chaucer with the rest of the Tales. For I have seene it in written hand in Iohn Stowes library in a booke of suche antiquity, as seemeth to have beene written neare to Chaucer's time.'

406. *Dr. Drake*: James Drake (1667–1707), medical practitioner and political

pamphleteer, to whom is ascribed *The Antient and Modern Stages survey'd. Or Mr. Collier's View . . . Set in a True Light*, 1699.

411. *Prior læsit*: Terence, *Eunuchus*, prol. 6.

428. *Baptista Porta*: Giovanni Battista della Porta (*c.* 1538–1615), whose *De Humana Physiognomonia* (1586) was the standard treatise on physiognomy.

442. *Choice*: perhaps a misprint for 'Chace' (Nichol Smith).

468–85. *But first*, &c. Prologue to *The Canterbury Tales*, ll. 725–42. Dryden's quotations and the text of the tales which he prints at the end of the *Fables* are drawn, with some alterations, from Speght's *Chaucer* (1687).

497–8. *Wincing she was*, &c. *The Miller's Tale*; *CT* (A), ll. 3263–4.

503. *not worth receiving*. Editors amend to 'not worth reviving'; but 'receiving' is retained in the 1713 edition, and the phrase may be understood as 'not worth taking trouble over'.

503. *the late Earl of Leicester*: Philip Sidney, third Earl (1619–98), who was highly favoured in Cromwell's service as Lord Lisle, and retired from public life at the Restoration. He succeeded to the title in 1677, and in his old age entertained literary men and provided a patronage which Dryden celebrates in the Dedication of *Don Sebastian*.

534–6. *There saw I Danè*, &c. *The Knight's Tale*; *CT* (A), ll. 2062–4.

539. *Milbourn*. See *infra*, l. 663, note.

542–7. *They suppose*, &c. Cf. *The Works of Virgil*, 'Postscript To the Reader', ll. 24–29.

555–7. *multa renascentur*, &c. Horace, *De Arte Poetica*, ll. 70–72.

558. *I have that reasonable Veneration*, &c. With this balanced attitude to archaism, cf. Dedication of *The Satires of Juvenalis*, ll. 383–92.

571. *some old Saxon Friends*. The 'profluvium of Saxonists' at Oxford were making substantial contributions to Anglo-Saxon scholarship in the last decades of the seventeenth century. Their leader was George Hickes, whose *Institutiones Grammaticae Anglo-Saxonicae* was published at Oxford in 1689, followed by his great *Thesaurus* in 1705. Prominent among them were Edmund Gibson, who edited the *Anglo-Saxon Chronicle* (1692), and Edward Thwaites, editor of the *Heptateuch* (1698). Which of them were Dryden's friends is unknown. He need not be taken, as by Ker, to refer to Rymer.

581. *Grandam Gold*. See *The Hind and the Panther*, iii. 149, note.

592. *Mademoiselle de Scudéry* was more than ninety in 1700; and Dryden's information is unlikely to be accurate. There is no trace of a version in medieval French—Dryden's 'old *Provencal*'—and nothing is known of any French translation of Chaucer until the nineteenth century.

652. *Dioneo e Fiametta*, &c. *Il Decameron*, VII. x, epilogue.

663. *one M——*: Luke Milbourne (1649–1720), at this time rector of Osmandiston, Norfolk, and lecturer of St. Leonard, Shoreditch. His translation of *Aen.* i (1687) had no success; and when Dryden's *Virgil* appeared, he attacked it acridly in *Notes . . . In a Letter to a Friend* (1698), adding his own

2064   *Commentary*

version of *Georgics*, i, for comparison. He ended: 'If I have turn'd Mr. *D*'s harsh words sometimes upon himself, he may remember, that besides his *Brother Poets*, he never spar'd a Clergyman, which perhaps might make the Hands the rougher of *Your Humble Servant*.' 'His outrages seem to be the ebullitions of a mind agitated by stronger resentment than bad poetry can excite, and previously resolved not to be pleased' (Johnson, i. 449).

    one B——: Sir Richard Blackmore (*c.* 1655–1729), the 'City Bard, or Knight Physician', was knighted by William III and appointed a court physician in 1697. His *Prince Arthur. An Heroick Poem. In Ten Books* (1695) contained a criticism of lewd poets in the preface, and 'a libel' on Dryden as one of the needy poets who throng the gate of the charitable Dorset (p. 167):

> *Laurus* amidst the meagre Crowd appear'd,
> An old, revolted, unbelieving Bard,
> Who throng'd, and shov'd, and prest, and would be heard.
> Distinguish'd by his louder craving Tone,
> So well to all the Muses Patrons known,
> He did the Voice of modest Poets drown.

Blackmore returned to the attack in *A Satyr against Wit* (1700); and Dryden retaliated in *To My Honour'd Kinsman, John Driden* (ll. 83 ff.) and in the Prologue to *The Pilgrim* (ll. 16 ff.). Tom Brown ridicules Blackmore as 'the worshipful graduate in the noble art of manslaughter': 'whatever you do, you must use him as the great ones have done, that is, flatter him and tell him he's the best man at heroics, in the present age, or to rectify your judgment he'll dismiss you with a pill that shall send you to a place where a great many bold tell-truths are gone before you' (*Amusements Serious and Comical*, ed. A. L. Hayward, 1927, pp. 17–18).

    672. *Ogilby*. See *Mac Flecknoe*, l. 102, note.

    694. *his two Poems*: *Prince Arthur*, and *King Arthur* (1697).

    697. *an Epick Poem on King Arthur*. See Dedication of *The Satires of Juvenalis*, ll. 614 ff.

    700. *the Whirl-bats of Eryx. Aen.* v. 400.

    715. *The Zeal of God's House*, &c. Ps. lxix. 9; John ii. 17.

    735–7. At Senef in Flanders, on 11 August 1674, the Prince of Condé pressed his advantage over the Prince of Orange's vanguard too far, and suffered heavy losses.

    743–4. *Demetri*, &c. Horace, *Sat.* I. x. 90–91.

    To Her Grace the Dutchess of Ormond. (Page 1463.) Lady Mary Somerset (1665–1733), eldest surviving daughter of Henry, Marquis of Worcester and first Duke of Beaufort, became Ormonde's second wife in 1685. Her father was created Duke of Beaufort in 1682, 'having been eminently serviceable to the king since his most happy restoration, in consideration thereof and his most noble descent from King Edward III by John de Beaufort, eldest son of John of Gaunt by Catherine Swynford'—an ancestry round which Dryden's fancy plays (ll. 19–31). In the summer of 1697 the duchess and her daughters paid their first visit to the family seat at Kilkenny, in Ireland, where they were welcomed with the enthusiasm which Dryden celebrates. Ormonde joined his family in October, and soon afterwards returned to England. They did not follow till May 1699. See *HMC Ormonde*, N.S., viii, introductory memoir. Derrick was told by some of Dryden's relations 'that his *Fables* obtained five hundred pounds from the dutchess of Ormond, a present not unsuitable to the magnificence of that splendid family' (Johnson, i. 408).

4. *leaves a doubtful Palm.* Cf. Juvenal, *Sat.* xi. 180–1:

> conditor Iliados cantabitur atque Maronis
> altisoni dubiam facientia carmina palmam.

14–18. *And then the fairest*, &c. Scott took these lines to refer to Blanche, wife of John of Gaunt, who was Chaucer's patron. Craik suggested, with better reason, that Dryden is speaking of Joan, Countess of Kent, whose third husband was the Black Prince, and who is 'commonly believed to be the Countess of Salisbury from whom the Order of the Garter, according to the well-known story, derived its name'.

29. *a new Platonick Year*: 'a cycle imagined by some ancient astronomers, in which the heavenly bodies were supposed to go through all their possible movements and return to their original relative positions (after which, according to some, all events would recur in the same order as before)' (*OED*).

48–50. *Portunus*, &c. Cf. *Astræa Redux*, l. 121, note.

51–52. *The Land*, &c. Cf. *Astræa Redux*, l. 253, note.

59. *bear the Reins.* Cf. Virgil, *Georgics*, i. 514: 'fertur equis auriga, neque audit currus habenas'.

70–79. *As when the Dove*, &c. Cf. Prologue to *The Unhappy Favourite*, ll. 1–8.

80–95. *When at Your second Coming*, &c. Cf. Prologue To *The Dutchess*, ll. 26–46.

118–19. *And where, imprison'd*, &c. Cf. Donne, *Of the Progresse of the Soule*, ll. 220–3:

> To'advance these thoughts, remember then, that she,
> She, whose faire body no such prison was,
> But that a Soule might well be pleas'd to passe
> An age in her.

125. *young Vespasian*: Titus Flavius Sabinus Vespasianus, who commanded the siege of Jerusalem, but lamented the destruction of the Temple.

130. *the Table of my Vow.* Sailors who had escaped shipwreck dedicated their garments to Neptune, sometimes with a picture of the event. Cf. Horace, *Od.* I. v. 13, *Sat.* II. i. 33; and Juvenal, *Sat.* xii. 26–28.

131. *Morley*: Christopher Love Morley, M.D., physician and medical writer.

133–4. *As once the Macedon*, &c. Dryden refers to the story of Alexander's dream of 'an Herb which cur'd *Ptolomy*' (cf. *The Second Satyr of Persius*, note 6).

Palamon and Arcite: or, The Knight's Tale, From Chaucer. In Three Books

(Page 1468)

Book I. Dryden's additions to his original here are calculated to heighten the passions of love, anger, and grief in his characters (e.g. details in ll. 40–46, and ll. 213–15, 354–7, 446, 522–3, 556); to reinforce statements and emphasize or extend arguments (e.g. ll. 73–74, 199–200, 278–9, 327–8, 333–4, 416–17, 492–5); and to give new colour, vividness, or precision to descriptive passages (e.g. ll. 114, 153–4, 185–7, 191–4, 220–2, 528–9). See further W. H. Williams, '*Palamon and Arcite* and *The Knight's Tale*', *MLR* ix (1914), 161–72 and 309–23.

89. *skriek'd.* Scott and later editors emend to 'shriek'd'; but cf. Defoe's 'Terrible Shrieks and Skreekings of Women' (*OED*) and Scots 'skriegh'.

109. *Argent Field*: translating 'white baner'. Cf. Earle, *Microcosmographie* (1628), 'A Herald': 'He seemes very rich in discourse, for he tels you of whole fields of gold and siluer, Or and Argent, worth much in French, but in English nothing.'

199–200. *Ev'n wondring Philomel*, &c. Cf. Kynaston, *Cynthiades*, 'To Cynthia on Concealment of her Beauty' (Saintsbury, ii. 160):

> Do not conceal thy heavenly voice,
> Which makes the hearts of gods rejoice,
> Lest Music hearing no such thing,
> The Nightingale forget to sing.

246. *the Dungeon of the Sky.* Here 'Dungeon' may mean simply 'tower'; but Dryden may have known the old astrological use: cf. Lydgate, *The Fall of Princes*, viii. 3102–5:

> Thus of Breteyne translatid was þe sunne
> Vp to þe riche sterri briht dongoun,—
> Astronomeeres weel reherse kunne,—
> Callid Arthuris constellacioun.

342–5. *Like Esop's Hounds*, &c. The new paragraph in *F* is misleading; Arcite's speech continues to l. 351. Dryden is following the paragraphing of Speght's text, which opens less ambiguously with 'We striuen, as did the houndes for the bone'. He quotes Aesop as the source of the story; but the origin of Chaucer's version is unknown. At l. 345, Dryden read 'cur' in Speght, where Chaucer manuscripts have 'kyte' (*CT* (A), l. 1179).

358. *Perithous.* Speght's spelling of 'Pirithous'.

404. *Loves extreamest Line.* W. H. Williams, in *MLR* vi (1911), 386, quotes Terence, *Eunuchus*, l. 640, as Dryden's source:

> saltem hoc licebit. certe extrema linea
> amare haud nil est.

But Dryden, with Terence's phrase in mind, adds the image of the sun of beauty, thinking of 'Line' as the circle of the terrestrial sphere farthest from the path of the sun.

421. *Fortune, Fate, or Providence*: 'Of purveyance of God, or of fortune' (Speght). Dryden's three nouns are not synonyms; they point to the medieval distinction, drawn from Boethius, between *providentia*, 'ipsa illa divina ratio . . . quae cuncta disponit', *fatum*, 'inhaerens rebus mobilibus dispositio per quam providentia suis quaeque nectit ordinibus', and the capricious force *fortuna* (*De Consolatione Philosophiae*, iv. 6 and ii. 1).

500. Dryden extends Chaucer's astrological references. A quartile aspect is the unfavourable relative position of two heavenly bodies which are 90° distant from each other.

522–3. *He rav'd*, &c. Dryden's elaboration (Chaucer, *CT* (A), ll. 1359–60). Cf. Spenser, *The Faerie Queene*, III. x. 17, 'He rau'd, he wept', &c.

539–40. *Uncomb'd his Locks*, &c. Translating 'in his gyre . . . nought comly like to louers malady' (Speght) where modern editors read '. . . nat oonly lyk the loueris maladye' (*CT* (A), ll. 1372–3).

Book II. Dryden's additions provide vivid detail (e.g. ll. 196–7, 532–3, 540–3, 546–7, 571–5), colour (e.g. ll. 27, 245, 619–22), and explanation, emphasis, or rhetorical finish (e.g. ll. 89–91, 149, 220–1, 265–6, 320–3, 656–8, 661–2). Arcite's song is freely embellished (ll. 54–60), and Palamon's speech to Theseus is graced with an apologia (ll. 287–93).

15–17. *A pleasant Beverage*. Chaucer's draught is a 'claree' made of wine, 'nercotikes and opye' (*CT* (A), ll. 1471–2). Dryden specifies the ingredients of 'clary' as he knows it—a mixture of wine, honey, and ginger.

34. *Style*. With this concrete use of 'style' (*stilum vertere*), cf. *The Medall*, ll. 22–23, and Butler, *Hudibras*, II. iii. 202.

42. *licks the dropping Leaves*, &c. Cf. Marvell, *Damon the Mower*, ll. 45–46:

> And, if at Noon my toil me heat,
> The Sun himself licks off my Sweat.

115–18. *Of such a Goddess*, &c. Dryden echoes Carew, *A cruell Mistris*:

> Of such a Goddesse no times leave record,
> That burnt the temple where she was ador'd.

119–20. *At this*, &c. Cf. Lucretius, *De Rerum Natura*, iii. 153–6.

364–5. *The Proverb holds*. Chaucer has 'Who may been a fool, but if he love?' (*CT* (A), l. 1799). Dryden clarifies the aphorism of Publilius Syrus on which this is based: 'Amare et sapere vix deo conceditur' (*Sent*. xxii). Cf. Tilley, L558.

414. *From out the Bars*: translating 'out of lystes'. 'The bars were the palisades of the lists' (Scott).

483. *Sigils*: occult devices said to have mysterious powers. Cf. *infra*, "The Flower and the Leaf", l. 606; Pope, *The Temple of Fame*, ll. 105–6.

515. *all bare below the Breast*. Noyes suggests that the sense requires 'above

the Breast'; but Chaucer's Venus 'fro the navele doun al covered was' (*CT* (A), l. 1957).

589. *Boars*: a misreading of Chaucer's 'beres' (ibid., l. 2018).

616. *One when Direct*, &c. Derived from a misleading note in Speght: 'The names of two figures in geomancy, representing two constellations in heaven. Puella signifieth Mars retrograde, and Rubeus Mars direct.' For an explanation of 'Geomantick Figures', see W. W. Skeat, *Works of Chaucer*, 1894, v. 82.

623. *manifest of Shame*. Cf. *Absalom and Achitophel*, l. 204, note.

634. *Caledonian*. Dryden's spelling of 'Calydon' is not consistent; cf. *infra*, 'Meleager and Atalanta', Argument, and ll. 1, 364.

Book III. Dryden's additions are numerous. He adds descriptive detail (e.g. ll. 92–93, 119–23, 468–74, 531–5, 552–5, 623–8, 782–5), increases the classical colouring of the story (e.g. ll. 99–100, 201–4, 669–72), and emphasizes the interest of the gods in Palamon and Arcite (e.g. ll. 439–42, 1141–7). He adds touches of romance and ceremony (e.g. ll. 36–37, 87, 488–93, 1016–17). He underlines, explains, and illustrates (e.g. ll. 151–2, 169–74, 308–12, 403–5, 502–5, 1066–77), and extends didactic passages (e.g. ll. 739–42, 808–35, 847–53, 889–92). He discards the vivid concrete detail of Chaucer's battle (*CT*(A), ll. 2601–7), and introduces a generalized account of his own (ll. 583–601).

17. *An Isle for Love*, &c. Cf. Songs from *King Arthur*, X, ll. 61–76.

35. *Jambeux*: not in Chaucer's description. Dryden probably introduced the term, as he was fond of doing, from Spenser (*The Faerie Queene*, II. vi. 29).

43. *Lion*: Speght. Chaucer manuscripts have 'griffoun' (*CT* (A), l. 2133). Cf. l. 57, where Dryden's 'Pards' and 'Bear' translate Speght, and manuscripts have 'the leoun or the deer' (*CT* (A), l. 2150).

65. *barb'rous Gold*: an imitation of Virgil, *Aen*. ii. 504. Cf. Milton, *Paradise Lost*, ii. 4, '*Barbaric* Pearl and Gold'.

67. *Thrace*: 'Trace' (Speght). The manuscripts have 'Tars' (*CT* (A), l. 2160), Tarsia or Tarsus.

72–77. Dryden reduces the startling colour contrasts which Chaucer makes in accordance with astrological requirements (see W. C. Curry, *Chaucer and the Medieval Sciences*, 1926, pp. 130 ff.). 'Ruddy' (l. 75) is derived from Speght, and is not a vivid substitute for 'rounde' (*CT*(A), l. 2168).

100. *honest*: glorious, comely. Cf. *Alexander's Feast*, l. 52.

104. *Posts*. 'Pots' is clearly an error. Dryden was familiar with the Roman custom of decorating door-posts for celebrations: cf. *The Sixth Satyr of Juvenal*, ll. 75, 320–1; *Examen Poeticum*, 'The First Book of *Ovid*'s Metamorphoses', ll. 760–3; *infra*, 'Cymon and Iphigenia', l. 561.

123. *flick'ring*. Dryden recollects the earlier description of Venus, 'above her heed hir dowves flikerynge' (*CT*(A), l. 1962).

129–44. *Creator Venus*, &c. Dryden's amplification of *CT* (A), ll. 2221–2, from Lucretius and Spenser. Cf. *Sylvæ*, 'Lucretius The beginning of the First Book', ll. 1–25; Spenser, *The Faerie Queene*, IV. x. 44 and 46:

Great *Venus*, Queene of beautie and of grace,
The ioy of Gods and men, that vnder skie
Doest fayrest shine, and most adorne thy place

.   .   .   .

The Lyons rore, the Tygres loudly bray,
The raging Buls rebellow through the wood,
And breaking forth, dare tempt the deepest flood,
To come where thou doest draw them with desire.

201–4. *But such they were*, &c. Dryden's addition. Cf. his note 20 to *The Sixth Satyr of Juvenal*.

208. *Mastless*. Chaucer manuscripts have 'ook cerial' (*CT* (A), l. 2290), evergreen, 'quercus cerris'. Dryden has been misled by Speght's impossible 'a crowne of a grene oke vnseriall'.

220. *the Vengeance of thy Darts*. For Chaucer's 'Acteon' (*CT* (A), ll. 2302–3) Dryden substitutes the legend of Niobe's children (*Iliad*, xxiv. 602–7).

388. *not to be outridden, though outrun*. A mistranslation of Speght, 'Men may the old out ren, but not out rede', i.e. men may outrun but not outwit the old (*CT* (A), l. 2449).

389. *Trin'd*. See *Annus Mirabilis*, ll. 1165–6, note.

411. *Bought Senates*, &c. Dryden's addition; doubtless alluding to the Revolution of 1688.

441–2. *The Gods came downward*, &c. Cf. *Astræa Redux*, ll. 153–4; *Annus Mirabilis*, ll. 61–64.

905. *dodder'd Oaks*. See *The Fifth Satyr of Persius*, l. 80, note.

927. *Mourning Bride*. 'The italics point the compliment to Congreve's tragedy . . . acted and published in 1697' (Noyes).

959–64. The descriptive phrases and epithets in this catalogue are added (cf. *CT* (A), ll. 2920–3). Dryden doubtless knew the catalogue in Statius, the ultimate source of *The Knight's Tale* (*Thebaid*, vi. 98–106); but it is more likely that he drew on Spenser's list of trees (*The Faerie Queene*, I. i. 8–9), which contains 'the Firre that weepeth still', 'the builder Oake', and 'the Laurell, meed of mightie Conquerours'. The spelling 'Eugh' was not uncommon in Dryden's time; and he had it before him in Spenser. 'The swimming Alder' is an imitation of Virgil's 'alnos primum fluuii sensere cauatas' (*Georgics*, i. 136).

1039. *subborn their Death*: procure it 'in a secret, stealthy, or underhand manner' (*OED*). Cf. *The State of Innocence*, v:

Those who by lingring Sickness lose their Breath,
And those who by Despair subborn their Death.

1076. *First vegetive, then feels, and reasons last*. 'The common division of the *Soul*, is into three principal faculties, *Vegetal*, *Sensitive*, and *Rational*, which make three distinct kind of living Creatures: *Vegetal* Plants, *Sensible* Beasts, *Rational* Men. . . . The inferior may be alone, but the superior cannot subsist without the other: so *Sensible* includes *Vegetal*, *Rational* both; which are contained in it (saith *Aristotle*) *ut trigonus in tetragono*, as a Triangle in a Quadrangle' (Burton, I. i. 2. 5). Cf. Aristotle, *De Anima*, ii. 3 ff.

1141-7. *Smil'd Venus*, &c. Dryden's addition, in the style of seventeenth-century epithalamial verse; and more appropriate to a pagan tale than is Chaucer's prayer for God's blessing on Palamon (*CT* (A), ll. 3099-3100). The two Cupids—Eros and Anteros—represent mutual love. Cf. their reconciliation by Hymen in the wedding masque *A Challenge at Tilt* (Jonson, vii. 394-5): 'You are both true CVPIDS, and both the sonnes of VENVS by MARS, but this the first-borne, & was called EROS: . . . yet he could not thriue and encrease alone. Therefore if shee affected his growth, VENVS must bring forth a brother to him, and name him ANTEROS: that with reciprocall affection, might pay the exchange of loue. . . . Since when, your natures are, that either of you, looking vpon other, thriue, and by your mutuall respects and interchange of ardor flourish and prosper; . . . This is the loue, that *Hymen* requires, without which no marriage is happie: . . . This is a strife, wherein you both winne, and begets a concord worthy all married mindes emulation, when the louer trans-formes himselfe into the person of his belou'd, as you two doe now.' See also Otto Kurz, 'Gli Amori de' Carracci', *Journal of Warburg and Courtauld Institutes*, xiv (1951), 226-7.

To My Honour'd Kinsman, John Driden, of Chesterton in the County of Hunting-don, Esquire. (Page 1529.) Dryden's cousin, John Driden of Chesterton (1635-1708), country gentleman and Member of Parliament for Huntingdon, showed great kindness to the poet in his last years. In March 1699 Dryden told Mrs. Steward that his cousin had sent him 'a turkey hen with Eggs, & a good young Goose; besides a very kind letter, & the News of his own good health, which I vallue more than all the rest; He being so noble a Benefactour to a poor, & so undeserveing a Kinsman, & one of another persuasion, in matters of Religion' (Ward, p. 112). Of this poem Dryden wrote to Montague: 'In the description which I have made of a Parliament Man, I think I have not onely drawn the features of my worthy Kinsman, but have also given my Own opinion, of what an Englishman in Parliament oughto be; & deliver it as a Memorial of my own Principles to all Posterity' (ibid., p. 120; cf. James Kinsley, 'Dryden and the Art of Praise', *ES* xxxiv (1953), 57-64). He thought the poem the best in the *Fables*; and his friends and 'the Town' seem to have agreed (Ward, pp. 123, 135). There was a family tradition that John Driden acknowledged the tribute with a gift of £500 (Malone, I. i. 325-6).

19-22. *Where, for a Year*, &c. Cf. Donne, *Loves Alchymie*, 11-12 ff.:

> So, lovers dreame a rich and long delight,
> But get a winter-seeming summers night, &c.

82-87. *Guibbons but guesses*, &c. On Gibbons, see *The Third Satyr of Persius*, l. 126, note; on Maurus (Blackmore) and Milbourne, see *supra*, Preface, l. 663, note. There is no need to suppose that in l. 85 Dryden confuses Blackmore with Milbourne, the translator of Maro (Noyes); '*Maro's* Muse' is the muse of epic poetry, outraged by Blackmore's experiments in heroic verse. With

Dryden's sentiments on the medical profession, cf. Garth, *The Dispensary* (1699), iii. 190–1, 'we . . . Who fill *Church-yards*, and who unpeople States'; and iv. 55–57, where Mirmillo (Gibbons) declares

> By this Right Arm what mighty Numbers fell.
> Whilst others meanly ask'd whole Months to slay,
> I oft dispatch'd the Patient in a Day.

The theme of *The Dispensary* is the opposition of the profit-making apothecaries to the College of Physicians, who provided free medical aid for the poor (cf. ll. 107–8, *infra*). When Dryden died, his body lay in state at the College of Physicians, and Garth spoke a funeral oration in Latin (Macdonald, p. 292).

140. *Munster.* See *Annus Mirabilis*, ll. 145–8, note.

142. *Our Foes . . . have Peace embrac'd*: the Peace of Ryswick (1697). William 'found his Reign grow so unacceptable to his people, by the continuance of the War, that he saw the necessity of coming to a Peace' (Burnet, ii. 202). When he sent this poem and the lines on the Duchess of Ormonde to Montague for criticism, Dryden expressed his fear that he had 'purgd them out of their Spirit; as our Master Busby, usd to whip a Boy so long, till he made him a Confirmd Blockhead. My Cousin Driden saw them in the Country; & the greatest Exception He made to them, was a Satire against the Dutch valour, in the late Warr. He desir'd me to omit it, (to use his Own words) out of the respect He had to his Soveraign. I obeyd his Commands; & left onely the praises, which I think are due to the gallantry of my own Countrymen' (Ward, p. 120). The Peace of Ryswick was followed by a dispute between King and Commons on the question of maintaining a standing army (see Burnet, ii. 205–7). Dryden's views on this matter, after his cousin's revision of the poem, are 'to be inferred from his panegyric on the navy, and his declamation against the renewal of the war' (Scott). Cf. *The Sixteenth Satyr of Juvenal*, Argument; and 'Sigismonda and Guiscardo', *infra*, ll. 596–605, note.

152. *Namur Subdu'd.* The taking of Namur by William's army in 1695 cleared the way for the peace of 1697. It was 'reckoned one of the greatest actions of the King's life, and indeed, one of the greatest that is in the whole History of War' (Burnet, ii. 153).

160–3. *When once the Persian King*, &c. For the account of Alexander's difficulties with his troops on the banks of the Ganges, and for the belief that he was the issue of Jove, Dryden draws on Plutarch. Cf. *Alexander's Feast*, l. 30, note.

188. *your gen'rous Grandsire*: probably Sir Erasmus Driden, also the poet's grandfather, who seems to have been 'one of those sent to prison on account of the loan-money, and liberated on the eve of the general election for Charles I's third parliament, 1628' (Christie). Malone's statement (I. i. 321) that the reference is to John Driden's maternal grandfather, Sir Robert Bevile, appears to be mere supposition.

Meleager and Atalanta. (Page 1535.) *Meta.* viii. 270–545. On Dryden's Latin texts, see *Ovid's Epistles*, introductory note. He made use of Sandys's *Ovid's Metamorphosis Englished* (1626) in translating Ovid for the *Fables*; only his more obvious debts are here noted.

1. *Caledonians*. See 'Palamon and Arcite', ii. 634, note.

60. *twice old Iolas*: 'Hyanteo Iolao' (l. 310). Iolas was rejuvenated by Hebe at the instigation of his friend Hercules (*Meta.* ix. 398–401).

108. *spend their Mouth*: give tongue on discovering the quarry. Cf. Shakespeare, *Henry V*, II. iv. 69–71:

> Turne head, and stop pursuit: for coward Dogs
> Most spend their mouths, when what they seem to threaten
> Runs farre before them.

127, 129. *Empalamos . . . Onesimus*. Perhaps misprints. Dryden's Latin texts have 'Eupalamon' and 'Enæsimus' (ll. 360, 362).

140. *ranch'd*. See *Æneis*, xi. 1184, note.

183. *The Strong may fight aloof*: 'licet eminus esse | fortibus' (ll. 406–7). Cf. Sandys (p. 160), 'The wise in valour should aloofe contend'.

191. *And through the Dog*, &c. Cf. Sandys (p. 160):

> [hit]
> A dog betweene his baying iawes: the wound
> Rusht through his guts, and naild him to the ground.

202. *Gires*. Ovid has 'dum saevit, dum corpora versat in orbem' (l. 416), paraphrased in the Delphin edition as 'dum furit, dum torquet corpus in gyrum'. Cf. Spenser, *The Faerie Queene*, II. v. 8, 'Or strike, or hurtle round in warlike gyre'.

363. *shoots out the Soul in Air*: '. . . inque leues abiit paulatim spiritus auras' (l. 524). Cf. the Delphin paraphrase, 'et spiritus paulatim disjectus est in tenuem aerem'.

402. *Who yearly*, &c. Dryden's addition, from a note in the Delphin edition.

Sigismonda and Guiscardo, from Boccace. (Page 1545.) *Il Decameron*, iv. 1. Dryden seems to have had before him not only the Italian text, but also the anonymous English version (1620) made partly from the Italian and partly from Antoine le Maçon's French translation of the *Decameron* (1545), and William Chamberlayne's *Pharonnida: A Heroick Poem* (1659), which contains an episode based on Boccaccio's tale. In *The First English Translation of the 'Decameron'*, 1953, H. G. Wright argues convincingly that John Florio was the author of the 1620 translation.

On the title-page of *1620* Boccaccio is described as the 'first Refiner of Italian Prose'; and Florio complains that earlier translations have not been 'beautified with his sweet Stile and Elocution of Phrase, neither savouring of his singular Moral Applications'. This may have been a challenge to Dryden (cf. Preface, *supra*, ll. 64–70). He owes some suggestions in characterization to Florio. The portrait of Tancred, distracted with grief and rage, speechless, and pacing through the night in an agony of mind (ll. 241–4, 254–8, 270–6, 289–91), reflects the Tancred of Florio, afflicted with 'Oppressions many and violent', rather than Boccaccio's tyrant 'dolente a morte'; and he is a more appropriate character for a Restoration romance. The excessive pathos in l. 304 is derived from Florio; and the lamentation of old age (ll. 325–38) is an expansion of Tancred's 'imagine what a heart-break this will be to me, so long as Life remaineth in this Poor, Weak, and Aged Body' in *1620*. Dryden's rhetorical play with the claims of nature and justice (ll. 354–65) is essentially Florio's version of Boccaccio's contrast between Tancred's paternal 'amore' and his kingly 'giustissimo sdegno'.

In Chamberlayne's poem (Saintsbury, i) the princess Pharonnida reads aloud a letter from her secret lover Argalia, and is overheard by her father, who has been asleep in concealment. Stricken with sorrow and rage, he rates her for her unfilial conduct and her choice of a lover; Pharonnida makes a bold defence; and he issues an ultimatum, and retires to plot Argalia's destruction. At some points, Dryden's story corresponds with Chamberlayne's, without reference to Boccaccio or Florio: the king retires to sleep in the heat of the day (ll. 195 ff.; *Pharonnida*, III. ii. 76–81); Chamberlayne provided Dryden with a tyrant in whom anger, grief, blood-lust, and calculating policy are joined (*Pharonnida*, III. ii. 94–99, 122–4, 189–93, 210 ff.); the strong language which Dryden's Tancred uses of the low-born Guiscardo (ll. 315–24) is anticipated in *Pharonnida*, III. ii. 140–4. See also *infra*, ll. 57–66, note.

It is possible that Dryden knew the Elizabethan tragedy of *Tancred and Gismund* (1591). His portrait of Tancred, delighting in bloody revenge, recalls the declamatory fury of Tancred in the play; and his emphasis on destiny (e.g. ll. 215, 224, 227–8, 242–9, 580–1) recalls one of the play's main themes.

This and Dryden's other translations from the *Decameron* are discussed in H. G. Wright, *Boccaccio in England from Chaucer to Tennyson*, 1957, pp. 265–77.

57–66. *ev'ry Day increas'd*, &c. Dryden develops Sigismonda's love more slowly and carefully than does Boccaccio. With his imagery of fire, cf. Florio: 'her affections being but a glowing spark at the first, grew like a Bavin to take flame'. Donne is the ultimate source of the conceit in ll. 63–64 (*The Extasie*, ll. 7–8); but cf. Chamberlayne's description of a secret love (*Pharonnida*, III. i. 109–12):

> Few 'mongst the observant wits o' the court yet knew
> (Though it with twisted eye-beams strengthened grew
> At every interview, and often dropped
> Some tears to water it). . . .

Chamberlayne was fond of the image (e.g. IV. i. 311, IV. ii. 544–52).

240–4. *But now he stood collected*, &c. Cf. *Absalom and Achitophel*, ll. 445–52.

292–6. *Who long expecting lay*, &c. Boccaccio's hero is taken as he leaves his mistress; Dryden's never reaches her. Dryden heightens the tension of the story at many points; and here he alters the sequence of events to balance the two pictures of a distracted father and an anxious daughter.

305–7. *O Sigismonda*, &c. Boccaccio has simply 'piangendo le cominciò a dire'. Cf. *Pharonnida*, III. ii. 123–8; Fairfax, *Godfrey of Bulloigne*, iii. 46; Milton, *Paradise Lost*, i. 619–21:

> Thrice he assayd, and thrice in spite of scorn,
> Tears such as Angels weep, burst forth: at last
> Words interwove with sighs found out thir way.

337–8. *my glorious Race is run*, &c. Cf. *Absalom and Achitophel*, ll. 268–9, note.

596–605. 'The dispute between William and his Parliament about his favourite Dutch guards, was obviously in Dryden's recollection' (Scott). See *supra*, 'To My Honour'd Kinsman', l. 142, note.

694. *by Infection wept*. Cf. 'Palamon and Arcite', ii. 310–14.

Baucis and Philemon. (Page 1565.) *Meta*. viii. 611–724. See 'Meleager and Atalanta', note. Dryden's additions here are few (ll. 57, 66–67, 76, 124–5, 135–6, 138).

20. *Phrygian Realms, my Grandsire's Government*. Ovid has (ll. 622–3):

> ipse locum vidi: nam me Pelopeia Pittheus
> misit in arva, suo quondam regnata parenti.

Dryden uses Cnipping's notes: '*Pelopeia*.] In Phrygiam, regnatam Tantalo Pelopis patri. *Pittheus*.] Trœzen & Pittheus Pelopis filii. . . . Fuit & Pittheus pater Æthræ quæ mater Thesei. Hunc tamen Lelegis patrem fuisse . . . .'

21–22. *Not far from thence*, &c. Cf. Sandys (p. 166):

> Hard by, a lake, once habitable ground;
> Where Coots and fishing Cormorants abound.

47. *Two Cushions stuff'd with Straw*. A 'little circumstance' drawn from Sandys. Ovid has 'textum rude' (l. 640).

56–57. *Kettle . . . little Seether*: 'parvoque . . . aheno' (l. 645). Sandys also translates 'kettle', which was currently used for 'cauldron' (cf. l. 106, *infra*; *The First Book of the Georgics*, l. 393).

98. *roasted rear*: lightly cooked. Sandys's phrase.

Pygmalion and the Statue. (Page 1570.) *Meta*. x. 243–97.

Cinyras and Myrrha. (Page 1573.) *Meta*. x. 298–524. Dryden extends his original for illustration or emphasis (e.g. ll. 20–21, 74–75, 146–8, 159–61, 262–3); and adds reflective commentary (ll. 52–57) and descriptive detail (e.g. ll. 127, 200–1, 272, 372–3).

143. *prepares to choak her Breath*: 'laqueoque innectere fauces | destinat' (ll. 378–9), which Sandys translates 'Resolu'd to choke her hated breath' (p. 205).

264. *Arctophylax*: 'Bootes' (l. 447). Cnipping gives the alternative name.

320. *the Moon hath mew'd her Horns.* Cf. Cleveland, *The King's Disguise*, l. 11: 'The Sun hath mew'd his Beams from off his Lamp.'

The First Book of Homer's Ilias. (Page 1583.) Dryden's additions emphasize the passion of his characters (e.g. ll. 223, 333–4, 361, 458–60, 484, 720), enliven the quarrel of Jove and Juno (ll. 697–700, 735–6, 752–3), and introduce a light comic strain at the close (ll. 807, 810, 814–15). At l. 233 he inexplicably omits Homer's lovely lines on Phthia (ll. 154–7), which are included in the translations he used.

77. *at Rovers*: at random. Cf. Dedication of *The Satires of Juvenalis*, l. 170. Chapman has here:

> Like night he rang'd the host, and rov'd
> (Apart the fleet set) terribly. . . .

118–20. *Ev'n tho' th' Offence,* &c. Homer, ll. 81–83. The figures are Dryden's, following Chapman:

> . . . When a King hath once mark'd for his hate
> A man inferior, though that day his wrath seems to digest
> Th' offence he takes, yet evermore he rakes up in his breast
> Brands of quick anger. . . .

336. *Tongue-valiant Hero.* Cf. *Æneis*, xi. 514, note.

365. *Two Centuries*: δύο μὲν γενεαὶ (l. 250), translated as 'ages' in Chapman and 'generations' in Ogilby. Dryden is following Ovid; cf. *infra*, 'The Twelfth Book of Ovid his Metamorphoses', l. 260.

585. *in the Deep*: ἐς 'Ωκεανὸν (l. 423). Ogilby distinguishes between the blameless Ethiopians in the west, and 'those of the East, who daily curst the rising Sun'. Dryden follows Chapman:

> Jupiter went yesterday to feast
> Amongst the blameless Æthiops in th' ocean's deepen'd breast.

632. *Cauls.* Ogilby, annotating Chryses's speech (*supra*, l. 63), says that only the thighs of sacrificed beasts were 'totally burnt, being wrapped in a double Caul or Leaf of Fat, to cause them to burn the clearer'.

803. *Skinker.* Cf. Case, *Praise of Musicke* (1586), 'That banquet of the gods where Vulcan plaid the skinker' (*OED*).

The Cock and the Fox . . . from Chaucer. (Page 1605.) Dryden develops Chaucer's attribution of human qualities to the poultry and the fox, and his mock-heroic treatment of Chanticleer (e.g. ll. 55–66, 73–77, 83–88, 124–5, 128–9, 138–9, 459–66, 480–8, 603–7, 631–8, 736–9). Other additions are ll. 326–41, 509–22, and 531–51; and a number of satirical touches (e.g. ll. 30, 169–70, 402–7, 561–3, 565–6).

3. *Dell*: 'dale' (*CT* (B), l. 4013).

55–66. *This gentle Cock,* &c. Chaucer's cock has simply seven hens, 'his sustres and his paramours' (*CT* (B), ll. 4056–7). Lines 63–64 refer to

Henry VIII's marriage with Catherine of Aragon, his brother's widow (cf. *The Hind and the Panther*, i. 351–69). Cf. Donne, *The Progresse of the Soule*, xx:

> Already this hot cocke, in bush and tree,
> In field and tent, oreflutters his next hen;
> He asks her not, who did so tast, nor when,
> Nor if his sister, or his neece shee be.

106. *Shrovetide-Cock*: a cock tied and pelted with stones on Shrove Tuesday.

156–9. *Choler adust*: 'the humour of malencolie' (*CT* (B), l. 4123). Dryden pedantically specifies the type of melancholy indicated by the symptoms. 'Choler adust becomes *æruginosa melancholia*, as vinegar out of purest wine putrified or by exhalation of purer spirits is so made, and becomes sowr and sharp; and from the sharpnes of this humor proceed much waking, troublesom thoughts & dreams, &c.' (Burton, I. i. 3. 3).

190. *Fumetery, Centaury, and Spurge*. Dryden simplifies Chaucer's catalogue of digestives (*CT* (B), ll. 4153–6). 'Fumetery' and 'Centaury' are discussed by Burton in several places; for 'spurge', which replaces Chaucer's more technical 'katapuce', see Browne, *Pseudodoxia Epidemica*, II. vii.

202–4. Dryden's addition. The first allusion is to *Iliad*, i. 63. In the second, the distinction is between the Roman Cato and the medieval school-book *Dionysii Catonis Disticha de Moribus ad Filium*, vulgarly ascribed to Cato.

254. *sacred hunger of my Gold*. Cf. Virgil, *Aen*. iii. 57, 'auri sacra fames'.

325–41. *Dreams are but Interludes*, &c. Cf. *The State of Innocence*, III, where Lucifer soliloquizes over the sleeping Adam and Eve:

> Their Reason sleeps, but Mimick Fancy wakes;
> Supplies her parts, and wild Idea's takes
> From Words and things ill-sorted and mis-joyn'd;
> The Anarchy of Thought and Chaos of the Mind.

Scott suggests that l. 328 should read 'A Court of Coblers, and a Mob of Kings'; but Dryden is thinking, in Hobbesian terms, only of the compound imagination which blends such disparate images as cobblers and kings (*Leviathan*, I. ii). With ll. 337–9, cf. Burton (II. ii. 5): '*Tully* notes, *for the most part our speeches in the day time, cause our phantasie to work upon the like in our sleep*,' which *Ennius* writes of *Homer: Et canis in somnis leporis vestigia latrat.*'

372–5. *By Quenda slain*, &c. Quenda and Bede are Dryden's additions. He errs in citing Bede, who belongs to the century before Kenelm; but he may have read the story in Milton's *History of Britain* (1670), IV, where the wicked sister Quendrid is mentioned.

480–90. *A Fox*, &c. Dryden turns the fox's hypocrisy to indirect satire on the puritans. With ll. 484–5, cf. *Absalom and Achitophel*, ll. 588–90.

501. *Gallick*, a pun ('gallus', a cock). Cf. *infra*, l. 636, where Chanticleer is derived from Brennus and Belinus, a leader and a divinity of the Gauls (Scott).

531–5. *The first so binds the Will*, &c. The distinction is between (i) deliberate, rational choice of a course of action, and (ii) 'spontaneous' or unreflective action in inevitable circumstances. The slaves do not initially choose whether to row or not; but constrained to work, they pull 'willingly' under the natural prompting of a 'prospect of the Shore'.

652. *proud beside, as solar People are.* Dryden's addition. 'Some men have peculiar Symptoms, according to their temperament and *Crisis*, which they had from the Starres and those celestiall influences. . . . If the *Sun* [domineers], they will be Lords, Emperors, in conceipt at least, and Monarchs, give Offices, Honors, &c.' (Burton, I. iii. I. 3).

659–60. *Ye Princes*, &c. See *Alexander's Feast*, l. 30, note.

686. *Native*: one born under a particular planet. The dream thwarted the fortunes of Chanticleer, a 'native' of the sun, through Saturn's influence.

728. *Talbot with the Band.* Dryden was misled by Speght's '*Talbot*, and eke garlonde'; Chaucer wrote of two dogs, Talbot and Gerland (*CT* (B), l. 4573).

752. *sagacious Hounds.* See *The Hind and the Panther*, ii. 5, note.

Theodore and Honoria, from Boccace. (Page 1626.) *Il Decameron*, v. 8. Dryden's additions emphasize the chivalry and devotion of Theodore (e.g. ll. 7–9, 18–19, 125–6) and the passion of the converted Honoria (ll. 419–24), and increase the ghostly horror of the vision (ll. 78–80, 90–99, 119–21, 271–3, 283). Dryden repeats the slaughter in ll. 300–9, where Boccaccio is content with 'il cavaliere . . . faccendo quello, che altra volta aveva fatto'. He adds the psychological analyses in ll. 220–30 and 344–79. The names of the characters are changed. Nastagio becomes Theodore (probably suggested by Teodoro in Boccaccio's preceding tale), Guido degli Anastagi becomes Guido Cavalcanti, and 'la giovane' is named Honoria. Byron praises 'Dryden's lay' in *Don Juan*, iii. 105–6.

90–96. *At once the Wind was laid*, &c. 'Terror is most usually caused, as *Plutarch* will have, *from some imminent danger, when a terrible object is at hand, heard, seen, or conceived.* . . . If one sense alone can cause . . . violent commotions of the minde, what may we think when hearing, sight, & those other senses are all troubled at once? as by some Earth-quakes, thunder, lightning, tempests, &c.' (Burton, I. ii. 4. 3).

115. *pinch'd*: bit. Cf. Spenser, *Minor Poems*, ed. E. de Sélincourt, p. 484.

123. *chear'd*: urged; a hunting term. Cf. Shakespeare, *A Midsummer Night's Dream*, IV. i. 127–30; Scott, *The Lady of the Lake*, i. 9.

189. *vers'd in*: occupied in, busy about (Lat. 'versari').

221–30. *But Dreams*, &c. Dryden's extension of 'gran pezza stette tra pietoso, e pauroso', based on Florio's translation (see 'Sigismonda and Guiscardo', *supra*, introductory note). There Anastasio stands 'hoodwinkt with his own Passions, not knowing the subtle Enemies cunning illusions in offering false suggestions to the sight, to work his own ends thereby'. Cf. Shakespeare, *Hamlet*, I. iv. 40 ff.

403–4. *The Precipice in sight*, &c. Cf. *The Rival Ladies*, v. ii:

As from some steep and dreadful Precipice,
The frighted Travellor casts down his Eyes,
And sees the Ocean at so great a distance,
It looks as if the Skies were sunk below him;
Yet if some Neighb'ring shrub (how weak soe'er)
Peeps up, his willing Eyes stop gladly there. . . .

Ceyx and Alcyone. (Page 1637.) Ovid, *Meta.* xi. 410–748.

51. *present, what I suffer only fear*: being with you, fear only what I am really suffering: 'nec, nisi quae patiar, metuam' (l. 442).

93. *hoist their Yards a-trip*: 'cornuaque in summa locat arbore' (l. 476). *A-trip*: swayed up. Here and in ll. 102–3 Dryden takes his technical terms from Sandys's translation (1626, p. 228).

133. *Like various Fits*, &c. An awkward translation of 'ipsa quoque his agitur vicibus Trachinia puppis' (l. 502).

351. *the steerage of his Wings.* See *Æneis*, iv. 376, note.

394. *Caull.* Ibid., l. 198, note.

395. *Her Nurse*, &c. The amended punctuation is required by the Latin: 'et altrici quae luctus causa roganti . . . ait' (ll. 683–4).

The Flower and the Leaf. (Page 1650.) Dryden's original, a fifteenth-century poem written apparently by a woman, is included as Chaucer's in Speght's edition. The text is printed in the Supplement to Skeat's edition of Chaucer, 1897, pp. 361 ff. Dryden elaborates decoratively (e.g. ll. 8–15, 29–32, 151–2, 195–6, 218–20, 261–2, 316–23, 377–8, 583–6, 591–3). He changes the knights and ladies into supernatural beings, partly by creating an atmosphere of mystery (e.g. ll. 62–65, 148–52, 203–6), and partly by frequent allusion to fairies and enchantments, culminating in ll. 480–501. His knights and ladies linger till dark, to dance fairy-like beneath the moon (see ll. 490–5); and the poet returns from her enchanted walk at dawn instead of, as in the original, 'nigh night'.

61. *Receptacle*: place of shelter.

155–6. *A Train less fair*, &c. '*Lactantius lib.* 14. *cap.* 15. *God sent Angels to the tuition of men; but . . . that mischievous all-commander of the Earth, and hot in lust, enticed them by little and little to this vice, and defiled them with the company of women: . . . Justin Martyr . . . &c.* to this sense make a twofold fall of Angels, one from the beginning of the world, another a little before the deluge' (Burton, III. ii. 1. 1).

233. *Charge*: a device borne on an escutcheon.

261–3. *The golden Fringe*, &c. See *Æneis*, v. 115–16, note.

341–3. *Symarrs*: mantles (cf. *Æneis*, iv. 196; *infra*, 'Cymon and Iphigenia', l. 100). *Gridelin*: a pale purple colour. The romantic associations of 'simar' are preserved by Byron (*The Giaour*, ll. 1272–5) and Scott: Rebecca in *Ivanhoe*, viii, wears 'a simarre of the richest Persian silk, exhibiting flowers in their natural colours embossed upon a purple ground'.

423–36. In the original poem, the Lady of the Leaf offers hospitality to the Lady of the Flower, and provides horses for her company; whereupon they all ride off. Dryden has the banquet supernaturally provided on the spot; and a moonlight dance follows before they disperse (ll. 453–6).

493. *Demogorgon.* He 'has not much propriety here, except as supplying a name of excellent sound' (Saintsbury). But Dryden had from Spenser the notion of Demogorgon as a primordial terror, 'Prince of darknesse and dead night' (*The Faerie Queene*, I. i. 37); and in the *Oedipus* of Dryden and Lee (III. i) Tiresias swears by Demogorgon's name, 'at which Ghosts quake'.

542–5. *Bows*: 'bowes . . . of the precious lawrer' (l. 512). Skeat emends to 'boughes'. The bow 'made no part of a knight's proper weapons. But it is curious how Dryden, having fallen into an error, finds out a reason for his false reading, by alleging, that the bows were borne as an emblem of strength of arm, valour, and victory' (Scott).

606. *Sigils.* See *supra*, 'Palamon and Arcite', ii. 483, note.

The Twelfth Book of Ovid his Metamorphoses. (Page 1666.) Dryden's additions are few and insignificant. He generalizes or reduces Ovid's catalogues (ll. 507–8, *Meta.* xii. 378–9; ll. 605–8, *Meta.* xii. 452–8).

154. *To wound him first*, &c. An annotation of Ovid, l. 112, based on Cnipping: 'Vulnus & auxilium. Thelephus rex Mysiæ transitu prohibiturus Græcos ad Trojam proficiscentes ab Achille vulneratus est. Vulnus ubi putrescebat, oraculo consulto responsum tulit, quærendum esse remedium ab eadem hasta. Conciliatus ergo Achilli, ærugine cuspidis sanatus est.'

811. *Warriour.* 'Warrious' is not impossible; but cf. *Æneis*, vii. 1095 and xi. 756.

818. *great in Homer*: interpreting 'totum quae gloria compleat orbem' (l. 617) with a note in Cnipping: 'A præstantissimis enim quibusque poëtis tam Græcis quam Latinis Achillis gesta fuere celebrata, sicque per totum terrarum orbem vulgata.'

The Speeches of Ajax and Ulysses. (Page 1688.) *Meta.* xiii. 1–398. Dryden's occasional additions sharpen the satiric flavour (e.g. ll. 100, 104, 110, 116, 129–30, 147).

147. *Tongue-valiant.* See *Æneis*, xi. 514, note.

338. *Vers'd.* See *supra*, 'Theodore and Honoria', l. 189, note.

The Wife of Bath her Tale. (Page 1703.) Dryden elaborates the fairy element in Chaucer's tale (e.g. ll. 5–15, 19–23, 211–14), and increases the hideousness of the hag-bride by giving her the attributes of a witch (ll. 226–8, 255–63, 329–33). He draws out Chaucer's slyness into a pervasive satiric humour (e.g. ll. 38–39, 51–54, 153–4, 160–4, 180–1, 187–92, 307–10, 315–16), and extends commentary and argument (e.g. ll. 61–68, 139–48, 396–403, 418–36).

5–6. *And where the jolly Troop*, &c. Cf. *The Hind and the Panther*, i. 212–13, note.

19–23. *In vain the Dairy*, &c. 'Our Fairies . . . have been in former times adored with much superstition, with sweeping their houses, and setting of a pail of clean water, good victuals, and the like, and then they should not be pinched, but find money in their shooes, and be fortunate in their enterprizes' (Burton, I. ii. I. 2). Cf. Richard Corbett, *Poems*, ed. Bennett and Trevor-Roper, pp. 49–50.

73. *Geneura.* This and similar forms of 'Guinevere' are to be found in Geoffrey of Monmouth's *Historia*, which Dryden read for *King Arthur* (1691).

104. *But, our Proffer*, &c. The Folio reading is faulty; but Christie's emendation is meaningless, and Warton and Noyes ignore the initial capital in 'Proffer'. It seems likeliest, despite the catalexis, that the compositor simply confused the word order.

194. *as a Bittour bumps within a Reed*: 'as a bitore bombleth in the myre' (*CT* (D), l. 972). Dryden accepts the alternative explanation of the bittern's cry, rejected by Sir Thomas Browne as a vulgar error: 'A Bittor maketh that mugient noise, or as we term it Bumping, by putting its bill into a reed' (*Pseudodoxia Epidemica*, III. xxvii). 'Bump' is a country word.

216. *featly footing.* Cf. Shakespeare, *The Tempest*, I. ii. 380.

372–3. The first line is the crone's, the second the knight's.

400–32. *No Father can infuse*, &c. Dryden fills out the argument with the help of Lucretius. With ll. 402–3, 421–3, and 429–32, cf. *De Rerum Natura*, iv. 1218–22, i. 1021–8, and iv. 1209–12.

434. *a dusky gleam of Sodom blue.* Cf. Spenser, *The Faerie Queene*, I. xi. 44:

> From his infernall fournace forth he threw
> Huge flames, that dimmed all the heauens light,
> Enrold in duskish smoke and brimstone blew. . . .

436. *the fair Mermaid*, &c. Horace, *De Arte Poetica*, ll. 3–4.

Of the Pythagorean Philosophy. (Page 1717.) *Meta.* xv. 1–484. Dryden works additional detail into his version (e.g. ll. 121–4, 165–6, and the picture of childhood in ll. 339–41); and he adds links and single lines for better finish (e.g. ll. 251–3, 274–5, 328–9, 413, 443, 496, 705–6).

330–3. *But when*, &c. Cf. *Annus Mirabilis*, ll. 869–72.

658. *Birth.* The emendation is supported by Sandys's rhyme, 'birth . . . Earth' at the same point (p. 315). Dryden drew many of his rhymes ready-made from Sandys.

The Character of a Good Parson. (Page 1736.) A paraphrase of Chaucer's portrait of the 'povre persoun of a toun' (*CT* (A), ll. 477–528), undertaken at the suggestion of Pepys (Ward, pp. 115–16). It is an oblique tribute to the non-juring clergy, and probably contains a eulogy of Bishop Ken. See James Kinsley, 'Dryden's *Character of a Good Parson* and Bishop Ken', *RES*, N.S., iii (1952), 155–8.

117–18. *The senseless Plea*, &c. An allusion to Dean Sherlock's *The Case of the Allegiance Due to Sovereign Powers* (1691), one of the most notable statements of the doctrine of passive obedience to William III, by an 'apostate' non-juror. See G. R. Cragg, *From Puritanism to the Age of Reason*, 1950, pp. 175 ff.

The Monument of a Fair Maiden Lady. (Page 1740.) The inscription on the mural tablet in Bath Abbey runs: 'Here lyes the Body of Mary, third Daughter of Richard Frampton of Moreton in Dorsetshire, Esqr and of Iane his Wife, sole Daughter of Sr Francis Cottington of Founthill in Wilts, who was Born Ianuary y^e J^st 167$\frac{8}{7}$. And Dyed after Seven Weeks sickness on the 6th of 7ber 1698. This Monument was Erected by Cath. Frampton, her second Sister and Executress in testimony of her Grief, Affection, and Gratitude.' The 'Epitaph' follows, with the signature 'By Mr. Dryden'. The inscription is weak in punctuation, particularly in final stops. It contains many of Dryden's characteristic spellings, e.g. 'layd . . . Cœlestial Mayd' (ll. 1–2), 'Ecclips'd' (l. 13), 'pierceing' (l. 14), 'rould' (l. 15), 'sully's' (l. 20), 'houre' (l. 31).

19–20. *All white*, &c. Cf. Donne, *An Anatomie of the World*, 'A Funerall Elegie', ll. 74–76:

> she soone expir'd,
> Cloath'd in her virgin white integritie,
> For marriage, though it doe not staine, doth dye.

Cymon and Iphigenia, from Boccace. (Page 1741.) *Il Decameron*, v. 1. Dryden expands, ornaments, and emphasizes (e.g. ll. 42–45, 58–60, 93–98, 104–6, 172–4, 331–6, 339–48, 458–61, 464–75, 615–24). He takes care over the psychology of Cymon (ll. 83–85, 112–16, 117–28, 133–48, 179–82). He represents him as a man of violent passion, raised suddenly from brutishness, and tries thus to make his conduct less unprincipled and more convincing than it is in the original (e.g. ll. 234–5, 238–41, 260–3, 300–3). He gives colour and realism to the character of Iphigenia (e.g. ll. 308–11, 318–21, 350–6, 366–8, 422–4). He increases the speed of the climax: Boccaccio's Cymon has three days to consider Lysimachus's proposal, but Dryden's lovers, men of action, decide to join forces on the wedding day itself. Vividness and spirit are added to the final scene (ll. 538–9, 560–8, 579–80, 598–9, 603–4, 607–8).

1–41. *Poeta loquitur*, &c. A reply to Collier. See *supra*, Preface, l. 132, note.

55. *Beauty in disgrace.* Cf. Patrick Hannay, *A Happy Husband* (1622), ll. 85–86 (Saintsbury, i. 681):

> . . . so demure, with such a lovely face,
> That beauty seem'd apparell'd in disgrace.

93–94. *Like Dian*, &c. Cf. Spenser, *The Faerie Queene*, II. iii. 31:

> Such as *Diana* by the sandie shore
> Of swift *Eurotas*, or on *Cynthus* greene,
> Where all the Nymphes haue her vnwares forlore,
> Wandreth alone. . . .

117–22. *Through the rude Chaos*, &c. Cf. Virgil, *Ecl.* vi. 31 ff.

289. *He reap'd the Field*, Cf. Virgil, *Aen.* xii. 662–4, and *Don Sebastian* (1690), I:

I mow'd a-cross, and made Irregular Harvest,
Defac'd the Pomp of Battel. . . .

309–11. *To seeming Sadness,* &c. Cf. *Absalom and Achitophel,* l. 472, note.
384. *shipwreck'd on the Ground.* Cf. *To the Pious Memory Of . . . Mrs Anne Killigrew,* l. 171.
399–408. *The Country rings around,* &c. Dryden's addition. The maintenance of a standing army was a serious issue between William and the Commons in 1697. 'Papers were writ on both sides . . .; it was urged, that since all our Neighbours were armed . . . nothing could give us a real security, but a good Body of regulated Troops; Nothing could be made of the Militia, chiefly of the Horse, but at a vast charge. . . . The word, *standing Army,* had an odious sound in *English* ears; So the popularity lay on the other side' (Burnet, ii. 206). With Dryden's description of the militia, cf. Tom Brown, *Letters from the Dead to the Living* (ed. A. L. Hayward, 1927, p. 239): '. . . our holiday heroes and custard-stormers of Cheapside, those merry burlesques of the art military in Finsbury Fields, who, poor creatures, never meant the destruction of any mortal thing but transitory roast-beef and capon'.

424. *So passive,* &c. A satiric reference to the Anglican doctrine of passive obedience. See *The Hind and the Panther,* iii. 134–43, note.
518. *With Love to Friend,* &c. Repeated from 'Palamon and Arcite'. i. 12.
561. *the Posts were crown'd.* See 'Palamon and Arcite', iii. 104, note.

Prologue, Epilogue, Song and Secular Masque from The Pilgrim, A Comedy

(Page 1758)

'Within this moneth', Dryden wrote to Mrs. Steward on 11 April 1700, 'there will be playd for my profit, an old play of Fletchers, calld the Pilgrim, corrected by my good friend Mr Vanbrook [Sir John Vanbrugh]; to which I have added A New Masque, & am to write a New Prologue & Epilogue' (Ward, p. 136). The date of performance is unknown. The title and opening lines of the *Secular Masque* refer to the turn of the century, but this is no ground for supposing that 'it was intended to have been produced on the 25th of March 1700, on which day the new year at that time began' (Malone, I. i. 331–2). If the story that Dryden died on the third night can be relied on (Malone, loc. cit.; Macdonald, p. 135), the first performance may be dated 29 April. There are two editions of 1700: one (presumed the first) in which the Song precedes the Masque, and another in which the order is reversed and a title-leaf printed for 'A Dialogue, and Secular Masque', possibly so that these pieces could be sold separately (Macdonald). *The Pilgrim* was advertised in the *London Gazette,* 13–17 June 1700. The variants in the 1701 text of the Prologue are obvious corrections.

Colley Cibber spoke both Prologue and Epilogue, this 'not being usually done by the same Person'. Vanbrugh gave him the Epilogue, 'which being written so much above the Strain of common Authors, I confess, I was not a little pleased with. And *Dryden*, upon his hearing me repeat it, to him, made me a farther Compliment of trusting me with the Prologue. This so particular Distinction was looked upon, by the Actors, as something too extraordinary' (Cibber, pp. 220–1).

Prologue. 3. *Tom Dove*: a bear. See Epilogue *To the King and Queen*, l. 24, note. 7–8. *The Fops*, &c. Cf. Prologue to *Cæsar Borgia*, ll. 7–8 and note.

16–19. *Quack Maurus*: Blackmore; see Preface to *Fables*, l. 663, note. Lines 16–17 are a 'libel'; Blackmore was an Oxford graduate. His 'Three Books' are *Prince Arthur* (1695), *King Arthur* (1697), and *A Paraphrase on the Book of Job* (1700).

29. *flounders in*. Gardner retains 'founders in', with the sense 'to sink or stick fast'; but this is difficult with 'in'.

35. *Hopkins*. See *The Second Part of Absalom and Achitophel*, l. 403, note.

39. *Merry Andrew*: a mountebank's assistant. Cf. Prior, *Poems on Several Occasions*, ed. A. R. Waller, 1905, p. 133.

41. *At leisure Hours, in Epique Song he deals*. Blackmore says in the Preface to *King Arthur* that the poem was composed 'by such catches and starts, and in such occasional uncertain hours as the business of my profession would afford me: . . . the greatest part . . . was written in coffee-houses, and in passing up and down the streets, because I had little leisure elsewhere to apply to it' (see Johnson, ii. 237 and notes).

52–53. *Traduc'd Two Kings*, &c. In 1687 Blackmore became one of the thirty Fellows added to the College of Physicians by James II's new charter; in 1697 he was knighted by William. 'The malignity of the wits attributed his knighthood to his new poem; but king William was not very studious of poetry, and Blackmore perhaps had other merit; for he says, in his Dedication to *Alfred*, that "he had a greater part in the succession of the house of Hanover than ever he had boasted" ' (see Johnson, ii. 236, 239–40).

Epilogue. 1. *the Parson*: Collier. See Preface to *Fables*, l. 132, note.

5–6. *a banisht Court*, &c. Cf. *To the Pious Memory Of . . . Mrs Anne Killigrew*, ll. 56–66; *Fables*, 'The Wife of Bath her Tale', ll. 61–68.

21. *Misses*: mistresses. See Epilogue to *Love Triumphant*, l. 15, note.

39. *the Trade of Love, behind the Scene*. See Epilogue *To The King and Queen*, l. 35, note.

41–42. *For while abroad*, &c. Repeated from Prologue to *The Disappointment*, ll. 55–56.

47. *Hains*: the comedian. See Prologue to *The Assignation*, l. 45, note; Epilogue to *Henry the Second*, l. 20, note.

Song of a Scholar and his Mistress: Probably written for the mad-house scene in Act III, where the scholar fancies himself to be Neptune stilling a storm.

9–11. *what's that I View*, &c. The corposant, or St. Elmo's Fire, is the light seen about the masts and sails of a ship in a storm, supposed to forecast calm and safety.

The Secular Masque. 'By the introduction of the deities of the chace, of war, and of love, as governing the various changes of the seventeenth century, the poet alludes to the sylvan sports of James the First, the bloody wars of his son, and the licentious gallantry which reigned in the courts of Charles II and James' (Scott). The music was written by Daniel Purcell and others (see Day, pp. 184–5). In l. 82 'there seems . . . to be a secret allusion to the exile of the beautiful queen of James II, so much admired by the Tory poets' (Scott). Cf. *Poetical Miscellanies: The Fifth Part*, 'The Lady's Song', ll. 7–12.

The Fair Stranger

(Page 1765)

This song is ascribed to Dryden in 'Gildon's Miscellany', *A New Collection of Poems On Several Occasions* (1701). Another version is printed as 'Witty Mr. Henningam's Song' in *Tixall Poetry* (1813; see *On The Marriage of Mrs. Anastasia Stafford*, introductory note). In *Tixall Poetry* (p. 374) Clifford says: 'There are also two very different copies of it in my MS. The Heveninghams were a Roman Catholic family . . . and resided at Aston, near Stone, in Staffordshire.' The Tixall heading indicates only that Henningham sang the song, and does not affect the question of authorship. BM Harl. MS. 1264 contains the only musical setting (ff. 78ᵛ–80; Day, pp. 185–6).

Lines on Tonson

(Page 1766)

Faction Display'd. A Poem (1704), which includes Dryden's lines on p. 15, is a satire on the Whigs by William Shippen (1673–1743). A letter from R. Powys to Prior, dated 14 July 1698, contains another version with the comment: 'Mr. Godfrey Kneller hath drawn at length the picture of your friend Jacob Tonson, which he shewed Mr. Dryden, who desired to give a touch of his pencil, and underneath it writ these three verses' (*HMC Bath*, iii, pp. 238–9). A different account is given by Malone: 'Tonson having refused to advance him a sum of money for a work on which he was employed, [Dryden] sent a second messenger to the bookseller, with a very satirical triplet; adding, "Tell the dog, that he who wrote these lines, can write more." These descriptive verses, which had the desired effect, by some means got

abroad in manuscript; and, not long after Dryden's death, were inserted in
FACTION DISPLAYED' (I. i. 525). Powys's letter suggests the truth of Malone's
statement that the epigram circulated in manuscript; but the rest of Malone's
account, for which he gives no authority, has the appearance of gossip.

2. *Judas-colour'd*: red; traditionally the colour of Iscariot's hair and beard.

Poems from Poetical Miscellanies: The Fifth Part

(Page 1767)

In addition to the poems which follow, Tonson included in this volume
(i) parts of the translation of *Ovid's Art of Love* which was published complete
in 1709; (ii) 'Upon the Death of the Earl of *Dundee*'; and (iii) reprints of the
verses to Charleton, *'Verses to her* Highness *the* Dutchess', and the Epilogue to
The Tempest.

Ovid's Amours. Book I. Elegy IV. 72. *Grubble*: grope, fondle.
88. *Coakes*: wheedle with caresses ('cokes', a simpleton).

On the Death of a Very Young Gentleman. 1-8. *He who cou'd view*, &c. Cf.
Eleonora, ll. 291-8, note.
23-25. *rarify'd . . . exhal'd.* Cf. *Eleonora*, ll. 303-8.

The Lady's Song. An inferior version was included in *Miscellaneous Works,
Written by His Grace, George, Late Duke of Buckingham* (1704), p. 122, as 'The
Beautiful Lady of the May. Written by Mr. Dryden, in the Year 1691'. 'The
obvious application of this song is to the banishment of King James, and his
beautiful consort Mary of Este' (Scott). Cf. 'The Secular Masque' from *The
Pilgrim*, note.

Song: 'High State and Honours.' The words of this song first appeared
anonymously in *The Compleat Courtier* (1683). Day (p. 134) gives a setting by
John Abell from *Choice Ayres and Songs* (1683), iv. 21.

Upon the Death of the Viscount Dundee

(Page 1777)

John Graham of Claverhouse, soldier and persecutor of the Covenanters,
was created Viscount Dundee by James II in 1688; and after attempting to
prop the sinking Jacobite cause in the Highlands, was killed at Killiecrankie
on 17 July 1689. The Latin elegy was by Dr. Archibald Pitcairne (1652-1713),
an Edinburgh physician: see *Scottish Poetry: A Critical Survey*, ed. James
Kinsley, 1955, pp. 97-98.

Ovid's Art of Love. Book I

(Page 1778)

On 30 August 1693 Dryden wrote to Tonson: 'I have translated six hunderd lines of Ovid; but I believe I shall not compasse his 772 lines under nine hunderd or more of mine' (Ward, p. 58). *De Arte Amandi,* i, runs to 772 lines in Cnipping's edition (Amsterdam, 1670). In December 1697 he wrote again to Tonson: 'You told me not, but the Town says, you are printing Ovid de Arte Amandi; I know my Translation is very uncorrect: but at the same time I know no body else can do it better, with all their pains' (Ward, pp. 98–99). Whatever truth there was in the rumour, nothing came of it. Tonson printed Dryden's versions of 'The Rape of the Sabines' and 'The Meeting of *Bacchus* with *Ariadne*' (ll. 111–51 and 590–635 in the complete translation) in *Poetical Miscellanies: The Fifth Part* (1704). In 1709 he published *Ovid's Art of Love. In Three Books. Together with his Remedy of Love. Translated into English Verse by Several Eminent Hands.* Book I of the *Art of Love* was 'Translated, some Years since, By Mr. *Dryden*'; II is anonymous, and III is by Congreve. The translation of *Remedia Amoris* is by Tate; and the book also contains versions of Ovid's *Medicamina Faciei* and *The Court of Love* from Stow's *Chaucer,* with Charles Hopkins's *History of Love,* made up mainly of 'imitations' of Ovid. Tonson, with Dryden's translation on his hands, seems to have intended first to dispose of it in miscellany pieces, and later to have decided to build up an erotic anthology from it. Some of Dryden's words and phrases indicate that he looked at Francis Wolferston's translation (1661), but his debt is inconsiderable.

31–32. *Nor Clio,* &c. Translating 'nec mihi sunt visae Clio Cliusque sorores | servanti pecudes vallibus, Ascra, tuis' (ll. 27–28) in the light of Cnipping's note on Ascra: 'Vicus est in Thespiis, juxta Heliconis partem: quam Dius & Pycimede, Hesiodi parentes incoluerunt, relicta patria Cuma.'

37–38. *I sing the Brothels,* &c.: 'nos Venerem tutam . . . canemus' (l. 33). 'Ignobiles fœminas, ad quas est aditus tutus: Quum è diverso ad nobiles periculosus sit' (Cnipping).

70. *Millions of Matrons.* Ovid, ll. 65–66, with 'iuvenes tibi *mille* placebunt' carried forward from l. 63.

74. *Concord's Fane:* 'ubi muneribus nati sua munera mater | addidit' (ll. 69–70). 'Sunt qui intelligant de templo Concordiæ. Mihi magis placet, intelligas de porticu Octaviæ' (Cnipping).

74–75. *that Proud Edifice,* &c.: 'porticus auctoris Livia nomen habet' (l. 72). Cnipping annotates: 'Domin. Porticus Livia, teste P. Victore, erat in tertia urbis regione, prope Suburram.'

81. *They mourn Adonis with Assyrian Rites:* 'Veneri ploratus Adonis' (l. 75). 'Intelligit autem hic Ovidius de templo Veneris, quæ ritu Assyrio Romæ colebatur cum Adonide, maxima veneratione' (Cnipping).

86–89. *And if the Hall it self,* &c.: 'et fora conveniunt... amori | flammaque in arguto saepe reperta foro' (ll. 79–80). 'The Hall' is Westminster Hall, with Palace Yard adjacent, where 'on your left-hand you hear a nimble-tongued painted sempstress ... and on your right a deep-mouthed cryer, commanding impossibilities, viz. silence to be kept among women and lawyers' (Tom Brown, *Amusements Serious and Comical,* ed. A. L. Hayward, 1927, p. 36).

103. *Berries.* A berry is 'a collection of burrows or warren. It still has that sense in Dryden's own county' (Sergeaunt).

110. *Some to undo, and some to be undone.* A witty improvement on 'ille locus casti damna pudoris habet' (l. 100), from Denham, *Coopers Hill,* l. 32.

120. *No Scenes in Prospect, no machining God.* Particularizing 'scaena sine arte fuit' (l. 106): 'at postea Claud. Pulcher scenam varietate colorum adumbravit' (Cnipping).

132. *the Word too was the Best.* Cf. Byron, *Don Juan,* ix. 55–57.

172–3. *the Statues of the Deities,* &c. Dryden prefers the reading 'at cum pompa frequens coelestibus ibit eburnis' (l. 147) to 'at . . . certantibus ibit ephebis'. 'Vide de hac Deorum pompa per Circum ferri solita ipsum Ovidium copiose agentem Amor. iii. 2' (Heinsius).

443. *dipt*: involved. Cf. Preface to *Fables,* l. 358.

564. *thou may'st ogle*: 'multa supercilio . . . loquare' (l. 498). See 'Another Epilogue' to *The Duke of Guise,* l. 26, note.

587. *free your Arm-pits from the Ram and Goat*: 'nec laedant nares virque paterque gregis' (l. 520), translated with Cnipping's reference to 'alæ sive axillæ, partes . . . sub brachiis'.

611. *clear*: drunk.

832–3. *That Colour,* &c. For 'hoc multi non valuisse putent' (l. 728). Dryden's text has 'hoc vultu', &c., with the note: 'ex hoc vultu colligant ac persuadeantur puellæ te non valere, & ægrum esse præ nimio sui amore.'

837. *Night-Cap*: 'palliolum' (l. 732): 'Qui enim infirmæ valetudinis erant, palliolis obnubebant caput' (Heinsius).

851. *Perithous.* See *Fables,* 'Palamon and Arcite', i. 358, note.

882. *Bug Words.* See Prologue to *The History of Bacon in Virginia,* l. 23, note.

Epitaph on the Monument of the Marquis of Winchester

(Page 1800)

John Paulet, fifth Marquis of Winchester, garrisoned his house at Basing, Hampshire, against the Parliamentary army from August 1643 till October 1645, when he was forced to yield. He 'had written, in every window of the house, with a diamond, the motto *Aymez Loyaulté.* The parliamentary leaders, incensed at this device, burned down this noble seat (a conflagration which Cromwell imputes to accident,) and destroyed and plundered property to the amount of L. 200,000' (Scott). He lived at Englefield in Berkshire after the Restoration, and died there on 5 March 1675.

Æsacus transform'd into a Cormorant

(Page 1801)

Ovid, *Meta.* xi. 749–95. These lines were first published in *Ovid's Metamorphoses in Fifteen Books. Translated by the most Eminent Hands*, 1717. The book has a Preface by Garth, who pays tribute to Dryden as 'one of the greatest Poets, that ever was upon Earth'; it contains a number of Dryden's translations from *Examen Poeticum* and *Fables*, and contributions by Addison, Congreve, Gay, Pope, and Tate.

Lines to Mrs Creed

(Page 1803)

Mrs. Elizabeth Creed was distantly related to the poet. Her grandfather, Sir John Pickering, married Dryden's paternal aunt Susan; and her great-grandfather, Sir Gilbert Pickering, was the brother of Henry Pickering, Dryden's great-grandfather on his mother's side. William Walcot, Mrs. Creed's great-grandson, told Malone that she resided 'many years in a mansion-house at Barnwell, near Oundle, in Northamptonshire', a pattern of industry and piety. 'Conversation one day after dinner, at Mrs. Creed's, running upon the or[igin of names], Mr. Dryden bowed to the good old lady, and spoke extempore the f[ollowing verses].' Mrs. Creed was responsible for the elaborate inscription on Dryden's monument at Tichmarsh in 1722. Malone, I. i. 339–42, 564–6.

'These verses,' says Malone, 'as well as the introductory account of the occasion that gave rise to them, are copied from an original paper now before me, written in an elegant female hand (probably that of one of her daughters); which was found in the cabinet of Mrs. Mary Walcot, late wife of William Walcot, of Oundle, M.D. and grand-daughter to Mrs. Elizabeth Creed.' The lacuna in l. 3 is due to an omission in the transcript.

Epitaph on Erasmus Lawton

(Page 1803)

The inscription on the mural tablet in the church of Great Catworth, Huntingdonshire, erected in memory of Dr. John Lawton and his wife Rose, Dryden's sister, ends thus: 'Mrs Lawton lived in this Town near 40 years | And died Lamented Decem 26. 1710. in the 77 Yeare of her age | Having first buried her only child Erasmus Lawton | on whom her Brother wrote these lines. . . .' The Epitaph was printed in James Prior's *Life of Edmond Malone*, 1860, p. 265.

On the Marriage of the Fair and Vertuous Lady, Mrs Anastasia Stafford, with that truly Worthy and Pious Gent. George Holman, Esq. A Pindarique Ode

(Page 1804)

Anastasia Stafford (1646–1719) was the fifth daughter of Viscount Stafford (1614–80), who was executed for complicity in the Popish Plot (see *Absalom and Achitophel*, l. 676, note). George Holman (1630–98), of Warkworth Manor in Northamptonshire, was a Catholic convert. The date of their marriage is not known; but since the poem was written after Dryden's conversion (see *The Hind and the Panther*, introductory note), and the inscription on Holman's memorial at Warkworth records that he died the father of nine children in 1698, the marriage probably took place between 1686 and 1688, and on or about Christmas (see stanza 1).

This poem 'By Mr Dryden' was first printed in *Tixall Poetry*, edited by Arthur Clifford in 1813 from a manuscript collection found in a trunk at Tixall Hall in Staffordshire, once the seat of the Catholic family of Aston (cf. *The Fair Stranger, supra*, note). The fourth division of *Tixall Poetry* consists, says Clifford, 'of such pieces, as I found totally unconnected with each other, and written on backs of letters, or other scraps of paper. . . . I have prefixed to them, a "Pindaric Ode," by Dryden; two small poems, by Sir Richard Fanshawe; one, by Sidney Godolphin; and one by Waller: all of which I found in the old trunk. . . . Of these "Miscellaneous Poems," it is evident, that many were written by individuals of the Aston family, and their friends; while others have been collected from a variety of volumes' (p. xiii). The collection included transcripts of the Songs from *The Indian Emperour* (p. 248) and *Secret-Love* (p. 146). Clifford suggests that Dryden would be likely to form an acquaintance with the leading Catholic families, among them the Staffords; and that a copy of his ode might well find its way to Tixall from Stafford Castle, four miles distant (p. 380). See B. H. Newdigate, in *The London Mercury*, xxii (1930), 438–42. The Tixall collection has now disappeared. The ode is obviously incomplete.

17. *From her, their glorious resurrection came.* 'Anastasia' means resurrection. The feast of St. Anastasia, martyr, is kept on Christmas Day.

54. *Bestow a bride upon his darling son.* Stafford's son John married Mary Southcote on 1 December 1682.

57–89. On the evidence of these lines, George Holman went abroad when the persecution of the Catholics began (ll. 75–78), helped to maintain other Catholic exiles (ll. 79–89), and was joined by Anastasia Stafford some time after 1681 (ll. 57–59)—possibly after James II's accession in 1685.

INDEX OF POEMS

* Plays of which Dryden is author or part author.

      * Plays of which Dryden is author or part author.

INDEX OF FIRST LINES